The Birds of Ohio

The Birds of Ohio

Completely Revised & Updated
with Ohio Breeding Bird Atlas Maps

∽

Bruce G. Peterjohn

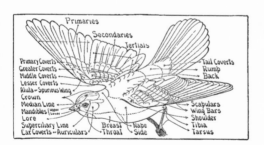

The Wooster Book Company
Wooster ℰ Ohio
2001

The Wooster Book Company

205 West Liberty Street
Wooster Ohio • 44691

ISBN 1-888683-88-0

Library of Congress Cataloging-in-Publication Data

Peterjohn, Bruce G.
   The birds of Ohio : with the Ohio breeding bird atlas / Bruce G.
   Peterjohn.—Rev. & updated
      p.   cm.
   Includes bibliographical references (p.)
   ISBN 1-888683-88-0 (trade paperback : alk. paper)
   1. Birds—Ohio. 2. Birds—Ohio—Geographical distribution. I. Title.

QL684.O3 P48 2000
598'.09771—dc21   99-058312

∞ This book is printed on acid-free paper.

To everyone working for the
conservation of birds in Ohio

The Birds of Ohio

Preface to the Second Edition

In the twelve years since **The Birds of Ohio** was published, some significant advances have occurred in our knowledge of the status and distribution of birds within the state. Publication of the Breeding Bird Atlas documented distributional changes in summer populations that had occurred since the 1930s and serves as the benchmark for comparisons with future changes. The atlas may have sparked a greater interest in some of the lesser-known summer residents, such as northern birds occupying hemlock forests, because the size and geographic ranges of their statewide populations have been better defined during the 1990s. The breeding biology of some of these species has also been the subject of detailed studies, providing the first insights into how these northern birds have adapted to life at the southern edge of their breeding ranges.

Outside of the breeding season, gulls remain a strong focal point of interest. Their winter status along Lake Erie has been well documented during the 1990s, and some of the rarer species are beginning to be discovered at a few inland locations. Hawk migration has also received considerable attention, with the recent recognition that under certain circumstances spring movements eastward along Lake Erie in Ashtabula County may equal the well-known migration along western Lake Erie. Shorebirds and warblers are well reported in seasonal summaries, but primarily in patterns that were well established during earlier decades.

While patterns of distribution and seasonal movements tend to be well documented for birds in most portions of the state, this information is limited for many unglaciated counties. Many other aspects of the life histories and breeding biologies remain poorly known. Most of the available information on the breeding chronologies of birds in Ohio is found within a few sources from the central and northeastern counties. I suspect that birds breed earlier in the southern counties than has been previously documented, but there are few published records to support this belief.

As I return to Ohio for periodic visits, the changes to the landscape are readily apparent. The ever-expanding urban areas are replacing agricultural fields and woodlands with housing developments. Rural counties are not spared from development, as roadsides are becoming increasingly populated while natural habitats are pushed farther from the roads. Recreational and urban development have transformed most of the Lake Erie shoreline into highly modified landscapes. Not every change has been harmful to wildlife, however, and the maturation of woodlands in eastern Ohio has benefited forest bird communities. More mature woodlands meant fewer successional fields, and most birds associated with shrubby habitats have declined during recent decades. Maintaining habitat diversity is the key activity for conserving healthy bird populations across Ohio, a fact that is as apparent in 2000 as it was in 1989.

Preface to the First Edition

Despite Ohio's reputation as a heavily urbanized state with extensive farmlands, it actually boasts a wide variety of habitats. This variety extends from the dry cedar barrens in Adams County near the Ohio River to the damp northeastern beech-maple forests in Ashtabula County, and from the forested hillsides in the southeastern unglaciated counties to the Lake Erie marshes in the northwest. This diversity of habitats is attributed to Ohio's location at the point of transition between the Appalachian highlands to the east and broad plains to the west. Not surprisingly, these diverse habitats attract a wide variety of migrant and resident birds to the state.

The composition of this avifauna has changed dramatically since the last comprehensive books describing the birds of Ohio were published in 1903. When William Dawson was writing his delightful volumes, birds such as Bewick's Wrens and Bachman's Sparrows were just beginning to invade Ohio. These species eventually established sizable populations, flourished for several decades, and then mysteriously vanished. When Lynds Jones' book was in preparation, heron populations had been decimated by the millinery trade, while waterfowl and shorebirds were suffering from market hunting. With adequate protection, these groups have recovered and some shorebirds may have become more numerous today than at any time in the past century. These examples are just a few of the many changes in Ohio's avifauna during the twentieth century, a pattern that has probably accelerated since 1940 as urban expansion and agricultural land-use practices continue to alter the state's habitats. Similar changes will undoubtedly occur in the future, and Ohio's avifauna of the twenty-first century will most likely be different from what we observe today.

This book is not intended to be a field guide. Instead, it was written to give an accounting of the present relative abundance and distribution of all species of birds that have been seen in Ohio and to provide some insight into their habitat preferences and breeding biology. In addition, I have chronicled the historical changes in abundance and distribution of many species since the late 1800s.

During the preparation of this book, I have relied on my own observations as well as the published and unpublished accounts of numerous observers. Interpretation of published and unpublished records is always a difficult process, especially when exceptionally large numbers, unseasonal dates, or difficult-to-identify species are reported without accompanying details. Although many of these records may be accurate, it is impossible to establish positively the veracity of undocumented sightings. When citing records in this book, I have admittedly taken a conservative stance and accepted only documented records or those reported by reputable observers and fitting established patterns of occurrence. The omission of published records does not necessarily imply the birds were misidentified, only that they were supported by less than convincing details. My intention was to report the accurate records, while putting the questionable sightings to rest. Today's birders should recognize the problems involved in the field identification of birds and strive to keep accurate and detailed records of their observations, including thorough descriptions of all unusual or unseasonal sightings. This information will prove invaluable for future researchers attempting to establish the veracity of sight records.

This book not only documents our knowledge of Ohio birds, but also demonstrates areas of ignorance. New species are being discovered within our borders almost annually, and there is much still to be learned about many of the species that are regularly recorded from the state. It is hoped that this book will stimulate studies of the more poorly known species in order to fill the gaps in our knowledge.

The relationship between habitat availability and the abundance of birds is obvious. Declining bird populations during the twentieth century are almost invariably caused by the loss of habitats. Habitat destruction has continued at an accelerated pace in recent decades, threatening to eliminate several vegetative communities and the wildlife associated with them. The issue of habitat preservation and wise use of our natural resources should be of the utmost importance to anyone interested in the welfare of birds. The maintenance of Ohio's diverse avifauna can be achieved only through the protection and conservation of all the state's natural habitats.

Introduction

An understanding of bird distribution patterns within Ohio requires knowledge of the state's physiography, vegetative communities, and climate. People unfamiliar with Ohio may think of it as a state whose large urban areas are surrounded by extensive cornfields and few redeeming natural features. Admittedly, portions of Ohio are heavily urbanized and other areas are intensively farmed, but the state still supports thousands of acres of woodlands, successional fields, and wetlands that are inhabited by diverse and abundant avian communities.

Ohio contains 41,263 square miles, extending approximately 210 miles north to south and 215 miles east to west. Elevations vary from 1,550 feet above mean sea level near Bellefontaine in Logan County to 450 feet at the mouth of the Great Miami River in Hamilton County. It has a continental temperate climate. Precipitation is distributed from mean annual levels of 31–33 inches in northwestern counties near Lake Erie to 41–44 inches in northeastern Ohio and the south-central counties. Snowfall is greatest within the "snowbelt" east of Cleveland, where it averages in excess of 100 inches annually in Geauga County. Average snowfall totals are more than 50 inches in other northeastern counties, but fewer than 20 inches are expected in counties bordering the Ohio River. Winter mean daily maximum temperatures approach or slightly exceed 32°F. Periods of cold weather are frequent and temperatures may drop below zero. The coldest temperature officially recorded was -39°F in Perry County on February 10, 1899. Summer temperatures normally peak during July, with mean daily maximums of 80–82°F in the northeastern counties and 88°F in southern Ohio. Temperatures seldom exceed 100°F, but have been recorded as high as 113°F in Gallia County on July 21, 1934.

The state is underlain by sedimentary rocks formed during the Paleozoic Era 600 million to 200 million years ago (Bownocker 1965). The oldest formations are under the western half of the state—primarily limestones, dolomites, and shales. The eastern counties are underlain by younger sandstones, shales, limestones, and coals.

The existing topography is a result of a series of glacial invasions during the Pleistocene epoch. Within the past two million years, at least eight glaciers covered portions of the state under as much as 5,000 to 8,000 feet of ice. These ice sheets covered Ohio for thousands of years, acting as giant bulldozers as they indelibly changed the landscape. Then they retreated. The most recent ice sheet, known as the Wisconsin glacier, melted 11,000 years ago, leaving the terrain that is visible today (Stout et al. 1943). The western half of Ohio is characterized by flat to rolling terrain known as till plains. Similar till plains are found in the northeastern counties. Unglaciated terrain is restricted to southern and eastern Ohio, where the hilly countryside has local relief of 100–400 feet and as high as 800 feet at bluffs along the Ohio River (Goldthwait et al. 1961).

These topographic features and the natural vegetative communities form five distinct physiographic regions. The avifauna of each region is different, and result in the diverse bird community that is known in the state. To better understand the reasons behind these bird distribution patterns, the physiographic regions are briefly described.

UNGLACIATED ALLEGHENY PLATEAU. An important feature influencing bird distribution in Ohio is the glacial boundary. South of this boundary, the topography is very hilly, with steep valleys dissected by small high-gradient streams. With its hilly terrain and relatively infertile soils, this portion of the Allegheny Plateau supports the most extensive woodlands in Ohio. Several woodland communities may be present, depending upon exposure. Upland mixed oak forests are found along the upper slopes and ridges, dominated by various oaks and hickories. Mixed mesophytic forests occupy the lower protected slopes. These forests are composed of beeches, oaks, elms, maples, tulip trees, cherries, and occasionally hemlocks. Lowland forests also have a mixed composition, including sycamores, elms, ashes, maples, cottonwoods, and willows (Gordon 1969).

Successional habitats are widely distributed where these forests have been cleared. Other habitats are relatively scarce within the rugged terrain. Farmlands tend to be small and are as likely to be devoted to pastures and hayfields as to cultivated crops. Wetlands are generally small and sparsely distributed, except where they have been created on reclaimed strip mines. Openwater habitats are largely restricted to reservoirs and portions of the Scioto and Muskingum Rivers. Most counties are sparsely inhabited, with the largest cities scattered along the Ohio River and its major tributaries.

Portions of Harrison, Tuscarawas, Coshocton, Guernsey, Belmont, Muskingum, and Morgan Counties have been modified by strip mining. The forests, farmlands, and other habitats were replaced by highly modified habitats. Unreclaimed strip mines are reverting to various successional habitats, frequently with altered drainage patterns creating wetlands in areas where these habitats were absent. In contrast, recent strip mines are reclaimed to rolling terrain covered with extensive grasslands.

GLACIATED ALLEGHENY PLATEAU. The glaciated Allegheny Plateau extends from Ashtabula and Medina Counties south to Ross County. Since glaciers covered this portion of the plateau, the terrain is less hilly (Goldthwait et al. 1961). This rolling terrain is more suitable for agriculture and urban development, and its natural habitats have been greatly modified. Woodlands tend to be smaller than the extensive forests characteristic of the unglaciated plateau.

Woodland communities are similar to the unglaciated hillsides, except within the northeastern counties, where beech-maple forests predominate (Gordon 1969). Woodland, edge, and successional habitats are interspersed with farmlands and urban areas, producing the greatest diversity of terrestrial habitats in any of the state's physiographic regions. Wetlands are widely distributed in the northeastern counties, although their acreage has decreased as a result of drainage, and marshes along the Killbuck Creek valley constitute the largest remaining wetlands in the interior of Ohio. Wetlands become sparse south of Ashland and Holmes Counties. Portions of Stark and Columbiana Counties have been modified by strip mining, but the glaciated plateau has not been subject to the severe modifications characteristic of some unglaciated counties.

BLUEGRASS REGION. Our smallest physiographic region lies at the western edge of the Allegheny Plateau in portions of Adams and Brown Counties, an extension of the Bluegrass Region of Kentucky. Its terrain is similar to the unglaciated counties, but the area is underlain by limestone and shale bedrock rather than sandstone. Plant communities and prevailing land use are similar to the unglaciated plateau. Dry exposed hillsides, however, support extensive fields overgrown with red cedars and a few other woody species (Gordon 1969).

LAKE PLAIN. A flat plain stretches along the south shore of Lake Erie. Only several miles wide from Ashtabula County west to Erie County, it then widens to cover most of northwestern Ohio. This plain was once the bottom of a larger lake formed during the retreat of the last glacier. As this glacial lake retreated, it left a plain with a slope of only two to three feet per mile, broken by a series of low sandy beach ridges.

With its flat terrain and poorly drained soils, this lake plain originally supported a vast wooded swamp known as the Great Black Swamp (Kaatz 1955). This swamp covered approximately 1,500 square miles, beginning near Fort Wayne, Indiana, and paralleling the Maumee River to Lake Erie. It supported an extensive elm-ash forest that flooded during spring, was mostly mud during summer and autumn, and froze in winter (Gordon 1969). Dry terrain was found along beach ridges and narrow strips of land bordering the larger rivers.

This inhospitable terrain was largely uninhabited until the mid-1800s when drainage projects rapidly destroyed the entire swamp, converting it to farmlands before 1900 (Kaatz 1955).

Other habitats originally found along the lake plain in northwestern Ohio included extensive wet prairies that were flooded during spring and supported dense grasses and other prairie vegetation later in the summer. Perhaps its most unique habitats were the Oak Openings west of Toledo, occupying a ten-mile wide strip of sandy land along a glacial beach ridge. These openings supported open oak-hickory forests interspersed with swamp forests, prairies, and marshes (Gordon 1969).

Today the lake plain is probably the most highly modified of Ohio's physiographic regions. The Great Black Swamp was transformed into the state's most productive and intensively cultivated lands. More than 90 percent of the land is farmed, with natural habitats restricted to isolated oak-hickory woodlots and narrow riparian corridors. Only the unproductive soils within the Oak Openings continue to support extensive natural habitats. Most of the lake plain east from Sandusky has undergone extensive urbanization. Undeveloped lands are generally farmed, although wooded habitats remain in portions of Lake and Ashtabula Counties.

TILL PLAINS. Till plains created by the Wisconsin and Illinoian glaciers cover the remainder of western Ohio. These plains have more topographic relief than the lake plain, becoming rolling hills along end moraines. The Wisconsin till plain extends south to Butler, Warren, Clinton, and Highland Counties (Goldthwait et al. 1961). Farther south, the Illinoian till plain was only slightly modified by the ice sheet, and the terrain becomes hilly.

Initially, these till plains supported extensive oak-hickory and beech-maple forests, with a few prairie openings (Gordon 1969). Their productive soils and relatively flat terrain allowed them to become valuable farmlands, and the forests were replaced by cultivated fields along the Wisconsin till plain, where only isolated woodlots remain. The original forests were also removed from the Illinoian till plain, but the hilly terrain is less suitable for agriculture. Second-growth forests, edge, and successional habitats are more widely distributed on this plain than in other counties in western Ohio. Wetlands were formerly widespread on the Wisconsin till plain, especially near the prairie openings, but similar habitats were scarce on the Illinois plain. These wetlands have largely been drained.

LAKE ERIE. No discussion of Ohio's physiography would be complete without mention of Lake Erie. Lake Erie is divided into three basins, two of which are associated with Ohio's waters. These basins have different physical characteristics that strongly influence the composition and abundance of their waterbird communities.

The Western Basin extends east to the Lake Erie islands and Cedar Point at the mouth of Sandusky Bay. The shallowest basin, it has an average depth of 25 to 35 feet and a maximum depth of 62 feet. At one time, this basin was bordered by extensive marshes. Every bay hosted abundant aquatic and emergent vegetation that fluctuated in response to changing water levels (Gordon 1969). These wetlands changed markedly during the twentieth century. Increased lake levels and concentrations of suspended sediments transformed these bays into large expanses of open water with little vegetation. Strong southerly winds or other periods with low water expose extensive mudflats. The wetlands have not entirely disappeared. Instead, most are diked to maintain relatively constant water levels and vegetative communities.

The Central Basin extends from the Lake Erie islands and Cedar Point east to Erie, Pennsylvania. This basin has an average depth of 61 feet and a maximum depth of 84 feet. In contrast to the Western Basin, the Central Basin is bordered by few sizable bays, wetlands, or exposed mudflats. Unlike the other Great Lakes, the south shore of Lake Erie does not have great quantities of sand and lacks extensive dune systems. Its beaches are narrow and frequently include much gravel.

The lakefront makes the greatest single contribution to the diversity and abundance of the state's avifauna. Large numbers of waterfowl, shorebirds, gulls, terns, and other water birds annually visit Lake Erie. But the lake's influence extends beyond attracting water birds. It serves as a migration corridor for hawks, funneling them around both ends of the lake because many species are reluctant to pass over large bodies of open water. Lake Erie also serves as the focal point of the annual songbird migration. Every spring, favorable winds produce phenomenal flights along the south shore, where songbirds gather to rest and feed before continuing their northward movements. Fall flights are generally not as spectacular, although sizable movements may be noted on northerly winds.

The habitats within Ohio were extensively modified during historic times. These changes were described by Trautman (1977, 1981), and I will only briefly summarize them. Not only have they had a tremendous influence on the expansion of many species into the state, but habitat modifications also affected the relative abundance of species that were already present.

The initial settlement of Ohio began during the eighteenth century, as the settlers encountered a largely forested state. The primeval forest was composed of stately oaks, "many of them six feet and more in diameter, towering up royally fifty and sixty feet without a limb; the shellbark hickories, and the glowing maples, both with tops far aloft; the mild and moss-covered ash trees, some of them over four feet through; the elms and beeches, the great black walnuts, and the ghostly-robed sycamores, huge in limb and body, along the creek bottoms" (Trautman 1977). Forest cover was not uniform, even in the southern and eastern counties, where a few openings were produced by storms or cleared by Indians. The northwestern and central counties supported numerous prairie openings, where grasses grew "as high as a horse's back" and woody vegetation was largely absent (Trautman 1977). At the beginning of the nineteenth century, Ohio was still largely undisturbed. An estimated 45,000 people inhabited the state in scattered settlements along large rivers and Lake Erie.

Ohio's human population expanded during the nineteenth century, to two million by 1850 and 4.1 million in 1900 (Trautman 1981), and greatly altered the state. Most virgin forests disappeared before 1860, except for the Great Black Swamp. The prairies disappeared as their productive soils were converted to farmlands. Many wetlands were drained for agricultural purposes. By the late 1800s, most of Ohio was actively farmed, with numerous small farm fields interspersed among brushy fencerows and occasional woodlots, even in the unglaciated counties (Trautman 1977).

The composition of Ohio's avifauna was radically altered during the nineteenth century. Species dependent on mature forests and other undisturbed habitats declined or disappeared. Other species benefited from these habitat changes, particularly birds occupying agricultural fields and shrubby edge habitats, and a number of species invaded Ohio.

The landscape continued to change during the twentieth century as Ohio's human population expanded to more than eleven million. Urban areas grew rapidly, converting farmlands and woodlands to residential areas. Agricultural practices became increasingly mechanized and dependent on pesticides, herbicides, and fertilizers to maintain production. The size of most farm fields increased, especially after 1940, eliminating many fencerows and woodlots. While farmlands formerly supported fairly abundant wildlife communities, today's farms are relatively barren and occupied by few species. Not all habitat changes were adverse; in the unglaciated counties, many farms were abandoned and the land reverted to second-growth woods.

Ohio's bird communities also continued to change. Only a few species spread into or disappeared from the state as compared with the more dramatic alterations that occurred during the 1800s. Instead, regional changes in bird populations reflected evolving patterns of habitat availability. In urban areas and intensively farmed lands, many species substantially declined. Conversely, most woodland birds increased along the unglaciated Allegheny Plateau as wooded acreages expanded.

Ohio is fortunate to have a fairly complete set of historical references describing its avifauna. The state was visited in the early 1800s by John James Audubon and Alexander Wilson, but their coverage was fragmentary and their writings contain many vague second-hand reports in addition to their personal observations. The first statewide investigation of the bird communities was performed by Dr. Jared Kirtland (1838). He was one of the prominent American naturalists of the mid-1800s, continuing his studies until his death in 1877. In the 1870s, Dr. J. M. Wheaton became Ohio's most prominent ornithologist. While his studies were largely restricted to central Ohio, his periodic observations from other areas, along with reports by other reliable naturalists allowed him to publish the *Report on the Birds of Ohio* (Wheaton 1882).

After Wheaton's untimely death, William Dawson and Lynds Jones were recognized as the most authoritative ornithologists in Ohio. Jones largely confined his studies to northern Ohio, while Dawson was based in Columbus. They independently published their accounts of Ohio's avifauna in 1903 (Dawson 1903, Jones 1903). Dawson left the state shortly after his book was published, while Jones actively contributed observations through the first decades of the twentieth century.

No comprehensive statewide publications appeared between 1903 and 1989 (Peterjohn 1989). Several annotated checklists briefly summarized statewide distribution patterns, most notably Borror (1950), Trautman and Trautman (1968), and Peterjohn et al. (1987). A number of regional publications thoroughly described the distribution and abundance of birds in portions of the state, produced by the most prominent naturalists and ornithologists of the twentieth century.

In northwestern Ohio, Lou Campbell studied birds along western Lake Erie, beginning in the 1920s, producing authoritative references for the Toledo area (Campbell 1940, 1968). Harold Mayfield, Milton Trautman, Laurel Van Camp, and others significantly contributed to these publications. The counties away from the lakefront received scant attention, except for Paulding, where Homer Price was an oologist into the 1930s and studied birds into the 1970s (Price 1935, 1972). In west-central Ohio, most activity was centered around Lake St. Marys, where Clarence Clark observed birds between the 1940s and 1960s (Clark and Sipe 1970).

Bird communities in southwestern Ohio were studied throughout the twentieth century. Ben Blincoe contributed observations from the Dayton area since the 1920s. His sightings, along with more recent reports, were summarized by Mathena et al. (1984). A number of naturalists were active in the Cincinnati area since the 1930s. Emerson Kemsies collaborated with Worth Randle to publish a comprehensive book on the area's avifauna (Kemsies and Randle 1953). Other naturalists, including G. Ronald Austing, Woodrow Goodpaster, and Karl Maslowski, also significantly contributed to our knowledge of bird distribution patterns.

For central Ohio, the classic reference on bird distribution is Milton Trautman's study on the birds of Buckeye Lake during the 1920s and 1930s

(Trautman 1940). More recent observations by Donald Borror, myself, Edward Thomas, Tom Thomson, Milton and Mary Trautman, and others documented changes in the area's avifauna since the 1940s.

In eastern Ohio, the Cleveland-Akron region has been extensively studied since the 1920s, culminating in the book produced by Arthur Williams (1950). Comprehensive annotated checklists compiled by Donald Newman (1969) and Larry Rosche (1988) updated the status of all species in this area. Jones' studies in Lorain and Erie Counties (Jones 1910, 1914) and Hicks' (1933a) monograph on the breeding birds of Ashtabula County are important historic references on the status of bird populations from the northeastern counties. Except for Hicks' (1937a) summary, the unglaciated counties have received relatively sparse coverage.

In addition to these regional publications, the distribution of breeding birds was the subject of several studies. Lawrence Hicks accumulated considerable breeding bird data during the late 1920s and 1930s that appeared in his monograph on the breeding birds of Ohio (Hicks 1935a). The first systematic survey of Ohio's breeding avifauna was the Breeding Bird Atlas, initiated during 1982 under the sponsorship of the Division of Natural Areas and Preserves within the Ohio Department of Natural Resources. Fieldwork for this project was completed in 1987 (Peterjohn and Rice 1991), providing a detailed basis for assessing future changes to the status and distribution of the breeding bird communities.

REFERENCES

Any book describing the birds of Ohio relies on these regional and statewide references for information on the historic status, distribution, and relative abundance of the state's avifauna. Numerous articles and notes in various peer-reviewed journals also provide significant information. Field observations from Ohio have been summarized since the first decades of the twentieth century in the National Audubon Society's publications: *Bird-Lore*, *Audubon Field Notes*, *American Birds*, and *Field Notes*, and their successor, *North American Birds*, published by the American Birding Association. These summaries have provided a wealth of material on bird distribution and abundance in Ohio, including many reports that were never published anywhere else. Since the late 1980s, *The Ohio Cardinal* has summarized seasonal observations from across the state, while regional publications such as the *Cleveland Bird Calendar,* and *The Bobolink* have also become important sources of information. All of these references were reviewed, as well as many other articles and notes that did not include material pertinent to this book.

Some unpublished information was also regularly utilized, especially my personal observations from every county between the late 1960s and 1991 and less frequent visits to the state during subsequent years. Other unpublished sightings were obtained from reports submitted to the *American Birds* regional editors during the 1970s and 1980s.

A few sources of information were not used in the preparation of this book, particularly sightings published in the newsletters of local Audubon Societies and natural history clubs. While many of these sightings may be accurate, they frequently lack supporting details and their veracity cannot be ascertained, or include sightings from two states but do not indicate the exact location of the reports. Beginning in the late 1990s, internet web sites have served as a means for improving communication and disseminating information between birders in the state. Many bird reports appearing on these sites are valid and subsequently appeared in the published literature. However, text and graphics files on these web sites can be easily modified and replaced, without documenting any changes that have been made. The historic value of web sites remains to be determined, because the long-term availability of this electronic information is uncertain. For these reasons, I avoided using information from internet web sites unless the reports also appeared in the published literature.

SPECIES ACCOUNTS

These accounts describe the abundance, distribution, and historic status of all birds positively recorded from Ohio as of December 31, 1999. Taxonomy and nomenclature follow AOU (1998, 2000). As described in Peterjohn (1989), species on the state list have been documented by specimens, identifiable photographs, or complete written descriptions prepared at the time of observation. Species lacking adequate documentation or thought to have escaped from captivity were excluded.

Decisions to include specific sightings within the species accounts were based on my assessment of the available information supporting each report, the relative difficulty of positively identifying the species in the field, the precedence for similar reports at statewide, regional, or larger geographic scales, and the abilities and reputations of the observer(s). Such subjective decisions are impossible to avoid in the preparation of any state bird book, and my views on the acceptability of records may differ from summaries published by records committees or other individuals. For example, assessing reports submitted by single observers poses a considerable challenge, especially when an observer repeatedly claims exceptionally large tallies of individuals, remarkably early or late sightings of migrants, and numbers of noteworthy rarities, all of which are very seldom confirmed by others. Unfortunately, Ohio's ornithological literature has a history of questionable single-observer sightings, dating from the late 1920s. My tendency was to exclude these reports unless they were based on extant specimens, high-quality photographs, or other solid evidence. My intent is to provide well-supported species accounts that serve as a solid basis for comparison with future sightings.

The categories used to describe status and abundance are those used by Peterjohn (1989):

ABUNDANT: Requires no special effort to locate, widely distributed, and conspicuous when present.

COMMON: Present in lesser numbers than indicated by "abundant", but nearly always found when searched for in the appropriate habitat and season.

FAIRLY COMMON: Not always found when searched for in the appropriate habitat, although frequently can be found with persistent effort.

UNCOMMON: Observed infrequently and found in small numbers, even in its preferred habitat.

RARE: Observed annually, but generally not more than a few times annually despite diligent efforts to locate in appropriate habitat.

CASUAL: Not observed annually but has an established pattern of occurrence.

ACCIDENTAL: Has single records or a very small number of records without an established pattern of occurrence.

EXTIRPATED: Formerly established populations in Ohio that disappeared from the state. Extant populations remain elsewhere in North America.

Use of these terms recognizes that abundance levels vary for the different groups of birds. Hence, songbirds might be considered "common" if 25–75 individuals are normally observed daily, while 5–10 hawks would constitute a "common" raptor.

Other terms used in the species accounts include:

PERMANENT RESIDENT: Resides in Ohio throughout the year.

SUMMER RESIDENT: Nests in Ohio and present primarily during the breeding season.

WINTER RESIDENT: Remains in Ohio throughout the winter months.

SUMMER VISITOR: Appears in Ohio during summer, but normally remains for only a few days or weeks. These species do not normally breed in the state. Summer visitors do not include species that regularly migrate through Ohio during summer.

WINTER VISITOR: Appears for only a few days or weeks during winter, but does not normally spend the entire season in the state. For example, species such as the House Wren that occasionally linger into December are treated as winter visitors since they normally disappear before the season is over.

Birds that normally migrate during early winter are treated as migrants rather than winter visitors.

The calendar year was divided into four seasons as follows: spring, March through May; summer, June and July; autumn, August through November; winter, December through February.

To facilitate discussion of avian distribution patterns, the state was subdivided into the following regions:

1. WESTERN LAKE ERIE: The Western Basin of Lake Erie, extending east to the Lake Erie islands and the mouth of Sandusky Bay; includes all lands within two miles of the lakefront.
2. CENTRAL LAKE ERIE: The Central Basin of Lake Erie, extending eastward from the Lake Erie islands and Cedar Point (Erie County); includes all lands within two miles of the lakefront.
3. NORTHWESTERN COUNTIES: All counties from the western border east to Erie, Huron, and Richland and from the northern border south to Paulding, Putnam, Hancock, Wyandot, and Crawford.
4. NORTHEASTERN COUNTIES: All counties north of the glacial boundary and from Lorain and Ashland east to the border.
5. UNGLACIATED COUNTIES: The southeastern portion of the state occupying the unglaciated Allegheny Plateau.
6. SOUTHWESTERN COUNTIES: All counties from the southern border north to Preble, Montgomery, Greene, and Clinton and west to the glacial boundary in Highland and Adams Counties.
7. CENTRAL COUNTIES: Franklin and Delaware Counties along with all contiguous counties and glaciated portions of Ross County.
8. WEST-CENTRAL COUNTIES: All counties from Van Wert, Allen, and Hardin south through Darke, Miami, and Clark.

For some species, the state was divided into northern, central, and southern thirds. Northern Ohio refers to the northwestern and northeastern counties; central Ohio refers to the west-central and central counties and the unglaciated plateau south through Muskingum, Guernsey, and Belmont Counties; and southern Ohio refers to the southwestern counties and unglaciated plateau north through Perry, Morgan, Noble, and Monroe Counties.

For some species, the state was divided into western and eastern portions. Western Ohio refers to the northwestern, west-central, central, and southwestern counties and eastern Ohio refers to the northeastern and unglaciated counties.

For species breeding in Ohio, maps from the Ohio Breeding Bird Atlas (Peterjohn and Rice 1991) accompany each species account to illustrate geographic patterns in distribution and allow access to information that is no longer in print. On these maps, priority block data are represented by squares, special areas data are shown by circles, and data for asterisked species collected outside of blocks or special areas are indicated by triangles. Hollow symbols represent "possible" breeding records, while the shaded symbols are "probable" and "confirmed" records; the atlas codes defining "possible", "probable", and "confirmed" status are provided in Peterjohn and Rice (1991). These maps have not been updated since their publication. Atlas maps were not included for a few species whose patterns of distribution markedly expanded after the 1980s, such as the Wild Turkey (*Meleagris gallopavo*); for species that established very small breeding populations after 1988, such as the Osprey (*Pandion haliaetus*) and Peregrine Falcon (*Falco peregrinus*); or for species that no longer breed in the state, such as the Little Blue Heron (*Egretta caerulea*).

Acknowledgments

This undertaking could not have been accomplished without the assistance of many birders and professional ornithologists scattered throughout Ohio. Special thanks are due to the other members of the former Ohio Bird Records Committee, Ray Hannikman, Jean Hoffman, Larry Rosche, and Elliot Tramer, whose previous review of innumerable sightings and research of historical records made this task much easier. I am also indebted to John Condit of The Ohio State University Museum of Zoology, Robert Kennedy at the Cincinnati Museum of Natural History, and Tim Matson at the Cleveland Museum of Natural History, who kindly allowed me to examine specimens at their museums. Ken Parkes at the Carnegie Museum of Natural History graciously provided information on specimens under his care. I am especially grateful to Dan Rice of the Ohio Department of Natural Resources, Division of Natural Areas and Preserves, for generously allowing access, prior to publication, to some of the data obtained for the **Ohio Breeding Bird Atlas**. I am also grateful to the hundreds of birders who participated in this endeavor.

Most important, observers throughout Ohio contributed significant sightings, either through their regular reports submitted to the seasonal summaries published in *American Birds* or in other correspondence. These observers include: Jon Ahlquist, J. Kirk Alexander, Matt Anderson, Ron Austing, Carole Babyak, Frank Bader, Robert Ball (deceased), H. Thomas Bartlett, Charles and Betty Berry, Kay Booth, W. William Brockner, Jerry Cairo, Lou Campbell (deceased), Cliff Cathers, Nancy Cherry, Bob Conlon, Dave Corbin (deceased), Joseph Croy, M. Owen Davies (deceased), Elinor Elder, F. W. Fais, Vic Fazio, Jim Fry, John Gallagher, Charles Gambill, Larry Gara, Bruce Glick, Robert Graham, Mary Gustafson, Ray Hannikman, Rob Harlan, Jim Haw, John Herman, Jim Hickman, Jim Hill, Chuck Hocevar, Jim Hoffman, Richard and Jean Hoffman, Judy Howard, James Ingold, Paula Jack, Tom Kemp, William and Nancy Klamm (Bill is deceased), Dennis Kline, Vernon Kline, Jean Knoblaugh, Tom LePage, Tony Leukering, Karl Maslowski, Charlotte Mathena, Jim McCormac, Steve McKee, Howard and Marcella Meahl (Howard is deceased), Dave Nolan, Reed Noss, Dave Osborne, Doug Overacker, J. Paul Perkins (deceased), A. Town Peterson, Dan Petit, Ken Petit,

Ed Pierce, John Pogacnik, Worth Randle (deceased), Bill Reiner, Frank Renfrow, Dan Rice, Larry Rosche, Ed Schlabach, Mark Shieldcastle, John Shrader, Dave Smith, Bruce Stehling, Dave Styer, Ethel Surman (deceased), Bert Szabo, Jerry Talkington, Merrill Tawse, Tom Thomson, Elliot Tramer, Don Tumblin, Carol Tveekrem, Laurel Van Camp (deceased), Norm Walker, Pete Whan, and Art Wiseman (deceased). My thanks to all these people; their contributions are reflected in the wealth of information made available to me.

Other individuals provided assistance in the preparation of the manuscript. I am very grateful to Bill and Mary Baum, retired librarians at the Cleveland Museum of Natural History, who graciously allowed me access to references under their care. Tom Bartlett, Dan Rice, and Jeff White also provided references that were not available from other sources. Dorothea Peterjohn spent many tedious hours entering most of the manuscript into the computer. Finally, Mary Gustafson provided invaluable assistance throughout the duration of the project, from providing references to entering manuscript to keeping me from destroying the computer after it scrambled a full disk of manuscript. In all likelihood, this book would never have been completed without her support.

I am also indebted to my parents, Dorothea and the late Alvin Peterjohn, who supported my interest in birds at an early age and tolerated it when it became an obsession. I must also express my deep appreciation to the late Evelyn Gordon, who had the patience to take me birding during my formative years and taught me the proper approach to the field identification of birds.

I am extremely grateful to a number of individuals for their important contributions towards the completion of this second edition, especially Dan Rice of the Ohio Department of Natural Resource's Division of Natural Areas and Preserves for permitting publication of the Breeding Bird Atlas maps. He also allowed access to unpublished data from surveys of riparian corridors along selected streams across Ohio. Steve McKee provided unpublished summaries of breeding bird surveys conducted in the Mohican State Forest during 1997. Larry Rosche and Dwight Chasar provided access to various reference materials and publications. Ken Brock made available copies of documentation materials for several noteworthy reports. Jon Dunn, Jim Fry, Bruce Glick, Cece Johnston, and Ed Schlabach made helpful contributions to this edition. My sincere thanks are extended to these individuals.

Hundreds of observers contributed significant sightings to various publications, reports that continue to expand our knowledge of the status and distribution of birds across the state. Many of these observers were individually acknowledged in the first edition, while others became active birders after 1988. These birders are too numerous to be individually listed here, but I want to acknowledge these extremely important contributions. Additionally, individuals serving as statewide and regional editors of Ohio bird sightings perform a difficult and thankless task, yet are creating a crucial historic record of ornithological information. During the 1990s, Matt Anderson, Ken Brock, Bob Conlon, Vic Fazio, Rob Harlan, Tom Kemp, Ed Pierce, Larry Rosche, and Bill Whan have devoted countless hours towards producing these summaries. I extend my thanks for their efforts, and hope that their contributions are recognized by birders across the state.

I also want to thank the staff at The Wooster Book Company for their support and assistance throughout the preparation of this edition. David Wiesenberg initiated the project and undertook the challenge of creating modern word-processing files from the old electronic files containing the first edition. He also prepared the versions of the Breeding Bird Atlas maps that appear in this edition. These significant contributions are greatly appreciated. Other staff members at The Wooster Book Company who contributed to the production and publication of this edition also deserve my thanks, especially Dennis Kline for his careful proofreading of the manuscript.

—Bruce G. Peterjohn

Species Accounts

Red-throated Loon *Gavia stellata* (Pontoppidan)

Red-throated Loons, like many other water birds, have benefited from the creation of reservoirs. Before 1955, these loons were casual to accidental migrants in Ohio, with most sightings from Lake Erie and the northern counties. The number of records increased during the late 1950s and early 1960s, mostly within the interior counties, where Red-throateds were repeatedly observed on new reservoirs. They have been annually reported since 1965. These increased sightings do not necessarily reflect expanding populations. They may only represent migrants that formerly flew over the state but presently rest and feed on the large lakes, as well as increased numbers of birders searching for migrant water birds on these habitats.

Red-throated Loons are casual to rare fall migrants on large lakes, with two to seven sightings statewide during most years. During the autumn of 1985, an exceptional flight produced at least 13 scattered individuals (Peterjohn 1986a). Most fall migrants are observed along central Lake Erie and on large reservoirs in the glaciated counties. There are very few records from unglaciated Ohio, while the scarcity of records from western Lake Erie is not easily explained. The earliest documented fall migrant was observed at Headlands Beach State Park on September 23, 1990 (Peterjohn 1991a), but they do not normally return until the second half of October. Most are reported during November, peaking between November 10 and 20, when as many as three Red-throateds have been found. Most reports consist of single loons, frequently stopping for only an hour or two before continuing their journey, although some may linger as long as a week. The last fall migrants normally depart by December 12–20.

Red-throated Loons have always been accidental midwinter visitors, with fewer than fifteen sightings between January and early March. Most winter records are along Lake Erie between Cleveland and Ashtabula, including a February 19, 1909, specimen at Ashtabula originally identified as a Pacific Loon (Borror 1950). Inland winter records are limited to loons on Summit Lake in Akron during 1959 and 1965 (Mumford 1959b, Petersen 1965b), at Caesar Creek Reservoir on January 6–19, 1991, and at Killdeer Reservoir on January 13–16, 1991 (Peterjohn 1991b). Most winter records are prior to 1966, when Red-throateds were still infrequently reported from Ohio, with only a single report during the 1980s and three during the 1990s.

Spring Red-throated Loons remain accidental to casual visitors, and are not discovered every year. These migrants appear between mid-March and mid-May and have remained through May 22–26 in northern Ohio. They are invariably solitary individuals, frequently in nonbreeding plumage, and mostly at inland reservoirs in the glaciated counties. There are no summer records.

Pacific Loon *Gavia pacifica* (Lawrence)

Pacific Loons breed across the Arctic tundra from Hudson Bay west to Alaska, and normally winter along the Pacific Coast of North America. They are also rare but regular migrants through the interior western states and casual visitors to the Great Lakes region, where they are most likely to appear during autumn (American Ornithologists' Union 1998). There are currently three acceptable records of this accidental visitor to Ohio. The first Pacific Loon was studied by many observers along Lake Erie at Huron on December 7–10, 1985 (Peterjohn 1986b). A nonbreeding individual was photographed at Alum Creek Reservoir on May 21–22, 1990 (Peterjohn 1990c). The third report was of a single loon observed at Caesar Creek Reservoir on November 24–26, 1996 (Conlon and Harlan 1996b). Careful examination of the large numbers of loons regularly migrating through Ohio will probably uncover additional records of this species.

Common Loon *Gavia immer* (Brünnich)

Few sounds are as enchanting as the calls of a Common Loon, which are mixtures of sharp cries, loud yells, and rolling laughter, unlike the notes of any other bird. They add a mysterious if not supernatural quality to the north woods, especially on a calm moonlit night. In states such as Ohio, where Common Loons do not breed, we have few chances to experience their magical charm, since these loons are normally silent during migration. Occasionally at sunset on a warm April day the laughter of a pair of loons may briefly resound across an Ohio reservoir.

Since breeding Common Loons are strikingly handsome, it is unfortunate they are in a such a hurry to reach their nesting areas. While a few early migrants appear between February 25–March 15, they normally return by March 20–30. Breeding adults are noted first and generally depart by April 15–20. The drab immature loons are regularly observed through May 5–15, and small numbers remain through the end of the month.

Common Loons are uncommon to fairly common spring migrants on large lakes. They are surprisingly scarce along Lake Erie, and greater numbers are observed on inland reservoirs in the central and northern counties. Most spring migrants are encountered in groups of 12 or fewer. Flocks of 25–50 are noteworthy, while the largest concentrations have totaled 75–112 loons.

Formerly accidental to casual summer visitors, reports of nonbreeding Common Loons increased during the 1990s. As many as 16–19 loons lingered into the summers of 1991 and 1997 (Harlan 1991b, Fazio 1997c), although fewer than ten were reported during most years. They prefer Findlay Reservoir, where a maximum of seven appeared in June 1991 (Harlan 1991b). However, they are generally rare in the northern half of the state and casual summer visitors elsewhere. Most disappear by June 15–25 and may represent very late spring migrants. Only four or fewer loons normally spend the entire summer in Ohio, usually as widely scattered singles or pairs. Most summering loons are immatures, but a few nonbreeding adults have been observed.

Common Loons are most numerous in autumn. Early loons noted between August 15 and September 15 may represent nonbreeding summer visitors. The first migrants normally appear between October 5 and 15, while large flights are not expected until the last week of October. The largest movements occur during November, when these loons become common to abundant along Lake Erie and fairly common to locally abundant on large inland lakes.

Along Lake Erie during November, it is difficult to scan from any vantage point and not see a loon. When winds are southerly, only 5–25 loons may be observed daily. Following passage of a cold front, northwesterly winds may produce flights of 75–300+ loons along the lakefront east from Huron. The largest movement totaled 938 past Headlands Beach State Park on November 18, 1989 (Peterjohn 1990a), while flights of 600–804 loons have been reported from other locations. These flights begin at dawn. While some loons fly low over the water, most are high in the air, frequently in groups of 5–50+ heading south or east. They continue to pass overhead for an hour or two after sunrise.

Away from Lake Erie, 3–20 loons are expected on large lakes throughout Ohio. Sizable movements may also be noted as tightly packed flocks visiting inland lakes for a few hours or perhaps a day, or as flocks of loons migrating over land. These flights are most noticeable in the central and northern counties, usually producing flocks of 35–100+ loons. Larger concentrations are possible, with a maximum of 430 at Clear Fork Reservoir, Richland County, on November 8, 1997 (Yoder 1997), and flocks of 200–300+ at other locations across the state.

During most years, numbers of Common Loons are greatly reduced by the first week of December. Most December sightings are of 1–8 loons, with occasional flocks of 15–40. Large inland flights are still possible, such as 357 in Delaware County on December 1, 1986 (Peterjohn 1987a), and several reports of 100–200 loons on lakes in southern Ohio. The last flocks disappear by mid-December, although scattered individuals will remain into the first half of January as long as open water remains available.

Even during mild winters, the last loons usually disappear by January 15–20. Accidental during midwinter, a few loons have attempted to overwinter, as indicated by February sightings at Cleveland, Columbus, Mahoning County, Salem (Columbiana County), and in Delaware County. With the exception of seven at Cleveland on January 15, 1932, and four along the Cleveland lakefront during the very mild weather of January and February

1998 (Rosche 1998a, Williams 1950), all midwinter sightings have been of single loons.

Pied-billed Grebe *Podilymbus podiceps* (Linnaeus)

Migrant Pied-billed Grebes can be found on Ohio's lakes, ponds, rivers, and marshes, preferring vegetated margins where suitable cover is readily available. However, they also frequent open water habitats far from any protective cover. Best known for their ability to dive quickly as danger approaches, Pied-billeds can instantly disappear under water but take flight only with considerable difficulty.

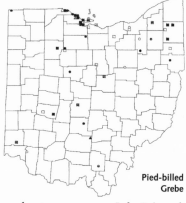

Pied-billed Grebe

Pied-billeds are uncommon to locally abundant and widely distributed migrants each spring and fall. They are least numerous on Lake Erie and within counties lacking sizable lakes and marshes. The timing of their migratory movements are fairly uniform across the state.

The first spring migrants appear between February 20 and March 5, as the ice disappears from lakes and marshes. Peak numbers are usually attained between March 25 and April 20, when normally ten or fewer grebes are observed daily. The largest flights are composed of 15–40 Pied-billeds, although Trautman (1940) reported as many as 50 at Buckeye Lake on several dates before 1940. Smaller numbers may be observed through May 10–20.

They are generally most numerous as fall migrants. The first Pied-billeds may appear during the last half of August; others pass through Ohio until freeze-up. The largest numbers are expected between September 25 and November 20. Fall flocks of 5–20 account for most sightings, but concentrations of 30–75 appear almost annually. The largest flights have been composed of 100–151 Pied-billeds. There are exceptions to this migration pattern. During some years, the largest flocks appear before October 1. In other years, no more than 10–15 individuals may be noted at any location. Influxes of 10–46 are regularly noted in December, when cold weather forces lingering grebes to pass through the state in search of open water. Otherwise, Pied-billeds are usually noted in groups of 1–5 during December.

During relatively mild winters, Pied-billeds become rare winter residents across the state; though they are never numerous, 1–6 may be noted daily. The largest flock totaled 40 at East Fork State Park (Clermont County) during

January 1999 (Whan 1999a). Some spend the entire winter on one lake, others only a few days in January and February. Subfreezing temperatures normally force most Pied-billeds to leave Ohio by December 24–January 15. During these periods of harsh winter weather, 1–12 grebes are regularly encountered at localities retaining open water, including Summit Lake in Akron, hot-water outlets along Lake Erie, and the Great Miami, Scioto, and Ohio Rivers in southern Ohio.

Breeding Pied-billeds are restricted to large marshes, particularly those exceeding ten acres in size where dense emergent vegetation is interspersed with small openings. Once nesting is underway, they become exceedingly shy and seldom stray from dense cover. Breeding grebes are surprisingly vocal, and their presence is regularly detected by their distinctive loud calls. Their nests are constructed of decaying vegetation, as mats tied to stalks of cattails or floating through the marsh. When they are not incubating, the adults cover the eggs with dead vegetation to hide them from predators and to keep them warm. While the earliest nest with eggs was discovered on May 3, downy young have been reported as early as May 17, indicating nest construction can occur during the first half of April. Along Lake Erie, young grebes are regularly observed by late May (Campbell 1940). They are fully grown by late June or early July. Unsuccessful adults will renest and some pairs may raise two broods. A number of nesting attempts have been discovered during July, and partially grown grebes have been reported as late as September 30, 1970, in Hancock County and November 1, 1972, at Magee Marsh Wildlife Area (Kleen and Bush 1973a, Phillips 1980).

Pied-billed Grebes have always been locally distributed summer residents. The largest breeding population occupied the marshes bordering western Lake Erie in Lucas, Ottawa, Sandusky, and Erie Counties, where Hicks (1935a) considered them common to abundant residents. Considerably fewer grebes nested elsewhere. Nesting grebes were recorded from all northeastern counties, where they were generally rare and irregular but became locally common near Cleveland and Youngstown. Pied-billed Grebes were sporadic nesters in central Ohio, with records from Buckeye Lake, Indian Lake, Lake Loramie, and Lake St. Marys, plus Delaware, Madison, Pickaway, and Franklin Counties (Hicks 1935a). In the unglaciated counties, grebes nested in Tuscarawas and Pike Counties (Henninger 1902, Hicks 1937a). The only change to their breeding distribution during the twentieth century was an expansion into the southwestern counties, beginning with a Dayton nesting record in 1955 (Mathena et al. 1984).

As a result of habitat destruction, numbers of breeding Pied-billed Grebes have declined since the 1930s. This decline is most apparent within the northeastern counties, where they have become casual to rare residents, with breeding confirmed or considered probable at only seven locations during the Breeding Bird Atlas (Peterjohn and Rice 1991). Along western Lake Erie, they remain fairly common residents, although midsummer drawdowns may be reducing their numbers. A concentration of 91 at Magee Marsh Wildlife Area on July 20, 1997, is exceptional, and includes breeding adults and young produced that summer (Fazio 1997c). Elsewhere, Pied-billeds tend to be opportunistic nesters, depending upon the availability of suitable habitats. They are very locally distributed and accidental to rare in the western half of Ohio, with as many as 4–6 pairs nesting at Big Island Wildlife Area (Marion County), Killdeer Plains Wildlife Area, Gilmore Ponds (Butler County), and Miami-Whitewater Forest during some years. However, these grebes are irregular at other locations (Peterjohn and Rice 1991). Along the unglaciated Allegheny Plateau, Pied-billed Grebes are accidental summer visitors, with the only recent records from Ross and Jackson Counties (Peterjohn and Rice 1991). While 100–200 pairs may reside along western Lake Erie, the inland population may not exceed 20–30 pairs during most years.

Horned Grebe *Podiceps auritus* (Linnaeus)

Migrant Horned Grebes prefer sizable bodies of water; the greatest numbers appear on Lake Erie and large reservoirs. They are not restricted to these habitats, however, and may be found wherever water birds congregate. This species has a reputation as an irregular and unpredictable migrant, numerous some years and scarce in others, with no apparent explanation for their fluctuations.

Their irregular migratory behavior is most evident during spring. Some years, these grebes are numerous throughout March and disappear by early April. In other years, sizable numbers may not appear until mid-April, or they may mostly bypass Ohio. The first Horned Grebes generally appear by February 25–March 5 and become widespread by March 15. Within the western half of Ohio, their northward movement usually peaks between March 15 and April 5. The largest flights in the eastern counties are usually noted during April. Most depart before April 25, although small numbers may remain into the first half of May. The last stragglers have lingered into the first week of June.

Within the northeastern counties, Horned Grebes become fairly common to locally abundant migrants. Their appearance is irregular along central Lake Erie, where they are nearly absent some years and numerous in others. The largest spring lakefront concentrations totaled 486 at Cleveland on April 4, 1970, and 467 on April 12, 1979 (Kleen 1979c, Petersen 1970c). Most sightings do not exceed 10–40. Larger flocks may appear on inland lakes, with maxima of 800 on Mosquito Creek Reservoir (Trumbull County) on April 16, 1977, and 606 on several lakes in Summit and Portage Counties on April 12–13, 1986

(Kleen 1977c, Peterjohn 1986c). Flocks of 100–300 Horned Grebes have appeared at other northeastern lakes, while daily totals normally are 10–25. These large flights have been recorded east to Lorain County (400 on April 9, 1979) and south to Carroll County (100 on May 1, 1955)(Brooks 1955c, Kleen 1979c).

Horned Grebes are generally uncommon to locally common migrants elsewhere. Spring totals are normally 5–20 daily. Larger flights are restricted to the glaciated counties, where 30–114 Horned Grebes have been observed on a few lakes.

These grebes are accidental nonbreeding summer visitors to the northern counties. Single June grebes have been reported from Toledo, Lorain County, and Mosquito Creek Reservoir; the only summering individuals have been noted from Cleveland during 1985 and Mahoning County in 1992 (Harlan 1992d, Peterjohn 1985d). The latter grebe was injured and could not migrate.

Fall Horned Grebes are more predictable than spring migrants. Extremely early migrants have appeared during August, although some of these individuals may have been nonbreeding summer visitors. The first migrants may return by September 25–October 10 and are regularly encountered by October 18–25. Their maximum abundance is achieved during November. Numbers decline during December, but small numbers remain as long as open water is available.

These migrants are most numerous along Lake Erie, where they are normally common to abundant along the entire lakefront. During most years, totals of 20–100+ develop during November. Larger concentrations of 150–600+ grebes are occasionally detected, although such flocks were scarce during the 1990s. The largest movements were noted at Cleveland: 958 on November 18, 1979, and 693 on November 26, 1978 (Kleen 1979a, 1980a). Periodically, fall Horned Grebes become inexplicably scarce and the largest flights total only 10–25.

They become uncommon to fairly common migrants on inland reservoirs. They are most numerous within the northern and glaciated central counties, where 5–30+ grebes may be tallied, and occasional flights of 80–200+ have been reported. Fewer Horned Grebes pass through the southern and unglaciated counties, where most fall totals are 20 or fewer.

The last fall migrants normally depart between December 20 and January 7. During some years, Horned Grebes are unreported after early January. In other years, a few scattered wintering grebes may be detected or small flights may be apparent during late January or early February. The direction of these midwinter movements is uncertain. In general, Horned Grebes are casual to rare winter visitors to hot-water outlets along central Lake Erie and accidental to casual visitors to all interior counties. Most winter records are of 1–6 grebes, with a maximum of 40 at East Fork State Park (Clermont County) during January 1999 (Whan 1999a). Most Horned Grebes appear for only a few days and are best characterized as temporary visitors rather than winter residents.

Red-necked Grebe *Podiceps grisegena* (Boddaert)

Ohio lies just outside the established Red-necked Grebe migration corridor through the Great Lakes, and these grebes have always been rare visitors. The number of reports has increased since the late 1980s, reflecting improved coverage of their preferred habitats during migration and several noteworthy movements into the state. Red-necked Grebes prefer large lakes and frequently forage far from shore. They are unlikely to be found in other habitats, except for migrants forced to land in fields after encountering inclement weather.

As fall migrants, Red-necked Grebes are casual to rare visitors along Lake Erie, mostly occurring within the Central Basin. They become casual migrants through the glaciated counties but are accidental elsewhere. These migrants are normally detected at one to five localities nearly every year. A large fall movement during 1989 produced 11 reports statewide, including eight from Lake Erie (Peterjohn 1990a). Most fall sightings are of 1–2 grebes.

The earliest fall migrants returned to Lake Erie in Lucas County on September 9, 1978, and the Cleveland area on September 16, 1945, and September 18, 1991 (Kleen 1979a, Peterjohn 1992a, Williams 1950). There are few other sightings prior to October 20–30. They are most likely to appear during November and December. Late migrants usually depart by December 20–25 but may linger into early January if open water remains available.

There are surprisingly few Red-necked Grebe sightings between January 7 and 25. However, these grebes fairly regularly appear in late winter, beginning during the last days of January and continuing throughout February. These late winter grebes are casual visitors along central Lake Erie and northeastern Ohio near Akron but are accidental elsewhere. They are normally detected during five to seven winters each decade, with only one or two sightings and a maximum of three grebes during most years.

A remarkable flight occurred during February 1994, when frigid temperatures completely froze the upper Great Lakes and forced large numbers of Red-necked Grebes to move south into the lower Great Lakes and Mid-Atlantic regions. Ohio was near the western edge of this movement, and there were an unprecedented 61 Red-necked Grebes reported statewide during the month, including 41 inland. The largest concentrations totaled 28 in Washington County on February 14 and 11 at Ashtabula on February 22, while smaller numbers were scattered across the western half of the state (Harlan 1994a). This invasion continued into the spring as the grebes returned northward.

More than 50 additional Red-neckeds were reported, with a maximum of seven at Summit Lake in Akron on March 20. Most departed by the first week of April.

Spring Red-neckeds are normally casual to rare migrants through the northeastern counties and along central Lake Erie but are generally accidental to casual elsewhere, least numerous along the unglaciated Allegheny Plateau. These migrants usually appear at four or fewer localities nearly every year. Most reports are of 1–2 grebes. Small flights are more frequent during spring, such as six at Dayton on April 20, 1924 (Mathena et al. 1984), seven scattered across Mahoning and Trumbull Counties between March 21 and April 10, 1959 (Hall 1959), at least 13 reported from nine locations in northern and central Ohio during March 5–25, 1962 (Graber 1962b), and a statewide total of 11 during spring 1996 (Conlon and Harlan 1996a). These migrants are most frequently reported between March 20 and April 15, although individuals have lingered through May 17, 1998, at Shalersville and May 20, 1926, near Columbus (Borror 1950, Rosche 1998b).

Red-necked Grebes are accidental summer visitors. The only acceptable record was provided by a molting male discovered at Lake St. Marys on August 9, 1940. It remained through August 14, when it was collected (Clark 1994b).

Eared Grebe *Podiceps nigricollis* Brehm

Eared Grebes were unrecorded from Ohio until 1941, when an individual was discovered at Holden Arboretum (Lake County) on April 21. This grebe was collected the following day (Godfrey 1943). Another Eared Grebe was collected on Lake Erie off South Bass Island on November 29, 1945 (Trautman 1946). There were a few additional sight records between 1941 and 1970. The number of sightings increased during the 1970s, and Eared Grebes have been annually reported since 1980.

Their status as spring migrants is obscured by difficulties in separating Eared Grebes from the considerably more numerous Horned Grebes, especially in transitional plumages. They were found at only two- or three-year intervals during the 1970s and 1980s, but were reported nearly annually during the 1990s. Spring Eared Grebes are apparently casual to accidental visitors throughout Ohio. Most reports are from the glaciated counties and Lake Erie. These migrants have been reported as early as March 6, but most confirmed sightings have been between April 10 and May 7, with stragglers through May 22–23. All records are of 1–2 grebes.

This species is an accidental summer visitor. The only report is of one photographed at Kyger Creek Power Plant in Gallia County on July 29–30, 1990 (Hall 1990d).

Eared Grebes are most frequently detected as fall migrants, with one to five sightings annually. They are rare along Lake Erie, usually as isolated individuals loosely associated with flocks of Horned Grebes. Fall migrants are casual to accidental elsewhere, with the majority of reports from the western half of the state. Most reports are of single grebes, although small flocks with as many as five have appeared on inland lakes. An early migrant was noted near Akron between August 20 and 24, 1981 (Peterjohn 1982a), and there have been three other sight records prior to October 1. Most sightings are between November 1 and December 7, with a few stragglers remaining along Lake Erie through December 20–27.

A small flock of Eared Grebes showed remarkable fidelity to the C.J. Brown Reservoir near Springfield. In 1982, four Eared Grebes were discovered there on November 13, remaining into early December (Mathena et al. 1984). In subsequent years through 1987, 3–5 grebes returned to this lake. Their numbers gradually diminished, and only one or two grebes survived into the 1990s. While the breeding and wintering areas of these grebes remain a mystery, their ability to find this reservoir each fall is a testimony to avian navigational skills.

There are only two confirmed midwinter records. An Eared Grebe was discovered on December 25, 1955, at Summit Lake in Akron and remained through February 26, 1956 (Newman 1969). It was observed by many as it wintered on the lake. The other Eared Grebe appeared at Caesar Creek Reservoir on January 30–February 1, 1992 (Peterjohn 1992b).

Western Grebe *Aechmophorus occidentalis* (Lawrence)

Before 1985, the identification of Western Grebes was straightforward. In 1985, however, its two morphs were recognized as distinct species, currently known as Western Grebe (*Aechmophorus occidentalis*) and Clark's Grebe (*A. clarkii*) (AOU 1985). These two species are very similar, requiring careful study to ensure correct identifications. While Western Grebes are the most likely member of this species complex to wander into eastern North America (AOU 1998), Clark's Grebes have appeared east to Illinois and could conceivably occur within Ohio. Hence, all "Western Grebe" sightings earlier than 1985 required reevaluation to determine which species actually appeared in the state.

On the basis of this reevaluation and several subsequent sightings, there are currently nine unequivocal records of this accidental visitor to Ohio. Single specimens were collected at Youngstown on October 28–30, 1913 (Fordyce 1914), and Columbus on April 25–May 13, 1964 (Thomson 1983). Four have been found along Lake Erie: one photographed at Bay Village (Cuyahoga County) on November 24, 1985 (Peterjohn 1986a), another documented in Ottawa County on May 11, 1986 (Peterjohn 1986c), one widely observed at

Rocky River (Cuyahoga County) on December 8–20, 1991 (Peterjohn 1992b), and one at Metzger Marsh Wildlife Area on March 22, 1997 (Fazio 1997b). A Western Grebe along the Maumee River near Waterville, Lucas County, on January 25, 1995 (Brock 1995b) and another at East Fork State Park between January 20 and April 21, 1999 (Armstrong 1999, Whan 1999a) established two of very few midwinter records from the Great Lakes region. One was reported from Clear Fork Reservoir on December 15–18, 1999 (E. Schlabach 1999). Four additional reports of *Aechmophorus* grebes probably pertain to this species: from Pippin Lake (Portage County) on March 30–April 5, 1959 (Newman 1969), Clear Fork Reservoir on April 8–12, 1975 (Kleen 1975c), Buckeye Lake on May 10, 1958 (Thomson 1983), and near Dayton on November 15–18, 1967 (Mathena et al. 1984).

Black-capped Petrel *Pterodroma hasitata* (Kuhl)

A storm along the Atlantic Coast in early October 1898 was thought to be responsible for the appearance of three Black-capped Petrels on the Ohio River near Cincinnati, October 4–5. While one petrel was recovered in Kentucky on October 4, two were found on the Ohio side of the river the next day. All were emaciated and died soon after their capture. One specimen is still preserved in the collection of the Cincinnati Museum of Natural History (Lindahl, 1899). Since these petrels regularly occur in the Atlantic Ocean off the southeastern United States (AOU 1998), a hurricane passing through that region and into Ohio could conceivably produce additional storm-driven records of this pelagic species.

Leach's Storm-Petrel *Oceanodroma leucorhoa* (Vieillot)

Like all storm-petrels, Leach's live on the open sea and normally come to shore only to nest. The presence of one in Ohio is a truly accidental event; this species has been found at fewer than a dozen locations in the interior of North America (AOU 1998). On May 16, 1929, a freshly killed Leach's Storm-Petrel was picked up from a Dayton street by a boy on his way to school. He gave this specimen to his teacher, Miss Winifred Nutting, who had the foresight to ensure its preservation. It is deposited in the Ohio State Museum of Zoology (Blincoe 1930). Its appearance in Ohio on this date is puzzling because there were no storms which might have blown it this far inland.

Northern Gannet *Morus bassanus* (Linnaeus)

Each spring, Northern Gannets return by the thousands to their North Atlantic nesting colonies. After fledging, most young gannets follow their parents to offshore feeding grounds. Occasional young gannets wander up the St. Lawrence River to the Great Lakes, continuing their journeys until they reach Lake Erie.

Ohio's first Northern Gannets were sighted near Cleveland on November 2, 1925, and November 10, 1929. The first specimen was collected at Cedar Point (Erie County) about November 15, 1931 (Williams 1950). There were no additional records until December 1947, when a small flight produced 1–5 gannets daily at Cleveland between December 6 and January 13, plus one record at Toledo (Campbell 1968, Williams 1950). Gannets also appeared at Cleveland during the winter of 1949–1950 (Mayfield 1950b). There were substantiated reports in 1967, 1969, 1976, and 1978. Their status improved in the 1980s, with sightings during seven years, but there were only four reports between 1990 and 1999. All confirmed records have been first-winter gannets during late fall and early winter; none of the spring and summer sightings of adults were supported by convincing details.

Northern Gannets are currently casual late fall and early winter visitors to central Lake Erie. There are at least 19 records between Huron and the Cleveland area. The earliest gannet appeared at Cleveland on November 2, but most sightings are between November 15 and December 15. These individuals usually wander along the lakefront and may appear at several locations over a period of several weeks. Most sightings are of single gannets, although multiple birds were detected during the winters of 1947–1948, 1949–1950, and 1982–1983. If Lake Erie remains open, a few gannets may remain through mid-January; one survived until February 18, 1950, at Cleveland (Mayfield 1950b).

Northern Gannets are accidental visitors to western Lake Erie, with only three published records: single individuals noted between December 6 and January 2. They are also accidental visitors to the interior of Ohio, where there are two reports. A first-winter gannet was intermittently observed at Cincinnati between December 7 and 24, 1967. Captured in a residential yard on the latter date, it had been banded at Bonaventure Island in the Gulf of St. Lawrence on September 9, 1967 (Petersen 1968a). On November 7, 1993, a first-year gannet was observed flying south along I-71 near Brunswick. What was most likely the same individual was found injured in Franklin County on November 10, and subsequently died in captivity (Brock 1994a).

American White Pelican *Pelecanus erythrorhynchos* Gmelin

American White Pelicans were apparently "irregular but not infrequent" visitors to Ohio between 1860 and 1910 (Clark and Sipe 1970, Trautman 1940). Although most early records are based on anecdotal accounts, reports of these distinctive birds are probably correct. Pelicans fairly regularly appeared at Lake St. Marys and Buckeye Lake before 1910, and occasionally there were sightings elsewhere in the western half of the state.

As their continental populations declined after 1910, fewer pelicans were detected in Ohio. They became accidental visitors, with only five published sightings between 1920 and 1940. Their status improved after 1940, especially along western Lake Erie, where Campbell (1968) cited records during twelve years between 1940 and 1967. Pelicans remained accidental visitors to all other areas. This status was maintained through the 1970s. Greater numbers appeared during the 1980s, with annual records since 1982. Their status in Ohio continued to slowly improve during the 1990s.

Throughout most of the twentieth century, White Pelicans were accidental spring migrants, averaging only 1–3 sightings each decade. Before 1940, spring pelicans were only reported from Lake St. Marys and Buckeye Lake. Between 1940 and 1990, most records were along western Lake Erie, with only three reports from other locations, including a flock of eight near Canton on May 19–20, 1945 (Ball 1946).

Their spring status changed during the 1990s, with 1–5 reports during most years after 1991. White Pelicans are currently rare along western Lake Erie and accidental to casual elsewhere, with recent reports scattered across the state except for the southwestern counties. The earliest spring migrant was reported from Lorain on March 7, 1996 (Conlon and Harlan 1996a), but there are few records earlier than mid-April. Pelicans are most likely to appear between April 20 and May 15, with late migrants into the first half of June. These sightings frequently are of single individuals, although small groups of 3–8 have been noted.

Reports of nonbreeding pelicans increased during the 1990s. They have become casual summer visitors along western Lake Erie, but remain accidental elsewhere. Inland summer sightings are restricted to Buckeye Lake, Lake St. Marys, the Cincinnati area, and the Maumee River in Lucas County. These nonbreeders may appear anytime between mid-June and early August. Some remain for only a few days, while others arrive in July and linger well into autumn. With the exception of six at Buckeye Lake on June 21, 1933 (Thomson 1983), all summer reports involve 1–2 birds.

Fall reports of American White Pelicans have increased slightly since the 1980s, producing four or fewer records annually. They have become casual to rare migrants along western Lake Erie but remain accidental elsewhere, most likely to appear within the western half of Ohio. These migrants may appear between the last half of August and mid-November. While there are sightings throughout September and October, in recent years most pelicans have been reported before September 15 or between October 15 and November 15. The latest migrant remained through December 19–20, 1999, in Mahoning County (Whan, in press). All substantiated fall sightings involve six or fewer pelicans.

Brown Pelican *Pelecanus occidentalis* Linnaeus

Normally confined to coastal habitats, Brown Pelicans occasionally wander into the interior of North America and have appeared at a number of locations scattered across the continent (AOU 1998). These wandering pelicans may be found on large lakes or small ponds. Some are driven inland by coastal storms, while others apparently move under their own volition.

An accidental visitor, the first documented Brown Pelican was found along Lake Erie at Bay Village on April 29, 1990 (Peterjohn 1990c). One or possibly more pelicans visited Ohio during 1991, when one photographed at Caesar Creek Reservoir on June 2 (Peterjohn 1992b) may have been the same individual reported from a borrow pit near Vanlue, Hancock County, on May 28 (Harlan 1991a). Perhaps the same pelican summered on Lake Erie that year, splitting its time between the offshore waters of Lake and Ashtabula Counties, Ohio, and Erie County, Pennsylvania (Hall 1991d, Peterjohn 1992a). The most recent report was of one briefly observed in Franklin County on September 18, 1996 (Brock 1997a), approximately two weeks after Hurricane Fran passed to the east of Ohio.

Double-crested Cormorant *Phalacrocorax auritus* (Lesson)

In the early 1800s, Double-crested Cormorants were regular migrants only along Lake Erie. The creation of canal reservoirs provided additional habitats, and breeding populations were established at Buckeye Lake and Lake St. Marys during the 1860s and 1870s (Clark and Sipe 1970, Trautman 1940). Although "large numbers" nested at Lake St. Marys, only 10–15 pairs made up the Buckeye Lake colony. Both colonies were subjected to indiscriminate hunting and egg collecting, and disappeared by the early 1880s.

Their status did not change appreciably between 1900 and the 1940s. Migrant cormorants were most often observed along Lake Erie, where they were uncommon to fairly common during spring and fall. The largest flocks seldom exceeded 10–20 birds. While small numbers may have lingered into winter at Cleveland (Williams 1950), there were very few winter records elsewhere along the lakefront. Migrant cormorants were uncommonly encountered at inland reservoirs.

During the 1950s, extensive use of DDT and other harmful pesticides proved disastrous for Double-crested Cormorants. The accumulation of pesticides in their tissues caused them to lay infertile or thin-shelled eggs. Relatively few young were produced, and populations significantly declined (Weseloh et al. 1995). Within Ohio, reduced numbers were not evident until the late 1950s. By 1965, cormorants became rare throughout the state, with fewer than ten sightings annually of 1–5 individuals.

Even after use of these pesticides was banned, cormorants remained relatively rare during the 1970s. Most reports were of widely scattered individuals or small flocks. An exception was a remarkable concentration of 600 observed near North Bass Island on October 28, 1970 (Campbell 1973). Their recovery during the 1980s was astounding, as the Great Lakes breeding population increased at a rate of nearly 29% per year (Weseloh et al. 1995). For example, a fall peak of 175 along western Lake Erie in 1981 increased to 1,100 by 1983 (Peterjohn 1984a). These increases continued throughout the 1980s and 1990s, producing unprecedented numbers along Lake Erie and on inland lakes.

Double-crested Cormorants are most numerous during autumn, especially along Lake Erie, a major staging area for the Great Lakes nesting population. Very abundant throughout the Western Basin of the lake, daily totals are normally 200–500+, while scattered flocks of 2,000–5,000+ are encountered annually. The largest reported concentrations are an estimated 15,000 near Kelleys Island on September 28, 1996 (Brock 1997a), and an aerial tally of 13,130 for the entire Western Basin on September 29–30, 1993 (Harlan 1994a). These cormorants are generally abundant migrants across the Central Basin of Lake Erie. Their abundance in Erie County is similar to the Western Basin, while from the Cleveland area eastward, the largest concentrations are normally 1,000–2,000+.

Within the interior of Ohio, fall migrants have become uncommon to locally abundant visitors across the state. Most inland sightings are of 25–100, with peak concentrations of 200–1,700+. Reports of 3,000–8,600 from locations in central and northern Ohio are exceptional.

Fall migration begins during the last half of August, and numbers rapidly increase by early September. Peak concentrations occur between September 20 and November 10. Their numbers are greatly reduced by late November, although flocks of 50 or fewer will remain across Ohio until freeze-up.

Formerly a casual winter visitor along Lake Erie and accidental elsewhere, the number of wintering cormorants increased during the 1990s. Small numbers regularly winter at hot-water outlets and other areas with open water along Lake Erie; generally ten or fewer per site, with maxima of 20–26. Away from Lake Erie, Double-crested Cormorants are accidental to locally rare winter residents, with the number of reports reflecting the severity of the weather conditions. They may be absent during the harshest winters, when few sources of open water remain available. Mild winters allow scattered individuals or groups of 2–13 to overwinter on lakes and large rivers, primarily in the southern half of the state, although their numbers tend to diminish as the season progresses.

Following mild winters, the first spring migrants may appear during the last half of February. However, they are not widely distributed until the last half of March. Peak numbers are expected during April and the first week of May. Most migrants depart by May 20, although some northward movement continues into the first half of June. Double-crested Cormorants are abundant spring migrants on Lake Erie, although not in the immense flocks reported during autumn. Between 100 and 300 may be counted daily and peak concentrations are normally 1,000–2,500+. They are uncommon to locally abundant within the inland counties, where fewer than 100 are encountered on most days and the largest flocks have totaled 300–730+.

Double-crested Cormorants have nested in Ontario waters of western Lake Erie since 1939 (Campbell 1968), producing scattered summer sightings in the Ohio portion of the lake into the 1970s. As the Ontario population increased, new colonies were established and produced annual summer records from Ohio since 1979. In June 1987, six pairs of cormorants built nests on Ottawa Wildlife Refuge (Peterjohn 1987d). Several of these pairs apparently laid eggs, although none of the nests were successful. In 1992, 180 pairs of cormorants nested on West Sister Island (Ashley 1992), the first successful breeding attempts in Ohio in more than a century. This colony rapidly expanded to 580 pairs in 1994, 1,480 pairs in 1995, and 1,380 pairs in 1997 (Harlan 1994d and 1995d, Cuthbert et al. 1997). Small numbers were also found nesting on Turning Point Island (Erie County), beginning in 1998 (Fazio 1999).

Nonbreeding cormorants are generally uncommon to fairly common summer residents along central Lake Erie and on large lakes in the northeastern counties. Most reports are of 20 or fewer daily, although flocks of 40–60 have been reported. These nonbreeders are accidental to uncommon in other portions of the state, where 35 or fewer cormorants have been noted at widely scattered locations. Some of these nonbreeders remain for the entire summer, while others linger for only a few days or weeks. A few pairs nested in Mercer County during 1998 (Fazio 1999), and additional inland breeding colonies will likely be established in the future.

Anhinga *Anhinga anhinga* (Linnaeus)

In November 1885, a specimen of this accidental visitor was collected on the Muskingum River near the village of Lowell in Washington County (Jones 1905). The circumstances surrounding this specimen record were never disclosed. Anhingas are occupants of wetlands, lakes, and rivers in the southeastern United States and have occasionally dispersed from their normal range after the breeding season (AOU 1998). The Ohio specimen was probably a result of this dispersal.

Magnificent Frigatebird *Fregata magnificens* Mathews

This accidental visitor from tropical oceans has appeared in Ohio on four occasions. The first Magnificent Frigatebird was collected in Fairfield County during spring 1880 by Emmet Adcock (Trautman and Trautman 1968). This specimen is no longer extant and there is no additional information to substantiate this record. Two specimens were recorded on consecutive days in 1967. One was found dead in a suburb of Cincinnati, Hamilton County, on September 29. The other was discovered by Thomas Nye at Clear Fork Reservoir, Richland County, on September 30. When collected the following day, it proved to be a greatly emaciated adult female in fresh fall plumage (Trautman and Nye 1968). The fourth Magnificent Frigatebird was photographed at East Harbor State Park on October 17, 1998.

With their ability to soar at high altitudes for long distances, Magnificent Frigatebirds occasionally wander far from their established range. They have been recorded along both coasts north to Alaska and Newfoundland and at a number of localities in the interior of North America (AOU 1998). These extralimital frigatebirds normally appear during summer and autumn and are frequently displaced by hurricanes, although such an event does not explain the presence of two in Ohio during late September 1967.

American Bittern *Botaurus lentiginosus* (Rackett)

At sunrise on a warm spring morning, a strange sound like a distant pump or a mallet driving a stake into the mud arises from a large marsh along western Lake Erie. It is instantly recognized as the territorial notes of an American Bittern, whose unique calls are not likely to be confused with any other noise coming from the marsh.

Nesting bitterns prefer large undisturbed wetlands whose dense vegetation is broken by scattered small pools. Occasionally they occupy bogs, large

American Bittern

wet meadows, and dense shrubby swamps. Nests have also been found in upland hayfields (Walker and Franks 1928). Their nests are platforms constructed of dead vegetation over shallow water. Within Ohio, nesting activities are initiated during May, and nests with eggs are expected between mid-May and mid-June. Most clutches hatch during June, and recently fledged young normally appear by late July (Braund 1939b, Campbell 1968, Price 1934b, Williams 1950).

At one time, the American Bittern's strange territorial calls were regularly heard in Ohio marshes. In the early 1900s, Jones (1903) considered them local summer residents wherever suitable swamps and bogs were found. Their numbers were declining by the 1930s. Hicks (1935a) cited summer records from only the northern and central counties. Breeding American Bitterns were common within the extensive marshes bordering western Lake Erie. They were uncommon to rare in every northeastern county south to Wayne, Stark, and Columbiana, with scattered records elsewhere south to Guernsey, Perry, Franklin, Champaign, and Mercer Counties.

Of all factors responsible for this decline, habitat destruction is undoubtedly the most important. Wetlands have been continuously drained and filled, especially within the interior counties. Remaining wetlands are mostly small, isolated areas or narrow strips of emergent vegetation; habitats unsuitable for nesting American Bitterns. Even where suitable marshes are available, spring and summer drawdowns are particularly detrimental to breeding bitterns.

These factors adversely affected bittern populations in subsequent decades. At Lake St. Marys, American Bitterns regularly summered through 1948, but all breeding habitat was eliminated by the early 1960s (Clark and Sipe 1970). Similar declines were evident in the northeastern counties. Despite occasional breeding records at new sites, such as a Carroll County nest in 1956 (Buchanan 1980), most nesting American Bitterns disappeared from the interior of Ohio by 1965. They also declined along western Lake Erie. Campbell (1968) cited an abrupt decline during 1945, followed by substantially reduced numbers. Despite slight increases between 1969 and 1973 (Campbell 1973), breeding bitterns remained alarmingly low through the 1980s. Their status did not change during the 1990s, and their statewide breeding population remains extremely small.

American Bitterns are rare summer residents within the western Lake Erie marshes in Lucas and Ottawa Counties, where the total population is no more than 10–20 pairs. They are casual to rare summer residents within the northeastern counties. Since 1980, scattered reports from Geauga, Summit, Portage, Trumbull, and Mahoning Counties indicate a small breeding population still remains, probably fewer than ten pairs. Other nesting American Bitterns sporadically reside at Big Island Wildlife Area (Marion County) and Springville Marsh (Seneca County). Elsewhere, American Bitterns are accidental to casual summer visitors, mostly within the northern half of the state, including a recent nesting record from Hancock County (Whan 1999b). There are also several sightings from the Cincinnati-Dayton area, a report from Lake Rupert (Vinton County) (Peterjohn and Rice 1991), and a report from Crown City Wildlife Area (Gallia and Lawrence Counties) (Whan 1999b).

When their continental populations were larger, migrant bitterns were more frequently encountered. Declining breeding populations have significantly diminished the numbers of migrants passing through Ohio. In spring, the first American Bitterns may appear during the last half of March, but are usually encountered by April 5–12. They are mostly noted between April 15 and May 10 as rare to uncommon migrants along western Lake Erie, casual to rare visitors to the glaciated counties, and accidental to casual along the unglaciated Allegheny Plateau. When populations were larger, 4–20 could be observed daily at some inland marshes and along western Lake Erie (Campbell 1968, Trautman 1940). Since 1960, most spring reports are of single bitterns, with maxima of 4–8. Migrant bitterns are not found only in wetlands; they have been flushed from pastures, fallow fields, and other upland habitats. One of the first American Bitterns I ever observed was perched 15 feet high in a spruce tree, looking very out of place in a residential neighborhood.

American Bitterns were formerly more numerous as fall migrants. Trautman (1940) reported peaks of 25–37 daily at Buckeye Lake during the 1920s and 1930s. Campbell (1968) observed similar numbers along western Lake Erie before 1940. In recent years, they have become casual to rare fall migrants along western Lake Erie and accidental to locally rare elsewhere, with most reports of only 1–2 daily. While migrants may appear by the last week of August, they are generally encountered between September 15 and October 10. Late bitterns may linger into November.

A few American Bitterns have attempted to overwinter in Ohio. Most winter sightings are from the western Lake Erie marshes, where they are casual visitors with at least thirteen records (Campbell 1968, 1973). Some of these bitterns survived into February. Away from these marshes, American Bitterns are accidental winter visitors, with a single December record from Youngstown, two winter sightings in the Buckeye Lake-Newark area, and at least six reports from the Cleveland area. Most of these winter sightings were before 1965, although one was found in the Cuyahoga Valley National Recreation Area on February 15, 1998 (Rosche 1998b).

Least Bittern *Ixobrychus exilis* (Gmelin)

At one time, Least Bitterns were locally common summer residents in Ohio. Bales (1911a) reported 14 nests in one Pickaway County marsh in 1907, and similar numbers were distributed in other wetlands within the northern and central counties during the early 1900s. Extensive marshes supported larger populations. Trautman (1940) considered Least Bitterns "the most numerous nesting heron" at Buckeye Lake during the 1920s and 1930s, estimating 40–90 nesting pairs annually. As many as 20 pairs nested at Lake St. Marys, and they were common in the marshes bordering western Lake Erie (Campbell 1940,

Clark and Sipe 1970). These numbers exhibited considerable annual variation, however.

By the mid-1930s, Least Bitterns were experiencing local declines, especially at inland marshes (Hicks 1935a). Despite these declines, Least Bitterns remained fairly common summer residents within western Lake Erie marshes. They were very locally distributed elsewhere, common at a few sites and rare within most counties south to Columbiana, Guernsey, Muskingum, Licking, Pickaway, Mercer, and Logan

Least Bittern

(Hicks 1935a, 1937a). Their declines were most apparent between 1935 and 1965, when wetland drainage activities were prevalent. Least Bitterns disappeared from many counties and even sizable populations at Buckeye Lake and Lake St. Marys declined substantially or were entirely eliminated. Nonetheless, breeding Least Bitterns spread into southwestern counties. Nesting pairs were first recorded in Montgomery County in 1935, Butler and Clermont Counties in 1938, and annually in Warren County since 1960 (Kemsies and Randle 1953, Mathena et al. 1984). Reduced numbers were also noted within the western Lake Erie marshes. This decline was obscured by annual fluctuations, but reasonably stable populations were maintained into the early 1960s (Anderson 1960, Campbell 1968). Campbell (1973) noted declines between 1969 and 1973; additional reductions continued into the 1980s, but their status did not significantly change during the 1990s.

Least Bitterns are currently uncommon residents of the western Lake Erie marshes, with 1–10+ pairs occupying every extensive wetland that is not annually drawn down. Away from western Lake Erie, they are very locally distributed and generally rare summer residents south to Columbiana, Carroll, Licking, Warren, and Hamilton Counties (Peterjohn and Rice 1991). As many as 11 males have been counted in Mentor Marsh (Lake County) (Peterjohn 1986c), and a few pairs are scattered within other northeastern counties. They are known from very widely scattered marshes elsewhere, with 1–4 breeding pairs at most sites and a maximum of eight at Miami-Whitewater Park (Hamilton County) in 1996 (Brock 1997b). These bitterns are mostly absent along the unglaciated Allegheny Plateau except for a few pairs in Specht Marsh (Carroll County) and a territorial male recorded in Ross County during 1986 (Peterjohn and Rice 1991).

Least Bitterns normally remain hidden among dense vegetation and are unlikely to be seen except as a small heron briefly flying over the cattails. On rare occasions, one may perch at the tops of cattails or quietly hunt at the edge of a small pool. Least Bitterns are not as vocal as their larger relative, the American Bittern, producing quiet cuckoo-like notes at dawn or dusk.

The earliest Least Bitterns returned to Dayton and western Lake Erie by April 10–11 (Mathena et al. 1984, Whan 1999a), but these birds do not normally appear until April 25–May 5. Most spring migrants and summer residents return during May, usually as 1–4 daily in recent years. When populations were larger, Trautman (1940) observed 20–60 Leasts at Buckeye Lake in late May. Their northward migration continues into the first week of June. Spring migrants are casual to rare away from nesting locations.

Least Bitterns begin nesting shortly after returning to their territories. Nest construction has been noted by May 9 and continues into June (Trautman 1940). Their nests are simple platforms of dried vegetation suspended between cattails 0.5 to 2.5 feet above water. They are rarely placed in dense shrubs (Bales 1911a). The first eggs are laid in mid-May and most clutches are complete by early June. Renesting efforts are responsible for nests with eggs through August 3 (Hicks 1933a, Trautman 1940). The young normally hatch by mid-June, although Trautman (1940) recorded young out of the nest by June 10. Dependent young have been noted until late July or early August.

Their fall migration begins in late July and apparently peaks between August 15 and September 10 (Trautman 1940). While these movements produced daily tallies of 5–25 bitterns before 1940, most recent fall sightings are of single individuals, with maxima of 4–8. These migrants are casual to rare in every county. The last migrants normally depart by October 3–7, except for a few stragglers into late October. The latest Least Bitterns were an injured bird in Cuyahoga County on November 12, 1996 (Conlon and Harlan 1996b), and singles in Ottawa and Lucas Counties through November 13, 1960, and December 27, 1970 (Campbell 1968, 1973).

The rare dark color phase known as "Cory's" Least Bittern has been substantiated only once within Ohio: a specimen was collected at Toledo on May 25, 1907 (Campbell 1968). There are also several undocumented sight records of this color phase.

Great Blue Heron *Ardea herodias* Linnaeus

This stately heron is a conspicuous component of our summer avifauna, frequently observed along streams, lakes, and marshes. Foraging Great Blues are the epitome of patience as they stalk their aquatic prey. As described by Dawson (1903):

"While standing knee-deep in the water of some pond or stream, awaiting its customary prey of minnows or frogs, it may remain for an hour as motionless as a bronze statue; then with a movement like lightning, the head is drawn back and suddenly shot downward, and a wriggling fish is transfixed on the spear-like beak. A deft toss of the head puts the fish up and transfers it to the inside, and the bird moves with quiet, measured step to another station …"

Great Blue Heron

Observations of feeding Great Blue Herons are taken for granted today, but they have not always been numerous and widely distributed residents in Ohio. Their numbers were greatly diminished by the millinery trade during the 1800s. Repeated persecution caused their disappearance from portions of the state (Jones 1903). Complete protection allowed them to recover during the early twentieth century. By the mid-1930s, Hicks (1935a) cited breeding records from thirty-three counties and historic records from thirteen others. He estimated the statewide population at 1,500–2,000 pairs, with heronries south through Warren, Franklin, Tuscarawas, and Trumbull Counties. However, a large heronry near Fremont supported 1,118 nests in 1935 (Campbell 1968), indicating that Hicks' population estimate was probably low.

Great Blue Heron populations continued to expand during subsequent decades, a trend documented on Breeding Bird Survey (BBS) routes since the mid-1960s (Sauer et al. 1998). A statewide survey of heron colonies was conducted during 1980–1981, producing reports of 89 colonies within 52 counties (Peterjohn and Rice 1991). This survey has not been repeated, but given increasing population trends, the number of colonies has undoubtedly increased during subsequent years. Our statewide population is not precisely known, but probably exceeds 5,000 pairs.

These herons are currently abundant summer residents along western Lake Erie. The huge heronry on West Sister Island supported a maximum of 2,400 nests in 1993 (Harlan 1994a), but declined to 1,400 pairs in 1995 (Harlan 1995d) due to competition with Double-crested Cormorants for nest sites. At least three other colonies near Sandusky Bay number in the hundreds of pairs (Peterjohn and Rice 1991). Summer totals of 50–150+ individuals may be regularly observed in this area. Considerably fewer herons breed elsewhere. Great Blues are fairly common to locally abundant summer residents throughout northern and central Ohio, with colonies in most counties south to Belmont, Hocking, Ross, and Darke (Peterjohn and Rice 1991). Most colonies support 10–75 pairs, while heronries with 100–300+ pairs are known from Buckeye Lake, Senecaville Reservoir (Noble County), Lordstown (Trumbull County), and Ashtabula County. Summer totals are of 5–30 herons daily within these counties, although counts of 100+ are possible near the larger colonies. Summering Great Blues become uncommon to fairly common in the southern counties. Regular sightings of ten or fewer herons daily indicate a few colonies probably exist within this portion of Ohio, but their locations have never been discovered.

Great Blue Herons may nest in tall trees near feeding areas, but many inland colonies are in isolated woodlots several miles from streams or lakes. A large heronry is an exciting place. Early in their nesting cycle, courtship displays are repeated, nests are reconstructed, and territorial strife is evident as they maneuver for prime nest sites. Later in the season, activities are more sedate, with the murmur of hungry young greeting each returning adult. Not all Great Blues nest in large colonies; some form heronries of only 2–5 pairs. These small colonies generally exist for only a few years, in contrast with the large colonies, which may remain intact for more than forty years when undisturbed.

The first clutches are laid shortly after the nest has been refurnished. Incubating adults have been noted by March 12 in central Ohio and the last half of the month along Lake Erie. Most pairs are incubating during April. Young herons normally hatch between late April and mid-May. Recently fledged young have been noted by June 23 but are most likely to appear during July. The last young herons may not leave the nest until mid-August.

Great Blue Herons return as soon as the ice melts from streams and lakes; by February 15–25 during warm seasons but not until mid-March in exceptionally cold years. Their northward movements peak between March 20 and April 15. Migrants may be noted through the first week of May. This migration seldom produces sizable movements. Along western Lake Erie, large concentrations may develop within drawndown marshes and 200–400+ herons have been counted in Ottawa and Lucas Counties.

Sizable concentrations are more likely to appear in late summer and autumn. Along western Lake Erie, fall flocks of 100–250 are observed annually, while as many as 400–1,000+ have gathered in a single drawndown marsh. Similar concentrations do not normally develop elsewhere; most observations are of 40 or fewer herons, with occasional flocks of 100–200. Maximum abundance is normally attained between July 15 and September 30, although Great Blues remain fairly common to abundant until late November. Individuals and groups of 5–20+ are regularly encountered until subfreezing temperatures force them to depart.

As winter residents, very few Great Blue Herons were reported before 1940. The few sightings were of scattered individuals or groups of 2–4. A report of 35 wintering Great Blues at Akron on January 20, 1935, was exceptional (Baird 1935a). Their wintering numbers have substantially increased during subsequent decades, especially in the 1990s, as their breeding populations have expanded. These numbers fluctuate annually depending upon the severity of the weather conditions, becoming most numerous during milder winters. Great Blue Herons are currently fairly common winter residents along western Lake Erie, where 5–20 may be observed daily. Concentrations of 50–120+ have been noted during some years, and Christmas Bird Count totals of 60–110 may occur in milder seasons. They are uncommon to fairly common along central Lake Erie, usually in groups of ten or fewer, with a midwinter maximum of 44 at Eastlake on February 5, 1994 (Brock 1994b). Away from Lake Erie, Great Blue Herons are generally uncommon to rare winter residents, with most sightings of 1–5 daily, although Christmas Bird Count totals of 25–50+ are possible during relatively mild seasons. Many inland birds disappear later in winter once the water freezes, and the largest midwinter concentrations have totaled 50–51 at several central Ohio sites in mid-January.

Great Egret *Ardea alba* (Linnaeus)

Watching an elegant Great Egret as it patiently forages within a marsh, quietly preens while standing on a muskrat house, or roosts in a tall dead tree, it is difficult to imagine anybody could shoot one for its breeding plumes. Yet, breeding egrets were regularly persecuted in the late 1800s, nearly causing their demise in North America. Before 1880, Great Egrets were "rather common" late summer visitors to Ohio (Wheaton 1882). But as the plume trade flourished, fewer egrets visited Ohio, and their late summer flights ceased before 1895 (Hicks 1931). By the turn of the twentieth century, they were rare visitors, no longer observed annually (Jones 1903).

Great Egret

Great Egrets remained sporadic visitors into the early 1920s. Beginning in 1924, they regained their status as regular late summer visitors, with four to fourteen sightings annually. These records were scattered across the state between mid-July and early December; only the western Lake Erie marshes hosted egrets each year (Hicks 1931).

In 1930, Ohio experienced its first Great Egret invasion of the twentieth century. This invasion produced sightings of 755 egrets from 110 localities in 45 counties (Hicks 1931). The largest concentrations totaled 55 in Portage County, 46 near Toledo, and flocks of 20–25 elsewhere. Late summer egrets were regularly reported throughout the 1930s, with invasions during 1933 and 1936. The 1933 movement brought a maximum of 190 egrets along western Lake Erie and 52 near Youngstown (Campbell 1940, Sim 1936b). In 1936, their invasion was most noticeable in the western counties, with early August totals of 64 at Lake Loramie and 212 at Lake St. Marys (Baird 1936c).

These late summer movements normally commenced during mid-July. Largest concentrations were noted between the first week of August and first week of September. Most departed by early October. Small numbers also appeared in spring, usually during the last half of April and May. A few remained through the summer.

The 1940s brought the first Great Egret breeding records. A single pair was discovered nesting within a Great Blue Heron colony along Sandusky Bay in Sandusky County during 1940 (Campbell 1947). In 1946, a colony of 25 pairs of Great Egrets was discovered on West Sister Island (Campbell 1968). Away from western Lake Erie, 1–2 pairs nested at Lake St. Marys between 1942 and 1944 (Clark and Sipe 1970). Their status was also changing as more egrets appeared during spring. However, they were still mostly known as late summer visitors, although the invasions of the 1930s were not repeated. Away from western Lake Erie, concentrations in excess of 15–20 egrets were exceptional.

Similar trends continued through the 1950s and 1960s. The western Lake Erie breeding population slowly grew to an estimated 125 nests on West Sister Island in 1959 (Campbell 1968). As many as 25 pairs nested at Winous Point (Ottawa County) through 1959, although only one pair remained in 1960 (Anderson 1960). As this breeding population increased, Great Egrets became numerous summer residents throughout the western Lake Erie marshes. Large concentrations occasionally developed, including 255 near Toledo on September 25, 1959 (Campbell 1968). Elsewhere, small numbers regularly appeared throughout Ohio each spring, while the late summer movements were reduced to a trickle. Concentrations in excess of ten egrets were exceptional away from western Lake Erie.

The Lake Erie breeding population continued to increase during subsequent decades, although the rate of increase slowed in the 1990s. Similar trends were less apparent away from western Lake Erie, especially within inland counties, where increased numbers were evident only since the late 1980s.

Great Egrets are currently common to abundant summer residents in the marshes bordering western Lake Erie. The first migrants normally appear between March 17 and 25 and most breeding egrets return by April 20–25. West Sister Island hosts the largest breeding colony, with an estimated 1,040 nests in 1991 increasing to 1,120 by 1995 (Harlan 1991b, 1995d). A second colony on Turning Point Island (Erie County) hosts 20–30 pairs. Single pairs occasionally nested at Winous Point near Sandusky Bay and in other heronries near the lake (Peterjohn and Rice 1991). Their breeding chronology is generally 2–3 weeks later than Great Blue Herons, although nests with large young have been reported as early as July 5 (Hicks 1944, Peterjohn and Rice 1991). Great Egrets are numerous until early October, with only small numbers normally remaining until early November. A concentration of 96 at Ottawa Wildlife Refuge on November 3, 1991, was exceptional for late autumn (Harlan 1992a).

Throughout the breeding season, daily totals of 30–60 egrets are possible along western Lake Erie. Spring flocks of 100–200 have developed in drawndown marshes. During August and September, flocks of 150–250 appear during most years, and 466 were counted at Ottawa Wildlife Refuge on September 21, 1978 (Kleen 1979a).

Along central Lake Erie, Great Egrets are rare to uncommon migrants, slightly more numerous during autumn. Spring migrants normally appear between March 25 and May 15, while fall egrets are most frequent from mid-August through late October, with a few lingering into November. In recent years, most reports are of 1–5 egrets. They are casual to rare nonbreeding summer visitors as scattered individuals along the Cleveland-Lorain lakefront.

Within the interior of Ohio, migrant Great Egrets are casual to uncommon during spring and casual to fairly common in autumn, generally most numerous in the glaciated counties. The timing of their inland migration is similar to their movements along central Lake Erie. Spring migrants are normally detected in groups of six or fewer, with occasional reports of 10–18. They are more numerous during autumn, when 15 or fewer appear at scattered sites and flocks of 20–30 can develop during some years. A flock of 64 migrating over Tuscarawas County on October 15, 1995, was the largest inland report in recent decades (Harlan 1996a).

Nonbreeding egrets are casually noted at inland lakes and marshes during summer, generally as isolated individuals. In 1996, a pair of Great Egrets was discovered nesting in a Great Blue Heron colony along the Scioto River in northern Pickaway County (Carver 1998). Summering egrets were also observed near that colony in 1998, the same year that another pair exhibited nesting behavior at a heronry in Butler County during late June. As the western Lake Erie breeding population continues to increase, additional inland nesting attempts are likely.

Great Egrets have always been accidental winter visitors to Ohio. Before 1970, the only published winter record was an egret observed near Peninsula (Summit County) on January 14, 1940 (Walker 1940a). Beginning in the 1970s, a few egrets lingered in the western Lake Erie marshes until freeze-up, normally disappearing by December 10–25. The mild winter of 1973–1974 allowed one to remain at Magee Marsh Wildlife Area through January 4 (Kleen 1974b). As many as seven egrets remained into January in 1982, 1983, 1987, and 1998, and one successfully survived the winter of 1982–1983 within these marshes (Peterjohn 1982b, 1983b). Away from western Lake Erie, a few Great Egrets have remained through December 10–19 and one was found in Holmes County through January 6, 1988 (Peterjohn 1988b).

Snowy Egret *Egretta thula* (Molina)

The historic status of Snowy Egrets was obscured by the inability of early ornithologists to correctly identify small white herons. Jones (1903) considered Snowy Egrets "rare and irregular" summer visitors during the nineteenth century, but others thought that many of the early sightings were probably of Little Blue Herons (Hicks 1931). In all likelihood, Snowy Egrets were casual late summer visitors during the 1800s, although there are no extant specimens to substantiate this belief.

Snowy Egret

After Snowy Egret populations were decimated by plume hunters during the last decades of the nineteenth century, this species seldom visited Ohio during late summer. Between 1900 and 1929, the only published records were single Snowies at Buckeye Lake in 1901 and near Youngstown during 1924 (Skaggs 1936b, Trautman 1940).

During the 1930s, the late summer invasions of southern herons produced a number of Snowy Egret sightings. These reports are plagued by misidentifications and their true status during this decade is uncertain. However, Snowies apparently appeared most years as visitors between late July and early October. Most confirmed sightings were of scattered individuals, while a few flocks of 3–7 Snowies were also reported. These sightings were usually from the northern half of Ohio.

During the 1940s and 1950s, Snowy Egrets sporadically appeared as scattered individuals or occasional flocks of 4–7. With the exception of a few spring sightings, they mostly appeared in late summer and early fall. In the mid-1950s, Snowy Egrets began to appear more regularly during spring, while the number of fall records became progressively fewer. This trend continued into the 1960s as the number of sightings noticeably increased along western Lake Erie, where Campbell (1968) cited fifteen records from the Toledo area between 1962 and 1967. This increase was not apparent elsewhere.

Their status changed after 1970 with the development of a small breeding population along western Lake Erie. Small numbers summered in these marshes as early as 1970–1973 (Campbell 1973). In 1978, a Snowy was observed making regular visits to the heronry on West Sister Island, but breeding was not established there until 1983, when two nests were discovered (Kleen 1978d, Peterjohn and Rice 1991). This population increased to 8–10 pairs by 1987, with similar numbers nesting there during most subsequent years (Harlan 1995d, Peterjohn and Rice 1991). A single Snowy frequented the Turning Point Island heronry in 1993 (Harlan 1994a) and a few pairs subsequently began nesting at that site.

Snowy Egrets are currently rare to locally uncommon summer residents in the western Lake Erie marshes. While they occasionally return during the first half of April, the first Snowies are usually encountered during April 25–May 7. Spring reports normally total five or fewer, with maxima of 11–18. Individuals or small flocks are occasionally observed throughout the summer. Their breeding activities normally commence during May and young fledge by late July or August. Once the young fledge, flocks of 3–7 Snowies regularly appear and as many as 11–20 have congregated during some years. These flocks usually remain until late September. Late migrants have been noted through October 25, 1993 (Harlan 1994a).

Away from western Lake Erie, the number of reports increased during the 1990s. Snowy Egrets are accidental to casual spring visitors, with most recent records from the western half of the state. They average 1–4 reports annually of widely scattered singles or pairs, although ten were noted near Waterville, Lucas County, on May 5, 1992 (Harlan 1992c). The earliest Snowy returned to Ashtabula County on March 31, 1962 (Graber 1962c), but most records occur between April 20 and May 20. They are accidental summer visitors, with three reports in June and two in July during the 1990s. Fall migrants have become nearly annual visitors away from western Lake Erie, producing 1–2 sightings during most years. They are accidental to casual in autumn as singles or groups of 2–4, primarily in the western half of Ohio. These migrants are most likely to occur between August 15 and October 5.

Little Blue Heron *Egretta caerulea* (Linnaeus)

A flock of Little Blue Herons roosting in a large dead tree silhouetted by an August sunset is a scene associated with the swamps of the southeastern United States. Yet it has also been observed in Ohio during periodic invasions of southern herons. No single factor adequately explains these mysterious irruptions of immature herons, although droughts combined with successful nesting seasons may contribute to them. While several species of herons are involved in these flights, the Little Blue Heron is one of the prominent components.

Little Blues have not always been regular visitors to Ohio. Although they visited the state during the nineteenth century, there are no specimen records to substantiate their presence, and identification problems obscured their status during this era. The millinery trade decimated populations of Little Blues and other herons during the late 1800s, and all southern herons were virtually absent from Ohio after the early 1880s.

With protection of their nesting colonies, their populations recovered and the first Ohio specimen was collected along the Scioto River in Pike County during August 1901. Other Little Blues were observed in Butler County at the same time (Henninger 1901, Hicks 1931). Between 1905 and 1920, they remained rare and very irregular visitors. During the 1920s, Little Blue Herons became regular late summer and early fall visitors, appearing in all portions of the state. Although their numbers fluctuated, there were as many as nineteen reports annually between 1924 and 1929 (Hicks 1931). They were most frequently encountered in flocks of six or fewer, with several reports of 11–13.

The 1930s were the decade of the southern heron, with immense movements during several years. Little Blues were the most frequently encountered southern invader, appearing in numbers that are almost inconceivable today. The largest invasion occurred between late July and early September of 1930. Hicks (1931) compiled reports from ninety-five localities in forty counties totaling 1,185 individuals. Only a small number of adults were encountered in flocks scattered across all portions of the state. During August, the largest flocks included 85 in Lucas County, 77 at Buckeye Lake, 52 in Holmes County, 45 in Portage County, 28 in Butler County, and 26 in Columbiana County (Hicks 1931, Marshall 1931). Another widespread movement occurred during 1934. While they were noted in all sections of the state, only a few large flocks developed, such as 62 at Youngstown and 37 at Dayton (Baird 1934c, Mathena et al. 1984). The last statewide movement occurred in 1939, but large concentrations developed only along western Lake Erie, with a maximum of 35 in Lucas County (Campbell 1940).

While Little Blues remained regular fall visitors during the 1940s, the massive invasions of the previous decade were not repeated. They were reported each year, mostly in groups of six or fewer. The largest flock totaled 20 in Hancock County in August 1949 (Philips 1980). In addition, adult Little Blues began to appear as irregular spring visitors. During the 1950s, numbers of fall visitors gradually declined and large concentrations were unreported. Conversely, spring records continued to accumulate. These trends continued through the 1960s, except for small movements during July and August 1963, 1965, and 1966. These movements produced flocks of 21 at Cincinnati and six at Dayton in late July 1965. Small numbers were reported throughout the state during late summer 1966 (Petersen 1965d, 1966c). Since the mid-1960s, Little Blue Herons have not staged any noticeable fall movements into Ohio, and the number of reports have gradually decreased in recent decades.

Little Blue Herons briefly established a very small breeding population along western Lake Erie, where they initially summered in these marshes in 1969 (Campbell 1973). During June 1978, adults were observed making daily flights to the heronry on West Sister Island. Two nesting pairs were documented on the island in 1983 (Kleen 1978d, Peterjohn 1983d). One or two pairs nested there through 1991 (Ashley 1992), but have been absent during subsequent years.

Little Blues are currently rare spring and fall visitors to western Lake Erie and accidental to rare elsewhere, least numerous in the southeastern counties. They normally produce one to five records annually each spring and fall, although they may be unreported during some seasons. In recent years as many as three Little Blues have been found along western Lake Erie, but only 1–2 have been noted at other locations.

While an exceptionally early migrant returned to Columbus on March 19, 1978 (Kleen 1978c), most spring arrivals are between April 20 and May 7. Except along western Lake Erie, spring Little Blues depart by May 20–27. Fall visitors may appear by mid-July, with peak numbers between July 25 and August 30. Most depart by September 10–15, with occasional stragglers into early October.

Tricolored Heron *Egretta tricolor* (Müller)

Tricolored Herons occupy coastal marshes along the Gulf of Mexico and the Atlantic Coast north to southern New England (AOU 1998). At one time, they rarely wandered even fifty miles inland. The appearance of Ohio's first record, a specimen collected in Ashtabula County on April 22, 1954, was astonishing because it represented one of the first Tricolored Herons ever noted in the Great Lakes region (Trautman and Trautman 1968). Since the late 1960s, these herons have demonstrated a greater tendency to wander away from coastal marshes. While they remain among the rarest herons within the interior of eastern North America, they have become rare but fairly regular visitors to the lower Great Lakes area.

Following Ohio's 1954 specimen, Tricolored Herons were unrecorded until 1971, when there were two sight records from marshes along western Lake Erie. Another was reported from these marshes during 1973 (Campbell 1973, Thomson 1983). There were single sight records elsewhere during 1976 and 1977. Beginning in 1979, this heron became a rare but regular nonbreeding summer visitor to the western Lake Erie marshes, where at least one was reported in every subsequent year except 1980, 1994, and 1999.

While a Tricolored appeared as early as April 18, 1971 (Campbell 1973), they usually return during May. The latest fall records are during the second week of September. In 1979, a Tricolored Heron was observed making regular flights to the West Sister Island heronry but nesting was not confirmed (Kleen 1979d). A Tricolored Heron also visited this heronry during the summer of 1986, but neither a mate nor a nest could be located (Peterjohn and Rice 1991).

Tricolored Herons are accidental visitors elsewhere. Other lakefront records are the Ashtabula County specimen plus four documented sight records in the Cleveland area. Inland sightings are limited to an undocumented record near Cincinnati on May 1, 1977 (Kleen 1977c), and single Tricoloreds near Pickerington on April 28–30, 1981 (Peterjohn 1981b), near Barberton (Summit County) on May 5, 1987 (Peterjohn 1987d), in Logan County on May 6, 1989 (Peterjohn 1989c), at East Fork State Park on April 18–19, 1991 (Peterjohn 1991c), and an immature at East Branch Reservoir (Geauga County) on August 21–29, 1993 (Harlan 1994a). Of these eleven records, seven are during spring, including an early migrant at Cleveland on April 6, 1986 (Peterjohn 1986c). There are single Cleveland area sightings during July, August, and September.

Cattle Egret *Bubulcus ibis* (Linnaeus)

Few birds have undergone such a dramatic and widely publicized range expansion as Cattle Egrets. Formerly native to Africa, they colonized South America and quickly spread through Central America and the Caribbean region to occupy much of North America. Their North American range expansion was most noticeable from the 1950s to the 1970s. Their populations apparently stablized, if not declined somewhat, during the 1980s and 1990s.

Ohio's first Cattle Egret was discovered near Columbus on May 23, 1958 (Nolan 1958c). Their next appearance was along western Lake Erie, with several reports from Ottawa and Lucas Counties during summer 1960 (Campbell

1968, Mumford 1960c). Spring 1961 produced a small flight along Lake Erie during May, including five at Toledo on May 6 and three at Conneaut on May 1 (Mumford 1961c). Cleveland's first Cattle Egret was recorded on April 27, 1962 (Newman 1969). The first records from Dayton and Youngstown occurred in 1966 (Hall 1966d, Mathena et al. 1984), at Lake St. Marys in 1967 (Petersen 1967b), and Marietta and Findlay in 1968 (Hall 1968a, Phillips 1980). During the 1960s, their appearances were very sporadic except along western Lake Erie, where there were at least nine records.

Cattle Egret

During the 1970s, Cattle Egrets established a regular pattern of occurrence within Ohio. Most appeared during spring, particularly along western Lake Erie, where they were annually recorded. Spring Cattle Egrets were casual to rare visitors elsewhere, although they were fairly regularly observed in all portions of the state. After spring migration ended, they disappeared except along western Lake Erie, where breeding was confirmed in 1978, when twenty nests were discovered on West Sister Island (Kleen 1978d). Fall migrants were regularly encountered along western Lake Erie, and flocks occasionally appeared there after 1975. Elsewhere, small numbers were very infrequently reported during autumn.

Their status did not appreciably change during the 1980s, although the number of sightings slowly declined after 1983. This trend continued into the 1990s, causing a reduction in the number of spring reports. The small breeding population on West Sister Island was maintained through 1989, but by 1992 this site was abandoned (Ashley 1992, Peterjohn 1990a). This population apparently shifted to the Turning Point Island heronry in Erie County, where nesting was initially recorded in 1984 and 20–30 pairs annually nested during the 1990s (Harlan 1994a, Peterjohn and Rice 1991).

Cattle Egrets are currently rare to uncommon spring migrants along western Lake Erie. Whereas spring flocks of 15–23 appeared during the 1970s and early 1980s, most sightings have been of eight or fewer since 1984. Spring Cattle Egrets are accidental or casual visitors elsewhere in Ohio. They may be completely absent some years or produce small flights in others, such as 1996 when they appeared in ten counties, with a maximum of 29 in Butler County on May 13 (Conlon and Harlan 1996a). They are normally found at three or fewer locations annually. Most recent sightings are from the glaciated counties, normally 1–5 individuals and occasional flocks of 7–13. The earliest migrant returned to Pickaway County by March 24, 1990 (Peterjohn 1990c), but they normally appear during April 15–25. Most spring sightings occur between April 25 and May 20, and late migrants can linger into the first week of June.

Cattle Egrets are normally restricted to western Lake Erie during summer, but are very infrequently encountered away from their nesting colony during late June and July. Summer reports invariably are of six or fewer egrets. Nesting activities are normally initiated by mid-May, and adults with young may be noted by early August.

During the last half of August and early September, the western Lake Erie population apparently congregates into one or two flocks. Since breeding has been restricted to Turning Point Island, these flocks have favored nearby portions of Erie, Sandusky, and Ottawa Counties. These flocks total 20–53 during most years, with a maximum of 75 in 1992 (Brock 1993a). The flocks normally disappear by early October, but stragglers fairly regularly remain into the first half of November, with reports into the first week of December during 1982 and 1983.

Cattle Egrets are accidental or casual fall visitors away from western Lake Erie and are not reported annually. Fall migrants can appear by the middle of July, but there are relatively few sightings before mid-October. Most fall records have been lingering egrets during November or the first week of December, normally scattered individuals but including small flocks with as many as seven egrets.

Foraging Cattle Egrets prefer upland fields rather than marshes. During spring they prefer wet meadows and pastures, where they supplement their insect diet with a few amphibians. Fall concentrations along western Lake Erie are found in dry grasslands and recently mowed fields where grasshoppers and other insects abound.

Green Heron *Butorides virescens* (Linnaeus)

Among our most widely distributed breeding herons, the diminutive Green Heron is found along small streams, rivers, marshes, and the margins of ponds and lakes throughout Ohio. They usually nest as isolated pairs and never frequent large colonies with other herons. Instead, they construct their loose platforms in dense bushes and small trees near water. If suitable low dense cover is unavailable, they place their nests at heights of forty to seventy-five feet in tall trees (Price 1934b, Williams 1950). Green Herons will rarely nest in loose segregated colonies of 5–20+ pairs (Campbell 1968, Hicks 1935a).

Nest construction begins in late April and continues into May. Nests with eggs have been discovered by April 26 but are usually reported between May

10 and June 20 (Trautman 1940). A few late pairs were incubating eggs during July (Williams 1950). The young fledge before they can fly, clambering about woody cover as they await the return of their parents with food. These young herons have left their nests as early as June 12 but normally appear between late June and early August (Trautman 1940).

Green Heron

In the early 1900s, Green Herons were common summer residents throughout Ohio (Jones 1903). In the 1930s, Hicks (1935a) described them as fairly common to abundant residents in every county. After 1940, wetland drainage and stream channelization significantly reduced their numbers, particularly in western Ohio. These declines continued into the 1990s, including a significant decrease in the statewide population since the mid-1960s based on BBS data (Sauer et al. 1998).

Despite their declining numbers, Green Herons remain uncommon to fairly common summer residents and were reported from every county except Van Wert during the Breeding Bird Atlas (Peterjohn and Rice 1991). They are most numerous within the northeastern counties and along western Lake Erie, where 4–8 may be observed daily. Nesting herons are least numerous within the intensively farmed western counties, where scattered individuals and pairs are infrequently noted, and in urban areas, where a few pairs nest along streams if undisturbed riparian habitats are available.

As spring migrants, a few Green Herons return remarkably early: to Cleveland by March 12 (Williams 1950) and other localities by March 25–30. Most years, migrants are first observed between April 10 and 20 and are widely distributed by April 28–May 5. They are uncommon to fairly common migrants in most counties. Most spring totals are currently five or fewer daily; the largest movements total 15–20 individuals, although there have been few spring reports exceeding ten in recent years. Most return by May 20, but a few late migrants may be noted through the end of the month.

Greater numbers of Green Herons pass through Ohio each autumn. Before 1965, fall concentrations of 30–50+ were encountered within the northern and central counties each year. The last movement of this magnitude was 55 at Newtown (Hamilton County) on September 16, 1979 (Kleen 1980a). During the 1980s and 1990s, the largest fall movements totaled 10–30 and even these concentrations have been scarce after 1984. In recent years, Green Herons have become fairly common fall migrants, with most sightings of six or fewer.

The first southward migrants are expected by July 20–30. In recent years, their maximum abundance is attained during August, with sharply reduced numbers by September 10–15. When populations were larger, sizable movements continued through mid-September. Small numbers normally remain through October 1–5, while a few stragglers linger into the first half of November during most years. When the weather is relatively mild, a few Green Herons survive into December, although they are accidental early winter visitors. One remained at Cleveland through January 1, 1942 (Williams 1950), but this species is not known to have overwintered in Ohio.

Black-crowned Night-Heron *Nycticorax nycticorax* (Linnaeus)

Black-crowned
Night-Heron

Black-crowned Night-Herons have nested in Ohio since 1867, when the first colony was discovered at Lake St. Marys (Clark and Sipe 1970). During the remaining decades of the nineteenth century, they became locally common summer residents near the few known colonies but were generally unreported elsewhere (Jones 1903). Unlike most other herons, Black-crowneds were not persecuted by the millinery trade, and their numbers remained stable into the 1900s.

Their Ohio breeding population expanded between 1915 and 1935 (Hicks 1935a). Nesting night-herons became established along western Lake Erie by 1920. At the same time, a number of new colonies were scattered across the western half of the state. These colonies varied in size from a few pairs to several hundred; many were short-lived. Despite their constantly changing locations, Hicks (1935a) cited at least nineteen colonies in Ottawa, Lucas, Paulding, Madison, Franklin, Fairfield, Champaign, Mercer, Logan, Shelby, Hamilton, Butler, Warren, Greene, Montgomery, and Erie Counties. While there were numerous sightings from the northeastern counties, no breeding colonies were discovered. The largest colonies included 1,000+ nests on West Sister Island, 500 nests at Lake Loramie (Shelby County), 300+ in Champaign and Greene Counties, and 200 near Cincinnati (Chapman 1931, Clark and Sipe 1970, Kemsies and Randle 1953, Mathena et al. 1984).

These populations remained fairly stable through the 1940s, and new colonies were reported from Hancock and Van Wert Counties (Phillips 1980,

Price 1972). The Black-crowned's status changed during the 1950s, particularly within the interior counties, where every small colony and several large heronries disappeared. The only new colony was composed of several pairs at the Cleveland zoo (Newman 1969). Trends of the western Lake Erie population were not apparent. The large herony on West Sister Island remained intact, and another large heronry was established on North Bass Island (Nolan 1955d). Meanwhile, other small colonies in Ottawa and Lucas Counties disappeared. During the 1960s, the last colonies away from western Lake Erie disappeared. Breeding was last recorded in Cincinnati in 1963 and Cleveland in 1966 (Newman 1969, Petersen 1964c). In Ottawa and Lucas Counties, only the West Sister Island heronry remained intact, with an estimated 1,200 pairs (Campbell 1968).

Following these declines during the 1960s, the Ohio Black-crowned Night-Heron population remained fairly stable until the late 1980s. The breeding population on West Sister Island has significantly declined, from 1,240 pairs in 1991 to 560 in 1995 and fewer than 200 pairs in the late 1990s (Harlan 1991b, 1995d). A smaller breeding population on Turning Point Island (Erie County) totaled approximately 100 pairs in the 1980s (Peterjohn and Rice 1991); Black-crowneds still nest there but their trends at this site are unknown. As the western Lake Erie population declined, several small colonies developed within the interior of Ohio. Five pairs nested at Gilmore Ponds in Butler County in 1989 (Peterjohn 1989d), and this colony has grown to 12–18 pairs. A colony along Mill Creek in Hamilton County was established in 1990 and supports similar numbers of breeding pairs (Peterjohn 1990d, Conlon and Harlan 1996a). Breeding has also been suspected in the Cleveland area and at Columbus (Harlan 1992d, 1995d).

Despite recent declines, Black-crowned Night-Herons remain fairly common to common summer residents of the marshes bordering western Lake Erie and Sandusky Bay. The first migrants normally return between March 22 and 27, but Black-crowneds do not become numerous until mid-April. Generally 5–20 are observed daily during spring and summer, although concentrations of 30+ may develop in favorable habitats. Larger flocks have occurred during late summer. While flocks of 100–300 were formerly encountered in these marshes, the largest recent concentrations have totaled 30–75. Their numbers gradually decline during September and October, with small flocks remaining through October 25–November 15.

Black-crowned Night-Herons usually nest in saplings, frequently at heights of less than 20 feet. Breeding activities are not necessarily synchronous. Some adults lay eggs as early as April 5, although most clutches are not initiated until late April or early May. Eggs may hatch by the first week of May and young may fledge before the end of the month (Campbell 1968, Franks 1928). Most young leave their nests during late June and July, while the latest remain until mid-August.

Although most Black-crowned Night-Herons winter in the southern United States, the Caribbean islands, and Central America, small numbers regularly overwinter at the Acme power plant in Toledo. This flock is generally composed of 20–40 night-herons, although 103 spent the winter of 1972–1973 and 50 were counted in 1993. Wintering Black-crowneds are casually observed within the western Lake Erie marshes, usually as isolated individuals, but small flocks of 5–10 have been reported.

Their status in Cleveland has recently changed. Beginning in 1993, Black-crowned Night-Herons were found to congregate along the lower Cuyahoga River (Harlan 1993c). Spring numbers peak during April, when 65–100 have been counted, while the largest fall flocks occur during November and may total 30–50. Elsewhere along central Lake Erie, Black-crowneds are rare to uncommon spring migrants, usually as five or fewer, with occasional reports of 10–30. These migrants are observed between March 25 and May 15. They are rare nonbreeding summer visitors, frequently as isolated immatures. Beginning in late July and continuing into September, they become uncommon to fairly common fall migrants and may appear as individuals or groups of 2–12. These migrants normally depart around mid-October. In the 1990s, Black-crowned Night-Herons proved to be locally distributed but regular winter residents at hot-water outlets scattered from Lorain to Ashtabula. Four or fewer are normally detected at each location, while the largest flocks peaked at 38 in Lorain during January 1993, and 21 at Cleveland in February 1997 (Brock 1997b, Harlan 1993b).

Within the interior counties, Black-crowneds were once uncommon to locally common summer residents. Flocks of 10–25+ herons were regularly noted near their breeding colonies but were sporadically detected elsewhere. Migrants were frequently observed, including flocks of 40 in Summit County on April 19, 1947, and 150 there on August 17, 1948 (Williams 1950). Since the late 1960s, these herons have been accidental to rare migrants in most inland counties, least numerous in unglaciated Ohio. Groups of six or fewer are sporadically encountered between April 5 and May 15, and August 10 and September 30. They become locally uncommon to fairly common near their colonies in the Cincinnati area, where flocks of 10–20 may be observed. Nonbreeding summer visitors are accidental to casual elsewhere, with a few recent reports of 1–6 from central and northeastern Ohio.

Black-crowneds have always been accidental to casual winter visitors within the interior of Ohio. When their populations were larger, winter records were widely scattered, with a maximum of 27 on the 1956 Dayton Christmas Bird Count. After very few records during the 1970s and 1980s, there were at least six inland winter reports during the 1990s, including two overwintering at Columbus during 1996–1997 (Fazio 1997a).

Yellow-crowned Night-Heron *Nyctanassa violacea* (Linnaeus)

Yellow-crowned Night-Herons were unrecorded from Ohio until 1928, when a nesting pair was discovered in the heronry at Indian Lake (Logan County) on May 16 (Walker 1928b). While breeding adults returned to this colony through 1932 (Hicks 1935a), the only other record before 1940 was an adult observed in the marshes bordering Killbuck Creek in Wayne County on April 25, 1931 (Bruce 1931).

Yellow-crowned Night-Heron

A northward range expansion became apparent during the 1940s, when vagrant Yellow-crowneds began to regularly appear within Ohio. Most records were from the northern half of the state, including sightings at Toledo in 1940 and Cleveland in 1945 (Campbell 1968, Williams 1950), usually single herons appearing for a few days between early May and early September. The only nesting record was a pair along Flatrock Creek in Paulding County between 1943 and 1946 (Price 1972).

A permanent breeding population was established in the 1950s. While vagrant records continued to accumulate from the northern half of the state, nesting Yellow-crowneds were restricted to the southern and central counties. Small colonies were established at Cincinnati and Dayton in 1953 and Columbus in 1954 (Austing and Imbrogno 1976, Mathena et al. 1984, Nolan 1954d). Sightings in other southern counties suggested the presence of additional colonies.

This northward expansion apparently halted in the 1960s. Except for a nesting pair at Youngstown in 1967 (Hall 1967), breeding Yellow-crowneds were restricted to traditional colonies at Columbus, Cincinnati, and Dayton. Regular observations in the Toledo area strongly suggested the possibility of a small breeding population (Campbell 1968). By the late 1960s, the statewide population may have started to decline. The Cincinnati nesting colony disappeared and the number of vagrant sightings was markedly reduced. This trend continued into the 1970s. Except for Cleveland's first nesting record in 1978 (Kleen 1978d), these herons were only infrequently encountered away from established colonies.

The status of Yellow-crowned Night-Herons did not appreciably change during the 1980s and 1990s. They remain accidental to locally rare summer residents within the southern half of the state. The only known populations at Dayton and Columbus total no more than 5–10 pairs in each area (Peterjohn and Rice 1991). Another nest was reported at Lake Logan in 1980 (Hall 1980). Other small nesting colonies probably exist, as evidenced by summer records from Belmont, Monroe, Morgan, Jackson, Ross, and Clinton Counties during the 1980s (Peterjohn and Rice 1991). In the northern half of Ohio, Yellow-crowneds are accidental to casual summer residents. In the Cleveland area, a nesting pair remained through 1982, but only isolated nonbreeders have been recorded there subsequently. Elsewhere in northeastern Ohio, summer reports are limited to Ashland County and near Spencer Lake Wildlife Area during the 1990s (Harlan 1994d). Toledo's first nest was discovered in 1994 (Brock 1994d), while summering Yellow-crowneds have been noted at other north-western Ohio locations from Kelleys Island west to the Maumee River in Wood County and south to Seneca County (Brock 1992d, Peterjohn and Rice 1991). The statewide breeding population is very small, perhaps fewer than 20 pairs, although there are probably more breeding pairs scattered across southern Ohio than are currently known.

Breeding Yellow-crowned Night-Herons are usually found along shallow rocky streams, where they feed on crayfish and small fish. While they will nest in mixed colonies with other herons, most Ohio nesting records are isolated pairs or small segregated colonies with 2–5 pairs. Their choice of nesting habitats varies from isolated woods and undisturbed parks to trees in residential yards. The urban colonies rank among the most stable. In fact, a Columbus colony in a residential neighborhood has been regularly occupied for more than twenty years, producing fledglings that have played with children's toys and neighborhood pets before departing for the Scioto River.

Resident Yellow-crowned Night-Herons return fairly early, appearing near Oxford (Butler County) by March 16, 1980 (Kleen 1980c), and Columbus by March 21, 1992 (Harlan 1992c). They normally appear during April. The largest spring flock totaled seven at Spring Valley Wildlife Area on May 5, 1996 (Brock 1996c). Nesting activities begin shortly thereafter, and complete clutch-es have been noted by the last week of April. Young normally hatch by late May or early June and fledge by early August. Small flocks of 8–13+ have been detected at Columbus and Dayton in August. These herons normally depart during September, although a few occasionally remain into the first half of October. There are no verified winter records for Ohio.

These herons are accidental visitors away from established and suspected colonies, producing one to five sightings annually in recent years. Spring records predominate, as isolated individuals during late April and May, although a few postbreeding visitors have appeared between late July and early September.

White Ibis *Eudocimus albus* (Linnaeus)

Like most ibis and herons, postbreeding White Ibis tend to wander north of their established nesting range in the southern United States. These movements have produced four records of this accidental visitor to Ohio. An immature White Ibis was discovered by Ben Blincoe at Englewood Dam near Dayton on August 20, 1964. This cooperative individual remained through August 31, was viewed by many observers, and was photographed for the local newspapers (Mathena et al. 1984). The second White Ibis also appeared in southwestern Ohio, visiting Spring Valley Wildlife Area on July 14, 1990 (Peterjohn 1990d). Ohio's third record was provided by an immature photographed along the Rocky River near Cleveland on July 19, 1993 (Brock 1993d). The fourth record was of 1–2 observed at Killdeer Plains Wildlife Area during July 7–15, 1998 (Brock 1998d). An adult White Ibis documented from Delaware Wildlife Area on May 7, 1997 (Fazio 1997b), established one of few spring reports from the Great Lakes region.

Glossy Ibis *Plegadis falcinellus* (Linnaeus)

While *Plegadis* ibis are instantly recognized by their long decurved bills and distinctive plumages, separating Glossy and White-faced Ibis poses a serious challenge. Only adults in breeding plumage are readily identified in the field when they can be carefully studied under good viewing conditions. Field identification of immatures and nonbreeding adults is accomplished only under ideal conditions, and many will never be satisfactorily identified. These identification problems have obscured the status of both *Plegadis* ibis within Ohio. Most sightings are believed to pertain to Glossy Ibis, but recent records of White-faced Ibis indicate that the identification of all individuals should be proved and not assumed. Unfortunately, many sightings of *Plegadis* ibis are accompanied by insufficient details to positively eliminate either species.

Ohio's first Glossy Ibis record was provided by two specimens collected at Cleveland in 1848 (one of these specimens is still in the Cleveland Museum of Natural History) (Williams 1950). They subsequently went unrecorded for nearly a century until three Glossies were discovered in Lucas County on May 30, 1943 (Campbell 1944). This sighting was followed by other Toledo area records in 1947 and 1952 (Campbell 1968). Their status abruptly changed during the 1960s. Previously considered accidental visitors, they were reported almost annually, with records from one to three localities during most years. This pattern of regular sightings continued through 1976. The number of records then diminished through the late 1980s, with only three confirmed sightings and five additional records of unidentified ibis. Reports of *Plegadis* ibis increased during the 1990s, with eight reports confirmed as Glossies and twelve records of unidentified ibis.

The majority of Glossy Ibis have been discovered along western Lake Erie in Ottawa and Lucas Counties. They are apparently casual visitors to this area, with more than twenty published records. They are accidental visitors elsewhere. There are at least five sightings in the Cleveland-Akron area, three records at Lake St. Marys, three in the Columbus-Buckeye Lake region, and single reports from Ashtabula County, Wayne County, Holmes County, Hueston Woods State Park, Mosquito Creek Lake, and Brown County.

Most of these ibis have been reported during spring, when they are most easily identified. The earliest arrival was noted at Hueston Woods State Park on April 7, 1971 (Kleen and Bush 1971a), while most spring sightings have been during May. Most records are of 1–3 ibis. The largest concentration totaled 21 in Ottawa County on May 5, 1962 (Graber 1962c). Away from western Lake Erie, the largest flock was five at Cleveland on May 14, 1973 (Kleen and Bush 1973c).

Midsummer sightings are restricted to western Lake Erie, mostly single nonbreeding ibis briefly observed during June. However, 1–2 Glossy Ibis frequented the Black-crowned Night-Heron colony at North Bass Island between June 26 and July 5, 1963 (Putnam et al. 1964). The breeding status of these ibis was never established.

There are fewer autumn records of *Plegadis* ibis and most lack sufficient details for positive identification. These fall reports are scattered between late July and November. Proven Glossy Ibis records are limited to five photographed in Ripley Township, Holmes County, on September 21–22, 1992 (Harlan 1993b), and single ibis reported from three locations between October 5 and November 7.

White-faced Ibis *Plegadis chihi* (Vieillot)

Western counterparts of Glossy Ibis, White-faced Ibis breed from the Great Plains and Great Basin south into Mexico. Wintering ibis are largely restricted to the Pacific and Gulf Coasts (AOU 1998). They are presently accidental visitors east of the Mississippi River, but their actual status is uncertain because of our inability to positively identify most immature *Plegadis* ibis in the field.

Ohio's first White-faced Ibis record was provided by a specimen collected at Lake Grant in Brown County on October 1, 1949. According to Kemsies and Randle (1953), the identity of this immature ibis was established by Harry C. Oberholser. A recent examination of this skin indicates that bill, tarsi, and feet characteristics resemble a White-faced Ibis, but soft-part coloration was not recorded at the time of collection.

The next record was provided by a breeding-plumaged adult photographed at Magee Marsh Wildlife Area (Ottawa County) on May 18–23, 1985 (Peterjohn 1985c). There were five additional reports during the 1990s, and some of the recent unidentified *Plegadis* ibis sightings might pertain to this species. The recent documented sightings of White-faced Ibis are one in Erie County on May 4, 1991 (Peterjohn 1991c), an immature photographed at Spencer Lake Wildlife Area on October 10–17, 1991 (Peterjohn 1992a), an adult in Delaware County on June 6, 1994 (Brock 1994d), four at Englewood Reserve on September 24–25, 1994 (Brock 1995a), and three at Salt Fork Reservoir on April 26, 1998, including a breeding-plumaged adult (E. Schlabach 1998).

Roseate Spoonbill *Ajaia ajaja* (Linnaeus)

Roseate Spoonbills only rarely wander from their established range during late summer and early autumn. Their North American populations are small and locally distributed from Florida to Texas, and the few extralimital sightings are usually from the southern states (AOU 1998). Spoonbills are accidental visitors elsewhere; hence, the appearance of a Roseate Spoonbill in Ohio is truly extraordinary. The only acceptably documented report is provided by an immature spoonbill discovered by Roger Emerling in a shallow pond near the Auglaize River in Defiance on September 24, 1986 (Peterjohn 1987a). The bird was observed at close range by Emerling and several other persons as it spent most of the late afternoon sleeping along the edge of the pond until it was flushed by a passing jogger.

Wood Stork *Mycteria americana* Linnaeus

Within the United States, Wood Storks nest in Florida, Georgia, and South Carolina. They also breed in Mexico and regularly wander north to Texas, Louisiana, and southern California. On rare occasions, they have strayed as far north as New Brunswick, the lower Great Lakes states, and South Dakota (AOU 1998). Most wandering storks are immatures discovered during summer and early autumn.

Wood Storks have always been accidental visitors to Ohio. The state's first confirmed visit was by an immature captured near Wilmington (Clinton County) on July 23, 1909 (Jones 1918). Held in captivity "for some days," it died shortly after its release. The next Wood Stork was also discovered in the Wilmington area, an immature captured along Todd's Fork on May 5, 1946. Obviously weak, it died shortly after it was taken into captivity (Hazard 1947).

The only other confirmed record was of two Wood Storks discovered in an Ashtabula County field on July 1–2, 1955 (Nolan 1955d). These storks were carefully observed during their brief visit. There have also been unverified sightings during the nineteenth century and in 1914, 1964, and 1986.

Black Vulture *Coragyps atratus* (Bechstein)

In the early 1800s, Black Vultures were residents of the southeastern United States. The northern edge of their range may have included southwestern Ohio. Audubon contended that they summered along the Ohio River at Cincinnati (Jones 1903), but he never substantiated his assertion and there were no corroborating sightings.

Black Vulture

Beginning in the 1870s, Black Vultures underwent a northeastward range expansion into southern Ohio. Langdon (1877) provided three Cincinnati area records, including the first specimen on January 1, 1877. They spread to Warren County by 1883, and the first Ohio breeding record was established there in 1891 (Hicks 1935a). Their expansion into other southern counties apparently occurred by the early 1900s, as evidenced by a specimen secured near Cadiz (Harrison County) on December 17, 1906 (Jones 1907). By the mid-1930s, Hicks (1935a) considered Black Vultures "very local" residents in southern Ohio, nesting in 12 counties. He estimated the total breeding population at 100 or fewer pairs of vultures. Along the unglaciated Allegheny Plateau, their breeding range extended north to Hocking, Athens, and Washington Counties (Hicks 1937a). Though "fairly common" in Hocking County, they were rare elsewhere. Another range expansion was noted in the 1950s, when a population became established in northeastern Licking County. First observed in 1952, they numbered as many as 90 in a roost there during the winter of 1957–1958 (Greider and Wagner 1960, Thomson 1983). While Black Vultures were reported from Licking County through the winter of 1981–1982, none were found there during the Breeding Bird Atlas (Peterjohn and Rice 1991).

Ohio's Black Vulture population increased during the 1990s, most notably within its established range in the southern counties. While small numbers were casually reported along the entire unglaciated plateau, the most noteworthy northward range expansion was the establishment of a population in the Tuscarawas, Holmes, Richland, and Knox Counties area. Initially reported from Holmes County in 1991 (Peterjohn 1991c), as many as 15 were counted at Pleasant Hill Reservoir during March 1992 and 49 in Knox County on February 14, 1993 (Brock 1992a, 1993b). Recent sightings have reported winter maxima of 20–35 from this area (R. Schlabach 1999b).

Black Vultures remain locally distributed residents in southern Ohio. They are uncommon to locally common along the edge of the Allegheny Plateau from Adams and Brown Counties north through Ross and Highland Counties to Hocking and Fairfield Counties (Peterjohn and Rice 1991). They are generally casual visitors elsewhere in the unglaciated counties, but became rare in the Marietta area during the 1990s. Black Vultures remain rare residents in southwestern Ohio. A few pairs regularly breed along the Little Miami River in Warren County, and they have sporadically nested at Hueston Woods State Park and in Hamilton County (Austing and Imbrogno 1976, Kemsies and Randle 1953, Peterjohn and Rice 1991).

The statewide nesting population has undoubtedly expanded beyond the 70–100 pairs estimated in 1991 (Peterjohn and Rice 1991). Roosts totaling 170 Black Vultures at Rocky Fork Lake, Highland County, on November 5, 1995 (Brock 1996a), 400 in Brown County on December 2, 1999 (Whan, in press), 82 in Ross County during December 1995 (Harlan 1996b), and 70 in Hocking County on February 7, 1982 (Hall 1982b) are indicative of current population levels. Away from known roost sites, eight or fewer Black Vultures are generally observed daily throughout the year. Many Black Vultures appear to be permanent residents, but their seasonal movements are poorly understood.

Black Vultures may wander during the nonbreeding season. These movements may extend twenty to more than fifty miles from known breeding locations. They casually appear north to Dayton, Columbus, and the Buckeye Lake area in glaciated Ohio, but remain accidental visitors to the northern counties. Reports from northeastern Ohio are limited to three sightings from Mahoning and Trumbull Counties during the 1950s (Brooks 1950c, 1956, 1959b), one at Hudson (Summit County) on May 30, 1966 (Newman 1969), and one at Headlands Beach State Park on March 31, 1991 (Peterjohn 1991c). Single Black Vultures have also wandered into northwestern Ohio to visit Seneca County on May 16, 1993 (Harlan 1993d), Magee Marsh Wildlife Area on April 29, 1994 (Harlan 1994c), and Marblehead (Ottawa County) on May 19, 1996 (Conlon and Harlan 1996a). While there are a few winter sightings, wandering Black Vultures are most likely to appear during March through May and late August through October. Most extralimital sightings are of 1–5 vultures, although ten were counted in Delaware County on October 10, 1984 (Peterjohn 1985a).

Black Vulture nests have been found within caves in sandstone cliffs, large hollow logs, abandoned buildings, and bare ground surrounded by boulders. Most pairs probably lay their eggs in March, placing them on the ground. The young normally hatch during the last half of April, after an incubation period of thirty-nine to forty-one days. They remain in the nest for more than two months and are fed a diet of regurgitated food (Thomas 1928a). The young vultures normally leave the nest in July. Renesting attempts are responsible for clutches during May and an extremely late attempt in July (Greider and Wagner 1960). The latter nest had young vultures in late August, which would not have fledged until late September or early October.

Turkey Vulture *Cathartes aura* (Linnaeus)

At sunrise, normally a time of peak avian activity, roosting Turkey Vultures have hardly stirred from their perches on tall dead trees. They remain at the roost until midmorning temperatures create thermals needed to maintain sustained flight. Masters at riding thermals, these vultures can soar effortlessly for many miles over fields, forests, rivers, and wetlands. Unlike Black Vultures, which locate food by sight, Turkey Vultures have a well-developed sense of smell, which they use to locate decaying animals from considerable heights.

Turkey Vulture

Migrant Turkey Vultures increased during the 1990s and have shown a tendency to return earlier to Ohio in recent springs. The first migrants regularly appeared during the first half of March in the 1980s, but small numbers are now observed anywhere in the state by February 15–25, except during severe winters. They become common to locally abundant migrants throughout Ohio by March 10–15. Sizable flights may occur along Lake Erie through mid-May, while individuals and small flocks continue to pass along the lakefront into the first week of June. This migration is most noticeable along Lake Erie, particularly on days with strong southwesterly winds. Few migrants are detected with northerly winds. Lakefront flights frequently total 200–350+, while the largest movements include 1,260 along western Lake Erie on April 2, 1994 (Harlan 1994c) and occasional reports of 500–850+ daily. Similar flights are not apparent away from Lake Erie. Inland spring totals normally are 10–50+ except at roosts, where 100–200+ may gather. The maximum inland spring count totaled

500 at East Fork Lake (Clermont County) on March 31, 1992 (Harlan 1992c). Turkey Vultures have always been widely distributed summer residents. Hicks (1935a) indicated they almost certainly nested in all but two counties. They became locally uncommon in northern Ohio but were numerous elsewhere. He recorded 114 roosts in eighty-one counties and estimated a statewide population of 3,650 vultures. Similar estimates are not available today, but their statewide populations have increased since the 1930s, reflecting similar trends throughout the Great Lakes region (DeVos 1964). Breeding Bird Survey data exhibit significant increases across Ohio since 1966 (Sauer et al. 1998), an indication that these trends have continued into recent years.

Turkey Vultures are currently fairly common to abundant summer residents except near urban areas, where they are normally absent. Summering vultures were reported from every county in the Breeding Bird Atlas (Peterjohn and Rice 1991). Breeding vultures are most numerous along the unglaciated Allegheny Plateau, with daily totals of 30–75+. They are least numerous within the intensively farmed western counties, where sightings seldom exceed 3–10 except near roosts. Summer roosts occur throughout Ohio, composed of nonbreeding vultures and breeding adults whose presence is not required at the nest. While numbers vary from evening to evening, 20–100+ vultures may congregate at these roosts.

Breeding Turkey Vultures are very timid around their nest sites and only occupy undisturbed areas. Within the western counties, breeding pairs inhabit large isolated woodlots. In southeastern Ohio, they prefer protected ledges or small caves on sheer rocky cliffs, but will also nest on the ground under rock ledges, beside boulders, in hollow logs, and in brush piles within extensive woodlands (Coles 1944). They will also occupy abandoned buildings (Buchanan 1980, Price 1934a). A few pairs have nested within large cavities in tall trees at heights of forty to sixty feet (Maslowski 1934, Price 1928b). Nests with eggs have been discovered as early as April 8 (Coles 1944), but most are recorded between mid-April and late May, with a few through mid-June. While some young vultures may remain at the nest into the first half of August, recently fledged young have appeared at roosts by the last week of June (Price 1934a, Trautman 1940, Williams 1950).

Their fall migration apparently begins by September 15–25, but the largest movements are generally noted during October. Fall Turkey Vultures do not congregate along Lake Erie, and large numbers of migrants are regularly reported only from the Oak Openings area of Lucas County. Fall totals of 10–50+ can occur in most counties, while movements over the Oak Openings may total 150–270 daily, with a maximum of 450 on October 13, 1993 (Harlan 1994a). Large concentrations can also appear at roosts, where 100–500+ have been counted at scattered sites across Ohio.

Turkey Vultures remain common to locally abundant fall migrants until the first half of November, with stragglers remaining into late November or December. As their populations expanded in recent years, the number of late sightings has also increased, and late November and December records have become annual occurrences since the 1980s.

Wintering vultures are locally fairly common near established roosts in southern Ohio. Turkey Vultures regularly form mixed roosts with Black Vultures, and 30–150+ may be encountered from Adams and Brown Counties north into portions of Ross, Fairfield, Hocking, and Morgan Counties. In addition, flocks of 45 or fewer have sporadically wintered in southwestern Ohio (Kemsies and Randle 1953). A large roost developed in northeastern Licking County during the 1950s and 1960s but has not been reported since 1982 (Graber 1962b, Nolan 1958b). In the 1990s, a roost developed in the Knox, Holmes, and Tuscarawas Counties area, where a maximum of 150 were counted in Knox County on February 14, 1993 (Brock 1993b). Turkey Vultures are casual to accidental midwinter visitors away from these roosts, although the number of reports increased markedly during the 1990s. Scattered individuals or small groups may appear for a day or two anywhere within the state during relatively mild seasons. Some of these vultures may be early migrants, especially on warm days in early February, taking advantage of southerly winds to begin their northward movements across Ohio.

Fulvous Whistling-Duck *Dendrocygna bicolor* (Vieillot)

Fulvous Whistling-Ducks have a North American breeding range restricted to Florida, coastal Texas, Louisiana, and very locally in southern California (AOU 1998). But they have wandered to many other states and Canadian provinces, appearing as individuals or small flocks anytime between early spring and late autumn.

Ohio has at least nine valid records of Fulvous Whistling-Ducks, six between 1962 and 1969, two in the mid-1970s, and only one documented report in subsequent years. Three spring sightings were during April: four in Butler County on April 11, 1974 (Kleen 1974c), one near Amherst (Lorain County) on April 13, 1964 (Newman 1969), and nine near Carey (Wyandot County) on April 24–25, 1975 (Kleen 1975c). Summer records are limited to two Fulvous Whistling-Ducks spending June 1967 at Killdeer Plains Wildlife Area (Wyandot County) (Thomson 1983), and a single bird briefly observed at Magee Marsh Wildlife Area on June 5, 1994 (Pierce 1994). Four fall records include Ohio's first specimen, collected by a hunter at Metzger Marsh Wildlife Area (Lucas County) on October 19, 1962. The next day, nine whistling-ducks appeared at nearby Toussaint Wildlife Area (Ottawa County) and three were shot by hunters (Campbell 1968). Other fall sightings are six near Ashland on November 21, 1963 (Petersen 1964a), and a flock of 12 noted in flight over Buckeye Lake on November 24, 1969 (Trautman 1978).

Greater White-fronted Goose *Anser albifrons* (Scopoli)

During the nineteenth century, Greater White-fronted Geese were apparently rare but fairly regular visitors to Ohio. Anecdotal accounts indicate that they occasionally appeared within the western half of the state, and specimens were collected east to Fairfield County (Clark and Sipe 1970, Trautman and Trautman 1968, Wheaton 1882). Overhunting greatly reduced their numbers during the late 1800s, and White-fronted Geese quit visiting Ohio before the turn of the twentieth century.

A 1926 specimen from Lake St. Marys was never substantiated, and the first acceptable modern record was provided by a flock of 42 near Painesville (Lake County) on March 30, 1930 (Clark 1946, Williams 1950). White-fronted Geese did not reappear until 1945–1949, when there were five sightings scattered across northern and western Ohio. They remained accidental during the 1950s, with only three reports. In the 1960s, Greater White-fronted Geese started to appear regularly east of the Mississippi River, producing increased sightings from Ohio. They were not annual visitors but were recorded nine times during this decade. An equal number of sightings was documented in the 1970s. These geese have been observed annually since 1980, with an increase in the number of reports during the 1990s.

Greater White-fronted Geese are now rare but regular spring visitors along western Lake Erie. There are normally one to three sightings each year of four or fewer geese, with infrequent flocks of 6–15. They are accidental to casual visitors elsewhere in western and northern Ohio, and are most likely to be found in areas where Canada Geese congregate in large numbers, such as Killdeer Plains Wildlife Area and flooded fields in southwestern Wayne County. These sightings usually consist of six or fewer geese, although a remarkable 97 appeared at Big Island Wildlife Area (Marion County) on March 16, 1985 (Peterjohn 1985c). Other large flocks include the 1930 report from Painesville, 62 in Wayne County on March 15, 1985, and 34 there on March 25–27, 1980 (Kleen 1980c, Peterjohn 1985c). They are accidental along the unglaciated plateau, where White-fronteds have been reported from Gallia, Muskingum, and Adams Counties, including flocks of 15–23. During some years, spring White-fronteds are unreported away from western Lake Erie, while in other years, they are found at four or more inland locations. The earliest migrants may return during the first half of February, but most records are between February 15 and March 25. The last migrants disappear by April 10–18.

Fewer Greater White-fronted Geese are detected during autumn, and they became regular fall visitors only during the 1990s. These migrants are casual to accidental across Ohio, and most likely to appear in the western half of the state. There is only one report from the unglaciated counties. Most fall records consist of four or fewer geese, with occasional flocks of 10–12. Sizable flights comprised approximately 100 passing over Lake County on November 11, 1962 (Newman 1969), and 90 at Killdeer Plains Wildlife Area on November 15–19, 1998 (Brock 1999a). The earliest migrant returned to Gallia County on October 2–9, 1988 (Hall 1989a), but most are observed during November.

The number of winter reports has also increased since 1990, although they are not annually detected during this season. Most of these records are during December and the first half of January, and may be very late fall migrants rather than wintering geese. However, a few Greater White-fronted Geese have overwintered in Ohio. They are casually encountered along western Lake Erie and accidental elsewhere, with most reports from the western half of the state. Four in Muskingum County on January 4, 1997, provide the only winter report from unglaciated Ohio (Fazio 1997a). Most records consist of four or fewer geese, although as many as 15 wintered at Pickerington (Franklin/Fairfield Counties) through February 15, 1997 (Fazio 1997a).

Most Ohio records of Greater White-fronted Geese pertain to the *frontalis* race, the most widely distributed race in North America. However, the Greenland race *flavirostris* has been reported on at least five occasions during winter, including well-documented sightings in the Ross-Pickaway county line area during December 30, 1984–January 6, 1985 (Peterjohn 1985b), and at Springfield on January 22–28, 1989 (Peterjohn 1989b). The field identification of this race is challenging under most circumstances, but *flavirostris* appears to be an accidental winter visitor to the state.

Snow Goose *Chen caerulescens* (Linnaeus)

Large flocks of Snow Geese regularly migrate along the Mississippi River valley and Atlantic Coast but unfortunately miss Ohio by several hundred miles. We must normally be content with isolated individuals and small flocks associated with Canada Geese. On rare occasions, however, strong winds displace migrating Snow Geese over Ohio, providing a marvelous spectacle for birders accustomed to observing these handsome geese in flocks of only 5–20 birds.

In the early 1900s, Snow Geese were rare migrants and not regularly detected in Ohio (Jones 1903). By the early 1930s, a few observers realized that flocks of Snow Geese occasionally flew over the state during their southward migration. These flocks were only briefly observed in passage, usually concentrated within a period of a few days, as noted at Buckeye Lake in 1924, Wooster in 1925, and Toledo in 1936 and 1937 (Campbell 1940, Stevenson 1928, Trautman 1940).

The first substantial flight was recorded between October 13 and 24, 1939; more than 1,000 Snow Geese were tallied at Toledo, and Hicks estimated at least 10,000 over Columbus on the evening of October 20 (Campbell 1940). Other flights were reported during the 1940s and early 1950s. Campbell (1968) cited noticeable flights along western Lake Erie in 1940, 1945, 1946, 1948, and 1949. The 1948 movement was particularly strong, producing concentrations of 3,200 at Toledo (Campbell 1968), "several thousand" at Cincinnati (Kemsies and Randle 1953), 500 at Lake St. Marys (Mayfield 1949a), and "flocks" at Youngstown (Brooks 1949). The October 1949 movement was only slightly less impressive. The largest flight occurred in late October 1952, with "huge" numbers at Cleveland and an estimated 150,000 (95% "blue phase") over Meander Creek Reservoir (Mahoning County) during a two-hour period on October 25 (Brooks 1953a, Nolan 1953a). This flight was not detected elsewhere. But just when these flights were becoming fairly regular, they abruptly stopped. Although Campbell (1968) reported a flight along western Lake Erie in 1960 and another movement was apparent in northwestern and central Ohio during October 1969 (Campbell 1973, Thomson 1983), no sizable statewide movements have been subsequently reported, even though there has been a substantial increase in the continental populations of Snow Geese in recent years.

Fall Snow Geese are most frequently reported along western Lake Erie, where they are uncommon to fairly common migrants. Some years flock sizes are 150–350+, while in others they number fewer than 50. They casually appear in the unglaciated counties, where most reports are of 1–3 geese and the largest flocks totaled 55–75. Elsewhere, Snow Geese are casual to locally uncommon fall migrants. Ten or fewer geese are regularly detected at Killdeer Plains, Lake St. Marys, and Mosquito Creek Wildlife Areas. Similar small flocks may appear at other western, central, and northeastern Ohio locations. Small movements are detected at two- to three-year intervals, producing scattered flocks of 30–200 Snow Geese in the western half of Ohio and along central Lake Erie. Since 1960, the largest concentrations away from western Lake Erie were 620 at Hoover Reservoir on October 21, 1969, and 600 at Findlay Reservoir on November 9–14, 1982 (Peterjohn 1983a, Thomson 1983).

The earliest fall Snow Geese returned to Ottawa Wildlife Refuge on September 4, 1994 (Harlan 1995a), and Lake St. Marys on September 5, 1964 (Clark and Sipe 1970). They normally appear during the first half of October. The largest flights are noted between October 15 and November 15, with the last migrants departing by December 15–January 7.

Most wintering Snow Geese are restricted to western Lake Erie, where they are rare to uncommon residents. Wintering numbers are variable but do not normally exceed 50. Flocks of 200–350+ are exceptional, but 475 spent the winter of 1948–1949 in Sandusky County (Campbell 1968). Away from western Lake Erie, Snow Geese are accidental to casual winter visitors, with few records from the unglaciated counties. Sightings usually are of 1–5 Snows mixed among large flocks of Canada Geese. Not every wintering Snow Goose fits this pattern. One immature survived the winter of 1964–1965 on the Ohio State University campus, grazing on grass along the Olentangy River. Larger inland wintering flocks are exceptional, such as 36 in Wayne County on January 3–23, 1997 (Fazio 1997a).

Spring migrants may appear during the first half of February, but their northward migration normally commences between February 25 and March 7. Most spring Snow Geese appear in March and depart by the first week of April. A few immatures and nonbreeders remain after April 15–20, and have lingered through May 15–31 at scattered locations and June 5, 1992, at Cleveland (Harlan 1992d).

Spring Snow Geese are generally uncommon migrants along western Lake Erie, where most flocks are composed of 5–50 and a maximum of 150–200 has been noted. Snow Geese are casual to locally uncommon spring migrants elsewhere in the western half of Ohio. Most reports are of 1–6 Snows, with sporadic flocks of 10–35. The largest spring flight totaled 3,000 near Cincinnati on February 29, 1948 (Mayfield 1948). Snow Geese are generally accidental or casual spring migrants through the eastern counties, becoming uncommon to rare at Mosquito Creek Wildlife Area and in southwestern Wayne County. Most eastern Ohio sightings are of 1–3 geese, with a few flocks of 20–40 and a maximum of 75.

Ohio's only summer record was provided by a single bird noted at Dublin (Franklin County) during July 18–31, 1995 (Harlan 1995d). This individual was presumably a nonbreeder.

Ross's Goose *Chen rossii* (Cassin)

Ross's Geese were formerly restricted to a limited breeding range in Arctic Canada. Migrants followed a narrow corridor through western North America to wintering grounds in California and southern Oregon. Since the 1970s, their populations have substantially increased. New breeding colonies have been established in the Arctic, and Ross's Geese are now regular migrants through the Great Plains to wintering areas in Texas. Small numbers have become rare but regular winter visitors among large Snow Goose flocks in eastern North America as well (AOU 1998).

Given this recent range expansion, the appearance of Ross's Geese in Ohio was expected. The first acceptable record was provided by one at Ottawa Wildlife Refuge on March 18–21, 1982 (Peterjohn 1982c). The second record came from Lake Rockwell (Portage County) between October 21 and November 12, 1989 (Peterjohn 1990a). There are at least twelve additional acceptable reports between 1990 and 1999, although Ross's Geese remain an accidental visitor across Ohio.

Of these fourteen reports, seven have been during spring: Ottawa Wildlife Refuge (two sightings), Marion-Wyandot Counties, Buck Creek State Park, Holmes County, Pickaway County, and Lake St. Marys. These records span the dates of February 9 through April 6. In addition to the Lake Rockwell bird, the other three fall reports are from Lake St. Marys, Killdeer Plains Wildlife Area, and Gallia County, between October 18 and November 29. The three winter records include one shot by a hunter near Marysville on January 1, 1990 (Anderson and Kemp 1991a), one in Lorain County on January 8–12, 1997 (Fazio 1997a), and one wintering in Jackson County during 1989–1990. This bird lingered through May 25 (Peterjohn 1990c, 1990d). With the exception of three Ross's Geese at Lake St. Marys on October 18, 1993 (Harlan 1995b), all reports pertain to single geese. Given their current population trends, additional sightings are expected.

Canada Goose *Branta canadensis* (Linnaeus)

Initially, Canada Geese were primarily migrants passing through Ohio to and from their Arctic nesting range. Small numbers occasionally wintered in southern and central Ohio during relatively mild seasons (Jones 1903). As spring migrants, flocks were regularly encountered along western Lake Erie but made very brief appearances elsewhere. Most spring flocks were composed of 50 or fewer geese, and concentrations in excess of 100–200 were exceptional (Campbell 1940, Trautman 1940). While larger numbers generally appeared each autumn, these movements lasted for only a few days. During some years, small flocks were detected along western Lake Erie and at a few inland lakes. In other years, sizable flights produced local concentrations of 500–1,000 geese. Trautman's (1940) estimate of 5,000 at Buckeye Lake on

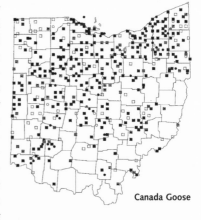

Canada Goose

October 21–22, 1925, was exceptional for that era.

These distribution patterns were maintained until the mid-1940s, when overhunting and poor reproductive success reduced Canada Goose populations to all-time low levels. Decisive action was necessary to prevent their disappearance. The first step was the establishment of refuges on their wintering grounds and along their migration corridors. Canada Geese quickly responded by changing their status within Ohio. Large flocks began to winter within the northern counties. For example, 2,000 spent the winter of 1948–1949 near Sandusky Bay in Sandusky County and an equal number wintered on Meander Creek Reservoir (Mahoning County) in 1949–1950 (Brooks 1950a, Mayfield 1949a). Similar flocks were reported during the 1950s. Numbers of migrants also increased dramatically. Canada Geese became numerous and widely distributed migrants, and flocks of 500–1,000+ were frequently noted.

Concurrent with the establishment of refuges, the development of a locally nesting Canada Goose population was undertaken. This program has produced nesting pairs at Lake St. Marys since 1953 and within the western Lake Erie marshes since 1955 (Campbell 1968, Clark and Sipe 1970). Initially, nesting geese were restricted to wildlife management areas. These populations spread throughout the state during the 1970s and 1980s.

As a result of this intensive management, a semidomesticated resident population has become permanently established. But successful management was achieved with a price. Unlike their warier brethren, our resident geese are accustomed to people and readily appear anywhere water is available. As this resident population expanded, it became a nuisance by befouling beaches and lawns and damaging corn and winter wheat crops. While the species still looks the same, the noble character formerly associated with a skein of migrant geese passing overhead has been tarnished.

Canada Geese are still most numerous as migrants. During spring, their northward movements are frequently apparent by mid-February and peak during March. Small migrant flocks may be encountered through April 15–25. As fall migrants, a few Canadas appear during the first half of September. The first large flights are normally associated with strong cold fronts between September 15 and 25, and peak between October 20 and November 15. Migrants are noted until freeze-up in January.

Canada Geese are fairly common to abundant migrants during spring and fall, more numerous during their southward migration. The largest concentrations appear along western Lake Erie, where 10,000–40,000+ congregate each year. Sizable flocks also accumulate at Lake St. Marys, Killdeer Plains, Mosquito Creek, and other wildlife management areas, regularly attracting 1,000–10,000+ geese. Canadas regularly visit most large lakes, marshes, artificial ponds and similar small bodies of water, and extensive flooded fields across Ohio. Flocks of 500–2,000+ may appear in all portions of the state, including major urban areas.

Numbers of wintering Canada Geese fluctuate annually, but they are most numerous during mild seasons, when open water is readily available. Canada Geese are locally abundant winter residents along western Lake Erie and at wildlife management areas across Ohio, regularly attracting 5,000–20,000+ geese. They are generally common to abundant winter residents elsewhere, and winter flocks of 200–2,000+ occur across the state.

Ohio's breeding Canada Goose population has greatly expanded since the mid-1980s. They were found in 81 counties during the Breeding Bird Atlas (Peterjohn and Rice 1991), and breed in every Ohio county today. They are locally uncommon residents in a few unglaciated counties but are fairly common to abundant elsewhere. Once the young geese hatch in late spring, daily totals of 100–500+ can be recorded across the state.

Breeding Canadas are found anywhere water is available, including extensive marshes, large lakes, small ponds, golf courses, along rivers and creeks, and in wooded swamps. They normally nest on the ground near water but readily accept "goose tubs" erected on ponds and marshes. Complete clutches are expected during the last half of March, and downy young can be found by mid-April. Nesting activities normally peak in April, and adult geese followed by downy young are a familiar sight during May and June.

Brant *Branta bernicla* (Linnaeus)

During the first half of the 1900s, Brant were accidental visitors to Ohio. There were only four published records, all during spring: a specimen taken at Indian Lake on March 29, 1905 (Fisher 1907b), a flock of 20 in Lake County on March 23, 1930, 36 in Lake County on March 9, 1924 (Williams 1950), and one at Buckeye Lake on May 30, 1902 (Trautman 1940). Beginning in the early 1950s, Brant became casual visitors, mostly as fall migrants along Lake Erie. They were observed at two- to three-year intervals through the mid-1970s, but during most years after 1976. These increased sightings are partially the result of more observers along Lake Erie. However, the complete absence of fall sightings prior to 1949 indicates their fall migration corridor may have shifted in recent decades.

Brant are currently rare fall migrants along central Lake Erie but casual visitors to the Western Basin. While migrants have been reported as early as October 6 (Campbell 1968), most pass along the lakefront between October 29 and November 18. The latest migrants are noted through mid-December. These reports are mostly of 1–4 Brant flying along the lakefront or feeding near a breakwater. Flocks of 26–69 are infrequently encountered. By far the largest flight occurred on November 11, 1985, when 290+ flew past Vermilion (Erie County) (Peterjohn 1986a). With the exception of 1985, when Brant were widely scattered along the lakefront, they have produced six or fewer sightings annually since the late 1970s.

Brant are accidental fall migrants away from Lake Erie. There are at least four records from the Columbus area, two records each from the Youngstown area, Akron, and Findlay Reservoir, and single sightings from Lake St. Marys, LaDue Reservoir, and Auglaize and Gallia Counties. These inland records coincide with movements along Lake Erie. With the exception of ten at LaDue Reservoir on November 22, 1990 (Peterjohn 1991a), these inland records are of four or fewer Brant.

Brant are accidental winter visitors, usually single individuals remaining for brief periods. Two at Belpre (Washington County) between December 5, 1995, and January 9, 1996, may have been late migrants (Hall 1996b). Other midwinter sightings include Cleveland area records between January 20 and February 15 during three winters, and one at Magee Marsh Wildlife Area on January 22, 1983 (Newman 1969, Peterjohn 1983b, Rosche 1988). The only Brant to overwinter in Ohio were singles observed at several Columbus area reservoirs during the winter of 1959–1960, at Lake St. Marys between November 20, 1966, and March 14, 1967, and along the Great Miami River between Middletown and West Carrollton on January 1–28, 1997 (Brock 1997b, Clark and Sipe 1970).

They remain accidental spring migrants through Ohio. Since 1950, inland spring records are limited to singles at Lake St. Marys on May 9, 1958 (Nolan 1958c), and Cincinnati between March 10 and April 2, 1994 (Harlan 1994c). There are also four recent sightings along Lake Erie during May: singles at two locations in the Western Basin and flocks of 27 at Ashtabula on May 20–25, 1956, and 28 at Crane Creek State Park on May 26, 1985 (Peterjohn 1985c, Thomson 1983). A Brant was also present in Erie County between March 12 and April 8, 1995 (Harlan 1995c).

Mute Swan *Cygnus olor* (Gmelin)

With its curved neck and arched wings, the Mute Swan is the epitome of grace as it quietly swims along the edge of a small pond. Its elegance made this European swan a favorite among waterfowl fanciers on this continent. Some captive swans escaped or were intentionally released and established feral populations in North America. The largest population is found along the Atlantic Coast from southern New England to North Carolina. Another is expanding across the Great Lakes region, and established a small breeding population in Ohio during the 1990s. These feral populations are normally resident, although Great Lakes swans undertake short-distance movements during winter.

In Ohio, Mute Swans were initially reported at Cleveland in 1936, Dayton in 1944, and Sandusky Bay in 1948 (Campbell 1968, Mathena et al. 1984, Skaggs 1936a). They were irregular visitors along Lake Erie and at Youngstown during the 1950s and have been regularly observed along the lakefront after 1962. They remained sporadic visitors to inland locations into the 1980s. Their status noticeably changed during the 1990s, as expanding populations allowed Mute Swans to become regular visitors across the state.

Mute Swans are currently uncommon to rare winter visitors along Lake Erie. They are most numerous between November and March, when they are generally observed in groups of eight or fewer, with occasional flocks of 12–30+. In November and early December, they are usually encountered along western Lake Erie and Sandusky Bay. When these marshes freeze, the swans move to open water along the lakefront. Spring thaws allow them to return to the western Lake Erie marshes.

Away from Lake Erie, Mute Swans have become casual to locally uncommon winter visitors. They are most frequently encountered in the northeastern counties, but small groups are likely to appear across the state. Wintering swans are generally present between early December and April, usually in groups of nine or fewer, although flocks of 12–23 have occasionally appeared in all portions of Ohio. Statewide estimates of as many as 91–93 Mute Swans during several winters of the 1990s indicate the current size of the winter population.

The first nesting record for Mute Swans in Ohio occurred in 1987, when a pair raised young along western Lake Erie in Lucas County (Peterjohn and Rice 1991). Small numbers have summered in the western Lake Erie marshes during subsequent years, although this breeding population totals fewer than ten pairs. Small numbers of breeding Mute Swans were also found on scattered lakes in the eastern half of Ohio during the 1990s. Some of these records pertain to swans that have been intentionally released, although nesting pairs in northeastern Ohio probably have a feral origin. The inland population is also currently fewer than ten pairs. Nonbreeders are casual to rare visitors to inland counties between May and September, usually in groups of four or fewer swans. As the Great Lakes population continues to expand, the statewide breeding population should be expected to increase.

Trumpeter Swan *Cygnus buccinator* Richardson

The former status of Trumpeter Swans in Ohio is poorly understood. Anecdotal accounts by early naturalists provide sketchy information on their former abundance, their migrations, and other aspects of their life history. Much confusion stems from an inability to distinguish Trumpeter from Tundra Swans, causing the validity of many sight records to be questioned. While there are no extant specimens to document the Trumpeter's occurrence in Ohio, a specimen taken on the Ohio River near Cincinnati (technically in Kentucky) during December 1876 supports claims of Trumpeter Swans migrating through the state (Kemsies and Randle 1953).

Trumpeter Swans once nested across the northern United States east to northern Illinois (Banko 1960). Since their wintering grounds included the central Atlantic Coast from southern New Jersey to North Carolina, migrants certainly passed through Ohio. Trumpeters were early spring migrants and probably peaked during March and early April. Their autumn flight extended from late October until freeze-up. Some Trumpeters also wintered along the Mississippi and lower Ohio Rivers upstream to southern Indiana. But despite assertions to the contrary (Jones 1903), there is no evidence to suggest Trumpeters wintered in southwestern Ohio.

As a result of overhunting and habitat destruction, Trumpeter Swans rapidly declined throughout the eastern United States. While they were reported to be regular migrants through Ohio during the early 1800s, they were encountered only occasionally after 1860 (Campbell 1940, Williams 1950). There were unverified reports of specimens taken near Ravenna and Lake St. Marys in the 1880s (Coale 1915). In the next decade, a Trumpeter was reported from Lorain on April 20, 1891, and there may have been several other sightings along Lake Erie (Jones 1903, Williams 1950). The last Ohio record was of a swan reportedly shot either April 18 or 19, 1900, near Wellston (Jackson County) (Henninger 1919).

During most of the twentieth century, Trumpeter Swans have been restricted to small populations in western North America (Banko 1960). Once seriously endangered, their numbers have substantially improved in recent decades. The few Ohio sight records prior to 1980 pertain to known escapes from captivity or swans of suspect origins. Beginning in the early 1980s, several state and provincial wildlife departments have attempted to establish Trumpeter Swans in the Great Lakes region. Swans from these programs may have contributed to the small number of recent reports of Trumpeters from Ohio, beginning with one during autumn 1988. However, a waterfowl propagator in Hancock County has also intentionally released small numbers of swans since 1993 (and possibly earlier) and is responsible for reports in that area and possibly elsewhere in the state.

Beginning in 1996, the Division of Wildlife initiated a Trumpeter Swan introduction program within Ohio. Swans have been released in the western Lake Erie marshes and at Killdeer Plains and Killbuck Marsh Wildlife Areas.

Most sightings have been at or near these release sites, although some individuals have wandered to scattered locations elsewhere in Ohio and adjacent states. While it is too early to know if this introduction program will be successful, and to predict the eventual distribution and abundance of this species in Ohio, the status of the Trumpeter Swan is rapidly changing at this time.

Tundra Swan *Cygnus columbianus* (Ord)

The distant calls of Tundra Swans may resemble barking dogs or perhaps a flock of geese. As they come closer, their distinctive resonant calls can be recognized before the Tundras become visible. Eventually, a flock of these magnificent birds passes overhead and lands in a field, providing the highlight of many March trips to western Lake Erie.

Ohio lies along the major migration corridor of Tundra Swans between their Arctic nesting grounds and wintering areas on the Atlantic Coast. During spring, this migration corridor crosses northern Ohio south to Wayne, Columbiana, Erie, Sandusky, Ottawa, and Lucas Counties. Spring Tundra Swans are mostly observed along western Lake Erie. The largest March concentrations totaled 5,500 in 1962 and 5,000 in 1930 in Ottawa and Lucas Counties (Campbell 1968). During most years, however, the flocks may not exceed 50–600. Their appearance at other locations along this corridor is more sporadic. Concentrations of 1,000 at Lake Rockwell on March 27, 1981, 600 in Trumbull and Ashtabula Counties on March 12–13, 1966, and 400 in Wayne County on March 29, 1980, are exceptional (Hall 1966b, Kleen 1980c, Peterjohn 1981b). Spring flocks usually total 20–150 in northeastern Ohio. The largest flocks tend to appear during unusually cold springs when most water remains frozen into March, while the fewest are found in relatively mild seasons.

While Tundra Swans are uncommon to locally abundant spring migrants along their northern Ohio corridor, surprisingly few appear elsewhere. They are accidental to rare migrants in the other counties, least numerous in southern Ohio. They are usually detected in groups of 3–10, with occasional flocks of 24–45.

The first spring migrants may return during February. Their passage is relatively rapid, mostly during March. Their numbers are generally reduced by the first week of April, although flocks have been reported as late as April 21. Nonbreeding immatures and other stragglers occasionally remain into May.

Tundra Swans are accidental summer visitors, with most reports during June. Campbell (1968) claimed "a few" June records from western Lake Erie, including two that summered at Cedar Point Wildlife Refuge in 1943. Single swans also summered in these marshes during 1991–1993 and 1999. Summer records away from western Lake Erie are limited to one or two Tundra Swans summering in Trumbull County during 1991 and 1992 (Harlan 1992a, 1992c), one at Killdeer Plains Wildlife Area through July 1, 1989 (Peterjohn 1989d), and several early June observations elsewhere in the northern half of the state.

Their fall migration is impressive across northern Ohio. Following a November cold front, large flocks fly eastward along Lake Erie, some passing over the shore while others are mere specks on the horizon. As evening approaches, these flocks move inland to settle on large lakes. Most rest only briefly, continuing their journey before dawn.

Although their numbers vary annually, Tundra Swans are generally more numerous during fall. This variability is most noticeable along western Lake Erie. Some years few swans visit these marshes, but other years produce concentrations as large as 13,000 on November 23, 1985 (Peterjohn 1986a). Elsewhere along Lake Erie, flights involving 1,000–5,000 swans are observed some years. Within northeastern Ohio south to Holmes and Tuscarawas Counties on the unglaciated Allegheny Plateau, migrant flocks of 200–500+ may appear following November cold fronts. The largest inland movements totaled 2,000 near Youngstown on November 4–5, 1961 (Hall 1962a), and a similar number over Akron on November 1, 1993 (Brock 1994a).

Tundra Swans are uncommon fall migrants through the northwestern and glaciated central counties. While flocks of 100–250 infrequently occur, Tundras are mostly encountered in flocks of 40 or fewer. Fall migrants are accidental to rare in southern and unglaciated central Ohio, usually as groups of ten or fewer, with occasional flocks of 20–30.

Early fall migrants have returned to Canfield by September 19, 1989 (Hall 1990a), and western Lake Erie by the first week of October, but Tundras do not normally appear until the last week of October. Large flights normally occur between October 29 and November 20. During some years, the entire Tundra Swan population may pass across Ohio during two or three days in November; in other years, defined movements accompany each cold front throughout the month.

Tundra Swans normally depart by late November. However, mild weather encourages swans to linger, and concentrations of 100–1,200 have remained along western Lake Erie until freeze-up. The last migrants normally depart by December 15–25, although their southbound movements will occur as late as January 10–20 during mild winters.

Wintering Tundra Swans were formerly exceptionally rare throughout Ohio. Beginning in the early 1960s, small numbers wintered in the western Lake Erie marshes during most years (Campbell 1968). These wintering numbers varied from just a few swans to a flock of 130 during the winter of 1982–1983 (Peterjohn 1983b). They were accidental winter visitors elsewhere in the state.

Midwinter sightings increased during the 1990s. Tundra Swans are currently rare to uncommon winter visitors along western Lake Erie, usually in flocks of 50 or fewer, with a maximum of 154 in Erie County on February 8, 1997 (Fazio 1997a). Wintering swans are casual to rare along central Lake Erie, usually in groups of four or fewer. They are generally accidental to casual winter visitors to inland lakes, producing four or fewer reports during most winters. Inland Tundras are most likely to appear in the northern half of the state, usually in groups of seven or fewer. However, the mild winter of 1996–1997 produced flocks of 14–21 swans at two inland locations and a maximum of 57 in Wayne County (Fazio 1997a). While some swans have wintered on inland lakes, others remain for only a few days.

Wood Duck *Aix sponsa* (Linnaeus)

Few ducks possess the beauty of a drake Wood Duck quietly perched on a log in a wooded swamp. This breathtaking sight is often taken for granted today, since Wood Ducks are numerous residents along streams, quiet backwaters of lakes, wooded swamps, and marshes throughout Ohio. But they have not always been so numerous. In fact, they were protected during several decades of the twentieth century after their populations were decimated by overhunting.

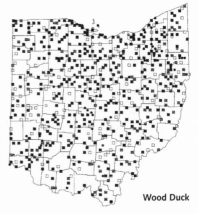

Wood Duck

By all accounts, sizable numbers of Wood Ducks graced the waterways of Ohio into the 1880s (Wheaton 1882). Their decline was fairly rapid; by 1900, Wood Ducks became rare at most localities (Campbell 1968, Henninger 1902, Trautman 1940). Further reductions were apparent by 1910–1915, when Wood Ducks essentially disappeared from most counties and the appearance of a small flock was noteworthy.

Their recovery was quite slow initially. By the mid-1930s, they remained uncommon to rare and very locally distributed summer residents. Hicks (1935a) cited breeding records from 47 counties; only four of these counties were in the southern third of the state. Wood Ducks were very rare to absent along the unglaciated Allegheny Plateau (Hicks 1937a). While some improvement was evident after 1935, populations remained depressed because of a shortage of suitable nesting cavities (Campbell 1940).

Beginning in the 1940s, the practice of providing nest boxes for Wood Ducks became widespread and their populations expanded. By the early 1960s, Wood Ducks regained their former abundance (Campbell 1968, Clark and Sipe 1970). Their numbers continued to improve, reflecting significant increases throughout the eastern United States after 1966 (Sauer et al. 1998).

Wood Ducks currently rank among the most widely distributed and numerous of Ohio's breeding waterfowl and nest in every county (Peterjohn and Rice 1991). They are generally fairly common to common summer residents, becoming locally uncommon within a few western counties. A canoe trip down any Ohio river invariably will turn up three to ten broods of Wood Ducks during June and July, even along streams in urban areas if mature riparian corridors remain intact. The densest populations are noted in managed marshes, where as many as 10–20 Wood Duck broods may be observed in a morning.

Wood Ducks nest exclusively in cavities, including artificial structures directly over water and natural cavities at heights of 50 feet or more. While they prefer to nest close to water, they have nested more than one-half mile from any stream or pond. Their nesting activities peak during May and the first half of June; nests with eggs have been reported through July 8 (Nolan 1954d). A few pairs breed earlier; recently hatched young have been observed in central Ohio as early as April 18. The first broods are usually noted during the last half of May and most are detected between early June and mid-August. Late nesting attempts produce partially grown young through September 5–14. After their young become independent, Wood Ducks frequently accumulate in flocks at evening roosts, preferring isolated buttonbush swamps and quiet backwaters along rivers.

With such a substantial breeding population, the beginning of fall migration is difficult to determine. Trautman (1940) reported southward movements by late August. In general, Wood Ducks remain fairly common to locally abundant fall migrants through October 15–25. Flocks of 15–35 may be encountered during the day, while 200–500+ may gather at evening roosts. Fall migrants are most numerous along Killbuck Creek in Wayne and Holmes Counties, where evening flights in excess of 1,000 can be witnessed during late September and early October. Their numbers noticeably diminish by early November and the last migrants usually depart by November 15. During their southward migration, Wood Ducks occasionally appear on large lakes and even occur along Lake Erie, where they may frequent sheltered bays.

At one time, Wood Ducks were accidental winter visitors. There were very few winter sightings before 1950, mostly near Toledo and Cleveland. As their breeding populations expanded, the number of winter records also increased, although they did not regularly overwinter until the early 1970s. Wood Ducks are now accidental to rare winter residents, most numerous in southern Ohio. Within the northern counties, winter reports are normally restricted to a small number of ponds and lakes that regularly host large numbers of waterfowl, mostly in the Cleveland-Akron area and occasionally at Castalia (Erie County). These winter records are normally of five or fewer ducks, with as many as 16–19 counted at Cleveland. Within the central and southern counties, small numbers are regularly found along the Scioto, Muskingum, Great Miami, and other large rivers. A few may also be mixed among flocks of wintering puddle ducks on reservoirs or ponds. These reports normally total five or fewer, with occasional flocks of 10–25.

The first spring migrants are expected in southern and central Ohio by February 20–March 5 and appear in the northern counties by the first week of March. Wood Ducks are widely distributed by March 15–25. This movement usually comprises pairs and small flocks of 10–20, with a few reports of concentrations of 50–120+. This northward migration continues into the last half of April, although late migrants are difficult to distinguish from residents.

Gadwall *Anas strepera* Linnaeus

In the nineteenth century, Gadwalls were numerous migrants until their numbers were reduced by overhunting during the 1880s (Trautman 1940). By 1900, Jones (1903) considered them rare migrants. Their status did not improve until the 1930s and 1940s. As their populations increased during the 1960s and 1970s, their breeding range expanded eastward into the Great Lakes region (DeVos 1964). These trends continued into the 1990s.

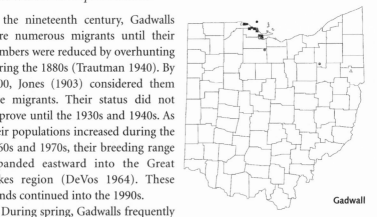

Gadwall

During spring, Gadwalls frequently associate with other puddle ducks in marshes, flooded fields, and the margins of large lakes. They are generally common to abundant along western Lake Erie and uncommon to locally common elsewhere. Along western Lake Erie, 40–75 may be observed daily and counts of 150–700+ are possible. Away from western Lake Erie, spring totals seldom exceed 30–50. The largest inland flocks totaled 200 at Youngstown and Cincinnati during the early 1950s (Brooks 1951a, Kemsies and Randle 1953). Spring migrants normally return during February and reach their peak abundance during March. Gadwalls are regularly encountered until mid-April, but most depart from interior counties by April 20–30, with a few lingering into May. Along western Lake Erie, their numbers decline during the last half of April, and the last migrants depart by May 5–15.

Despite several anecdotal accounts, there were no confirmed Ohio summer records during the nineteenth century. The first summering Gadwalls were reported from Pymatuning Lake during 1938, although they were probably nonbreeders (Walker 1938b). They also remained into June in northeastern Ohio during 1952 (Brooks 1952b). Most summer records have been since 1960. Along western Lake Erie, 1–2 pairs summered at Magee Marsh Wildlife Area between 1962 and 1964, but nesting was not confirmed (Campbell 1968). They did not regularly summer within Ottawa and Lucas Counties until the mid-1970s but have nested annually since 1979 (Kleen 1979d). Breeding has not been confirmed at any inland location, while small numbers of individuals and pairs have appeared at scattered sites in the northern half of the state.

While small flocks of 5–18 Gadwalls are infrequently reported along western Lake Erie between June and early August, these flocks are probably nonbreeders and molting males. Some years, fewer than ten pairs reside in the marshes; as many as 15–30 pairs may be present in other years (Peterjohn and Rice 1991). The few confirmed breeding records indicate that nesting is initiated in May, since most broods are reported during the last half of June and July.

The first fall migrants normally return to the western Lake Erie marshes by September 10–25 and become common by mid-October. While aerial surveys produced estimates of 12,310 on November 14, 1994, and 19,650 on November 1, 1996 (Harlan 1995a, Fazio 1997a), such numbers are not apparent from the ground. Ground observations in autumn indicate greater numbers than during spring along western Lake Erie, where the largest concentrations total 400–800+ and 75–200 may be observed daily. This status is maintained into the second half of November, with smaller numbers remaining until freeze-up.

Elsewhere, they are generally uncommon to fairly common fall migrants. Most flocks total 50 or fewer, with occasional concentrations of 100–200+. Along central Lake Erie, Gadwalls are relatively scarce until November or early December. In the interior counties, they are mostly encountered between mid-October and early December.

Gadwalls were rare winter residents before 1940. As their breeding populations expanded, wintering numbers increased. After freeze-up, Gadwalls are currently uncommon to rare visitors among large flocks of Mallards and American Black Ducks. Flocks of 20–45 have congregated at scattered locations across the state. Many of these flocks disappear by mid-January; others have overwintered. The largest winter concentration was 125 near Sandusky during February 1947 (Mayfield 1947a).

Eurasian Wigeon *Anas penelope* Linnaeus

Ohio's first Eurasian Wigeon was collected at Buckeye Lake on March 29, 1902 (Jones 1903). Others were noted in the Sandusky Bay area between April 18 and 20, 1904 (Deane 1905). By the 1920s, additional records indicated they were rare but fairly regular migrants through Ohio. In the mid-1940s, Hasbrouck (1944) cited at least forty-two records, the most from any interior state. Thirty-nine were spring migrants; only two were fall sightings, and one was an early winter observation. Eurasian Wigeon were most frequently noted from the late 1930s to the early 1950s, when they averaged two to six sightings annually. Since 1960, only one to three observations have occurred most years.

Eurasian Wigeon are rare but fairly regular spring migrants through the western Lake Erie marshes, producing as many as three sightings annually of single males among flocks of American Wigeon. They are accidental to casual spring migrants elsewhere, producing three to ten records each decade since 1960, mostly in the northeastern counties (30+ sightings) and in central Ohio near Columbus (22+ sightings). A few scattered records come from other northern counties, seven from the Cincinnati-Dayton area, three from the unglaciated counties, and one from Lake St. Marys. Most reports are of single males, although four were noted in Canton on April 19, 1935, and three appeared in Columbus on March 22, 1959 (Baird 1935c, Mumford 1959b). A few return by February 20–March 5, but most are observed between March 15 and April 20. Stragglers lingered near Toledo through May 31, 1942, and at Cleveland until May 27, 1967 (Campbell 1968, Flanigan 1968).

There are only thirteen records of this accidental fall visitor; ten in the northeastern counties and three along western Lake Erie. Except for a red-phased female in Erie County on October 22, 1988 (Peterjohn 1989a), these sightings are single males molting into their distinctive breeding plumage. They have appeared as early as September 14, 1980, at Lake Rockwell (Portage County) (Kleen 1981), but most are noted during the last half of October and November.

Eurasian Wigeon are accidental winter visitors. Single males observed at Buckeye Lake between December 30, 1938, and January 3, 1939, and Rocky River (Cuyahoga County) on January 2, 1991, may have been late fall migrants rather than wintering birds (Anderson and Kemp 1991b, Trautman 1940). Single males spent the winters of 1947–1948, 1963–1964, and 1994–1995 at Castalia (Campbell 1968, Harlan 1995c).

American Wigeon *Anas americana* Gmelin

As they pass overhead, American Wigeon are immediately recognized by their distinctive whistled calls. They are equally unmistakable on the ground. These wigeon readily join mixed flocks with other puddle ducks or occasionally form large segregated flocks. They are likely to be observed wherever waterfowl congregate.

Early spring migrants, American Wigeon return with the first warm days of February. Maximum abundance is attained between March 10

American
Wigeon

and April 7. Spring wigeon are abundant along western Lake Erie, where concentrations of 100–500 are frequent and flocks of 1,000–2,500+ may be encountered. Larger concentrations are exceptional, although as many as 20,000 were estimated on March 18, 1971 (Campbell 1973). Along central Lake Erie and in most northern and glaciated central counties, wigeon are fairly common to common migrants, but flocks seldom exceed 50–250. They become locally abundant at a few localities; at Big Island Wildlife Area (Marion County) and in Wayne County concentrations of 400–1,000+ may appear. Spring migrants are least numerous in the southern and unglaciated counties, where they are locally rare to fairly common. Flocks seldom exceed 20–75 except for occasional concentrations of 300–450 in southwestern Ohio (Kemsies and Randle 1953, Mathena et al. 1984). Small flocks and individuals are regularly noted through the end of April. Most depart by May 5–10, except along western Lake Erie where a few may remain into June.

American Wigeon rank among the rarest summer residents within the western Lake Erie marshes. Small numbers have summered there since the 1930s, most of them nonbreeders. Before 1960, the only nesting attempt was confirmed in 1936 (Campbell 1968). Beginning in the early 1960s, wigeon expanded their breeding range eastward (DeVos 1964), resulting in small numbers of breeding pairs along western Lake Erie since 1962 (Campbell 1968). They are currently rare summer residents, and the entire breeding population is probably fewer than five pairs during most years (Peterjohn and Rice 1991). While nesting has almost certainly occurred, there have been no confirmed breeding attempts since 1970. Their breeding chronology has not been established in Ohio. Nonbreeders are rare visitors to these marshes, normally in groups of 1–6. Molt migrations may produce larger concentrations, including 50 at Cedar Point National Wildlife Refuge (Lucas County) on June 21, 1980 (Kleen 1980d), and other flocks of 28–30.

Elsewhere, American Wigeon are accidental to casual summer visitors in the northern half of Ohio. There are several summer records at Cleveland, and a pair nested there in 1967 to establish the only breeding record away from western Lake Erie (Flanigan 1968). They have also summered at Pymatuning Lake in 1938 (Walker 1938b), Seneca County in 1984, and Portage County in 1985 (Peterjohn and Rice 1991). Other individuals have remained for only a few days at scattered localities.

During fall, the first American Wigeon return to western Lake Erie by August 25–September 5. Sizable concentrations are encountered by late September or early October. Although their numbers fluctuate annually, wigeon remain common to abundant migrants through early December. Some years, the largest flocks are composed of 100–300, while 800–4,000+ may appear in other years. The largest fall concentrations totaled 10,000 at East Harbor State Park on November 13, 1948, and aerial surveys of 15,355 on October 22, 1966, and 18,700 on November 2, 1994 (Campbell 1968, 1973; Harlan 1995a).

Away from western Lake Erie, American Wigeon normally return by September 15–25 and flocks may appear during mid-October. These migrants are locally rare to fairly common. Fall concentrations are generally 25–100, with occasional flocks of 200–400 in the central and northeastern counties. Larger flocks are exceptional, although 2,500 congregated at Pymatuning Lake during 1936 and 1938 (Baird 1936d, Walker 1938c).

Freezing temperatures during December or early January force most wigeon to migrate. Winter residents are generally casual to rare and locally distributed. Their numbers have slowly increased since the early 1960s. A flock of 100–180+ normally winters at Castalia, while 15–40 are found near Columbus. Elsewhere, scattered individuals may be found among large wintering flocks of Mallards and American Black Ducks across the state.

American Black Duck *Anas rubripes* Brewster

In every aspect of their life history, behavior, and habitat requirements, American Black Ducks are similar to Mallards. As a result of extensive hybridization between these species, some ornithologists regard them as conspecific. Black Ducks have not fared well in competition with Mallards during the twentieth century, and have declined across much of their range as Mallard populations have increased.

Before 1940, American Black Ducks were the most numerous wintering puddle ducks in Ohio (Campbell 1940, Trautman 1940). Their relative abundance began to change during the 1940s, and Mallards outnumbered American Black Ducks at Buckeye Lake by the winter of 1952–1953 (Nolan 1963b). Similar trends were apparent at other localities and continued into the 1990s.

Despite declining populations, American Black Ducks remain uncommon to abundant winter residents on large lakes, marshes, and streams throughout Ohio. Most numerous along western Lake Erie, especially portions of Sandusky Bay, their numbers vary with the severity of the weather. Totals of 500–2,000+ are frequent, and larger concentrations are possible. Aerial surveys have estimated 20,000–37,500+ during many winters (Campbell 1973). The largest flocks are frequently noted between December 15 and January 15 but may be substantially reduced by February.

Elsewhere, the largest concentrations appear in the northern and glaciated central counties, where flocks of 100–1,500+ gather each year. Reservoirs in the southern and unglaciated counties normally host flocks of 50–250+. Similar flocks regularly winter along central Lake Erie. In counties lacking large lakes, flocks of American Black Ducks are composed of only 5–30 scattered along streams. These numbers represent a substantial decline from former wintering populations, when flocks of 500–2,500+ were regularly reported from the glaciated counties.

Spring migration begins during February and peaks in March. Along western Lake Erie, American Black Ducks remain numerous through April 5–15 and small flocks are regularly observed into the first half of May. Elsewhere, small flocks are noted through April 7 and only stragglers after April 10–20. These migrants are abundant along western Lake Erie, although daily totals are normally 50–200 and seldom surpass 500–1,000. They become uncommon to locally abundant migrants elsewhere, with most counts of 30 or fewer, and occasional flocks of 50–250.

In the mid-1930s, American Black Ducks were common summer residents along western Lake Erie (Hicks 1935a). They were rare to uncommon and locally distributed within the northeastern counties south to Columbiana County. Scattered breeding pairs were sporadically encountered south to Mercer, Shelby, Logan, Franklin, Fairfield, Guernsey, and Carroll Counties (Hicks 1935a, 1937a).

Along western Lake Erie, this population remained stable into the 1960s (Andrews 1952, Campbell 1968). Campbell (1968) cited an average of 14 nesting pairs at Magee Marsh Wildlife Area, with a maximum of 28 pairs in 1961. Anderson (1960) estimated 20 pairs at Winous Point in 1960. Their numbers were declining elsewhere. A few pairs nested in the northeastern counties, but they disappeared from other counties except for nesting records in Butler County before 1953, Carroll County in 1962, and Jefferson County in 1974 (Buchanan 1980, Kemsies and Randle 1953).

While small numbers of American Black Ducks nested within the western Lake Erie marshes during the 1980s (Peterjohn and Rice 1991), this population almost completely disappeared during the 1990s. They have become casual to rare summer residents in these marshes. They may not be present every year, and the entire breeding population probably totals fewer than ten pairs. Summer records are accidental to casual elsewhere in northwestern Ohio, with isolated breeding attempts confirmed in Wood, Seneca, and Sandusky Counties during the Breeding Bird Atlas (Peterjohn and Rice 1991). Within northeastern Ohio, American Black Ducks remain casual to locally rare summer visitors, with scattered reports south to Carroll County and Killbuck Marsh Wildlife Area (Peterjohn and Rice 1991). Except for 3–5+ pairs breeding near Lake Rockwell (Portage County), confirmed nesting records are infrequent and many reports pertain to nonbreeders.

Nesting American Black Ducks are usually found in large marshes or isolated ponds bordered by emergent vegetation. Their territorial activity starts by late March and peaks in mid-April, when the first clutches are laid (Andrews 1952). Most nests are located on dikes or in grasslands adjacent to marshes and have been discovered during May. While downy young have been observed as early as May 5, most broods are noted in June and July (Campbell 1968).

When populations were larger, American Black Ducks regularly undertook a substantial molt migration into the western Lake Erie marshes, and as many as 1,000 were counted by the first week of August (Campbell 1968). Similar flights have not been apparent in recent years, when their numbers have slowly accumulated during the last half of August and September. They normally become numerous during the first half of October. Peak concentrations are expected during November and the first half of December, when 500–5,000+ may be tallied from the ground and aerial surveys may count 20,000–50,000+.

Away from western Lake Erie, American Black Ducks are casually encountered during August and the first half of September. The first migrants normally appear within the northern and central counties between September 15 and 25 and in southern Ohio during the first half of October. Peak concentrations are expected in November and the first half of December. Fall flocks of 200–2,000+ are regularly reported in the northern and central counties. Flocks of 25–300+ may appear in the southern and unglaciated counties.

Mallard *Anas platyrhynchos* Linnaeus

At the turn of the century, Jones (1903) described Mallards as "locally common migrants, but absent from many localities and mostly seen in small flocks." Breeding pairs were irregularly reported from the southern half of

Ohio but were "more common and very local" elsewhere. While most puddle ducks declined after the early 1900s, the adaptable Mallard substantially increased. In the mid-1930s, Hicks (1935a) considered Mallards common summer residents in the western Lake Erie marshes. They were uncommon to rare and very locally distributed elsewhere in the northern half of Ohio but were absent from the southern half. This population noticeably increased in the 1940s and 1950s, as pairs expanded into the southern

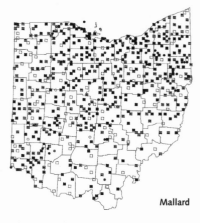

Mallard

counties. Mallards released from game farms augmented these expanding populations (DeVos 1964). By the mid-1960s, nesting Mallards were found in most counties. Their statewide breeding population significantly increased during subsequent decades (Sauer et al. 1998).

Mallards are currently common to abundant summer residents within the marshes bordering western Lake Erie, where their relative abundance was estimated at 20–25 pairs per square mile before 1952 (Andrews 1952). Similar densities are encountered today except in drawndown marshes. In addition, nonbreeders and molting males regularly form flocks of 50–500+ as early as the first half of June. Away from western Lake Erie, Mallards are fairly common to common summer residents. They are numerous throughout the glaciated counties, where daily totals of 5–50+ are expected. They are more locally distributed in unglaciated Ohio, although breeding pairs are found in every county (Peterjohn and Rice 1991).

Breeding Mallards usually nest in upland grassy cover adjacent to ponds and marshes. A few nests may be placed more than a mile from water. They normally nest on the ground but some have used tree cavities. Most pairs establish territories in late March or early April. Nests have been discovered during the last week of March but first clutches are normally laid by mid-April (Andrews 1952). Renesting efforts are responsible for clutches through mid-June. The first broods have hatched by the last week of April, although most appear between May 15 and June 15. Partially grown young may be regularly observed through the first half of August.

Fall migrants are apparent along western Lake Erie by August 20–30, although flocks may not be encountered within the interior counties until the last half of September. The largest numbers usually appear between October 25 and December 15. These flocks may remain until freeze-up in January.

These migrants are most numerous along western Lake Erie, where 1,000–5,000+ may appear by early September. As many as 10,000–20,000 are expected on aerial surveys during mid-October, with peak concentrations of 40,000–75,000+ in November and early December. A remarkable 113,000+ were tallied along western Lake Erie on December 18–19, 1996 (Fazio 1997a). From the ground, the largest flocks seldom exceed 5,000–12,000. Their numbers decline during the last half of December, although 25,000–40,000+ have been estimated on aerial surveys into early January.

Fall migrants are common to abundant away from western Lake Erie, least numerous in the unglaciated counties. Inland flocks seldom exceed 100–500 during September, and concentrations of 500–1,000+ normally appear by mid-October. Peak numbers are expected between November 15 and December 15, producing local flocks of 3,000–15,000 in the glaciated counties but normally less than 1,500 in southeastern Ohio. The largest flocks frequently appear immediately before freeze-up and may remain into the first half of January.

Before 1940, wintering Mallards were outnumbered by American Black Ducks throughout Ohio. Their status began to change in the late 1930s along western Lake Erie (Campbell 1940). Increased numbers were apparent elsewhere during the 1940s and 1950s as Mallards became the most numerous wintering puddle ducks. Mallards are currently fairly common to abundant winter residents. The largest concentrations are expected along western Lake Erie, where 8,000–20,000+ may winter in the marshes. Elsewhere, winter flocks of 500–5,000+ may develop in the glaciated counties, while totals seldom exceed 300–500 in unglaciated Ohio.

Their spring migration begins during the first warm days of February. These movements peak during March, when they become common to abundant migrants. The last flocks normally depart by April 25–May 5. Spring concentrations of 500–4,000+ may appear on large lakes, marshes, and flooded fields throughout Ohio. Larger flocks are unusual. Along western Lake Erie, concentrations of 1,000–7,000+ may be observed from the ground, while aerial surveys produce estimates of 20,000–40,000+.

Blue-winged Teal *Anas discors* Linnaeus

These attractive ducks have always been among our more numerous migrant waterfowl. Regularly encountered in most counties, Blue-winged Teal generally avoid the open waters of large lakes in favor of sheltered backwaters, flooded fields, marshes, and small ponds. Their numbers fluctuate in response to habitat conditions in the prairies of the central United States and Canada. While poor habitat conditions on the prairie breeding grounds are responsible for substantially reduced populations during the 1980s, improved breeding habitat conditions in the 1990s have produced increased numbers of migrants passing through Ohio.

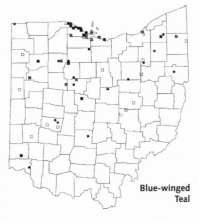

Blue-winged Teal

Blue-winged Teal remain fairly common to locally abundant spring migrants, least numerous along the unglaciated Allegheny Plateau. Local concentrations of 200–500+ may develop in any glaciated county but are most regularly encountered along western Lake Erie. Most spring reports total 25–150. A few have appeared north to Lake Erie by February 22–23, but the first migrants normally return by March 5–15. Their maximum abundance is normally attained during April. Small flocks and scattered pairs pass through most counties until May 20–25.

Breeding Blue-winged Teal have always been most evident within the northern third of Ohio. In the mid-1930s, Hicks (1935a) considered them fairly common residents within the western Lake Erie marshes. They were rare and locally distributed elsewhere in northern Ohio, with records from most northeastern counties south to Wayne and Columbiana, and from Defiance, Huron, and Ashland Counties. The only other breeding teal were recorded at Lake St. Marys, Indian Lake, and in Holmes and Tuscarawas Counties. Of these inland sites, only Lake St. Marys supported a sizable population (Clark and Sipe 1970).

Their breeding range expanded in subsequent decades. The first Columbus broods were reported in 1942 (Hicks 1945c). Nesting was confirmed in Hamilton, Butler, and Brown Counties by 1953, and the first Dayton nest was discovered in 1963 (Kemsies and Randle 1953, Mathena et al. 1984). Nesting populations were also increasing along western Lake Erie, with 129 breeding pairs estimated at Magee Marsh Wildlife Area in 1966–1967 and similar numbers in other marshes (Anderson 1960, Campbell 1968). This range expansion ended during the 1970s and fewer breeding pairs have been evident since 1980.

Blue-winged Teal remain fairly common summer residents along western Lake Erie, where breeding pairs occupy all suitable marshes. Elsewhere, the number of summer records exhibits considerable annual fluctuations. They are casual to locally uncommon within the other northern counties. As many as 5–10 pairs are regularly found in Seneca and Summit Counties, and along the Killbuck Creek marshes in Wayne and Holmes Counties, but scattered pairs are sporadically encountered in other locations (Peterjohn and Rice

1991). In glaciated central and southern Ohio, nesting Blue-winged Teal are accidental to casual summer visitors, except at Big Island Wildlife Area (Marion County) and Gilmore Ponds (Butler County), where 1–5 pairs are present during most years (Harlan 1991b, Peterjohn and Rice 1991). Summering teal are largely absent from the unglaciated Allegheny Plateau, where nesting has been confirmed from Tuscarawas, Carroll, and Vinton Counties (Harlan 1991b, Peterjohn and Rice 1991).

Nesting Blue-wingeds prefer extensive marshes and large ponds bordered by dense emergent vegetation. Their nests are placed in upland grassy cover near these habitats. Most pairs establish territories by April 20–30 (Andrews 1952). Nests with eggs have been recorded as early as April 30–May 1, but most are discovered during May and early June. The first broods appear by June 15–25. Renesting attempts are responsible for clutches through July 31 and adults accompanied by partially grown young on August 25 (Campbell 1968, Phillips 1980).

These teal are the first waterfowl to begin their southward migration. Flocks frequently return by July 20–30 and are widely distributed by mid-August. This movement peaks between August 25 and September 30 but noticeably diminishes during the first half of October. Along western Lake Erie, small numbers regularly remain through November 3–10, with occasional stragglers later in the month. Elsewhere, Blue-wingeds normally depart by October 15–27 and there are few records after November 1.

Fall teal are common to abundant along western Lake Erie, where concentrations of 100–1,000+ regularly develop. Aerial surveys conducted in early September may produce estimates of 5,000–9,000+ (Harlan 1994a). They become uncommon to locally abundant migrants within the other glaciated counties. Flocks of 500–900+ may appear, although daily totals generally do not exceed 50–200. These migrants are rare to fairly common along the unglaciated Allegheny Plateau, mostly in flocks of 30 or fewer.

Although these teal normally depart long before the onset of winter, mild weather has prompted a few to linger into early December. They become accidental visitors after December 5–10. The few confirmed winter records are invariably single teal, frequently birds crippled during the hunting season. There are only three reports of Blue-winged Teal remaining after early January. Trautman (1940) reported one observed intermittently at Buckeye Lake throughout the winter of 1931–1932, another reportedly spent the winter of 1982–1983 at Magee Marsh Wildlife Area (Peterjohn 1983b), and one was observed at Castalia between January 8 and February 7, 1995 (Harlan 1995b).

Cinnamon Teal *Anas cyanoptera* Vieillot

In North America, these attractive teal breed primarily on lakes and marshes in the western United States and Canada. Their winter range extends from California and the southwestern states into Mexico. Cinnamon Teal are most numerous west of the Rocky Mountains but regularly migrate through the Great Plains. They are generally accidental visitors anywhere east of the Mississippi River (AOU 1998).

Cinnamon Teal are most conspicuous during spring. Seven of Ohio's eight confirmed records are distinctive breeding males that associated with Blue-winged Teal. The first Cinnamon Teal was collected at Buckeye Lake in Fairfield County on April 4, 1895 (Trautman 1940). Fifty-six years later, another appeared at Kellogg Pond near Cincinnati between March 20 and 31, 1951, and courted several female Blue-wingeds (Kemsies and Randle 1953). Drake Cinnamons were also discovered at Magee Marsh Wildlife Area on May 11, 1980 (Kleen 1980c), Delaware Wildlife Area between April 19 and 26, 1986 (Peterjohn 1986c), Wayne County on April 9–15, 1989, Ottawa County on April 14, 1989 (Peterjohn 1989c), and at Spring Valley Wildlife Area on April 25–26, 1996 (Brock 1996c). Additionally, several apparent Cinnamon X Blue-winged Teal hybrids have been reported during spring.

As fall migrants, Cinnamon Teal retain their drab eclipse plumage and are very similar to Blue-wingeds. In addition, some Blue-wingeds become stained with iron oxides and can superficially resemble a breeding drake Cinnamon Teal. Given these identification problems, there is only one confirmed fall record from Ohio. A Cinnamon Teal was shot by a hunter at Magee Marsh Wildlife Area on November 5, 1980. This specimen is on display at the wildlife area.

Northern Shoveler *Anas clypeata* Linnaeus

Even in their obscure eclipse plumages, Northern Shovelers are instantly recognized by their oversized bills. These bills are very effective strainers of plant and animal matter from shallow water along the margins of ponds, wetlands, and flooded fields. While shovelers regularly associate with other puddle ducks, their unique feeding apparatus allows them to occupy a niche of their own.

A few early spring migrants return in late February, but Northern Shovelers are not expected until March 7–15. The largest numbers appear between March 15 and April 15 and most depart by May 5–10. A few stragglers linger into June, mostly along western Lake Erie. Even though they are widely distributed, spring shovelers are seldom encountered in sizable flocks. They are most numerous along western Lake Erie, appearing as fairly common to common migrants in flocks of 20–50, with occasional concentrations of 100–500+. Elsewhere, shovelers are generally uncommon to fairly common migrants through the glaciated counties and rare to uncommon along the unglaciated Allegheny Plateau. These migrants are mostly observed in flocks of 40 or fewer, with infrequent concentrations of 50–150+. The largest inland flocks totaled 200–350.

Northern Shoveler

The first breeding shovelers were reported along western Lake Erie in the 1930s (Trautman 1935a). Nesting pairs in these marshes were most evident in 1936 and 1937, probably drought-displaced birds from central North America (Campbell 1940). Shovelers produced few summer sightings in the 1940s and early 1950s, but by the late 1950s summering shovelers returned to western Lake Erie as part of an eastward range expansion (DeVos 1964). They were considered "a definitely established nesting species" in the Winous Point marshes in 1960 and have summered annually in the Magee Marsh Wildlife Area-Ottawa Wildlife Refuge complex since 1960 (Anderson 1960, Campbell 1968).

Northern Shovelers are currently rare summer residents in marshes bordering western Lake Erie. Fewer than ten pairs are present during most years, although 20–30 pairs may occur during years of peak abundance (Peterjohn and Rice 1991). These summer records are of individuals or family groups. The few confirmed breeding records indicate that clutches are laid during May and hatch by mid-June. Family groups remain intact until late July or early August.

Away from western Lake Erie, Northern Shovelers are accidental summer visitors in the northern and central counties. Confirmed breeding records are limited to a brood in Delaware Wildlife Area (Marion County) on June 22–23, 1956 (Stewart 1957), a pair in Seneca County in 1993 (Harlan 1993d), an unsuccessful nest on Killdeer Plains Wildlife Area (Wyandot County) during May 1984 (Peterjohn and Rice 1991), and a nest at Pymatuning Lake in 1936 (Baird 1936c). A pair was suspected of nesting at Big Island Wildlife Area (Marion County) during 1983 (Peterjohn and Rice 1991). Other summer records from these localities and at Evans Lake (Mahoning County) (Brooks 1950d) are thought to be nonbreeders.

Relatively few Northern Shovelers migrate through Ohio each autumn. These migrants are uncommon to fairly common along western Lake Erie but uncommon to rare elsewhere. Fall shovelers are mostly observed in groups of ten or fewer, with occasional concentrations of 30–75. The largest ground counts produced tallies of 500–750+, while aerial surveys along western Lake Erie seldom produce estimates of more than 400–600. The first migrants may return during August with flocks of Blue-winged Teal. Shovelers regularly appear along western Lake Erie during the first half of September but are sporadically observed elsewhere until October. Most are reported between October 10 and November 20, with another small movement immediately before freeze-up in December.

By early January, only a few wintering shovelers remain. These winter residents are regularly observed only at Castalia, where numbers increased during the 1990s and as many as 100–140 were counted (Harlan 1995b). They are casual to accidental winter residents elsewhere, mostly 1–6 among large flocks of puddle ducks. Small flocks have wintered during relatively mild seasons, including 33 at Buckeye Lake throughout the winter of 1931–1932 and 50 at Magee Marsh Wildlife Area in 1982–1983 (Peterjohn 1983b, Trautman 1940).

Northern Pintail *Anas acuta* Linnaeus

During the nineteenth and early twentieth centuries, Northern Pintails were the most numerous puddle ducks (Jones 1903, Wheaton 1882). While precise counts are unavailable, anecdotal records indicate that they easily surpassed Mallards in abundance. Their numbers were declining in the 1890s, and pintails became less numerous than Mallards by the early 1920s (Trautman 1940). This trend continued during subsequent decades.

Northern Pintail

Pintails are currently common to abundant spring migrants along western Lake Erie but have become uncommon to locally common in the glaciated counties and rare to uncommon on the unglaciated Allegheny Plateau. Along western Lake Erie, flocks of 100–1,000+ can be observed during most years and as many as 5,000 have been reported (Campbell 1968). Fewer pintails migrate along central Lake Erie, where flocks seldom exceed 25–50. Inland migrants are most numerous in the northeastern and glaciated central counties. Pintails once gathered into local flocks of 400–1,000+ and as many as 3,000 were counted at Youngstown on March 24, 1934 (Baird 1934b). In recent years, pintails mostly appear in groups of 50 or fewer, with occasional flocks of 100–500. Smaller numbers migrate through other interior counties; flocks of 100–300+ were formerly observed but reports in excess of 50–75 are unusual today. The only exception is the mouth of the Great Miami River (Hamilton County) where "hundreds" may congregate.

Relatively early migrants, pintails regularly appear during February and become most numerous between March 7 and April 7. Away from western Lake Erie, their numbers noticeably decline by mid-April and very few stragglers remain after May 1. In the western Lake Erie marshes, small flocks are regularly observed through late April; late migrants frequently remain through May 10–20.

Northern Pintails were formerly irregular summer residents in the western Lake Erie marshes. Most early records were probably of nonbreeders, although nesting was confirmed in 1930 and 1937 (Campbell 1968, Hicks 1935a). Between 1949 and 1952, approximately two percent of summering ducks along western Lake Erie were pintails (Andrews 1952). However, most were nonbreeders and there were few additional confirmed nesting attempts. Since 1960, pintails have been rare summer residents, with a breeding population of fewer than ten pairs during most years (Peterjohn and Rice 1991). Most summer records from these marshes are nonbreeders or ducks returning to molt, producing flocks as large as 100 (Anderson 1960). Breeding pintails prefer to nest in grassy cover near large undisturbed wetlands. The few breeding records indicate that nesting activities are initiated during May; most family groups are observed in June (Campbell 1968, Hicks 1935a).

Away from western Lake Erie, Northern Pintails are accidental summer visitors to the northern and central counties. Most are nonbreeders, although there are nesting records at Pymatuning Lake (Ashtabula County) during 1936 and 1937 (Baird 1936c, Walker 1937a), and broods were discovered at Killdeer Plains Wildlife Area in 1986, and Delaware Wildlife Area in 1989 (Peterjohn and Rice 1991). Nesting has also been attempted in Seneca County in 1984 and near Dayton in 1990 (Peterjohn 1990d, Peterjohn and Rice 1991).

As fall migrants, pintails are decidedly most numerous in the western Lake Erie marshes. The first migrants usually return during the last half of August. They are commonly encountered by late September in flocks of 50–500+. The largest concentrations are discovered during November, including aerial estimates of 13,325 on November 11, 1960, and 26,425 on November 2, 1994 (Campbell 1973, Harlan 1995a), while 6,500 were estimated from the ground on November 27, 1948 (Campbell 1968).

Fall pintails are rare to uncommon migrants elsewhere. In recent years, most reports are of 30 or fewer, with infrequent flocks of 100+. Earlier in the twentieth century, fall flocks of 100–400 were regularly noted in the central and northeastern counties. These migrants may appear during the last week of August, although they are not regularly observed until September 15–25. Most appear during the last half of October and November.

By mid-December, most pintails have departed for their wintering grounds. Mild weather allows flocks to linger into the first half of January. But once the marshes and lakes freeze, they become casual to locally uncommon winter residents across Ohio. Individuals and small flocks are found among the large associations of wintering puddle ducks. A few also regularly over-winter at Castalia. Numbers are usually fewer than 10, with occasional reports of 15–25.

Green-winged Teal *Anas crecca* Linnaeus

Green-winged
Teal

The first Green-winged Teal may appear during February, but normally spring migrants return by March 3–7. This movement peaks between March 10 and April 7. During these weeks, Green-wingeds are common to abundant migrants along western Lake Erie, where 50–400+ may be observed. Larger concentrations are exceptional. They become uncommon migrants along central Lake Erie, and flocks seldom exceed 10–20. Spring Green-wingeds are uncommon to fairly common migrants within the northern and glaciated central counties, where daily totals of 5–50 are expected. These teal become locally abundant at preferred localities such as Big Island Wildlife Area (Marion County) and southwestern Wayne County, where 100–300+ may congregate. They are least numerous in the southern and unglaciated counties, becoming uncommon to rare migrants in flocks of 5–100. Numbers noticeably decline by mid-April. Green-wingeds largely depart from interior counties by April 25–30, although a few linger into the first week of May. Along western Lake Erie, small numbers regularly remain through May 15–22.

As summer residents, Green-winged Teal are largely restricted to marshes bordering western Lake Erie. Summering pairs were initially recorded there in 1934, and the first breeding attempt was confirmed in 1937 (Campbell 1940). Despite sporadic summer sightings, the next nesting record was established in 1954 (Campbell 1968). Summering records became more frequent in the late

1950s, with another nest discovered in Ottawa County during 1960 (Anderson 1960). Breeding pairs were regularly noted at Magee Marsh Wildlife Area between 1962 and 1967 (Campbell 1968), and their numbers slowly increased after 1970.

Green-winged Teal are currently rare summer residents within the western Lake Erie marshes. The entire population may total 10–20 pairs during most years, although as many as 25–50 pairs may be present during years of peak abundance (Peterjohn and Rice 1991). Small numbers of nonbreeders may also spend the summer in these marshes. Away from western Lake Erie, Green-winged Teal are accidental summer residents. There are confirmed nesting records from Pymatuning Lake (Ashtabula County) in 1937 and possibly 1938 (Walker 1937a, 1938b), Berlin Reservoir in Mahoning County in 1953 (Brooks 1953d), near Pickerington in Franklin County in 1981 (Peterjohn 1981c), Barberton (Summit County) sporadically after 1985 (Peterjohn 1988d, Peterjohn and Rice 1991), and in Seneca County in 1993 (Brock 1993d). Summering Green-winged Teal have also been discovered at Killdeer Plains and Big Island Wildlife Areas and in Gallia and Paulding Counties, although nesting has not been confirmed.

Nesting teal are restricted to extensive wetlands where open water is interspersed with emergent vegetation. Their nests are placed on dikes or in grassy fields near these marshes. The few breeding records indicate that nesting activities begin in late April or early May. Most broods are observed in June or early July, although small young at Berlin Reservoir were discovered on August 2 (Brooks 1953d).

While 125 Green-winged Teal were noted in Lucas County on July 1, 1983, this concentration comprised male teal returning to molt. Other "molt migrations" involved flocks of 20–40+. Fall Green-wingeds may appear along western Lake Erie and scattered inland localities between July 25 and August 7. By mid-August, fall migrants are regularly mixed among flocks of Blue-winged Teal passing through the state.

Along western Lake Erie, 1,500 Green-winged Teal were observed at Ottawa Wildlife Refuge on September 6, 1981, but they do not normally become common migrants until September 20–25. Fall migrants are most numerous during October and November. The largest concentrations totaled 3,300–3,750+ from the ground and an aerial estimate of 24,595 on October 13, 1994 (Harlan 1995a). Fall Green-wingeds are usually observed in flocks of 50–500+. They normally depart during December, although as many as 75–250 have been counted through December 15–21.

Their inland passage peaks between October 5 and November 15. These migrants are generally rare to uncommon in most counties, becoming locally fairly common at a few preferred localities. Most fall totals are 5–40, with infrequent flocks of 50–100+ and maxima of 200–250+. Numbers of inland migrants noticeably decline during the last half of November, although small numbers linger until freeze-up.

Unlike most other puddle ducks, Green-winged Teal do not regularly winter in Ohio and become accidental to casual visitors after early January. Trautman's (1940) observations of small numbers regularly wintering at Buckeye Lake in the 1920s and 1930s have not been evident elsewhere. Wintering teal are most likely to be noted during mild years. They are most often reported from the western Lake Erie marshes, but midwinter records are scattered across the state in groups of ten or fewer.

Most of our Green-winged Teal are members of the North American race, *A. c. carolinensis*. The European race, *A. c. crecca*, is an accidental visitor. The few Ohio records of this race include a specimen collected at New Bremen (Auglaize County) on March 18, 1910 (Walker 1931), and documented sightings of males at Buckeye Lake on March 6, 1932 (Trautman 1940), near Pickerington (Franklin County) on March 18–30, 1976, and near Sugarcreek during February 5–27, 1999 (R. Schlabach 1999a). Undocumented records near Youngstown during the springs of 1933, 1935, and 1938 could pertain to the same individual (Baird 1935b, Borror 1950, Walker 1938a).

Canvasback *Aythya valisineria* (Wilson)

In the early 1900s, shallow bays along western Lake Erie supported abundant vegetation. Cattails formed dense patches over the exposed bars, while deeper water supported extensive mats of pondweeds, eelgrass, and other aquatic plants. These bays provided abundant food for waterfowl and served as major staging areas during migration. The most notable migrant was the Canvasback, forming large rafts over the eelgrass beds. A sizable proportion of the Atlantic Coast wintering population passed through these marshes each spring and fall.

Conditions within these bays changed dramatically during the twentieth century. Most aquatic and emergent vegetation disappeared as a result of rising lake levels and increased suspended sediments in the water. As the food supply was reduced, waterfowl declined. Puddle ducks still abounded in diked marshes along western Lake Erie, but these marshes were less suitable for Canvasbacks. While flocks of Canvasbacks still appeared on Lake Erie each year, most moved to Lake St. Clair and other locations where aquatic vegetation was still plentiful. The introduction of zebra mussels into Lake Erie has improved water clarity, which resulted in the reestablishment of beds of aquatic vegetation during the 1990s, producing a resurgence in Canvasback populations.

Along western Lake Erie, large numbers of migrant Canvasbacks were observed into the 1930s, including concentrations of 11,000 on March 24, 1939, 7,800 on March 21, 1937, and 5,000 on November 7, 1936, and November 24, 1935 (Baird 1937, Campbell 1968). Their decline became evident in the 1940s and continued into the 1980s. Deteriorating habitat quality on their breeding and wintering grounds contributed to this decline. Improving water quality and increased breeding populations during the 1990s allowed their numbers to approach their former abundance.

Canvasbacks are early spring migrants, regularly appearing during February, and migrant flocks are observed throughout March. Largest numbers appear during cold springs when open water is limited. Warm March temperatures allow Canvasbacks to rapidly pass through the state.

Spring migrants are most numerous along western Lake Erie, where they are common to abundant. Peak concentrations of 500–2,000 are reported most years and flocks of 3,000–5,000+ are less frequently encountered. An aerial estimate of 24,744 on February 18–20, 1997, is indicative of their recent recovery (Fazio 1997). Elsewhere along the lakefront, Canvasbacks are fairly common to locally abundant migrants. When the lake is mostly ice covered, flocks of 200–600+ appear at hot-water outlets from Huron eastward. Concentrations seldom exceed 50–200 once the ice disappears.

Away from Lake Erie, spring Canvasbacks are mostly reported from the northern half of Ohio, where they are uncommon to fairly common migrants, and daily totals are usually 25–150. While flocks of 300–600 occasionally appear, concentrations of 500–1,000 are regularly noted only in southwestern Wayne County. Migrant Canvasbacks are rare to uncommon migrants in the southern half of Ohio, mostly reported in flocks of 50 or fewer.

Most spring Canvasbacks depart during the first half of April. While there are few inland sightings after April 25, stragglers remain along western Lake Erie into early May and the last migrants usually depart by May 7–15.

Summering Canvasbacks are casually encountered along western Lake Erie but are accidental elsewhere. Most records are during June and may represent very late migrants. Single birds have summered at Toledo, Metzger Marsh Wildlife Area, and Cleveland, and remained at Columbus through July 1, 1982 (Campbell 1968, Flanigan 1968, Harlan 1992). There are no confirmed nesting records.

As fall migrants, Canvasbacks are currently fairly common to locally abundant along western Lake Erie, where the largest flocks normally total 100–500. An aerial estimate of 7,275 on November 30, 1993, is indicative of their improved numbers during the 1990s (Harlan 1994a). They are uncommon in the northern and central counties and casual to rare in southern Ohio. Daily totals are generally fewer than 20, with occasional flocks of 50+. These migrants may return during the last half of October, but most are encountered during November.

Lake Erie Canvasbacks tend to be widely distributed during winter. Severe weather during December has caused large numbers to appear in the Toledo area, including 10,206 on the 1976 Christmas Bird Count. Most years, these concentrations do not develop until January or early February. Wintering Canvasbacks are most numerous on Maumee Bay, where 3,000–5,000 regularly appear and as many as 8,500 and 10,000 were reported during the winters of 1976–1977 and 1990–1991, respectively (Kleen 1977b, Peterjohn 1991b). Smaller flocks are noted elsewhere along the lakefront wherever open water is available, usually 50–250, with occasional concentrations of 500–1,000+. These wintering Canvasbacks are primarily adult males. In the interior counties, most Canvasbacks depart by December 10, although a few may remain as long as open water is available. They are accidental to casual midwinter visitors and do not regularly overwinter at any location. Most inland wintering reports are during mild seasons, invariably scattered individuals or flocks of fewer than 10.

Redhead *Aythya americana* (Eyton)

Large flocks of Redheads once used Maumee and Sandusky Bays along western Lake Erie as migration staging areas, especially during spring. But most flocks shifted to other locations with the disappearance of aquatic vegetation from these bays. Redhead numbers also fluctuated in response to changing habitat conditions on their breeding and wintering grounds. Droughts during the 1930s and 1950s caused their numbers to plummet, but they recovered with the return of

Redhead

favorable water conditions. Their populations slowly declined after 1970, with the drainage of prairie wetlands and a series of dry years. The return of favorable habitat conditions on their prairie breeding grounds allowed their populations to increase during the 1990s.

Redheads are among the first waterfowl initiating spring migration. The first February thaw usually prompts their return. Flocks are normally present by the first week of March. They remain plentiful throughout the month and occasionally into early April. The last Redheads depart by April 15–20, with occasional stragglers into early May.

The largest concentrations develop during unusually cold seasons. In warm years, Redheads pass rapidly through Ohio and large flocks are infrequently noted. These migrants are most numerous along western Lake Erie, where they are common to abundant. Daily totals of 100–700 are possible, with peak concentrations of 1,500–3,000+. The largest flock totaled 7,575 near Toledo on March 6, 1961 (Campbell 1973). Elsewhere, they are generally fairly common to common spring visitors to lakes and large marshes. Along central Lake Erie, flocks of 500–1,000 may develop while the lake is frozen. Once the lake thaws, Redheads are mostly encountered in flocks of 200 or fewer. Inland lakes may host flocks of 50–600, and occasional concentrations of 800–1,200 have appeared in the glaciated counties. These large flocks have been noted in the southwestern counties only after large reservoirs were constructed in the 1940s (Kemsies and Randle 1953, Mathena et al. 1984).

Fall Redheads are considerably less numerous than spring migrants. They are uncommon to fairly common along Lake Erie and on large inland lakes. In recent years, fall flocks mostly totaled fewer than 50, with occasional reports of 100–300. Aerial estimates along western Lake Erie may peak at 3,000–5,000+ during some years. Late August Redheads may represent summering individuals, since the first fall migrants do not normally return until October 5–15. This migration normally peaks between October 20 and November 20. At inland lakes, numbers of migrants are considerably reduced by early December. December migrants are more frequently encountered along Lake Erie, although flocks seldom exceed 100 unless the lake becomes partially frozen.

Wintering Redheads are primarily restricted to Lake Erie, where they are uncommon to common residents, most numerous within the Central Basin. Their numbers are most plentiful when open water is restricted to hot-water outlets. Under these conditions, flocks of 200–1,000+ may develop during January and February. When the lake does not freeze, only small flocks are scattered along the entire lakefront. At inland localities, Redheads may linger until the lakes freeze over in early January. However, overwintering ducks are regularly observed only at Castalia, where 10–12 are present most years. Elsewhere, small numbers are casually encountered along the Scioto and Great Miami Rivers, but Redheads remain on large lakes only during mild seasons.

Nesting Redheads recently expanded into the Great Lakes region (DeVos 1964). This range expansion was responsible for Ohio summering records since the late 1930s. Breeding was confirmed in 1961, when four nests were discovered at Magee Marsh Wildlife Area. As many as 11 pairs nested in this marsh through 1967 (Campbell 1968).

Redheads are currently rare summer residents in the western Lake Erie marshes. This population probably does not exceed 6–18 pairs during most years (Peterjohn and Rice 1991). Very little information is available on their nesting chronology. Most broods have been observed during late June and July. These nesting ducks prefer extensive and deep marshes where open water is interspersed with emergent vegetation.

Away from western Lake Erie, Redheads are accidental summer visitors. There are two inland breeding records: a pair that raised a brood in Seneca County during 1984 and several pairs that summered at Big Island Wildlife Area (Marion County) between 1983 and 1986, with breeding confirmed during the last year (Peterjohn and Rice 1991). Nonbreeding summer visitors are mostly reported from the northern half of the state, including summering pairs at Pymatuning Lake during the late 1930s (Walker 1938a). The only summer record from southern Ohio was one in Hamilton County on July 15, 1973 (Kleen 1973).

Ring-necked Duck *Aythya collaris* (Donovan)

Unlike most diving ducks, Ring-neckeds prefer inland bodies of water. Spring migrants are considerably more numerous on reservoirs, borrow pits, ponds, and marshes than on Lake Erie. At the height of their spring movements, Ring-neckeds are fairly common to abundant through most inland counties, becoming locally uncommon in southern and unglaciated Ohio. Inland flocks of 50–500 are frequent and concentrations of 1,000–2,000+ are periodically reported. They are most plentiful in the northeastern counties, where 3,000–3,200 were estimated on Mogadore Reservoir during several springs in the 1990s and 3,000+ visited Killbuck Marsh Wildlife Area on March 21, 1998 (E. Schlabach 1998). They are also common spring migrants in the western Lake Erie marshes. The largest flocks usually total 250–400, with a maximum of 8,400 in Ottawa and Lucas Counties on March 16–17, 1997 (Fazio 1997b). They are uncommon migrants on Lake Erie, normally observed in flocks of 50 or fewer.

The first migrants normally return in February and early March. Large flocks usually appear by March 15. Ring-neckeds remain numerous until mid-April, while small flocks frequently linger through the end of the month. The last migrants generally depart by May 5–10, but a few remain into late May.

Ring-necked Ducks are accidental to casual nonbreeding summer visitors that normally disappear by June 15–25. These summer records are restricted to the northern half of Ohio. Most reports are of isolated individuals, although 1–4 summered in Portage and Seneca Counties and Lake St. Marys during the 1990s. Pairs have also lingered well into June in the western Lake Erie marshes, at Pymatuning Lake, Castalia, and Killdeer Plains Wildlife Area (Campbell 1968, Harlan 1995d, Peterjohn 1986d, Walker 1938a). While breeding behavior has been observed, there are no confirmed nesting records.

The preference for inland localities is more pronounced in autumn. Fall migrants are generally fairly common to abundant on inland lakes, most numerous in the northeastern counties. Flocks of 50–700 are noted during most years, while as many as 1,000–1,750 have been detected on several central and northeastern lakes. Ring-neckeds are fairly common to common within the western Lake Erie marshes, where aerial surveys may produce estimates of 1,000–2,000+. They are uncommon along the lakefront, where flocks in excess of 50 are noteworthy. A few fall migrants return by the last week of September, but the first migrants normally appear during October 1–10. The largest movements are expected between October 15 and November 15, usually associated with cold fronts or immediately before a full moon (Trautman 1978). Small flocks normally remain until freeze-up in late December or early January, although as many as 100–200 have been counted on lakes in the southern half of Ohio during early winter in the 1990s.

As winter residents, Ring-necked Ducks are rare and very locally distributed in the northern counties. Fewer than 15 overwinter at Castalia, and individuals may appear at hot-water outlets along Lake Erie. They are accidental to casual winter visitors elsewhere. They may appear on large lakes during mild seasons; the largest wintering flocks have totaled 10–15.

Tufted Duck *Aythya fuligula* (Linnaeus)

A few Tufted Ducks have been detected in recent years among large flocks of scaup migrating and wintering along the Great Lakes and Atlantic Coast. Since Tufted Ducks normally breed across Europe and northern Asia, it is generally assumed that these vagrants reach Alaska from Siberia and join the scaup in their transcontinental migrations. Sightings not fitting this pattern of vagrancy are usually dismissed as escapees, for Tufted Ducks are commonly kept in captivity.

Within Ohio, there is only one record generally accepted as a wild Tufted Duck. An adult male was discovered by Tom LePage in the harbor at Lorain on March 3, 1980. This duck, associating with a flock of 1,000–2,000 Greater Scaup, was seen intermittently through March 14 (Kleen 1980c).

Males showing characteristics of Tufted Ducks have been discovered on two other occasions: at Cleveland on April 2–5, 1996, and Killbuck Marsh Wildlife Area on March 21, 1998 (Peterjohn 1989c, E. Schlabach 1998). Photographs of the Cleveland duck indicate that it was most likely a Tufted Duck X scaup hybrid, since a number of field marks were intermediate between these two species. The Killbuck Marsh duck had a noticeably reduced tuft on its head, also indicating a hybrid origin.

Greater Scaup *Aythya marila* (Linnaeus)

Identification of Greater Scaup posed an insurmountable challenge to most early ornithologists, who did not attempt to distinguish between the two scaup. These identification problems resulted in conflicting statements concerning their status. Trautman (1935a) cited only one specimen and "a few" reliable sight records of Greater Scaup; he considered them rare migrants that mostly passed north of Ohio. In contrast, Williams (1950) described Greaters as uncommon winter visitors at Cleveland, citing flocks as large as 300–400. As the ability to correctly identify Greater Scaup improved, their distribution and relative abundance along Lake Erie became well established. They proved to be fairly numerous winter residents and may outnumber Lesser Scaup during some years.

Greater Scaup are most numerous within central Lake Erie from Lorain eastward. The earliest fall migrant was reported from Lake County on September 30, 1990 (Peterjohn 1991a), but the first migrants normally appear during the last week of October or early November. They remain fairly scarce until mid-December, when they become fairly common to locally abundant winter residents. During some years, large flocks may not appear until January or February. They are least numerous during warmer winters, when daily totals seldom exceed 100–200. When the lake is mostly ice covered, flocks of 2,000–3,000+ have been reported from the Lorain-Cleveland lakefront. Their spring migration is most pronounced when Lake Erie remains ice covered into March. Under these conditions, flocks of 1,000–2,500+ have appeared between March 5 and 20. When the lake is open, spring concentrations seldom exceed 50. Numbers noticeably decline by the last week of March. Only a few Greaters are encountered during April, although late migrants have been reported through mid-May.

Greater Scaup are uncommon to common migrants and winter residents along western Lake Erie. Most observations are of 40 or fewer, with occasional flocks of 100–200+. Concentrations of 1,000–3,000+ have been reported in early March when the lake is mostly covered with ice. Timing of their spring and fall movements coincides with their passage elsewhere along Lake Erie.

Greater Scaup are casual to rare migrants and winter visitors on large lakes throughout the interior of Ohio, least numerous in the unglaciated counties. Most inland reports total six or fewer, although flocks as large as 50–79 have been reported during migration and 10–15 in midwinter. Fall migrants may appear by November 5, but most are noted between November 15 and January 15. They normally depart when the lakes freeze. While there are scattered inland records during mild winters, Greater Scaup do not regularly overwinter at any location. Spring migrants mostly appear before March 21. There are few reliable records after April 15. The only Ohio summer records are from inland locations: a female summered at Oberlin Reservoir during 1989, and one remained in Gallia County through July 16, 1988 (Hall 1988, Peterjohn 1989d).

Lesser Scaup *Aythya affinis* (Eyton)

Lesser Scaup are among the most numerous and widely distributed of Ohio's diving ducks. Especially in spring, flocks are fairly common to abundant visitors to small farm ponds, borrow pits, large reservoirs, and Lake Erie. Spring migrants are most numerous along western Lake Erie, where large flocks traditionally congregate in Maumee Bay. Peak numbers usually total 2,000–10,000 annually, with maxima of 20,000 on April 8, 1934, 40,000 on March 25, 1996, and 80,000 on April 10, 1994 (Campbell 1940, Conlon and Harlan 1996a, Harlan 1994c). Similar numbers occasionally appear off the Marblehead Peninsula in Ottawa County, where as many as 20,000–40,000 have been estimated in 1988 and 1990 (Harlan 1994c). Lesser Scaup are also abundant spring migrants through central Lake Erie, most numerous during cold seasons when open water is limited. Peak numbers total 4,000 along the Cleveland-Lorain lakefront, but most flocks are of 300–1,500. Warm spring weather allows these scaup to disperse along the entire lakefront, mostly in flocks of 200 or fewer. Within the interior counties, spring Lesser Scaup are most numerous in northern and central Ohio, where flocks of 300–1,000 are frequent and 2,000–2,500 have concentrated at several locations. In the southern and unglaciated counties, flocks mostly total 100–500, with occasional reports of 750–1,000.

The first Lesser Scaup return in February or early March. Large flocks appear by the second week of March and remain through mid-April. Small flocks are regularly observed through the first week of May. Most depart by May 12–18 except along western Lake Erie, where they may remain into early June. These late migrants normally are individuals or pairs, although a flock of 100 remained at Toledo as late as June 9 (Campbell 1968).

In the early 1900s, summering Lesser Scaup were regularly reported from inland lakes, sometimes "considerable numbers of both sexes" (Jones 1903). Most were nonbreeders and cripples from spring hunting seasons. A few breeding records were established, including a Franklin County brood in 1919 and reports from Lorain, Summit, and Stark Counties (Hicks 1935a, Jones 1903, Kimes 1912). Small numbers were also encountered along western Lake Erie, including an Erie County brood in 1907 and another near Toledo in 1918 (Campbell 1968, Henninger 1910b).

Summering scaup have declined on inland lakes, with relatively few records since the 1920s. They are currently accidental or casual summer visitors, with most reports from the northern and central counties. While Clark and Sipe (1970) reported nest construction at Lake St. Marys, no eggs were produced. The only recent inland nesting record was provided by a female with ten young at Stony Lake in Carroll County during 1954 (Brooks 1954c). Along Lake Erie, nonbreeding scaup have always been accidental summer visitors to the Central Basin. Their status along western Lake Erie was uncertain. While Hicks (1935a) claimed a breeding population "was rather definitely established in Lucas, Ottawa, and Sandusky Counties," Campbell (1940, 1968) thought these scaup were mostly nonbreeders and cited only one nesting record in 1937. This discrepancy was never resolved. In any event, numbers of summering scaup in the western Lake Erie marshes declined after 1940. They are currently casual nonbreeding summer visitors; there are no confirmed nesting records since 1937.

The few breeding reports provide little insight into their nesting ecology in Ohio. They apparently preferred large lakes and marshes with open water interspersed among emergent vegetation. The few broods were observed during June.

Fall migrants normally return to Lake Erie during the first week of October. Within the Western Basin, they become numerous by mid-October and remain common until early December. Most fall concentrations total 500 or fewer, with occasional flocks of 1,000–2,000. Aerial surveys estimate 15,000–20,000+ scaup during most years, and as many as 105,730 scaup (probably of both species) on November 30, 1993 (Harlan 1994a). In the Central Basin, they become abundant during mid-November or later, when large flocks accumulate along the Cleveland-Lorain lakefront. These flocks increase during early winter and may approach 500–2,000+ birds.

Within the interior counties, fall Lesser Scaup prefer large lakes. The first migrants return by October 5–12. As Trautman (1978) noted, their peak movements are usually associated with clear nights and favorable winds immediately before a full moon. These flights may occur between mid-October and mid-November. Most scaup pass through the state in only two to five days. These flights produce flocks of 100–1,000 ducks on most reservoirs; as many as 2,400 have been reported on one lake. Many more fly over Ohio than land on its lakes. Trautman (1978) witnessed flights of 10,000+ scaup in a single day over Buckeye Lake. Numbers of migrants noticeably decline by late November, although small flocks may remain until freeze-up.

Wintering Lesser Scaup are fairly common to abundant residents along Lake Erie. They are most numerous during cold winters, when open water is restricted to hot-water outlets. At such times, flocks of 1,000–5,000 may develop along the Cleveland-Lorain lakefront. Milder winters allow these scaup to spread along the entire lakefront, normally in flocks of 100–200 or fewer. Concentrations of 1,000–1,500+ may be noted along the Western Basin during these warmer seasons (Campbell 1968, 1973). Inland Lesser Scaup become accidental to locally rare residents after January 10–15. They are infrequently reported at open water throughout the state, usually scattered individuals or flocks of 15 or fewer.

King Eider *Somateria spectabilis* (Linnaeus)

Since the late 1940s, King Eiders have been casual fall migrants along Lake Erie, most frequently recorded east from Huron. The earliest migrant returned to Lake County on October 22, 1989 (Peterjohn 1990a), and there are a few records during the first half of November. The majority of eiders appear between November 15 and December 25. These sightings mostly are of 1–3 eiders, with infrequent small flocks of 5–7, usually females or immature males.

While most King Eiders eventually depart for the Atlantic Coast, they are accidental winter visitors to central Lake Erie, with records from the Cleveland-Lorain lakefront during 1948–1949, 1959–1960, 1981–1982, and 1992 (Mayfield 1949b, Newman 1969, Peterjohn 1982b, 1992b). These winter sightings are of 1–3 eiders remaining into late January, although one survived until March 27, 1960, at Cleveland.

These eiders are accidental spring visitors to Lake Erie. The five records probably pertain to individuals that wintered along the Great Lakes. These records are from Erie County eastward, of single eiders observed between March 4 and April 20, including an adult male observed at two Lake County sites on March 4–10, 1996 (Brock 1996c). The same male probably reappeared in Lake County during March 1998 (Rosche 1998b).

King Eiders were observed more frequently in recent decades, reflecting better coverage by birdwatchers along Lake Erie. Before the late 1940s, they were unknown except for a few anecdotal accounts. Between 1947 and 1979, these eiders averaged two to five sightings each decade. During the 1980s, they were unrecorded only in 1986 and produced as many as four sightings annually. However, they were reported during only five years in the 1990s.

King Eiders are accidental fall visitors away from Lake Erie. There are three records from central Ohio: three eiders at Buckeye Lake (Fairfield County) on December 2, 1926 (Trautman 1940), a Franklin County specimen collected November 26, 1960 (Trautman and Trautman 1968), and an unspecified report on November 11, 1895 (Borror 1950). The only other acceptable inland record is an eider shot along the Ohio River near Cincinnati on January 2, 1971 (Thomson 1983).

Common Eider *Somateria mollissima* (Linnaeus)

Identification of female and immature eiders is difficult. Because most eiders recorded from Ohio have been in these plumages, uncertainty over whether they were Common or King Eiders has obscured the status of both species. Unless specimens were collected, identification of sight records has been viewed with some suspicion.

In recent years, better optical equipment and identification information has permitted the accurate identification of most eiders under good viewing conditions. If recent records accurately represent their status, then Common Eiders are accidental fall or early winter visitors to Ohio. There are no extant specimens. The only confirmed record is of one eider discovered by Jim Hoffman at the former White City Beach in Cleveland on October 9, 1978 (Kleen 1979a). This bird was viewed by many other observers, and diagnostic photographs were taken by Richard Hoffman.

There are a number of questionable unconfirmed records. A possible Common Eider was shot at Buckeye Lake on November 11, 1895, but the specimen disappeared before its identity was confirmed (Trautman 1940). Since 1947, there have been at least ten reports from the Cleveland-Lorain lakefront and two from Toledo, none of them accompanied by written descriptions or photographs conclusively establishing their identities. It is conceivable that most, if not all, of these records pertain to King Eiders.

Harlequin Duck *Histrionicus histrionicus* (Linnaeus)

In eastern North America, wintering Harlequin Ducks are normally found along rocky jetties and seacoasts, with a few regularly appearing on the Great Lakes. Since inland Harlequins are accidental away from the Great Lakes, Ohio's first sighting was unexpectedly from the Dayton area. An unmistakable adult male was discovered on the Great Miami River near West Carrollton (Montgomery County) on February 13, 1949. It was observed foraging within the river's swift currents for more than an hour (Mathena et al. 1984).

There are five other records from the interior of Ohio, three of these from the Springfield-Dayton area. A female was discovered at Veterans Park in Springfield on December 27, 1980, and remained through mid-January 1981; an immature male was found below the dam at Eastwood Lake (Montgomery County) on December 18, 1983 (Mathena et al. 1984); and another immature male was noted along the Great Miami River in Dayton on January 14, 1996 (Harlan 1996b). Two immature males were shot by hunters on West Branch Reservoir (Portage County) on November 8, 1995 (Conlon and Harlan 1996b). One was reported from Hoover Reservoir on November 27, 1997 (Fazio 1998). A tame male reported from Zanesville between mid-March and June 20, 1999, regularly accepted handouts and was likely an escapee from captivity.

Along Lake Erie, the first record was a specimen collected in Ottawa County on November 2, 1951 (Campbell 1968). The first Cleveland sighting was in 1955 (Newman 1969). Harlequins averaged one record every two or three years along the lakefront into the 1970s but have been recorded annually since 1977.

Harlequin Ducks are casual to rare fall migrants along Lake Erie, with one to three reports during most years. Most sightings are from the Central Basin, with relatively few detected in Ottawa and Lucas Counties. These fall records are distributed between October 29 and the first week of January, but generally occur between November 10 and December 15. They are casual winter visitors. These winter sightings are primarily from the Cleveland-Lorain area, where a total of 7–10 were scattered along the lakefront during 1988–1989 (Peterjohn 1989b), but three or fewer are found during most winters. These winter records were very sporadic before the mid-1980s, but occurred in eight years between 1988 and 1999. Harlequin Ducks are accidental to casual during spring, when the few sightings are scattered between early March and April 20. These spring sightings frequently pertain to individuals that wintered along Lake Erie and occur on average of every two to four years. All lakefront observations have been of 1–3 Harlequins.

Harlequin Ducks are accidental summer visitors. The first record was provided by a male originally discovered at Lorain on January 8, 1968. After wintering in the harbor, this individual never migrated and was last reported on August 26, 1968 (Flanigan 1968). A second summer record was provided by an eclipse male discovered at Cleveland on August 6, 1991, which remained through autumn (Peterjohn 1992a).

Surf Scoter *Melanitta perspicillata* (Linnaeus)

The status of Surf Scoters changed dramatically during the twentieth century. They were accidental or casual visitors to Ohio before 1940 and were annually reported beginning in the 1950s. Small numbers were recorded each year through the 1970s. The number of sightings increased markedly during the 1980s and 1990s. While Surfs were formerly the least numerous scoter within Ohio, they are currently the most frequently encountered scoter and have replaced White-wingeds as the winter scoter on Lake Erie.

Surf Scoters are currently rare fall migrants along western Lake Erie and rare to uncommon through the Central Basin. Most sightings are of ten or fewer, with occasional flocks of 20–35. Several flights during the 1990s produced reports of 50–200+ from the Central Basin. Away from Lake Erie, Surf

Scoters are casual fall visitors to the glaciated counties and accidental elsewhere. Inland scoters are usually detected at 1–6 locations each autumn. Most inland sightings are of five or fewer scoters, with occasional flocks of 10–12, frequently associated with mixed flocks of diving ducks.

The earliest fall migrants have returned to Lake Erie by September 28–30, but Surf Scoters normally appear along the lakefront between October 7 and 17. Their movements peak between October 20 and November 15. They usually depart by the first week of December, although stragglers remain into early January. On inland lakes, the earliest Surfs appear by October 5–12. The majority are detected between October 15 and November 15, while a few stragglers linger into the last half of December.

Their winter status changed dramatically during the 1990s. Surf Scoters have become casual to locally uncommon winter visitors along the lakefront, most numerous in the Cleveland-Lorain area. While flocks of 20–57 have been reported during the first half of January, these flocks do not normally remain for the entire winter. Most midwinter reports are of five or fewer scoters, with a few groups of 8–13. Surf Scoters are accidental winter visitors away from Lake Erie. Most sightings are during the first half of January, although single scoters have twice overwintered in the Columbus area. The largest inland winter flock was five at Hueston Woods State Park on January 3, 1991 (Peterjohn 1991b).

Fewer Surf Scoters pass through Ohio as spring migrants. They averaged only three to six spring sightings per decade prior to 1980, but have become annual spring visitors since the late 1980s. They are rare migrants along Lake Erie and accidental to casual inland, least numerous within the unglaciated counties. Spring migrants appeared at as many as six to ten inland sites during some years of the 1990s. Most reports are of five or fewer scoters, with maxima of 62 along Lake Erie and 23 at Eastwood Lake (Montgomery County) on April 25, 1996 (Conlon and Harlan 1996a). The earliest spring migrants appear during the last week of February and early March, but most are noted in April. Small numbers have lingered into the last half of May in northern and central Ohio.

An accidental visitor to Ohio after late May, there are currently two summer records. A single Surf Scoter at Mosquito Lake on June 4–9, 1997 (Brock 1997d), may have been a very late spring migrant. A male at Lake St. Marys on July 4–13, 1991, was obviously a nonbreeder (Harlan 1991b).

White-winged Scoter *Melanitta fusca* (Linnaeus)

At one time, White-wingeds were regarded as the most numerous scoter within Ohio. This status is not necessarily true today, because their numbers have declined since the 1970s while the other scoters have increased.

As fall migrants, White-wingeds are rare to uncommon along Lake Erie, more frequently encountered within the Central Basin. They can be scarce some years and fairly numerous in others. Most fall reports are of 1–8, with infrequent flocks of 12–20. The only reliably reported fall flight totaled 55 at Cleveland on November 8, 1979.

Away from Lake Erie, White-winged Scoters have become casual fall visitors to the glaciated counties and accidental in unglaciated Ohio, producing 1–6 reports most years. These records usually are of six or fewer, with occasional flocks of 8–12. The largest reported inland flock was composed of 21 at Buckeye Lake (Trautman 1940). Trautman (1978) noted that they usually appear after calm, clear, frosty nights.

While White-winged Scoters have returned to Cleveland by August 25, 1985, and September 2, 1944 (Peterjohn 1986a, Williams 1950), there are no other sightings before October 1. The first fall migrants normally appear during October 5–15 along Lake Erie and October 15–25 at inland lakes. There are generally two poorly defined peaks to their fall passage: between October 20 and November 10, when White-wingeds are most likely to visit inland lakes and small flocks appear along Lake Erie; and between November 25 and December 15, when greater numbers appear along Lake Erie but only scattered individuals inland. White-winged Scoters continue to pass through the state until December 25–January 10.

Small numbers of White-winged Scoters regularly spend the winter along Lake Erie. When the lake remains open, wintering scoters are scattered along the entire lakefront. Extended cold weather forces them to concentrate at hot-water outlets. White-wingeds are casual winter residents along the Western Basin but are rare to locally uncommon along central Lake Erie. Most winter reports are of six or fewer, with occasional flocks of 8–19. The largest flock totaled 25 at Cleveland on February 5, 1949 (Mayfield 1949b).

Few White-wingeds overwinter away from the lakefront. They are accidental midwinter visitors to interior counties, with scattered records across the state. While small numbers regularly winter along the Ohio River, these scoters seldom venture into Ohio's limited portion of the river. Most midwinter records are of 1–2 appearing for only a few days. The only inland winter flock totaled eight at Columbus on January 31, 1959 (Mumford 1959b).

Fewer White-winged Scoters visit Ohio as spring migrants. They are casual to rare migrants along Lake Erie, most numerous within the Central Basin during March, but with sightings scattered along the entire lakefront later in the season. The number of lakefront records exhibits marked annual variability, with only one or two sightings some springs and six to ten reports in others. Most reports are of eight or fewer, although sizable movements have produced maxima of 186 at Cleveland on March 10, 1990, and 36–50 in western

Lake Erie on April 27–28, 1962 (Campbell 1968, Peterjohn 1990c). Inland White-winged Scoters are accidental to casual spring visitors to large lakes, primarily in the glaciated counties, producing one to five records most years. These records normally are of three or fewer scoters. Small flocks of 6–13 appear infrequently.

Their spring migration is fairly protracted. Small numbers may appear during the last half of February, but the majority of spring records are during March. Flocks irregularly appear during April and occasionally remain into early May. Stragglers have been noted through May 31 at Cleveland and June 3–4 in western Lake Erie (Campbell 1968, Peterjohn 1984c).

Black Scoter *Melanitta nigra* (Linnaeus)

The status of Black Scoters dramatically changed during the twentieth century. Before 1940, they were accidental visitors across the state. The number of sightings increased during the 1940s, especially along Lake Erie. However, Black Scoters did not become annual visitors until the 1950s, usually as groups of three or fewer, although a "small flight" developed in Ottawa and Lucas Counties during October 1952 (Campbell 1968). Most sightings were along Lake Erie; these scoters remained accidental visitors to inland lakes. This status was maintained through the 1970s.

Beginning in the early 1980s, numbers of Black Scoters noticeably increased. Along Lake Erie, small flocks appeared most autumns and an exceptional movement occurred during November 1985. Small numbers were regularly detected on inland lakes. Two factors contributed to these increased sightings: greater numbers of birdwatchers discovered migrants that previously passed through the state undetected, and there may have been a shift in their migration corridor.

Black Scoters are currently rare fall migrants along western Lake Erie but uncommon visitors to the Central Basin. Most lakefront reports are of 1–6 individuals, with occasional flocks of 10–20. Larger flights of 50–70 are infrequently encountered. The largest movement was noted during November 1985, when a remarkable 600 congregated in the Huron-Vermilion area on November 11, and flocks of 41–85 briefly appeared at other localities within the Central Basin (Peterjohn 1986a).

On inland reservoirs, Black Scoters are casual to rare fall migrants through the northern and glaciated central counties and accidental elsewhere, producing one to five records annually. Sightings usually are of five or fewer individuals. The largest inland flocks were composed of 15 on Bass Lake near Dayton on November 28, 1967, and 12 at LaDue Reservoir on October 24, 1995 (Harlan 1996a, Mathena et al. 1984).

Fall Black Scoters have returned to Lake Erie by October 4–5, but normally appear during October 15–20. They are mostly observed between October 25 and November 15. At inland lakes, Black Scoters are generally detected between October 20 and November 20.

Winter Black Scoters are restricted to Lake Erie, where they are casually encountered through January 5–20. These scoters normally disappear when the lake freezes over, and may represent very late fall migrants. A few individuals have overwintered along the Cleveland-Lorain lakefront (Peterjohn 1989b). All reliable winter records are of three or fewer Blacks, usually at hotwater outlets.

Considerably fewer Black Scoters pass through Ohio as spring migrants. They infrequently appear between February 25 and March 20, in association with large flocks of diving ducks. They are more likely to be detected during April and have remained as late as June 1, 1998, at Headlands Beach State Park (Brock 1998d). These migrants are accidental to casual visitors, as likely to appear on inland lakes as Lake Erie. There are sightings from all portions of the state, invariably of six or fewer individuals. Spring Black Scoters are generally recorded during 2–6 years each decade.

Long-tailed Duck *Clangula hyemalis* (Linnaeus)

Long-tailed Ducks have always been irregular migrants and winter visitors to Ohio. They can be nearly absent some years but occur at widely scattered localities in other years, while sizable flights appear at rare intervals. Numbers of these handsome ducks have markedly declined since the early 1900s, perhaps reflecting a shift in their winter distribution or reduced populations throughout the Great Lakes.

In the early 1900s, Jones (1903) thought their irregular appearance was governed by weather conditions, noting that Long-tailed Ducks occasionally became "decidedly numerous anywhere along the lakefront and may venture well inland to the Ohio River." These movements were frequently followed by several years without any records. The only indication of the size of these movements is provided by Trautman's (1940) report of "several hundred" at Buckeye Lake during the spring of 1912. Similar flights have not been apparent since 1920, with only Ashtabula regularly hosting small flocks of Long-tailed Ducks along Lake Erie. December flocks of 15–40+ were reported between the 1930s and 1950 but have not appeared in subsequent years.

Long-tailed Ducks are currently rare to uncommon fall migrants along Lake Erie, more numerous within the Central Basin. During most years, there are three to ten or more sightings scattered along the lakefront. They become casual fall visitors to large lakes within the interior of Ohio, where the fewest records are from the southern and unglaciated counties. While they are not annually detected on any lake, there are usually up to seven inland sightings each autumn. All recent fall records are of 1–8 Long-tailed Ducks.

The earliest fall Long-tailed Duck returned to Cleveland on October 1, 1981, and Dayton on October 10, 1968 (Mathena et al. 1984, Rosche 1992). There are few other records before October 25–30. Most are observed between November 10 and December 7. This southward movement continues through January 5–15, but it is difficult to distinguish late migrants from winter visitors.

Wintering Long-tailed Ducks are mostly restricted to Lake Erie, where they are casually recorded within the Western Basin and rare elsewhere. The number of winter lakefront records is variable, with two to five reports most years and infrequent small flights producing ten or more sightings. Since the early 1950s, these winter records have mostly been of eight or fewer Long-tailed Ducks.

Away from Lake Erie, Long-tailed Ducks are accidental to casual winter visitors. They visit large lakes if open water is available but also frequent large rivers. These ducks usually remain for only a few days, although several have spent the entire winter (Kemsies and Randle 1953). Inland Long-tailed Ducks are as likely to appear in the southern counties as in northern Ohio, with most reports of three or fewer individuals. The largest winter flocks included 14 near Dayton on January 13, 1946 (Mathena et al. 1984), 12 on the Maumee River near Toledo between February 10 and March 11, 1934 (Campbell 1940), and nine specimens collected near Waverly (Pike County) between February 7 and 18, 1899 (Henninger 1902).

Spring Long-tailed Ducks begin to move north during March but are mostly observed between March 25 and April 20. All large flights have been detected during April. Stragglers have remained through May 7 at Cincinnati and May 12–27 within the northern and central counties.

Spring Long-tailed Ducks are normally accidental to locally rare migrants, as likely to appear on inland reservoirs as Lake Erie. During most years, there are one to ten records of six or fewer Long-tailed Ducks scattered across the state. Several times each decade, this species stages a noticeable "flight." These movements may take the form of many individuals widely scattered across Ohio. In 1984, there were at least 14 records along Lake Erie and eight at various inland lakes, mostly of 1–5 individuals; the largest flock totaled 12. Other flights produce one or two large flocks but few records elsewhere. The 1986 flight was responsible for April 13 flocks of 24 in Summit and Portage Counties and 14 at Killdeer Plains Wildlife Area (Peterjohn 1986c). The largest spring flock in recent decades appeared at LaDue Reservoir (Geauga County) on April 15, 1972, where 53 Long-tailed Ducks presented an impressive sight (Thomson 1983).

Bufflehead *Bucephala albeola* (Linnaeus)

Buffleheads are feisty little ducks very capable of successfully competing with larger waterfowl. Surprisingly hardy, they winter wherever open water is available, easily withstanding the midwinter rigors on Lake Erie. The handsome males have a distinctive black and white plumage, including a small white crest which they erect during their nuptial displays before the plainer females. Like Common Goldeneyes, they do not let harsh winter weather deter them from their courtship displays.

Fall Buffleheads have appeared in Cleveland as early as August 12, 1983 (Rosche 1992), but this sighting and others along Lake Erie during late August and early September probably pertain to nonbreeders. The first migrants usually return to Lake Erie by October 15–25 and to most inland lakes by the first week of November. They are generally fairly common to locally abundant migrants on large lakes during November and December. The largest fall flocks total 275–900+ along western Lake Erie, 350 at Rocky Fork Lake on November 11, 1997, and 258 at Mosquito Lake on November 9, 1996 (Fazio 1998, Hall 1997a), while flocks of 80–150+ are occasionally encountered. Daily totals are usually 35 or fewer. Only wintering birds remain after early January.

Wintering Buffleheads are generally uncommon to fairly common along Lake Erie. During open winters, they are spread along the entire lakefront as small flocks of ten or fewer ducks. Harsh weather forces them to congregate at hot-water outlets, and as many as 100–250 have been counted. Buffleheads linger on inland lakes as long as open water is available. During warm winters, they become casual to rare residents, with 20 or fewer at widely scattered lakes. Most winters, Buffleheads are generally absent from the interior counties, except at Castalia and Summit Lake in Akron, where a few individuals remain throughout the season.

Spring Buffleheads are as likely to appear on small ponds and borrow pits as large lakes. They tend to be numerous in northeastern Ohio, where several large flights have been encountered, including 500 at Youngstown on April 19, 1932, and 658 in Summit and Portage Counties on April 13, 1986 (Baird 1932c, Peterjohn 1986c). Concentrations of 200–500+ may also appear on western Lake Erie. Spring totals of this fairly common to common migrant usually are 50 or fewer elsewhere. The first spring migrants appear as soon as open water is available. Largest numbers are normally reported between March 15 and April 15. Stragglers are regularly noted during the first half of May, particularly in the northern half of the state. There are very few records after May 25. Buffleheads lingering at Buck Creek State Park through June 22, 1991 (Peterjohn 1991d), Cleveland through June 29, 1984 (Rosche 1992), and Ottawa Wildlife Refuge through July 10, 1988 (Peterjohn 1988d), furnish the latest summer records.

Common Goldeneye *Bucephala clangula* (Linnaeus)

One of the hardiest diving ducks, Common Goldeneyes survive wherever open water is available. They are not deterred by Ohio's winter weather, ignoring subzero temperatures and biting wind chills as they blithely feed, preen, and perform courtship displays in these conditions as they might on a warm March day. Their tolerance for cold weather allows the Common Goldeneye to be one of our latest returning fall waterfowl. Along Lake Erie, unusually early migrants have appeared during September or early October, but they normally return during October 25–November 5. Concentrations seldom exceed 20–100 during November. Relatively cold weather produces large wintering flocks by December 5–10, while warm temperatures may delay the arrival of sizable concentrations until January.

Away from Lake Erie, the first fall Common Goldeneyes appeared at Mogadore Reservoir (Portage County) on October 2, 1985, and Lake St. Marys on October 10, 1945 (Clark and Sipe 1970, Peterjohn 1986a). They normally return during the first half of November. Fall migrants are generally most numerous in the northeastern counties, becoming fairly common to locally abundant on large reservoirs between November 20 and December 20. Flocks of 50–200 are expected, and larger concentrations, such as 1,500 at Mosquito Creek Reservoir on December 1, 1984, have been infrequently encountered. Considerably fewer pass through the other counties, where they are uncommon to fairly common migrants and fall flocks seldom exceed 10–75. This inland migration continues until freeze-up.

Wintering Common Goldeneyes are common to abundant residents along Lake Erie. During the 1990s, large concentrations regularly developed in the Western Basin, particularly Maumee Bay, where aerial totals include estimates of 15,057 in January 1994 and 12,206 in January 1996 (Harlan 1994b, 1996b). Counts from the ground have peaked at 4,800–7,000, but most reports are flocks of 100–1,000+. When the Western Basin freezes, many of these goldeneyes move to the Central Basin, although similar movements may also occur in relatively mild winters. Along central Lake Erie, daily totals of 50–300+ are expected, and concentrations of 1,000–2,500+ occasionally develop along the Cleveland-Lorain lakefront.

These wintering numbers have substantially increased since 1900. At that time, Jones (1903) thought Common Goldeneyes did not winter along Lake Erie. As late as the 1940s, only small flocks regularly wintered at Cleveland (Williams 1950). Improved wintering numbers between the 1950s and 1980s probably resulted from increased availability of small fish, while the establishment of zebra mussels throughout the lake may be a factor in the large winter concentrations reported during the 1990s.

Wintering Common Goldeneyes are rare to locally fairly common residents inland. Small numbers regularly winter throughout Ohio, usually 1–20 goldeneyes, with occasional flocks of 30–60. The largest inland wintering concentrations totaled 100–300 in the Columbus area.

Their spring migration commences during February, producing flocks of 25–100+ on inland lakes and 100–1,000+ along Lake Erie. Larger concentrations are infrequently observed: 350 near Cincinnati on February 27, 1937 (Kemsies and Randle 1953), 1,000 at Columbus on February 28, 1974 (Thomson 1983), 6,000 at Lorain on March 10, 1984 (Peterjohn 1984c), and 7,000 on Maumee Bay on March 7, 1993 (Harlan 1993c). These large flocks normally depart by March 15 on inland lakes and March 20–25 from Lake Erie. Smaller numbers are expected through April 1–5 within the interior counties and along Lake Erie until April 15. Stragglers occasionally remain through May 15–21 in the northern half of the state.

Common Goldeneyes are accidental nonbreeding summer visitors. Summer records are limited to single individuals in the Toledo area in 1934, 1937, and 1992 (Campbell 1940, Brock 1992b); near Dayton on July 13, 1959 (Mathena et al. 1984); and at Cleveland on July 28, 1984 (Peterjohn 1984d).

Barrow's Goldeneye *Bucephala islandica* (Gmelin)

Based on their status elsewhere along Lake Erie, Barrow's Goldeneyes are expected to be casual or accidental winter visitors and early spring migrants along the Ohio lakefront. Recent records conform to these expectations. Since 1980, there have been documented sightings of single Barrow's Goldeneyes at Lorain between January 7 and 10, 1984 (Peterjohn 1984b), Eastlake on March 8–9, 1986 (Peterjohn 1986c), in Ottawa County on February 11, 1987 (Peterjohn 1987b), Lorain on February 20, 1988 (Peterjohn 1988c), Avon Lake (Lorain County) between February 28 and March 1, 1993 (Brock 1993b), and Ashtabula on February 28, 1994 (Harlan 1994b). The only sight record during the previous decade was an adult male at Avon Lake between February 6 and 28, 1972 (Kleen and Bush 1972b). Although details are unavailable, this bird was viewed by many observers and its identification is almost certainly correct.

Historic accounts include a number of unsubstantiated sightings from the Cleveland-Lorain lakefront, western Lake Erie between Sandusky Bay and Port Clinton, and southern Ohio. The veracity of these reports cannot be adequately assessed. Since female and immature Barrow's Goldeneyes are easily confused with the more numerous Common Goldeneyes, there is a strong possibility some of these birds were misidentified.

Hooded Merganser *Lophodytes cucullatus* (Linnaeus)

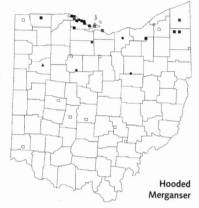

Hooded Merganser

This exceptionally attractive duck is usually found on wooded ponds, swamps, streams, and lakes. On occasion, the Hooded, our smallest merganser, joins other diving ducks resting on large lakes, but it is more likely to occur in small segregated flocks, where the brilliantly colored males are outnumbered by the somber females and immatures.

Spring Hooded Mergansers are uncommon to locally common visitors, becoming rare on Lake Erie. Most records are of 20 or fewer, with infrequent flocks of 30–60. The largest concentrations have totaled 100–150 during the 1990s. This migration normally begins between February 20 and March 7 and peaks during March 15–April 10. Fewer migrants are detected through April 20–25, with stragglers lingering into the first half of May.

Small numbers of Hooded Mergansers nested in the northern half of Ohio during the nineteenth century (Clark and Sipe 1970, Trautman 1940). This population was eliminated by overhunting before 1900. There were very few summer records between 1900 and 1930. Beginning in 1930, individuals appeared on large lakes scattered across the northern and central counties. Hicks (1945c) cited totals of 2–14 Hoodeds each summer after 1930. Many were nonbreeders, but nesting was documented at Pymatuning Lake, in Franklin County, and along western Lake Erie in Ottawa and Lucas Counties. Their status did not change until the early 1970s, when the number of summer records began to increase. Hooded Mergansers became regular residents along western Lake Erie, while scattered individuals were detected elsewhere. Their statewide breeding population slowly expanded during the 1980s and 1990s, and is greater than the 40–70 pairs estimated by Peterjohn and Rice (1991) from Breeding Bird Atlas data.

Hooded Mergansers are currently uncommon to fairly common summer residents along western Lake Erie, where as many as 6–10+ breeding pairs may be found in most large marshes. They are uncommon residents in northeastern Ohio and casual to rare residents within other glaciated counties. While 3–5 pairs may breed at preferred locations, most inland nesting reports are of scattered pairs. These mergansers are accidental summer visitors to the unglaciated counties, where there are no confirmed nesting records.

Nonbreeding mergansers may appear at any time, but females with broods are mostly observed during May and June. Wandering family groups of 3–6 Hoodeds may appear during August and early September at locations where they did not nest.

Hooded Mergansers nest in cavities but also utilize Wood Duck boxes. Most recent nests have been discovered in boxes, and their use of these structures has contributed to their expanding breeding population. Their nesting activities begin during April, with most clutches hatching by mid-May, although recently hatched young have been reported through late June (Campbell 1968, Hicks 1945c, Peterjohn and Rice 1991).

Hooded Mergansers attain their maximum abundance as fall migrants. They appear during the last half of October and generally peak during November, when they become uncommon to locally abundant across Ohio. While most localities support 40 or fewer, flocks of 100–250 visit inland lakes each autumn. The largest concentrations total 400–650 and are most likely to be found in the northeastern counties. Subfreezing temperatures cause most Hooded Mergansers to depart by December 15–25, with stragglers remaining into early January. Mild weather sometimes allows flocks of 20–150+ to remain until mid-January.

Hooded Mergansers are generally rare but regular winter residents at hot-water outlets along Lake Erie, where 1–5 may be observed among the mixed flocks of diving ducks. At inland locations, they are rare winter residents along the Scioto, Muskingum, and other large rivers, and casual visitors to large lakes, most likely during mild seasons. Most inland reports are of four or fewer, although as many as 63 wintered at Columbus during 1995, and 20–48 have been noted there in other winters of the 1990s (Harlan 1995b).

Common Merganser *Mergus merganser* Linnaeus

Unfortunately, this handsome duck has generally declined in numbers throughout the twentieth century. Clark and Sipe (1970) reported a gradual reduction at Lake St. Marys after 1910. In southwestern Ohio, Common Mergansers were common migrants at Dayton before 1950 and at Cincinnati until the early 1950s (Kemsies and Randle 1953, Mathena et al. 1984). Flocks of 200–400 were reported from Dayton between 1943 and 1946. In central Ohio, spring flocks of 100–200 were regularly observed and there were 1,000 at O'Shaughnessy Reservoir (Delaware County) on March 11, 1940, and 2,000 at Buckeye Lake on March 20, 1924 (Trautman 1940, Walker 1940b). Numbers declined during the 1950s, and these mergansers have been scarce since 1962 (Graber 1962b). Within the northeastern counties, spring flocks of 200–400 were observed into the early 1950s but have not appeared since 1960.

Along Lake Erie, wintering and migrant Common Mergansers were regularly observed in considerable numbers through 1950. Then their appearance became erratic. For example, 10,000+ wintered at Cleveland in 1951–1952 but only 40 during 1954–1955 (Nolan 1955b). This pattern of unpredictable winter abundance continued into the 1980s, but sizable concentrations were noted along Lake Erie during most winters of the 1990s.

Common Mergansers are currently fairly common to abundant winter residents along Lake Erie. While they have been reported as early as the last week of September, the first migrants are normally expected during October 27–November 10. Flocks of 100+ normally appear in December.

Along western Lake Erie, Common Mergansers are most numerous between December 20 and January 15. Concentrations of 5,000–9,000+ are indicative of the large numbers which may congregate, although 50–300 are usually observed daily and the largest early winter flocks seldom exceed 500–2,000+ (Campbell 1968, Thomson 1983). Once the lake freezes over, flocks of 20–200+ may remain at isolated pockets of open water.

Along central Lake Erie, large flocks frequently appear between January 20 and February 15, and may represent birds moving in from the Western Basin. The largest recent concentrations were noted during the severe winters of 1976–1977 and 1977–1978, with maxima of 7,000–10,000 along the Cleveland-Lorain lakefront. In other years, 50–300 are expected daily and the largest flocks total 2,000–4,000+.

Common Mergansers initiate their northward movements during the last half of February. Lakefront concentrations are expected between February 25 and March 15, producing occasional flocks of 1,000–2,000 in the Central Basin and 1,000+ along western Lake Erie. However, most flocks total 50–400. They usually depart from Lake Erie during the last half of March, with small flocks remaining through April 7–15 and occasional stragglers into May.

Considerably fewer Common Mergansers visit inland lakes and large rivers, where their distribution and relative abundance are fairly uniform across the state. They normally return by November 5–15 and are regularly observed during December, when they become uncommon migrants. Fall flocks are normally composed of 25 or fewer. Most depart by early January when the lakes freeze. As winter residents, Common Mergansers are rare to uncommon on large rivers and casual to rare on large lakes wherever open water is available. Winter flocks have been composed of 5–30 during recent years. They are most numerous as spring migrants, becoming fairly common on large lakes between February 25 and March 15. The largest recent flocks have totaled 75–120, but most reports are of 40 or fewer. These migrants normally depart by April 1–5 in the southern and central counties and April 15 in northern Ohio. A few have been reported into the second half of May.

Common Mergansers are accidental nonbreeding summer visitors along western Lake Erie, with reports in 1928, 1939, and 1984 (Campbell 1968, Peterjohn 1984d). These sightings are of single mergansers, several of which apparently summered. They have also lingered through June 5, 1993, in the Cleveland area (Brock 1993d). The only inland record was provided by a Common Merganser summering at Buckeye Lake in 1925 (Trautman 1940). While a breeding attempt was reported from the Grand River in Lake County during 1996, this report was never adequately verified.

Red-breasted Merganser *Mergus serrator* Linnaeus

Fall flocks of Red-breasted Mergansers along Lake Erie can be awe-inspiring. Beginning at sunrise, these flocks fly low over the water, some days to the east and other days to the west, depending on wind direction. They continue to pass along the lakefront all day, although the greatest numbers are seen in early morning and late afternoon. I once witnessed an evening flight stretching across the entire horizon and continuing for more than ten minutes, easily exceeding 100,000 individuals, with additional flocks flying by as the sunlight disappeared from the sky. But most flocks are composed of 20–500+ mergansers, forming rafts of 1,000–15,000+ when actively feeding on small fish in a frenzy of activity.

Despite careful observations from shore, our understanding of their movements is poor. As Red-breasted Mergansers fly along the lakefront at rates of 5,000–20,000+ individuals per hour, many questions arise. Do they move from one Ohio locality to another, or do their movements extend around the entire western end of the lake? Are these movements only daily flights in search of food, or are they part of their seasonal migrations? While these questions cannot be answered, one point is clear; each fall, Lake Erie hosts a sizable proportion of the North American population of Red-breasted Mergansers.

Fall Red-breasted Mergansers are most numerous between the Lake Erie islands and Cleveland; daily totals of 10,000–50,000+ are regularly observed there during November, and numbers approaching 250,000 have been estimated on several occasions. They are also numerous east of Cleveland, although totals seldom exceed 5,000–10,000. West of the islands, they may be scarce some years and abundant in others. They may occasionally rival their status in central Lake Erie; an aerial survey estimated 210,000 within the Western Basin on November 29, 1985 (Peterjohn 1986a).

These immense numbers have not always staged on Lake Erie. In the early 1900s, Jones (1909) seldom observed flocks of more than 100–200 at Cedar Point (Erie County). Williams (1950) reported only small flocks at Cleveland into the 1940s. Large numbers were regularly observed near the western Lake

Erie islands by 1950 (Nolan 1955a), but huge flights within the Central Basin were not evident until the 1960s. These flights continued into the 1990s, as evidenced by an estimated 220,000 at Sandusky on November 14, 1992 (Brock 1993a). However, the introduction of zebra mussels has dramatically changed the ecology of Lake Erie, which is influencing the fish populations that support these mergansers. Should their prey populations decline, then the numbers of Red-breasted Mergansers staging on Lake Erie will likely diminish in the future.

As fall concentrations increased along Lake Erie, fewer Red-breasted Mergansers appeared on inland reservoirs. While Trautman (1940) regularly observed flocks of 200–500 on Buckeye Lake during the 1920s and 1930s, similar numbers have not been evident in recent decades. These mergansers are currently uncommon to locally common fall migrants on large reservoirs throughout Ohio. Most inland reports are of 30 or fewer, with infrequent flocks of 50–200; the largest inland flocks totaled 600–850+ in recent decades.

Along Lake Erie, the first migrants may appear by the last week of September but are usually noted between October 3 and 10. Maximum abundance is attained between October 22 and November 30. On inland reservoirs, the first mergansers are expected by October 20–30, but most sightings are during November. The large Red-breasted Merganser flocks normally disappear by December 7. When the weather is relatively mild, flocks in excess of 50,000 have remained on Lake Erie into the second half of December, although 1,000–5,000 are more typical December totals.

Numbers of wintering Red-breasted Mergansers fluctuate considerably along Lake Erie. They may be relatively scarce some winters, with no more than 20–50 at any locality, but numerous in other winters, when concentrations of 1,000–2,000 may develop. These wintering mergansers are normally fairly common to abundant visitors within the Central Basin, particularly at hot-water outlets along the Lorain-Cleveland lakefront. They are rare to fairly common winter residents within the Western Basin, where the largest flocks may total 30–100 individuals.

On inland reservoirs, small numbers of Red-breasted Mergansers remain until December 20–January 10. During most winters, Red-breasted Mergansers are unreported from inland locations after early January. They become accidental to casual visitors during mild winters, when the few widely scattered records are of single mergansers.

Spring migration begins in late February or early March. While 192 were counted at Hueston Woods State Park in early February, 1975 (Kleen 1975b), the largest numbers are usually present between March 25 and April 25. Most migrants depart by May 5–10, although some linger through May 25–June 10, especially along Lake Erie.

While Red-breasted Mergansers are common to abundant spring migrants along Lake Erie, they do not appear in the immense numbers noted each autumn. The largest spring flocks are composed of 1,000–4,200+, and daily totals frequently do not exceed 50–500. They are uniformly distributed along the lakefront. Within the interior counties, Red-breasted Mergansers are uncommon to locally abundant migrants on large reservoirs, most numerous in the western half of the state. Spring concentrations of 20–100+ appear on most lakes, and flocks of 300–500 are regularly noted. Larger concentrations are noteworthy: 1,500 at Bresler Reservoir (Allen County) on April 11, 1992 (Harlan 1992c), 1,000 at Findlay Reservoir (Hancock County) on April 16, 1983, and 700 near Cincinnati during late March 1978 (Kleen 1978c).

Red-breasted Mergansers are casual to rare summer visitors along Lake Erie, with scattered reports of 1–3 individuals along the entire lakefront most years. While they frequently disappear by early July, some have survived into autumn. Summering Red-breasteds are accidental to casual nonbreeding visitors on inland reservoirs, mostly during June in the northern half of the state, although one summered at Buckeye Lake in 1929 and another at Hoover Reservoir in 1992 (Harlan 1992d, Trautman 1940). While there is a report of a partially grown Red-breasted Merganser at Cleveland during June, 1982 (Peterjohn 1982d), this sighting lacks sufficient evidence to establish a confirmed nesting record for Ohio.

Ruddy Duck *Oxyura jamaicensis* (Gmelin)

For waterfowl, Ruddy Ducks are fairly late spring migrants, normally appearing by March 5–15. Their movements peak between March 25 and April 15, but numbers are diminished by April 20–25 and most depart by May 10.

Along western Lake Erie, spring Ruddies are common to abundant migrants. When their populations were larger, impressive flocks staged on Maumee Bay and elsewhere within the Western Basin: 20,000 estimated in Lucas County on April 19, 1951, and

Ruddy Duck

26,660 tallied during an aerial survey in 1962 (Campbell 1968, Mayfield 1951b). But most reports before 1970 were of 300–2,000. Since 1970, the largest flocks usually contain 100–500, while concentrations of 2,000–5,000 are exceptional.

Ruddy Ducks are common to abundant spring migrants within the northeastern counties, fairly common along central Lake Erie, and uncommon to locally common on large lakes in other counties. Along central Lake Erie, most spring sightings are of 30–250 Ruddies. Within the inland northeastern counties before 1970, spring flocks of 1,500–2,000+ were occasionally noted at Youngstown and smaller flocks elsewhere. Since 1970, the largest concentrations total 500–900+ during most years, while flocks of 30–200 are expected during April. Large spring concentrations are sporadically reported elsewhere. Ruddy Ducks like Findlay Reservoir (Hancock County); 1,500 were estimated on April 16, 1983, and smaller flocks appear most years (Peterjohn 1983c). A flock of 500 at Senecaville Reservoir on April 12, 1970, was exceptional for southeastern Ohio (Hall 1970b), while no more than 250 have been reported near Columbus. Ruddy Ducks mostly pass through the southern and central counties in flocks of 6–12, and daily totals seldom exceed 35–75.

Ohio's first nesting Ruddy Ducks were discovered at Pymatuning Lake in Ashtabula County, where a brood was observed in 1935 (Hicks 1935a). One pair nested there in 1936 and summered in 1938 (Baird 1936c, Walker 1938b). Except for occasional nonbreeding individuals, summer Ruddy Ducks were unrecorded until 1961 and 1962, when nesting pairs were discovered at Magee Marsh Wildlife Area (Campbell 1968). Summering or nesting Ruddy Ducks have resided within the western Lake Erie marshes in subsequent years, part of an eastward range expansion (DeVos 1964).

Ruddy Ducks are now rare summer residents along western Lake Erie. This summering population includes small flocks of 5–12 nonbreeders as well as scattered nesting pairs, probably fewer than 20 (Peterjohn and Rice 1991). Ruddy Ducks are accidental to casual summer visitors within other glaciated counties. While most records are isolated nonbreeders, nesting was established in Hamilton County on July 15, 1973 (Kleen 1973), Big Island Wildlife Area (Marion County) on July 4, 1986, Cleveland on August 1, 1987 (Peterjohn and Rice 1991), and Barberton in 1988 (Peterjohn 1988d).

Nesting Ruddies normally prefer large undisturbed marshes where open water is interspersed among emergent vegetation. Their nests are placed within vegetation near water. The few confirmed breeding records indicate that nesting activities begin during May or early June. Most broods are observed during July or early August when the young are already fairly large.

Fall Ruddy Ducks are most numerous along western Lake Erie. As recently as the 1970s, flocks of 5,000–7,000 were noted off Lucas County, and an aerial survey estimated 24,660 in Ottawa and Lucas Counties on November 30, 1962 (Campbell 1973). During the 1980s and 1990s, the largest flocks totaled 500–1,000 and daily counts were mostly 50–250. They are also common to abundant fall migrants through the inland northeastern counties. Large flocks were occasionally noted at Youngstown, with 2,000 on November 22, 1958, and 3,000 on November 7, 1949 (Brooks 1950a, 1959a). In recent years, the largest flocks are composed of 500–1,500+, although most reports total 50–300. They are fairly common to common migrants through central Lake Erie, where flocks of 30–200 are regularly noted and the largest concentrations are 500–1,100. They become uncommon to locally common fall migrants elsewhere. The largest concentrations include flocks of 500–1,000+ on reservoirs in Allen and Hancock Counties and 300 near Columbus. Sightings generally total 25–100 in the northwestern and central counties and fewer than 30 in the southern and unglaciated counties.

A few Ruddy Ducks may appear during August and the first half of September, but the first fall migrants normally return to Lake Erie by September 25–October 2 and inland lakes by October 3–10. Largest movements generally occur during the last half of October and November. Some years Ruddy Ducks remain numerous into the first half of December. Lakefront flocks of 600–1,100 have been reported as late as December 19–23. Other years their numbers diminish by the last week of November. The last flocks normally disappear by December 25.

Few Ruddy Ducks winter within Ohio. They are rare but regular residents along Lake Erie, especially the Cleveland-Lorain lakefront, where 1–8 winter at hot-water outlets. They also regularly overwinter on Summit Lake in Akron. Numbers there are usually no more than 10–20, although 100 were counted on January 3, 1995 (Harlan 1995b). Ruddy Ducks are accidental to casual winter residents away from these locations, with only a few reports of scattered individuals during relatively mild seasons.

Osprey *Pandion haliaetus* (Linnaeus)

For most people, their first encounter with an Osprey is a memorable experience. This large raptor suddenly appears over a lake or river, effortlessly riding the winds as it searches for food. It briefly hovers over a school of fish swimming near the surface of the water. By folding its wings, the Osprey drops out of the sky in a spectacular plunge as it attempts to catch its prey. It is usually unsuccessful and quickly rises from the water to resume its hunt. After repeating this sequence several times, the Osprey finally captures a fish, takes it to a perch, and consumes it.

Unfortunately, the experience of observing hunting Ospreys was almost eliminated from most of North America. Their populations were greatly reduced by pesticide contamination during the 1950s and 1960s. By the late 1960s, Ospreys were rare migrants, with only four to eight sightings from Ohio during their annual migrations. This decline was reversed just in time. The use of harmful organochlorine pesticides was banned during the late 1960s, while intensive management practices were undertaken to increase the breeding success of the remaining adults. Their recovery was widely apparent by the late 1970s, and increasing population trends continued into the 1990s.

Ospreys are generally uncommon to fairly common migrants, becoming locally rare in counties lacking sizable lakes and rivers. They may become locally common along western Lake Erie during spring. While the first spring Ospreys have returned as early as March 7–15, they are usually encountered during the first half of April. Their spring passage peaks between April 15 and May 15, when as many as three or four are observed on inland lakes and rivers, and small flights of 6–12 may occur along western Lake Erie. The largest daily movements along western Lake Erie totaled 19–25 during the 1990s. Similar numbers have not been reported from central Lake Erie. A remarkable inland tally of 18 Ospreys was reported at East Liverpool (Columbiana County) on May 1, 1965 (Hall 1965). Numbers decline during the last half of May, although nonbreeders may remain into June.

Ospreys are more widely reported during fall. Migrants may appear during the last week of July, mostly nonbreeders or unsuccessful adults, but are normally encountered by August 20–30. They are most frequently observed between September 10 and October 15, usually as daily totals of five or fewer. No large flights have been reported in autumn. Most depart by the first week of November, although a few have lingered into the first week of December.

During winter, Ospreys are normally scattered from the southern United States into South America (AOU 1998). Midwinter sightings from the Great Lakes region have generally been dismissed as misidentifications. Within Ohio, there have been a number of Osprey sight records between mid-December and mid-February. None of these records was substantiated by a specimen, photograph, or corroboration by multiple observers, leaving the state without a well-documented midwinter record. While lingering Ospreys could remain into late December or January during mild winters, such reports should be accompanied by thorough documentation in order to better substantiate their status as winter visitors in Ohio.

At one time, small numbers of Ospreys may have nested regularly within Ohio. During the nineteenth century, Kirtland (1838) reported a nesting pair near the city of Poland (Mahoning County). Small numbers regularly summered along Lake Erie, where a nest was claimed for Erie County (Hicks 1935a). They may have also nested at Buckeye Lake and Lake St. Marys (Hicks 1935a, Trautman 1940). After the turn of the century, a pair of Ospreys nested at Lake St. Marys in 1913 but did not return in subsequent years (Henninger 1916). One pair reportedly summered along the Scioto River in Pike County between 1928 and 1930, although a nest was never discovered (Hicks 1935a).

A pair constructed a nest at Buckeye Lake in 1941 but were shot before their eggs hatched. Another pair reportedly constructed a nest at Burr Oak State Park (Athens County) several years later.

Beginning in the 1980s, Ospreys became regular summer visitors in Ohio. Most appear at inland reservoirs, producing as many as 4–10 sightings annually. These birds may remain for a few days or several weeks. The first recent indication of nesting behavior was provided by an unmated Osprey in Belmont County which started to build nests during 1985 and 1986. Neither structure was completed (Peterjohn and Rice 1991). In 1989, West Virginia started an Osprey hacking program along the Ohio River at Blennerhassett Island (Hall 1991d). This program, and similar programs in adjacent states, released numbers of young Ospreys within this region and contributed to an increased number of summer reports from Ohio during the 1990s. An Osprey nest was built near Belpre (Washington County) along the Ohio River in 1994, but no eggs were laid (Hall 1994d). Ohio's first recent successful nesting attempt occurred near Rayland (Jefferson County) in 1995 (Hall 1995d). This nest has remained active in subsequent years, and additional nesting pairs have become established at Berlin Reservoir, Salt Fork Lake, and in Butler County (Brock 1997c, E. Schlabach 1998). If Osprey populations continue to increase, then additional nesting pairs and summering individuals should be expected in the future.

Swallow-tailed Kite *Elanoides forficatus* (Linnaeus)

With their present North American breeding range restricted to the southeastern United States, it is difficult to imagine that these elegant raptors formerly resided in Ohio. Yet, accounts from early naturalists indicate that Swallow-tailed Kites probably nested in the state during the first half of the nineteenth century. Their distribution may have been decidedly local; there were reports from Portage, Stark, Crawford, Marion, Pickaway, Fayette, and Ross Counties (Hicks 1935a). These kites were also described as "quite common" in Warren County, and there is a specimen from Cincinnati (Kemsies and Randle 1953, Mathena et al. 1984).

In all likelihood, Swallow-tailed Kites were disappearing from Ohio at the time of these initial sightings. For example, Kirtland (1838) found "considerable numbers" in Portage and Stark Counties during 1835, but none could be located in 1838. Kirkpatrick described them as "once numerous in Crawford County and still found occasionally" in 1858, a statement coinciding with Wheaton's (1882) belief that the kites disappeared as a "regularly occurring species" during the 1850s. Kirtland (1838) speculated that cold weather during several summers of the 1830s may have been responsible for this decline.

Habitat destruction and persecution may also have eliminated some populations.

Following their disappearance as summer residents, Swallow-tailed Kites became accidental visitors. During the last half of the nineteenth century, confirmed reports are limited to specimens taken in Licking County on August 22, 1878, and Ross County on August 29, 1898 (Hicks 1935a). In the twentieth century, a Swallow-tailed Kite was discovered in flight over fields east of Fremont on May 26, 1975 (Kleen 1975c), another was briefly observed near Austinburg (Ashtabula County) on June 16, 1989 (Peterjohn 1989d), and one was found in Holmes County on September 6, 1997, and was viewed by many birdwatchers through September 18 (Yoder 1997).

Mississippi Kite *Ictinia mississippiensis* (Wilson)

In the eastern United States, Mississippi Kites are found from the Carolinas across the Gulf Coast states and north along the Mississippi River to southern Missouri and southern Illinois (AOU 1998). This breeding range slowly expanded northward after the mid-1960s, and the number of extralimital kites also increased. Small numbers of Mississippi Kites now regularly wander north to the Great Lakes and New England states during late spring and early summer.

Mississippi Kites are accidental late spring and summer visitors to Ohio, with nine confirmed sightings of single individuals between May 11 and July 4, almost invariably immatures. Ohio's first Mississippi Kite was discovered by Frank Bader and Milton Rinehart on May 13, 1978, as it soared over Greenlawn Cemetery in Columbus (Thomson 1983). Others were observed over Oak Openings (Lucas County) on May 16, 1982 (Thomson 1983), along western Lake Erie in Lucas County on May 11, 1985 (Peterjohn 1985c), at Fort Loramie on June 4, 1987, and in Delaware County on June 23–24, 1987 (Peterjohn 1987d). During the 1990s, an immature was photographed in Ashtabula County on June 7, 1992 (Brock 1992b), one was observed at Metzger Marsh Wildlife Area (Lucas County) on May 19, 1996 (Brock 1996c), one appeared at Toussaint Wildlife Area on May 17, 1997 (Fazio 1997b), and one was discovered at Cuyahoga Valley National Recreation Area on July 4, 1999 (Rosche 1999b).

Bald Eagle *Haliaeetus leucocephalus* (Linnaeus)

Few birds command the respect shown large birds of prey. While falcons are renowned for their aerial maneuverability and Goshawks for their stealth, no raptor matches an eagle for its noble character. This demeanor was described by Herrick (1924c) during his studies of nesting Bald Eagles along Lake Erie:

When standing before us in full sunshine either bird presented an admirable picture of strength and self-reliance, every feather which clothed its powerful form lying unruffled in its place; its white head and tail cut off, as it were, from its trim, compact body; its yellow shanks and toes and corn-colored bill-hook were in sharp contrast with the plumage and the darker polished talons; while those restless yellow eyes in the male showed that no one was trusted, and as plainly in his mate that from no one would any nonsense or interference be tolerated.

The south shore of Lake Erie has always supported a breeding Bald Eagle population. When Ohio was initially settled, breeding eagles were regularly spaced along the entire lakefront, but disappeared from the more populated sections during the nineteenth century. They have not nested in Cuyahoga County since the 1800s, and the last lakefront nests in Lorain and Ashtabula Counties were during the 1930s (Hicks 1933a and 1935a, Williams 1950). Since the 1940s, this population has been restricted to Sandusky Bay and western Lake Erie.

Bald Eagles were always sporadic summer residents in the interior of the state. Trautman (1940) cited anecdotal accounts of nesting at Buckeye Lake during the 1800s, although they did not nest there in the twentieth century. At least one pair nested at Lake St. Marys through 1909, with occasional breeding attempts through 1925 (Clark and Sipe 1970, Price 1934a). A pair also nested at Indian Lake in 1906 (Fisher 1907a). The proliferation of reservoirs during the twentieth century encouraged a few additional attempts: at Lake Rockwell (Portage County) in 1935 (Williams 1950), Charles Mill Reservoir in 1950 (Mayfield 1950c), and near Youngstown during 1954 and 1966 (Brooks 1955a, Hall 1966b). A pair of eagles nested along Indian Creek in Butler County during 1953 (Kemsies and Randle 1953).

Between 1955 and 1966, the Ohio Bald Eagle population remained stable at 11–15 pairs. However, very few young eagles were successfully fledged. The nesting pairs had become contaminated with the residues of DDT and other related pesticides that caused them to lay infertile eggs, or eggs with thin shells that broke under the weight of the incubating adults. Since eagles are long-lived, the population did not decline immediately, but as the adults died, they were not replaced. This population declined to 4–5 pairs by 1979, and these pairs were still producing few young (Kleen 1975d, 1979d). At this time, the Ohio Division of Wildlife began to intensively manage the remaining pairs by monitoring nests, protecting breeding adults from disturbance, and transplanting young eagles into the nests of sterile adults to supplement natural reproduction. These actions, along with the natural recovery of eagle populations after DDT and other harmful pesticides were banned, allowed the statewide population to increase to 12 pairs by 1989 (Peterjohn 1989d). In the interior counties, a pair nested at Mosquito Creek Reservoir since 1981 (Peterjohn and Rice 1991).

The statewide breeding population markedly increased during the 1990s, to 20 nests in 1992, 33 in 1996, and 57 in 1999 (Brock 1996d, Harlan 1992d, Whan 1999a). Along Lake Erie, nesting Bald Eagles remain confined to Erie, Sandusky, Ottawa, and Lucas Counties. Inland pairs are now scattered across the northern half of the state, most numerous around large lakes in northeastern Ohio. Single pairs are scattered south to Delaware, Knox, and Coshocton Counties.

Most information on the nesting biology of Bald Eagles along Lake Erie was gathered by Francis Herrick in the 1920s (Herrick 1924a, 1924b, 1924c, 1924d). These breeding Bald Eagles remain within their territories throughout most of the year, sometimes abandoning them for brief periods during midwinter. Most of their activities are centered around their nests—immense structures maintained and reused for many years. Undoubtedly, the largest eyrie built in North America was located near Vermilion. Initially constructed in 1891, it was used continually through 1925, when the tree it was in collapsed (Herrick 1924b). While some pairs maintain only one nest, others build several and use them in alternating years. Nest building usually occurs during fall and early spring through mid-March. While some nests are near the lakeshore, others are more than a mile from Lake Erie. These nests are generally fifty to eighty-five feet above the ground, although one pair reportedly attempted to nest on the ground (Kleen 1976c).

The first eggs are laid by late February during advanced seasons or mid-March during relatively cold years. The young hatch by mid-April and the adults care for them for more than two months. Fledging, described by Herrick (1927), normally occurs during the last week of June or first week of July.

Bald Eagles have fairly well-defined migrations along Lake Erie during spring and fall, movements that became evident during the 1990s with the recovery of their continental populations. Similar movements were noted before eagle populations started to decline during the 1950s. Along western Lake Erie, they are currently fairly common to common during both migrations. Spring migrants are observed between late February and mid-April with a smaller peak in May. Totals are usually 12 or fewer daily, with peak counts of 20–25. These tallies include both migrant and resident eagles. Their fall migration extends between late August and mid-November, producing counts similar to those reported during spring. Along central Lake Erie, Bald Eagles are rare to uncommon migrants; generally seven or fewer are noted daily during the same migration periods as farther west along the lakefront.

Their movements through the interior counties are poorly defined, and Bald Eagles may be encountered almost anywhere at any time of the year. They are casual to locally uncommon visitors during spring and fall, most numerous in northeastern and central Ohio and least numerous in the unglaciated counties. Most reports are of three or fewer, although 13 congregating at Mosquito Creek Wildlife Area on April 10, 1997, may have included both migrant and resident eagles (Hall 1997c). Their spring migration has two poorly defined peaks. The first occurs between February 20 and March 20, and the second during May. As fall migrants, small numbers of eagles drift through the state, with the majority of reports during October and November. Away from inland nesting locations, Bald Eagles are casual to rare nonbreeding visitors and are most likely to be found as scattered individuals in the northern half of Ohio.

Numbers of wintering Bald Eagles increased dramatically throughout Ohio during the 1990s. While 15 or fewer eagles may have wintered within the interior of Ohio during the late 1980s, this population grew to 100–150 eagles by the late 1990s. They can be locally fairly common to common winter residents along western Lake Erie, where peak daily counts are 15–25, and at Mosquito Creek Lake, where maxima of 10–14 have been noted. Elsewhere, they are casual to locally uncommon winter residents, with as many as 6–12 eagles reported from scattered localities south to the Ohio River, but 1–3 are tallied at most locations.

Northern Harrier *Circus cyaneus* (Linnaeus)

On a warm April morning, a male Northern Harrier catches a thermal and soars into the blue sky. He appears to be gaining altitude in order to continue his migration. All of a sudden, he folds his wings and rockets toward the earth, only to pull up at the last second and give a loud call. This performance is repeated again and again, as this male is displaying for a female perched in a grassy field below.

Northern Harrier

At one time these displays were regularly observed between late March and early May in the northern two-thirds of Ohio, where harriers were locally common summer residents (Hicks 1935a). They were most numerous in northwestern Ohio. Campbell (1968) described them as "one of the more common breeding hawks" near Toledo and Price (1934a) thought they "probably equaled the total number of all other hawks" in Paulding County. They were generally rare in most other counties, although local populations were found south to Montgomery, Fayette, Pickaway, Fairfield, Muskingum, Guernsey, Harrison, and Jefferson Counties. Harriers were absent from southern Ohio except for isolated nesting attempts in Jackson and Vinton Counties (Hicks 1935a, 1937a).

Even in the mid-1930s this breeding population was declining. Hicks (1935a) and Trautman (1940) noted that numbers of harriers were already "much reduced," a result of habitat destruction and persecution. Additional declines were noted during the 1940s, especially near Toledo and in eastern Ohio (Buchanan 1980, Campbell 1968). By the mid-1950s, nesting harriers disappeared from most counties and became very scarce in northwestern Ohio (Campbell 1968, Phillips 1980, Price 1972). Isolated pairs remained at only a few widely scattered locations.

Their status did not change between the mid-1950s and the late 1980s. While the Breeding Bird Atlas uncovered a few additional nesting pairs, Northern Harriers remained casual to rare and very locally distributed summer residents in northern and central Ohio. The statewide breeding population was thought to total 15–25 pairs (Peterjohn and Rice 1991). The number of summering harriers increased slightly during the 1990s, although relatively few breeding attempts were confirmed. Many summer reports pertain to nonbreeders, so the size of this breeding population is difficult to estimate. Recent reports indicate that the statewide breeding population may now be in the range of 20–30 pairs.

Summering Northern Harriers are currently rare residents along western Lake Erie and in the northeastern counties of Ashtabula, Trumbull, Portage, and Lake. Breeding pairs and summering harriers are casual to locally rare in other northern and central counties south to Wyandot, Seneca, Wood, Henry, Madison, Clark, Clinton, Belmont, and Muskingum. They are generally accidental in the southern counties. Peterjohn and Rice (1991) cited summer records south to Butler, Clinton, and Noble Counties, and they resided in Clermont County as recently as 1976 (Kleen 1976c).

Breeding harriers prefer wet meadows, wet prairies, and the grassy margins of wetlands (Campbell 1968, Trautman 1940). As these habitats disappeared, they occupied upland pastures, hayfields, cultivated oat fields (Price 1934a), and in recent years, reclaimed strip mines. Their nests are placed on the ground, often in the middle of rose tangles in wetlands. In upland grasslands, harriers prefer large undisturbed fields without woody cover. While nests have been discovered as early as April 28 (Williams 1950), most are reported during the last half of May, with the young hatching by mid-June. The earliest fledglings are noted by July 1, although most appear during the last half of July or early August (Campbell 1968, Trautman 1940). Renesting attempts may produce clutches as late as July 15 (Walker and Franks 1928). These late attempts seldom fledge young.

Northern Harriers disperse widely after the breeding season and begin to appear away from nesting localities by July 25–August 20. Their fall migration consists of a gradual southward drift through Ohio. While they are most numerous in September and October, migrating harriers may be noted into the first half of January. Fall observations are usually 1–6 harriers daily; large fall movements have never been reported.

Numbers of wintering Harriers also declined during the twentieth century. They were formerly one of the most numerous wintering hawks in central and northern Ohio, and as many as 50–75 could be counted at a single roost (Campbell 1968, Trautman 1940, Williams 1950). This decline was gradual, reflecting changing land-use patterns and a significant reduction in breeding populations throughout eastern North America (Robbins et al. 1986, Sauer et al. 1998). Since the 1940s, the conversion of grasslands to cultivated fields and the practice of fall plowing has contributed to further reductions in their populations.

Northern Harriers are now uncommon to locally common winter residents throughout Ohio, where most reports are of 1–8 daily, with peak counts of 10–15. Harriers regularly congregate at Killdeer Plains Wildlife Area, Maumee Bay State Park, and the Ross-Pickaway county line area, but roosts may form in other counties. As many as 25–40 have been counted at roosts in central and western Ohio in recent years. Rodents form the bulk of their winter diet, and the numbers of wintering harriers reflect the abundance of this prey. When rodents are plentiful, large numbers of harriers may remain in Ohio. When rodents are scarce, most harriers move elsewhere, and even preferred wintering sites host only 3–8 daily.

Northern Harriers form communal roosts during winter in grasslands and fallow fields where weeds and grasses provide protection from the harsh conditions. As dusk approaches, they appear from all directions. They fly low over the roosting field, and while a few may pounce on prey, most just quietly fly over the field. At first only one or two, then four or five, and perhaps as many as 12–15 may be visible at once. Antagonistic behavior occurs if two hawks approach too closely, but they are more likely to be harassed by Short-eared Owls leaving their daytime roosts in the same field.

Their spring migration is poorly defined within the interior counties, where harriers simply depart from their wintering sites. Inland totals are generally eight or fewer daily through mid-April, with very few after May 1. Spring migration is more apparent along Lake Erie, where the first migrants are noted by March 3–10, and others continue to move along the lakefront through May 20. The largest flights, normally between March 20 and April 20, may be composed of 25–50 harriers daily.

Sharp-shinned Hawk *Accipiter striatus* Vieillot

As thermals develop during the mid-morning hours, Sharp-shinned Hawks emerge from the woodlands where they spent the previous evening. Mostly as individuals, but occasionally in groups of two or three, these migrant hawks soar higher and higher until they are hardly more than pinpoints in the sky. After attaining sufficient altitude, they take advantage of tail winds and continue their journey over Ohio.

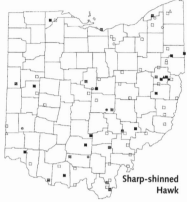

Sharp-shinned Hawk

Sharp-shinneds are normally most numerous during spring. While their passage is generally associated with southerly winds, migrants may be encountered under almost any condition except hard rains. Their northward migration begins with the first favorable winds in late February, and they become widely distributed by March 10–20. Large flights may occur by early April but are most likely between April 20 and May 7. They normally depart by May 20 except along Lake Erie, where non-breeders may appear through June 5.

Spring Sharp-shinneds are fairly common to abundant along Lake Erie. Favorable conditions regularly produce flights of 30–60 and occasionally 100+. The largest flights totaled 400+ Sharp-shinneds over Lucas County on April 26–27, 1969 (Campbell 1973), and 170–228 on several dates. With unfavorable conditions, fewer than five are noted daily. These hawks are rare to uncommon migrants through the interior counties, where most sightings are of 1–3 and the largest movements total 10–15.

Their southward migration is less conspicuous. Fall migrants are uncommon to rare in most areas, normally encountered as scattered individuals, with occasional groups of 3–6. Defined movements occur through the western Lake Erie islands, where hawks moving south from Point Pelee in Canada "island hop" across the western end of the lake. Sharp-shinneds passing around the western end of Lake Erie also regularly appear over the Oak Openings area of Lucas County. Fairly common to common migrants through these areas, northerly winds may produce flights of 40–80, although 20 or fewer are counted on most days.

The earliest fall Sharp-shinneds return to northwestern Ohio by the last week of August but are expected in most counties by September 10–20. These migrants are mostly observed between September 25 and October 20. This movement continues into November, but it is difficult to distinguish late migrants from wintering hawks.

At one time, Sharp-shinned Hawks were casual to rare winter residents throughout Ohio, mostly restricted to woodlands, wooded fencerows, and dense thickets. Given their secretive habits, their abundance may have been greater than the few reports indicated. Since the mid-1970s, wintering Sharp-shinneds have started visiting urban and rural residences to capture small songbirds at feeders. The number of winter sightings has markedly increased, and they have become rare to uncommon winter residents, invariably as scattered individuals.

Their status as summer residents also fluctuated during the twentieth century. Hicks (1935a) considered breeding Sharp-shinneds rare and very locally distributed residents, with records from forty-eight counties, mostly in the eastern half of Ohio. Recognizing their secretive behavior, he realized they might be more numerous than these sight records indicated. Beginning in the late 1940s, this population underwent a gradual decline that continued through the 1960s. This reduction was believed to be the result of pesticide contamination. By 1970, very few nesting pairs remained within Ohio, but after the harmful pesticides were banned, Sharp-shinned Hawks quickly recovered. Recent sightings indicate they have regained their former abundance. Most summering Sharp-shinneds are discovered along or near the Allegheny Plateau in eastern Ohio, where they are rare to locally uncommon residents (Peterjohn and Rice 1991). They become accidental to casual residents in the western half of Ohio, with few confirmed breeding records after 1970, although nests near Cincinnati and Toledo indicate small local populations exist. Nesting Sharp-shinneds are not easily detected, and Ohio probably supports more pairs than are currently known.

Nesting Sharp-shinned Hawks occupy wooded habitats varying from young second-growth woods to mature forests. They are seldom observed over open fields, and do not normally venture into residential areas. They prefer to nest in conifers but will also occupy large deciduous woodlots. Nests with eggs have been reported between mid-May and early June; an exceptionally late nest in Ashtabula County was found on July 12, 1928 (Hicks 1933a). Recently fledged young have been reported during July.

Cooper's Hawk *Accipiter cooperii* (Bonaparte)

Stealthy hunters of birds and occasionally mammals, Cooper's Hawks are found wherever their prey congregates. These crow-sized raptors prefer woodlands, wooded fencerows, and similar habitats, where they adeptly pursue their prey through dense cover. Cooper's Hawks may also be observed pursuing blackbirds through their marshy roosts, Mourning Doves in cornfields, and songbirds at backyard feeders.

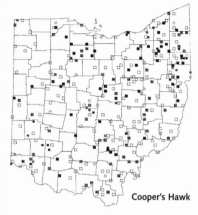

Cooper's Hawk

In the early 1900s, Cooper's Hawks were widespread residents (Jones 1903). Despite frequent persecution, they were among our more numerous breeding hawks. Campbell (1968) considered them "second numerically only to Marsh Hawks [Northern Harrier]" as summer residents at Toledo. Populations remained stable during the first decades of the twentieth century despite local declines resulting from habitat destruction (Trautman 1940). In the mid-1930s, Hicks (1935a) considered Cooper's Hawks rare to common residents within every county, most numerous along the unglaciated Allegheny Plateau.

Their numbers declined during the 1940s, and breeding pairs disappeared from many localities during the 1950s (Buchanan 1980, Campbell 1968, Clark and Sipe 1970). By the early 1960s, these formerly widespread residents were reduced to scattered nesting pairs. While habitat destruction contributed to this decline, the major cause was eventually shown to be pesticide contamination of the adults. After use of these pesticides was banned, this decline was halted during the early 1970s (Robbins et al. 1986). Cooper's Hawks remained scarce through the end of the decade, but improved numbers became apparent between 1980 and 1983. By 1985, they once again became widely distributed residents, and populations continued to increase into the 1990s.

Cooper's Hawks are now rare and locally distributed summer residents within intensively farmed western Ohio, but become uncommon to locally fairly common in the southern and eastern counties, where wooded habitats are widely distributed (Peterjohn and Rice 1991). Breeding pairs are present in most counties, even in western Ohio where summer records are of isolated individuals or adults accompanied by young.

Nesting Cooper's Hawks prefer pine plantations but also occupy second growth deciduous woods (Mutter et al. 1984, Price 1941). Pairs will nest in small groves of trees if suitable dense cover is present. Their nests are placed at heights of twenty to eighty feet, frequently in the principal forks of large trees. Breeding pairs are most evident during their courtship displays in April, but become secretive once their breeding activities begin. Nests are constructed in

April or early May and clutches have been reported between April 21 and May 30 (Williams 1950). Most young Cooper's Hawks hatch during the last half of May and remain in the nest through late June or the first half of July (Campbell 1968, Trautman 1949). Renesting attempts are responsible for small young in the nest through July 21 (Hicks 1933a).

Numbers of wintering Cooper's Hawks also increased after the early 1970s, reflecting the recovery of continental breeding populations. They are currently widely distributed in habitats varying from deciduous woods to rural farmlands to urban residential areas. They are uncommon to fairly common across Ohio. Most reports are of three or fewer, although 4–8 may be encountered daily at preferred localities.

The expansion of wintering Cooper's Hawks into urban areas began during the 1980s. Their stealth and hunting skills are useful in surprising songbirds at feeders. Many are immatures, whose hunting skills may not be fully developed; the adults are more likely to be found in woodlands.

As a result of their substantial breeding and wintering populations, the migratory movements of Cooper's Hawks are poorly defined. These movements are most apparent during spring, especially along Lake Erie, where they become fairly common to locally common migrants between late February and April 25, with smaller numbers appearing through mid-May. The largest flights were reported before 1945; 100 were counted along western Lake Erie on March 19, 1942 (Campbell 1968). Since 1960, the largest movements have been composed of 20–45, with ten or fewer counted on most days. Within the interior counties, migrant Cooper's Hawks are mostly reported as three or fewer during March and April.

The southward migration normally consists of scattered individuals throughout Ohio. No sizable flights have been reported, with daily maxima of 6–8 over the Oak Openings area of Lucas County. This movement begins during the last half of September and is most apparent between September 25 and November 1. Smaller numbers may appear during December, as the birds search for suitable winter territories.

Northern Goshawk *Accipiter gentilis* (Linnaeus)

This impressive raptor is a resident of northern coniferous and mixed forests. Its breeding range extends south to the upper Great Lakes and the mountains of Pennsylvania, West Virginia, and northern New Jersey (AOU 1998). Remarkably wary, the Northern Goshawk is renowned for its stealth and hunting prowess. With luck and perseverance, one may be viewed perched near the trunk of a tall tree, watching the surroundings for prey.

Goshawks were once considered accidental or casual winter visitors, with about one sighting every two or three years. Since 1968, there have been at least one or two reports every year, indicating that goshawks are rare winter visitors to northern Ohio and accidental to casual elsewhere. Undoubtedly more of these wary birds occur within Ohio than are positively identified.

This species also undertakes periodic movements away from its normal breeding range. These flights occur at ten-year intervals and are correlated with cyclical lows in its prey populations. The most pronounced flights were noted during the winters of 1972–1973 and 1982–1983. The latter flight produced at least sixteen winter sightings within Ohio and additional migrants during spring and fall. Smaller "echo" flights frequently appear during the winter following an invasion, but these flights normally produce fewer than six sightings.

During invasions, a few goshawks are reliably reported as early as mid-October; all earlier sight records most likely are misidentifications. They usually appear during November, when migrants are casually encountered near western Lake Erie or over the Oak Openings area of Lucas County. Fall migrants are accidental elsewhere in the state.

As winter visitors, goshawks are mostly reported from the northern tier of counties and northeastern Ohio south to Akron and Youngstown. They usually wander farther south only during pronounced invasions, when there may be scattered sightings south to the Ohio River. Goshawks may be discovered anytime during winter. Most inhabit extensive woodlands, but a few visit small woodlots, wooded parks within cities, and even backyard bird feeders.

Their spring migration is most evident along western Lake Erie, where one or two goshawks are reported during March of most years. Greater numbers pass along the lakefront following pronounced invasions, but usually no more than five or six sightings of single birds. Spring migrants are accidental elsewhere, primarily during March. A few late migrants have appeared in April, and the latest acceptable records from northern Ohio are through April 23–28.

Harris's Hawk *Parabuteo unicinctus* (Temminck)

This accidental visitor from the southwestern United States has appeared in Ohio only once. About December 24, 1917, one of a pair of Harris's Hawks was collected in Pickaway County, approximately four miles southwest of Harrisburg. T.M. Earl (1918) noted that these birds were "reported to be molesting poultry and had killed one or two." The specimen, an adult, is in the Ohio State University Museum of Zoology, and there is no excessive feather wear or other indication that the bird had been kept in captivity.

While some extralimital records of Harris's Hawks have been dismissed as birds that escaped from captivity (AOU 1998), this explanation does not necessarily apply to the Ohio record. The sport of falconry was not as widely practiced in this country in 1917 as it is today, and captive birds were not as readily available. More important, Harris's Hawks are known to wander occasionally during late fall and early winter (AOU 1998), the season when the pair appeared in Ohio. While the origins of this pair will never be conclusively proven, the evidence suggests that the Ohio record represents truly wild birds.

Red-shouldered Hawk *Buteo lineatus* (Gmelin)

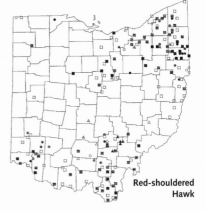

Red-shouldered Hawk

Without a doubt, the Red-shouldered Hawk is the most handsome of our resident buteos. A striking raptor with red underparts, rusty shoulders, and a black and white barred back, this hawk is equally impressive as it perches quietly in a tall tree or soars overhead. Unfortunately, encounters with this beautiful hawk have become too infrequent in recent decades.

In the early 1900s, Red-shouldereds were the most numerous large hawk within Ohio (Jones 1903). Breeding pairs were most frequently observed in the northern and central counties. Some were permanent residents but many migrated south each fall, producing an influx of wintering Red-shouldereds into southern Ohio. In the mid-1930s, Hicks (1935a) cited summer records from seventy counties, noting that they were most frequently observed in the northern third of the state, and absent or very rare within most unglaciated and some southwestern counties. Their numbers were declining, however, since they were described as uncommon to rare and locally distributed in most areas. Trautman (1940) recorded 22 nesting pairs at Buckeye Lake between 1922 and 1924 but only four pairs by 1933. Similar declines were evident throughout the western half of Ohio (Price 1934a).

These declines continued during subsequent decades. At Toledo, Red-shouldereds were greatly reduced by the mid-1950s and only 2–3 pairs remained in 1968 (Campbell 1968). These hawks essentially disappeared from most northwestern and glaciated counties by 1970. A sizable but declining population remained near Cincinnati (Austing and Imbrogno 1976). Surprisingly, populations remained stable in the northeastern counties

(Newman 1969), and Red-shouldereds were increasing along the unglaciated Allegheny Plateau. These trends continued through the mid-1970s, but populations stabilized after 1980.

Of all factors contributing to this decline, habitat destruction was most important. These hawks occupy mature lowland woods, hunting within these woods or along the margins of fields and wetlands, where they chiefly prey upon amphibians, reptiles, and birds during summer, and mammals and birds in winter. Within the glaciated counties, most lowland forests were cleared, beginning in the 1920s, while many remaining forests are too small and disturbed to support nesting Red-shouldereds. Pesticide contamination may have also reduced breeding populations in suitable habitats.

Fortunately, some lowland forests remain intact and are occupied by breeding Red-shouldereds. These habitats are most prevalent in the northeastern counties and along the unglaciated Allegheny Plateau, where they are uncommon to rare residents. They are scarce to absent near large cities and within extensively strip-mined areas from Tuscarawas, Harrison, and southern Jefferson Counties south to Perry, Morgan, and Washington Counties (Peterjohn and Rice 1991). Red-shouldered Hawks are uncommon and locally distributed summer residents in the southwestern counties north to Montgomery and Warren. They are accidental to locally rare residents within the northwestern and glaciated central counties, where the number of breeding pairs may not exceed 10–20.

Red-shouldered Hawks place their nests from forty to seventy-five feet high in large trees and may use these platforms for several years. Nest construction takes place during March, and the first eggs may be laid during the last week of the month (Trautman 1940, Williams 1950). While most young hatch by late April or early May, nests with eggs have been reported as late as May 18 (Braund 1940a). The earliest fledglings are reported during the last week of May but normally appear in June or early July.

Wintering Red-shouldereds also declined since the 1920s. As recently as the early 1960s, these wintering hawks were regularly detected in swamp forests and along wooded riparian corridors throughout Ohio. By the mid-1960s, they disappeared from most northwestern and glaciated central counties. Small numbers were regularly observed elsewhere. Numbers in the northeastern counties increased during the 1990s, but similar trends are not evident elsewhere.

Red-shouldereds are now rare to uncommon winter residents in most southern and eastern counties. Most winter records are of three or fewer, although as many as 6–10 may be tallied in northeastern Ohio. Within the glaciated central and northwestern counties, these hawks are accidental or casual winter visitors, averaging one or two sightings annually since 1970.

Their migratory movements are most noticeable in spring, when the first migrants may appear on strong southerly winds during February. Most migrants are detected during March, with smaller numbers through April 10–20 and occasional immatures passing along Lake Erie through the last week of May.

This northward passage is most evident along Lake Erie, where Red-shoulderds become fairly common to common migrants. On March days with strong southerly winds, kettles of 20 or more adults create quite a spectacle. Before 1950, sizable numbers appeared each spring, and the largest flight totaled 800 near Toledo on March 19, 1942 (Campbell 1968). In the 1990s, as many as 80–125 daily were counted along western Lake Erie and 161 at Conneaut on March 21, 1997 (Brock 1997c). Most reports are of 25 or fewer during March and only singles after April 15. Red-shouldereds are rare to locally uncommon spring migrants away from Lake Erie; most inland reports are of scattered individuals.

Their fall migration is poorly defined in most areas. These migrants are generally rare to locally uncommon as scattered individuals, although 18+ were counted in Trumbull County on October 19, 1992 (Hall 1993a). They become fairly common migrants over the Oak Openings of Lucas County, where the peak daily flights have totaled 20–33 in recent years. A few immature Red-shouldereds appear during August, but they probably represent wandering young raised in the state. Most fall migrants are detected between October 1 and November 15.

Broad-winged Hawk *Buteo platypterus* (Vieillot)

Broad-winged Hawks are renowned for their spectacular flights each spring and autumn as they move back and forth between their winter range in Central and South America and their breeding territories in the deciduous forests of eastern North America. Ohio is fortunate to share in this spectacle, although the appearance of sizable flocks is not as predictable as their movements elsewhere.

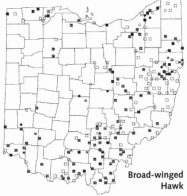

Broad-winged Hawk

The first spring arrivals are normally resident pairs returning to the southern and eastern counties between April 5 and 15. A few migrants may appear north to Lake Erie by the first week of April but are expected during April 15–20. Their northward migration peaks between April 20 and 30. Smaller numbers pass through Ohio until May 10–20, with stragglers along Lake Erie through June 7.

These spring movements are most pronounced along Lake Erie, where Broad-wingeds become fairly common to abundant migrants. During some years, the largest movements are composed of only 100 or fewer Broad-wingeds. Other years produce flights of 300–500. On rare occasions, immense flights appear, including 4,500 on April 26–27, 1969, 2,012 on April 20, 1992, and 2,000 on April 25, 1984, in Lucas County (Brock 1992a, Campbell 1973, Peterjohn 1984c); 1,200 at Cleveland on April 24, 1961 (Mumford 1961c); and 1,230–1,377 at Conneaut. These flights occur on strong southwesterly winds; unfavorable winds produce only 3–20 daily. Away from Lake Erie, Broad-wingeds are generally uncommon to fairly common migrants and six or fewer are expected daily. The largest inland spring flights total 80–300 in the eastern counties.

As summer residents, Broad-wingeds gradually increased since 1900. In the mid-1930s, Hicks (1935a) reported that nesting pairs were largely restricted to eastern Ohio, where they were locally distributed from Lake and Trumbull Counties south along the entire unglaciated plateau. More than a dozen pairs inhabited several counties, although most supported only a few pairs. The largest populations were found in northeastern Ohio and along the Ohio River between Monroe and Meigs Counties. Elsewhere, Hicks (1935a) cited nesting records only from Williams County, although a few pairs also resided at Cincinnati (Kemsies and Randle 1953). Their numbers slowly improved during subsequent years as woodlands matured within the unglaciated counties. This expansion eventually resulted in scattered pairs in the glaciated central and northwestern counties during the 1970s.

Broad-winged Hawks are now uncommon to fairly common summer residents along the Allegheny Plateau. Usually noted as scattered pairs, a total of ten within Mohican State Forest in 1997 may be representative of their breeding abundance in heavily wooded portions of the state. They become more locally distributed in northeastern Ohio, especially near large cities. Within southwestern Ohio, Broad-wingeds are uncommon residents in counties bordering the Ohio River and rare elsewhere. They are least numerous within the glaciated central and northwestern counties, where they are accidental to locally rare summer residents. A few pairs nest in Lucas, Fulton, and Williams Counties, as well as near Columbus, but summering Broad-wingeds are absent from most of western Ohio (Peterjohn and Rice 1991).

Nesting Broad-wingeds occupy extensive mature upland woods. Their nests are placed in the crotches of large trees at heights of 30 feet or more. Nest construction begins during the last half of April in southern Ohio but not until May near Lake Erie. Complete clutches are expected between early May and mid-June. Most young hatch in June and fledge by late July or early August.

In fall, large numbers of Broad-wingeds migrate around western Lake Erie, but after passing through southeastern Michigan they disperse across a broad front as they head toward Texas. Those hawks migrating around eastern Lake Erie move along the Appalachian Mountains and miss Ohio entirely. As in spring, these fall movements are quite variable. During some years, they miss Ohio. In other years, migrant Broad-wingeds become briefly numerous, particularly within the western counties.

Fall Broad-wingeds are uncommon to locally abundant migrants through northwestern Ohio, where most movements are reported from the Toledo area. The largest flight totaled 2,000 over Oregon (Lucas County) on September 21, 1982 (Peterjohn 1983a); flights of 1,500–1,600 passed over the Oak Openings area of Lucas County during several years of the 1990s. Flocks of 100–500 are detected most years (Campbell 1968). Elsewhere in western Ohio, Broad-wingeds are rare to locally abundant migrants. Large kettles may appear in any county but are most frequently encountered in the Cincinnati-Dayton area. These kettles usually total 35–200, with occasional concentrations of 300–500+. Within the central third of the state, Broad-wingeds are casual to rare fall migrants. Small flocks are infrequently noted, and the largest movement totaled 250 at Columbus on September 17, 1978 (Thomson 1983). Small flocks and individuals are casual to uncommon fall migrants through the eastern counties.

A few migrant Broad-wingeds are encountered during August, including a kettle in Ottawa County on August 28, 1957 (Nolan 1958a). While small numbers of migrants are observed between September 5 and 15, the largest flights almost invariably occur between September 15 and 25. October migrants are usually groups of six or fewer; 100 at Cincinnati was exceptional on October 24, 1987 (Peterjohn 1988a). The last fall migrants usually depart by October 10–15, with a few stragglers lingering through the end of the month. The latest reliable fall sighting was at Buck Creek State Park on November 14, 1995 (Harlan 1996a).

There have been a number of winter Broad-winged Hawk sightings, mostly on Christmas Bird Counts. These sightings are invariably misidentifications; there are no substantiated winter records. Since Broad-wingeds normally winter in Central and South America, it is very unlikely they would appear within Ohio during this season.

Swainson's Hawk *Buteo swainsoni* Bonaparte

Ohio currently has two acceptable sight records of Swainson's Hawk. An immature was discovered at Magee Marsh Wildlife Area in Lucas County on July 1, 1983. It was viewed in flight for several minutes and may also have been observed on several later dates (Peterjohn 1983d). The second record was provided by a light-phased adult carefully studied as it migrated past Maumee Bay State Park (Lucas County) on April 6, 1991 (Schlabach 1991). None of the other sight records from Ohio is adequately documented.

Swainson's Hawk is a migratory raptor whose breeding range encompasses most of western North America. It nests east through the plains states, while a small disjunct population is located in northern Illinois (AOU 1998). In recent years, these hawks have proven to be very rare but regular migrants wherever large numbers of hawks congregate in eastern North America, and the appearance of one along western Lake Erie during spring was not unexpected.

This species normally winters in South America, although small numbers may also occur in southern Florida and south Texas (AOU 1998). Winter records from other portions of North America are generally dismissed as misidentifications or hawks escaped from captivity (Browning 1974). Ohio has a winter record of an adult photographed in Ottawa County on February 14, 1984 (Peterjohn 1984b). Based on its unseasonal occurrence and several broken primaries, this hawk may have escaped from captivity and does not constitute an acceptable record (Peterjohn et al. 1987).

Red-tailed Hawk *Buteo jamaicensis* (Gmelin)

As it effortlessly rides the midday thermals, a Red-tailed Hawk surveys its territory below. For most Red-taileds, this territory consists of open farmlands, grassy roadside edges, and successional fields. Upland woods are essential, especially tall mature trees where they place their bulky nests. The Red-tailed may soar high in the sky, enjoying its free ride over the countryside, but most hunting is performed from perches closer to the ground.

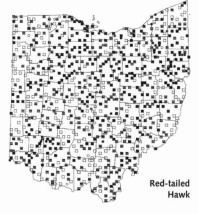

Red-tailed Hawk

The sight of soaring Red-tailed Hawks is now a fairly common occurrence in most counties during the breeding season. Although regularly encountered, they are never numerous and summer totals seldom exceed 6–15 daily. They are least numerous along the wooded hillsides of southeastern Ohio and in urban areas, where breeding pairs become locally uncommon (Peterjohn and Rice 1991).

Their nests are normally placed at heights of thirty feet or more in tall trees. These nests may be reused for several years, with fresh material added before each attempt. The oldest nests often become prominent features of barren winter woodlots. Nest construction has been reported as early as January 24 and may continue into April (Campbell 1968). The first clutches may be laid by March 11–17, although most are initiated in late March or early April. Most young hatch in May and fledge by late June, with early nests producing fledglings by May 23 (Williams 1950). Some pairs renest if their first clutch fails, producing nests with eggs through May 31 and recently fledged young in early August (Campbell 1968).

While Red-tailed Hawks are presently our most numerous breeding buteo, they have not always had that status. They were widely distributed before 1900, but their numbers were greatly reduced by persecution and habitat destruction during the first decades of the twentieth century. Their populations reached their lowest levels in the 1920s and 1930s, when Red-taileds were uncommon residents in southeastern Ohio and rare to locally absent elsewhere (Hicks 1935a, 1937a). Today, it is difficult to imagine that no Red-taileds nested at Buckeye Lake between 1920 and 1940 (Trautman 1940). Their numbers slowly improved during the 1940s, although they remained locally rare in western Ohio into the early 1950s (Kemsies and Randle 1953). Substantially greater numbers were apparent after the mid-1950s, and populations continued to increase into the 1990s (Robbins et al. 1986, Sauer et al. 1998).

Most Red-tailed Hawks are permanent residents. Some migrate south for the winter, but the proportion of migratory pairs appears to be fairly small. Resident birds are joined by sizable numbers migrating south from Canada and the upper Great Lakes states. Their fall migration is poorly defined except over the Oak Openings of Lucas County, where 273 were counted on November 13, 1994, and flights of 70–135 appear during most years (Harlan 1995a). The first migrants are detected by mid-September (Trautman 1940). Most appear between October 15 and November 20, with a second influx during December.

As winter residents, Red-tailed Hawks are fairly common to common throughout Ohio. Except in the extreme northeastern counties, wintering numbers are greater than the breeding population. As many as 10–20 may be observed daily in most counties, while 30–40+ are possible at favored localities such as the Killdeer Plains Wildlife Area. Wintering Red-taileds prefer fallow fields and corn stubble, especially if bordered by wooded fencerows or woodlots (Bildstein 1987). These wintering hawks are very beneficial, since they prey mainly on rodents and other small mammals.

With the return of moderate temperatures in February, Red-taileds begin their northward passage through Ohio. Their wintering numbers diminish within the interior counties by mid-March. While their inland spring migration is poorly defined, large numbers regularly pass along Lake Erie. The largest lakefront flights occur between March 7 and April 25. With favorable winds, 50–250+ may be counted along western Lake Erie, with maxima of 423 on April 2, 1994, and 406 on March 23, 1982, over Lucas County (Harlan 1994c, Peterjohn 1982c). Along the Central Basin, most counts total 30–75 and the largest flights may be composed of 100–200+. Migrants continue to pass along Lake Erie through May 10–20, usually in totals of 40 or fewer. These later migrants are almost exclusively immatures.

The vast majority of Red-tailed Hawk sightings in Ohio pertain to the race *borealis*, which is widely distributed in eastern North America. However, several other races may occur as accidental or casual winter visitors. Very pale Red-taileds showing characteristics of the *kriderii* race have been occasionally reported, primarily from the western half of the state, with sightings east to Tuscarawas County (Peterjohn 1989b). Dark morph Red-taileds have also been occasionally encountered; some have been identified as the western race *calurus*, although individuals of the *harlani* race could potentially appear within Ohio.

Rough-legged Hawk *Buteo lagopus* (Pontoppidan)

One of the better Ohio locations to observe and study these winter residents is the reclaimed strip mines of Muskingum County. The area's grassy hayfields and pastures with abundant rodent populations provide ideal wintering habitats for these hawks. Unlike Red-taileds, which normally hunt from tall perches, Rough-leggeds are adept at hunting on the wing or from the tiny upper branches of young saplings.

In these strip mines, Rough-legged Hawks are fairly common winter residents, with daily totals of 5–20+ and a maximum of 51 during the 1998–1999 winter. Similar numbers may be found at localities scattered along the edge of the unglaciated Allegheny Plateau from Columbiana and Holmes Counties south to Adams County. Rough-leggeds are also fairly common winter residents at Killdeer Plains Wildlife Area and along western Lake Erie; daily totals are generally six or fewer at these locations. Elsewhere, they are casual to locally uncommon winter residents, most frequently reported from the northern half of the state and least numerous in the southeastern counties bordering the Ohio River.

These wintering numbers are variable, reflecting the cyclical fluctuations of prey populations on their Arctic breeding grounds and Ohio winter territories.

Large numbers of breeding Rough-leggeds combined with sizable winter rodent populations have produced several pronounced "flights." The largest may have occurred during the winter of 1964–1965, when 50 Rough-leggeds were observed between Magee Marsh Wildlife Area and Port Clinton in Ottawa County (Campbell 1968). Flights during the winters of 1974–1975 and 1975–1976 produced Christmas Bird Count totals of 72 and 87, respectively, in the vicinity of Kingston. Smaller flights producing maxima of 20–24 were reported during the winters of 1929–1930, four winters during the 1930s, and the winter of 1944–1945 (Campbell 1968, Trautman 1940). Conversely, small breeding populations combined with a scarcity of rodents can cause this species to be relatively rare throughout Ohio.

Rough-legged Hawks are the only eastern buteos to regularly exhibit melanism. The black Rough-leggeds with their silver underwings are particularly appealing. Unfortunately, they compose only 10–25 percent of our wintering population. This proportion may increase during pronounced "flights," when melanistic birds may outnumber light-phased individuals.

While fall Rough-leggeds have been reported as early as late August, these records are considered doubtful in the absence of substantiating details. A few have been noted in the northern counties between September 20 and 30, but these early migrants are extremely rare. The first Rough-leggeds normally return during October 20–November 10. Their fall migration is mostly individuals filtering through the state. The only detectable movement usually accompanies the onset of harsh winter weather during December. However, many of these hawks do not establish territories, so the size of the wintering population is not known until January 5–10.

Their spring migration is equally poorly defined as most individuals quietly move northward. Unlike many other hawks, Rough-leggeds are not afraid to migrate over open water and readily fly across Lake Erie. Spring migrants congregate along western Lake Erie, where maxima of 16–23 have been reported. Elsewhere, the largest spring flight totaled 20 over Lake County on April 27, 1919 (Williams 1950). Rough-leggeds regularly remain until April 5–15. Most later individuals are recorded along Lake Erie, although a small number of records are scattered across Ohio during the first half of May. The latest migrant passed over Ottawa County on the unusual date of May 27, 1979 (Kleen 1979c).

Rough-legged Hawks are accidental summer visitors, with only three records. Campbell (1968) reported one on West Sister Island in western Lake Erie on June 16, 1948. Another Rough-legged was reported from Cleveland on July 26, 1978 (Rosche 1992), while an injured hawk was captured at Cincinnati on July 25, 1981 (Peterjohn 1981c).

Golden Eagle *Aquila chrysaetos* (Linnaeus)

Golden Eagles have always ranked among the rarest hawks visiting Ohio. In North America, this magnificent raptor is largely confined to the western half of the continent, and breeding pairs are widely distributed from Alaska south into Mexico. Only a few nesting pairs are known from eastern North America, where they are primarily migrants and winter residents (AOU 1998).

Their historic status is obscured by the inability of early observers to distinguish between Golden Eagles and the more numerous Bald Eagles. While there are nineteenth-century specimens to support some reports, the confirmed records are too few to determine their status before 1900. After 1900, Golden Eagles were primarily accidental or casual visitors. Trautman's (1940) report of seven Ohio specimens between 1922 and 1933 may be indicative of their statewide abundance before 1940. The number of records remained fairly constant through the 1970s, with five to eight sightings per decade. Their numbers increased during the 1980s and 1990s, reflecting similar trends throughout eastern North America. They became annual visitors during the 1980s, and produced 5–15+ sightings annually by the late 1990s.

Before 1940, the number of Golden Eagle winter records was nearly equal to the observations of migrants. Since 1940, their winter records have been reduced to one to six confirmed sightings each decade. They are presently accidental winter residents, appearing anytime between the last half of December and mid-February. They prefer upland locations but may be found near large lakes. Winter records usually are of singles, although two may have spent the winter of 1947–1948 near Toledo (Campbell 1968). They have been reported from localities scattered across the state, with most sightings from the northern and central counties.

Since 1980, Golden Eagles have been rare spring migrants along western Lake Erie, producing 1–4 records during most years. They are casual spring migrants along central Lake Erie and accidental through all interior counties, with one to three records annually away from western Lake Erie during the late 1990s. All spring reports are of 1–2 eagles. Early migrants have passed along Lake Erie by February 19, but they are not expected until the last half of March. These migrants are most likely to appear between April 10 and May 5, with stragglers through May 20.

The number of fall records noticeably increased during the 1990s. Golden Eagles have proven to be rare migrants over the Oak Openings area of Lucas County, where 1–7 are reported during most years. They are casual fall visitors along western Lake Erie and accidental elsewhere, producing one to seven reports annually away from the Oak Openings. These migrants have been reliably observed as early as October 12, but most sightings are during November.

A few may pass through Ohio into the first half of December. Most fall sightings have been of 1–2 eagles, but an exceptional seven were tallied over western Lucas County on October 31, 1998 (Kemp 1997).

There have been a few Golden Eagle reports during July and August, but none of these summer records has been acceptably substantiated. They most likely pertain to misidentified Bald Eagles.

American Kestrel *Falco sparverius* Linnaeus

The adaptable American Kestrels have thrived despite Ohio's changing land-use patterns. They undoubtedly increased as the virgin forests were replaced by open farmlands, and have been widely distributed ever since. Their populations fluctuated during the twentieth century, with local declines attributed to reductions in the availability of suitable nest sites. As natural cavities disappeared, kestrels quickly took advantage of man-made structures and are the only hawks reg-

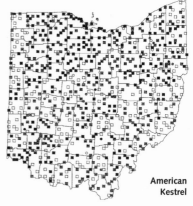

American
Kestrel

ularly found along urban freeways, the intensively farmed fields of western Ohio, and the mixed rural habitats of the unglaciated counties.

While some kestrels maintain their territories throughout the year, most do not. Their status as uncommon to locally common permanent residents hides a fairly complex pattern of seasonal movements within the state.

As summer residents, American Kestrels are widely distributed in every county (Peterjohn and Rice 1991). They become locally uncommon in intensively cultivated western Ohio, where most woody vegetation has been eliminated and nesting cavities are scarce. Kestrels are fairly common to common elsewhere. Summer totals seldom exceed 5–12 before the young fledge in midsummer. These populations have increased since the mid-1960s, a trend exhibited throughout eastern North America (Sauer et al. 1998).

American Kestrels are our only hawks to nest in cavities. When natural cavities are unavailable, they use a variety of other sites, including nest boxes, eaves of buildings, freeway signs, Purple Martin houses, church steeples, and a squirrel nest (Mathena et al. 1984, Phillips 1980, Thomson 1983). Their courtship displays are observed as soon as warm temperatures return in late February and early March. Clutches are normally produced in April, although renesting attempts have been recorded into the first week of June. Within the southern counties, recently fledged young may appear by May 25–June 5, but elsewhere they are normally evident during the last half of June (Trautman 1940, Williams 1950). Late broods have been recorded through August 27 (Campbell 1940).

Wintering kestrels are currently widely distributed, but somewhat less numerous in the snowbelt of northeastern Ohio. They are fairly common to locally common winter residents, with 5–15 daily in most counties, although 20–35+ may be tallied in favorable habitats. Their winter numbers are greatest during December and early January. February declines are attributable to harsh weather some years, but similar declines have been noted during mild seasons.

Wintering kestrels are most numerous in open farmlands, where fence posts, telephone wires, and tall trees provide convenient perches. They regularly hunt near rural residences (Bildstein 1987). They also show an affinity for the grassy rights-of-way along interstate highways. Hovering kestrels are a familiar winter sight along urban and rural highways, invariably facing into the wind as they search the grassy strips for rodents.

Since breeding and wintering kestrels are so numerous, their migratory movements are difficult to discern. Spring migrants are most evident along Lake Erie, where these falcons regularly follow the lakeshore. The first migrants appear by March 5–15 and their northward passage continues through May 10–20. Kestrels normally trickle along the lakefront at rates of 1–10 daily. Movements of 20–30+ may occur on late March or April days with southwesterly winds, and the largest flights have totaled 85 at Cleveland on April 15, 1993, and 54–63 at Conneaut (Harlan 1993c). Within the interior counties, their spring migration is mostly an influx of breeding pairs between February 20 and March 20.

Their southward migration begins during September and continues into December. This movement is poorly defined in September and October, except over the Oak Openings area of Lucas County, where 15 or fewer migrants are noted most days and a maximum of 57 were observed on October 15, 1995 (Harlan 1996a). The first noticeable statewide influx is usually apparent between November 1 and 15. Another influx normally occurs between November 25 and December 15 and is largely composed of wintering individuals. Fall totals normally are fewer than ten daily except during influxes, when 15–30+ may be recorded.

Merlin *Falco columbarius* Linnaeus

Slightly larger than kestrels but considerably more powerful and graceful in flight, Merlins look like miniature Peregrines as they deftly chase a flock of shorebirds over a mudflat. Migrant Merlins are occupants of open marshes, fields, and shorelines, usually providing unsatisfactory glimpses of small fleet falcons disappearing across the countryside. On rare occasions, they hunt from tall perches, warily scanning the terrain below for shorebirds, songbirds, or other prey to be captured after a short spectacular chase.

Merlins have always been rare migrants through Ohio. Along with several other hawks, their populations declined during the 1950s and 1960s as a result of pesticide contamination. Their populations rebounded shortly after the pesticides were banned and have increased throughout the 1980s and 1990s.

Merlins are currently rare to uncommon spring migrants along Lake Erie, where 1–5 individuals may be observed daily. Away from the lakefront, they are casual to rare spring migrants, normally as scattered individuals within the glaciated counties. A total of 11 noted along the Ohio River near Washington County during spring 1993 may indicate regular migration along that body of water (Hall 1993c), but similar numbers have not been apparent at other inland locations. The earliest spring Merlins appear between February 20 and 25, but there are relatively few records before March 15. Most are observed between March 20 and May 10. A few migrants linger into the last half of May, with the latest reports from western Lake Erie on June 6, 1943, and June 8, 1993 (Campbell 1968, Harlan 1993d).

Fall Merlins are rare to uncommon migrants along Lake Erie, in numbers that are comparable to spring. They are casual to rare visitors to the interior counties, least numerous along the unglaciated Allegheny Plateau. Small numbers regularly pass over the Oak Openings of Lucas County, but most inland reports are of scattered individuals, with daily maxima of 2–3. The earliest fall migrant was reported along western Lake Erie on August 23, 1942 (Campbell 1968). There are a few additional late August reports, but they normally return by September 7–15. Most fall migrants are detected between September 15 and October 20, with scattered records into the last half of November.

Formerly accidental winter visitors, the winter status of Merlins changed markedly during the 1990s. They have become rare to almost uncommon winter residents of the Cleveland-Akron area, where as many as four have been observed at a roost in Bath (Summit County) (Harlan 1994b), and Merlins may be reported from a total of 4–8+ locations each year. They are casual to rare winter residents elsewhere, with most reports of widely scattered individuals from the northern half of the state. These wintering Merlins are most likely to be found in urban or semiurban areas, although a few have been observed in open farmlands.

At one time, Ohio may have hosted a small breeding population within the extreme northeastern counties. Kirtland reported a nesting pair in Cuyahoga County before 1858, including specimens of two juveniles (Williams 1950).

During the twentieth century, summering Merlins were reported from the Rocky River gorge in Cuyahoga County in 1923 and 1934 and along the Grand River gorge in Lake and Ashtabula Counties and the Conneaut Creek gorge in Ashtabula County between 1928 and 1932 (Hicks 1933a, 1935a, Williams 1950). Few details are available for these sightings and some identifications may be questionable. Hicks (1933a) claimed fourteen summer records from Ashtabula County, including "an immature," but no nest was ever discovered. In fact, there are no indisputable breeding records from Ohio. No summering Merlins have been reported after 1934. If a small breeding population once existed, it apparently disappeared during the 1930s. During the late 1990s, a few single-day reports in mid-June and July probably pertain to nonbreeders or migrants.

Gyrfalcon *Falco rusticolus* Linnaeus

Gyrfalcons are residents of the Arctic tundra across North America and Eurasia. While most reside there throughout the year, small numbers wander southward during winter. A few regularly appear in the upper Great Lakes states and Canada, occasionally wandering south to New England and the lower Great Lakes (AOU 1998).

Within Ohio, Gyrfalcons are casual winter visitors along western Lake Erie, where there are at least seven confirmed records since 1950 and an equal number of unconfirmed sightings. They prefer the western Lake Erie marshes, with their open flat terrain and abundant waterfowl. They are accidental visitors elsewhere, with specimen records from Fayette County on January 30, 1907 (Henninger 1911a), Wood County on December 10, 1942 (Campbell 1968), and Lorain County on October 29, 1992 (Harlan 1993b). Documented sight records are from Lorain on October 22, 1983 (Peterjohn 1984a), Headlands Beach State Park (Lake County) on February 10, 1996 (Brock 1996b), and Paulding County, where one spent the 1995–1996 winter and was observed by many birders (Dunakin 1996). There are also unverified sightings from Youngstown, Hamilton County, and near Coldwater (Mercer County). Most appear between November 20 and January 30.

There are few records of migrant Gyrfalcons from Ohio. Fall sightings are during October: the two from Lorain County and a very early migrant in Lucas County on October 3, 1971 (Campbell 1973). The only spring records are singles observed along western Lake Erie on March 14, 1982, and March 26, 1967 (Campbell 1968, Peterjohn 1982c). The wintering bird in Paulding County was last observed on March 16, 1996 (Conlon and Harlan 1996a).

Peregrine Falcon *Falco peregrinus* Tunstall

No other raptor produces the excitement generated by a hunting Peregrine. Its stoop is awe-inspiring, while its speed, maneuverability, and raw power are unrivaled as it pursues its intended victim over a marsh or lake. Most birds are extremely wary of this fleet falcon, and its presence is frequently detected by the panic-stricken flight of waterfowl and shorebirds before the soaring Peregrine comes into view.

At one time, this magnificent raptor appeared doomed to extinction in North America. Its breeding populations were decimated by pesticide contamination between the 1940s and 1960s, resulting in the disappearance of the subspecies nesting in the eastern United States and southern Canada. This decline produced a reduction in the numbers passing through Ohio. Campbell (1968) cited 52 records from Toledo between 1927 and 1939 but only one record annually between 1940 and 1967. Fortunately, Peregrine populations slowly recovered after use of these pesticides was banned during the 1960s.

This natural population recovery was supplemented by Peregrines "hacked" into the wild to establish breeding pairs in cities. These Peregrine introduction programs were initiated in nearby states during the 1980s, and were responsible for the establishment of a resident pair in Toledo by 1987, which produced young in 1988 (Peterjohn and Rice 1991). An introduction program was operating in Ohio by 1989, which contributed to the appearance of breeding pairs in most major cities within the state during the 1990s. The breeding population increased to six pairs in 1993 and 12 pairs by 1997; these pairs have been found in Toledo, the Cleveland-Akron-Elyria area, Columbus, Cincinnati, Dayton, Lima, and Youngstown (Peters 1998). Since natural nesting sites do not exist within Ohio, breeding Peregrines are restricted to nesting on tall buildings within large cities. The number of pairs will increase as long as management activities provide suitable nest sites on buildings and ensure the survival of young birds produced in urban settings.

Peregrine Falcons are currently rare and very locally distributed summer residents, most likely to be found in or near the large cities where breeding pairs have become established. After the young birds fledge from nests in Ohio and adjacent states in mid-July, single Peregrines may appear throughout the state, although most late summer records are from the glaciated counties. Before the resident Peregrines began to appear in Ohio during the mid-1980s, they were strictly accidental summer visitors, with only a single acceptable report: one was noted at Cedar Point Wildlife Refuge (Lucas County) on July 31, 1930 (Campbell 1968).

Their winter status has also changed markedly as a result of these introduction programs. Historically, Peregrine Falcons were accidental winter visitors, with most reports during December or early January from the glaciated counties. Virtually all substantiated wintering falcons were reported before 1940. Most were recorded in large cities, where they roosted on downtown buildings and subsisted on a diet of pigeons (Kemsies and Randle 1953). With the establishment of resident pairs in the mid-1980s, Peregrines have become rare but very locally distributed winter residents in large cities across the state. Wintering numbers include resident pairs and young birds prospecting for suitable territories. They remain accidental or casual winter visitors away from these large cities, although single Peregrines have been detected at scattered locations, where they usually remain for only a few days before disappearing.

Numbers of migrant Peregrines increased during the 1990s, reflecting the continued recovery of native populations and birds produced by the introduction programs. They are currently rare to uncommon spring migrants along Lake Erie, where most reports are of 1–3 in passage along the lakefront. They are accidental to locally rare spring migrants elsewhere, least numerous in the southern and unglaciated counties, producing 5–10+ sightings annually of scattered individuals.

Spring migrants may appear as early as February 20–March 15; these early migrants were probably from introduction programs in the midwestern states. Arctic-breeding Peregrines tend to migrate later, perhaps appearing as early as March 25–April 15. Most are detected between April 20 and May 15, with a few lingering through the end of the month.

As fall migrants, a few Peregrines may appear between August 15 and September 10, although these migrants probably represent young birds produced by local introduction programs. Arctic-breeding Peregrines generally return by September 15–20 and most pass through Ohio between September 25 and October 20. Their southward passage continues into November, but it may be difficult to distinguish late migrants from resident individuals.

Fall Peregrines are most numerous along Lake Erie, becoming uncommon in the western Lake Erie marshes and rare to locally uncommon elsewhere. Numbers are generally comparable to spring, although as many as 3–4 may be observed daily along western Lake Erie. They are accidental to rare migrants through the interior counties, where most are noted at large reservoirs and marshes where waterfowl and shorebirds congregate or in passage over the Oak Openings area of Lucas County. These sightings are usually of single falcons, least numerous within the southern and unglaciated counties.

Prairie Falcon *Falco mexicanus* Schlegel

Prairie Falcons are normally associated with the vast open plains of western North America from southern Canada south into Mexico. In recent years, they have been rare but regular winter visitors east to Iowa, Missouri, and Illinois, but accidental farther east (AOU 1998).

Ohio has one confirmed record that fits this established pattern of vagrancy. A wounded Prairie Falcon was recovered from the Rickenbacker Air

Force Base in southern Franklin County on January 21, 1983 (Peterjohn 1983b). It was captured and transported to the Ohio State University Veterinary School for rehabilitation, where it was noted to have fresh plumage and antagonistic behavior towards humans, which is indicative of a wild falcon rather than one recently escaped from captivity.

There is one additional published sight record. A Prairie Falcon was discovered entangled in a fence and captured near Oberlin, Lorain County, on September 20, 1940 (Jones 1941). The bird's plumage and behavior were not described, however, and whether or not this individual escaped from captivity cannot be ascertained.

Gray Partridge *Perdix perdix* (Linnaeus)

In the early 1900s, populations of native Ohio game birds were greatly reduced. Wild Turkeys and Greater Prairie-Chickens were extirpated, Ruffed Grouse were restricted to the southeastern counties, and Northern Bobwhite fluctuated erratically in response to severe winter weather. Only introduced Ring-necked Pheasants were thriving. Having succeeded with pheasant introductions, Ohio wildlife personnel introduced Gray Partridge to establish another game species in the state.

Approximately 2,000 Gray Partridges were liberated statewide between 1909 and 1916. These partridges quickly disappeared from southern and eastern Ohio but thrived in the northwestern and west-central counties. Following a rapid increase, the first hunting season occurred in 1917 (Westerkov 1956). Additional releases between 1924 and 1930 totaled 7,000 partridges (Hicks 1935a). These releases resulted in increased numbers in western Ohio but did not establish sustained populations in the southern or eastern counties.

Ohio Gray Partridge populations undoubtedly peaked during the early 1930s. Densities estimated at 25+ birds per square mile were recorded in portions of Fulton, Lucas, Defiance, Henry, Wood, Paulding, Putnam, Hancock, Van Wert, and Allen Counties (Hicks 1935a). Elsewhere in western Ohio, partridges were locally distributed and uncommon to rare in every county east to Erie, Crawford, and Delaware, and south to Preble, Montgomery, Clinton, and Highland. These numbers were maintained through 1937 but noticeably decreased by 1940 despite additional releases of 8,420 partridges in western Ohio. An estimated 110,000 partridges remained during the autumn of 1939 (Westerkov 1949).

Partridge populations declined rapidly during the 1940s. By 1948, they virtually disappeared from northwestern Ohio. Most remaining partridges were locally distributed in Madison, Fayette, Champaign, Clark, Miami, and Darke Counties (Westerkov 1956). These remnant populations quietly disappeared during the 1950s and early 1960s. Their disappearance is partially obscured by reintroduction efforts during the 1960s (Thomson 1983), producing sightings near Utica (Licking County) through 1965 and at Lake St. Marys in 1969. Elsewhere, the last partridges were reported from Toledo in 1962 (Campbell 1968), Dayton in 1966 (Mathena et al. 1984), and Madison County in January 1968. Local landowners indicated they remained in Madison County into the early 1970s. Reports from west-central Ohio during the 1980s are the result of several birds released by landowners (Peterjohn and Rice 1991). Barring further reintroductions, Gray Partridges have become extirpated within Ohio.

Gray Partridges are occupants of open farmlands, preferring flat or rolling terrain with sandy soils, numerous shrubby fencerows, and grasslands interspersed among small farm fields (Westerkov 1949). They tolerated severe winter weather as long as adequate food could be secured. Most nests were located in pastures and hayfields. When suitable grasslands were unavailable, Gray Partridges nested along roadsides and ditches and in small fallow fields. Nesting normally began during the first half of May and most young hatched during the last half of June and early July. Their nesting success was generally low. Most nests in hayfields were destroyed by mowing, and predation rates were high along roadsides (Westerkov 1949). Renesting attempts were frequent, resulting in nests with eggs as late as August 9 (Baird 1936c).

Why did Gray Partridges disappear from Ohio? Changing agricultural land-use patterns were the most prominent factor. The trend toward large fields devoted to corn and soybean monocultures largely eliminated their preferred habitats. Instead of undisturbed grasslands, they were forced to nest in hayfields or along roadsides, where they experienced poor breeding success. Clay soils posed additional problems: following rains, clay particles frequently encased their feet in mud balls, reducing their mobility and producing excessive mortality of small chicks. Simply stated, Gray Partridges were not well suited for Ohio's changing habitats during the twentieth century.

Ring-necked Pheasant *Phasianus colchicus* Linnaeus

This gaudy game bird was introduced after populations of our native grouse, quail, and turkeys were severely depleted or extirpated during the late 1800s. The first Ring-necked Pheasants were released in 1896 and became established in ten counties by 1903 (Jones 1903). In 1913, following establishment of other small populations (Trautman 1940), state agencies undertook an ambitious program to establish Ring-necked Pheasants throughout Ohio. Large numbers were liberated in all portions of the state, estimated at 10,000–25,000 annually between 1923 and 1935 (Hicks 1935a, Leedy and Hendershot 1947). These releases established sizable populations in some counties but failed where suitable habitats were unavailable.

Ring-necked Pheasants peaked during the late 1930s and early 1940s (Leedy and Hendershot 1947). They were common to abundant residents in western Ohio from Fulton, Lucas, and Ottawa Counties south to Hardin, Union, and Marion Counties. Estimates of 35,500 in Lucas County and 175,000+ in Wood County during 1939 provide an indication of their sizable populations (Campbell 1940, 1968). They were generally common permanent residents east to Cuyahoga and Wayne Counties, and south to

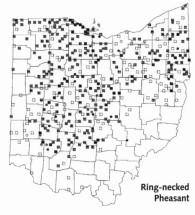

Ring-necked
Pheasant

Preble, Greene, Fayette, and Pickaway Counties. Pheasants became uncommon to rare in other northeastern and southwestern counties (Leedy and Hendershot 1947). Although they were released within the unglaciated counties, permanent populations never became established. Hicks (1937a) considered them uncommon to fairly common residents in Coshocton, Tuscarawas, and Pike Counties. In other unglaciated counties, they were mostly observed only immediately following releases.

By the mid-1940s, pheasants were declining despite annual releases. These trends continued through the 1970s, but statewide populations have been fairly stable since 1980 (Sauer et al. 1998). Among the contributing factors, changing agricultural land-use practices were the most important. The trend toward large fields devoted to cultivated crops eliminated many pastures and hayfields occupied by nesting pheasants. Remaining hayfields were subject to more frequent mowing, increasing mortality of incubating females and destroying many nests. Fall plowing reduced the amount of food available during winter. These factors, combined with excessive mortality during the severe winters of the 1970s, reduced pheasants to a fraction of their former abundance.

Even though their numbers are greatly reduced, the Ring-necked Pheasant's breeding range has not changed appreciably since the 1940s. They are currently uncommon to fairly common residents in northwestern and west-central Ohio and rare to locally uncommon in the southwestern and northeastern counties (Peterjohn and Rice 1991). Daily totals seldom exceed 3–12 pheasants. Along the unglaciated Allegheny Plateau, small populations exist in portions of Coshocton, Holmes, Tuscarawas, Carroll, Harrison, and Jefferson Counties, where pheasants are rare to locally uncommon residents (Peterjohn and Rice 1991). A few pheasants are found near the glacial boundary elsewhere in the southeastern counties.

Pheasants are most numerous in flat open farmlands where grassy fields and cultivated crops are interspersed with woodlots. They seldom enter wooded habitats except to find cover during severe winter weather. Pheasants are usually associated with grasslands, the grassy borders of wetlands, and fallow fields. They regularly feed in harvested grain fields in autumn and winter but usually do not wander far from cover.

During winter, pheasants frequently associate in loose flocks composed of a few males and many females. When populations were larger, winter flocks of 25–50+ were encountered in western Ohio. With the approach of spring, these flocks break up and breeding activities are initiated. The males mate with as many females as are attracted by their courtship displays. After mating, the females search for suitable cover for their nests, preferring hayfields and lightly grazed pastures, although they also nest along roadsides, ditch banks, fencerows, and wheat fields if grasslands are unavailable. The first clutches are laid in late April but most are produced during the first half of May. These clutches normally hatch by mid-June, and young pheasants remain with the hens into August. Their nesting success is fairly poor; many nests are lost to predators or mowing of hayfields and roadsides (Leedy and Hendershot 1947). Females will renest if their first clutch is destroyed, producing nests with eggs through August 4 and partially grown young through mid-September (Phillips 1980).

Since Ring-necked Pheasants are still released each year, it is doubtful they will disappear from Ohio in the near future. In most counties, however, their outlook is not bright. Today's farmlands provide marginal habitats, with critical shortages of grasslands for nesting and suitable cover for wintering pheasants. These trends are not irreversible, but it is doubtful that the immense populations of the 1930s and 1940s will ever be reestablished.

Ruffed Grouse *Bonasa umbellus* (Linnaeus)

"With the warm days of late March, small groups of grouse which have wintered together, disperse," F.B. Chapman and colleagues noted in 1952. They then describe what follows this dispersal.

The males begin to drum and courtship is under way. The most spectacular event of courtship is the drumming by the cock Ruffed Grouse. Standing on a fallen log, rock, or other prominence, he beats the air rapidly with his wings with a forward and upward movement that produces a sound not unlike the 'thump, thump, thump' of a far distant farm tractor. When approached by the female bird who has been attracted from her wintering territory not far away, the male bird often deserts the drumming log, and struts slowly and deliberately toward his prospective mate with tail spread fanwise and the black 'ruffs' on the neck puffed out to the fullest extent.

To experience these displays, one must visit the woodlands of eastern Ohio. Ruffed Grouse are locally rare to fairly common residents east of a line extending through eastern Cuyahoga, Medina, Wayne, Richland, Knox, Licking, Fairfield, Ross, Highland, Brown, and Clermont Counties (Stoll and McClain 1986). In northeastern Ohio, grouse are most numerous in Geauga, Ashtabula, and Trumbull Counties but are rare and declining elsewhere. They are widely distributed along the unglaciated Allegheny

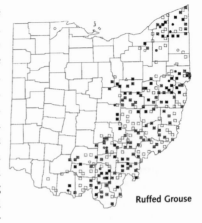

Ruffed Grouse

Plateau except for areas extensively disturbed by strip mining (Peterjohn and Rice 1991). They become rare and very locally distributed in adjacent glaciated areas. The only recent range expansion into glaciated Ohio was evident in portions of Adams, Brown, and southern Clermont Counties (Stoll and McClain 1986).

Ruffed Grouse were not always restricted to eastern Ohio. When the state was initially settled, they were sparingly distributed throughout the mature virgin forests. After 1800, the transformation of these forests into younger woodlands was beneficial for grouse. Their populations increased dramatically and peaked between 1850 and 1875 (Trautman 1977). Habitat destruction and market hunting exacted a tremendous toll as their numbers sharply declined by 1885. After market hunting ceased, habitat destruction continued to decimate populations. Grouse disappeared from Lake St. Marys prior to 1900 (Clark and Sipe 1970), Seneca County in 1892 (Henninger 1906), and Buckeye Lake and Lorain County by 1900 (Jones 1903, Trautman 1940). With their disappearance from Toledo by 1908 (Campbell 1968), grouse were extirpated from glaciated western and central Ohio.

Grouse were scarce in eastern Ohio during the first decades of the twentieth century. In the 1920s and 1930s, many abandoned farms were reverting to brushy habitats and woodlands, allowing their populations to recover. By 1952, they were reestablished throughout their present range (Chapman et al. 1952). At the same time, small remnant populations in Butler and Warren Counties disappeared (Stoll and McClain 1986).

In addition to this natural recovery, the Ohio Division of Wildlife attempted to reestablish grouse in northwestern Ohio. Small numbers were released in the Oak Openings of Lucas and Fulton Counties and on Kelleys Island in western Lake Erie during the 1950s. These releases produced regular sightings through the mid-1960s (Campbell 1968). However, the absence of recent records indicates these introductions were not successful.

Grouse populations were reasonably stable through the early 1980s, although some declines were apparent during the 1990s. Recent evidence suggests that Ohio grouse are subject to cyclical fluctuations in abundance. Although long-term data are unavailable to conclusively establish these trends, indices of grouse abundance show relatively high numbers during the early 1970s and early 1980s followed by sharp declines in the mid-1970s and mid-1980s (Stoll and McClain 1986). These cyclical fluctuations occur independently of hunting pressure and habitat changes.

Grouse are most numerous in young second-growth deciduous woods supporting dense bushes and tangles interspersed with scattered openings. They are seldom found more than a short flight from dense cover. In winter, grouse prefer woodlands with dense honeysuckle and greenbrier tangles and a few conifers (Chapman et al. 1952). Lower hillsides and valley slopes are preferred over dry ridges.

In mature woods and other marginal habitats, Ruffed Grouse are normally encountered as widely scattered individuals. In preferred habitats, totals of 5–10+ are possible. While they are mostly observed as individuals, small groups of 3–10 may be noted in prime cover during winter.

The low thumps of drumming grouse vibrate across the hills of southeastern Ohio during late March and April. These displays may continue into early June. Most females mate during April. Full clutches have been reported as early as April 10, although most nests are initiated during late April and May. Most young hatch in June and the young follow the hens for the next few months (Chapman et al. 1952). Reproductive success is greatest during warm dry summers; cool wet weather during June causes extensive mortality of young grouse.

During fall, family groups break up as the grouse move to their winter territories. Similar movements occur in spring when they wander in search of suitable breeding habitats. These birds seldom move more than two miles and are considered permanent residents. An occasional grouse may wander considerable distances and appear in unlikely places. There are at least two recent records from Cincinnati, Columbus, and Cleveland. One of the Columbus records was a grouse captured in a garage. In Cleveland, a grouse appeared in a small downtown park along the lakefront (Kleen 1980a). Similar movements are responsible for reports of single grouse from Caesar Creek Reservoir (Warren County) on March 20, 1993 (Harlan 1993c), and another near Tiffin on March 4, 1995 (Harlan 1995c).

Greater Prairie-Chicken *Tympanuchus cupido* (Linnaeus)

Few other native game birds match the ritualistic spring courtship displays of the Greater Prairie-Chicken. With the advent of warm weather in late March, groups of 10–30 males assemble on their display grounds—patches of bare soil and short grasses which these grassland grouse have used for decades. Their courtship antics are best described by Oberholser (1974):

> At dawn and dusk, males dance, boom, and spar. Frenzied birds space themselves about ten yards apart. Each cock inflates the golden air sacs on his neck, erects and spreads his tail, and raises the neck tufts as he stamps madly on the ground, booms loudly, springs, and whirls in the air, and intermittently charges his neighboring rivals. Usually one or two males mate with most of the hens which are attracted to the edge of the display ground.

These displays were undoubtedly witnessed by the first settlers inhabiting prairie openings in Williams, Fulton, Lucas, and Wood Counties in northwestern Ohio and the scattered prairies in Erie, Crawford, Wyandot, Marion, Union, Madison, Fayette, and Pickaway Counties (Hicks 1935a). Anecdotal accounts indicated that populations also existed in the southwestern and west-central counties. In the 1830s, these prairie-chickens were apparently numerous in the northwestern counties, although they were probably rare and very locally distributed in north-central and central Ohio (Kirtland 1838). Near Toledo, Campbell (1968) cited historical accounts of "more than 500" and "thousands" of prairie-chickens, apparently during the 1830s, an indication of the sizable numbers in some northwestern counties.

Despite these substantial populations, there is virtually no information concerning their life history within Ohio. Greater Prairie-Chickens were permanent residents and undoubtedly nested, although no nests were ever described.

As their name implies, prairie-chickens were restricted to extensive grasslands, a habitat preference responsible for their demise within Ohio and perilous decline throughout most of their range. As the original prairies were converted to cultivated fields, the prairie-chickens disappeared. Their decline apparently occurred during a span of only several decades. The last Greater Prairie-Chicken in central Ohio was reported "seven miles west of Columbus" on November 16, 1868 (Wheaton 1879). The populations in northern Ohio largely disappeared by the 1870s, with only a few isolated sightings as late as 1880 (Campbell 1968). This species was undoubtedly extirpated before 1900.

Beginning in 1925, scattered reports by hunters and local landowners indicated that prairie-chickens had returned to Ohio. The few documented reports included sightings from Ottawa County in 1928, Lucas County in 1932 and 1934, and Wood County in 1934 (Campbell 1968, Trautman 1935b), apparently isolated and wandering individuals. No courtship displays or nesting behavior was observed, and the assertion by Hicks (1935a) of "reestablished populations in Fulton, Henry, and Wood Counties" is almost certainly an exaggeration. These birds probably wandered south from Michigan, where prairie-chickens were still well established. Similar movements were reported elsewhere in the Great Lakes region (DeVos 1964). However, this range expansion was short-lived; no Greater Prairie-Chickens were reported from northwestern Ohio after 1934. Reintroductions were attempted in Marion County during 1933 and nesting was reported there in 1934 and 1935 (Hicks 1935a). These birds disappeared by 1937 and no other reintroductions have been attempted.

Wild Turkey *Meleagris gallopavo* Linnaeus

"In all the United States," A. M. Wright (1915) declared, "no state had more turkeys than Ohio and her neighbors." If anecdotal accounts by the first settlers are believed, a phenomenal number of Wild Turkeys inhabited Ohio during the eighteenth century. They were regularly encountered in flocks of 30–50+ during winter and as scattered individuals at other times of the year.

As soon as the first permanent settlers arrived, turkey populations began to decline. Unrestricted harvests decimated populations; by 1822, turkeys were scarce near Chillicothe. Ten years later, none could be found near Mansfield (Wright 1915). Similar local extirpations were apparent elsewhere. By the 1850s, habitat destruction in combination with overharvesting resulted in the extirpation of Wild Turkeys from most counties. They were scarce in the Cleveland area by 1864, with very few reliable reports in subsequent years (Williams 1950). Turkeys were scarce in southwestern Ohio after 1845, disappearing from Warren County in the early 1860s and Cincinnati before 1870 (Langdon 1879, Mathena et al. 1984). In central Ohio, the last sightings from Buckeye Lake were between 1853 and 1870 (Trautman 1940). Despite their declining populations, no attempts were made to prevent their extirpation. The last northeastern Ohio records were from Ashtabula County "about 1880" (Hicks 1933a). In northwestern Ohio, they disappeared from Seneca County by 1880 (Henninger 1906), Paulding County "about 1880–1885" (Price 1935), and Toledo by 1892 (Campbell 1968). Their extirpation from the southern counties was poorly described, but Henninger (1902) thought they disappeared from Scioto and Pike Counties before 1900. While Jones (1903) hoped a few remained in southern Ohio, his optimism was unfounded, and Wild Turkeys were almost certainly extirpated before 1900.

To reestablish turkey populations during the twentieth century, wild birds were transplanted into suitable habitats and protected until breeding populations developed. The first Wild Turkeys were released in southeastern Ohio in February 1956 (Donohoe and McKibben 1973). Similar releases were attempted in every subsequent year, and sizable populations were eventually established in the southeastern counties (Donohoe et al. 1983). Releases within the glaciated counties were started in the 1980s, initially in Ashtabula County. These releases were also successful, and turkeys were transplanted to a number of locations in the central and western counties during the 1990s.

The distribution of Wild Turkeys has expanded considerably since the Breeding Bird Atlas of the 1980s (Peterjohn and Rice 1991). In 1994, they were found in 60 of the 88 counties (Harlan 1994c), and their breeding populations have expanded in subsequent years. They are now uncommon to common residents throughout the unglaciated Allegheny Plateau and within rural portions of the northeastern counties, where 5–15+ males are heard on warm spring mornings and winter flocks of 15–50+ are regularly encountered. Christmas Bird Count totals of 150–400+ were reported during the 1990s. In southwestern Ohio, they have become fairly common to common residents in the counties bordering the Ohio River east of Cincinnati but are rare to uncommon elsewhere.

In northern Ohio, they are rare to locally uncommon residents west to Erie, Huron, Richland, and Morrow Counties. Their distribution is still decidedly local in other northern and western counties, reflecting where individuals have been recently released; they are absent in some counties and generally rare elsewhere. Their populations are rapidly increasing in glaciated Ohio, however, and Wild Turkeys will likely establish sizable breeding populations in most counties during the twenty-first century. As an indication of the rate of population growth, Donohoe et al. (1983) estimated a statewide population of 7,677 during 1982. This population had expanded to an estimated 77,000 by 1993 (Harlan 1994c).

During winter, most turkeys congregate in flocks composed of several hens, their broods, and a number of adult males. These flocks roam across a territory of several square miles searching for food in woodlands, pastures, and harvested fields. When winter weather is severe, they may visit feedlots.

While some flocks remain intact through mid-April, most break apart by the last days of March. Male turkeys become intent on acquiring a harem, and dominant males are frequently surrounded by 5–8+ females. Most first-year males seldom, if ever, mate. The males maintain their breeding territories into May and are still gobbling on warm calm mornings through mid-May, but normally fall silent before the end of the month.

During the breeding season, Wild Turkeys are normally found within extensive woodlands, although females and their broods visit woodland edges, pastures, and other open fields. Most female turkeys are fertilized by April

15–25 and immediately lay eggs in nests located on the ground in dense cover, frequently at woodland edges. For such a large bird, their nests are surprisingly difficult to locate. Most clutches hatch in late May or early June and the young remain with the hen throughout summer and fall. Renesting attempts have produced recently hatched young through the last week of June. Like other gallinaceous birds, young turkeys acquire the ability to fly at an early age and can follow their mother into trees to avoid people or predators.

Northern Bobwhite *Colinus virginianus* (Linnaeus)

Northern Bobwhites were probably absent from Ohio until the nineteenth century. The creation of open farmlands, combined with a series of relatively mild winters, allowed them to expand into the Great Lakes region during the 1840s and 1850s (DeVos 1964). By the 1860s, bobwhites were established in most counties, and their whistled calls were familiar sounds in Ohio's farmlands.

Northern
Bobwhite

Their statewide population peaked between 1875 and 1900. Anecdotal accounts indicated that remarkable numbers inhabited most counties. Terms such as "very common" and "abundant" described bobwhites at Buckeye Lake and Lake St. Marys (Clark and Sipe 1970, Trautman 1940), while Campbell (1968) cited 1,000 at Toledo in 1893. This abundance resulted from very favorable land-use practices. Farm fields were small with interspersed grasslands and cultivated crops bordered by brushy fencerows and woodland edges, nearly ideal quail habitats.

Bobwhite populations fluctuated considerably during the first decades of the twentieth century. The first major decline was noted in 1912–1913, followed by similar declines in the winters of 1917–1918 and 1928–1929 (Kendeigh 1933, Trautman 1940). These declines were largely the result of excessive mortality during severe winter weather. Unfavorable weather during the nesting season also reduced their reproductive success. However, these declines generally lasted for only a few years.

Following the severe winter of 1928–1929, bobwhites gradually increased and reached their "peak for the twentieth century" in 1935. At that time, Hicks (1935a) described them as common to abundant residents in most counties, least numerous in extreme northeastern Ohio. He estimated their statewide abundance at 20 pairs per square mile, while winter totals of 50–100+ were frequently noted in southern and central Ohio.

Severe weather during the 1935–1936 winter decimated quail populations, and such large densities have not been attained subsequently (Baird 1936a). Cyclical fluctuations continued during the 1940s and 1950s, but each population peak was achieved at progressively smaller densities. As Trautman (1940) predicted, declining numbers were inevitable as agricultural land use became more intensive. Increased field size, removal of fencerows, conversion of grasslands to cultivated crops, and fall plowing substantially reduced quail populations. Along the unglaciated Allegheny Plateau, secondary succession also contributed to this decline.

By 1960, Northern Bobwhites became uncommon and locally distributed residents in northern Ohio (Campbell 1968, Newman 1969). They were common only within some southern counties. These populations continued to decline in the 1960s and early 1970s, especially in the western counties. Remaining quail populations were virtually eliminated by the harsh winters of 1976–1978. Their numbers declined by more than 90 percent, and bobwhites disappeared except for small locally distributed populations in the southern and eastern counties. Fortunately, the following winters were less severe and their numbers slowly grew during the 1980s. Some declines were evident during the 1990s, but statewide population trends remained stable during the 1980–1996 period (Sauer et al. 1998).

Their statewide distribution has not appreciably changed since the Breeding Bird Atlas (Peterjohn and Rice 1991). Northern Bobwhites are uncommon to fairly common residents of southern Ohio from Washington and Athens Counties west to Indiana and north to the Dayton area. Calling bobwhites are regularly heard during summer, when 4–10+ may be counted daily. Totals of 20–30+ are possible during winter. Bobwhites are locally distributed in eastern Ohio south of the snowbelt. They are rare in many eastern counties, becoming uncommon residents from Trumbull and Portage Counties south to the glacial boundary. Tallies of 1–8 are possible during summer. They are casual to rare in the remainder of Ohio, where widely scattered pairs and coveys survive in favorable habitats.

Bobwhites raise only one brood annually. Their nests are placed on the ground, usually in pastures, hayfields, and fallow fields. Most clutches are laid during May and early June. While recently hatched young have been reported as early as April 27 (Williams 1950), they are expected between mid-June and mid-August. Bobwhites renest until they successfully hatch a brood. Nests with eggs are possible through the first half of August, and recently hatched young have been reported through mid-September. Extremely late broods were discovered on October 7 at Salem and November 1 at Dayton (Mathena et al. 1984, Walker 1939c).

What does the future hold for Northern Bobwhites in Ohio? As Kendeigh (1933) stated:

> The whole problem of increasing the population of Bobwhite reduces down to the establishment and expansion of habitat areas containing suitable cover and food ... where given proper protection and habitat, and when the climate is favorable, the species is capable of rather rapidly increasing its numbers by natural reproduction. With the increase in abundance, the birds must of necessity expand their areas into new and favorable regions.

Unless current land-use practices are reversed, bobwhites will be largely restricted to portions of southern and eastern Ohio in future years.

Yellow Rail *Coturnicops noveboracensis* (Gmelin)

Few birds are as elusive and secretive as Yellow Rails. Experts at hiding in grasses and sedges, they normally forage under dense vegetation and are rarely observed at the exposed edges of marshes. When disturbed, they would rather run than take flight and easily disappear under thick cover. Considerable luck is required to catch a glimpse of this shy bird as it vanishes into cover.

The status of Yellow Rails within Ohio is not precisely known. Given their wintering grounds along the Gulf Coast and breeding range extending from northern Michigan and Minnesota to Hudson Bay (AOU 1998), they undoubtedly pass through Ohio each spring and fall. However, only a very small percentage of these migrant rails will ever be detected.

Most migrant Yellow Rails have been reported during spring, with one to three records of single individuals during most years. They are accidental or casual visitors to most counties, except unglaciated Ohio, where there are no published records. While migrants have been reported between March 31 and May 31 (Clark and Sipe 1970, Flanigan 1968), they usually occur in two peaks. The first extends between April 15 and May 5 and may include birds in passage to more southerly nesting grounds. The second peak, May 15–30, may be rails breeding in northern Canada. Two factors are responsible for the preponderance of spring records. First, Yellow Rails are more likely to be calling during this season; they are most vocal at night, when rails can occasionally be lured into view. Second, vegetation within their preferred wet meadows is not as dense and the rails are slightly more visible.

Yellow Rails average only one report every two to four years during autumn. They probably return in August and depart by mid-October, although most records are during October. There are two November reports: an injured bird captured at Dayton on November 8, 1975, and a sight record from LaDue Reservoir (Geauga County) on November 11, 1979 (Kleen 1980a, Mathena et al. 1984). Their fall distribution pattern is similar to spring, except for one captured in Tuscarawas County on September 21, 1991, which provides the only record for the unglaciated counties (Peterjohn 1992a). Fall migrants occasionally appear in unlikely habitats. There are several records of Yellow Rails flushed from dry hayfields. During 1952 and 1954, they were also discovered in a cultivated cornfield near Oxford (Butler County) (Nolan 1953a, 1955a). As many as seven Yellow Rails may have been present in this field during 1952.

At one time, Yellow Rails may have been very local and rare summer residents at several extensive sedge meadows, but their status cannot be accurately assessed from the few records. The only nest was collected in Pickaway County during 1909 (Hicks 1935a). Breeding was indicated at the former Pymatuning Bog, where an adult was observed in July 1928 and a "half grown immature" was located on August 9, 1932 (Hicks 1933a). An adult was killed in the former Huron Bog (Huron County) on July 16, 1928, but nesting was not confirmed (Hicks 1935a). The destruction of these bogs during the 1920s and 1930s eliminated suitable nesting habitats for Yellow Rails in Ohio. The most recent summer record was provided by a calling rail in Lake County between June 25 and July 5, 1944 (Williams 1950).

Black Rail *Laterallus jamaicensis* (Gmelin)

The smallest and most elusive of all rails, Black Rails are very seldom observed in the dense wetland vegetation where they prefer to live. They readily walk under matted grasses and easily disappear among cattails. While the males produce a distinctive "kick-kee-doo" quite unlike the calls of other rails, Blacks are vocal only at night. Even tape-recorded calls may not persuade them to venture away from dense cover.

There are few satisfactory sightings of Black Rails from Ohio, and thus their distribution and relative abundance have never been conclusively established. The first records were seven specimens collected from Hamilton County between 1890 and 1893, all in May (Kemsies and Randle 1953). Twentieth century records are of widely scattered individuals, averaging one to four reports each decade. These rails have been recorded from all portions of the state except the unglaciated counties and are accidental visitors throughout Ohio.

Most Black Rails are discovered during spring, with at least thirteen modern sightings in addition to the nineteenth century specimens. The few confirmed spring Black Rails have appeared during April and May, without a defined pattern to their movements.

The only documented summer record is provided by a singing male in the Irwin Prairie Nature Preserve (Lucas County) June 15–23, 1980 (Kleen 1980d), but sightings at Buckeye Lake on June 10, 1923, and Mentor Marsh (Lake

County) on July 21, 1965, are also probably accurate (Newman 1969, Trautman 1940). Summer records from Lake St. Marys in 1912 and 1915 are based on less than satisfactory evidence. These sightings are of single individuals, and nesting has never been established. Nevertheless, Black Rails could conceivably breed within Ohio. At one time, a small and locally distributed summer population was established in several midwestern states (AOU 1998). Black Rails are most likely to be discovered in extensive wet meadows and wetlands dominated by dense grasses and sedges where standing water is only several inches deep.

Black Rails are least numerous as fall migrants. There are only three published sight records, two in the Toledo area and one in Paulding County (Campbell 1968, Price 1940b); all were single individuals observed between August 30 and October 1.

King Rail *Rallus elegans* Audubon

The largest rails in Ohio, Kings are as adept at hiding in marshlands as their smaller brethren. When undisturbed, they can be surprisingly tame and may forage at the edge of a marsh for many minutes. Except when they are nesting, King Rails are also very vocal; their deep hoarse calls formerly resonated across Ohio wetlands. As described by Trautman (1940):

King Rail

> In the dusk of spring evenings the reiterated "umph-umph-umph" note could be heard coming from the swamps and marshes, and often the birds, presumably the males, could be seen uttering their calls. It was interesting to watch them as they stood in some small opening in the marsh or swamp, or under a rosebush or blackberry bush, and emphasized each "umph" with a grotesque jerk of the head.

Although it is difficult to believe today, Kings were once the most numerous nesting rails in many Ohio counties. In the mid-1930s, they were widely distributed within the western Lake Erie marshes, where Campbell (1968) considered them common summer residents. In suitable inland marshes, King Rails became locally common. Trautman (1940) estimated 45–50 pairs breeding at Buckeye Lake, while similar numbers were reported from Lake St. Marys (Clark and Sipe 1970). Elsewhere within the northern and central counties, they were rarely encountered as isolated pairs, with breeding records from forty-two counties south to Darke, Pickaway, Harrison, Guernsey, and Muskingum (Hicks 1935a, 1937a). King Rails were accidental to casual summer residents in the southern counties, with isolated nesting attempts in Scioto, Adams, Butler, Warren, Hamilton, and Montgomery Counties (Hicks 1935a, Kemsies and Randle 1953, Mathena et al. 1984).

Nesting rails preferred cattail marshes but were also found in buttonbush swamps, wet prairies, marshy pools in swamp forests, and rose tangles in wet meadows (Trautman 1940). They generally initiated their breeding activities slightly later than other resident rails (Andrews 1973). Their nests were constructed during May, either on the ground or as a platform above standing water (Trautman 1940). The earliest clutches were reported by May 10, although most nests with eggs were noted during the last half of May. Adults accompanied by small young were expected between late May and early August.

Their migrations were always poorly defined. Resident Kings occasionally returned during the first week of April but normally appeared during April 16–25. Most returned in early May, although a few migrants were noted through the end of the month (Campbell 1968, Trautman 1940). Spring King Rails were apparently accidental to rare migrants away from known breeding sites. In autumn, most Kings quietly disappeared from their breeding territories during September. Small concentrations were sporadically encountered, including 21 at Lake St. Marys on August 3, 1936, and 20 along western Lake Erie on September 3, 1948 (Baird 1936c, Campbell 1968). Most fall reports were of isolated Kings in their nesting marshes and as accidental to rare migrants elsewhere. They were fairly regularly observed through September 20–30, with infrequent stragglers into late October.

They were casually noted in the western Lake Erie marshes during winter. Campbell (1968) cited records of 1–3 Kings during seven of thirty-nine winters, mostly in December and early January, although a few may have overwintered. There were no winter records elsewhere.

During the 1930s, King Rails were noticeably declining. These declines were most apparent in inland counties, where wetlands were rapidly disappearing (Trautman 1940). These trends accelerated in subsequent years. Most isolated nesting pairs disappeared during the 1940s, and the large populations at Lake St. Marys and Buckeye Lake vanished by the 1950s (Clark and Sipe 1970). A few pairs remained in northeastern Ohio marshes, with nesting at Youngstown in 1963 and Geauga County in 1965 (Hall 1963b, Newman 1969).

Along western Lake Erie, they remained common summer residents through 1952 but then precipitously declined. By 1960, only a few pairs remained in these marshes (Anderson 1960, Campbell 1968). This decline was partially the result of drought conditions during several summers, as well as habitat destruction. However, they also inexplicably disappeared from suitable marshes. Kings became our rarest breeding rail, and Trautman felt they were "on the verge of extirpation in Ohio" during the early 1960s (Mumford 1961a).

Their status has not changed appreciably since the early 1960s. King Rails are now rare summer residents of western Lake Erie marshes in Ottawa and Lucas Counties. They may be found in only one to three marshes some years, but when water levels are favorable, as many as 11 adults have been reported from eight Lake Erie marshes (Peterjohn and Rice 1991). This breeding population probably does not exceed 10–25 pairs. The inland King Rail population has virtually disappeared. Since 1970, they have occasionally summered at Big Island Wildlife Area (Marion County), where nesting was confirmed in 1989 (Peterjohn and Rice 1991). This species is an accidental summer visitor elsewhere. While nesting has not been confirmed in northeastern Ohio since the 1960s, suitable wetlands remain, and a very small breeding population might be overlooked.

Away from the nesting locations, King Rails are accidental to casual migrants. The timing of their migratory movements has not changed. All recent records consist of single rails. They are strictly accidental winter visitors. The most recent winter records are single Kings discovered on the Buckeye Lake Christmas Bird Count on December 27, 1965, and one banded in Ottawa County on January 1, 1980 (Kleen 1980b).

Virginia Rail *Rallus limicola* Vieillot

Unlike King Rails, which nest in a variety of wetlands, breeding Virginias prefer dense cattail marshes covering several acres. Small openings are not essential, while water depths of 0.5 to 1.5 feet are preferred (Andrews 1973). Virginias also occasionally occupy large wet meadows, but they avoid small wetlands and narrow fringes of cattails bordering ponds, except during migration.

Virginia Rails have always been locally distributed summer residents.

Virginia Rail

Hicks (1935a) described them as "rather common" in the western Lake Erie marshes and at several unspecified inland reservoirs. They were rare and very locally distributed elsewhere, especially within the western counties. Their breeding range extended south to Columbiana, Carroll, Guernsey, Perry, Pickaway, and Butler Counties.

Like other marshland birds, Virginia Rails have generally declined in numbers as a result of habitat destruction. These declines are most apparent within the interior counties. In the marshes along western Lake Erie and the northeastern counties that still host sizable breeding populations, Virginias may be the most numerous resident rails. In eastern Ohio, where strip mining has created some sizable marshes, Virginia Rails have locally increased. Their statewide breeding distribution has not changed substantially since the mid-1930s. Nesting Virginias are most numerous along western Lake Erie, where they occupy every suitable wetland as fairly common residents. Breeding Virginias are also uncommon to fairly common in the northeastern counties south to Columbiana, Stark, and Wayne. In the remainder of northern Ohio, they become casual to rare and locally distributed, with the fewest reports from the western tier of counties (Peterjohn and Rice 1991).

Elsewhere, Virginia Rails are casual to rare and locally distributed summer residents. Small populations occupy preferred marshes, such as Spring Valley Wildlife Area (Greene and Warren Counties) and Big Island Wildlife Area (Marion County), but most other reports are of scattered individuals and pairs. They are least numerous along the southern unglaciated Allegheny Plateau, where a summering bird in Jackson County during the 1980s and a juvenile in Gallia County in 1991 provide the only recent evidence of breeding (Hall 1991d, Peterjohn and Rice 1991).

Most Virginia Rail nests are expertly concealed among dense emergent vegetation (Andrews 1973). They may be domed structures on the ground, or platforms 1.5 feet above shallow water (Williams 1950). Nest construction begins during the first half of May, and most eggs are laid before the end of the month. The young normally hatch in June and remain with their parents until August (Andrews 1973, Williams 1950). A remarkably early nesting record was established by an adult Virginia Rail accompanied by a small downy chick at Spring Valley Wildlife Area on April 23, 1983 (Mathena et al. 1984). Renesting attempts produce clutches as late as July 10 (Campbell 1968). While breeding rails are easily detected when they are establishing territories, they become inconspicuous once the adults begin incubating. They remain silent and furtive until their young are fully grown.

They remain inconspicuous through autumn, and their fall migration is poorly defined. Migrants are occasionally flushed from upland fields and a few have appeared in cities, looking out of place among downtown office buildings (Kemsies and Randle 1953). Most fall migrants are detected in wetlands, where they are rare to uncommon throughout Ohio and daily totals seldom exceed 1–4. Their southward migration begins by the last week of August. Most depart by October 5–10, although stragglers are reported into November (Trautman 1940).

Virginia Rails are surprisingly hardy, and a few have attempted to overwinter. Before 1960, wintering Virginias were only encountered once or twice a decade. They have been observed more frequently since 1960, averaging one record every two or three years through the 1980s but were reported annually during the 1990s. Whether these increased numbers of winter reports are the result of greater effort to locate this secretive species or an increase in the numbers of rails attempting to overwinter in Ohio is unknown. Virginia Rails now appear to be casual to locally rare winter residents along western Lake Erie and in the marshes along the Killbuck Creek valley (Holmes County). They are generally accidental winter visitors elsewhere, except at Spring Valley Wildlife Area, where they are casually reported. Most winter sightings are of 1–3 rails, although nine were reported at Spring Valley Wildlife Area on February 23, 1992 (Harlan 1992b). They are mostly reported during December and early January, although a few have survived until spring.

Migrant Virginias are most conspicuous during spring. Seldom numerous, they are generally uncommon to fairly common migrants across Ohio. Normally, 1–6 are noted daily, and the largest flights produce concentrations of 15–20. They have appeared as early as March 3–13 across the state. The first migrants regularly appear by April 5–15. Spring migrants are most numerous between April 25 and May 10, and only summer residents remain after May 25.

Sora *Porzana carolina* (Linnaeus)

Without a doubt, Soras are our most numerous migrant rails. Every cattail marsh, wet meadow, and pond margin hosts their share of Soras each spring and fall. While a few may be observed as they lurk among the vegetation, their true abundance can only be ascertained by encouraging the rails to call. Tape-recorded calls, loud noises, and throwing rocks into the marsh prompt them to respond with their distinctive descending whinnies, whistled notes, or sharp "keeks."

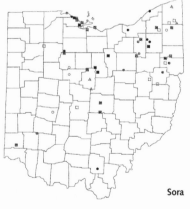

Sora

In spring, remarkably early Soras have appeared north to Lake Erie by March 20–30. They normally return during April 10–17 and are most numerous between April 27 and May 15. These migrants are common along western

Lake Erie, where 25–65+ may be noted daily. They are uncommon to fairly common elsewhere, becoming locally common at a few large inland marshes. Daily totals of 3–15+ may be noted away from western Lake Erie, with infrequent concentrations of 20–60. One hundred Soras at Mentor Marsh on May 1, 1976 (Thomson 1983), and 96 in Hamilton County on May 5, 1996 (Brock 1996c), are exceptional. Only summer residents remain by June 1.

The distribution of breeding Soras has not changed greatly since the 1930s. Hicks (1935a) described Soras as uncommon to rare residents within the western Lake Erie marshes. Small numbers were scattered across twenty-seven other northern and central counties south to Columbiana, Stark, Holmes, Licking, Pickaway, Champaign, and Mercer. Soras are still largely confined to this range, although there has been a slight southward expansion. Isolated pairs have nested or summered at Spring Valley Wildlife Area, another Greene County marsh, and near Cincinnati in southwestern Ohio, and in Carroll, Harrison, Tuscarawas, Jackson, and Washington Counties along the unglaciated Allegheny Plateau (Hall 1988d, Kleen 1976c and 1979d, Mathena et al. 1984, Peterjohn and Rice 1991).

While their breeding range remained fairly constant, their relative abundance was markedly altered. Along western Lake Erie, Hicks (1935a) considered Soras local and irregular summer residents, "greatly outnumbered" by other rails. As late as the 1960s, Campbell (1968) cited reduced numbers of Soras in these marshes. Their status must have changed abruptly; he considered them "the most numerous of all rails" along western Lake Erie in the early 1970s (Campbell 1973). Breeding Soras are presently fairly common residents in every extensive marsh in Ottawa, Lucas, Sandusky, and Erie Counties. Similar increases were not apparent elsewhere, as inland breeding populations declined as a result of habitat destruction. Breeding Soras are uncommon residents in northeastern Ohio, but become casual to rare and locally distributed elsewhere in the northern and central counties (Peterjohn and Rice 1991).

Breeding Soras occupy extensive marshes, usually the grass and sedge borders of cattail marshes or large wet meadows (Andrews 1973). Sora nests are placed on the ground in dense grassy cover. Their breeding activities begin during the first half of May, and most nests with eggs are reported between May 13 and June 16 (Trautman 1940, Williams 1950). Renesting attempts are responsible for clutches into early July. Young Soras may hatch during the last week of May, but most broods are observed in June and July. Parents with their broods are observed into the first half of August.

As soon as their young become independent, Soras initiate their southward migration. While a few migrants may appear by July 15–20, they become widely distributed by August 15–20. This movement largely takes place during September. The last migrants normally depart by October 10–15, with occasional stragglers through mid-November. Numbers of fall Soras fluctuate considerably. These migrants are most numerous along western Lake Erie, where 184 were counted on October 4, 1983, and 64 on September 7, 1983 (Peterjohn 1984a). Peak fall counts usually total 10–40 daily. Away from western Lake Erie, Soras become uncommon to fairly common migrants, in numbers similar to spring. The largest inland fall concentrations are 40–60. While most Soras pass through wetland habitats in autumn, a few have been found in upland fields.

Soras are accidental winter visitors. The first winter records were from Dayton on December 16, 1941, and December 10, 1948 (Mathena et al. 1984). There was also a sighting at Youngstown during the winter of 1952–1953 (Brooks 1953b). After 1960, winter Soras were reported on four occasions along western Lake Erie, twice in southwestern Ohio, and once in Athens County. All winter sightings were single individuals, noted as late as January 22–24 (Brock 1998b, Campbell 1968).

Purple Gallinule *Porphyrula martinica* (Linnaeus)

This colorful gallinule is largely restricted to the Gulf coastal plain, with a few pairs nesting north to western Tennessee and the Carolinas (AOU 1998). However, Purple Gallinules have an uncanny knack for appearing at unexpected locations at unexpected times, and may wander north to the Great Lakes and Canadian Maritime Provinces during any season.

The first Ohio specimen was collected near Circleville on May 10, 1877, a "flight year" that also produced four spring records from Cincinnati (Kemsies and Randle 1953, Wheaton 1877). There were few records between the 1890s and 1950, but Purple Gallinules have averaged three to six sightings each decade since 1950.

Purple Gallinules are most likely to appear during spring, when they are accidental to casual visitors, with at least twenty-eight published records across Ohio. These sightings include nine records from Cincinnati (six in the 1800s); five reports from the Dayton area; three records each at Cleveland and Columbus; and single sightings from the Sandusky Bay area, Circleville, Washington Court House (Fayette County), Wayne County, Lorain, Seneca County, Proctorville (Lawrence County), and Fulton County. Most reports are of single gallinules, although a remarkable six were found in Montgomery County on March 18, 1989 (Peterjohn 1989c). They have been noted as early as the last half of March, but most appear between April 20 and May 20.

These extralimital gallinules are mostly detected in wetlands or on small ponds bordered by emergent vegetation. They may also appear in unexpected locations. One of two gallinules found in Lorain County on April 18, 1980, was discovered swimming along the shore of Lake Erie (Kleen 1980c), and several have been found in residential areas miles from any water. While some remain for only one or two days, others linger for weeks.

Several lingered into summer, including one during June 1964 at Cincinnati and another through June 25, 1962, near Cleveland (Newman 1969, Petersen 1964c). There are also several unconfirmed summer records from the western Lake Erie marshes. The most surprising summer record was the discovery of a pair on Baumgartner's Pond in southern Franklin County in May 1962. Their nest was discovered on June 15 and contained seven eggs on June 17. These eggs hatched between July 4 and 8, and the young gallinules were regularly observed into August (Trautman and Glines 1964). This pair provided the only confirmed breeding record from Ohio.

Purple Gallinules are strictly accidental visitors during other seasons. The only fall records are a specimen found near Lake Erie in Erie County on September 2, 1894 (Tuttle 1895), and an injured gallinule discovered in Cleveland Heights on September 24, 1992 (Brock 1993a). This species has also appeared once during winter. A Purple Gallinule was encountered at a Mansfield residence on February 21, 1983; it was alive when captured but died in captivity (Peterjohn 1983b).

Common Moorhen *Gallinula chloropus* (Linnaeus)

Common Moorhens suffered from the destruction of wetlands at Lake St. Marys, Buckeye Lake, Indian Lake, and other inland marshes during the twentieth century. Substantial numbers nested in these wetlands during the 1930s (Hicks 1935a), but they largely disappeared by 1960 (Clark and Sipe 1970, Trautman 1940). Common Moorhens are now rare and locally distributed summer residents in the inland counties of glaciated central and western Ohio. Fewer than 100 pairs reside south to

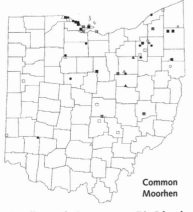

Common Moorhen

Hamilton, Warren, and Fairfield Counties. Small populations occupy Big Island Wildlife Area, Springville Marsh (Seneca County), and Spring Valley Wildlife Area. Scattered pairs are distributed in other suitable wetlands, although most counties lack breeding moorhens (Peterjohn and Rice 1991).

Moorhens remained fairly common to common residents in the marshes bordering western Lake Erie through the 1980s. Their numbers fluctuated considerably, from six or fewer reported daily in years of scarcity, to 10–20+ in years of maximum abundance. In suitable marshes, densities of 4.6 pairs per hectare have been recorded, and more than 60 pairs occupied a single marsh (Anderson 1960, Brackney and Bookhout 1982). In marginal wetlands, breeding densities approach one pair in five hectares. Brackney and Bookhout (1982) estimated approximately 1,200 breeding pairs in these marshes during 1978. Beginning in the late 1980s, numbers started to noticeably decline along western Lake Erie. This trend continued through the 1990s, and Common Moorhens have become uncommon summer residents, with daily totals of four or fewer, and are absent from some marshes where they formerly nested. No recent estimates of total population size are available.

Moorhens are widely distributed within northeastern Ohio marshes (Peterjohn and Rice 1991). They are locally common residents in the wetlands bordering Killbuck Creek in Wayne and Holmes Counties but are generally uncommon to fairly common elsewhere. While 10–15+ may be observed in large marshes, most wetlands support three or fewer pairs.

In the unglaciated counties, they were unknown as summer residents until strip-mining activities and expanding beaver populations created suitable wetlands. They have become accidental to locally rare summer residents in these counties. Summering moorhens were reported near Senecaville Lake in 1966 and in isolated marshes in Ross, Guernsey, Perry, Holmes, and Tuscarawas Counties after 1982 (Brock 1997d, Hall 1966d, Peterjohn and Rice 1991).

Moorhens breed in extensive marshes, where they furtively swim along the vegetated margins. When undisturbed, they are readily observed swimming and picking food from the surface of the water. They prefer marshes with approximately 50 percent open water, interspersed with emergent vegetation (Brackney and Bookhout 1982). Small numbers are also found in semipermanent marshes and shrub-dominated wetlands. Their nests are placed in dense vegetation near open water, either anchored to vegetation or floating (Trautman 1940). Along western Lake Erie, clutches have been laid as early as May 2, with a peak during the last half of the month (Brackney and Bookhout 1982). Renesting attempts have been recorded through July 10. Recently hatched young have been observed by June 7 but are most frequently noted during late June and July (Trautman 1940). Most young become independent by mid-August. Renesting attempts produce small downy young as late as August 28 and juveniles through October 21 (Brooks 1959a).

Spring migrants are mostly resident pairs returning to their nesting territories. Moorhens become accidental or casual visitors away from breeding locations. Migrants have returned to western Lake Erie as early as March 20 but normally appear by April 15–20 (Campbell 1968). They attain their nesting densities during the first half of May. Late migrants have been detected into the first week of June.

The largest concentrations are reported during autumn, and are generally groups of adults joined by their independent young. As many as 20–35+ moorhens have been counted at a single location, although most fall totals are of ten or fewer daily. Their southward movements largely occur during September and the first week of October. Most depart by October 15–20. Stragglers have lingered into November at several locations and December 9, 1949, near Cleveland (Flanigan 1968).

On three occasions, Common Moorhens survived into midwinter in Ohio. One was discovered at Magee Marsh Wildlife Area on January 5, 1953 (Campbell 1968), and another remained in Butler County through January 21, 1991 (Peterjohn 1991b). Two were discovered near Cuyahoga Falls in late December 1959 and remained through February 28, 1960 (Flanigan 1968, Mumford 1960b).

American Coot *Fulica americana* Gmelin

No other native water birds receive as little respect as American Coots. Their relative abundance, plain plumage, and typically unwary behavior combine to make them invisible to most observers, who regularly ignore these slate-gray birds awkwardly swimming in tightly packed flocks across large lakes.

Coots are common to abundant migrants. They are equally at home on large reservoirs, small ponds, and marshes, feeding at the surface or with their peculiar brief dives. The first

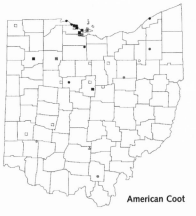

American Coot

coots return during February or early March as the ice melts from lakes and marshes. They become numerous by March 15–20 and remain conspicuous through May 3–7. Flocks of 50–500 are possible on all large lakes and marshes. Concentrations of 1,000–2,000+ may appear along western Lake Erie and within the northern and western counties. The largest spring flocks totaled 4,000 along western Lake Erie and 10,000 at Buckeye Lake on April 17, 1936 (Baird 1936b). Fewer remain through May 15, while stragglers linger into early June.

Numbers of migrant coots noticeably declined between the mid-1970s and early 1990s. This decline was largely attributed to poor wetland conditions and habitat destruction on their breeding grounds in central North America. Most spring flocks totaled 500 or fewer during these years, although their numbers improved in the 1990s as more favorable habitat conditions returned to their breeding range.

During summer, nonbreeding coots are casually encountered on large lakes, small ponds, and marshes throughout Ohio. Most are reported from the glaciated counties, with very few summer records along the unglaciated Allegheny Plateau. Individuals observed for a few days in June could be very late migrants. Others have appeared during July and remained into August.

Ohio also supports a breeding coot population whose distribution changed substantially during the twentieth century. In the mid-1930s, American Coots were common summer residents within the western Lake Erie marshes. They nested in northeastern Ohio, with scattered records from Ashtabula, Stark, Wayne, Mahoning, and Columbiana Counties (Hicks 1935a). Breeding coots were also reported from Williams and Franklin Counties, Lake St. Marys, Indian Lake, and Buckeye Lake. Of these latter locations, coots were "rather common" and regularly nested only at Lake St. Marys (Clark and Sipe 1970).

Breeding coots remained common along western Lake Erie into the early 1960s, but reduced numbers were reported later in the decade (Campbell 1968). Spring and summer drawdowns continued to reduce their numbers into the 1980s. Away from western Lake Erie, the breeding populations at Lake St. Marys and in the northeastern counties largely disappeared during the 1950s and 1960s. But breeding coots were recorded from Hancock and Lake Counties in northern Ohio, while a nest at Lake Grant (Brown County) on June 21, 1949, established the first southern Ohio breeding record (Kemsies and Randle 1953, Phillips 1980, Williams 1950).

American Coots are now fairly common residents in the western Lake Erie marshes, but are irregular and locally distributed summer residents in other glaciated counties. In northeastern Ohio, summering coots are casually encountered, with few recent breeding records. In northwestern Ohio away from Lake Erie, coots have casually nested in Seneca County, and the only other recent nesting record is from Putnam County (Peterjohn and Rice 1991). Within the central and southwestern counties, small breeding populations of 8–30+ pairs occupy Big Island Wildlife Area and Gilmore Ponds (Butler County) during most years (Peterjohn 1989d, Peterjohn and Rice 1991). Isolated pairs occasionally nest in other central counties, but the only other recent breeding reports from the southwest are limited to Hamilton County. There are no published nesting records along the unglaciated Allegheny Plateau, although summering pairs in Ross and Jackson Counties are suggestive of breeding (Peterjohn and Rice 1991).

Breeding coots prefer permanent marshes where open water is interspersed with emergent vegetation. Their nests are simple platforms constructed a few inches above the water within dense cover. Some coots begin nesting in April;

downy young have been observed by May 11 at Big Island Wildlife Area. Most pairs nest during May and June, while dependent young may be noted into early August. Late nesting attempts produced dependent young in Hancock County through August 26–27 (Phillips 1980), and a small chick in Mahoning County on September 19, 1978.

A few early fall migrants return during late August and early September, but the first coots normally appear by September 15–25. Their numbers peak between October 10 and November 25, when they become more numerous than during spring. The largest fall concentrations occur along western Lake Erie, where 1,000–8,000+ may gather, and aerial surveys produce estimates of 12,000+ (Campbell 1968, Harlan 1994a). On central and northwestern Ohio reservoirs, as many as 1,800–4,000+ have been noted, but most reports are of 700 or fewer (Thomson 1983, Trautman 1940). Elsewhere, flocks of 50–500+ may appear, while concentrations of 1,000–2,000 are unusual.

Cold November weather causes most coots to migrate, and only small flocks remain until freeze-up. Conversely, mild weather may allow flocks of 100–500+ to linger into late December. Subfreezing temperatures eventually force most coots to leave Ohio.

Their wintering numbers increased during the 1990s. American Coots are now uncommon winter residents along Lake Erie, with groups of 5–20+ frequenting most sheltered areas with open water. They are casual to uncommon and locally distributed elsewhere. Similar numbers regularly winter at Castalia, Columbus, and along large rivers in the southern half of the state, while Summit Lake in Akron may host a flock of 30–50+. Relatively mild winters entice larger flocks to remain as long as open water is available, including 150–180 at Buckeye Lake through the winter of 1931–1932 and 720 at Wellington Reservoir (Lorain County) on January 31, 1998 (Rosche 1998a, Trautman 1940).

Sandhill Crane *Grus canadensis* (Linnaeus)

In eastern North America, Sandhill Cranes primarily nest from northern Ontario south to Michigan, Wisconsin, and Minnesota, with a few pairs scattered within the southern Great Lakes states (AOU 1998). During their fall migration, most of these cranes congregate at Jasper-Pulaski Wildlife Area in northwestern Indiana; smaller numbers accumulate at other staging areas in Indiana and southern Michigan. From these areas, they fly to their wintering grounds in Florida. They reverse this route each spring (Walkinshaw 1960). Ohio lies on the eastern edge of this migration corridor, and the number of cranes passing over the state depends upon the prevailing wind directions and the size of this breeding population.

Most Sandhill Cranes are observed in passage over Ohio. Since their loud guttural calls carry for miles, they may be heard long before they are seen. Their unmistakable trumpeting announces that a flock is about to pass overhead. These migrants may be mere specks soaring on midday thermals, or they may appear suddenly at low altitudes, necks and legs outstretched as they quickly proceed on shallow wingbeats.

Sandhill Crane

Until the extensive bogs and wetlands were converted to agricultural fields, small numbers of these cranes nested in northern Ohio. Campbell (1968) cited accounts of 12–15 pairs breeding in the Oak Openings of Lucas and Fulton Counties around 1875. "Many juveniles" were reported from this area but no nests were ever discovered. This population disappeared around 1880. Other cranes nested in the bog that once covered much of southwestern Huron County. One or two pairs summered in this bog through 1926, and an unmated crane remained in the area through 1931 (Hicks 1935a). Summering cranes were also reported from Erie, Crawford, and Ashtabula Counties by Hicks (1935a), although breeding was never confirmed.

The demise of Ohio's nesting population reflected the Sandhill's population trends throughout eastern North America during the nineteenth and early twentieth centuries, as overhunting and habitat destruction significantly reduced their numbers. Even with complete protection, they did not begin to improve until the mid-1940s. Except for the Huron County breeding pairs, Sandhill Cranes were accidental visitors to Ohio between 1900 and 1940. They averaged one to three sightings a decade, mostly near Lake Erie, with one fall sighting from Buckeye Lake.

Judging from numbers staging at Jasper-Pulaski Wildlife Area, the Sandhill Crane population apparently doubled between 1945 and 1955 (Mumford and Keller 1984). This increasing population produced additional records from Ohio. Cincinnati's first modern record was established in 1948, and the second central Ohio sighting was reported that year (Borror 1950, Kemsies and Randle 1953). A flock of 28 flew over Toledo during October, 1949 (Campbell 1968), but Sandhill Cranes remained casual visitors to the western half of Ohio through the 1950s. This population expanded dramatically between 1955 and 1975, as evidenced by an exponential increase in numbers staging in Indiana (Mumford and Keller 1984), producing greater numbers of sightings from

Ohio. This trend continued into the 1990s and resulted in the reestablishment of a small breeding population within the state.

Migrant Sandhills are most frequently encountered in autumn. They are now rare to locally uncommon migrants in western Ohio, most frequently reported south from the Springfield area and along western Lake Erie. They normally appear in flocks of 75 or fewer, with occasional groups of 100–300+. Fall migrants are casual to rare visitors to the other glaciated counties. In central Ohio, most reports are of 25 or fewer, with occasional flocks of 60–100+. A concentration of 450 at Deer Creek Reservoir on November 20–22, 1995, was exceptional (Harlan 1996a). In the northeastern counties, most reports are of five or fewer, with occasional groups of 10–20+. They are accidental fall migrants on the unglaciated Allegheny Plateau, where the few records are concentrated at the northern margin of the plateau.

A few cranes have appeared along western Lake Erie during early August, probably wandering nonbreeders. The first migrants are expected during mid-October and most pass through the state during November and the first half of December. During mild seasons, their southward movements may continue into the first week of January.

Before 1984, there was only one undocumented winter record from the state. In 1984, a Sandhill Crane was observed near Pickerington (Franklin County) during the first half of January (Peterjohn 1984b). There have been winter crane records during most subsequent years, and they have become casual winter visitors to the southwestern counties but remain accidental elsewhere. Most reports are of individuals or small groups appearing for a few days during January, and could be very late fall migrants. A few have overwintered, including one in Knox County during 1986–1987 (Peterjohn 1987b), another at Mosquito Creek Wildlife Area (Trumbull County) during 1987–1988 (Hall 1988b), and two near Pleasant Hill Reservoir (Richland County) during 1991–1992 (Peterjohn 1992b).

The first spring migrants have returned as early as February 10–15 during mild seasons but normally appear during the last week of the month. Most are observed between March 5 and April 15, with scattered nonbreeders appearing during May. These migrants are uncommon through the southwestern counties and rare to uncommon elsewhere in western Ohio. Spring flocks tend to be smaller than in autumn, generally 30 or fewer, with infrequent groups of 50–80+. Spring migrants are rare in the northeastern counties, in numbers comparable to autumn, but are casual in the other glaciated counties and accidental along the unglaciated Allegheny Plateau. During most springs, a total of 50–100 cranes are reported from Ohio.

After the breeding population disappeared, the only Ohio summer record was provided by a Sandhill Crane in Union County during 1954. This nonbreeding individual was discovered on June 21 and remained into August (Nolan 1954c). In 1985, a pair of cranes summered in Wayne County, where nesting was suspected but not proven. They returned to the same area in 1986, but nesting was not confirmed until 1987 (Peterjohn and Rice 1991). They have summered in the area during subsequent years, and the number of breeding pairs in Wayne and Holmes Counties grew to three by 1997 (Kline 1997). Since 1990, Sandhill Cranes have become casual summer visitors in the other northeastern counties, with records scattered from Ashtabula and Geauga Counties west to Lorain County. While some reports are of individual cranes, others involve pairs of birds in areas where nesting has been suspected. To date, the only confirmed nesting attempts are from locations in Wayne and Holmes Counties.

Northern Lapwing *Vanellus vanellus* (Linnaeus)

One of the most unexpected species to ever occur within Ohio, a Northern Lapwing was discovered by Martin McAllister in a winter wheat field near West Union (Adams County) on December 29, 1994. This striking and unmistakable bird was studied by a number of bird watchers as it foraged in the field, until the morning of the next day when it took flight and disappeared to the south (Whan 1994).

Northern Lapwings are native to Eurasia and are normally found in open fields, pastures, wet meadows, and similar habitats. They are casual visitors to northeastern North America, where most records are scattered along the Atlantic Coast from Canada south to New York (AOU 1998). The Ohio record represents the first lapwing to be encountered well within the interior of this continent.

Black-bellied Plover *Pluvialis squatarola* (Linnaeus)

As spring migrants, Black-bellied Plovers normally return after they acquire their breeding plumage. Small flocks of these handsome plovers add a touch of class to flooded fields, drawndown marshes, and other habitats attracting shorebirds. These spring migrants are mostly encountered along western Lake Erie in Ottawa and Lucas Counties, where they are fairly common to common visitors and flocks of 5–30+ are regularly observed. Favorable conditions attract large flocks; as many as 125–250 have been reported from a single field.

Along central Lake Erie, Black-bellied Plovers are rare to uncommon migrants and most reports are of 12 or fewer. Away from the lakefront, these plovers are casual to locally uncommon migrants through all glaciated counties. The largest flocks are most likely to be encountered in northern Ohio, where 75–95 have been noted in Wayne County on several occasions and 92 were reported from Seneca County. In the glaciated central and southwestern counties, 10–35 make up the largest flocks. Most inland sightings are of 15 or fewer. Along the unglaciated Allegheny Plateau, Black-bellieds are accidental spring visitors, with only a few reports of scattered individuals.

Late March sightings likely pertain to misidentified American Golden-Plovers. The earliest confirmed report is April 6, 1997, at Headlands Beach State Park (Brock 1997c). Others have returned by April 17–25, but there are relatively few sightings before May. They are most likely to be observed between May 7 and 23, with late migrants lingering through June 7–12.

Nonbreeding plovers have been reported only from Lake Erie. They are casual summer visitors to Ottawa and Lucas Counties, where 1–6 are infrequently noted during June. Most remain for only several days, although a few linger for a week or longer (Campbell 1968).

The earliest fall migrants return to western Lake Erie by July 5, but they are not expected along the lakefront until the last week of the month. Black-bellieds are most numerous along Lake Erie between August 5 and October 10. Most depart by October 30, with a few remaining into November. Away from the lakefront, Black-bellieds appear during August 12–20 and are widely distributed in September. Timing of their departure is similar to the Lake Erie migrants. Adult Black-bellieds predominate through August. Most depart by early September, although a few have been noted as late as September 25. A juvenile along Lake Erie on August 4 was exceptionally early; they normally appear by the last week of August.

Black-bellied Plovers are uncommon to fairly common migrants along Lake Erie and rare to locally fairly common migrants at drawndown reservoirs within the inland glaciated counties. Along the unglaciated Allegheny Plateau, they are mostly accidental or casual migrants, although they may become locally uncommon visitors to the few localities regularly attracting numbers of shorebirds. Along Lake Erie, most fall reports are of 20 or fewer, with infrequent concentrations of 30–50. Flocks in excess of 100 are exceptional. At inland localities, only ten or fewer make up most fall sightings, and 22–50 compose the largest flocks.

The latest migrants normally disappear by November 15–25. Unusually mild weather allowed single plovers to linger into the first half of December at Toledo, Cleveland, Youngstown, and Columbus, and late December in Columbiana County. These accidental early winter visitors invariably depart before January 1.

American Golden-Plover *Pluvialis dominica* (Müller)

American Golden-Plovers were numerous migrants during the nineteenth century until their populations were decimated by market hunting. At the turn of the twentieth century, these handsome plovers were reduced to "hardly more than casual visitors" (Jones 1903). Their recovery started slowly, with the first increases evident by the 1920s (Trautman 1940). Populations did not fully recover until the 1940s and 1950s.

Spring American Golden-Plovers normally migrate through the central United States en route to their breeding territories on the Arctic tundra. These migrants are most numerous within the plains states and along the Mississippi River valley. The eastern edge of this migration corridor extends to western Ohio, where prevailing winds and other factors cause them to be plentiful some years and scarce in others.

Spring plovers are most numerous in western Ohio along a migration corridor extending east to Erie, Huron, Crawford, Marion, Union, and Madison Counties and south to Pickaway, Fayette, Clark, Miami, and Darke Counties. Golden-Plovers are generally fairly common to abundant spring migrants along western Lake Erie and uncommon to locally abundant within other counties. Flocks of 20–200 may be encountered throughout this corridor, and concentrations of 500–1,000+ appear some years. Larger flocks are less frequently observed: 6,000 near Bowling Green on May 10, 1940 (Walker 1940c); 5,000 on May 2, 1950, and 4,000 on April 24, 1954, in the Toledo area (Campbell 1968); 3,000 in Marion County on April 26, 1986; and 2,500 in Pickaway County on April 2, 1967.

American Golden-Plovers are uncommon to rare spring migrants through southwestern Ohio, where most reports are of 30 or fewer, but flocks of 200–400 have appeared on several occasions (Kemsies and Randle 1953, Mathena et al. 1984). Groups of 5–15 are locally rare to uncommon in southwestern Wayne County, the only location within eastern Ohio regularly hosting spring Golden-Plovers. They are accidental to casual visitors within all other eastern counties and along central Lake Erie.

Spring migrants prefer damp plowed fields and moist margins of flooded fields. The earliest American Golden-Plovers returned to Dayton by March 4 and Lake St. Marys by March 8 (Clark and Sipe 1970, Mathena et al. 1984). There are few other sightings before March 20. The first flocks are normally detected by April 5–15 and maximum abundance is attained between April 20 and May 10. Their numbers diminish by May 15 and only a few late migrants remain along western Lake Erie into late May. One lingered at Killdeer Plains Wildlife Area through June 6, 1994 (Campbell 1968, Harlan 1994d).

As fall migrants, most adult American Golden-Plovers head towards the Atlantic Coast before initiating a transoceanic flight to South America. Some juveniles also follow this route but others pass through the central United States. Hence, their fall distribution pattern is different than spring's. Fall migrants are most numerous along Lake Erie, becoming uncommon to locally common. Lakefront reports mostly total 20 or fewer, with occasional flocks of 40–100. Larger concentrations are restricted to the Toledo area, where 800 were counted on October 3, 1976, and 500 on October 27, 1940 (Campbell 1968, Thomson 1983). They become uncommon to fairly common migrants within the northern and glaciated central counties, normally 15 or fewer, with infrequent flocks of 20–50. Concentrations of 100–300 have appeared at several locations in the western half of the state. These plovers are least numerous within the southern and unglaciated counties, becoming accidental to locally rare migrants, and fall flocks never exceed 6–10.

These fall migrants regularly visit mudflats bordering drawndown reservoirs, dredge disposal sites along Lake Erie, sod farms, mowed hayfields, pastures, grassy fields bordering airports, and harvested croplands. The earliest Golden-Plovers returned to Lake Erie by July 1–5. They normally appear along the lakefront during July 27–August 12. The largest flocks are expected during September and the first half of October. They normally depart by November 1. Most migrants are adults through the first week of September, and a few may remain as late as September 21–28. The first juveniles appear by the last week of August and become widespread by mid-September. Within the interior counties, there are few July sightings. The first migrants frequently return during the last half of August. Peak numbers are attained during September, and these migrants normally become scarce after October 15.

Their status as late fall migrants is obscured by the difficulty of distinguishing Golden-Plovers from Black-bellieds. While Golden-Plovers have been confirmed during the first half of November, these individuals normally depart by November 10–17. Documented early winter reports are limited to an injured Golden-Plover at Metzger Marsh Wildlife Area on December 3, 1994 (Harlan 1995b), and one in partial breeding plumage along the Maumee River near Maumee (Lucas County) on January 3, 1995 (Brock 1995b).

Snowy Plover *Charadrius alexandrinus* Linnaeus

In North America, Snowy Plovers occur in two distinct populations. One population resides along the Gulf of Mexico, primarily in portions of Florida and Texas, while the other breeds at scattered locations in the western United States and winters along the Pacific Coast (AOU 1998). This species is known to wander from this established range, and vagrants have been reported from a number of locations in eastern North America. Hence, the discovery of a Snowy Plover at Headlands Beach State Park on May 13, 1993, was not unexpected (Hannikman 1993). This bird remained for the entire day, allowing close observations by numerous bird watchers and was photographed.

The fact that Snowy Plovers were recorded on four additional occasions between 1993 and 1995 is more surprising. These records are of single individuals near Lake Erie in Lucas County: at Ottawa Wildlife Refuge on August 1–7, 1993; on September 11-13, 1993, and July 15, 1995, at Metzger Marsh Wildlife Area; and at both Maumee Bay State Park and Metzger Marsh Wildlife Area between August 9 and September 15, 1995 (Brock 1994a, 1995d, and 1996a; Harlan 1994a and 1996a). Despite this flurry of reports, Snowy Plovers remain accidental visitors to Ohio.

Wilson's Plover *Charadrius wilsonia* Ord

The only acceptable Ohio record for Wilson's Plover is a bird collected at the former sand spit on Cedar Point (presently Cedar Point National Wildlife Refuge), Lucas County, on June 17, 1936. This adult male was "in good condition" (Campbell 1968). Its appearance, not due to stormy weather conditions, was unexpected; there are very few confirmed inland records in the United States. The normal breeding range for Wilson's Plover is along the Gulf and Atlantic Coasts north to Virginia (AOU 1998).

Semipalmated Plover *Charadrius semipalmatus* Bonaparte

This small plover is a regular visitor to mudflats, flooded fields, drawndown marshes, and other habitats attractive to shorebirds. It prefers damp mud and exposed gravel bars for feeding. Its presence may be detected by its distinctive plaintive call, easily recognized among the hoarse notes and sharp whistles produced by other shorebirds.

An incredibly early Semipalmated Plover was observed at Cleveland on March 18, 1986 (Hannikman 1986). Other early migrants have been noted during the first half of April, but they are not expected until April 27–May 5. Their maximum abundance is normally attained between May 12 and 25. These migrants usually depart from inland counties by May 30 but frequently remain along Lake Erie through June 5–10.

These migrants are fairly common to common near western Lake Erie in Ottawa and Lucas Counties, where totals of 20–75+ are noted most years and concentrations of 100–200+ may develop if conditions are favorable. Their appearance elsewhere is more erratic. Spring Semipalmateds are uncommon to fairly common migrants along central Lake Erie and rare to locally fairly common within northern and glaciated central Ohio. They become accidental to uncommon in the southwestern and unglaciated counties. Away from western Lake Erie, spring totals frequently are 1–10 daily, with occasional flocks of 15–50. Larger concentrations are noteworthy: 74 at Cleveland on May 18, 1986, and 115 at Big Island Wildlife Area on May 18, 1987.

Nonbreeding Semipalmated Plovers are casual visitors along western Lake Erie and accidental along central Lake Erie. Campbell (1968) cited six summer records in Ottawa and Lucas Counties between 1932 and 1937. In subsequent decades, they averaged one record every two to four years. These records are of single plovers, some remaining for only a few days, while others have lingered through June.

Along Lake Erie, fall migrants may appear during the last week of June but are expected during July 8–12. Semipalmated Plovers become numerous by July 20–25. Their return to the interior counties is generally later. While inland migrants have been noted as early as June 26, they normally appear by July 25–August 15. Numbers of fall migrants diminish in all areas by the first week of October and most depart by October 10–20. A few individuals remain into early November, but none have been recorded after November 14 (Campbell 1968, Williams 1950). Most fall migrants are adults through mid-August. A few adults remain into September, some as late as September 20–30. The first juvenile plovers return to Lake Erie by August 9 but normally appear by August 15–22.

Fall Semipalmated Plovers become fairly common to common along Lake Erie and uncommon to fairly common at inland habitats attracting migrant shorebirds. The largest flocks appear along western Lake Erie in Ottawa and Lucas Counties, where as many as 350–450+ have been reported on several dates. Flocks of 100–200+ occur most years when suitable habitats are available, although daily totals normally are 5–40. Along central Lake Erie, fall totals seldom exceed 5–20 and flocks in excess of 100 are noteworthy. Inland locations seldom attract more than 3–30 Semipalmateds. The largest inland concentration was 200 at Lake St. Marys on September 1, 1910 (Henninger 1911b). A flock of 45 at Spring Valley Wildlife Area was remarkably late on October 25, 1987 (Peterjohn 1988a).

Piping Plover *Charadrius melodus* Ord

Perhaps no bird is more symbolic of Great Lakes beaches than this little plover. Its light brown and white plumage blends so well with the dry sand that it is nearly invisible until it scurries down the beach. And, unfortunately, the plight of the Piping Plover reflects the deteriorating condition of the Great Lakes beaches. High lake levels have eroded these beaches, while remaining areas are subjected to increased recreational use. These factors so reduced the Great Lakes Piping Plover population that it is now classified as endangered. Approximately 20 pairs nest on the Great Lakes; the sighting of a Piping Plover has become a noteworthy event, and its plaintive call is rapidly becoming only a memory.

Although nesting had been suspected for many years, the first Ohio breeding pairs were discovered at Cedar Point (Erie County) at the turn of the twentieth century (Jones 1903). Subsequently, breeding Piping Plovers were discovered in Lucas, Ottawa, Erie, Lorain, Lake, and Ashtabula Counties. This population peaked during the 1920s and early 1930s. Although their numbers fluctuated annually, as many as 26 pairs were estimated along the lakefront between 1925 and 1935 (Hicks 1938a). This population was reduced to only six pairs by 1937, and the last documented nesting attempt occurred at Cedar Point National Wildlife Refuge (Lucas County) in 1942 (Campbell 1968).

Breeding Piping Plovers were restricted to the largest beaches and sand spits devoid of vegetation, with as many as six pairs nesting at a single location. Despite excellent camouflage of the eggs and young and the constant attention of vigilant adults, their nesting attempts were frequently unsuccessful. Nests with eggs were mostly recorded between May 20 and late June, with renesting attempts producing clutches through July 18. Adults with young were observed between June 16 and August 4 (Campbell 1940, 1968).

When Lake Erie supported a nesting population, Piping Plovers were regularly observed during migration. With the extirpation of this breeding population and substantial declines in other portions of the species' range, numbers passing along Lake Erie have noticeably declined since 1940. Piping Plovers are now casual spring migrants along the entire lakefront, averaging one sighting every three to four years. Recent records are individuals or pairs noted between April 15 and May 15, with a maximum of four during a single season. Fall Piping Plovers were regularly reported into the early 1960s but became casual to rare migrants along Lake Erie since the mid-1970s. They presently average one sighting every two to three years. Adult plovers may return by the second week of July and depart by early August. Juveniles generally appear during the last half of August and may be noted through September. Late migrants were noted in the Toledo area through November 5, 1966, and November 5, 1995 (Campbell 1968, Harlan 1996a), and at Lorain until November 24, 1969 (Rosche 1992). Most recent fall sightings are individuals, although a remarkable flock of 15 was reported from Lorain on August 24, 1963 (Newman 1969).

Piping Plovers have always been accidental spring migrants and accidental to casual fall visitors to the interior of Ohio. The majority of inland sightings are from the Columbus area, where they normally appear once or twice each decade. They are least numerous in southern Ohio, with no records from the unglaciated Allegheny Plateau. All records are of single individuals. The timing of their spring passage coincides with the migration along Lake Erie. Fall reports are almost exclusively of juvenile plovers during the last half of August and September.

Killdeer *Charadrius vociferus* Linnaeus

The first warming trend of February produces the first returning Killdeers. These early arrivals rapidly spread across the state. They usually become common and widely distributed by March 5–10. These migrants are mostly small flocks of 3–20, producing daily totals of 30–75. The largest flights total 100–225 in central Ohio and along Lake Erie.

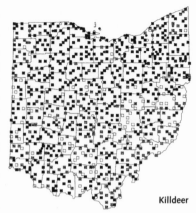

Killdeer

The last migrants are usually detected during the first half of April. By that time, Killdeers become fairly common to common residents throughout Ohio. Since they prefer short-grass meadows, pastures, and edges of cultivated fields, Killdeers are most numerous within the intensively farmed western counties, where 10–30 are noted daily. In the more heavily forested southeastern counties, daily totals seldom exceed 5–15. Urban areas support the fewest nesting Killdeers, with scattered pairs in vacant lots, parks, cemeteries, and along large streams. This adaptable plover has also nested on Lake Erie beaches, dikes in marshes, golf courses, and gravel-covered roofs.

Nesting begins early; nests with eggs have been reported by March 24 near Cincinnati, March 25 at Findlay, and March 31 at Cleveland (Kleen 1974b, Phillips 1980, Williams 1950). First clutches are normally laid during April. Some downy young appear by the last week of April but most are encountered during May or early June. Killdeers may raise two broods each summer, although some late nests may be produced by adults unsuccessful in their initial breeding attempts. Many clutches are reported during June and the first week of July, while small young are repeatedly observed throughout July. Adults accompanied by partially grown young have been reported through August 19.

Breeding Killdeers have been widely distributed residents since the nineteenth century. Their populations are still increasing. Breeding Bird Surveys indicate significant statewide increases since 1966, despite temporary reductions following severe winters (Sauer et al. 1998).

Flocks of Killdeers congregate during the last week of June, and their fall migration is underway by July 4. These migrants are numerous on exposed mudflats bordering lakes and marshes, but flocks are also observed in dry agricultural fields. Fall migration normally peaks between early July and mid-

October, when flocks of 30–250 are expected throughout Ohio and totals of 300–450+ occur during most years. Larger concentrations are infrequent, but as many 1,000–1,600 have been estimated at sites in the northeastern counties, central Ohio, and along western Lake Erie. They are regularly encountered until mid-November. While November concentrations are usually 30 or fewer, occasional large movements produce flocks of 50–100 in the northeastern counties through November 18–21 and 200–300 at central and southern Ohio reservoirs as late as November 22–28. Small numbers remain until the lakes and mudflats freeze. The last migrants may not depart until December 25–January 15. While most December sightings total six or fewer, as many as 20–60 have been noted into the second week of January during mild winters.

Killdeers are normally casual winter visitors after mid-January. They have become slightly more numerous after 1990, reflecting the relatively mild winters of that decade. Wintering birds are not regularly observed at any location, although 6–12 usually appear somewhere in the state each year, the majority in the southern and central counties. The largest reported late January flocks total 14–18.

Black-necked Stilt *Himantopus mexicanus* (Müller)

During the nineteenth century, anecdotal accounts indicate that these distinctive shorebirds may have been fairly regular visitors to the lower Great Lakes area. Accounts from Ohio include assertions that "one or two were seen every year prior to 1900" at Lake St. Marys, and that Black-necked Stilts were "repeatedly taken" along Lake Erie (Clark and Sipe 1968, Williams 1950). The only specific records are a Cincinnati area sighting in 1879 and a specimen taken in Cuyahoga County on October 24, 1881 (Kemsies and Randle 1953, Wheaton 1882). This specimen is no longer extant.

Black-necked Stilts were decimated by overhunting during the late 1800s and became rare throughout the United States. While their populations recovered in the western states, eastern populations remained small and locally distributed along the Gulf and Atlantic Coasts north to Delaware (AOU 1998). They are accidental visitors elsewhere in eastern North America.

During the twentieth century, there were only two Black-necked Stilt records from Ohio before 1980. One was reported from Lake St. Marys on May 27, 1967 (Petersen 1967b). Although details are unavailable, correspondence from Jim Hill and other observers indicates it was correctly identified. A road-killed stilt was reportedly found in Cleveland Heights on August 15, 1941 (Williams 1950). The specimen was not preserved. Given its unlikely location in an urban area and the absence of supporting details, this record appears to be questionable. Continental stilt populations have been expanding their

North American range since 1980 (AOU 1998), and this expansion has led to at least five additional sightings from Ohio. One stilt was discovered in a drawndown marsh at Magee Marsh Wildlife Area on July 18, 1981 (Peterjohn 1981c). Another stilt was found at Ottawa Wildlife Refuge on May 22–23, 1989, but was rumored to have been present elsewhere along western Lake Erie earlier in the month (Peterjohn 1989c). A Black-necked Stilt found in Ottawa County on August 5–16, 1989, may have been the same individual reported in May (Peterjohn 1990a). One stilt at Killdeer Plains Wildlife Area on May 23, 1995, provided the second inland report for the twentieth century (Harlan 1995c). In the autumn of 1995, two stilts were observed at Metzger Marsh Wildlife Area on September 15, while one was photographed at Conneaut during November 7–19 (Harlan 1996a).

American Avocet *Recurvirostra americana* Gmelin

While American Avocets are common and widely distributed in the western United States, the appearance of this distinctive shorebird is still a noteworthy event in many eastern states. Their past status in Ohio is uncertain. They undoubtedly migrated through the state during the nineteenth century but were apparently rare and irregularly observed. There were only a few widely scattered records, with the last specimen collected at Lake St. Marys in 1882 (Hicks 1937b). Shortly thereafter, avocets were decimated by market hunting and virtually disappeared from eastern North America.

During the first four decades of the twentieth century, American Avocets were accidental visitors to Ohio. Except for two vague records in 1907 and another in 1914, they were unrecorded until 1936, when one was observed near Toledo on September 6 and a specimen was collected at Ashtabula on September 21 (Campbell 1968, Hicks 1937b). During the 1940s, only single avocets were discovered near Sandusky Bay in 1944 and 1946 (Campbell 1968, Mayfield 1947a). Their status improved in the 1950s, when they were detected at a frequency of one to three sightings every other year, producing the first recent records from Columbus, Dayton, Lake St. Marys, and Pymatuning Lake. Avocets have been annually reported since 1963, including the first recent records from Cleveland and the unglaciated counties. During these years, they were as likely to appear at inland locations as along Lake Erie. In the 1970s, avocets established their present migration patterns.

Avocets are now erratic spring migrants. They are generally rare along western Lake Erie but accidental to casual elsewhere. The first migrants have been noted by April 14–15 and most appear between April 20 and May 15. Late migrants may remain into the first week of June. They may be absent some years and appear as widely scattered individuals in others. Flocks are infrequently discovered along western Lake Erie: 82 in Erie County on April 23, 1988 (Peterjohn 1988c); 42 near Sandusky on April 28, 1974 (Thomson 1983); and 32 at Oregon (Lucas County) on April 22, 1985 (Peterjohn 1985c). Small flocks have appeared at interior locations: 40 at Athens on April 15, 1987, and 18 on April 23, 1970 (Hall 1970b, Peterjohn 1987c); 16 in Fairfield County on May 3, 1980 (Thomson 1983); 14 at Paint Creek Reservoir on April 18, 1976 (Kleen 1976c); 13 at Headlands Beach State Park on April 16, 1994 (Brock 1994c); 12 at Findlay on May 12, 1975 (Kleen 1975c); and ten in Licking County on April 21, 1974. Spring avocets are generally observed in groups of six or fewer.

American Avocets are accidental summer visitors. Most June records pertain to late spring or early fall migrants. However, an avocet in the Winous Point marshes (Ottawa County) on June 21, 1944, was considered a non-breeding summer visitor (Campbell 1968).

Fall avocets are rare to uncommon migrants along the entire lakefront, producing three to twelve sightings each fall since the late 1970s. Adult avocets normally appear between the first week of July and early August. Most reports are of individuals along the Western Basin and groups of 14 or fewer in the Central Basin. Most juveniles pass along Lake Erie between August 10 and October 15, with a few remaining into November, usually in groups of 1–3, with occasional flocks of 6–10. One noted on the Toledo Christmas Bird Count on December 20, 1998, provides the only winter report for the state.

Within the interior counties, American Avocets are accidental to casual fall migrants. There may be no inland sightings during some years and two to five in others. A few adult avocets appear during July and early August but most inland records are juveniles in August and September. Late migrants may linger into November. Fall avocets have been detected in all portions of Ohio, usually as widely scattered individuals. The largest concentrations totaled 12 at Dayton on August 27, 1957 (Mathena et al. 1984); 11 at Stonelick Lake (Clermont County) on August 12, 1977; 11 at Killdeer Plains Wildlife Area on July 30, 1983 (Peterjohn 1983d); and eight at Rocky Fork Lake on the late date of November 2, 1995 (Harlan 1996a).

Greater Yellowlegs *Tringa melanoleuca* (Gmelin)

With their long legs and loud whistled calls, both species of yellowlegs are immediately recognized among a mixed flock of shorebirds. Distinguishing between Greaters and Lessers is fairly easy when they are together, but identifying a single yellowlegs is more difficult. Fortunately, both species are common migrants, allowing observers to become familiar with their diagnostic field marks.

As spring migrants, Greater Yellowlegs return slightly earlier than their smaller relatives. The earliest Greaters appeared in central Ohio by February 21, 1925, Wayne County by February 23, 1998, and along Lake Erie by the first week of March (Borror 1950, R. Schlabach 1998). They normally return by March 25–April 5. Their maximum abundance is expected between April 15 and May 7. Except for a few nonbreeders, the last Greaters normally depart by May 25–June 5.

Spring Greater Yellowlegs are widely distributed throughout Ohio. The largest flocks frequently form along western Lake Erie, where they are common migrants and 10–40 may be noted daily. Large concentrations are unusual, although 250 gathered near Toledo on May 2, 1943 (Campbell 1968). Elsewhere, Greaters are uncommon to fairly common visitors to flooded fields, marshes, and pond margins. Their numbers fluctuate considerably in response to habitat availability. During some years, they are fairly scarce and observed in flocks of 4–20. In other years, Greaters may be widely distributed, with occasional flocks of 40–140. The largest inland spring flock totaled 200 at Newtown (Hamilton County) on April 23, 1994 (Harlan 1994c).

While most Greater Yellowlegs breed in the boreal forests of Canada and Alaska, a few nonbreeders have summered in Ohio. These nonbreeders are casually encountered along Lake Erie, especially in the Western Basin and near Cleveland. Nonbreeding Greaters are accidental inland and have been detected at Lake St. Marys and in Summit County (Clark and Sipe 1968, Fazio 1999).

As fall migrants, Greater Yellowlegs are uncommon to fairly common visitors to mudflats bordering marshes and reservoirs within the interior counties. Inland Greaters are generally observed in flocks of 12 or fewer, with occasional concentrations of 20–50. Along Lake Erie, Greaters become fairly common to common migrants. Flocks of 80–140 have been reported, although most fall observations total fewer than 30.

The first fall migrants return to Lake Erie by June 23–30 but are not expected until July 12–22. They become widely distributed by early August. Adult Greaters usually remain through August 15–25, when the first juveniles normally appear. These juveniles are regularly observed through late October. During most years, the last juveniles leave between November 5 and 15, although occasional stragglers linger until late November. Mild weather allows a few Greaters to remain into December, and they have been noted on several Christmas Bird Counts. The only January record is of a single Greater near Cincinnati on January 15, 1951 (Kemsies and Randle 1953).

Lesser Yellowlegs *Tringa flavipes* (Gmelin)

Lesser Yellowlegs are among our more numerous and widely distributed shorebirds. Spring migrants prefer edges of marshes and ponds, flooded fields, and other shallow-water habitats. In autumn, they are mostly found on exposed mudflats bordering lakes, drawndown marshes, and gravel bars along large rivers. During both migrations, Lessers are considerably more numerous than their larger relatives.

Their spring arrival averages one or two weeks later than the Greaters'. Lesser Yellowlegs were reported from Cincinnati in "late February" (Kemsies and Randle 1953), but few sightings come before March 15–20. Migrants frequently appear during the first week of April. The largest movements normally occur between April 20 and May 15. Most inland migrants depart by May 20–25, although small numbers linger along Lake Erie until June 3–7.

Spring migrants are fairly common to common in most counties, becoming locally abundant when habitats are plentiful. They are most numerous along western Lake Erie, where flocks of 20–100+ are regularly noted and occasional concentrations of 300–500 develop. Elsewhere along Lake Erie and in the glaciated counties, flocks mostly contain 10–60 Lessers, with infrequent groups of 100+. The largest concentrations away from western Lake Erie totaled 400 at Buckeye Lake on April 26, 1928 (Trautman 1940), and 300 in the Cincinnati area during several years. Spring Lessers are least numerous in the unglaciated counties; most reports there are of 5–30.

Nonbreeders have remained in Ohio throughout June as scattered individuals. Most are observed along western Lake Erie, where Campbell (1968) considered them "regular" visitors, although they have only been casually reported in recent decades. They are accidental summer visitors elsewhere, with most reports from the northern half of the state.

Lesser Yellowlegs are among the first shorebirds migrating south each fall. Migrants frequently return to Lake Erie during the last week of June and are regularly observed by July 5–10 across the state. They become common migrants along the lakefront by July 15, but large inland numbers appear during July 22–27. They remain fairly common to locally abundant across Ohio until mid-October. The last migrants normally depart by November 7. Unlike Greater Yellowlegs, which are regularly observed during November, there are very few sightings of Lessers after November 10–15. Singles have lingered as late as December 7, 1985, in Gallia County (Hall 1986b), and this species has been reported from Christmas Bird Counts along western Lake Erie. Adult Lessers comprise most fall migrants until mid-August and depart by August 22–27. Juveniles usually return during the first week of August but become numerous by August 15–20.

Fall migrants are most numerous along western Lake Erie, where 30–200 are regularly noted and flocks of 300–500+ are infrequent between mid-July and early October. The largest concentration totaled 1,700 in Ottawa County on July 20, 1982 (Peterjohn 1982d). Along central Lake Erie and the glaciated counties, fall Lessers are mostly noted in groups of 50 or fewer, although concentrations of 100–200 may be observed. A report of 500 at Berlin Reservoir on September 19, 1997, is exceptional (Yoder 1997). These migrants are least numerous in unglaciated Ohio, where most flocks total 10–25 and concentrations of 50–100 are exceptional.

Spotted Redshank *Tringa erythropus* (Pallas)

Among the large numbers of shorebirds regularly migrating across Ohio, a few accidental Eurasian species have been detected. One, the Spotted Redshank, was discovered by Larry Rosche and Elinor Elder among a small flock of Lesser Yellowlegs at the dredge disposal basin in Huron on August 28, 1979 (Kleen 1980a). This unmistakable wader was an adult retaining most of its breeding plumage. As frequently happens with migrant shorebirds along Lake Erie, this flock rested in the basin for only a few minutes. There are no other acceptable sight records from Ohio.

Spotted Redshanks are accidental visitors in North America outside Alaska. The few extralimital records are primarily scattered along both coasts (AOU 1998).

Solitary Sandpiper *Tringa solitaria* Wilson

The Solitary Sandpiper is one of few shorebirds equally at home along a small rocky stream in Brown County and on a mudflat adjacent to Lake Erie. In fact, migrant Solitaries are more numerous through the interior counties than along the immediate lakefront. They prefer small shallow streams, quiet backwaters along large rivers, shallow marshes, and margins of small ponds, although they also visit mudflats with other shorebirds.

During spring, Solitary Sandpipers appear anywhere there is standing water, including shallow ditches and small vernal pools. They are uncommon to fairly common migrants across the state. While a few overflights may appear between March 27 and April 5, Solitary Sandpipers normally return by mid-April. Peak numbers are encountered between April 20 and May 10. As their name implies, they are frequently observed as individuals, but also form small flocks. Spring totals are normally fewer than ten daily, with occasional totals of 25–50. The largest movement occurred April 24, 1948, when an estimated 500 flew over Buckeye Lake (Mayfield 1948). Most migrants depart by May 20–25.

Nonbreeding Solitaries occasionally linger into the first half of June, and fall migrants regularly return before the end of the month. These June records prompted early ornithologists to believe that Solitaries nested in Ohio, and one even claimed to have discovered a nest on the ground. This assertion was erroneous. Solitaries nest in the boreal forests of Canada and Alaska, exhibiting the surprising habit of laying their eggs in abandoned songbird nests in trees.

The first fall arrivals are expected June 25–30. Between mid-July and the first week of September, Solitaries become uncommon to common migrants in every county. While they are slightly more numerous than during spring, daily totals are usually fewer than 15 and seldom exceed 25–40. The largest fall concentrations total 60–77. Fall migrants usually are adult Solitaries until the last week of July when the first juveniles appear. Juveniles predominate by mid-August. Numbers of migrants decline during the first half of September and only stragglers remain into October. There are two November records: November 5, 1930, in central Ohio and November 19, 1927, at Cleveland (Borror 1950, Williams 1950).

Willet *Catoptrophorus semipalmatus* (Gmelin)

During the nineteenth century, Willets were regular migrants through Ohio, described as "local and regular in some numbers" along Lake Erie and "uncommon to rare" elsewhere (Hicks 1937d). Their numbers were drastically reduced by overhunting during the late 1800s. Between 1900 and 1937, Willets were reported every two or three years, and Hicks (1937d) cited seventeen records of 32 individuals. Their status changed during the 1950s, and Willets have been observed annually since 1959. Numbers of migrants steadily increased through the late 1970s but remained stable in subsequent years.

This large stocky shorebird with its distinctive wing pattern presents an unmistakable image as it lands on a mudflat to feed. Nevertheless, this species has been misidentified. Undocumented reports of flocks during March or October seem questionable when compared with known migration patterns, and unseasonable Willets should always be carefully identified.

Willets are rare spring migrants along Lake Erie, averaging two to five reports annually. These migrants are mostly observed from Huron westward, with fewer sightings east to Cleveland. Most lakefront observations are of 1–2 Willets; flocks are unusual, although groups of 11–18 have appeared during several years. Spring Willets are accidental to casual migrants through the interior counties. They do not regularly appear at any locality, although there are usually one to four inland sightings of individuals or small flocks visiting a marsh or flooded field for a few hours or perhaps a day. The largest flocks totaled 21 in Hamilton County on April 30, 1990 (Peterjohn 1990c); 18 at Dayton on May 1, 1983 (Mathena et al. 1984); 17 in Washington County on April 17, 1997 (Hall 1997c); and 10–15 at other locations scattered across the state. These migrants are most likely to appear between April 25 and May 5, with smaller numbers returning by mid-April and others remaining into the first days of June.

Willets are rare to uncommon fall migrants along the entire lakefront. They may appear by June 20–25, but most flocks of adult Willets are encountered during July 1–15 within the Central Basin, including reports of 10–24 from the Cleveland-Lorain lakefront. Fewer adults are recorded later in July and are mostly replaced by juveniles in early August. Three or fewer Willets are normally detected during August, but occasionally large flocks appear, such as 50 at Cleveland on August 21, 1976 (Kleen 1977a). Most Willets depart by September 10. There are a few confirmed October and November sightings, including lingering individuals through November 5–13 along western Lake Erie.

Within the interior counties, Willets are accidental to casual fall migrants and are not detected annually. There are very few records of adult Willets during July; a flock of 12 along the Little Miami River near Cincinnati on July 5, 1971, was exceptional (Kleen and Bush 1971b). Most inland sightings are of scattered juveniles during August and the first half of September, with occasional groups of 3–4. These Willets are most likely to be observed in the northeastern and glaciated central counties. Very few have been detected in the unglaciated counties, where six at Beach City Dam (Tuscarawas County) on August 19, 1997, were remarkable (Yoder 1997).

Spotted Sandpiper *Actitis macularia* (Linnaeus)

Anyone floating down an Ohio river or boating on its lakes has observed these small shorebirds. Spotted Sandpipers are mostly noted as they forage at the water's edge, preferring quiet backwaters, riprapped shorelines, and exposed gravel bars. Breeding adults are easily identified by their spotted underparts and habit of constantly teetering as they walk along the shore. When flushed, Spotties emit their distinctive *peet-weet-weet* call notes as they fly with stiff fluttering wingbeats just above the water.

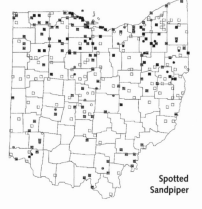

Spotted Sandpiper

Breeding Spotted Sandpipers are widely distributed in Ohio, with records from 76 counties during the Breeding Bird Atlas (Peterjohn and Rice 1991). Pairs are most frequently observed along Lake Erie, where they are fairly common residents. Summer totals seldom exceed 5–12. They are more locally distributed within the interior counties, where nesting pairs are encountered on creeks, rivers, lakes, ponds, and gravel pits. These sandpipers are fairly common residents along large rivers, in numbers approaching those along Lake Erie. They are casual to uncommon elsewhere, least numerous in the southern counties, where most reports are of scattered pairs.

Their statewide distribution patterns did not appreciably change during the twentieth century. In 1935, Hicks (1935a) recorded nesting pairs in every county. However, their population levels have probably declined since 1960, when fewer Spotties have been evident on lakes receiving heavy recreational use and along some rivers.

Spotted Sandpipers usually place their nests in herbaceous cover within fifty feet of water, although one pair nested on the face of a cliff overlooking Lake Erie (Williams 1950). Nests with eggs are mostly reported during the last half of May and June. Renesting attempts produce a few July clutches (Campbell 1968, Trautman 1940, Williams 1950). Adults with dependent young are expected between the last week of May and late July, although small young have been reported as late as August 8 (Campbell 1968).

The earliest Spotted Sandpipers are overflights, appearing in Cleveland by March 20, 1976 (Rosche 1992), and other localities by March 27–30. The first migrants normally return by April 15–23. Their northward migration normally peaks between April 28 and May 20; small numbers may pass along Lake Erie through June 7. Spring Spotties are most numerous along Lake Erie, where they are locally common visitors. The largest flights total 70–80, but most reports are of 5–35. Within the interior counties, they are generally uncommon to fairly common migrants; the largest movements total 25–30, but most reports involve ten or fewer.

Their southward passage begins by July 12–18. Fall migrants are most numerous between July 25 and August 25, with smaller numbers regularly noted through September. The last Spotted Sandpipers normally depart between October 15 and 27. A few stragglers remain into November, and there are at least three December sight records from Lake Erie.

Fall Spotted Sandpipers are most numerous along Lake Erie. Daily sightings of these fairly common to common migrants normally are of 5–20; the largest flights involve 70–75. They are uncommon to fairly common migrants through the interior counties. Most inland records total 3–15. Only Trautman (1940) regularly reported as many as 40–60 at Buckeye Lake during the 1920s and 1930s.

Upland Sandpiper *Bartramia longicauda* (Bechstein)

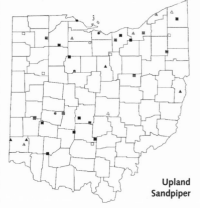

Upland Sandpiper

Shortly after dawn on a mid-April morning, the grasslands bordering many Ohio airports come alive. Amid the cheerful whistles of meadowlarks and lisping songs of Savannah Sparrows, a moderate-sized brown shorebird issues his distinctive whistle, proclaiming the surrounding grasslands as his breeding territory. As its name implies, the Upland Sandpiper is associated with grasslands, pastures, and prairies—preferring grasslands where the vegetation eventually reaches a height of one to two feet. Flat open terrain is favored, with fence posts, telephone poles, and tall trees serving as convenient sites for the male to declare his territory. Many generations of Upland Sandpipers have returned to Ohio, established territories, and raised their young. But over the years, they have witnessed changes in land-use patterns detrimental to their survival.

When Ohio was initially settled, Upland Sandpipers were restricted to prairie openings. Their populations expanded as the virgin forests were replaced with farmlands, and they became fairly common residents in many counties during the 1800s. They remained numerous until the last decades of the century when increased cultivation and market hunting considerably reduced their numbers (Trautman 1940).

At the turn of the twentieth century, Jones (1903) considered Upland Sandpipers fairly common residents in most counties, although they were "rather less common" along the southern border of Ohio. In the mid-1930s, Hicks (1935a) cited nesting records from 76 counties but noted that Uplands were absent or very rare in most southwestern counties and along the unglaciated Allegheny Plateau. The most significant declines were apparent between 1940 and 1960; breeding sandpipers disappeared from many counties, although a few pairs spread into several southwestern counties (Osborne and Peterson 1984). Changing agricultural practices were responsible for these declines, especially the conversion of grasslands to cultivated crops. Remaining grasslands were frequently unsuitable; pastures were overgrazed and hayfields mowed too frequently. These declines continued into the 1990s, but at a slower rate.

In 1981, breeding Upland Sandpipers occupied 30 counties (Osborne and Peterson 1984), usually widely scattered pairs in southwestern, central, and northeastern Ohio. Very few remained in northwestern and west-central Ohio, and they were absent along the unglaciated Allegheny Plateau. Nearly three-quarters of these sandpipers occupied grassy fields bordering airports. A similar distribution was evident during the Breeding Bird Atlas, with widely scattered records from 28 counties (Peterjohn and Rice 1991). Except for Uplands occupying a reclaimed strip mine in Jefferson County, these records were restricted to the glaciated counties. Few new breeding locations were reported during the 1990s, although a possible nesting pair in Pike County was noteworthy on the unglaciated Allegheny Plateau (Harlan 1993d). The size of the statewide breeding population was estimated at approximately 100–200 pairs in the 1980s (Peterjohn and Rice 1991), which may be a reasonable estimate today.

Upland Sandpipers begin nesting shortly after their territories are established. Their nests are shallow scrapes in the ground, expertly hidden among dense grasses. Most clutches are laid during the first half of May and hatch by early June. The young sandpipers remain with their parents into July (Campbell 1968, Trautman 1940, Williams 1950). A few pairs have nested early, producing small young by May 7 (Trautman 1940). Renesting attempts produce nests with eggs through June 20 (Price 1972).

When their populations were larger, Upland Sandpipers exhibited well-defined migrations through Ohio. After the early 1960s, these migrants became scarce in most counties; Uplands are now seldom encountered away from nesting locations. The earliest Upland Sandpiper returned to Oxford (Butler County) on March 18, 1982 (Peterjohn 1982c). There are few additional March sightings, mostly before 1940. They normally return by April 8–15 in the central and southern counties and April 15–22 in northern Ohio. In recent years, the largest spring flocks are composed of 4–10; concentrations of 20–30 were regular before 1940. Most Uplands return during April, but a few may pass along Lake Erie until May 10–15.

After their young become independent, Upland Sandpipers form small flocks prior to their fall migration. These flocks are usually observed at airports and pastures. By mid-July, the first migrants are heading south and their distinctive "putty-put-put" call notes may be heard as they pass overhead. This migration mostly occurs between July 25 and August 20, with smaller numbers remaining through September 10–20. When populations were larger, a few migrants remained into October, with the latest sightings at Columbus on October 11, 1932 (Borror 1950); Lake St. Marys on October 16, 1953 (Clark and Sipe 1970); and in Pike County on October 23, 1898 (Henninger 1902).

At one time, a few migrant Uplands were usually heard each August evening; occasionally "hundreds" were counted (Trautman 1940). Fall flocks were periodically encountered in grassy pastures, mowed clover fields, and harvested wheat fields. These flocks were composed of 20–50 and largely confined to the western half of the state, especially near western Lake Erie. A few flocks also congregated in the northeastern counties, including 31 in Lorain County on July 19, 1964, and 26 at Youngstown during July 1954 (Brooks 1954c, Petersen 1964d). The largest fall movement totaled 200 at Columbus on August 8, 1926 (Trautman 1928).

Since the mid-1960s, fall Uplands have become casual to rare migrants throughout Ohio, and very few are heard as they pass overhead. Small flocks of 10–20 are infrequently encountered in the western half of the state. Larger flights are limited to western Lake Erie in Ottawa and Lucas Counties, where 48 were counted on August 12, 1983, and a remarkable 96 on July 25, 1985 (Peterjohn 1984a, 1985d).

Eskimo Curlew *Numenius borealis* (Forster)

During the last half of the nineteenth century, unrestricted market hunting had disastrous effects on every species of shorebird. Perhaps no species suffered greater losses than the Eskimo Curlew. This diminutive curlew was a common spring migrant through the Mississippi Valley and the plains states, and fall migrants congregated along the Atlantic Coast between New England and Newfoundland (AOU 1998). Nearly hunted to extinction before they received protection during the late 1800s, most other shorebirds eventually recovered. However, Eskimo Curlews remained inexplicably scarce. Only small flocks and scattered individuals were sporadically observed through the early 1960s. Since then, a few sightings by reputable observers indicate that Eskimo Curlews survive in very small numbers, but their prospects remain bleak.

The former status of Eskimo Curlews in Ohio is poorly known. While nineteenth-century accounts suggest that they may have been regular migrants, there is no specific information concerning numbers of individuals or the timing of their migrations. Given their known migration corridors, Eskimo Curlews probably were not regular spring migrants through Ohio. Their presence during spring was only mentioned by Wheaton (1882), who described them as "not common" migrants but cited no specific records. If they occurred at all, Eskimo Curlews were probably casual or accidental spring visitors to the western counties.

Eskimo Curlews may have been regular fall migrants in Ohio, at least near Lake Erie from Sandusky Bay eastward. Winslow stated that they "were not rare" migrants in the Cleveland area during the mid-1800s (Williams 1950), while Wheaton (1882) considered them to be "not common" fall migrants. Most of these migrants appeared during September. Eskimo Curlews also occasionally visited the interior counties, where they were accidental or casual migrants. Inland records include a specimen (no longer extant) from Cincinnati during September 1878 and an unspecified sight record from Columbus (Kemsies and Randle 1953, Wheaton 1882). The date of the last specimen or sight record from Ohio is unknown, but it undoubtedly was before 1900.

Whimbrel *Numenius phaeopus* (Linnaeus)

Whimbrels are readily recognized by their large size, long decurved bills, and well-marked head patterns on otherwise nondescript plumages. While they occasionally visit mudflats and flooded fields with other shorebirds, they prefer upland grassy fields, drained marshes, and grassy dikes, where they readily blend into a background of dried vegetation.

Spring migration takes many Whimbrels from the Atlantic Coast across the Great Lakes to the tundra of Alaska and Canada. Though regularly observed along the north shore of Lake Erie, they are scarce in Ohio. Whimbrels are casual spring visitors to the northeastern counties south to Mahoning, Summit, and Wayne, and rare migrants along the entire lakefront. Since 1980, they average one to five sightings annually, generally individuals or groups of 2–7. Large flocks are infrequently noted along Lake Erie: 80 at Ashtabula on May 23, 1959 (Mumford 1959c); 42 at Cleveland on May 28, 1949 (Mayfield 1949b); and 80 in the Toledo area on May 20, 1934, and 75 on May 21, 1976 (Campbell 1968, Thomson 1983). A few flocks have also been detected in the interior northeastern counties: 101 in Wayne County on May 26, 1984 (Peterjohn 1984c); 42 over Medina County on May 26, 1985 (Peterjohn 1985c); and several flocks of 11–14. Whimbrels are accidental visitors away from this corridor, with only five reports from central Ohio, two from the southwestern counties, and single observations from Findlay, Tuscarawas County, and Dillon Reservoir (Muskingum County). These records are of single individuals, except for 12 at Findlay Reservoir on May 30, 1981 (Peterjohn 1981b), 27 at Cowan Lake (Clinton County) on May 21, 1995, and a remarkable 106 at Killdeer Plains Wildlife Area on May 24, 1995 (Harlan 1995c).

The earliest Whimbrels have been noted during April 16–19. The first migrants normally appear during May 5–12 and most spring sightings are recorded between May 20 and 30. Late migrants may remain into the first week of June.

Whimbrels are accidental nonbreeding summer visitors along western Lake Erie. Campbell (1968) reported a summering Whimbrel between May 28 and June 24, 1933, and a group of 3–4 through June 15, 1935. The only recent summer record was one periodically observed in Lucas County through July 5, 1985 (Peterjohn 1985d).

As fall migrants, Whimbrels are rare to locally uncommon along the entire lakefront, producing two to ten sightings annually. These migrants may return by June 27–July 7 but are expected by July 15–25. All migrants are adults through the first half of August. Juveniles appear by the end of the month; most are noted between August 25 and September 20, with a few lingering into the third week of October. These migrants mostly appear in groups of ten or fewer. The only sizable flocks have been reported from Headlands Beach State Park, where 104 were noted on September 8, 1990, 44 on August 19, 1990 (Peterjohn 1991a), and 30 on September 5, 1988 (Peterjohn 1989a). Fall Whimbrels are accidental visitors away from Lake Erie. Six reports from the eastern half of the state include four sightings from the northeastern counties and singles at Newcomerstown on October 16, 1977, and near Salem on October 16, 1981 (Hall 1978, 1982a). A flock of 20 near Ravenna on August 24, 1999, was exceptional (Rosche 1999b). The inland records from the western half of Ohio are limited to two sightings in the Columbus area and single records from Lake St. Marys and Paulding County.

Between July 10 and 18, 1988, a white-rumped Whimbrel was observed along the Maumee River near Toledo (Peterjohn 1988d). The heavily barred underwings, breast streaking that extended to the legs, and the lightly barred rump were suggestive of the Siberian race *variegatus*, establishing one of very few records of any Eurasian race of Whimbrel from the Great Lakes region.

Long-billed Curlew *Numenius americanus* Bechstein

The early status of Long-billed Curlews in Ohio is clouded with uncertainty. Anecdotal accounts provided by Kirtland, Wheaton, and others indicated they may have been rare migrants during the nineteenth century (Jones 1903), but no specimens or descriptions are available to support any of these records. Because these observers had difficulty distinguishing Long-billed Curlews from Whimbrels, nineteenth century sightings are considered questionable.

Modern observers also have problems separating these two species, and most recent sightings of Long-billed Curlews proved to be Whimbrels. There are only three acceptable sight records, two from central Ohio during late May. The first Long-billed Curlew was discovered by Milton Trautman and others at O'Shaughnessy Reservoir in Delaware County on May 22, 1926 (Trautman 1940). The second was observed by Jim McCormac at Killdeer Plains Wildlife Area on May 25, 1983 (Peterjohn 1983c). Another Long-billed Curlew was discovered by Aaron Hershberger in Holmes County on October 1, 1999. It was photographed prior to its departure on October 2 (Glick 1999b).

Long-billed Curlews nest on dry short-grass prairies of the western United States and prairie provinces of Canada (AOU 1998). They migrate through the western states to wintering areas along the Pacific Coast and the Gulf Coast of Texas. In recent years, they have been very rare but regular migrants along the Atlantic Coast.

Hudsonian Godwit *Limosa haemastica* (Linnaeus)

Hudsonian Godwits were almost exterminated by market hunters during the nineteenth century. The few nineteenth century records from Ohio were before 1879, when their populations were still relatively large. Even after hunting ceased, their recovery was very slow. There were only five Ohio sight records between 1900 and 1930. Slightly improved numbers during the 1930s included the first Hudsonians at Toledo and Youngstown in 1932 (Campbell 1968, Skaggs 1932). This slowly increasing population produced very occasional sightings until the mid-1960s, when Hudsonians began to appear regularly along western Lake Erie, including a large flight during 1967. Dramatic improvements during the 1970s brought a pronounced flight along western Lake Erie in 1975 and increased sightings in the remainder of the state. Their status as regular fall migrants has been maintained since 1980.

During spring, Hudsonian Godwits are generally rare east of the Mississippi River. Since 1970, they are casual spring migrants along western Lake Erie, where they are reported once every three to five years. They are accidental spring visitors elsewhere, with 2–3 sightings in central Ohio, Cincinnati, and the Cleveland-Lorain area, and single records at Lake St. Marys and Findlay. All spring records are of 1–3 Hudsonians observed between May 14 and June 6.

Many adult Hudsonian Godwits undertake a remarkable fall migration, flying directly from Canada to South America. Some juveniles undertake a similar nonstop migration, but others stop in the Great Lakes states and along the Atlantic Coast.

Fall Hudsonian Godwits are mostly observed near western Lake Erie, where they are generally rare to uncommon migrants. There are few records of adults during July and early August. Most migrants are juveniles appearing as early as the last week of August but most frequently between September 20 and October 15. The 1967 flight brought 63 to Ottawa Wildlife Refuge on October 7 (Campbell 1968). The largest movement occurred in 1975, when 143 were observed at Ottawa Wildlife Refuge on September 28, and 90 on October 5 (Kleen 1976a). Smaller flights during 1974, 1976, 1983, and 1985 produced flocks of 30–40. During other years, Hudsonians are detected in flocks of ten or fewer. While they normally depart by October 30–November 5, 12 remained at Ottawa Wildlife Refuge through November 8, 1982, and one lingered there until December 3, 1982 (Peterjohn 1983a, 1983b).

Hudsonian Godwits are casual to accidental fall migrants elsewhere in Ohio. They are most likely to appear along central Lake Erie, at large reservoirs near Columbus, and within the northeastern counties. Sightings are mostly juveniles between late August and mid-October, either individuals or groups of seven or fewer. Flocks include 24 at Cleveland on September 10, 1984 (Hannikman 1984); 21 at C.J. Brown Reservoir (Clark County) on August 26, 1979 (Mathena et al. 1984); and several reports of 12–17. A few remained as late as November 23–24 in Seneca County and Cleveland. None have been reported from the southwestern counties or the unglaciated Allegheny Plateau.

Marbled Godwit *Limosa fedoa* (Linnaeus)

Marbled Godwits occasionally passed through Ohio during the nineteenth century, producing records from Cleveland, Columbus, Cincinnati, Buckeye Lake, and possibly elsewhere. After their populations were decimated by over-hunting, they largely disappeared from eastern North America by the early 1880s.

The twentieth century's first Marbled Godwits were recorded in 1925, when five visited O'Shaughnessy Reservoir near Columbus (Trautman 1940). They became accidental to casual visitors, averaging three to five sightings per decade through the mid-1960s. Most records were from western Lake Erie and large reservoirs in the northeastern counties. Their status improved in the late 1960s, especially along Lake Erie during autumn, and they have been annually reported since 1971.

Marbled Godwits are now casual to rare spring migrants along western Lake Erie. They are unrecorded during dry seasons but produce one to three reports when habitats are abundant, usually of single godwits. Away from western Lake Erie, Marbled Godwits are accidental spring migrants, with at least fourteen records scattered across the state. Except for eight at Caesar Creek Reservoir on April 26, 1998, and nine at Delaware Wildlife Area on May 1, 1997 (Brock 1998c, Fazio 1997b), these records pertain to only one or two individuals. Throughout Ohio, the earliest migrants have been reported between April 8 and 15. Most are detected between April 28 and May 20, with a few late migrants remaining into early June.

Summering Marbled Godwits are accidental visitors along Lake Erie. Except for a single godwit at Cleveland on June 11–12, 1978 (Kleen 1978d), these records are restricted to Ottawa and Lucas Counties. As many as three nonbreeders reportedly summered during 1981, 1982, and 1983 and remained through mid-June 1985. While territorial behavior was reported in 1982, no nest was located (Peterjohn 1982d).

Marbled Godwits are mostly observed as fall migrants along Lake Erie. Within the Western Basin, they are generally rare to locally uncommon, producing one to six reports annually. Most sightings are of three or fewer, with occasional flocks of 4–8. From Huron eastward, these godwits are rare visitors, with one to three records annually. Most reports are of 1–3, but small flocks are possible and a remarkable 16 visited Cleveland on July 4, 1983 (Peterjohn 1983d).

Away from Lake Erie, these godwits remain accidental fall migrants. There are at least eight inland records from the northeastern counties and four from the glaciated central counties, but none have been noted in other portions of the state. All inland records involved single Marbled Godwits.

Along Lake Erie, the first migrants appear during the last days of June and are fairly regularly noted by July 3–12. They may be noted anytime between mid-July and September. Later migrants are restricted to western Lake Erie, where Marbleds occasionally linger through November 5–6 and one was reported on December 30, 1994 (Harlan 1995b). Most inland records occurred between August 15 and October 25, but a crippled bird remained at Lake St. Marys through November 14, 1992 (Harlan 1993a).

Ruddy Turnstone *Arenaria interpres* (Linnaeus)

Ruddy Turnstones are not likely to be misidentified in their attractive breeding plumage. Even their somber juvenal plumage is not readily confused with any other shorebird in eastern North America. During both migrations, Ruddy Turnstones occur anywhere shorebirds congregate, although they prefer beaches, breakwaters, and mudflats along Lake Erie. Spring migrants also regularly visit flooded fields and drawndown marshes along western Lake Erie.

As spring migrants, these turnstones are normally among the later shorebirds passing through Ohio. While single turnstones were discovered along Lake Erie in Lorain County on March 31, 1912, and at Cleveland on April 8, 1951 (Flanigan 1968, Jones 1914), these unusually early sightings may pertain to wintering individuals. There are very few records earlier than May 1. The first turnstones are expected May 5–10, with the largest movements between May 20 and June 5. The last migrants may not depart until June 10–15.

Although their numbers fluctuate annually, spring Ruddy Turnstones are most numerous along western Lake Erie. They are fairly common to common migrants, becoming locally abundant when flooded fields are widely distributed. Spring flocks of 15–50+ are regular, and peaks of 100–200 are reported during most years; the largest flocks total 350–800. Along central Lake Erie, they are generally uncommon migrants, as flocks of 5–15. Within the interior counties, they are absent some years but may be scattered across the state in others. Spring Ruddy Turnstones are accidental to locally rare migrants through the northern and glaciated central counties, most numerous in northeastern Ohio. While most inland sightings are of ten or fewer, an impressive 125 were discovered in Wayne County on May 17, 1978 (Kleen 1978c), and 82 at Lake St. Marys on May 17, 1997 (Brock 1997c). They become accidental to casual migrants within the southern and unglaciated counties, where most reports are of 1–2 turnstones and the largest flocks total 10–15.

A few nonbreeding Ruddy Turnstones have summered and are accidental along western Lake Erie in Ottawa and Lucas Counties (Campbell 1940, 1968). They have not been reported anywhere else in the state.

The first fall Ruddy Turnstones normally return to Lake Erie between July 20 and 30 and are regularly observed by the first week of August. Adult turnstones appear through the last week of August. The first juveniles have been observed by August 18–23 but become numerous during September. Most depart by October 10–20; late migrants may remain into November.

Fall turnstones are distributed along the entire lakefront as uncommon to fairly common migrants. Most records total 15 or fewer and the largest concentrations are 30–55. Within the interior counties, relatively few adults are discovered during autumn. Most records are of juveniles between August 20 and October 15. These migrants are normally casual to rare at large reservoirs in the northern and glaciated central counties, becoming accidental to casual within southern and unglaciated Ohio. Inland records invariably are of 1–5 turnstones.

A few Ruddy Turnstones have lingered into winter along the Cleveland-Lorain lakefront. Single turnstones remained through December in 1974, 1982, and 1993, and as late as January 12, 1968, at Lorain (Petersen 1968a). The only wintering turnstones were observed at Cleveland between December 25, 1974, and February 23, 1975, and at Lorain through March 12, 1989 (Kleen 1975b, Peterjohn 1989b). Both individuals disappeared with the onset of warmer temperatures.

Red Knot *Calidris canutus* (Linnaeus)

Large flocks of Red Knots regularly gather along Delaware Bay each spring, feeding on horseshoe crab eggs and gaining weight in preparation for the remainder of their northward migration. As they head towards their Arctic nesting grounds, some regularly pass over the Great Lakes region. Although most fly directly to the tundra, a few visit locations in between.

Within Ohio, spring Red Knots are mostly observed near western Lake Erie in Ottawa and Lucas Counties as rare migrants averaging three or fewer sightings annually. Most spring records are of individuals or groups of 2–8. Larger flocks are exceptional: 150 at Bay Point (Ottawa County) on May 26, 1956 (Campbell 1968); 49 at Ottawa Wildlife Refuge on May 17, 1980 (Kleen 1980c); and 15–35 on a few occasions.

Red Knots are casual spring migrants along the lake's Central Basin, with a few records of one or two, primarily from the Cleveland lakefront. They are accidental spring visitors to the interior counties, with scattered records from northern Ohio west to Seneca County and from central Ohio near Columbus. Most inland sightings are of one or two knots. The only sizable flocks were 60 in Wayne County on May 19, 1983 (Peterjohn 1983c); 47 in Seneca County on May 18, 1984 (Peterjohn 1984c); and 17 in Wayne County on May 19, 1997 (Brock 1997c).

The earliest spring knots appear by May 10–11, and most are observed between May 16 and 28. A few migrants are detected through the first week of June and infrequently as late as June 11–17.

Red Knots are accidental nonbreeding summer visitors along western Lake Erie. Individuals reported on June 26, 1954, and through July 1, 1985, were thought to be nonbreeding visitors rather than migrants (Campbell 1968, Peterjohn 1985d).

Red Knots are more likely to be observed during autumn. These migrants are rare to uncommon along the entire lakefront. The first fall migrants may return by July 15–20 and are regularly observed by August 5–15. Most are noted between August 20 and September 15, with smaller numbers through mid-October. They become very rare after October 20, with a few November records along western Lake Erie and a late knot near Toledo on December 1, 1935 (Campbell 1968). Adults pass along the lakefront through the last week of August. Juveniles normally appear during the last half of August.

Lakefront fall migrants can be scarce some years, with fewer than six sightings of scattered individuals. In other years, knots become fairly regular migrants with ten to twenty or more records, mostly of six or fewer, with occasional concentrations of 8–13. A flock of 43 at Cleveland on September 9, 1984, was exceptional (Peterjohn 1985a).

Red Knots are generally accidental fall migrants away from Lake Erie, becoming casual visitors to Hoover Reservoir near Columbus and Lake St. Marys. Fall records from the southern counties are limited to four sightings from the Dayton-Cincinnati area and two in Gallia County. Fall knots are usually detected at one to three inland localities each year, mostly as scattered individuals, although small flocks of 3–7 have been infrequently observed. The largest inland fall concentration totaled 21 at Lake St. Marys on October 10, 1956 (Clark and Sipe 1970). While a few adults have been observed in August, most inland records are juveniles between August 25 and October 15. Late migrants have lingered through November 3–10.

Sanderling *Calidris alba* (Pallas)

Renowned for their incessant chasing of waves on coastal beaches, Sanderlings are also familiar visitors to the Great Lakes. They are rare to uncommon spring migrants along Lake Erie, frequently mixed among flocks of Dunlins and Ruddy Turnstones. Most sightings are of 15 or fewer; 120 at Lorain on May 25, 1997, were exceptional (Rosche 1997b). Within the interior counties, they are accidental to casual migrants across the state, in flocks of 8–25 or fewer. The earliest Sanderlings returned to Cleveland on March 27, 1988, and April 12, 1986 (Rosche 1992). Other early arrivals are noted at lakefront sites and Columbus by April 22–23. They are expected to appear by May 10–15. Most sightings are during the last half of May, with a few lingering through June 7.

Sanderlings are accidental nonbreeding summer visitors. The only mid-summer record is of two at Toledo on June 17, 1933; these may have been very late spring migrants (Campbell 1968).

Fall migrants are more numerous, becoming fairly common to common visitors along Lake Erie, most frequently noted in the Central Basin. Most reports are of 20 or fewer, with infrequent concentrations of 30–85. The largest flock was discovered on the Maumee River near Toledo: 225 on October 10, 1937 (Campbell 1968). Considerably fewer Sanderlings visit mudflats adjoining reservoirs within the interior counties. They are uncommon to fairly common fall migrants through the northern and glaciated central counties, mostly observed in groups of eight or fewer, with occasional flocks of 15–20. The largest inland concentration was 50 at Lake St. Marys on September 24, 1909 (Clark and Sipe 1970). Within the southern and unglaciated counties, fall Sanderlings are accidental to locally rare visitors. Most sightings are of five or fewer and the largest flocks total 8–11.

Along Lake Erie, the earliest fall migrants return by July 4–7 but normally appear during July 20–25. Their maximum abundance is usually attained between August 20 and October 10. Smaller numbers may remain through November 15–20. Adult Sanderlings make up this migration through mid-August, but they depart by the end of the month. The first juveniles arrive by August 9 and predominate by the first week of September. Within the interior counties, few Sanderlings are recorded before August 8–15. They are mostly observed between August 28 and October 5 and normally depart by October 20–25. A few have lingered into November.

Sanderlings have survived along Lake Erie into early winter, producing at least seven December records of single individuals. The latest Sanderlings remained through January 11, 1979, at Lorain and January 2, 1960, at Ashtabula (Hannikman 1979, Mumford 1960b), but none have overwintered.

Semipalmated Sandpiper *Calidris pusilla* (Linnaeus)

For most birders, their first encounter with small sandpipers, or "peeps," is with an assemblage of look-alike species scattered across a mudflat in autumn. Identifying these species is a challenge and a source of frustration, even for experienced observers. Separating them requires careful study, and the first step is to become familiar with the more common species. Among the most numerous of the "peeps" are the Semipalmated Sandpipers.

Semipalmated Sandpipers are found wherever shorebirds congregate. They are fairly late migrants during spring, with a few reports during the last days of April but normally not until May 3–7. Maximum numbers are encountered between May 15 and 30. Small flocks are frequently observed during the first week of June, especially along western Lake Erie. Late migrants depart by June 10–15, although occasional nonbreeders have summered along the lakefront.

Spring Semipalmateds are most numerous along western Lake Erie, where they are common to abundant migrants and daily totals of 50–300+ are noted during May. When suitable habitats are plentiful, concentrations of 700–1,000+ have been reported. They are common visitors elsewhere along the lakefront, usually not exceeding 100 daily. Inland Semipalmateds are fairly common to common migrants through the northeastern counties, where most reports are of 50 or fewer and the largest flock totaled 1,000 at Barberton on May 27, 1986 (Peterjohn 1986c). They are rare to uncommon migrants in the unglaciated counties but fairly common at other inland locations, although concentrations seldom exceed 15–50.

Fall migrants are generally common to abundant along the entire lakefront. Daily tallies are normally 50–100+. Larger concentrations may total 1,000–1,500 along western Lake Erie and 200–300 in the Central Basin, with a maximum estimate of 3,500 at Turtle Creek Wildlife Area on July 23, 1994 (Harlan 1995a). Inland migrants are rare to fairly common at most localities, least numerous in the unglaciated counties and southwestern Ohio. The largest inland flock totaled 900 at Lake St. Marys on September 1, 1910 (Henninger 1911b). Concentrations of 100–200 have appeared in central Ohio but seldom exceed 20–75 elsewhere.

Along Lake Erie, the first adult Semipalmateds have returned during the last week of June and are expected by July 7–15. They remain numerous until mid-August. Juveniles arrive by August 3–10 and become the predominant members of flocks during the last half of the month. Largest flocks normally appear between July 20 and September 7. Most depart before the end of September. Timing of the inland migration is similar, except that adults are relatively scarce. Phillips (1975) demonstrated that these sandpipers are early fall migrants, seldom remaining in the Great Lakes region past the first week of October. The latest Ohio specimen was collected in Lucas County on October 11, 1937 (Campbell 1940), and the latest documented sight record is from Lake St. Marys on October 24, 1992 (Brock 1993a).

Western Sandpiper *Calidris mauri* (Cabanis)

Ohio's first Western Sandpiper was a female reported August 10–11, 1914, near North Lima (Mahoning County) (Young 1914). By the 1920s and 1930s, Western Sandpipers were shown to be rare but regular fall migrants, with most reports of three or fewer mixed among flocks of Semipalmated Sandpipers. Trautman's (1940) observation of 12 at Buckeye Lake on September 4, 1929, was remarkable for that era. Their status remained unchanged until the 1970s, when Western Sandpipers were found to be more numerous than previous records indicated.

Their spring status has been obscured by many misidentifications, and their true abundance remains to be determined. Western Sandpipers are apparently casual spring migrants along western Lake Erie and accidental to casual elsewhere in northern and western Ohio. They are unrecorded from the remainder of the state. These migrants are mostly observed as individuals or groups of 2–4. The earliest Western returned to Lucas County on March 30, 1938 (Campbell 1968). Most early April records of Semipalmated Sandpipers probably pertain to Westerns. Most spring Westerns have been reported during the last half of May. A few lingered into the first week of June but none have summered.

As fall migrants, adult Westerns are largely restricted to Lake Erie, with a few sightings from the northern and glaciated central counties. They may return during the first week of July; 20 at Paulding on July 1, 1991, is remarkable anywhere in the state (Harlan 1991b). Most are noted between July 15 and August 7. Juvenile Westerns appear after August 15 and are more widely distributed. Their maximum abundance is normally attained between September 15 and October 15. Most depart by October 27. A few stragglers may remain into November. There are only a few early December records, with the latest at Cleveland through December 14, 1984 (Hannikman 1985).

Fall migrants are most numerous within the northern half of Ohio, particularly along Lake Erie from Huron westward and at reservoirs in the central counties. Westerns are rare to locally fairly common migrants at these locations. Most fall sightings are of 1–15. Along Lake Erie, the largest flocks totaled 75 at Ottawa Wildlife Refuge on September 21, 1986, and 40 at Huron on September 4, 1981 (Peterjohn 1982a, 1987a). Peak inland concentrations were 50 at Hoover Reservoir on September 18, 1982, and 30 at Lake St. Marys on

August 15, 1987 (Peterjohn 1983a, 1988a). Within the southern and unglaciated eastern counties, they are casual to locally uncommon migrants in groups of 1–10.

Red-necked Stint *Calidris ruficollis* (Pallas)

The appearance of this Old World sandpiper is one of the most remarkable sightings in Ohio. An adult Red-necked Stint in breeding plumage was discovered by Jon Ahlquist, Paul Savage, and Ralph Browning at Walnut Beach in Ashtabula on July 21, 1962. Along with a flock of approximately 50 Least and Semipalmated Sandpipers, it remained at the beach until the next day (Ahlquist 1964). It was carefully studied and photographed. When compared with specimens at the National Museum in Washington D.C., the photographs positively eliminated all similar sandpipers.

Red-necked Stints breed in Siberia and northwestern Alaska and normally winter from India east to New Zealand (AOU 1998). Outside Alaska, North American records of Red-necked Stints are limited to a small number of sightings along both coasts. The Ohio sighting provides the only record from the Great Lakes region.

Least Sandpiper *Calidris minutilla* (Vieillot)

Our smallest "peeps" are also among the more numerous of the shorebirds passing through Ohio each spring and autumn. Least Sandpipers are found wherever shorebirds congregate, including flooded fields, drawndown marshes, and mudflats bordering large lakes. They prefer to feed on bare damp mud but also forage in shallow water and on dry mud with sparse vegetation.

The earliest spring migrants are reported during the first week of April, but the first Leasts normally appear between April 23 and 30. Their peak movements are expected May 5–18. Their numbers diminish by May 25, with a few stragglers lingering into early June along Lake Erie.

These migrants are most numerous along western Lake Erie, where they are common to locally abundant during May. Spring totals usually are 10–50, with occasional concentrations of 100–200+. Within the Central Basin, they are uncommon to fairly common migrants and daily totals seldom exceed 15–30. Within the interior counties, spring migrants can be scarce during dry seasons and widely distributed in wet years. Spring Leasts are generally uncommon to fairly common migrants through the glaciated counties. Daily totals are usually 30 or fewer, although concentrations of 70–250+ are infrequently encountered in central and northeastern Ohio. Least Sandpipers are normally casual to rare along the unglaciated Allegheny plateau, where most spring totals are of ten or fewer.

A few nonbreeders have spent the summer along Lake Erie, Buckeye Lake, Lake St. Marys, and at Barberton (Campbell 1968, Clark and Sipe 1970, Peterjohn 1989d, Trautman 1940). They are casually reported along western Lake Erie and accidental elsewhere, mostly as individuals, although small groups of 2–6 have been noted near Toledo (Campbell 1940).

Fall Least Sandpipers are fairly common to abundant migrants along Lake Erie and fairly common to common visitors to inland reservoirs in the glaciated counties. These migrants become rare to locally fairly common in unglaciated eastern Ohio. Along Lake Erie, most fall reports are of 10–50, with occasional concentrations of 75–150+. Larger flocks are restricted to the Western Basin, where 300–500 have infrequently congregated. Within the glaciated counties, most locations support 30 or fewer, with occasional flocks of 50–75. Larger concentrations include 100–200+ in central Ohio on several dates and 300 at Lake St. Marys on September 1, 1910 (Henninger 1911b). In unglaciated eastern Ohio, most fall flocks total 15 or fewer and the largest concentrations seldom exceed 30–40, although as many as 100–125 have been noted.

Along Lake Erie, fall Leasts invariably appear between June 25 and July 4 and become common by July 15–22. They remain numerous through October 5–15. The timing of their fall movement is similar at most inland localities, where they may not become numerous until the last half of August. These flocks are dominated by adults through the first week of August. The first juveniles are expected between July 25 and August 3 and make up the majority of fall migrants after August 10–15. Few adults are found after August 20.

The last fall migrants normally depart between October 25 and November 10. During relatively mild autumns, scattered individuals and small flocks may linger through the end of November and occasionally into December and early January. Along Lake Erie, these early winter records are restricted to a few sightings along the Western Basin. At inland locations, Leasts have been noted through December 3, 1989, in Gallia County (Hall 1990b); December 13, 1953, at Youngstown (Brooks 1954a); December 27, 1957, at Tappan Lake (Harrison County) (Brooks 1958); and January 6, 1985, at C.J. Brown Reservoir (Clark County) (Peterjohn 1985b). Wintering records are restricted to C.J. Brown Reservoir, where four were noted on January 16, 1983, and two were regularly observed through February 13 (Peterjohn 1983b). One observed there on March 9, 1991, was also believed to have wintered locally (Peterjohn 1991c).

White-rumped Sandpiper *Calidris fuscicollis* (Vieillot)

White-rumpeds are among the last sandpipers to pass through Ohio each spring. They may return during the first week of May but frequently do not appear until May 10–15. Their migration peaks between May 18 and June 7. Small flocks and individuals are casually reported through June 20–July 5, but whether these birds are late migrants or nonbreeders is not certain.

Spring White-rumpeds are most numerous along western Lake Erie, where they become uncommon to fairly common in late May. They are mostly observed in flocks of 5–15, with occasional concentrations of 25+. The largest spring flight was noted in 1971, when 200 visited Magee Marsh Wildlife Area on May 23 (Thomson 1983). Considerably fewer pass along the Central Basin, where they are rare migrants in groups of 12 or fewer. Within the interior counties, White-rumpeds may be absent during dry seasons, but when suitable habitats are plentiful they are rare to locally uncommon migrants in the northern and glaciated central counties. These migrants mostly appear in groups of ten or fewer; occasional flocks of 15–25 have been reported. The largest inland concentration totaled 55 in Wayne County on May 17, 1978 (Kleen 1978c). These spring migrants are accidental to casual visitors to the southern and unglaciated counties, mostly in groups of 1–5, with a maximum of 15.

As fall migrants, the first adult White-rumpeds normally return in mid-July and may remain through August 5–15. There are relatively few sightings during the last half of August, and juveniles normally appear during the first week of September. Most juveniles are observed between September 10 and October 15. Stragglers have lingered into the first half of November. One along Lake Erie near Huron on November 24–29, 1984, was exceptionally late (Peterjohn 1985a).

Fall White-rumpeds are rare to locally uncommon migrants along Lake Erie and within the northern and glaciated central counties. Adults are mostly found along Lake Erie in groups of five or fewer. Juveniles are evenly distributed in these counties, mostly in groups of six or fewer, with occasional flocks of 8–25. The largest flocks were detected in the northeastern counties: 40 at Mosquito Creek Reservoir on September 24, 1949, and near Youngstown on October 8, 1950 (Brooks 1950a 1951a). Fall White-rumpeds are accidental to casual migrants in the southern and unglaciated counties, mostly in groups of five or fewer.

Baird's Sandpiper *Calidris bairdii* (Coues)

Although Baird's Sandpipers associate with mixed flocks of "peeps," they seldom join Leasts and Semipalmateds to forage on wet mud or in shallow water. Instead, Baird's prefer to feed on dry mud and exposed flats covered with short vegetation, and may be found on sod farms, golf courses, and recently mowed hayfields.

Within Ohio, Baird's Sandpipers are almost exclusively fall migrants, most numerous along Lake Erie and within the glaciated central and northern counties. They become uncommon to locally fairly common migrants through these localities, mostly in groups of six or fewer, although small flocks of 10–15 periodically appear. The largest reported concentration was 34 at Turtle Creek Wildlife Area on August 19, 1994 (Harlan 1995a). Within the southern and unglaciated counties, they are accidental to locally rare migrants, in groups of four or fewer.

Except for a few sightings of adults during July, primarily along western Lake Erie, nearly all fall records are juveniles. Along Lake Erie, Baird's Sandpipers are very sporadically encountered between July 16 and August 10. Their fall migration normally peaks between August 20 and September 20, and they become rare after October 10. Timing of their inland passage is similar, though there are few confirmed sightings before August 10.

Most Baird's Sandpipers depart by early October, but a few remain later into autumn. Jehl (1979) contends that late fall and early winter records are most likely misidentifications, but growing evidence suggests that Baird's Sandpipers may linger until conditions become unsuitable for foraging. Since 1980, carefully identified Baird's Sandpipers have been noted into November during at least ten years. Combined with sight and specimen records from previous decades, these observations suggest that they may be casual migrants during November, as single individuals associating with other lingering shorebirds. Relatively mild weather allows a few Baird's to remain into early winter. The latest confirmed records are a specimen collected at Cedar Point Wildlife Refuge (Lucas County) on December 16, 1939 (Campbell 1968), and single sandpipers photographed at Huron on December 11, 1979 (Kleen 1980a); Alum Creek Reservoir on December 19–20, 1982; and C.J. Brown Reservoir through January 2, 1983 (Peterjohn 1983b).

This species' status as spring migrants has been obscured by numerous misidentifications. There are no spring records documented by specimens or photographs and very few acceptable sight records, such as one at Lake Rockwell (Portage County) on May 4, 1990 (Peterjohn 1990c). Based on known distribution patterns, these sandpipers are expected to be accidental spring visitors and could appear between the last days of March and mid-May. Whenever a spring Baird's Sandpiper is encountered, it should be thoroughly documented to help establish their spring status.

Pectoral Sandpiper *Calidris melanotos* (Vieillot)

Pectoral Sandpipers are familiar and widely distributed migrants, as likely to appear on flooded farm fields and mudflats bordering inland reservoirs as along Lake Erie. Their spring numbers exhibit considerable annual fluctuations. Large flocks may be regularly encountered across the state, especially during relatively wet seasons. But spring migrants can become scarce in drier seasons.

Spring Pectorals are generally fairly common to abundant migrants, except along central Lake Erie and the unglaciated Allegheny Plateau, where they become uncommon visitors. Within most counties, spring flocks are normally composed of 10–40, with occasional flocks of 100–500. Larger concentrations are most likely to appear in southwestern Wayne County and along western Lake Erie, where as many as 1,000–2,500 have been reported. Along central Lake Erie and the unglaciated counties, few flocks exceed 50.

The earliest spring migrants have returned by February 23–28, but they normally do not to appear until March 20–30. Their northward movements peak during April, although large flocks remain along western Lake Erie into the first week of May. The last Pectorals normally depart by May 15, with a few lingering through May 25–30.

A few nonbreeders have spent part of the summer within Ohio. These accidental summer visitors are primarily restricted to western Lake Erie, where Campbell (1968) reported "several" records—individuals noted for only a few days in mid-June and crippled birds remaining most of the summer. One was also noted at Killdeer Plains Wildlife Area on June 18, 1994 (Brock 1994d).

Fall Pectoral Sandpipers are fairly common to locally abundant migrants along Lake Erie. Flocks of 20–50 are regularly noted, with local concentrations of 100–200. Larger flocks are restricted to Ottawa and Lucas Counties, where 500–1,000+ have occasionally congregated. Within the interior counties, Pectoral Sandpipers are generally uncommon to locally common visitors, least numerous along the unglaciated Allegheny Plateau. Most inland reports are of 50 or fewer but 100–350+ have gathered at favorable habitats. The largest inland fall flock totaled 850 at Killdeer Plains Wildlife Area on August 16, 1991 (Harlan 1992a).

The first fall migrants have been noted during June 26–July 7. They become numerous along Lake Erie by July 15–22 and at most inland areas by August 10–20. While sizable lakefront movements have been evident by late July, the largest statewide concentrations appear during September, when juvenile Pectorals pass through Ohio. Small flocks are regularly noted through the end of October, and the last migrants normally depart by November 10–15. A few stragglers have remained into the first week of December, and there are reports from Christmas Bird Counts at Wooster and along western Lake Erie.

Sharp-tailed Sandpiper *Calidris acuminata* (Horsfield)

Sharp-tailed Sandpipers nest in Siberia and migrate along the western Pacific Ocean to wintering areas in the Southern Hemisphere. Like several other Asian shorebirds, Sharp-taileds have appeared in North America, primarily disoriented juveniles in autumn. These sandpipers regularly appear along the Pacific Coast of the United States and Canada, and occasionally wander into interior North America. A handful of records come from the Great Lakes region and along the Atlantic Coast (AOU 1998).

This accidental visitor has been discovered twice as a fall migrant in Ohio. Larry Rosche discovered a juvenile Sharp-tailed Sandpiper in the Gordon Park impoundment at Cleveland on October 6, 1984. It was banded the following day and remained through October 23 (Peterjohn 1985a). Another juvenile was discovered by John Szanto and Mike Bolton at Metzger Marsh Wildlife Area on December 1–2, 1990, but could not be subsequently relocated (Harlan 1991b).

Purple Sandpiper *Calidris maritima* (Brünnich)

To find these rare visitors to Ohio, one must visit jetties, breakwaters, and rocky shorelines along Lake Erie during late autumn and early winter. With perseverance, one may encounter them as they forage among moss-covered rocks at the water's edge. Because they are normally tame, they may be closely approached. However, Purple Sandpipers are easily overlooked as they search for food among large boulders.

During the nineteenth century, Purple Sandpipers were considered accidental visitors. Since the beginning of the twentieth century, they have proven to be rare fall migrants along the south shore of Lake Erie. They are never numerous and have produced one to eight sightings annually since the late 1960s. Most records are from the Central Basin, especially the Lorain-Cleveland area, where they have been regularly observed since 1916 (Williams 1950). In the Western Basin, they have been periodically encountered since 1943 (Campbell 1968), with most sightings from rocky shores along the western Lake Erie islands.

The earliest migrant was a specimen collected at Cleveland on the exceptional date of September 11, 1883 (Swales 1918). While a few Purple Sandpipers appear as early as mid-October, most pass through Ohio between November 5 and 25. Others appear between December 15 and January 7, corresponding with the freeze-up of inshore habitats along the lake. The latest migrants normally depart by mid-January. Most sightings are of 1–2 individuals, although small flocks of 4–6 are rarely encountered. Purple Sandpipers usually do not associate with other shorebirds, but there are always exceptions.

Certainly the most unusual behavior was exhibited by a Purple Sandpiper associating with a flock of starlings at Cleveland during December 31, 1977, to January 7, 1978. This sandpiper foraged with the starlings along the lakefront and was observed roosting with them on a building on one occasion (Hannikman 1978).

Despite their annual appearance as fall migrants, few Purple Sandpipers winter in Ohio. They are accidental after mid-January, because during most years their preferred habitats become enveloped in a thick layer of ice. Since the 1940s, the six definite wintering records are along the lakefront between Avon Lake and Ashtabula.

Their status during spring is uncertain. Wintering birds have been observed through March 21–22, 1949, at Cleveland and April 17, 1992, at Ashtabula (Harlan 1992c, Williams 1950). Additionally, there are a total of three reports from Lake Erie and Castalia during May (Dister 1995), none of which are supported by adequate documentation.

Accidental away from Lake Erie, there are three documented inland records of Purple Sandpipers during autumn. Single sandpipers were discovered at Ferguson Reservoir near Lima on November 29, 1985 (Peterjohn 1986a), Lake St. Marys on November 12, 1988 (Peterjohn 1989a), and Metzger Reservoir near Lima on November 12–13, 1994 (Dister 1995).

Dunlin *Calidris alpina* (Linnaeus)

A migrant flock of Dunlins presents an impressive spectacle as these sandpipers perform their aerial acrobatics over a flooded field near western Lake Erie. They twist and turn in unison, alternately exhibiting their reddish backs and black belly spots. These maneuvers are regularly observed along western Lake Erie, an important staging area for Dunlins in passage from the Atlantic Coast to Arctic nesting grounds.

Along western Lake Erie, spring Dunlins return as early as the first week of April, although they normally appear during April 15–25. While flocks of 100 or more have been noted by April 6, the largest concentrations are normally encountered between May 5 and 25. When flooded fields or drawndown marshes are available, spring migrants become abundant, and concentrations of 1,000–3,000+ may be observed. When these habitats are scarce, the largest flocks are composed of 100–500. Their numbers are noticeably reduced by the last week of May, although flocks of 100+ have remained into the first week of June.

These large spring flocks do not normally visit other portions of the state. Dunlins are fairly common migrants in small numbers along central Lake Erie, but their appearance within the interior counties is irregular and dependent upon habitat availability. Spring migrants are generally casual to uncommon and locally distributed in the northern and glaciated central counties, becoming accidental to rare in southern and unglaciated Ohio. Away from western Lake Erie, spring Dunlins are normally observed in flocks of 25 or fewer, with occasional concentrations of 35–60. An exceptional 500 appeared in Seneca County in 1984. Timing is similar to the movements along western Lake Erie, but early arrivals have appeared by March 19–22.

Nonbreeders are casual to rare summer visitors along Lake Erie, primarily within the Western Basin (Campbell 1968, Newman 1969), and may appear anytime between mid-June and mid-August. The only inland summer Dunlins have been reported from Lake St. Marys (Clark and Sipe 1970).

Fall Dunlins are widely distributed along the entire lakefront and on mud-flats bordering large reservoirs, generally as fairly common to abundant migrants. Concentrations of 1,000–1,500+ have appeared along western Lake Erie. However, most fall flocks are composed of 50–250 in northern and central Ohio, with occasional congregations of 300–500+. Smaller numbers visit reservoirs in the southern and unglaciated counties, where the largest flocks seldom exceed 25–75.

The first fall migrants normally appear along Lake Erie by September 18–25 and within the interior counties by September 25–October 2. Large flocks are observed by mid-October. Most depart during the last half of November but flocks may infrequently remain into December. The latest flock totaled 225 at Ashtabula on December 27, 1952 (Nolan 1953b). Occasional stragglers and small groups linger into the first week of January, and a few have overwintered during relatively mild winters. Successful wintering attempts include 1–3 in the Toledo area during 1931–1932 (Campbell 1968) and 4–5 at Lorain during 1997–1998 (Rosche 1998a). Others have remained through February 28, 1998, at Pleasant Hill Reservoir (R. Schlabach 1998); February 20, 1960, at Hoover Reservoir (Mumford 1960b); and February 13, 1983, at C. J. Brown Reservoir (Peterjohn 1983b).

Curlew Sandpiper *Calidris ferruginea* (Pontoppidan)

Within North America, Curlew Sandpipers are primarily rare summer residents in Alaska and rare migrants along both coasts. In recent years, a few have also been observed as migrants through the Great Plains and Great Lakes regions (AOU 1998). Ohio's first Curlew Sandpiper was discovered in Thompson Township, Seneca County, on May 16, 1984 (Peterjohn 1984c). Other spring migrants were discovered in Carroll Township, Ottawa County, on May 7–12, 1985 (Peterjohn 1985c), and in Erie County on May 4–7, 1995 (Brock 1995c). Fall migrants have been noted at Cleveland on July 15–19, 1984

(Peterjohn 1984d), and at Ottawa Wildlife Refuge on August 10, 1993 (Brock 1994a). All records were adults in breeding plumage. The spring migrants were associated with large flocks of Dunlins. Fall Curlew Sandpipers should pass through Ohio before Dunlins return.

Stilt Sandpiper *Calidris himantopus* (Bonaparte)

Stilt Sandpipers, greatly reduced by overhunting during the nineteenth century, were very rare throughout Ohio in the early 1900s. With adequate protection, their numbers subsequently improved. By 1940, Stilts became fairly common fall migrants along western Lake Erie (Campbell 1940). Elsewhere, they were regularly encountered at only a few localities in the central and northeastern counties. They became widespread fall migrants within the northern half of Ohio by the early 1960s. Their numbers steadily increased through the 1970s but remained fairly stable after 1980.

Stilt Sandpipers normally pass through the central United States during spring migration. They are not annually recorded from Ohio but are usually observed three years out of four. Spring migrants are casually encountered along Lake Erie, mostly within Ottawa and Lucas Counties. They are also casual spring migrants in central Ohio near Columbus. Spring Stilts are generally accidental elsewhere. The earliest Stilt Sandpiper returned to Seneca County by April 9, 1991 (Peterjohn 1991c). Most are observed during the first three weeks of May and depart by May 25–30. These migrants are normally encountered in groups of seven or fewer.

In most Ohio counties, Stilt Sandpipers are strictly fall migrants, appearing wherever shorebirds congregate. They usually forage in shallow water, wading belly deep and frequently immersing their heads and necks as they probe like dowitchers for invertebrates in the soft mud.

As fall migrants, their numbers vary from year to year, mostly in response to habitat availability. Fall Stilts are most numerous along western Lake Erie, where they are fairly common to common migrants. Although they are normally noted in groups of 30 or fewer, flocks in excess of 50 appear during most years, with a maximum of 200 on July 23, 1994 (Harlan 1995a). They are uncommon to fairly common elsewhere along the lakefront, generally in flocks of 15 or fewer. Concentrations of 40+ are exceptional east of Erie County.

Within the interior of Ohio, Stilt Sandpipers are generally uncommon to fairly common migrants in the northern and glaciated central counties. They become casual to locally uncommon in the southwestern and unglaciated counties. Inland totals are normally ten or fewer daily, with occasional flocks of 20–40. By far the largest inland concentration was 150 at Killdeer Plains Wildlife Area during September 9–17, 1983 (Peterjohn 1984a).

While the first fall migrants may return to western Lake Erie by July 1, they are not regularly encountered along the lakefront until July 10–17. The largest concentrations usually occur in August and early September. These migrants are largely adult Stilts through the first week of August; juveniles become prevalent by the third week of the month. At inland localities, adult Stilts are rarely encountered; most sightings are of juveniles after mid-August. Throughout Ohio, most Stilts depart by October 12–22, although 15 remained at Hoover Reservoir until October 23, 1984. Occasional stragglers have lingered through November 5–10, and an injured bird survived until November 23, 1997, at C.J. Brown Reservoir (Fazio 1998).

Buff-breasted Sandpiper *Tryngites subruficollis* (Vieillot)

A highlight of the fall shorebird migration is the appearance of this attractive bird, which often acts more like a plover than a sandpiper. Buff-breasteds generally avoid the shoreline mudflats preferred by most other sandpipers in favor of dry fields, golf courses, sod farms, and dried mud covered with short vegetation. Their buff-colored plumage provides surprisingly good camouflage against a background of dried mud or dead grasses, and Buff-breasteds are easily overlooked as they quietly forage.

As fall migrants, Buff-breasted Sandpipers are generally rare in northern Ohio, most frequently recorded near Lake Erie. They are also rare fall visitors to drawndown reservoirs near Columbus. They are casual to accidental migrants through the other counties. The earliest fall migrants have been noted during July 30–August 7 but these early arrivals are very rare. Most Buff-breasted Sandpipers are juveniles appearing between the last week of August and late September. Only a few stragglers remain into the first week of October; an exceptionally late migrant lingered at Cleveland through October 24–28, 1981 (Peterjohn 1982a), and an injured bird frequented Lake St. Marys until November 4–5, 1989 (Peterjohn 1990a). Buff-breasteds are generally recorded at six or fewer localities most years, although they occasionally produce twelve or more statewide sightings. Most reports are of 1–3, with occasional groups of 6–7. Flocks of 15–22 are very infrequent; most have been noted in northeastern Ohio. By far the largest flock totaled 78 in a mowed clover field in Ottawa County on September 12, 1985 (Peterjohn 1986a).

Buff-breasteds have always been rare migrants. While they were fairly regularly recorded near Toledo during the 1920s and 1930s (Campbell 1940), there were relatively few sightings elsewhere until the 1950s and 1960s. These greater numbers may reflect increased populations or increased efforts to locate this attractive shorebird.

In spring, Buff-breasteds are normally restricted to a migration corridor through the Great Plains. They are accidental anywhere east of the Mississippi River. There are only two documented spring records from Ohio. A flock of seven was discovered near Harpster, Wyandot County, on June 11, 1966, and observed at close range for nearly twenty minutes as they fed in a plowed field (Phillips 1967). One was found near Barberton (Summit County) on May 28, 1990 (Peterjohn 1990c).

Ruff *Philomachus pugnax* (Linnaeus)

Ohio's first record of this Eurasian shorebird was a specimen taken at Buckeye Lake on November 10, 1872 (Wheaton 1877). Another specimen was secured from the same area on April 28, 1878 (Borror 1950). No other Ruffs were recorded until one appeared along western Lake Erie near Toledo on August 1, 1956 (Campbell 1968). This sighting signaled a change in their relative abundance, since there were at least five reports during the 1960s, eight records in the 1970s, twelve in the 1980s, and thirteen in the 1990s.

The earliest spring Ruffs appeared by March 27–April 3, but there are few April records. Most northward migrants are detected during May, with sightings as late as May 23–28. Of twenty-four spring records, twelve are from western Lake Erie, where Ruffs have become casual visitors. They are accidental spring migrants elsewhere, with five records from central Ohio, an equal number of sightings in Wayne County, and single reports from Seneca County and Cleveland. Spring observations have been of single individuals except during 1985 when at least three Ruffs were discovered in Ottawa County between May 4 and 11 (Peterjohn 1985c). The majority of these sightings are of males in their distinctive breeding plumages.

The earliest fall Ruff returned to Killdeer Plains Wildlife Area on June 27, 1982 (Peterjohn 1982d). Most fall migrants have been noted during August and September, with only two October records from western Lake Erie and the November 10 specimen from Buckeye Lake. Ruffs are casual fall migrants in the vicinity of Lake Erie east to Huron, with at least thirteen published records. They are accidental fall visitors elsewhere, with single documented records from Dayton, Buckeye Lake, Killdeer Plains, and Cleveland. All fall sightings have been of single individuals.

Short-billed Dowitcher *Limnodromus griseus* (Gmelin)

At one time, dowitchers were classified as one species. Their identification was straightforward and their status was well defined. The splitting of dowitchers into Short-billed and Long-billed species posed serious identification problems. As a result, there have been many misidentifications, and the status of both species within Ohio was obscured until the 1970s.

Spring Short-billeds generally arrive later than Long-billeds. The earliest reported arrivals are April 12–14, but Short-billeds normally appear during the first week of May. This movement peaks between May 7 and 23. While stragglers linger along Lake Erie through June 10, none have summered.

Spring Short-billeds are most numerous along western Lake Erie, where they are fairly common to abundant migrants. During some years, the largest flocks are composed of 30–40 dowitchers; 100–300+ may congregate in other springs. Short-billeds are rare to uncommon spring migrants along central Lake Erie, mostly as flocks of 15 or fewer. Their appearance within the interior counties is related to habitat availability, with the largest numbers discovered during relatively wet seasons. They are casual to locally uncommon migrants through the northern and glaciated central counties. While most records are of 20 or fewer, flocks of 50–150 occasionally appear. In the southern and unglaciated counties, they are accidental to casual migrants. Most sightings are of 1–6, although as many as 40 have been reported near Cincinnati.

Fall migrants regularly appear along Lake Erie during June 27–July 4. By July 10–15, they are common to abundant along western Lake Erie and fairly common to common elsewhere along the lakefront. The largest concentrations appear in Ottawa and Lucas Counties, with 6,400 at Winous Point on July 20, 1982 (Peterjohn 1982d); 1,500 at Magee Marsh Wildlife Area on July 9, 1983 (Peterjohn 1983d); and 1,500 at Turtle Creek Wildlife Area on July 23, 1994 (Harlan 1995a). Most reports total 30–200 along western Lake Erie and 10–75+ within the Central Basin. July migrants are exclusively adults; they are replaced by juveniles during the first half of August. While Short-billeds remain fairly common to common along Lake Erie through September 15, flocks seldom exceed 50–300 along western Lake Erie and 5–40 within the Central Basin during August and September. Most depart by September 25–30, with a few lingering into early October. The latest fall migrant was a juvenile in Erie County on October 22, 1988 (Peterjohn 1989a).

Within the interior counties, adult Short-billed Dowitchers have appeared as early as June 30, but there are relatively few reports until the first half of August, when the juveniles normally appear. Inland Short-billeds are mostly observed between August 10 and September 15. A late Short-billed lingered at Lake St. Marys through October 12, 1986 (Peterjohn 1987a), but there are very few confirmed sightings after October 1. As along Lake Erie, inland October dowitchers are most likely Long-billeds.

Fall Short-billeds are rare to locally fairly common migrants through the northern and glaciated central counties. Most sightings are of 20 or fewer, but 136 were at Hoover Reservoir on September 17, 1974 (Thomson 1983), and 75 at Barberton on July 26, 1985. They are accidental to locally uncommon fall migrants through the southern and unglaciated counties, mostly in groups of 12 or fewer.

The vast majority of Ohio sightings pertain to the *hendersoni* race, which regularly migrates across the interior of North America (AOU 1957). Dowitchers showing characteristics of the *griseus* race have been reported from Metzger Marsh Wildlife Area (Lucas County) on May 23, 1992, and May 17, 1995 (Harlan 1992c, 1995c). This race normally migrates along the Atlantic Coast, and has been reported on very few occasions from the interior of North America.

Long-billed Dowitcher *Limnodromus scolopaceus* (Say)

The status of Long-billed Dowitchers in Ohio was also obscured by identification problems. Since the 1970s, our ability to distinguish them from Short-billed Dowitchers has improved tremendously and produced an understanding of the Long-billed's distribution and migration patterns across the state.

Spring Long-billed Dowitchers tend to migrate earlier than Short-billeds, appearing as early as March 8, 1987, in Seneca County (Peterjohn 1987c). Most records are scattered between March 20 and April 30. A few Long-billeds have been reliably identified along Lake Erie during the first week of May. Hence, most Long-billeds depart before the Short-billeds arrive.

Spring Long-billeds are accidental to casual migrants throughout the state. They are not regularly observed at any locality but are usually detected at one to three locations during most years. They are most likely to appear near Lake Erie but have been noted in all portions of Ohio except the unglaciated counties. Most spring reports are of 1–3 Long-billeds.

As fall migrants, Long-billed Dowitchers are considerably more numerous along western Lake Erie in Ottawa and Lucas Counties than in the remainder of the state. The first adults may return by July 20–30 but most appear in August. As many as 100 have been noted at Metzger Marsh Wildlife Area by the first week of August, and these numbers may increase to 250–400+ by the end of the month. These adults undergo their postbreeding molt along western Lake Erie, and usually remain through late September or early October. Juvenile Long-billeds have returned as early as August 28 but are not expected until September 7–15. A flock of 90 juveniles at Ottawa Wildlife Refuge on September 10, 1983, was exceptionally early, because they normally appear in numbers during October. The largest October concentrations normally total 100–350+. These numbers are substantially reduced by November 15. The last Long-billeds usually depart by November 20–25, with late migrants through December 7.

Long-billed Dowitchers are rare fall migrants elsewhere along Lake Erie. There are very few records of adults during late July and August. Juveniles are usually observed between September 20 and November 7 in groups of five or fewer. A few late migrants have lingered into early December.

Away from Lake Erie, Long-billeds are accidental to locally rare fall migrants. Most sightings are of 1–5 juveniles in the western half of Ohio between September 20 and November 7. A few migrants remain later in the month. The largest inland flock totaled 16 at Big Island Wildlife Area on October 27, 1984.

Common Snipe *Gallinago gallinago* (Linnaeus)

Common Snipe

Common Snipes occupy marshes, bogs, wet meadows, and ditches, where they can readily take refuge in dense vegetation. Their subtly patterned plumage provides excellent camouflage as they quietly probe in the soft mud for worms and other invertebrates. When approached, snipes frequently crouch over the mud, relying on their cryptic coloration to hide them from predators. Should danger approach too closely, they flush with an explosive takeoff followed by a rapid zigzagging flight.

During spring migration, snipes are common to abundant within the marshes bordering western Lake Erie. Tallies of 20–50 daily are regular and flights of 75–100+ appear most years. The largest movements total 150–235. Their spring movements are more erratic elsewhere. Snipes are fairly common to locally abundant migrants through all glaciated counties. Spring totals are usually 5–25 daily, with occasional concentrations of 40–75. Larger flights produce 100–125 in central Ohio and 150–200 in the southwestern counties. Fewer pass through the unglaciated Allegheny Plateau, where they are uncommon to fairly common migrants and daily totals are usually 15 or fewer, with maximum counts of 30–65.

Throughout Ohio, the first spring migrants normally return between March 5 and 15. Common Snipes are most numerous between March 25 and April 30. They depart from most interior counties by May 10–15. A few late migrants may linger along western Lake Erie through May 20–25.

While most Common Snipes silently pass through Ohio each spring, a few males undertake their spectacular courtship displays, flying in endless large circles high over a marsh. As they dive through the air, the wind vibrates their outer tail feathers to produce a diagnostic low booming sound. A single snipe may display for an hour or longer, providing a spectacular show witnessed too infrequently in Ohio.

These displaying males are normally migrants, but on rare occasions, Common Snipes have summered and nested. These summering snipes continue their courtship displays well into June. The few nests with eggs have been reported between April 28 and May 30, and adults accompanied by partially grown chicks have been noted through July 11 (Baker 1946, Campbell 1968, Hicks 1933a). Common Snipes establish their summer territories in marshes and wet meadows composed of grasses, sedges, and rushes. Except for displaying males, snipes are very secretive during summer. Their nests are nearly impossible to find, cleverly concealed on the ground in dense cover.

A small summering population has always existed in northeastern Ohio. Hicks (1933a) recorded snipes from twelve Ashtabula County locations, including 16 pairs in the former Pymatuning Bog. Summering snipes were sporadically encountered in Trumbull, Mahoning, and Portage Counties before 1935 (Hicks 1935a). Habitat destruction reduced this population by the early 1930s. Common Snipes are now casual to rare summer residents in northeastern Ohio south to Portage, Summit, and Columbiana Counties (Peterjohn and Rice 1991). They are reported from three or fewer locations during most years, and the entire population may total only 5–10 pairs. Snipes are also rare summer residents in the Oak Openings area of Lucas County, where one to three pairs are present during most years (Peterjohn and Rice 1991). Their current status in the western Lake Erie marshes is uncertain. They were formerly rare summer residents (Campbell 1968, 1973), but none were detected during the Breeding Bird Atlas and this population may have disappeared (Peterjohn and Rice 1991). They are accidental summer visitors elsewhere in northern Ohio, where nesting was confirmed near Cleveland in 1963 and Lorain County in 1967 and 1978 (Flanigan 1968, Petersen 1967c). Common Snipes are accidental nonbreeding summer visitors within the central counties. They have summered in Tuscarawas and Carroll Counties, where nesting is suspected but was never proved (Buchanan 1980, Peterjohn and Rice 1991). A few additional June records from other central counties may have been migrants.

As fall migrants, snipes occupy the same wetlands favored during spring, although a few join other shorebirds on mudflats. Their southward migration may begin by July 7–10 within the northern and central counties. However, the first migrants are normally expected during July 20–August 10. Their maximum abundance is normally attained between September 15 and October 25, although flocks may appear throughout November. Most depart by mid-December. These migrants are most numerous within the western Lake Erie marshes, where they are fairly common to locally abundant. Fall totals are usually 5–25 daily, with occasional concentrations of 30–60. As many as 100–150+ have been encountered on a few occasions. Elsewhere, snipes are uncommon to locally common migrants. Most reports are of 12 or fewer, with infrequent concentrations of 30–90+. These migrants are widely distributed within the glaciated counties but are scarce along the unglaciated Allegheny Plateau.

Subfreezing temperatures force most Common Snipes to depart for warmer climates. Small numbers winter along ditches and at springs where open water is always available. Snipes are rare winter residents within the southern and central counties and casual to rare in northern Ohio. Most sightings are of individuals, with occasional flocks of 4–6. Mild weather has enticed as many as 10–17 to remain into January.

Eurasian Woodcock *Scolopax rusticola* Linnaeus

This accidental visitor to North America is mostly known from nineteenth-century specimens from New England and eastern Canada. Outside this region, Eurasian Woodcocks have been reported only from Alabama and Ohio (AOU 1998). The Ohio record is one of very few during the twentieth century. On November 6, 1935, G. F. Dixon shot an unusually large woodcock along the banks of a stream in Newbury Township, Geauga County. He also shot several American Woodcocks that day, which were noticeably smaller. After reading an account of this exceptional woodcock in a local newspaper, John Aldrich of the Cleveland Museum of Natural History examined the remains of the bird. He obtained an incomplete skeleton, lacking head, wings, and feet, and noted that the bird's weight was ten ounces compared with five to seven ounces for a typical American Woodcock. After comparing the skeletal material with American Woodcock bones, Aldrich concluded the bird was a Eurasian Woodcock, an identification corroborated by Harry Oberholser (Aldrich 1936).

This skeletal material was deposited in the Cleveland Museum of Natural History, but is no longer present in the museum's collections and its whereabouts are unknown. The identification of these remains can be questioned, since these bones were never directly compared with bones from Eurasian Woodcocks. Additionally, Aldrich was unable to examine any plumage characteristics, as well as the head and bill and other features that would have confirmed that the bird was a woodcock and not some other species of shorebird. Until the skeletal material can be relocated, the occurrence of Eurasian Woodcock in Ohio cannot be conclusively established at this time.

American Woodcock *Scolopax minor* Gmelin

As darkness approaches each March evening, "peenting" noises are produced by unseen birds in abandoned fields, woodland edges, and other brushy habitats across Ohio. While the sound resembles the call of a nighthawk, March is much too early for that species. Instead, these noises are produced by courting male American Woodcocks. The "peenting" calls are associated with their courtship dance, performed on patches of short grass or bare soil. After the dance is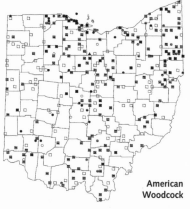

American
Woodcock

completed, the male takes flight, spiraling upward in ever smaller circles, with his stiff outer primaries producing a unique twittering sound. Higher and higher he flies until he passes from sight. After reaching his zenith, he quickly descends, with his spiraling flight producing a different but equally diagnostic set of twittering notes as the wind rushes through his wings. He lands at the same location from which he departed, only to repeat these displays until darkness falls.

These courtship displays can be regularly witnessed, for American Woodcocks are fairly common to locally common spring migrants in most counties. These migrants are widely distributed in the eastern third of the state, especially the northeastern counties near Lake Erie, but become scarce in intensively cultivated western Ohio. Most reports are of eight or fewer, with occasional concentrations of 12–18. Larger flights are unusual, although 40–50 have been reported near Columbus and 100+ in northeastern Ohio.

Spring woodcocks invariably return with the first warm days of February and early March. This early migration is not without risks. Deep snow cover and prolonged subfreezing temperatures can cause considerable mortality. Migrants may appear during the first half of February in mild winters, but are normally expected between February 20 and March 5. Peak numbers are expected between March 10 and 30 and the last migrants depart by April 10–15.

The courtship displays are continued by resident males into May or June. A courting male was reported as late as July 14 at Cincinnati (Kemsies and Randle 1953). Their nesting activities begin by mid-March in central Ohio and late March within the northern counties (Trautman 1940, Williams 1950). These early nests are abandoned if inclement weather returns. Most woodcock nests are discovered during April; clutches through mid-June probably represent renesting attempts. Later clutches are restricted to Ashtabula County, where Hicks (1933a) cited three July records and hatching eggs on August 7, 1928. Downy young woodcocks have been discovered by the first week of April. Most appear between mid-April and mid-May (Trautman 1940). The earliest broods fledge by late June, but others are noted into early August.

Breeding woodcocks prefer damp brushy fields, woodland edges, open moist woods, and the brushy margins of ponds. Their nests are also reported from orchards, patches of grass between fences, steep grassy banks planted with pines, and oat fields (Braund 1939a). Incubating females rely on their cryptic plumage to avoid detection, and allow a very close approach before flushing.

Woodcocks have been widely distributed summer residents since 1900, when Jones (1903) regarded them as fairly common in most counties. Hicks (1935a) cited summer records from eighty-four counties, with the greatest numbers in northeastern, southeastern, and central Ohio. Woodcocks were very local in most western counties. Their breeding populations declined in subsequent decades as a result of habitat loss (Straw et al. 1994).

Despite these declines, American Woodcocks remain widely distributed summer residents and were recorded from eighty-six counties during the Breeding Bird Atlas (Peterjohn and Rice 1991). They are generally fairly common residents in northeastern Ohio. They become uncommon to fairly common along the unglaciated Allegheny Plateau and in most southwestern and central counties. Breeding woodcocks are uncommon to fairly common from the Oak Openings area of Lucas and Fulton Counties eastward across northern Ohio, but are generally rare to uncommon in other west-central and northwestern counties. Most reports are of ten or fewer daily. Their movement patterns are fairly complex. Once the males abandon their territories, they may wander widely. Young woodcocks may also move considerable distances after fledging. Individuals may appear anytime during July or August at locations where they did not nest.

Woodcocks are less conspicuous during autumn and are more often encountered by hunters than birders. Southward migrants may appear by late August and are widely noted during the last half of September (Trautman 1940). The largest numbers are expected during October, when woodcocks become uncommon to fairly common migrants, most numerous within the northeastern counties. Most fall reports are of 1–5 daily. Large flights are possible; Hicks (1933a) recorded 100+ in Ashtabula County on twelve occasions during the 1920s and early 1930s. In recent years, the largest flight totaled 50 at Cincinnati on October 15, 1979 (Kleen 1980a). They are regularly observed through mid-November.

A few woodcocks may remain until they are forced southward by extended subfreezing temperatures. There are occasional sightings through December 15–25, but American Woodcocks are accidental visitors after January 1. The few midwinter records include a courting male at Cincinnati on January 16 (no year provided—Austing and Imbrogno 1976); one in Washington County on January 23, 1996 (Harlan 1996b); a wintering bird in Westerville (Franklin County) on February 13–21, 1985 (Peterjohn 1985b); and one near Mt. Vernon on January 14, 1999 (R. Schlabach 1999a).

Wilson's Phalarope *Phalaropus tricolor* (Vieillot)

Wilson's Phalaropes were not always regular migrants through Ohio. Their numbers were decimated during the 1880s, and these phalaropes were exceptionally rare in the early 1900s (Jones 1903). Their status did not improve until the 1930s. Campbell (1940) considered them "fairly regular but not numerous" migrants at Toledo, with 14 recorded between 1931 and 1936. Away from western Lake Erie, they remained accidental migrants until the 1950s and 1960s, when small numbers were regularly encountered in most portions of Ohio during fall migration. Their numbers increased during the 1970s, reaching a peak between 1978 and 1983. This increase corresponded with an eastward expansion of their breeding range. Numbers of migrants have declined somewhat since 1983.

Spring Wilson's Phalaropes are most numerous along western Lake Erie, where they are rare to uncommon migrants, usually in groups of six or fewer. An exceptional flight produced 47 at Magee Marsh Wildlife Area on May 10, 1978 (Kleen 1978c). Elsewhere in the western half of Ohio and along central Lake Erie, they are casual to rare, in groups of three or fewer, with a maximum of ten at Cincinnati on May 6–8, 1978 (Kleen 1978c). They become accidental in eastern Ohio. The earliest spring migrants appear by April 10–15, but there are few April records. Most are noted between May 7 and 21, with stragglers through June 3–7.

Fall Wilson's Phalaropes are also most numerous along western Lake Erie, where they have become uncommon migrants since 1990. Daily counts usually total six or fewer, with maxima of 10–14. Between 1978 and 1983, concentrations of 20–35 occasionally frequented suitable habitats in Ottawa and Lucas Counties. They are now rare migrants in groups of six or fewer along central Lake Erie. Adult Wilson's are normally noted along the lakefront between June 25 and July 20 but are replaced by juveniles during the last half of July. Largest concentrations develop between August 1 and September 7. The last migrants normally depart by September 25–October 7. Two exceptionally late phalaropes were documented from Toledo on November 20, 1987 (Peterjohn 1988a).

At inland localities, Wilson's Phalaropes are rare fall migrants in central Ohio but accidental to casual elsewhere and least numerous in the unglaciated counties. They are normally encountered as scattered individuals, mostly juveniles between July 20 and September 25. The latest fall records include singles documented from Lake St. Marys on November 7, 1982, and Pickerington (Franklin County) on December 4, 1981 (Peterjohn 1982b, 1983a).

Their recent eastward range expansion produced breeding records east to New England (AOU 1988), and was responsible for Ohio's only confirmed nesting attempt. During June 1980, two female and at least two male Wilson's Phalaropes nested at Magee Marsh Wildlife Area in Ottawa County. A nest with four eggs was discovered on June 4, but these eggs disappeared by June 20. Another male and at least two young were located on June 22 (Shieldcastle 1980). One pair summered in the wildlife area during 1981 but nesting was not established (Peterjohn 1981d). A possible nesting attempt at Ottawa National Wildlife Refuge during June 1988 was never confirmed (Peterjohn and Rice 1991). There were several additional mid-June records from northern Ohio, but these adults were probably very early fall migrants.

Red-necked Phalarope *Phalaropus lobatus* (Linnaeus)

Numbers of Red-necked Phalaropes markedly increased during the twentieth century. Before 1930, they were accidental visitors, with no more than six sightings from the entire state (Campbell 1938). The number of records increased during the 1930s, when Trautman (1935a) claimed they were "not as rare as generally supposed." This trend continued into the 1940s, generally as sporadic appearances of widely scattered fall migrants. The first sizable fall movement was near Youngstown, where a maximum of 23 appeared on September 5, 1949 (Brooks 1950a). This flight was not evident elsewhere and was not repeated during the next two decades. These phalaropes were casual fall migrants during the 1950s, and did not become annual visitors until the early 1960s. That decade produced regular observations of 1–6 phalaropes each autumn and occasional spring migrants. Additional increases were apparent in the 1970s, and small flights were detected during several autumns. Their status has not changed since 1980.

Red-necked Phalaropes are casual to rare spring migrants along western Lake Erie, with one to three sightings most years, usually of four or fewer, with a maximum of 8. They are accidental to casual spring visitors to the northern and glaciated central counties, producing four to seven records each decade. Most sightings involve one or two phalaropes, with a maximum of eight near Barberton between May 27 and June 1, 1986 (Peterjohn 1986c). They are unrecorded from southwestern and unglaciated Ohio. Their northward passage is normally very rapid; many remain for only a few minutes or hours. The earliest confirmed migrants appear by May 7–10. They are most likely to be observed between May 15 and 25. Few linger into June, although there are records as late as June 11, 1938, from central Ohio and June 11, 1992, from Paulding County (Borror 1950, Harlan 1992d).

As fall migrants, Red-necked Phalaropes are scarce some years, with only a few scattered individuals along Lake Erie and none inland. Other years produce scattered records across the state. Small flights occur during one to three years each decade, producing small flocks along Lake Erie and four to nine inland reports.

Fall migrants are rare to uncommon along Lake Erie, most numerous within the Western Basin. Most reports are of six or fewer on exposed sand bars, dredge disposal areas, and drawndown marshes. Flights produce flocks of 21–26 along western Lake Erie and 10–11 at Cleveland. Away from Lake Erie, Red-necked Phalaropes are casual to rare fall visitors within the northern and glaciated central counties, most likely to appear near Columbus and at northeastern lakes. Except for the 1949 flight at Youngstown, the largest inland flocks totaled 11 at Mosquito Creek Lake on September 8, 1945, and ten at Lima on August 29, 1974 (Kleen 1975a, Williams 1950). Most reports are of three or fewer. These phalaropes are accidental to casual fall visitors to the southwestern counties and along the unglaciated Allegheny Plateau, with only two or three sightings each decade of 1–4 individuals.

The earliest fall migrants return to western Lake Erie during the last half of July. They usually appear between August 10 and 20 and most are observed through October 7. A few stragglers have been reliably reported into the first week of November; later reports most likely refer to misidentified Red Phalaropes. At inland localities, Red-neckeds return by August 10–15 but most are observed between August 25 and September 25. A few linger until October 15–20.

There are no acceptable winter Red-necked Phalarope records from Ohio. Reports of single Red-neckeds from Toledo and Cleveland during January were accompanied by insufficient details to positively eliminate Red Phalaropes. Their appearance at this time of year is very unlikely.

Red Phalarope *Phalaropus fulicaria* (Linnaeus)

Along Lake Erie, Red Phalaropes are usually discovered in the relatively quiet waters along piers, breakwaters, and harbors. Few are found on the open waters of the lake, where they are easily overlooked. At inland localities, Reds occur mostly along shorelines rather than the open waters of reservoirs.

Before 1940, Red Phalaropes were accidental visitors, with only ten published records, all along Lake Erie and in the central counties near Columbus (Campbell 1938, Trautman 1940). There were few additional records into the 1960s. Since 1965, this phalarope has been annually recorded, a result of more thorough coverage by birdwatchers along Lake Erie and inland reservoirs during the late autumn months when this species is most likely to occur.

Red Phalaropes are now rare fall migrants along central Lake Erie and casual to rare visitors to the Western Basin. During most years, there are two to four reports scattered along the lakefront. Once or twice each decade, small flights develop and as many as ten sightings may occur. All substantiated reports are of 1–3 Reds; an undocumented flock of 30+ during mid-September seems very questionable. Exceptionally early fall Reds appeared at Cleveland on August 27, 1981, and September 3, 1982 (Peterjohn 1982a, 1983a). The first migrants normally appear during September 20–30. Individuals may be noted during October and November, but most are discovered between November 10 and 25. Fall migration continues into the first half of December.

Away from the lakefront, these phalaropes are casual fall visitors near Columbus, averaging two or three sightings each decade. They are accidental fall visitors elsewhere, with at least eleven records scattered across the glaciated counties. The only record from the unglaciated Allegheny Plateau is a specimen collected in Jefferson County on September 15, 1945 (Buchanan 1947). Inland reports are usually of single phalaropes, although three appeared near Buckeye Lake on September 27, 1968 (Thomson 1983). Most are detected between September 12 and October 15, with a few through November 15.

While Reds are the hardiest phalaropes, most eventually depart for the Atlantic Coast. The last sightings occur as the lake freezes between December 25 and January 7. While a few have lingered into late January, there is only one record of an overwintering Red Phalarope: at Cleveland from January 1 through March 31, 1955 (Newman 1969).

Red Phalaropes are strictly accidental spring visitors. March records are limited to the overwintering phalarope at Cleveland and one at Mosquito Creek Wildlife Area (Trumbull County) on March 15, 1983. This phalarope was exceptionally early and may have overwintered in the Great Lakes area (Peterjohn 1983c). Other spring records are single phalaropes at Wright-Patterson Air Force Base near Dayton on May 2–6, 1953 (Rogers 1955); Bresler Reservoir near Lima on May 12, 1976 (Kleen 1976c); and Cleveland on May 22, 1977 (Kleen 1977c).

Pomarine Jaeger *Stercorarius pomarinus* (Temminck)

Jaegers pose some of the most difficult identification challenges of all North American birds. While most adult jaegers can be readily identified, immatures of all three species exhibit considerable variability in their plumages. There are few characteristics that consistently separate them. Even experts regularly disagree over the identity of immature jaegers, and it is not unusual to have a single individual accused of being all three species.

Very few adult jaegers appear in Ohio, and many sightings of immatures are based on less than satisfactory evidence. The few specimen records provide only fragmentary data. Hence, our understanding of their status is poor, although observations during the 1990s have helped to define the timing of their fall movements and relative abundance. As our ability to identify immature jaegers improves, future observations may alter our current understanding of their status in Ohio.

Pomarine Jaegers are casual to rare fall migrants along Lake Erie, with the majority of reports from the Central Basin. Five or fewer individuals are reported during most years, but flights in 1988 and 1996 produced totals of 15–20 scattered along the lakefront (Brock 1997a, Peterjohn 1989a). Most records are of single jaegers, but small flights occasionally produce groups of 3–4. While adults have been reported during August, immature Pomarines tend to migrate later than the other jaegers and are unlikely to appear before mid-October. Most acceptable reports are during November and December.

Pomarines are accidental fall visitors away from Lake Erie. The only confirmed inland records are an immature collected at Lake St. Marys on October 17, 1964 (Clark and Sipe 1970), and another at East Fork State Park (Clermont County) during October 30–November 15, 1999 (Whan, in press). Single Pomarines were reported from Lake St. Marys on October 15, 1966, and at Lake Rockwell (Portage County) on September 30, 1973, but substantiating details are unconvincing.

Because Pomarines have the most northerly winter distribution of all jaegers, they are the species most likely to appear on the Great Lakes after mid-December. However, any winter jaeger should be identified on the basis of its characteristics and not assumed to be a Pomarine. A few have lingered along Lake Erie into January during mild winters, but these jaegers usually depart by January 15–25. The only indication of Pomarines wintering in Ohio is an adult and an immature discovered at Fairport Harbor (Lake County) on February 28, 1998 (Rosche 1998a).

Pomarine Jaegers are accidental spring visitors to Lake Erie, where the two reports are from the Cleveland area. In 1997, up to five immatures were noted at Cleveland between April 10 and May 10 (Rosche 1997b). The other record was provided by the winter birds at Fairport Harbor, where the adult was observed through April 5, 1998 (Brock 1998c).

The only summer record is provided by a subadult discovered on a farm field near Fresno (Coshocton County) on June 22, 1999. It was observed and photographed as it rested during the evening of a warm, clear day, but departed by the next morning (Troyer 2000).

Parasitic Jaeger *Stercorarius parasiticus* (Linnaeus)

If sight records were accurate, Parasitics would be the most numerous autumn jaegers along Lake Erie. It is not safe, however, to assume that any fall jaeger is a Parasitic. Instead, all jaegers should be carefully identified to obtain a more accurate understanding of the migration patterns and relative abundance of the three species.

Like many birds largely restricted to Lake Erie, Parasitic Jaegers were more regularly observed since 1980 than during previous decades, probably a result of more thorough coverage by birdwatchers. Before 1980, they were considered accidental to casual fall migrants along the entire lakefront, averaging two to four sightings per decade. Campbell (1968) cited six Toledo area records between 1931 and 1968. Williams (1950) and Newman (1969) reported a similar number from the Cleveland area, except in 1945 when as many as three were observed "almost daily" between October 2 and December 8 (Williams 1950). The continuous sightings suggested that a considerable number of jaegers were involved in this flight.

Since 1980, Parasitic Jaegers have been observed annually along Lake Erie, with one to six sightings every autumn. The only recent flight occurred in 1996, when at least 16 were reported along the entire lakefront (Brock 1997a). These sightings indicate that Parasitics are rare fall migrants through the Central Basin and casual visitors to the Western Basin. All recent records have been of 1–3 jaegers, most of them briefly observed in migration. While migrants have been reported as early as July 26, these early sightings have not been adequately documented. Confirmed Parasitics have appeared during the last half of August; the majority of Lake Erie sight records are in September, with another peak in November. A few have been reported during the first half of December, but their status in December remains to be positively determined. Single immatures in the Cleveland area on January 11 and 12, 1997, provide the only documented winter records (Brock 1997b). They are accidental fall migrants away from Lake Erie. The only confirmed inland record is a specimen collected at Buckeye Lake on September 2, 1919 (Trautman 1940).

The only spring record is a specimen recovered from a field near Lebanon (Warren County) in "late March or early April" 1880. This specimen now resides in the Cincinnati Museum of Natural History. Jones (1903) indicates that this jaeger appeared "after a week of stormy weather," but no other details are available concerning its presence at this time of the year.

Long-tailed Jaeger *Stercorarius longicaudus* Vieillot

The rarest jaegers to appear along the Great Lakes, Long-taileds are also the most difficult to identify. Some immature Long-taileds are very similar to immature Parasitics and their positive identification requires careful study at close range, while other immature Long-taileds are more easily identified in the field. The Long-tailed's fall migration tends to be slightly earlier than the movements of the other species, primarily in August and September, when few observers are searching for jaegers.

Long-tailed Jaegers are accidental visitors to Ohio. The initial confirmed records were specimens of immatures obtained during autumn. Ohio's first Long-tailed Jaeger was collected at Buckeye Lake on September 5, 1928 (Trautman 1940). The second was an injured jaeger discovered along a rural road near Ashtabula on October 18, 1956; it died in captivity (Novotny 1961). The third was a sick jaeger found in a residential yard in Parma on September 13, 1960. It too died in captivity (Newman 1969).

Between 1989 and 1999, there were a total of six documented sight records of Long-tailed Jaegers from Lorain to Headlands Beach State Park in the Central Basin of Lake Erie. All sightings were of single immatures between the dates of September 2 and 23 (Brock 1996a, Hannikman 1992, Harlan 1995b, Metcalf 1998). Advances in the field identification of immature jaegers have contributed to the increased number of recent reports from central Lake Erie. These reports may indicate that Long-tailed Jaegers are more regular migrants across the Great Lakes than the earlier records indicate.

Laughing Gull *Larus atricilla* Linnaeus

Laughing Gulls are very common and widely distributed residents along the Gulf of Mexico and the Atlantic Ocean north to Maine (AOU 1998). Before 1950, only a few wandered into the interior of North America, mostly storm-driven birds following hurricanes. Since the early 1970s, wandering gulls have become regular visitors to the Great Lakes region.

Within Ohio, the status of Laughing Gulls has been obscured by difficulties distinguishing them from Franklin's Gulls, especially during the 1950s and 1960s. Our ability to correctly identify Laughing Gulls has recently improved, allowing for a more accurate assessment of their current status.

Ohio's first Laughing Gull was collected along Lake Erie at Fairport Harbor on May 19, 1951 (Newman 1969). The second was a juvenile collected at South Bass Island on September 12–14, 1953 (Trautman 1956). In 1963, at least one visited Lorain on July 7–9 (Newman 1969). Single gulls were noted in Lake County on May 24, 1964, and May 28, 1969 (Newman 1969, Petersen 1969). One appeared near Toledo on July 9, 1972 (Campbell 1973), and Laughing

Gulls have been reported along Lake Erie in every subsequent year. The first inland records were confirmed during the 1970s. Only 1–3 Laughing Gulls were annually reported during the 1970s. The number of sightings gradually increased during the 1980s to five to ten reports during most years. This status has not changed since 1990.

Laughing Gulls are now rare spring visitors along Lake Erie and produce two to four sightings during most years. The only noticeable spring flight occurred in 1990, with at least 20 reports scattered along the lakefront (Peterjohn 1990c). The earliest appeared at Oregon (Lucas County) on February 21–27, 1987 (Peterjohn 1987b); this individual may have wintered somewhere on the Great Lakes. The first migrants may return by March 27–April 1, but most records are during May. All sightings are of 1–2 Laughing Gulls. They are accidental spring visitors to inland lakes, with at least nine substantiated records from the southern half of the state.

Most summering Laughing Gulls are found along Lake Erie, where they are casual to rare visitors. Adults or immatures may be encountered anytime during June and July as individuals or in groups of 2–3. One summering at Lake St. Marys during 1991 and two June records from Buck Creek State Park provide the only inland reports during this season. The only indication of breeding was provided by a female Laughing Gull discovered within a large Ring-billed Gull colony at Oregon. In 1984, this unmated female built a nest and incubated eggs between May 21 and June 11. A female Ring-billed Gull also shared this nest. The Laughing Gull eggs disappeared in mid-June and this attempt was unsuccessful (Tramer and Campbell 1986). This female Laughing Gull returned to the colony every year through 1987, never acquiring a mate but building nests and laying eggs each spring. None of her attempts is known to have been successful. However, a hybrid Laughing X Ring-billed Gull appeared in this colony during 1986, leading to speculation that hybrid offspring may have been raised one year (Peterjohn and Rice 1991).

As fall visitors, most Laughing Gulls are observed between early August and mid-October. They are very unusual after mid-November, although a few have lingered along Lake Erie into the first week of December and one was photographed at East Fork Lake (Clermont County) on December 22, 1990 (Anderson and Kemp 1991b). These migrants are rare along Lake Erie, with the majority of records from the Central Basin. Two to four lakefront sightings are reported during most autumns. They are accidental to casual visitors to inland reservoirs, with approximately twenty-two confirmed records since 1977 from scattered locations in the glaciated counties.

While most fall sightings are of 1–2 Laughing Gulls, an unprecedented influx produced flocks of 18 at Cleveland and ten at Lorain on August 12, 1985, and smaller numbers scattered along the lakefront into October. This influx also produced 12 at C.J. Brown Reservoir and one at Lake St. Marys on September 2 (Peterjohn 1986a). No meteorological conditions readily explained this movement of Laughing Gulls into Ohio.

Franklin's Gull *Larus pipixcan* Wagler

Ohio's first Franklin's Gull was collected at Buckeye Lake on October 15, 1906 (Trautman 1940). This specimen provided the only record until the late 1920s and 1930s, when small numbers were discovered along Lake Erie, and Campbell (1968) considered them uncommon but regular migrants in the Toledo area. During these years, they were described as "rare and accidental" at Cleveland (Williams 1950). The only inland record was near Columbus on October 10, 1937 (Borror 1950). Fewer Franklin's Gulls were observed during the 1940s and 1950s, perhaps reflecting less intense coverage by birdwatchers. The first spring migrants and nonbreeding summer visitors were recorded during these decades, however. Their status gradually changed after 1960. As gulls dramatically increased along Lake Erie, a few Franklin's regularly associated with large flocks of Bonaparte's and Ring-billeds. The number of inland records also increased, although inland Franklin's Gulls remained accidental through the mid-1970s.

Since 1975, spring Franklin's Gulls have been casual to rare migrants along Lake Erie and produce one or two sightings during most years. They are accidental visitors to the interior counties; of approximately twenty inland records, the only sighting from unglaciated Ohio was at Senecaville Reservoir on April 23, 1981 (Hall 1981b). These migrants appear as early as the first week of April, but most are observed between May 5 and 25, in groups of three or fewer.

Nonbreeding Franklin's Gulls are casual summer visitors along Lake Erie and are not observed annually. These nonbreeders are mostly observed in the Cleveland-Lorain area; surprisingly few are found in the Western Basin. Most records come during July and early August, usually of immature gulls. Away from Lake Erie, Franklin's Gulls are accidental summer visitors, with sightings from Alum Creek Reservoir, Buck Creek State Park, and Caesar Creek Reservoir since 1978.

As fall migrants, Franklin's Gulls are uncommon to rare along Lake Erie between Toledo and the Cleveland area but become casual farther east, producing two to four reports during some years and twelve or more in others. These migrants are normally recorded in groups of seven or fewer, mostly immatures, between September 20 and November 30. Away from Lake Erie, they are casual to rare migrants at reservoirs in the western and central counties. They average one to four inland sightings each year, with most records of

1–3 immatures between September 25 and November 15. A few large flocks have been observed, including 35 at Alum Creek Reservoir on October 28, 1984 (Peterjohn 1985a); 25 at Buck Creek State Park on October 12, 1991 (Peterjohn 1992a); and several groups of 14–24. Within the eastern counties, Franklin's Gulls are accidental fall migrants, with very few confirmed records.

In November 1998, a strong storm swept across the Great Plains and pushed unprecedented numbers of Franklin's Gulls into Ohio. The total number of gulls that passed through the state will never be known. At least several hundred individuals were scattered across the western counties, including several flocks of 15–28+, and along the lakefront east to the Cleveland area, where a maximum of 47 were reported from Lake County on November 21 (Rosche 1998c).

Along Lake Erie, Franklin's Gulls are casual to rare early winter visitors, mostly scattered individuals along the Cleveland-Lorain lakefront. They are accidental early winter visitors to inland lakes in the glaciated counties. Most depart during the first half of December, with occasional reports through December 25. There are very few confirmed sightings along Lake Erie after January 1, although one survived at Cleveland through late February, 1964 (Petersen 1964b).

Little Gull *Larus minutus* Pallas

Our smallest gull is an immigrant from Europe, first reported in North America around the turn of the twentieth century. Little Gulls did not become regular visitors for several decades. Initially, they were winter residents, but as their numbers increased, they were noted throughout the year. The first North American nesting records were established along the Great Lakes during the 1960s.

Ohio's first Little Gull was a thoroughly described adult discovered along Lake Erie at Fairport Harbor on December 24, 1923 (Doolittle 1924b). The next record came on December 23, 1947, when one was noted along the lakefront in Ashtabula County (Borror 1950). Little Gulls also appeared in 1949: a wintering bird near Cleveland and a spring migrant visiting a reservoir near Columbus (Borror 1950, Williams 1950). During the 1950s, they became sporadic visitors along central Lake Erie. The first Toledo area record was furnished in 1960 (Campbell 1968), and this species has been annually reported from Lake Erie in subsequent years. Numbers apparently peaked between 1975 and 1983.

Along Lake Erie, Little Gulls are mostly fall migrants and early winter visitors. Their fall migration exhibits two defined peaks, reflecting the movements of Bonaparte's Gulls, with whom they normally associate. The earliest Little

Gulls appear between July 20 and September 10, with a few individuals remaining through the end of the month. There are few additional records until the last week of October, when Little Gulls appear among the developing flocks of Bonaparte's. Little Gulls generally attain their maximum abundance during the last half of November and December.

Within the Central Basin, these migrants are casual to rare before late October, usually as scattered individuals. During November, they become rare to uncommon visitors, most frequently observed at river mouths. Most reports are of five or fewer, but occasional groups of 8–18 have been encountered, primarily before 1990. Along the Western Basin, Little Gulls are casual migrants, with most sightings of 1–3 during November.

During winter, Little Gulls are regularly observed as long as Lake Erie remains open and flocks of Bonaparte's Gulls frequent the lakefront. They normally leave the Western Basin before December 30 and the Central Basin between December 30 and January 15. Before January 15, this species is a casual to locally uncommon visitor, in groups of nine or fewer. They become casual visitors after January 15, although as many as 5–6 have overwintered during mild seasons. Twenty-six Little Gulls tallied in Lake County on February 27, 1999, represents a remarkable winter total anywhere on the Great Lakes (Hannikman 1999).

As spring migrants, they are casual to rare visitors within the Central Basin and accidental in Ottawa and Lucas Counties. Most sightings are of single gulls, with very infrequent concentrations of 6–10. These migrants mostly appear between March 20 and April 25, with a few lingering through May 20–27.

While Little Gulls have nested elsewhere on the Great Lakes (AOU 1998), there has been no evidence to suggest breeding in Ohio. They are accidental summer visitors along Lake Erie. The few summer records are restricted to the Cleveland-Lorain lakefront, mostly 1–3 immatures during the first half of June. Sightings during the first half of July may pertain to early fall migrants.

Away from Lake Erie, Little Gulls are accidental visitors. Four inland records are of single spring migrants: at O'Shaughnessy Reservoir (Delaware County) on March 22, 1949 (Thomas and Hengst 1949); along the Great Miami River in Hamilton County on March 30, 1978 (Kleen 1978c); at Lake St. Marys on May 14, 1984 (Peterjohn 1984c); and at Lake Rockwell on April 13, 1986 (Peterjohn 1986c). The only inland fall record is a specimen collected at Buckeye Lake on November 7, 1970 (Trautman and Trautman 1971), while one at East Fork State Park (Clermont County) during January 22–29, 1999, provides the only inland winter record (Brock 1999b).

Black-headed Gull *Larus ridibundus* Linneaus

This rare European visitor, like the Little Gull, associates with large flocks of Bonaparte's Gulls along Lake Erie; it has never been observed away from the lake in Ohio. But unlike Little Gulls, Black-headeds resemble Bonaparte's and are easily overlooked, especially when resting on the water.

Black-headed Gulls have a relatively brief history within the state. The first one was observed at Cleveland on December 13, 1965, and may have been the same gull noted at Lorain during the following month (Newman 1969). There were at least seven sight records between 1965 and 1974, while Black-headeds averaged one to four sightings annually during 1978–1988. They produced at least eight records during the 1990s. These increased sightings are correlated with similar trends in eastern North America since the late 1970s and greater efforts to locate unusual gulls along Lake Erie.

Most Black-headed Gulls are encountered between mid-November and mid-January as casual visitors to the Central Basin and accidental within the Western Basin. They become accidental visitors later in winter, with most records from the Central Basin. Spring migrants are accidental along the entire lakefront between March 13 and April 6. The only confirmed summer records are from Cleveland between July 23 and August 4, 1978, and at Ottawa Wildlife Refuge on July 11, 1991 (Harlan 1991b, Kleen 1978d). All sightings are of single gulls.

Bonaparte's Gull *Larus philadelphia* (Ord)

Unlike the larger gulls, with their loud raucous calls and aggressive behavior, the small Bonaparte's has a gentle and agreeable manner, much like a tern elegantly picking small fish from the surface of the water or capturing them with short plunges. The Bonaparte's flight pattern is graceful but deceptive; even gale-force winds do not deter its movements along the lakefront. Its aerial prowess allows it to make an honest living off fish. The Bonaparte's Gull is not a scavenger and avoids dumps and parking lots where its larger relatives congregate.

Bonaparte's Gulls were common lakefront migrants throughout the twentieth century. Fall and early winter concentrations of 8,000–15,000 were reported at Toledo and Cleveland since the 1930s (Campbell 1968, Williams 1950). Their populations underwent a dramatic increase during the 1960s. As early as 1967, 41,000 were reported on the Lorain Christmas Bird Count. Flocks numbering in the thousands are scattered along the lakefront each autumn, because the south shore of Lake Erie serves as a major staging area for Bonaparte's Gulls during fall migration. The largest reported flocks include an estimated 75,000 along the Cleveland lakefront during December 1984 and in excess of 100,000 frequenting the Cleveland-Lorain lakefront in November 1986 (Peterjohn 1985b, 1987a).

Fewer Bonaparte's Gulls pass through Ohio during spring. Along Lake Erie, the first migrants return between March 15 and 25 and are fairly common to common by the end of the month. They are most numerous during April, normally in flocks of 25–300. Large concentrations are infrequent and usually restricted to the Central Basin, where flocks of 1,500–4,500 have been reported. They remain locally common migrants until early May but most depart by May 15. Small numbers of nonbreeders linger through the end of the month.

Within the interior counties, spring migrants may be uncommonly encountered in flocks of only 10–25 some years but fairly common to locally common with flocks of 50–200+ in other years. Inland concentrations of 400–500+ are unusual, and 1,500 in Hancock County on April 13, 1995, are exceptional (Harlan 1993c). They are most numerous on large lakes in the northern and glaciated central counties; only small flocks are expected in southern and unglaciated Ohio. Timing is similar to the movements along Lake Erie, but with fewer sightings after May 15.

Between late May and mid-July, nonbreeding Bonaparte's Gulls are normally rare visitors along Lake Erie, usually in groups of ten or fewer, but infrequently in larger flocks, such as 500 at Toledo on July 5, 1931, 200 at Magee Marsh Wildlife Area on June 25, 1995, and 100 at Lorain on June 20, 1964 (Campbell 1968, Harlan 1995d, Petersen 1964d). They may remain for a few days or the entire summer. Summering Bonaparte's are accidental to casual visitors to inland lakes in the glaciated counties, generally as isolated individuals, with a maximum of 15 at Killdeer Plains Wildlife Area on July 8, 1995 (Harlan 1995d).

Their fall migration has two defined peaks, corresponding with their movements elsewhere along eastern Lake Erie and the Niagara River (Beardslee 1944). During the last half of July, flocks of adult Bonaparte's Gulls accumulate along central Lake Erie from Lorain eastward. Although their abundance and timing varies from year to year, flocks of 300–800+ may appear by July 20–25 and remain into early September. The largest concentrations have numbered 1,500–3,000 in Lake County. This early migration may also produce concentrations of 20–250 at Huron and 10–50 in the Western Basin. They remain accidental to casual visitors to inland lakes during these months, in groups of nine or fewer.

Along the Central Basin, numbers of Bonaparte's decline during late September, although flocks of 10–50 may still be encountered. They do not become abundant again until November, when the size of their migration varies. During some years, the largest flocks total only 300–2,000+. In other years, more than 50,000 may congregate in one harbor. These numbers are maintained into December. Within the Western Basin, Bonaparte's increase during October and peak in November. Their numbers are generally smaller than farther east, with most reports of 200–2,500 and the largest concentrations total 10,000–15,000. These flocks normally depart during the last half of December. Sizable concentrations remain into January in the Western Basin only during mild winters.

Inland, fall Bonaparte's Gulls are mostly observed between October 20 and December 10, with peak numbers during November. They are generally most numerous during the years they are least abundant along Lake Erie. During years of maximum abundance, most inland flocks total 25–75, with occasional concentrations of 300–500+ and totals of 1,300–1,600+ from Mosquito Creek Reservoir (Trumbull County). Maximum flock size is normally 15–50 during years when they are scarce. Their statewide distribution is similar to spring migration. These gulls depart inland reservoirs during the first half of December, although a few individuals and small flocks may remain until freeze-up. There are very few inland records after January 10. They overwinter on inland lakes only during exceptionally mild seasons, as has occurred at Buckeye Lake and Senecaville Reservoir (Hall 1974b, Trautman 1940).

Bonaparte's Gulls are casually observed along western Lake Erie after early January and are expected only during mild winters. These wintering Bonaparte's are normally observed as individuals or small flocks, although 300 overwintered at Toledo during 1931–1932 (Campbell 1940). The number wintering within the Central Basin is also related to the weather conditions. Most Bonaparte's depart when the lake freezes over, usually by mid-January, although a few stragglers may overwinter even when little open water is available. Large flocks may remain throughout mild seasons: 20,000 during the winter of 1982–1983 at Cleveland (Peterjohn 1983b); as many as 35,000 there through January 24, 1987 (Peterjohn 1987b); and 25,000 there through February 5, 1989 (Peterjohn 1989b). These concentrations often abruptly disappear with the onslaught of winter weather, even during mid-February, as occurred in 1989. Once they have left, Bonaparte's Gulls remain scarce along Lake Erie until the first spring migrants return in March.

Heermann's Gull *Larus heermanni* Cassin

The appearance of a Heermann's Gull in Ohio is one of those events that seemingly could never happen but did. A single individual was detected along Lake Erie near Detroit, Michigan, during the winter of 1979–1980. It subsequently wandered into Ohio, where it was discovered at Lorain on February 12, 1980, by John Pogacnik and Jim Fry (Kleen 1980b). This distinctive gull was periodically observed through March 12, when it had assumed adult breeding plumage. The same individual returned to Lorain the following winter. Initially discovered on December 20, 1980, it was infrequently observed into February (Peterjohn 1981a). This sighting is unprecedented for eastern North America. Heermann's Gulls are normally restricted to the Pacific Coast from Mexico to southern British Columbia and seldom stray more than a mile or two inland (AOU 1998). The presence of a Heermann's Gull in Ohio raises the intriguing questions of how it reached the Great Lakes and where it spent the breeding seasons.

Mew Gull *Larus canus* Linnaeus

To some, gull identification is an exercise in futility. The variable plumages, similarly-appearing species, and enormous numbers overwhelm the capabilities of many observers. To others, gulls present the challenge of discovering and identifying a rarity among thousands of individuals of common species. Within Ohio, Mew Gulls are accidental visitors and a prized species of the serious gull watcher. There are five accepted records: four from Lake Erie, consisting of a first-winter bird discovered at Lorain on November 29, 1981 (Peterjohn 1982a); an adult at Huron on December 7, 1985 (Peterjohn 1986b); a first-winter bird at Eastlake during December 11–25, 1989 (Peterjohn 1989b); and another first-winter bird photographed at Fairport Harbor on March 6–17, 1998 (Brock 1998c). The only inland report is an adult Mew Gull on the Maumee River in Lucas County on January 2–3, 1995 (Brock 1995b). When racial identification has been possible, all of these Mew Gulls have been of the North American race *brachyrhynchus*. In North America, Mew Gulls are mostly restricted to the Pacific Coast during winter. Their breeding range extends from Alaska south to British Columbia and northern Saskatchewan (AOU 1998). Other races are distributed across northern Eurasia.

Ring-billed Gull *Larus delawarensis* Ord

"I have searched for this gull in vain," mourned Lynds Jones (1903) as he described the demise of Ring-billed Gulls during the late 1800s. The millinery trade nearly extirpated them from the Great Lakes between 1882 and 1900. At the turn of the twentieth century, they were "rare everywhere in the state" (Jones 1903), a status nearly impossible to imagine today.

Ring-billed Gulls were scarcely reported from Ohio until the 1920s, when flocks of 5–30 visited Lake Erie and large inland lakes, with infrequent concentrations of 100+ each spring and fall. The few wintering gulls were mostly restricted to Lake Erie. Summering Ring-billeds were unknown (Trautman 1940, Williams 1950). Between 1935 and 1940, immature Ring-billeds began to summer along the lakefront, mostly near Toledo, where as many as 300 were regularly encountered (Campbell 1940). Larger numbers congregated in August and September, with occasional flocks of 1,000+ at Toledo and Cleveland. Lakefront Christmas Bird Count totals gradually increased from 100+ in 1930 to 500+ by 1940. Similar increases were apparent at inland lakes, where they were mostly known as migrants and rare winter residents; summering gulls on inland lakes were not recorded until 1940 (Walker 1940c). These trends continued through the 1950s. Nonbreeding Ring-billeds were regular summer visitors along the lakefront but remained a novelty inland. Migrant flocks of 1,000–5,000 were regular along Lake Erie and would occasionally appear within the northeastern counties. Wintering numbers were also improving, although Ring-billeds were outnumbered by Herring Gulls on most Christmas Bird Counts.

Ring-billed Gull populations exploded along Lake Erie during the 1960s as the birds discovered new food sources at dumps, shopping centers, and cultivated fields, and also fed on a greatly expanded gizzard shad population in Lake Erie. As early as 1961, more than 30,000 Ring-billeds were estimated on the Lorain Christmas Bird Count. This number increased to 76,000 by 1965. Concentrations of 5,000–20,000+ were encountered elsewhere within central Lake Erie each autumn and winter. Numbers of summering Ring-billeds also increased and resulted in the first two nests on a spoil island in Maumee Bay in 1966. This colony expanded to 50 pairs in 1967 (Campbell 1968). Away from Lake Erie, flocks of 50–500+ regularly appeared at large lakes across Ohio, although larger concentrations were exceptional. Small numbers of nonbreeding gulls remained at these lakes each summer. Similar trends continued through the 1970s (Dolbeer and Bernhardt 1986). Autumn and early winter concentrations of 10,000+ at Toledo and 50,000–75,000 along the Cleveland-Lorain lakefront appeared most years. The most dramatic increase was in the nesting population. Only 6–55 pairs nested in Maumee Bay between 1968 and 1970; this small colony was subsequently abandoned (Campbell 1973). Nesting gulls established another colony in Oregon (Lucas County) in 1975, expanding from 200 pairs in 1977 to 2,000 in 1979 (Kleen 1979d). The Lake Erie population reached a plateau in the 1980s and remained fairly stable in subsequent years. Numbers at inland locations continued to increase during the 1990s.

The most spectacular concentrations appear along Lake Erie each autumn. Their numbers usually increase during the last half of July and form flocks of 500–2,000+ at scattered localities. They increase gradually between August and mid-October, but concentrations in excess of 2,000–10,000+ are unusual during these months. Immense numbers appear in November, when 10,000–50,000+ may congregate near the mouths of bays and large rivers. Peak numbers are frequently attained between November 20 and December

25, when 100,000+ gather along the Cleveland-Lorain lakefront, 25,000–50,000+ appear at the mouth of Sandusky Bay, and 5,000–20,000 are noted elsewhere. These numbers normally decrease with the advent of winter weather in January.

During mild winters, Ring-billeds are scattered along the entire lakefront and are the most numerous gulls. Local concentrations of 10,000–50,000+ are possible, but daily totals frequently do not exceed 2,000–5,000+. When the lake freezes, wintering Ring-billeds are most numerous in the Central Basin. Flocks of 10,000–30,000+ may congregate around hot-water outlets, but these concentrations do not normally remain intact throughout the winter. They are most prevalent in harsh weather with strong north winds but disperse on sunny days with south winds. They can also vanish for several weeks in midwinter, when their whereabouts become a mystery.

Their spring migration is unremarkable. The large winter flocks usually disperse in February and Ring-billeds become widely distributed by early March. Flocks of 1,000–3,000+ are expected in March. Larger concentrations are unusual, although movements involving 10,000–20,000+ have occurred during some years. Daily totals seldom exceed 500–700 after mid-April except near nesting colonies.

Breeding Ring-billed Gulls were formerly restricted to the large colony at Oregon where 3,600+ nests were estimated in 1983 and similar numbers were present through the 1980s. A small colony was briefly established near the mouth of Sandusky Bay in Ottawa County in 1983 (Peterjohn and Rice 1991). The Oregon colony was abandoned in 1992 (Harlan 1992d). New colonies were then established at several localities in the Cleveland area during the 1990s, where as many as 8,600+ nesting pairs were estimated in 1997 (Fazio 1997b). A large colony was also formed at Ashtabula (Harlan 1996a). Nonbreeding gulls are common to abundant residents elsewhere along the lakefront, but flocks seldom exceed 300–500.

These nesting colonies are normally located on spoil islands or dredge disposal areas, where their nests are placed on the ground among herbaceous cover. In recent years, undisturbed natural nest sites have become scarce, and Ring-billed Gulls have developed the habit of nesting on the graveled rooftops of large buildings, which may be located several miles from the lakefront (Dwyer et al. 1996). Along Lake Erie, nesting activities begin in late March and the first clutches are produced by mid-April. The first young hatch by mid-May and attain flight by the first week of July. Late nesting attempts produce incubating adults through early July and dependent young into the last half of August (Peterjohn and Rice 1991).

Away from Lake Erie, Ring-billed Gulls are common to abundant migrants along large rivers and reservoirs. The first fall migrants normally appear during the last half of August and become numerous by early October. Peak concentrations are expected between October 20 and January 1. Flocks of 100–500+ are found in many counties, and concentrations of 1,000–2,500+ gather on large lakes across Ohio. Spring numbers tend to be smaller, and concentrations in excess of 1,500 occur less frequently than in autumn. Spring migrants usually appear in February and are most prevalent between March 15 and April 20. Flocks of immature gulls regularly linger throughout May.

Their inland wintering numbers increased significantly during the 1990s, as Ring-billeds learned to forage in parking lots, landfills, and other urban environments, and are no longer restricted to the vicinities of large lakes. They are fairly common to abundant winter residents across Ohio, but become locally rare to uncommon along portions of the unglaciated Allegheny Plateau. Nightly roosts of 1,000+ may gather on large lakes near cities, while landfills may host 1,500–5,000+, but daily totals are usually less than 250 in most areas.

Summering Ring-billed Gulls also increased on inland lakes during the 1990s. They are fairly common to locally abundant across the state, least numerous in the unglaciated counties. Summer flocks of 200–300+ may occur on large lakes, but summer totals are mostly 100 or fewer. The expanding breeding population along Lake Erie produced a nesting attempt from the interior of Ohio. In 1994, a small colony was discovered in a quarry near Findlay (Harlan 1994d). The number of nesting pairs was not precisely determined, but probably totaled fewer than 50.

California Gull *Larus californicus* Lawrence

California Gulls normally reside in the western half of North America, breeding east to North Dakota and wintering along the Pacific Coast (AOU 1998). In recent years, small numbers have also regularly wandered eastward to the Great Lakes, where they associate with large flocks of Herring and Ring-billed Gulls. Within Ohio, the first acceptably documented record was provided by an adult at Huron on November 24–25, 1979 (Kleen 1980a). There were at least twenty additional sightings during the 1980s and 1990s, indicating that this species is a fairly regular visitor to the state, although it is not reliably reported every year.

California Gulls are casual visitors to the Central Basin of Lake Erie, where reports are nearly equally divided between fall migrants and winter visitors. The earliest fall sighting is of a first-year gull in Lake County on October 30–November 6, 1988 (Peterjohn 1989a), but most reports occur between November 11 and December 7. Winter records are scattered throughout the season, and California Gulls have been found wherever large numbers of gulls congregate. Records during March probably pertain to gulls that wintered on Lake Erie. One at Cleveland on April 29, 1987, is the only spring migrant discovered in Ohio (Hannikman 1987).

This species is accidental elsewhere in the state. The absence of reports from western Lake Erie is surprising, especially since there are two documented records of adults from inland locations. One California Gull was discovered at Oberlin Reservoir (Lorain County) on November 29, 1985 (Peterjohn 1986a), and another was observed by many birders at Pleasant Hill Reservoir (Richland County) on November 3–23, 1990 (Peterjohn 1991a).

Herring Gull *Larus argentatus* Pontoppidan

The factors responsible for the incredible increase of Ring-billed Gulls along the Great Lakes also benefited Herring Gulls. Today, it is difficult to imagine that Herring Gulls were relatively scarce along Lake Erie in the early 1930s. For example, Christmas Bird Counts reported 100–300 then, as compared with the tens of thousands encountered today. Even though they were relatively scarce, the first signs of their impending increase were already apparent.

Nesting Herring Gulls were initially recorded from western Lake Erie in 1926, when they were discovered on the Chicken Islands in Ontario (Williams 1950). Small colonies were established on other Canadian islands but did not appear in Ohio until 1945, when six nests were located on Starve Island (Campbell 1968). This population rapidly expanded. By the early 1950s, they spread to every suitable western Lake Erie island. They colonized Maumee Bay by the mid-1960s and eventually spread to other portions of the lake.

As this breeding population expanded, Herring Gulls underwent corresponding increases during other seasons. Concentrations in excess of 1,000 were occasionally reported by the late 1930s, with a maximum of 3,250 on the 1939 Toledo Christmas Bird Count. During the 1940s, large flocks were possible, such as the "inestimable" numbers at Cleveland in January 1948 (Williams 1950). As their populations exploded in the late 1950s and early 1960s, flocks of 5,000–10,000+ regularly appeared along the Cleveland-Lorain lakefront. This rapid expansion continued through the mid-1970s, when concentrations of 10,000–50,000+ were noted. Their numbers remained fairly stable in subsequent years (Dolbeer and Bernhardt 1984). Declines were evident in some Great Lakes breeding populations since the 1980s, but numbers nesting on Lake Erie increased into the 1990s (Dolbeer et al. 1990, Dwyer et al. 1996, Scharf and Shugart 1998).

Herring Gulls are now common to abundant permanent residents along Lake Erie, most numerous during winter. Before freeze-up in late December or January, they are distributed along the entire lakefront, and concentrations of

1,000–5,000+ are expected. Inclement weather may produce flocks of 10,000–20,000+, with occasional concentrations of 50,000+ as the lake freezes.

Once Lake Erie has frozen, their distribution patterns change. Most Herring Gulls leave the Western Basin and congregate at hot-water outlets near Cleveland. Flocks of 5,000–40,000+ appear at these outlets during January and February. Even when the lake is frozen, their movements are not readily explained. These large concentrations may be present for several weeks, then vanish overnight and fewer than 100 gulls may remain. During some years, they never come back, while in others, they may be absent for a few days or weeks and just as mysteriously return. Where they go and why they leave has never been explained. During mild winters when the lake remains open, Herring Gulls are distributed along the entire lakefront, mostly in flocks of fewer than 2,000.

With the advent of warming temperatures in February and early March, the winter flocks rapidly disperse along the entire lakefront. By mid-April, they attain their summer distribution patterns. Except for occasional flights of 3,000–5,000+ during March, flocks in excess of 500–2,000 are unusual during spring.

As summer residents, Herring Gulls are most numerous in western Lake Erie, where they breed at every available undisturbed site on the Lake Erie islands, as well as Maumee Bay, Sandusky Bay, and protected areas on the mainland. In 1990, this population was estimated at approximately 6,400 pairs, with 4,250 nests in Sandusky Bay (Dolbeer et al. 1990, Scharf and Shugart 1998). Most of these colonies are composed of fewer than 200 pairs, although as many as 2,964 have been estimated on Turning Point Island near Sandusky (Dolbeer et al. 1990). Smaller numbers nest in the Central Basin, where scattered small colonies have formed between Avon Lake and Ashtabula (Scharf and Shugart 1998). This population is still growing, but currently totals fewer than 1,000 pairs (Dwyer et al. 1996). Away from these colonies, Herring Gulls are generally observed as flocks of 50–400 nonbreeders during summer.

Most Herring Gull colonies form on small sparsely vegetated islands, but they also occupy more densely vegetated areas on the mainland (Peterjohn and Rice 1991). In addition, Herring Gulls have developed the habit of breeding in goose-nesting structures in the western Lake Erie marshes. This habit was first noted in 1974, and pairs are now scattered across most marshes (Hoffman 1983). Herring Gulls also nest on the gravel roofs of buildings, which has greatly increased the availability of suitable nest sites in urban areas, especially along central Lake Erie. At least ten colonies formed on roofs in the Cleveland area during the early 1990s (Dwyer et al. 1996).

Herring Gulls return to their colonies by late March or early April and claim a nest site. The first eggs are laid by mid-April, although some pairs may not begin nesting until May. The first young hatch by mid-May and fledge in early July. Late nesting attempts produce small young as late as the first week of July (Peterjohn and Rice 1991), and these young may not fledge until August.

After the breeding season, Herring Gulls become widely distributed along Lake Erie. Increased numbers are evident by August, and flocks in excess of 1,000 normally appear by mid-October. Their numbers increase through November, although immense flocks usually form with the advent of cold weather in December.

While Herring Gulls increased along Lake Erie, numbers appearing on inland lakes declined in portions of the state. At one time, they were the most numerous inland gulls, and flocks of 100–300 were widely reported except in the unglaciated counties (Mathena et al. 1984, Trautman 1940). These numbers gradually declined during the 1950s. Since the early 1960s, Ring-billed Gulls have substantially outnumbered Herrings on most inland lakes.

Their current abundance at inland locations is directly related to the distance from Lake Erie. Inland Herring Gulls are numerous in the northeastern counties, making daily flights from Lake Erie to lakes from southern Lorain County east to the Akron-Kent area. Flocks of 100–300+ appear on many northeastern lakes, and larger flocks visit bodies of water close to Lake Erie, especially during late fall and early winter. Similar numbers move upstream along the Maumee River across Lucas County, while concentrations of 1,000–5,000+ visit landfills within the counties bordering the lake. These large concentrations are not apparent in central and southern Ohio, where lakes seldom support more than 10–30 Herring Gulls. Occasional flights produce flocks of 50–100+ in central Ohio and along the Ohio River.

The largest inland spring movements, mostly adults, occur in February and early March, coinciding with the thawing of reservoirs. Immatures migrate between March 20 and May 1, with a few nonbreeders remaining through the end of the month.

Summering Herring Gulls were formerly unusual in the interior of Ohio, with very few published records before 1960. As the Great Lakes breeding population expanded, inland nonbreeders also increased. They are now rare to uncommon summer visitors throughout Ohio, in groups of six or fewer immatures. In addition to nonbreeders, small numbers of Herring Gulls have attempted to breed on goose-nesting structures at several inland lakes. The first inland nesting attempt was at Lake Rockwell (Portage County) in 1981 (Peterjohn 1981c). One or two pairs began to nest at Mosquito Creek Reservoir in 1983 (Peterjohn and Rice 1991). By 1991, nesting Herring Gulls had been noted at inland locations in every northeastern county except Medina (Peterjohn 1991d). This population remains small, and probably totals fewer than 30 pairs. The only other inland nesting report is of a pair that may have bred at Lake St. Marys in 1985 (Peterjohn and Rice 1991).

The first fall migrants may return to inland lakes by mid-August, and normally appear during September. Fall Herring Gulls become widespread by mid-October and are regularly observed on these lakes until they freeze.

Once the lakes freeze, most inland wintering Herring Gulls are found in the northeastern counties at dumps, parking lots, and other foraging sites away from the lakefront. Numbers moving inland vary considerably from year to year, depending on the conditions along Lake Erie, but daily totals seldom exceed 100–300 except at landfills. Away from northeastern Ohio, Herring Gulls are casual to locally uncommon winter visitors, with most records of 15 or fewer along large rivers and lakes in the southern half of the state, although larger groups may gather at landfills.

Thayer's Gull *Larus thayeri* Brooks

Before 1973, this species was considered to be a race of the Herring Gull. Its distinguishing characteristics were poorly understood and the only Ohio record was provided by a first-winter specimen collected at South Bass Island by Milton Trautman on February 26, 1946 (Trautman 1956). In 1973, Thayer's Gull was elevated to the status of a full species. Several years passed before the subtle field marks distinguishing this species from Iceland and Herring Gulls were described in the literature. Once birders became familiar with these field marks, Thayer's Gulls were regularly observed among the large winter gull flocks along Lake Erie. The first sight records were during the winter of 1977–1978 (Kleen 1978b). They have been reported in every subsequent year, indicating that they were probably overlooked during previous decades.

In the 1990s, the taxonomic status of Thayer's Gull became uncertain again. Individuals with intermediate characteristics were observed, which may indicate that some populations or perhaps all Thayer's Gulls may be better treated as a race of the Iceland Gull, rather than as a separate species (AOU 1998). Additional field studies on their Arctic breeding range are necessary to resolve these taxonomic issues. The field identification issues within the Thayer's-Iceland Gull complex are more difficult than previously thought, and the status of Thayer's Gull in Ohio should be viewed as tentative until these taxonomic questions are answered.

Thayer's Gulls are generally rare winter residents along Lake Erie, in association with large flocks of Herring Gulls. They are only casually encountered during mild winters as isolated individuals. In contrast, they may become locally uncommon visitors to hot-water outlets along the Cleveland-Lorain lakefront during severe winters. As many as six Thayer's Gulls have been reported under these conditions. Most recent records are from Huron eastward, reflecting the normal midwinter distribution of gulls. There are few sightings from the Western Basin, which normally freezes over before most Thayer's Gulls arrive on Lake Erie.

Early returning Thayer's Gulls have been reported by the first week of November. They are casually encountered until the lake freezes over, when they are most likely to be observed between mid-January and mid-February. They quickly depart when the lake begins to thaw, usually during the last half of February. Most leave by March 5-20, although immature Thayer's Gulls exhibit a tendency to linger into spring. Since 1980, there are at least five acceptable May records, with the latest individual remaining at Cleveland through May 19, 1985 (Peterjohn 1985c).

Away from Lake Erie, Thayer's Gulls are casual winter visitors along the Maumee River near Waterville. Single gulls have been observed there during three winters, beginning in 1994–1995 (Harlan 1995b). A Thayer's Gull was also observed in flight heading towards an inland landfill in the Cleveland area during the winter of 1993-1994 (Harlan 1994b). These records pertain to gulls that moved a short distance inland from Lake Erie. This species is accidental elsewhere in the state, with only one documented report: a first-winter bird at Buck Creek State Park during November 9-17, 1996 (Brock 1997a).

Iceland Gull *Larus glaucoides* Meyer

Unlike Thayer's Gulls, Iceland Gulls have been known as winter residents along Lake Erie since the nineteenth century (Wheaton 1882). Between the 1880s and 1960s, they were among Ohio's rarest gulls, with very infrequent sightings along the lakefront. Beginning in the early 1960s, Iceland Gulls have been fairly regular members of the lake's midwinter gull concentrations.

Their status along Lake Erie is similar to Thayer's Gulls, except that Icelands tend to be slightly less numerous. They are rare winter residents from Lorain eastward but are only casually encountered within the Western Basin. Iceland Gulls are most numerous during cold winters, when large numbers of gulls congregate at hot-water outlets. Under these conditions, generally 1–2 frequent each outlet; concentrations of 3–5 are unusual. During mild winters, single Icelands are only casually encountered anywhere on Lake Erie.

Iceland Gulls tend to arrive slightly later and depart earlier than Thayer's Gulls. There are relatively few sightings during November, and the first Icelands are expected between mid-December and early January. Most are observed between mid-January and the third week of February but disappear as soon as the lake begins to thaw. Unless ice conditions prevail into March, Iceland Gulls are casual visitors after the first week of the month. There are very few records of lingering Icelands, although singles remained at Conneaut through May 2, 1992 (Harlan 1992c), and Cleveland until May 6, 1984 (Peterjohn 1984c). Midsummer and early fall sight records from Lake Erie have not been adequately substantiated; these reports may pertain to misidentified worn or leucistic Herring Gulls.

The status of Iceland Gulls at inland locations has been better defined since the late 1980s. They have proven to be rare visitors along the Maumee River in the Waterville area, usually as single gulls, but with a maximum of four during the winter of 1993–1994 (Harlan 1994b). They are accidental upstream from Waterville to the Independence Dam (Defiance County), where one was observed on January 23, 1994 (Harlan 1994b). In the Cleveland area, single Icelands have been occasionally observed in flight between Lake Erie and inland landfills. They are accidental away from landfills in the northeastern counties, where the only documented report is one at Lake Rockwell on January 1, 1995 (Harlan 1995b). Iceland Gulls are accidental visitors away from the northern counties, where the only acceptable sighting is one at Buckeye Lake between December 26, 1937, and January 1, 1938. This second-winter Iceland was carefully studied and the description eliminates all similar species (Trautman 1940).

Lesser Black-backed Gull *Larus fuscus* Linnaeus

The Lesser Black-backed Gull is a Eurasian species regularly reported from North America since the 1960s. The North American population of these gulls has gradually increased, and they have become regular visitors along the Atlantic Coast and Great Lakes (AOU 1998). There are no North American breeding records, but development of a breeding population seems likely as their numbers increase.

Ohio's first Lesser Black-backed Gull was discovered at Cleveland on January 20, 1977 (Kleen 1977b); singles also appeared at Lorain and Eastlake that winter, and one wandering individual may have produced all three sightings. Lesser Black-backeds have been recorded in every subsequent year. Initially, they were discovered among the large wintering flocks at hot-water outlets. By the early 1980s, individuals were also detected during autumn and spring. The first report of multiple Lesser Black-backeds was in November 1981 at Lorain (Peterjohn 1982a).

Lesser Black-backed Gulls are accidental nonbreeding summer visitors to Lake Erie. The confirmed sightings are limited to single gulls at Huron through July 31, 1988 (Peterjohn 1988d); Lorain on June 29, 1997 (Rosche 1997c); Oregon (Lucas County) on August 7, 1981 (Peterjohn 1982a); and Cleveland on August 9, 1989 (Peterjohn 1990a). The latter two individuals may have been very early fall migrants, because other Lesser Black-backeds have appeared during the last half of August. There are relatively few sightings before October 20. Lesser Black-backeds become casual to locally uncommon migrants along Lake Erie during November and December. Most fall reports are of four or fewer.

Wintering Lesser Black-backeds are mostly observed at hot-water outlets along central Lake Erie, where they are rare to locally uncommon. Most sightings are of single gulls, although as many as five have gathered at a single location. They are casual to rare winter visitors within the Western Basin, reflecting a shortage of open water and large gull concentrations during most years.

After the winter gull flocks disperse in February or early March, Lesser Black-backeds become casual to rare spring visitors along Lake Erie. Spring migrants are usually noted as single individuals, primarily during March and early April, with late migrants through April 28–May 11.

Away from Lake Erie, Lesser Black-backed Gulls are casual to rare fall and winter visitors along the Maumee River near Waterville, where the earliest record is on August 17, 1988 (Peterjohn 1989a). They are accidental visitors to other inland locations. In the northeastern counties, the first report was of an adult at Summit Lake in Akron during February 20–26, 1978 (Hannikman 1978). There were ten additional reports from northeastern inland lakes during the 1990s: three in autumn, three in winter, and four during spring. The latest was found at Oberlin Reservoir on April 10, 1997 (Rosche 1997b). Elsewhere, single Lesser Black-backed Gulls have been documented from Columbus on December 26, 1990 (Peterjohn 1991b); Pleasant Hill Reservoir (Richland County) on April 12–14, 1991 (Peterjohn 1991c); Clear Fork Reservoir (Richland County) on October 20, 1996 (Conlon and Harlan 1996b); and East Fork State Park (Clermont County) during September 5–26, 1997 (Fazio 1998).

Slaty-backed Gull *Larus schistisagus* Stejneger

In North America, Slaty-backed Gulls are primarily known as nonbreeding visitors to western Alaska. Like most large gulls, they have shown a tendency to wander from their normal range, which extends from the western Bering Sea south along the western Pacific Ocean. They have been reported from scattered locations between British Columbia and the Great Lakes (AOU 1998).

The only report from Ohio is of an adult Slaty-backed Gull discovered at Eastlake on December 28–29, 1992. Probably the same individual was photographed at Lorain on February 8, 1993 (Brock 1993b). While the mantle color of this gull was paler than some Slaty-backed Gulls, it is within the range of variability exhibited by this species (Gustafson and Peterjohn 1994). All other characteristics were consistent with the identification as a Slaty-backed Gull. While the taxonomy and identification of large dark-mantled gulls remain the topics of considerable debate, the Ohio individual matches the characteristics of a Slaty-backed Gull as this species is presently defined.

Glaucous Gull *Larus hyperboreus* Gunnerus

Early ornithologists did not record this species, and its status during the nineteenth century is uncertain. Small numbers of Glaucous Gulls may always have wintered along Lake Erie. The first confirmed Ohio records were in the 1930s, when lakefront observers regularly noted small numbers, particularly near Toledo. Their numbers increased through 1947 (Campbell 1968, Mayfield 1943). They became inexplicably scarce after 1947 and there were relatively few sightings until the late 1950s. By the winter of 1959–1960, winter gull populations were increasing rapidly along the entire lakefront. As birders sifted through the large flocks, they regularly encountered small numbers of Glaucous Gulls. As many as 2–8 were discovered on Christmas Bird Counts within the Central Basin that winter. When gull populations expanded during the 1960s and 1970s, Glaucous sightings underwent a corresponding increase. Their wintering numbers and distribution along Lake Erie have stabilized since 1980.

Glaucous Gulls may be scarce during mild winters when the lake does not freeze but are regularly observed during cold weather when open water is restricted to hot-water outlets. While there are a few sightings during September and early October, these gulls are accidental early fall visitors. These early records are of immature gulls that may have summered on the Great Lakes. The first winter residents normally return during the last half of November, and most are observed between mid-December and mid-February. They may be regularly observed into March during cold winters. The last gulls normally depart by March 25–April 15, although a few immatures casually remain through May 5–15. Glaucous Gulls are accidental summer visitors. There are at least four acceptable June records from Lake Erie, including a specimen collected at Cedar Point Wildlife Refuge (Lucas County) on June 6, 1937, and an immature in Lucas County on June 22, 1983 (Campbell 1968, Peterjohn 1983d). One was periodically observed at Conneaut into July 1992 (Harlan 1992d), and one appeared at Cleveland on August 7, 1977 (Rosche 1992).

Within the Western Basin, Glaucous Gulls are most prevalent immediately before freeze-up in December and early January and when the ice is breaking up during February and early March. They are scarce in midwinter, especially during harsh weather when the lake is mostly frozen. They are casual to rare winter visitors in this basin and daily totals seldom exceed 1–4. In the Central Basin, they are most numerous between early January and late February when the lake is normally frozen. They become locally uncommon to fairly common winter residents during harsh winters, particularly along the Cleveland-Lorain lakefront, when as many as 10–20 may congregate at hot-water outlets. Fewer Glaucous Gulls are observed during mild winters, when 1–6 may be sporadically encountered.

Away from Lake Erie, Glaucous Gulls are casual to rare winter visitors to the Maumee River near Waterville, where as many as 4–5 have appeared during some winters. They are also casual to rare winter visitors to landfills near Lake Erie in the northeastern counties, accounting for periodic reports from Oberlin Reservoir (Lorain County) east to the Cleveland area. They are accidental visitors farther inland, where sightings are limited to single gulls at Akron on February 8–9, 1959, and February 21, 1981 (Mumford 1959b, Peterjohn 1981a); at Lake Rockwell on January 1, 1995 (Harlan 1995b); in Seneca County on April 6–10, 1981 (Peterjohn 1981b); the Indian Lake Christmas Bird Count in 1966; at Lake St. Marys on January 18, 1958 (Clark and Sipe 1970); Kokosing Lake (Knox County) on January 10, 1998 (R. Schlabach 1998); and Cincinnati on February 14–15, 1979 (Kleen 1979b). Three appeared at Dayton on January 16, 1999 (Brock 1999b).

Great Black-backed Gull *Larus marinus* Linnaeus

Great Black-backed Gulls benefited from changing conditions along the Great Lakes during the twentieth century. In the 1800s, they were described as occasional visitors to Lake Erie, with few specific records (Wheaton 1882). They were discovered with greater frequency during the 1920s but did not become annual winter visitors until 1935–1939 (Campbell 1968, Williams 1950). Winter populations slowly increased in the 1940s, when most sightings were of 1–4 gulls, and the largest winter flocks totaled 14–24 (Mayfield 1943, Williams 1950). In the 1960s, Great Black-backeds increased dramatically along the Atlantic Coast and the eastern Great Lakes (DeVos 1964). Similar trends were evident in Ohio. Midwinter concentrations in excess of 100 were no longer extraordinary and 350 were estimated at Toledo in December 1967 (Campbell 1968). These populations grew during subsequent decades, and Great Black-backed Gulls are now fairly common to abundant winter residents along Lake Erie, their distribution patterns differing between the Western and Central Basins.

Fall migrants are normally evident in the Western Basin by the last half of August, but flocks of more than 50–75 are unusual before early November. They markedly increase between November 15 and December 10. The largest numbers occur during late December and early January, when the lake and Sandusky Bay begin to freeze. Daily totals of 100–300+ are expected, and more than 1,000 were reported on the 1986 Gypsum Christmas Bird Count. Once the Western Basin freezes, midwinter concentrations are normally 25–100, and flocks in excess of 200 are unusual. When the ice in western Lake Erie breaks up in February or early March, large numbers of Great Black-backeds return to this basin. Their spring concentrations are restricted to March, producing daily totals of 75–200+. Most depart by mid-April, but small numbers of immatures are regularly encountered into May.

Within the Central Basin, Great Black-backed Gulls normally return during late July and August, and flocks of 75–150+ have been discovered by the last half of August. Similar numbers may be found through November, but daily totals are usually fewer than 50. Larger flocks appear when the harbors and bays freeze. They are normally most numerous between early January and late February, when flocks of 250–500+ congregate at hot-water outlets. Concentrations of 800–1,000+ were reported during the 1990s. Their numbers decrease when the ice breaks up, and flocks in excess of 100–250 are unusual after mid-March. Most depart by mid-April, with small numbers lingering into May.

Summering Great Black-backed Gulls were unknown along Lake Erie until single gulls appeared near Toledo in 1944 and at Cleveland in 1947 (Campbell 1968, Williams 1950). There were few additional summer records until the mid-1960s, when small numbers of immatures appeared along western Lake Erie. They have regularly summered within the Western Basin since the mid-1970s, but became regular summer visitors to the Central Basin only during the 1990s. Great Black-backed Gulls are now rare to locally fairly common nonbreeding summer visitors along the entire lakefront. Most sightings are of ten or fewer; the largest flocks total 50 along western Lake Erie and 20–75+ at several locations in the Central Basin. They are mostly immatures but a few nonbreeding adults have been noted.

As the Lake Erie population increased during the 1990s, the number of reports from inland locations has shown a similar trend, especially within the northern counties. They are presently casual to rare visitors along the Maumee River upstream to the Waterville area, where the first record occurred on February 18, 1934 (Campbell 1940). In the northeastern counties, small numbers apparently visit inland landfills and have been periodically noted south to Oberlin Reservoir (Lorain County), the Akron area, and Lake Rockwell (Portage County). Most are found during winter, but one lingered at Lake Rockwell through May 27–28, 1996 (Conlon and Harlan 1996a). Other sightings from northern Ohio include two reports from the Mansfield area and single records from Youngstown, Wayne County, Mosquito Creek Reservoir,

Huron County, and Seneca County. In central Ohio, the first documented inland Great Black-backed Gull was an immature at Buckeye Lake on November 19, 1933 (Trautman 1940). There are at least four reports from the Columbus area, where a maximum of three occurred during the 1993–1994 winter (Harlan 1994b). Other records include another sighting from Buckeye Lake and one from Buck Creek State Park. The only acceptable report from unglaciated Ohio is of one at Tappan Lake on May 17, 1998 (E. Schlabach 1998), while one at Dayton on January 16, 1999, provides the only report from southern Ohio (Brock 1999b).

Sabine's Gull *Xema sabini* (Sabine)

Sabine's Gulls are usually observed as individuals migrating across open oceans or adults on their Arctic breeding grounds. For many years, these boldly patterned gulls appeared only accidentally in the interior of North America. Since the late 1960s, they have been rare but fairly regular fall migrants across the Great Lakes. Within Ohio, there were only four sightings before 1970 and three records between 1970 and 1979. But in the 1980s, there were observations during eight years and they were detected at a similar rate in the 1990s. This increased number of sightings probably reflects expanded coverage by birdwatchers along the lakefront.

The best opportunity to observe a Sabine's Gull comes during October storms along Lake Erie, when strong northwesterly winds blow the birds onshore. These gulls are recognized by their distinctive wing patterns as they quickly fly along the lakefront, frequently with small flocks of Bonaparte's Gulls. A storm on October 3, 1987, produced four Sabine's Gulls at Vermilion and three in the Cleveland area (Peterjohn 1988a). However, not every movement is associated with storms. The largest flock, one adult and seven immature gulls, was observed at Huron on September 15, 1984, an overcast day with light winds (Peterjohn 1985a).

Sabine's Gulls are casual to rare fall migrants along Lake Erie, principally from Huron eastward. Most sightings are of single individuals, primarily immatures. The earliest migrants returned to Lorain by September 2–5, while late birds may be observed through November 10–20, but most are noted between September 25 and October 20. Despite these gulls' distinctive characteristics, two Christmas Bird Count records have to be questioned because they lack any documentation.

They are accidental fall migrants through the interior of Ohio. Three fall records are from central Ohio: Buckeye Lake on October 9, 1926 (Trautman 1940); Hoover Reservoir on October 4, 1970 (Thomson 1983); and Deer Creek Reservoir on October 11–12, 1987 (Peterjohn 1988a). Other sightings come from Lake Milton (Mahoning County) on September 21, 1940 (Walker 1940e); Lake St. Marys on October 20, 1956 (Clark and Sipe 1970); Hueston Woods State Park between November 3–13, 1985 (Peterjohn 1986a); and in Seneca County on September 22–27, 1991 (Peterjohn 1992a). A report from the Ohio River may not pertain to the limited portion of the river within Ohio's boundaries.

On January 21, 1989, a first-winter Sabine's Gull was discovered at Cleveland. Remarkably, this individual remained there into April, and provided the first confirmed winter record of Sabine's Gull from North America (Rosche and Hannikman 1989). It was rediscovered at Lorain on May 7, and was periodically observed along the lakefront between Lorain and Headlands Beach State Park during that summer (Peterjohn 1989d). It remained in the Lorain area into November (Peterjohn 1990a).

Black-legged Kittiwake *Rissa tridactyla* (Linnaeus)

Despite anecdotal nineteenth-century accounts along Lake Erie, Ohio's first confirmed Black-legged Kittiwake was a specimen collected at Buckeye Lake on November 7, 1925 (Trautman 1926). This species then went undetected until single kittiwakes appeared at Cleveland in 1944 and 1947 (Williams 1950). Since there were only two additional sight records through 1965, Trautman and Trautman (1968) considered them accidental visitors to the state. Their status changed during the mid-1960s. Between 1966 and 1977, kittiwakes were observed in all but three years. They have been annually observed since 1977. More thorough coverage by birdwatchers along Lake Erie probably contributed to the increased numbers detected during recent decades.

Black-legged Kittiwakes are now rare late fall visitors to central Lake Erie but casual migrants along the Western Basin. There are usually one to five sightings along the lakefront each autumn of 1–2 kittiwakes. The earliest confirmed kittiwakes appear during the last week of October, but most sightings are between November 10 and December 15. Kittiwakes are accidental late fall visitors away from the lakefront, with two sightings each from C.J. Brown Reservoir, the Columbus area, and the Dayton area. Single kittiwakes have been recorded at Buckeye Lake, Lake St. Marys, Clear Fork Reservoir (Richland County), and Findlay. A report of kittiwakes from the Ohio River near Marietta may not have been in the Ohio portion of the river. Inland kittiwakes are observed between October 25 and December 28.

Most kittiwakes disappear from Lake Erie between December 30 and January 20. Wintering kittiwakes are casually encountered along the Cleveland-Lorain lakefront but are accidental elsewhere, including a possible January sighting from Dayton (Mathena et al. 1984). All winter records are of

1–2 individuals. Some remain for only a few days, while others linger through the winter.

Spring kittiwakes are accidental visitors to Lake Erie, with one record in the 1970s and six since 1980. These records are mostly of single kittiwakes along the Cleveland-Lorain lakefront during March, although one remained through April 13, 1975 (Kleen 1975c). These are most likely kittiwakes that wintered on the Great Lakes. Spring records from western Lake Erie are limited to a sighting of four in Ottawa County on March 28, 1985, with one intermittently observed through May 2 (Peterjohn 1985c). The only inland spring record is from Beaver Creek Reservoir (Seneca County) on March 20, 1990 (Peterjohn 1990c).

Black-legged Kittiwakes are accidental summer visitors, with only one record from Lake Erie. One was observed at Lorain on June 9 and 19, 1989, and provided the fortunate observers with a unique opportunity to study simultaneously a Little Gull, Sabine's Gull, and Black-legged Kittiwake in their first-summer plumages (Hannikman 1989).

No matter when these birds appear, most satisfactory sightings are of first-year kittiwakes. There are only four acceptable records of adults, beginning with one at Cleveland on November 15, 1986 (Peterjohn 1987a). The other three adults were discovered in the Central Basin between December 7 and February 3.

Ross's Gull *Rhodostethia rosea* (MacGillivray)

Normally associated with coastal habitats, river deltas, and marshy tundra in Arctic areas, Ross's Gulls seldom wander to more temperate climates. In North America, they are most frequently observed as fall visitors to the Arctic coast of Alaska, although a few pairs attempted to nest near Churchill, Manitoba, during the 1980s and 1990s. They are accidental visitors elsewhere on the continent, and have wandered south to the mid-Atlantic states, the Great Lakes, and inland locations in the northern United States (AOU 1998). Wandering Ross's Gulls frequently associate with Bonaparte's Gulls, and the fact that Lake Erie hosts immense numbers of Bonaparte's each autumn has motivated birders to search through these flocks for this rare denizen of Arctic oceans. Ross's Gulls have been discovered twice. On December 14, 1997, Craig Holt observed an adult at Conneaut. No photographs were obtained, but the bird was carefully described (Brock 1999a). On November 15, 1998, Larry Rosche and Ray Hannikman discovered a Ross's Gull among a flock of Bonaparte's Gulls at Headlands Beach State Park. The gull remained offshore for several hours and was studied by numerous observers, but drifted out of view once the strong northwesterly winds subsided in late morning (Rosche 1998c).

Ivory Gull *Pagophila eburnea* (Phipps)

Few North American birds can withstand the rigorous conditions favored by Ivory Gulls. They breed on barren islands high in the Arctic. During winter, they favor the pack ice covering northern oceans, although they occasionally appear along the Atlantic Coast south to New Jersey. They are accidental visitors to interior North America, where they have wandered south to Tennessee, but most sightings have been near the Great Lakes (AOU 1998). This species has appeared in Ohio only once. An adult Ivory Gull was discovered by Jim Hoffman along the Cleveland lakefront on December 17, 1975. Apparently forced to shore by inclement weather, it associated with other gulls at the hotwater outlet of a power plant. It was closely studied and photographed by a number of observers through December 19 but departed as soon as weather conditions moderated (Hammond 1975).

Caspian Tern *Sterna caspia* Pallas

With loud rasping calls, Caspian Terns announce their presence as they fly along the shores of Lake Erie. The largest terns in the world, the breeding adults are impressive with their large crimson beaks and sharp black caps as they plunge into the lake for small fish. These birds are taken for granted today, but Caspian Terns have not always been regular visitors to Ohio. Decimated by the millinery trade during the nineteenth century, they were considered rare stragglers in the early 1900s (Jones 1903). Their numbers recovered, and a flock of 200 was reported near Toledo by 1928 (Campbell 1968). Large flocks did not appear in the Central Basin until the 1970s. The Great Lakes breeding population has steadily increased since the 1970s (Scharf and Shugart 1998a), a trend that has produced improved numbers across Ohio.

Along Lake Erie, Caspian Terns are fairly common to locally abundant spring migrants. The earliest returned to Sandusky Bay by March 13, 1982 (Peterjohn 1982c), but they usually appear during April 5–10. They are most numerous during the last half of April, when 30 or fewer are normally observed daily, with occasional flocks of 50–300+. The largest spring concentration totaled 586 at Lorain on April 24, 1996 (Brock 1996c). Most depart by May 22–28, but an unusually late flock of 150 appeared at Oregon (Lucas County) on May 27, 1986 (Peterjohn 1986d).

Within the interior counties, spring Caspians are rare to uncommon migrants at large lakes in the glaciated counties, becoming casual to rare on the unglaciated Allegheny Plateau. Most observations are of six or fewer, with infrequent flocks of 10–20. Their timing is similar to movements along Lake Erie, with most sightings between April 12 and May 15. While Trautman

(1940) noted late May flights at Buckeye Lake before 1940, these movements have not been evident in recent years.

Caspian Terns do not breed along Lake Erie, although colonies are established on other Great Lakes (Scharf and Shugart 1998). Nonbreeders are rare along the Ohio lakefront, usually in groups of six or fewer. Flocks with as many as 25 infrequently appear in late June. Nonbreeding Caspians are accidental to casual summer visitors in the interior counties. They are mostly observed in groups of four or fewer at reservoirs in the northern half of the state, with a few south to the Ohio River.

The first fall migrants return to Lake Erie by mid-July and are regularly noted after July 20. These migrants frequently include adults accompanied by dependent young; the shrill cries of begging Caspians become a familiar greeting for adults returning with a meal. Caspian Terns are normally fairly common to locally abundant migrants along the lakefront, but can be scarce during some years. They are most numerous in August and the first half of September, when flocks of 50–250 frequently develop. The largest concentration totaled 450 at Huron on August 28, 1983 (Peterjohn 1984a). Most daily totals are 25 or fewer. Small numbers are regularly noted through October 20–25. There are few November records, but Caspians have remained through November 18–20. The only December sight record is not accompanied by substantiating details.

In the interior counties, Caspian Terns are casual to locally uncommon fall migrants, least numerous in unglaciated Ohio. They appear at the same time as migrants along Lake Erie. Most observations are of 1–8 during August and September, although several flocks of 18–36 have appeared in the northeastern counties. The last inland migrants normally depart during October, but a few linger into the first half of November.

Royal Tern *Sterna maxima* Boddaert

Royal Terns are normally associated with coastal habitats. In eastern North America, their nesting range extends along the Gulf of Mexico and Atlantic Coast north to New Jersey. Small numbers of Royal Terns have wandered into the interior of the continent as far as the Great Lakes region (AOU 1998). Ohio's only acceptable record is of an adult Royal Tern discovered by Tom LePage at Lorain on July 8, 1995. The bird was observed with a small flock of Ring-billed Gulls and several Caspian Terns, but disappeared shortly after its discovery. The same individual was rediscovered there on July 20–21, and was photographed and studied by numerous birders (LePage 1995).

Common Tern *Sterna hirundo* Linnaeus

Perhaps no bird attests to the health of the Great Lakes ecosystem better than the Common Tern. A healthy tern population is indicative of healthy lakes that support abundant prey and suitable undisturbed nest sites, while environmental problems are reflected by declining numbers of terns. Unfortunately, the impact of people on the Great Lakes has threatened Common Terns in ways we are only beginning to understand.

Common Tern

Common Terns were originally abundant summer residents along western Lake Erie (Courtney and Blokpoel 1983). Their numbers remained fairly constant until the late 1800s, when populations were reduced by the millinery trade. When this trade ended, terns recovered very quickly. By the early 1900s, Jones (1909) estimated 3,000 nesting pairs and 1,500 nonbreeders on western Lake Erie islands in Ohio and Ontario.

Regular disturbance at some nesting colonies forced Common Terns to expand to the mainland, where their first nests were located in 1928 (Campbell 1968). These mainland colonies suffered greater disturbance by egg collectors and mammalian predators, and none achieved long-term success (Campbell 1968, Hicks 1935a). By 1939, an estimated 1,000–2,000 pairs nested on the western Lake Erie islands and 1,000–5,000 at mainland locations. Their reproductive success was poor and some years no young terns were raised.

In the 1940s, mainland colonies were abandoned but large colonies remained on several islands. The expansion of nesting Herring Gulls within western Lake Erie proved disastrous for Common Terns. The gulls usurped the tern colonies on Starve and Rattlesnake Islands in Ohio and the Chicken Islands in Ontario, where Common Terns have not nested since the mid-1950s (Campbell 1968). Newly created dikes and dredge disposal sites in Maumee Bay provided temporary replacements for their lost colonies. Some of these colonies were fairly successful but all were short-lived; either nesting gulls or dense vegetation forced the terns to find new sites. These colonies moved around Maumee Bay during the 1950s and 1960s, and as many as 5,000 nesting terns were still present in 1967 (Campbell 1968).

These colonies declined to 1,250 nests in 1968 and 1,000 in 1970 (Campbell 1973). High lake levels eliminated them in 1971. No terns nested until 1975, when a colony was established at a dredge disposal basin along Maumee Bay (Shields and Townsend 1985). At least 350 pairs nested at this site, experiencing good success in 1975 and 1976 but raising few young between 1977 and 1979. Their last successful year was 1980, when 147 young were banded. This colony subsequently declined and no nesting terns returned in 1983 (Kleen 1980d). Common Terns reappeared in 1986 and have nested during subsequent years, but only as a small number of pairs at a few sites in Lucas and Erie Counties (Peterjohn and Rice 1991).

Their status at inland locations reflected their changing abundance along Lake Erie. During the 1920s and 1930s, migrants regularly visited every large lake. Trautman (1940) observed as many as 600 at Buckeye Lake during spring, while flocks of 100+ were not unusual in autumn. Smaller flocks were reported elsewhere, including 50–75 in the Cincinnati-Dayton area during spring (Kemsies and Randle 1953, Mathena et al. 1984). Migrant Common Terns declined in the 1940s and 1950s. Since 1960, inland flocks in excess of 30–40 have been very infrequently encountered.

While Common Terns have been reported as early as March 29–April 5, they normally appear during April 20–30. They are widely distributed by May 5–10. Spring migrants are noted throughout May and occasionally into mid-June. Common Terns are now uncommon to fairly common spring migrants along Lake Erie. Before their populations declined, as many as 5,000 assembled in the Western Basin during May (Baird 1931a). These large concentrations have not been reported since the 1940s. Between 1970 and the mid-1980s, the largest spring flocks were generally composed of 50–200. The 1,500 at Lorain on May 16, 1983, is exceptional for recent years (Peterjohn 1983c). Since the mid-1980s, most spring flocks total 30 or fewer, with a maximum of 580 at Lorain on May 15, 1996 (Conlon and Harlan 1996a). Within the interior counties, spring Common Terns are mostly observed at large lakes, but occasionally visit ponds and borrow pits. They are now casual to uncommon migrants, mostly noted in groups of ten or fewer, with infrequent flocks of 15–25. The largest recent inland flock is 250–300 at Marietta on May 7, 1963 (Hall 1963a).

Breeding Common Terns are restricted to western Lake Erie at two sites between Sandusky and Toledo. This breeding population fluctuated between 60 and 180 pairs during the 1990s (Cuthbert et al. 1997, Peterjohn 1990d). Their colonies have been located on small islands, dredge disposal sites, dikes, and beaches, although they occasionally nested on muskrat houses in marshes when their populations were larger (Campbell 1940, 1968). Adults return to these colonies by early May. Eggs are laid as early as May 7, and young may hatch by the first week of June (Campbell 1968, Shields and Townsend 1985). If their first clutch is destroyed, Common Terns will renest, and nests with eggs have been reported through August 4. These late nests rarely produce young.

When their first clutches are successful, young Common Terns may appear with their parents during the last half of July.

Away from these breeding colonies, Common Terns are casual to rare summer visitors along Lake Erie, mostly as scattered individuals. While nonbreeders once were observed regularly within the interior counties, the number of midsummer records has declined since the mid-1950s. Nonbreeding terns are now accidental to casual summer visitors to all inland lakes, usually single terns or groups of four or fewer.

Despite declining populations, Common Terns continue to use the south shore of Lake Erie as a major staging area before their fall migration, remaining for several weeks to more than a month (Blokpoel et al. 1987). They do not remain at one location but move along the entire lakefront from the Cleveland area westward. The first fall migrants return to Lake Erie between July 15 and 25 and become locally common by August 7–10. Flocks of 500–2,000 appeared during most years through the 1980s but became less regular during the 1990s. Before 1980, the largest flocks totaled 3,300 at Cleveland on September 21, 1969; 4,000 at Ottawa National Wildlife Refuge on September 2, 1979; and an estimated 8,000 there on September 4, 1974 (Thomson 1983). Since 1980, the 3,700 in Lucas County on September 18, 1988, easily surpasses other recent totals (Peterjohn 1989a). After October 15, flocks are usually composed of fewer than 100 terns, although a remarkable 500 appeared at Cleveland on November 15, 1960 (Mumford 1961a). Most depart by November 5–15.

Since most Common Terns winter in oceans south of the United States (AOU 1998), their presence along Lake Erie in late November or early December may seem surprising. Given the numbers congregating along Lake Erie each fall, a few late migrants should be expected. Small flocks of 10–20 have been observed through November 24, but most late migrants are single terns, occasionally healthy adults but usually immatures in poor condition. Most stragglers disappear during the first half of December. When the weather is relatively mild, they may remain through December 15–25 and an adult specimen was taken at Lorain as late as December 30, 1892. Despite December sightings every two or three years, Common Terns have not been reported later than January 2.

Within the interior counties, Common Terns are now casual to locally uncommon fall migrants at large lakes, least numerous in unglaciated Ohio. Most records are of ten or fewer, with occasional flocks of 20–30. The largest recent inland concentration was 100 at Hoover Reservoir (Delaware County) on September 8, 1981. These migrants mostly appear between mid-August and late September. When populations were larger, small numbers would remain through October 15–20. The latest migrants have been reported through November 11–17.

Arctic Tern *Sterna paradisaea* Pontoppidan

Few birds match the long-distance migrations of Arctic Terns. In North America, they breed across the tundra of Alaska and northern Canada and locally along the Atlantic Coast south to Massachusetts. Migrants normally occur far offshore of both coasts. These terns winter in southern oceans off Antarctica (AOU 1998). In recent years, small numbers have proved to be casual migrants through the Great Lakes region. While most inland migrants are recorded during late May or early June, Ohio's first sighting of this accidental visitor was an adult in its fall migration. This Arctic Tern was discovered along Lake Erie at the Huron pier on July 27, 1980, by myself and Don Tumblin. It was closely studied and photographed while resting among a flock of Common and Forster's Terns (Kleen 1980d). During this observation, a small earthquake startled both the terns and the observers, allowing us to compare its diagnostic wing pattern with the other species. The second record was provided by two adults discovered at Alum Creek Reservoir on June 5, 1993 (Brock 1993d). These terns visited the lake during a day of inclement weather.

Forster's Tern *Sterna forsteri* Nuttall

In the early 1900s, Forster's Terns were apparently casual visitors, with very few substantiated records. Difficulties in distinguishing Forster's from Common Terns undoubtedly contributed to the paucity of nineteenth-century records from Ohio (Jones 1903). Their status did not improve until the 1930s, when observers became more adept at identifying terns and discovered Forster's Terns along western Lake Erie. The first Toledo area records were in 1933, and they became regular fall migrants by the end of the decade, with a maximum of 45 on October 18, 1937 (Campbell 1940). They remained accidental visitors elsewhere.

Their numbers gradually improved during the 1940s and 1950s in the western third of Ohio. Forster's Terns were regularly observed at Lake St. Marys after 1940 and Cincinnati after 1948 (Clark 1944a, Kemsies and Randle 1953). Along western Lake Erie, flocks of 100+ were noted during the 1950s, with a maximum of 200 in 1958 (Campbell 1968). Surprisingly few terns were reported from central and eastern Ohio.

During the 1970s and 1980s, Forster's Terns became regular migrants along the lake's Central Basin, particularly in autumn. As many as 132 were counted at Lorain on August 24, 1987 (Hannikman 1987b). For comparison, flocks of 200–400 regularly appeared along western Lake Erie, where the largest concentration totaled 1,000 in Sandusky Bay on September 15, 1968 (Campbell 1973). Within the interior counties, small numbers regularly passed through western and central Ohio but remained noteworthy in the eastern counties. Their numbers continued to increase during the 1990s, and Forster's Terns are now more numerous than Common Terns at many inland and some lakefront locations.

Forster's Terns are slightly earlier spring migrants than Commons. They have returned by March 25–26, and frequently appear during the first week of April. In recent years, any tern appearing before mid-April is most likely a Forster's. Their largest numbers are expected between April 20 and May 20; they become scarce after June 1. They are now uncommon to locally common migrants along Lake Erie, least numerous east of Cleveland. The largest lakefront flock totaled 375 at Lorain on May 17, 1997 (Fazio 1997b), but most reports are of 50 or fewer. Away from Lake Erie, Forster's Terns are generally rare to uncommon spring migrants in the glaciated counties and casual to rare elsewhere. Most are detected on large lakes but may also appear on ponds and borrow pits. Inland reports generally are of ten or fewer, with as many as 38 at Killdeer Plains Wildlife Area on May 18, 1995, and 15 in the unglaciated counties (Harlan 1995c).

Forster's Terns do not breed in Ohio, although they nest as close as Lake St. Clair (AOU 1998). Nonbreeding terns are rare summer visitors along the lakefront from Lorain westward, mostly as groups of five or fewer, although as many as 35–70 have gathered in the Central Basin. They are accidental to casual summer visitors away from Lake Erie, most likely to appear in the western half of the state, in groups of three or fewer.

As fall migrants, Forster's Terns are common to abundant along western Lake Erie. They associate with large flocks of Commons, and concentrations of 200–600+ Forster's appear east to Huron. Away from these concentrations, Forster's are mostly observed in flocks of 50 or fewer. They become uncommon to fairly common in the Central Basin, where most reports are of 30 or fewer, with occasional flocks of 50–100. Lakefront migrants have returned during the last week of June but usually appear by July 15–20. Large flocks may be encountered by mid-July but are more likely between August 10 and October 7. Their numbers normally diminish by October 20, but as many as 200 remained near Toledo through November 5 (Campbell 1973). The last migrants usually depart by November 10–15; a few linger into the first week of December. Within the interior counties, their fall status is similar to spring. They are usually encountered in groups of six or fewer, although a flock of 30 was reported at C.J. Brown Reservoir on October 20, 1985. While they may appear between early July and early November, most are observed during August 10–October 1.

Although Forster's Terns are the hardiest North American terns, there are few winter records from Ohio. The only documented sightings are of single terns at Cleveland on January 6–8, 1983, and at Headlands Beach State Park on January 13, 1990 (Peterjohn 1983b, 1990b).

Least Tern *Sterna antillarum* (Lesson)

Within the interior United States, breeding Least Terns are normally associated with the Mississippi and Missouri River systems. Most nest along large rivers in the plains states from Montana and North Dakota to northern Texas. There are also colonies scattered along the Mississippi River north to southern Illinois and along the lower Ohio River to southwestern Indiana (AOU 1998). Given this breeding range, Least Terns are not expected to wander regularly into Ohio.

During the twentieth century, Least Terns were unrecorded until 1924, when five appeared at Buckeye Lake on May 28 (Trautman 1940). The next record was from Toledo on September 16, 1934 (Campbell 1940). They have subsequently averaged two to six sightings a decade.

Least Terns are accidental spring visitors, with eleven records scattered across Ohio. Two sightings are in April: one near Gallipolis on April 16, 1972, and three at Evans Lake (Mahoning County) on April 23, 1950 (Brooks 1950c, Hall 1972b). The remaining records occur between May 10 and 30; 1–5 terns at Painesville, Cleveland, Lucas County, Lake St. Marys, Logan County, Pickerington (Franklin County), Buckeye Lake, Marietta, and Cincinnati.

There are only three summer records: adults at Gilmore Ponds in Butler County on July 1, 1951; in Lorain on June 18, 1997; and in Hamilton County on June 14, 1999 (Kemsies and Randle 1953, Brock 1997d, 1999d). All were nonbreeders.

As fall migrants, Least Terns are accidental to casual visitors along Lake Erie. Since 1934, there are at least twelve records along the lakefront—six in Ottawa and Lucas Counties, and six between Huron and Cleveland. All sightings are of single terns, two between July 11 and 17 and the remainder from August 14 to September 16. They are accidental fall migrants through the interior counties, with only six records: two terns collected in Hamilton County in 1878, and singles reported at Lake St. Marys in 1953 and 1965, at Buck Creek State Park in 1976, and reservoirs near Columbus in 1980 and 1987, mostly in late August and early September. A late adult was noted at Alum Creek Reservoir on September 23, 1980 (Kleen 1981).

Their status during the nineteenth century is uncertain. While there is only one published specimen record, both Jones (1903) and Dawson (1903) considered them rare migrants and implied that they had declined during recent decades. Least Terns were greatly reduced by the millinery trade, and their distribution and relative abundance may have been substantially different during the 1800s.

Large-billed Tern *Phaetusa simplex* (Gmelin)

The appearance of a Large-billed Tern in Ohio is one of the most unlikely events in our ornithological history. This unmistakable tern was observed at Evans Lake in Mahoning County on May 29, 1954. It was discovered resting on a sandbar with Caspian and Common Terns by Vincent McLaughlin, Evan Dressel, and William Findley (McLaughlin 1979). This sighting provided only the second North American record, the first occurring in Illinois during 1949 (AOU 1998). Large-billed Terns are normally found along rivers and freshwater lakes in northern and central South America east of the Andes Mountains. They are partially migratory and wander to the coast during the austral winter (AOU 1998). Since extralimital sightings are few in North America, these Large-billed Tern records have been questioned. However, this species is unknown in captivity and its appearance in Ohio corresponds with its seasonal movements in South America.

Black Tern *Chlidonias niger* (Linnaeus)

Marshes along western Lake Erie support breeding bird communities found nowhere else in Ohio, and no bird is a better indicator of the health of these wetlands than the Black Tern. These handsome terns breed in only the most diverse and least disturbed wetlands. The adults gracefully forage over open water, hawking insects and capturing small fish for their young, which are found in nests placed on muskrat houses or piles of debris hidden among cattails. Adult Black Terns are very protective, aggressively attacking all intruders approaching too close to their eggs or broods.

Within the western Lake Erie marshes, Black Terns normally initiate their nesting activities during the last half of May. The first clutches are laid by May 20–June 10. Most young terns hatch by late June, although flying young have been reported as early as July 4 (Campbell 1940, 1968; Henninger 1910b). Renesting attempts produce clutches through the first week of July.

Breeding Black Terns were formerly common residents in the marshes of Ottawa, Lucas, Erie, and Sandusky Counties and on North Bass, Middle Bass, and Kelleys Islands (Campbell 1968 Hicks 1935a). Through the early 1960s, nesting terns occurred in every large marsh, with as many as 26 pairs found in a single wetland (Anderson 1960). They declined rapidly between 1965 and 1975 (Campbell 1973, Peterjohn and Rice 1991). By the late 1970s, breeding terns were restricted to only two or three marshes during some years and four to six in others, depending upon habitat conditions. The total population was no more than 25–40 pairs during the 1980s (Peterjohn and Rice 1991). Their numbers were still declining, and by 1991, breeding Black Terns had disappeared from the western Lake Erie marshes (Scharf 1998). Nesting may have occurred in 1993 and 1999, but Black Terns have become sporadic summer residents in these marshes.

Black Terns occasionally nested elsewhere in northern Ohio. Jones (1914) reported breeding pairs in Lorain County around the turn of the twentieth century but provided little specific information. In Ashtabula County, Hicks (1933a) reported single nesting pairs during 1928 and 1932; they also nested at Pymatuning Lake in 1936 (Baird 1936c). The only Mahoning County breeding record was of two nests discovered in July 1959 (Brooks 1959a). A small colony was established at Cleveland in 1958, when 14 pairs and three nests were noted. This colony totaled 20 pairs in 1959 but only three pairs and two nests in 1960 (Newman 1969). There have been no nesting attempts away from western Lake Erie since 1960.

Nonbreeding Black Terns were once regularly encountered at inland reservoirs. Trautman (1940) considered them uncommon summer visitors to Buckeye Lake in the 1920s and 1930s. Clark and Sipe (1970) claimed they were fairly common nonbreeding visitors to Lake St. Marys. Numbers of nonbreeders also declined after 1960, and Black Terns are now accidental summer visitors to the interior counties.

As their breeding populations declined, numbers of migrant Black Terns underwent a corresponding decrease. They were formerly common spring migrants. Trautman (1940) reported 10–50 daily at Buckeye Lake before 1940, with maxima of 300–700 during late May and early June. They were common migrants at Lake St. Marys, where 200 were reported on May 18, 1952 (Clark and Sipe 1970). Kemsies and Randle (1953) reported a large movement through western Ohio on May 12, 1951, with 100 in Butler County and flocks on most ponds and flooded fields north to Lake St. Marys. Black Terns are now casual to rare spring migrants in most counties, usually noted in groups of five or fewer, with occasional concentrations of 8–12. The earliest migrant appeared at Paulding Reservoir by April 18, 1997 (Fazio 1997b), but most are observed between May 10 and June 5.

As fall migrants, Black Terns formerly congregated along Lake Erie. Although they were normally observed in flocks of 20 or fewer, larger concentrations developed during most years. The largest flocks formed in the 1940s in the Western Basin, where Campbell (1968) reported 1,500 on July 19, 1941, and August 26, 1944. By the mid-1970s, these concentrations mostly appeared between Huron and Cleveland. While 1,000 were reported from Cleveland during August 1982 (Peterjohn 1983a), these flocks diminished rapidly during the 1980s. Only 160 were counted in August 1986 (Peterjohn 1987a), and by 1989, fall migrants had almost completely disappeared along Lake Erie. Black Terns are now generally casual to uncommon fall migrants along the entire lakefront, with most sightings of ten or fewer. The largest flock reported during the 1990s totaled 120 at Metzger Marsh Wildlife Area on August 13, 1996 (Conlon and Harlan 1996b). The first fall migrants may appear by mid-July. Although flocks occasionally form by the end of the month, most migrants are detected during August and the first week of September. Most Black Terns depart by September 20–30. A few late migrants have remained through October 31–November 14.

Fall Black Terns were less numerous within the inland counties. Trautman (1940) reported "generally less than 60 per day" at Buckeye Lake before 1940, with a maximum of 120. Smaller numbers were reported at other lakes, although they were generally regarded as fairly common to common migrants until the late 1950s. These migrants subsequently declined, and became accidental to rare visitors to inland lakes, least numerous in the unglaciated counties. Most recent sightings are of groups of six or fewer, with infrequent concentrations of 15–28. A flight on August 14, 1994, produced flocks of 20–35+ at three lakes in central Ohio (Harlan 1995a). They normally appear in August and early September, with late migrants through the end of the month.

Thick-billed Murre *Uria lomvia* (Linnaeus)

Except during the breeding season, Thick-billed Murres normally spend their lives on the northern oceans. On rare occasions, strong storms have produced dramatic inshore movements of murres; some have even wandered considerable distances inland. The most famous flight of Thick-billed Murres followed an early December storm off New England in 1896. This storm scattered murres along the Atlantic Coast south to South Carolina and inland as far as Iowa. The first Ohio specimens were captured at Fairport Harbor on December 18 and Sandusky on December 19. By the end of the month, reports along Lake Erie totaled four murres in Lorain County, three in Erie County, two in Lake County, and one in Ashtabula County (Jones 1903). Others may have occurred in Ottawa County. Given these numbers reported by only a few observers, the magnitude of this inland movement must have been substantial. Similar circumstances produced a smaller flight during December 1907 that resulted in specimens taken at Sandusky on December 1 and inland near Jefferson (Ashtabula County) on December 22 (Moseley 1908, Sim 1907). Moseley (1908) also related accounts of two murres taken to taxidermists and of hunters shooting four others. The last Ohio record of this accidental visitor was not related to any storm. One was observed closely by Doolittle (1924a) on December 12, 1920, as it swam in Lake Erie at the entrance to Fairport Harbor.

Black Guillemot *Cepphus grylle* (Linnaeus)

Black Guillemots are residents of the North Atlantic and Arctic Oceans and seldom wander from their established range (AOU 1998). With few extralimital sightings, including a very small number of reports from inland locations, the appearance of one in Ohio is extraordinary. An immature Black Guillemot was discovered by William and Nancy Klamm at Cleveland on November 8, 1990. This bird spent several days in a harbor, but was found dead on November 11. On this guillemot, the white-tipped outer secondaries and more extensive white primary coverts suggested that it belonged to either the race *mandtii* or *ultimus*, indicating an origin from Arctic Canada rather than the Atlantic Ocean (Peterjohn 1991a).

Long-billed Murrelet *Brachyramphus perdix* (Pallas)

The Long-billed Murrelet is a native of the northeastern Pacific Ocean, with a breeding range extending from Russia to northern Japan (AOU 1998). This species regularly wanders outside of this range and has produced a number of records across North America since 1979 (Mlodinow 1997). Ohio's only Long-billed Murrelet was discovered by Dan Webb at Beaver Creek Reservoir (Seneca County) on November 12, 1996. This cooperative bird remained on the lake through November 18, was viewed by more than 300 observers, and diagnostic photographs were taken (Fazio and Webb 1997).

Ancient Murrelet *Synthliboramphus antiquus* (Gmelin)

Ancient Murrelets, normally occupants of the northern Pacific Ocean, exhibit a tendency to wander into the interior of North America. There are a number of records east to the Great Lakes Region (AOU 1998), primarily during late fall and early winter. The appearance of two of these accidental visitors in Ohio is not completely surprising, except that they provide one of very few spring records outside their normal range. On March 28, 1951, Herb Nielson noticed two small birds swimming in front of his commercial drag seine operating in Sandusky Bay near the Bay Bridge in Erie County. One flew away, but the other dived and drowned in the fishing net. The specimen was saved and deposited in the Ohio State Museum of Zoology (Handley 1953).

Atlantic Puffin *Fratercula arctica* (Linnaeus)

In North America, Atlantic Puffins normally nest along the Atlantic Coast south to Maine and spend the remainder of the year in the Atlantic Ocean.

Except during the breeding season, they are seldom observed from shore. A specimen from the western end of Lake Erie is one of only two reports from the Great Lakes region and the westernmost record from the interior of North America (AOU 1998). An immature puffin was discovered by Henry Kohler on the driveway of his residence in Oregon (Lucas County) on November 18, 1980. Emaciated and unable to fly, it was given to the Toledo zoo. Despite efforts to save it, the puffin died four days later (Kleen 1981).

Rock Dove *Columba livia* Gmelin

As a result of their close association with people, Rock Doves, or domestic pigeons, are among the most widely distributed birds in the world. Remarkably adaptable, they thrive wherever people have modified the surroundings. In this country, large flocks occupy every city, roosting on buildings and living on food provided intentionally or unintentionally by people. They are equally at home in farmlands, roosting on barns and feeding on waste grain in fields.

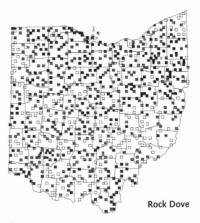

Rock Dove

Since Rock Doves are ignored by most birdwatchers, little information is available on their general biology in Ohio. The feral population was established from pigeons that escaped or were released from captivity. Timing of these releases was not documented, but feral pigeons were present in most large cities during the nineteenth century. They rapidly spread to small towns and rural farmlands. By the 1930s, Rock Doves were well-established residents throughout Ohio (Campbell 1968, Clark and Sipe 1970, Williams 1950).

Rock Doves are common to abundant permanent residents in most counties, becoming locally fairly common in rural southeastern Ohio. They are most numerous in large cities, where flocks of 100–200+ roost on buildings and more than 3,000 have been counted on Christmas Bird Counts. Smaller flocks are found in rural farmlands, where 100–400+ may be tallied daily. In the southeastern counties, daily totals seldom exceed 10–60 except in cities. Persecution and clean farming practices have produced a slight decline in the Ohio breeding population since 1966 (Sauer et al. 1998).

Although they are nonmigratory, Rock Doves undertake local movements. These movements are most noticeable in autumn, when large flocks leave urban areas to feed in harvested farm fields. At Columbus, flocks may fly up to forty miles to find waste grain, leaving their urban roosts at dawn and returning at sunset.

The success of Rock Doves results from their fecundity. Pigeons breed throughout the year; nests with eggs or young are as likely in January as June. A pair may raise four or more broods annually. In urban areas, most nests are placed on buildings, although a few pairs breed in tree cavities (Peterson 1986). Bridges, grain elevators, barns, and other farm buildings are also regularly used for nest sites.

Despite their close association with people, a few pigeons have reverted to more natural habitats and behavior. In southeastern Ohio, they may occupy sheer rocky cliffs bordering steep ravines and highway cuts. Pairs nest in crevices on the cliffs and forage in nearby woods and fields, a lifestyle reminiscent of wild Rock Doves in Europe rather than our domesticated street-wise pigeons.

Mourning Dove *Zenaida macroura* (Linnaeus)

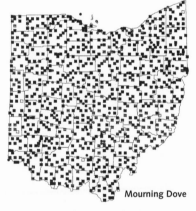

Mourning Dove

Most people are familiar with Mourning Doves, either as visitors to bird feeders, nesting pairs in residential shrubbery, or winter flocks feeding in farm fields. Gentle and tame, these doves benefited from their close association with people. Mourning Doves expanded during the nineteenth century, as the original forests were replaced by agricultural fields. Their breeding populations were well established by the late 1800s (Wheaton 1882). Hicks (1935a) described them as common to abundant summer residents in every county, a status that is applicable today. In fact, their populations have increased throughout eastern and central North America since 1966 (Sauer et al. 1998). These populations are subject to declines after unusually severe winter weather but quickly recover with the return of normal weather conditions.

Breeding Mourning Doves are most numerous near residences. Elsewhere, they are mostly found in edge habitats bordering open fields. Uniformly distributed across Ohio, daily totals of 50–150+ are expected along roadside surveys in early summer. They begin breeding with the first warm days of February and early March, although many early nests are abandoned if the weather turns sharply colder. Their breeding activities normally peak between mid-April and late July (Trautman 1940, Webb 1949). Many pairs make four or more nesting attempts annually, and these activities may continue into autumn; recently fledged young have been noted through early November (Campbell 1968). A few pairs have even produced clutches during December and January (Kleen 1980a, Trautman and Trautman 1968).

The nests are nothing more than a platform of loosely placed twigs. Nonetheless, doves successfully raise young in more than 50 percent of their attempts (Webb 1949). Their nests may be placed as high as forty feet but are usually less than twelve feet high. Conifers are their preferred nest sites, although other dense trees and shrubs will suffice. Ground-nesting doves have been recorded in sphagnum bogs, dry cattail swamps, cutover woods, and red cedar-covered hillsides. They have also nested on limestone outcrops, eroding streambanks, bales of wire, buildings, squirrel nests, and abandoned robins' nests (Roads 1931, Webb 1949).

While their summer status did not change during the twentieth century, their winter numbers increased dramatically. In the early 1900s, Mourning Doves were rather rare winter residents throughout northern Ohio (Jones 1903). In the central counties, they were uncommon residents, and large flocks were only observed during warm winters (Trautman 1940). Large numbers of wintering doves were only expected in southern Ohio. Their numbers gradually improved in the 1930s and 1940s, although wintering doves were mostly confined to cities in northern Ohio (Webb 1949). By the early 1960s, wintering Mourning Doves were established in every county.

Mourning Doves are now fairly common to abundant winter residents, most numerous in the farmlands of western and central Ohio and near cities. Winter totals of 100–1,000+ may be encountered in these areas. They are less numerous in eastern Ohio, where winter totals seldom exceed 25–100. Except for individuals visiting feeders, wintering Mourning Doves are normally encountered in flocks of 20–200+. These flocks usually feed on waste grain and weed seeds in farm fields. Mechanized crop harvesting leaves greater quantities of waste grain, contributing to their expanding winter populations (Hennessy and Van Camp 1963). Each evening, they gather at roosts in dense conifers, thick brush, deciduous trees, or on the ground in dense grassy cover.

While many of Ohio's Mourning Doves are permanent residents, others spend the winter in the southern United States. Their spring migration starts in late February and early March in southern Ohio and mid-March along Lake Erie (Webb 1949). This migration continues through April 15–25. Their fall migration begins in late July and peaks during August and September. The last migrants depart by early December. As their winter populations increased, these migratory movements became less obvious and produced few detectable influxes in recent decades.

Passenger Pigeon *Ectopistes migratorius* (Linnaeus)

At one time, Passenger Pigeons were the most numerous of all North American birds. Their continental population was estimated at three to five billion individuals. As many as two billion may occasionally have congregated into a single flock (Blockstein and Tordorff, 1985). Tales of their immense flocks filled the diaries of early settlers, accounts that are unimaginable today. As stated by Dawson (1903):

> During their passage the sun was darkened and the moon refused to give her light. The beating of their wings was like the voice of thunder, and their steady on-coming like the continuous roar of Niagara. Where they roosted, great branches, and even trees two feet in diameter, were broken down beneath their weight, and where they nested, a hundred square miles of timber groaned with the weight of their nests or lay buried in ordure.

Passenger Pigeons nested, roosted, and migrated in large flocks, mostly feeding on the mast of oak, beech, and chestnut trees. Because mast production is unpredictable, the pigeons were nomadic in order to take advantage of available food supplies. Large flocks would frequently fly hundreds of miles until they found an abundant mast crop, remaining in that area until the crop was depleted. This pattern of nomadic wanderings was most apparent during late summer and fall. As winter approached, many pigeons migrated to the southern states and continued their nomadic movements (Blockstein and Tordorff 1985).

Millions of nesting pairs normally congregated into huge colonies covering at least thirty square miles (Schorger 1955). Perhaps fewer than a dozen large colonies existed in eastern North America, with only scattered nesting attempts elsewhere. With their dependence upon suitable mast crops, the locations of these colonies varied annually. However, one enormous colony normally formed somewhere in Michigan or Wisconsin (Blockstein and Tordorff 1985). Their nesting activities were highly synchronous and most pairs laid their single egg on the same day. These activities were initiated in late March or early April and the young fledged by June.

Despite the radically changing landscape in eastern North America during the nineteenth century, Passenger Pigeons remained abundant through the mid-1800s. Local declines were evident by the 1860s, but their populations did not precipitously decline until 1871–1880. Of the factors contributing to their eventual extinction, overhunting at the nesting colonies was probably the most important (Blockstein and Tordorff 1985). During this decade, better communication and transportation allowed market hunters to decimate every large pigeon colony. Within a single decade, these incredibly abundant birds were reduced to a mere fraction of their former numbers. Nesting success within the remaining small colonies was very poor, resulting in their extinction in the wild by 1900.

Anecdotal accounts indicate that Passenger Pigeons probably resided within Ohio throughout the year but were most numerous during spring and summer (Schorger 1955). Their spring movements were evident in late February and March. While nesting records were scattered across the state, a large colony regularly formed near Buckeye Lake into the 1850s. These pigeons spread out over the entire central Ohio area to feed during the day (Trautman 1940). Nesting was also recorded from Fulton, Pickaway, Morrow, Wayne, Medina, Columbiana, Trumbull, Portage, Geauga, Ashtabula, Mercer, Darke, Highland, and Huron Counties (Hicks 1933a, 1935a). The pigeons roosted at or near these colonies throughout the summer until they departed in September or October (Schorger 1955). Their winter status was imprecisely known, although flocks were occasionally noted.

The Ohio breeding population noticeably declined during the 1850s. By the early 1870s, few nesting pigeons remained. Large migrant flocks still appeared during the 1860s and early 1870s, with the last recorded large flight near Berkey (Lucas County) in 1876 (Campbell 1968, Kemsies and Randle 1953). Their numbers were substantially reduced by 1880, and most counties recorded their last pigeons between 1880 and 1890. There were very few sightings during the 1890s, and the last pigeon collected in the wild was shot near the Pike-Scioto county line on March 24, 1900 (Hicks 1935a). This species became extinct when Martha, a captive Passenger Pigeon at the Cincinnati zoo, died on September 1, 1914.

The extinction of the Passenger Pigeon prompted a number of eulogies, none more fitting than an essay by Aldo Leopold (1947):

> There will always be pigeons in books and in museums, but these are effigies and images, dead to all hardships and to all delights. Book-pigeons cannot dive out of a cloud to make the deer run for cover, nor clap their wings in thunderous applause of mast-laden woods. They know no urge of seasons; they feel no kiss of sun, no lash of wind and weather; they live forever by not living at all.

Common Ground-Dove *Columbina passerina* (Linnaeus)

Common Ground-Doves are occupants of arid, shrubby habitats from the southern United States south to northern South America. They are known to regularly wander north of this range, and vagrants have appeared north to the Great Lakes region and New England in eastern North America (AOU 1998). These vagrants are most likely to appear during late summer and autumn. Ohio's only report is of a Common Ground-Dove discovered by Jared Mizanin at the Brecksville Reservation (Cuyahoga County) on November 5–6, 1999

(Mizanin 1999). The bird was well observed and photographed as it fed for several hours near a parking lot in the park.

Carolina Parakeet *Conuropsis carolinensis* (Linnaeus)

As the only native parrots in eastern North America, Carolina Parakeets were residents from the Ohio River valley to the Gulf of Mexico. Although their exact abundance will never be known, Carolina Parakeets were widespread and regularly encountered during the eighteenth and early nineteenth centuries. Their demise closely paralleled the disappearance of the virgin forests. Because most of the limited information about these parakeets is gleaned from anecdotal accounts of early naturalists and settlers, it is difficult to separate fact from fiction concerning their life history, behavior, and distribution.

During the early 1800s, Carolina Parakeets reportedly "occurred in numbers" in the southern Ohio counties bordering the Ohio River east to the Scioto River. They were most numerous near Cincinnati. Alexander Wilson traveled along the Ohio River during February and March 1811, observing flocks of parakeets at the mouths of the Great Miami and Little Miami Rivers (Wheaton 1882). McKinley (1977), however, believes that the resident population was relatively small and these sizable flocks only sporadically visited Ohio.

These parakeets frequented bottomland forests along large rivers. They roosted and presumably nested in large hollow trees. While historic accounts implied that Carolina Parakeets nested in Ohio, there is little supporting evidence other than a "former nesting tree" in Butler County shown to Dury and Langdon in the mid-1800s (Hicks 1935a). This tree was actually a roosting site, and there are no indisputable nesting records (McKinley 1977). While the parakeets were apparently nomadic in their search for food, they resided within Ohio throughout the year. Severe winter weather took its toll. More than one early account described entire flocks perishing within their roosting trees after unusually harsh weather (Hicks 1935b).

Their former status is more conjectural elsewhere in Ohio. They probably resided within bottomland forests along Ohio River tributaries upstream to Chillicothe on the Scioto River and Piqua (Miami County) along the Great Miami River (Dawson 1903, McKinley 1977). Small flocks occasionally wandered north to the Columbus area but were not regular residents. They seldom wandered into the southeastern counties, although flocks were reportedly observed at the mouth of the Little Hocking River (Athens County) and possibly Marietta (McKinley 1977).

These parakeets may have appeared infrequently in northern Ohio, but most of the records are based on less than satisfactory evidence. Audubon related an account of their occurrence near the mouth of the Maumee River shortly after 1800 (Campbell 1940), but this account was questioned by McKinley (1977). In northeastern Ohio, small numbers of parakeets may have resided in the Tuscarawas River basin. A sighting near Tallmadge (Summit County) is apparently valid, although the reported date of 1853 is probably erroneous. There are no other undisputed records from the northeastern counties; an 1863 specimen from Cleveland was most likely an escaped pet (McKinley 1977).

Available evidence indicates that Carolina Parakeets were declining during the early nineteenth century. Audubon visited Cincinnati in 1831 and reported that numbers had "markedly decreased." Only a few scattered individuals remained (Hicks 1935a). In all likelihood, the resident population disappeared between 1835 and 1840, with only occasional visits by small flocks after 1840 (Wright 1912). The last Ohio record of wild parakeets was a flock of 25–30 at Columbus during July 1862 (Wheaton 1882). A parakeet collected at Newark on October 9, 1884, was believed to be an escaped cage bird (McKinley 1977).

Carolina Parakeets normally fed on the fruits of hackberry, beech, oak, sycamore, and other trees, as well as grape, cocklebur, and a variety of other natural foods (Wright 1912). They also fed in orchards and croplands, a habit that resulted in their widespread persecution. Moreover, these parakeets were regularly kept as pets and, in later years, became victims of the millinery trade. This widespread persecution, combined with habitat destruction, resulted in their extinction. The last wild specimen was taken in Florida on March 12, 1913. The Cincinnati zoo kept the last captive specimen, which died on February 21, 1918 (AOU 1998).

Black-billed Cuckoo *Coccyzus erythropthalmus* (Wilson)

Within most Ohio counties, Black-billeds are the least numerous resident cuckoos. However, their status is somewhat obscured by difficulties distinguishing them from Yellow-billed Cuckoos. Although perched cuckoos at reasonable distances can be readily identified, many are only briefly observed in flight and their field marks are not discernible. Others are not observed at all; their identification is based on vocalizations, some of which are easily confused.

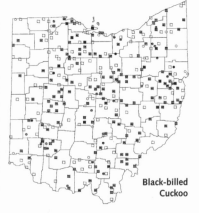

Black-billed
Cuckoo

Breeding Black-billed Cuckoos are most often detected in northern Ohio. They are generally fairly common residents in the northeastern counties. They are never numerous, and summer totals seldom exceed 4–6 daily within these counties. They are also locally fairly common summer residents near Toledo. Elsewhere in northwestern Ohio, they are uncommon to rare residents, least numerous within intensively cultivated farmlands. They are generally uncommon and locally distributed residents in the central counties, becoming locally rare within west-central Ohio. Central Ohio totals seldom exceed 1–3 daily. Nesting Black-billeds are rare residents throughout southern Ohio, mostly encountered as widely scattered pairs. Despite their relative scarcity in central and southern Ohio, breeding Black-billeds were reported from eighty-five counties during the Breeding Bird Atlas project (Peterjohn and Rice 1991). Their numbers may have declined during the 1990s, but Breeding Bird Survey data shows no significant trends for the statewide population (Sauer et al. 1998).

Black-billed Cuckoos may exhibit marked annual fluctuations in abundance. Summering pairs can be scarce some years and mostly restricted to the northern counties. In other years, they are more widely distributed. These fluctuations are not necessarily correlated with annual changes in Yellow-billed Cuckoo populations.

Statewide distribution of Black-billed Cuckoos changed considerably since the 1880s. Wheaton (1882) considered them very common residents throughout Ohio. By the turn of the twentieth century, however, Jones (1903) noted they were "decidedly less common than Yellow-billeds." In the mid-1930s, Hicks (1935a) cited summer records from eighty-four counties, noting that Black-billeds were locally distributed in most portions of the state and were most numerous within the eastern counties. They outnumbered Yellow-billeds along the Allegheny Plateau north to Washington, Morgan, and Hocking Counties (Hicks 1937a). The fewest summering Black-billeds were found in western Ohio, where they were "absent from large areas" (Hicks 1935a). Little information was available on their subsequent population trends.

Nesting Black-billeds are found in second-growth woods, woodland edges, and wooded riparian corridors. In Ashtabula County, Hicks (1933a) noted a preference for aspen thickets near swamps. While they are frequently found near water, Black-billeds also occupy upland woods. Their nests are placed at heights of two to six feet in dense shrubs and saplings. Most nests with eggs are reported during the last half of May and June, with young cuckoos fledging by late July or early August (Campbell 1968, Williams 1950). Late clutches have been reported through August 15; a nest with young through September 5; and adults with dependent young through September 20 (Campbell 1968, Harlan 1996a, Yoder 1997).

Spring Black-billeds may arrive slightly earlier than Yellow-billeds, although the northward movements of both species are frequently simultaneous. The earliest Black-billed returned to Oxford (Butler County) on April 19, 1982 (Peterjohn 1982c). Other early migrants have been noted by April 25–30. They regularly appear during May 6–15 and are generally most numerous between May 15 and June 10. During some years, they may be absent until the last half of May, and their brief migration mostly occurs during June. Black-billed Cuckoos are normally uncommon to fairly common spring migrants. Most reports are of five or fewer daily, with maxima of 8–12.

Black-billeds are uncommon to rare fall migrants in every county; most sightings are of 1–6. This southward movement begins during the last half of August and continues through September. Late individuals remain into the first half of October. Black-billeds are accidental after October 25. The only November records are of a single Black-billed at Canton on November 1, 1953, and two at Cleveland on November 13, 1954 (Nolan 1954a, 1955a).

Yellow-billed Cuckoo *Coccyzus americanus* (Linnaeus)

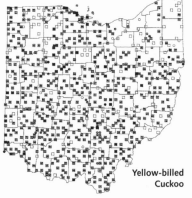

Yellow-billed
Cuckoo

Few birds are as erratic in their seasonal migrations, relative abundance, and distribution patterns as Yellow-billed Cuckoos. During some years they may be very plentiful, in others fairly scarce. Occasionally they do not appear in numbers until midsummer. The factors responsible for these fluctuations have never been satisfactorily established.

While overflights have appeared as early as April 21–23, Yellow-billed Cuckoos are traditionally late migrants, with few records before May 2–7. Some years, they are fairly numerous by the second week of May. In other years, they are absent until May 18–24 and become widespread during June. In general, their northward passage peaks between May 20 and June 7. This migration probably continues through mid-June, although late migrants are difficult to distinguish from residents. Yellow-billeds are fairly common to common spring migrants, normally totaling 1–8 daily, with occasional flights of 10–20.

Yellow-billed Cuckoos are difficult to observe as they sit motionless in tall trees, concealed by the abundant foliage. They are mostly detected by their distinctive loud, throaty calls. Breeding Yellow-billeds occupy a variety of woodland edge and successional habitats. They prefer brushy woodland borders and shrubby corridors adjacent to streams and lakes but also inhabit open second-growth woods, roadside thickets, moist scrubby fields, and brushy fencerows (Trautman 1940, Williams 1950). Their nests are usually placed four to eight feet high in dense saplings and thickets. Most nests with eggs are discovered during June and July, with a few as early as May 28–30 (Campbell 1968, Mathena et al. 1984). Late clutches are occasionally reported during August. Trautman (1940) discovered a nest with eggs on September 20, 1929; the young fledged on October 3. Another late nest with young was noted near Dayton on September 19, 1925 (Mathena et al. 1984). Most young cuckoos fledge between mid-June and early August.

Yellow-billed Cuckoos are widely distributed summer residents, fairly common to common in most counties (Peterjohn and Rice 1991). They are most numerous in the southern and unglaciated counties, where 5–15+ may be counted daily. Daily totals are 3–8 elsewhere. The statewide breeding population has significantly declined since 1980 (Sauer et al. 1998), but the factors responsible for these trends have not been determined. Despite these recent declines, their breeding abundance and distribution have not appreciably changed since the early 1900s (Hicks 1935a, Jones 1903).

Yellow-billed Cuckoos remain fairly conspicuous throughout August, the month their southward migration begins. In central and northwestern Ohio, they may attain their maximum fall abundance in August, regularly feeding on woolly bear caterpillars. By the first week of September, their southward migration is well underway. These cuckoos become inconspicuous, and many migrants are overlooked. Fall Yellow-billeds are generally uncommon to fairly common migrants, most numerous along western Lake Erie, where as many as 10–25 may be observed daily. Fall totals seldom exceed 1–8 elsewhere. The last migrants usually depart by October 5–13. A few remain well into October and there are November sightings from all portions of the state. The latest cuckoos have been noted through November 11, 1931, at Columbus (Borror 1950); November 17, 1975, at Hueston Woods State Park (Kleen 1976a); November 19, 1972, at Toledo (Campbell 1973); November 24, 1985, at Cleveland (Peterjohn 1986a); and December 8, 1990, in Hamilton County (Peterjohn 1991b).

Smooth-billed Ani *Crotophaga ani* Linnaeus

Unlike Groove-billed Anis, which have a well-established pattern of vagrancy in North America, Smooth-billed Anis seldom wander from their limited range in Florida. A few individuals have wandered north along the Atlantic Coast to North Carolina (AOU 1998). The appearance of a Smooth-billed Ani in Ohio was unexpected. An emaciated freshly-dead ani was brought by a cat to a house in Westlake (Cuyahoga County) on November 25, 1993. The specimen was taken to the Cleveland Museum of Natural History, where its identity was confirmed as a first-year male (McLean et al. 1995).

Groove-billed Ani *Crotophaga sulcirostris* Swainson

Although Groove-billed Anis are widely distributed in Central and South America, they have a limited breeding distribution in the United States. Nesting Groove-billeds are mostly found in southern Texas, with small numbers extending northward along the Gulf Coast to western Louisiana (AOU 1998). Despite this limited nesting range, these anis exhibit a tendency to wander considerable distances during autumn, appearing north to the Great Lakes and in most eastern and southwestern states.

These anis are accidental fall visitors to Ohio, observed on four occasions. The first was discovered by Karl Bednarik, Laurel Van Camp, and Jack Brown at the Crane Creek State Park/Magee Marsh Wildlife Area in Ottawa and Lucas Counties on October 20, 1963. The bird, collected that day, furnished one of the first confirmed records from the Great Lakes region (Campbell 1968). The second ani appeared at the Holmes County farm of Vernon Kline in mid-October 1972. During its month-long visit, it became very tame and began to accept food from people. Eventually, its natural foods disappeared and the bird was fed a diet of thirty grasshoppers and one hundred mealworms daily (Kleen and Bush 1973a). It was taken into captivity on November 17 and given to the Cleveland zoo. Ohio's third ani was discovered by myself at Alum Creek Reservoir (Delaware County) on the early date of August 10, 1980 (Kleen 1981). The most recent ani subsisted on persimmons at the Arlene Brown farm near Owensville (Clermont County) during October 1981. It was regularly observed into early November and sporadically through the end of the month (Peterjohn 1982a).

Barn Owl *Tyto alba* (Scopoli)

Barn Owls invaded Ohio during the mid-1800s, after the forested countryside was largely converted to farmlands. The first Ohio specimen was collected from the Cincinnati area around 1861 (Langdon 1879). There were few additional records before 1880, mostly in central Ohio between 1873 and 1878 (Wheaton 1879). Wheaton (1882) cited only six records, but these secretive owls were probably more numerous than these few records indicated.

Their population expanded considerably during the 1880s and 1890s, reaching Lake Erie by 1891 (Jones 1909). At the turn of the twentieth century, Jones (1903) considered them locally common residents in southern Ohio but generally rare elsewhere. They were probably most numerous along the lower Scioto River valley, where Henninger (1902) described them as fairly common and well-established residents.

Breeding populations probably peaked in the 1930s and early 1940s. Hicks (1935a) recorded nesting Barn Owls in eighty-four counties before 1935, describing them as rare to very common but locally distributed, least numerous in the northern tiers of counties. Their overall abundance was

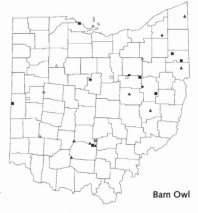

Barn Owl

summarized by his statement that Barn Owls were the "second most numerous owl in most of the state, rivaling Screech-Owls in a few counties."

Their decline was initially apparent in northern Ohio by the late 1940s. Campbell (1968) noted a severe decline near Toledo in the 1950s; at the same time, considerably fewer Barn Owls were observed at Cleveland (Newman 1969). Similar declines were occurring in the central and southern counties. In the 1960s, Barn Owls disappeared from a number of counties and became rare in many others. Local populations still survived; five nests produced 33 young in Ottawa and Lucas Counties in 1960 and 19 owls were banded at Cincinnati in 1964 (Mumford 1960c, Petersen 1964d). By the end of the decade, these populations were declining or had disappeared (Austing and Imbrogno 1976, Campbell 1968). During the 1970s, small populations remained in the Killbuck Creek valley in Wayne and Holmes Counties, the plains of the Ross-Pickaway county line area, and grasslands in Mahoning and Columbiana Counties. Additional breeding pairs were occasionally reported from other locations. Their status and statewide distribution patterns did not change during the 1980s, when 10–20 pairs were present annually (Peterjohn and Rice 1991).

An Ohio Division of Wildlife management program that provides nest boxes near suitable foraging habitats produced a modest recovery during the 1990s, with 40 pairs present statewide in 1998. Additional pairs nesting in natural cavities were probably overlooked. Barn Owls are now rare summer residents along the glacial boundary from Columbiana County south to Ross and Highland Counties. Only widely scattered pairs are present elsewhere in the state. Many locations are traditionally used, especially where nest boxes are provided, while other sites are occupied for only one or two years.

Nesting Barn Owls occupy undisturbed structures, including tree cavities, barns, silos, water towers, attics of houses, and church steeples. Their nests are usually placed within one mile of pastures, hayfields, and other grasslands, where the adults capture rodents for themselves and their broods. Barn Owls produce large clutches and raise as many young as they can feed. Their nesting activities frequently begin in mid-April and most clutches are complete by mid-May. Nests with young are mostly reported in June and July, with young fledging by mid-August. Barn Owls are opportunistic breeders and may nest during any month if rodents are plentiful. Nests with eggs have been reported between March 17 and September 3 (Campbell 1973, Phillips 1980). Later nesting attempts are indicated by November nests with young at Cleveland, Columbus, and Cincinnati and four-week-old young at Dayton on December 3, 1961 (Mathena et al. 1984).

Most Barn Owls are not permanent residents in Ohio. Their migratory movements were regularly noted before 1960 but have not been evident in recent years. As spring migrants, most Barn Owls appear between March 15 and April 15. They are presently casual visitors to migrant traps along Lake Erie and near Columbus, but there are few recent spring records elsewhere. Their fall migration apparently occurs in late September and October. These migrants do not regularly appear at any locality. Even when populations were larger, this migration was largely overlooked. During November 1917, however, many appeared in the southern half of the state and an estimated 200 were shot in central Ohio (Earl 1934).

A few Barn Owls overwinter in Ohio, roosting in dense pines and abandoned buildings and hunting in grassy fields. These wintering owls are most numerous in southern and central Ohio, where they were rare to uncommon residents before 1960 but accidental to casual in recent years. They have always been accidental winter residents in northern Ohio. Wintering Barn Owls are susceptible to considerable mortality caused by periods of snow cover and cold temperatures and may starve if deprived of food for only three or four days (Stewart 1952).

Of the factors contributing to their dramatic decline within Ohio, changing land-use patterns were critical. Many grassy pastures and hayfields were converted to cultivated fields. Near urban areas, grasslands were turned into housing developments. Suitable nest sites were also lost when many abandoned buildings were torn down (Colvin 1985). However, other factors were probably involved, since Barn Owls disappeared from areas where suitable habitats were still available.

Eastern Screech-Owl *Otus asio* (Linnaeus)

While their name evokes images of ear-piercing screams, Eastern Screech-Owls actually produce quiet, tremulous whistles. With their unobtrusive habits and camouflaged plumage, their whistled calls may provide the only clues to their presence, because they normally spend the daylight hours hidden in tree cavities or dense cover. Eastern Screech-Owls occur in both gray and red color phases. Intermediate phases are rare. The gray phase predominates in most of Ohio, although the red phase is equally abundant in the southern counties (Owen 1963). In northwestern Ohio, gray-phased owls make up 75 to 90 percent of the population (Van Camp and Henny 1975). This

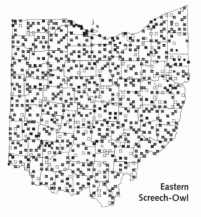

Eastern
Screech-Owl

phase more readily survives the extended periods of cold weather and snow cover encountered at the northern edge of their range.

Eastern Screech-Owls are our most numerous resident owls. Concentrated efforts to locate them on Christmas Bird Counts provide an indication of their actual status, such as 112 on the Waterville-Whitehouse count on January 6, 1982. In most counties, these owls are fairly common to common permanent residents. They become uncommon only in the northeastern counties of Lake, Geauga, Ashtabula, and Trumbull, where they are subject to considerable mortality during harsh winter weather.

Screech-Owl populations have remained fairly stable wherever suitable habitats exist. They experienced long-term declines in some western and central counties where most woodlots were replaced by cultivated fields. In addition, Screech-Owls are subject to short-term fluctuations in response to unusually severe winter weather. The winters of 1976–1978 reduced nesting populations by nearly 50 percent in Ottawa and Lucas Counties (Kleen 1978d). Similar declines were evident in other counties, but their numbers recovered by the early 1980s.

Eastern Screech-Owls are found anywhere suitable cavities are available. In addition to deciduous woods, they regularly reside in orchards, wooded pastures, shaded residential areas, and wooded streambanks. While they occupy interiors of extensive forests, Screech-Owls prefer small woodlots, wooded edges adjacent to fields, and open park-like habitats (Trautman 1940). Most Screech-Owls nest in natural cavities, but they also use man-made structures. Along western Lake Erie, they regularly usurp nest boxes provided for Wood Ducks. An enterprising pair of Screech-Owls nested in a Purple Martin house in Carroll County, successfully raising a brood in 1944 (Buchanan 1980).

Most life history information is provided by Van Camp and Henny (1975), who studied a Screech-Owl population in Ottawa and Lucas Counties for more than thirty years. Egg laying normally begins about March 15, with a few pairs nesting as early as March 5. Most clutches contain three to six eggs; a nest with ten eggs in 1967 was probably produced by two females. The first young normally hatch between April 11 and 20. Young Screech-Owls fledge in late May or early June. Approximately 86 percent of the nests successfully produce an average of three to four young. Breeding may begin slightly earlier in the southern counties, and a small young owl reported from Cuyahoga County on March 19, 1991, was from an exceptionally early nest (Peterjohn 1991d). Screech-Owls may renest if their first attempt is unsuccessful. Renesting efforts produced nests with young through July 10 and adults with dependent young on August 18 (Campbell 1968, Williams 1950).

Their diet varies seasonally, depending on the availability of prey. In winter, Screech-Owls subsist on small mammals and occasional birds. During spring, nests with young Screech-Owls correspond with the peak passage of migrant songbirds through Ohio. Along western Lake Erie, nearly two-thirds of their spring diet is migratory birds. Insects and other invertebrates make up the bulk of the summer and autumn diet. In addition to terrestrial prey, small quantities of fish and crayfish are regularly taken throughout the year (Van Camp and Henny 1975).

Screech-Owls seldom wander from established territories. Banding studies indicate that most young owls remain within twenty miles of their birthplace (Van Camp and Henny 1975). A few wander considerable distances, however. A young Screech-Owl banded in northern Ohio in May 1957 was recovered in Michigan, 145 miles northwest of its banding site, the following December.

Great Horned Owl *Bubo virginianus* (Gmelin)

The most powerful of our predatory birds, Great Horned Owls readily capture prey as large as adult skunks. They have the advantage of striking silently and swiftly at night. Other raptors are not immune from their predation. Even Bald Eagles abandon their eyries to nesting Great Horneds rather than risk an injurious confrontation. They rank as the top predatory bird, fearing no other creatures except people.

Their reputation as ruthless hunters almost led to their extermination from Ohio. During the first decades of the twentieth century, Great Horned Owls were subject to intense persecution. Shot on sight, these fairly common residents became very rare in many areas. By the 1930s, they were eliminated near every city and were rare throughout the western half of Ohio. Great Horneds were uncommon only along the unglaciated Allegheny Plateau (Hicks 1935a).

Great Horneds received protection during the early 1940s and their population levels immediately improved. These increases were first apparent in eastern Ohio, where more owls were noted in Carroll and Jefferson Counties by 1945 and in most northeastern counties by 1950 (Buchanan 1980, Williams 1950). Improved numbers were apparent at Toledo after 1948, with 19 pairs located in Ottawa County by 1955 (Campbell 1968, Nolan 1955d). Similar increases were noted in the central counties during

Great Horned
Owl

the 1950s. They remained rare in the southwestern and west-central counties, with only 2–3 pairs in the Cincinnati area during 1953 and very few Dayton area sightings before 1960 (Kemsies and Randle 1953, Mathena et al. 1984). Within these counties, their numbers did not improve until the early 1960s, as exemplified by 56 Great Horneds tallied at Cincinnati in 1964 (Petersen 1964d).

Since 1970, these owls have been uncommon to locally common residents throughout Ohio. They are least numerous in the unglaciated counties, where they are largely restricted to riparian corridors and the vicinity of farms or other clearings. They are widely distributed elsewhere. As many as 3–8 may be recorded daily in most counties, and Christmas Bird Count totals of 15–20+ are occasionally reported.

Great Horned Owls require undisturbed woodlots and riparian corridors with large trees for nesting, and nearby open fields for hunting. They do not occupy extensive mature forests. Great Horneds have moved into residential areas, especially where parks or streams provide nest sites, and hunt in residential yards from chimneys or large trees. Their preferred habitats remain the open farmlands of rural Ohio, where many woodlots are interspersed among agricultural fields.

Great Horned Owls are the first birds to begin nesting each year. Their territories are established in autumn, and a duet of hooting owls frequently breaks the quiet of a cool October evening. Nesting activities are normally initiated by the last week of January and early February, even when the ground is snow covered and temperatures are well below freezing. They occupy suitable cavities if they are available but also readily usurp Red-tailed Hawk and Great Blue Heron nests, even heron nests in the middle of large lakes. The young hatch in late February and early March. By the last half of April, the young owls are sufficiently mobile to climb among the branches of trees, though they are unable to fly. In mid-May, most owlets are capable of flight but retain much of their down, looking like large fuzz balls among the vegetation. Like all owls, Great Horneds raise only one brood but will renest if the first clutch is unsuccessful. Renesting attempts produce nests with eggs as late as May 12 and recently fledged young through June 16 (Campbell 1973, Price 1934a).

Snowy Owl *Nyctea scandiaca* (Linnaeus)

Wherever they appear, Snowy Owls are certain to attract attention. Mostly diurnal in their habits, they are likely to be observed during the midday hours as they hunt from low perches or the ground. These large owls are remarkably tame, normally inhabiting the Arctic tundra and infrequently encountering people. Although Snowies hunt over open fields, they regularly turn up in the middle of cities, perched on a large building and oblivious to the commotion on the street below.

Snowy Owls normally winter north of Ohio, where they subsist on lemmings and other rodents. Lemming populations undergo severe declines every three or four years, and then the owls move southward in search of food, producing sizable winter invasions into the Great Lakes region.

While Snowy Owls probably periodically invaded Ohio during the nineteenth century, the only reported flight was in the winter of 1858–1859 at Cleveland (Williams 1950). During the twentieth century, the first reported flight occurred in the winter of 1926–1927, producing at least 138 sightings across the state (Thomas 1928b). An invasion during the winter of 1930–1931 produced 126 statewide sightings (Hicks 1932b). A smaller flight was noted in the winter of 1933–1934. The 1941–1942 winter produced 100–150 reports from the Cleveland area but smaller numbers elsewhere (Williams 1950). The owl flight of 1945–1946 was mostly limited to 66 records from the Toledo area (Campbell 1968, Snyder 1947). Another flight during the 1949–1950 winter resulted in northeastern Ohio reports of at least 30 specimens from Cleveland and 11 sightings in Trumbull County (Brooks 1950b, Mayfield 1950b). Sizable numbers also appeared along western Lake Erie and south to Cincinnati (Kemsies and Randle 1953).

The first Snowies appeared in the last days of October and early November, but the majority were reported during December and January. Snowy Owls were first detected along Lake Erie, with sizable numbers in the northwestern or northeastern counties, depending upon the origin of the flight. After remaining along Lake Erie for a few days or weeks, they moved inland. Interior sightings were widely scattered, with most from the northern and central counties. Their spring flight produced only scattered sightings during March and April and occasional stragglers into May.

Their winter distribution patterns have apparently changed since 1950. While these owls still undergo periodic invasions, the magnitude of their flights is considerably reduced. Defined movements in the winters of 1953–1954, 1960–1961, 1974–1975, 1980–1981, and 1991–1992 produced only 20–30 statewide sightings. Their appearance is no longer confined to these movements and "echo flights" the following winter. Instead, Snowy Owls annually appear in Ohio. During some years, these reports are restricted to two or three sightings along Lake Erie; other years may produce five to seven lakefront reports and two or three inland.

Snowy Owls are now rare to uncommon winter visitors along Lake Erie. They are normally encountered as scattered individuals, although 2–3 may be observed at preferred locations. Larger numbers appear during invasions; the largest tally was 20 along an eleven-mile drive across Ottawa County on February 20, 1950 (Campbell 1968). Wintering Snowies are casual to accidental visitors to the interior of Ohio, where sightings invariably are of single owls, with the fewest reports from the unglaciated counties.

The timing of their movements has not changed in recent years. The earliest Snowy Owl returned by October 3, 1981 (Peterjohn 1982a), but they normally appear during November or December. Considerably fewer Snowies return north each spring, primarily between March 5 and April 10. Occasional stragglers linger into May, with the latest confirmed sightings in Licking County through May 23, 1997, and at Columbus on May 24, 1968 (Fazio 1997b, Thomson 1983). There is one unconfirmed June record from Lake Erie.

Most Snowy Owls appearing in Ohio are immatures that have poorly developed hunting skills. Many cannot capture enough food to sustain themselves and perish during winter, accounting for the relatively small numbers of spring migrants. One Snowy Owl provided a unique opportunity to observe its hunting techniques. During November 1980, it regularly visited Wildwood Park in Cleveland to feed on rats along the lakefront. Each evening, the rats boldly wandered around a lighted beach and parking lot as the owl hunted them from light poles, building roofs, and once from the hood of a birder's car. Even though the rats were plentiful, this young owl made a half dozen or more strikes each evening before eventually succeeding in capturing one.

Northern Hawk Owl *Surnia ulula* (Linnaeus)

Northern Hawk Owls are residents of boreal forests across Canada and Alaska (AOU 1998). Like all northern owls, they undergo periodic southward movements during winter in response to shortages of prey. Their movements are less predictable than the invasions of Snowy Owls and composed of considerably fewer individuals. These movements are normally evident in southern

Canada, the upper Great Lakes states, and northern New England, but a few owls wander south to New Jersey, northern Ohio, and Iowa (AOU 1998). The only confirmed Northern Hawk Owl record in Ohio is provided by a specimen collected at Pepper Pike (Cuyahoga County) on November 10, 1927 (Williams 1950). This specimen is believed to be the unlabeled Northern Hawk Owl in the collection at the Cleveland Museum of Natural History. Four undocumented sight records from northern Ohio are believed to be correctly identified. These owls appeared at Northfield between December 24, 1940, and January 6, 1941 (Williams 1950); at Cleveland on March 2, 1957 (Newman 1969); at Lorain on January 2–20, 1968 (Petersen 1968a); and near Maumee (Lucas County) on January 16, 1978 (Thomson 1983). There are three questionable published sightings from the northeastern counties and an anecdotal account from southeastern Ohio.

Burrowing Owl *Athene cunicularia* (Molina)

Burrowing Owls breed in open grasslands of central and western North America from southern Canada to Mexico. The eastern boundary of their range extends from the Dakotas south to Texas, with a disjunct population in Florida (AOU 1998). Like many migratory species, Burrowing Owls occasionally stray from this range and wander east to Ohio and southern Ontario. There are two sight records from Ohio. The first owl was discovered by Homer Price near Payne in Paulding County in early October 1944. While the details are sketchy, the bird's behavior leaves little doubt it was correctly identified. It was observed on four occasions as it roosted in a field tile along the bare bank of a ditch. When flushed, it flew into a harvested soybean field, where it walked considerable distances and attempted to hide under clumps of soybean straw (Price 1946). Another Burrowing Owl was closely studied by Sandra Zenser in Carroll Township, Ottawa County, on April 5–6, 1981 (Peterjohn 1981c). It too was discovered roosting in a drainage tile along a ditch. It was fairly tame, allowing examination of all diagnostic field marks. When approached, it was as likely to run into the adjacent fields as to take flight.

Barred Owl *Strix varia* Barton

Shortly after sunset on a calm evening in early March, the distinctive calls of a Barred Owl carry across a forested hillside in eastern Ohio. Its mate responds, initiating an eerie duet composed of traditional calls and various deep throaty notes, raucous shrieks, and other unusual sounds. These Barred Owls are courting and will shortly start raising their young. Their nest site has already been selected, most likely a cavity within a large hollow tree. Nesting Barred Owls on rare occasions also use abandoned hawk, crow, and squirrel nests

(Williams 1950). While nests with eggs have been reported during February in southwestern Ohio (Kemsies and Randle 1953), most clutches are laid in March and hatch by mid-April. Young Barred Owls have left the nest by April 23 but are most evident in the last half of May and June (Trautman 1940, Williams 1950). Barred Owls require extensive mature woodlands with numerous hollow trees for nesting and roosting. They prefer mesic habitats, especially wooded swamps, floodplain woods, large poorly drained woodlots, and protected hillsides. They are likely to be found in other habitats only during winter, when they roost in pine groves.

Barred Owl

Barred Owls were initially distributed throughout the virgin forests covering Ohio. As these forests were cleared, their numbers declined dramatically and they became locally rare by the mid-1800s. With the maturation of second-growth forests, their populations expanded during the last decades of the nineteenth century (Trautman 1940). By the early 1900s, the Barred Owl was "the most common large owl" in most counties (Jones 1903). In the mid-1930s, they were widely distributed. Hicks (1935a) cited breeding records from seventy-five counties, noting that they were absent only in some western counties where extensive mature woodlands were unavailable. Their relative abundance varied depending upon the availability of suitable forests. They were locally rare in all portions of the state, even along the unglaciated Allegheny Plateau, where many woodlands were too young to support resident owls (Hicks 1937a). Their populations were also experiencing local declines, particularly in glaciated counties (Clark and Sipe 1970, Trautman 1940).

Several factors contributed to their changing relative abundance since 1950. Habitat destruction eliminated suitable woodlands, particularly within the intensively farmed western and central counties. Barred Owls are also unable to compete with Great Horned Owls. Near most large cities and in many western and central counties, nesting Barred Owls were replaced by Great Horneds during the 1950s and early 1960s. Not every change has been detrimental. The maturation of woodlands along the unglaciated Allegheny Plateau expanded their breeding populations.

Barred Owls are now uncommon to fairly common permanent residents throughout the eastern half of Ohio and the southwestern counties, becoming locally rare near large metropolitan areas (Peterjohn and Rice 1991). They are the most numerous large owls within the rural southeastern counties; 1–8 can be detected each evening, perhaps more if mature woodlands are extensively distributed and tapes are used to elicit responses. Barred Owls are uncommon residents in northern Ohio from Huron and Crawford Counties west to Hancock and Allen Counties, but become rare to absent in most other west-central and northwestern counties.

While Barred Owls reside within their territories throughout the year, some dispersal takes place between September and November, when the young owls search for suitable unoccupied territories. Some movements also occur during spring, primarily in March; single Barreds very infrequently appear at migrant traps in central Ohio and along Lake Erie. There is no evidence to suggest regular migratory movements within Ohio.

Great Gray Owl *Strix nebulosa* Forster

Nocturnal visitors from Canadian boreal forests, Great Gray Owls undergo periodic southward invasions in response to food shortages. Most appear in the upper Great Lakes region and New England states; on rare occasions, they wander south to Ohio and New Jersey (AOU 1998). Most Ohio Great Gray Owl reports were from the nineteenth century. Unfortunately, most of these records were anecdotal and do not provide basic information such as specific locations and dates. Although nineteenth-century specimens were supposedly collected in Geauga and Clark Counties (Jones 1903, Williams 1950), neither can be located today. The only verified record is a specimen collected by C. C. Allen near Hubbard in "November or December about 1898." This information was provided by the collector in 1943, when the specimen resided in the Mill Creek Museum in Youngstown. This specimen was obtained by the Ohio State University Museum of Zoology on February 19, 1976, but was retained in Milton Trautman's private teaching collection until it was rediscovered by Mary Gustafson and John Condit in 1990.

During the twentieth century, there is one sight record, a Great Gray discovered by Milton Trautman on Starve Island off the Marblehead Peninsula in Ottawa County on October 30, 1947. He carefully observed and described the owl as it perched in a tree, constantly harassed by Herring Gulls (Trautman 1956).

Long-eared Owl *Asio otus* (Linnaeus)

These secretive owls are mostly known as winter residents in Ohio. They spend the daylight hours roosting in dense cover, preferring conifers twenty-five to forty feet high. If pine plantations are unavailable, Long-eareds roost within young deciduous woodlots containing numerous grapevines or other tangles.

They also roost in abandoned fields where groves of young hawthorns, Osage oranges, and other trees provide dense cover. At night, Long-eareds hunt over open fields, capturing large numbers of rodents and a few birds.

Long-eared Owl

As a result of their secretive behavior, their true abundance during winter has never been conclusively established. Many more owls are present than are ever discovered. Long-eareds are casual to rare and very locally distributed winter residents throughout Ohio. Most recent reports are from the glaciated counties. Winter roosts normally total 2–6 Long-eared Owls, with occasional congregations of 10–20+. Their wintering numbers are subject to considerable fluctuations in response to prey availability. An example is provided by owls wintering in the Cincinnati area during 1949–1950 and 1950–1951. In the first winter, at least 50 Long-eareds wintered in eight roosts within a 177-square-mile area around Cincinnati. Only two were discovered in the same area during the following winter (Kemsies and Randle 1953, Randle and Austing 1952). In recent decades, five to twelve or more roosts are discovered during winters of normal abundance, while only two to five roosts are noted when numbers are relatively low.

Their migratory movements are also poorly understood. Long-eareds are casual to rare migrants throughout Ohio during spring and fall. The only regular indication of these movements is the appearance of small numbers of Long-eareds along Lake Erie and at a Columbus cemetery.

Based on the abandonment of their winter roosts, Long-eareds may initiate their northward migration during the last week of February. Most wintering owls disappear during March, when Long-eareds are most likely to appear at migrant traps. These migrant reports generally are of only 1–3 owls. A few migrants may appear through April 5–15 in all portions of the state. Sightings as late as April 20–30 are largely confined to Lake Erie. May records most likely pertain to summer residents.

Their fall migration is largely undetected. The few September sightings may apply to summering owls. The first migrants may arrive during the last half of October, although most fall Long-eareds appear in November. Their winter roosts normally develop between November 10 and 25 but may increase in size throughout December. Except at roosts, most fall sightings are of solitary owls.

Our knowledge of their summer distribution and relative abundance is fragmentary. Summer records indicate that Long-eareds are sporadic and accidental to casual residents. Breeding pairs are not regularly reported from any locality. In the mid-1930s, nesting records from glaciated Ohio were limited to Williams, Ashtabula, Champaign, Paulding, Portage, Geauga, Erie, Huron, Lorain, Ashland, Van Wert, and Mercer Counties (Clark and Sipe 1970, Hicks 1933a, 1934b, 1935a). The only record from the unglaciated Allegheny Plateau was from Tuscarawas County (Hicks 1935a). Southern Ohio's only summer report was an anecdotal nineteenth-century account from Cincinnati (Kemsies and Randle 1953).

There were relatively few summer records in subsequent decades, although the first southern Ohio nesting pairs were discovered at Dayton during 1950 and 1962 and at Cincinnati in 1954 and 1960 (Austing and Imbrogno 1976, Mathena et al. 1984). The only recent breeding record from the unglaciated Allegheny Plateau was in Jefferson County in 1967 (Buchanan 1980). Other breeding records were mostly from the Toledo area and near Youngstown (Campbell 1968, Hall 1967). During the 1980s, the few reports were confined to the northern half of the state, with confirmed nests in Wayne, Wyandot, and Mahoning Counties and summer records from Seneca, Lucas, Geauga, Portage, and Columbiana Counties (Hall 1988d, Kleen 1980d, Peterjohn and Rice 1991). In the 1990s, the only evidence of breeding was reported from Killdeer Plains Wildlife Area, where a nest with young was discovered in 1993, and breeding behavior was noted in 1995 (Harlan 1995d, 1996a).

Nesting Long-eareds use abandoned crow and hawk nests, preferably in pine plantations. Where suitable conifers are unavailable, they breed in young deciduous woodlots with dense woody vegetation and many grape tangles (Van Camp and Mayfield 1943). Nests with eggs have been reported between March 16 and April 19. The young hatch during the last half of April and are usually observed in the nest during May. Only Hicks (1933a) reported nestlings as late as July 8. Most young owls leave the nest by early June.

Short-eared Owl *Asio flammeus* (Pontoppidan)

As sunset approaches on a calm January day, several harriers sail over a grassy field before settling into their winter roost. Their low flight flushes another raptor, which has spent the day roosting in this grassy cover. This second raptor, with its irregular flight pattern, is immediately recognized as a Short-eared Owl. The owl may briefly harass the harrier but then flies to a nearby fence post, where it remains for many minutes, swiveling its head as it scans the surrounding fields and occasionally produces a bark-like yelp. As darkness falls, it takes flight over grasslands in pursuit of small rodents, which form the bulk of its diet.

The interesting and frequently amusing behavior of this charismatic owl can be observed nightly at localities scattered across the state. Although these wintering owls are very locally distributed, they are generally rare to uncommon residents, least numerous in the northeastern counties. Along the Allegheny Plateau, they are found on reclaimed strip mines that provide extensive grassland habitats. Their wintering numbers exhibit marked annual fluctuations in response to prey availability. During some years, they are decidedly scarce, with the largest roosts totaling only 5–10 owls. In other years, they are fairly numerous, with roosts of 10–35+ scattered across Ohio. Large influxes produce infrequent totals of 50–80+ and a maximum of 100 at Killdeer Plains Wildlife Area on January 20, 1967 (Thomson 1983).

Based on historic accounts (Bales 1911a, Jones 1903, Trautman 1940), their populations substantially declined throughout western and central Ohio during the twentieth century. These declines resulted from the conversion of grasslands into cultivated fields. During the 1990s, however, their wintering numbers improved, as some suitable grasslands were created by the Conservation Reserve Program. Since 1960, wintering Short-eareds increased within the unglaciated counties, where reclaimed strip mines provide extensive new habitats.

In recent years, most Short-eareds are reported from wintering locations. There are very few records of migrants, except along Lake Erie. Wintering numbers diminish with the advent of warmer temperatures in February and early March, although small numbers may remain in the northern half of the state through mid-April. Sightings after April 20–28 may pertain to summer residents. Records of spring migrants are of five or fewer owls.

Short-eareds have appeared in Brown County by August 23 and Toledo by September 7 (Campbell 1968, Kemsies and Randle 1953), but these owls may have been wandering summer residents. The first fall Short-eareds normally return to Lake Erie by September 25–October 10 and to the central and southern counties by October 25–November 7. Most reports are of single owls, with a few groups of 5–8 along the lakefront. During some years, their numbers peak in early December and noticeably decline before the end of the month. In other years, large concentrations develop in early January and remain until spring.

Ohio lies at the southern edge of the Short-eared Owl nesting range in North America (AOU 1998). These owls have always been accidental to casual and very sporadic summer residents, averaging three to six sightings each decade since the 1920s. Many summer records are sightings of single owls whose breeding status is unknown. Confirmed nesting reports are exceptionally rare, usually at or near sites where they congregated during the previous winter. They rarely summer at any area for more than two consecutive years.

Before 1940, nesting Short-eared Owls were reported from Paulding, Marion, Pickaway, Ross, Ashtabula, Mercer, and Van Wert Counties (Hicks 1933a, 1935a); the Youngstown area (Baird 1932d); Buckeye Lake (Trautman 1940); and Huron County (Walker and Franks 1928). Between 1960 and 1988, breeding Short-eareds were only confirmed in Lucas, Wyandot, and Pickaway Counties; summering birds at Cleveland and in Holmes and Muskingum Counties were suspected of nesting (Gibbons 1966, Peterjohn and Rice 1991). Since the completion of the Breeding Bird Atlas, Short-eared Owls nested in Jefferson County in 1989, 1990, and possibly subsequent years (Hall 1990c, 1991c); Killdeer Plains Wildlife Area in 1995 and possibly in 1997 (Brock 1995d); and Muskingum County in 1997 and 1998 (Kline 1997, E. Schlabach 1998). As many as five adult owls summered at the latter location. The breeding status of owls observed in Coshocton, Tuscarawas, Seneca, and Wayne Counties is uncertain.

Breeding Short-eareds prefer extensive wet meadows but also nest in fallow fields and clover fields (Clark 1975, Gibbons 1966, Trautman 1940). Price (1972) reported a Paulding County nest in a mixed sedge meadow and brushy swamp. Their eggs are laid in shallow depressions on the ground, well concealed among the adjacent vegetation. Nests with eggs have been reported by April 3 and with small young by April 19 (Price 1934a). However, most nests with eggs are discovered between mid-April and mid-May, and young owls normally fledge in June and early July.

Boreal Owl *Aegolius funereus* (Linnaeus)

As their name implies, Boreal Owls are occupants of the boreal forests of Canada, Alaska, and the Rocky Mountains of the western United States. Like the other northern owls, Boreal Owls occasionally wander south of their established range during winter, in response to shortages of prey. These movements bring owls south to the upper Great Lakes region and northern New England (AOU 1998). Because of their very secretive habits, the southward extent of these movements has never been well defined. Ohio's only Boreal Owl was discovered by Judy Reimer after it had been chased into a window of her Lake County home on April 5, 1997. The stunned owl was taken to the Lake County Metroparks Wildlife Center for rehabilitation, where it was determined to be a second-year female. It was released on April 9 (Brock 1997c). This report is one of the most southerly records of Boreal Owl from North America (AOU 1998).

Northern Saw-whet Owl *Aegolius acadicus* (Gmelin)

In a group renowned for inconspicuous behavior, the diminutive Northern Saw-whets easily achieve the distinction of being our most secretive owls. They are experts at choosing hiding places where they are not likely to be discovered, especially dense tangles and conifers. A remarkably tame owl, Saw-whets normally watch people as they pass only a few feet away rather than take flight. Hence, they rank as the least known of our migratory owls, and there is much to learn about every aspect of their life history.

Their fall migration has never been well defined in Ohio. These migrants are mostly detected along Lake Erie, where Saw-whets are casual to rare most years. They become accidental to locally rare fall migrants throughout the interior counties. While the earliest migrants have been discovered in northern and central Ohio by September 27–28, most are reported between October 15 and November 20. Banding studies at Killdeer Plains Wildlife Area indicate that their southward movements continue into December or January during some years (Stahler et al. 1991). Fall sightings are normally of 1–2 owls, although 21 were banded at Killdeer Plains Wildlife Area and ten at Cincinnati during a single migration (Peterjohn 1982a, Stahler et al. 1991).

While Northern Saw-whet Owls winter throughout Ohio, they are rare residents within the central and southwestern counties and accidental to casual elsewhere. The fewest records are from the northeastern and unglaciated counties. Wintering Saw-whets can be almost absent during some years and widely distributed in others. This variability is most evident in banding studies undertaken by Ron Austing and others at Cincinnati for nearly 30 years. During some winters, only 1–2 Saw-whets can be located, despite extensive searches of suitable roosting sites. In other winters, as many as 24 have been banded (Mumford 1960b, Peterjohn 1982b, Randle and Austing 1952). In southwestern Ohio, wintering owls usually roost in pine trees but may be discovered in honeysuckle tangles and dense red cedars. They normally choose trees near the edges of groves, or isolated trees slightly removed from large plantations, preferring upland sites and avoiding steep ravines (Randle and Austing 1952). Their diet is mostly *Peromyscus* mice.

These owls are most apparent during their northward migration. Spring migrants regularly appear at migrant traps near Lake Erie, where they become rare to locally uncommon. While records are normally of isolated individuals, small flights of 5–7 are infrequently reported along western Lake Erie. Spring Saw-whets are rare but regular migrants at Columbus but are generally accidental to casual elsewhere. Inland records are mostly of scattered individuals, although 3–5 have been discovered in a Columbus cemetery. A few early migrants appear by the first week of February, especially along Lake Erie. Most Saw-whets are observed between March 10 and April 7. Within the interior counties, there are very few records after mid-April. Occasional late migrants are noted along Lake Erie through May 2–17.

Most summering Northern Saw-whets were recorded before 1940. Hicks (1935a) considered them locally distributed summer residents but regularly overlooked, citing records from Williams, Paulding, Licking, Portage, Geauga, Lake, Ashland, Knox, Holmes, Muskingum, Guernsey, Tuscarawas, and Mercer Counties and a May sighting near Cincinnati. Additional nesting owls were recorded from Franklin and Ashtabula Counties (Hicks 1933a, 1934b). Most records were of isolated nesting attempts during a single year. Only Ashtabula County may have supported a regular breeding population; adult Saw-whets were recorded from seven locations between 1928 and 1932 (Hicks 1933a). In recent decades, summering Saw-whets have sporadically appeared in the Cleveland area, with confirmed nesting attempts in Lake and Cuyahoga Counties in 1946, 1964, 1982, and 1995 (Brock 1995d, Newman 1969, Peterjohn and Rice 1991, Williams 1950). They also nested at Toledo in 1966 (Campbell 1968). A pair occupied a nest box in the Oak Openings during early May 1978, although this box was removed before the owls could nest. The only other recent nesting record was at Youngstown in 1979 (Hall 1979). A calling individual at Mohican State Forest during June 8–16, 1992, was suggestive of a breeding attempt (Brock 1992b). While these few records indicate that Northern Saw-whet Owls are accidental or casual summer residents in Ohio, their true status remains to be determined.

Summering owls have been found in mesic second-growth woods, especially where pines or hemlocks are mixed with the deciduous vegetation, but most recent records have been in shaded residential areas. They normally breed in cavities but will occupy nest boxes. Their nesting activities probably begin during late March and April; recently fledged young have been reported as early as May 24, with most records in June or the first week of July (Hicks 1934b).

Common Nighthawk *Chordeiles minor* (Forster)

When Ohio was initially settled, Common Nighthawks were probably rather rare and locally distributed summer residents. A few pairs nested on gravel bars along large rivers, exposed rock outcrops, and in prairie openings. But their habitat preferences dramatically changed during the nineteenth century, as breeding nighthawks readily adapted to the numerous flat roofs available in cities. Their breeding populations rapidly expanded and the "peenting" calls of territorial nighthawks became a familiar evening sound. By 1900, pairs occupied every Ohio city (Jones 1903).

Their status did not appreciably change during most of the twentieth century. Hicks (1935a) cited summer records from 117 cities in seventy-four counties, as well as "natural habitats" in Adams, Erie, and Ottawa Counties.

Breeding pairs were unrecorded from scattered rural counties along the unglaciated Allegheny Plateau and locally in western Ohio. This distribution pattern was still apparent during the 1980s, when summering nighthawks were detected in eighty counties on the Breeding Bird Atlas (Peterjohn and Rice 1991). However, their populations were probably declining at that time, a trend that continued into the 1990s, when breeding pairs disappeared from many small towns and have become scarce in most large cities. Common Nighthawks are now uncommon residents in large cities and uncommon to rare in smaller towns. They are largely absent from the rural countryside, but a few pairs may inhabit open hillsides in southeastern Ohio and several abandoned quarries near western Lake Erie.

Common Nighthawk

In their natural habitats, Common Nighthawks nest on the ground, relying on their cryptically-colored plumage to hide them from predators. Urban nighthawks are more visible on gravel-covered roofs, but the absence of predators allows them to successfully raise young. While nesting activities probably begin during late May in southern Ohio, most clutches are reported between June 1 and July 17, with a few late attempts into the first week of August (Dexter 1956a, 1961, Williams 1950). Young nighthawks may hatch by mid-June and fledge by the last days of the month (Dexter 1952), but most fledge during July, with late nests producing fledglings through August 19.

Their northward migration is largely resident nighthawks returning to their breeding territories. Most spring reports are of ten or fewer individuals. The largest movements total 15–25 in southern and central Ohio and 45–50 along western Lake Erie. While Common Nighthawks have been reported during the last half of March, none of these exceptionally early sightings are adequately substantiated. The earliest confirmed nighthawks returned between April 16 and 25. They normally appear during the first week of May, and territorial males are widely distributed by May 10–20.

In contrast, Common Nighthawks stage a remarkable southward migration. The first migrants are normally solitary individuals during the last days of July and more frequently between August 5 and 15. During the last half of August, small flocks of 10–30 appear each evening, migrating just above the treetops or briefly forming swirling flocks as they forage on flying insects. This movement peaks between August 25 and September 7, when flocks of 50–200+

appear in the evening sky, occasionally mixing with Chimney Swifts and swallows. The large flights end abruptly and only small migrant flocks are noted after September 12–15. The last migrants normally depart by October 5–15, and a few stragglers linger into the last half of October. Most November sightings are not acceptably documented, but this species has been reliably reported through November 13, 1988, at Dayton (Peterjohn 1989a).

During late August and early September, nighthawks become fairly common to locally abundant migrants. Most reports are of 10–100 daily, while local movements of 200–600 are occasionally encountered. Exceptionally large movements have produced estimates of 5,000 at Cincinnati, 3,500 in Portage County, 3,000 at Columbus, and 1,000–2,000 at Akron, Toledo, Cleveland, and in Holmes County. This status was maintained into the early 1990s, but since 1993, the number of fall Common Nighthawks passing through Ohio has been noticeably reduced. The largest flights have totaled only 200–500+, and most reports are of fewer than 50 daily. The reduced numbers of fall migrants in Ohio probably reflects a significant decline in nighthawk populations across eastern North America (Sauer et al. 1998).

Chuck-will's-widow *Caprimulgus carolinensis* Gmelin

To record Chuck-will's-widow within Ohio, a visit to the lower Ohio Brush Creek valley in southern Adams County during May or June is a necessity. Drive the narrow county roads in this valley, looking for open vistas next to hillsides covered with young red cedars. After finding a suitable location, wait patiently for darkness to fall, while listening to the evening sounds of rural southern Ohio. First, a nighthawk calls off in the distance, followed by the repetitive song of Whip-poor-wills. Finally, a Chuck-will's-widow adds its distinctive voice to the evening chorus.

Chuck-will's-widow

Hearing a Chuck-will's-widow is rather easy, since they are fairly common residents within this valley. Seeing one is a different story. While males may sing from the tops of cedars, they remain hidden among the foliage and are remarkably difficult to observe. With considerable luck, one may be discovered sitting on a county road, its eyes glowing a brilliant golden orange in the headlights of an approaching car.

Even though Chuck-will's-widows have resided in this valley since the 1930s, surprisingly little information is available on their migration and breeding biology. They normally arrive during the last half of April and establish territories by mid-May, preferring old fields overgrown with young red cedars. Nesting is probably initiated during the last half of May, judging from the few reports of adults accompanied by young during July. There are relatively few records after the males cease singing, but Chuck-will's-widows probably remain into September.

Ohio's first Chuck-will's-widows were discovered in Adams County on May 14, 1932. At least eight males were recorded four days later (Thomas 1932). A survey estimated 25–30 pairs along Ohio Brush Creek in Tiffin and Jefferson Townships in 1935 (Hicks 1935a). The next survey, in 1985, counted at least 60 male Chuck-will's-widows in Adams County, most of them along Ohio Brush Creek north to Green and Meigs Townships, with a few isolated males elsewhere (Peterjohn and Rice 1991).

While the majority of Ohio's Chuck-will's-widows are found in the Ohio Brush Creek valley of Adams County, they are casual to rare and very locally distributed summer residents elsewhere along the unglaciated Allegheny Plateau east to Washington County. Single pairs nested in Highland County during 1984 and Pike County in 1985. During the 1980s and 1990s, summering males were noted at locations in Scioto, Gallia, Hocking, Vinton, Lawrence, and Washington Counties (Fazio 1997b, Hall 1989d, Peterjohn and Rice 1991).

Chuck-will's-widows are casual to accidental visitors in the southwestern counties, where specimens were collected near Dayton on May 1, 1933, and in Clermont County on May 20, 1945 (Kemsies and Randle 1953, Mathena et al. 1984). Other published records include a Hamilton County male in June, 1954 (Nolan 1954d); a female captured in Butler County on May 1, 1974 (Kleen 1974c); a singing male at Charleston Falls Park near Dayton on May 20, 1982; and a territorial male returning to Germantown Reserve (Montgomery County) during the summers of 1981–1983 (Mathena et al. 1984).

Chuck-will's-widows are accidental visitors elsewhere. There are two records from the central counties: a singing male in Franklin County on June 7, 1952, and one observed at Greenlawn Cemetery in Columbus on May 2, 1983 (Gilbert 1953, Peterjohn 1983c). In Tuscarawas County, two summered at one location in 1995 and one returned to this site on May 3–10, 1996 (Brock 1995c, Conlon and Harlan 1996a). The only northwestern Ohio records are singing males at Maumee (Lucas County) on June 23, 1978, and at Maumee Bay State Park on May 17, 1992 (Harlan 1992d, Kleen 1978d).

Whip-poor-will *Caprimulgus vociferus* Wilson

As the summer sun sets over the hills of southeastern Ohio, the evening songbird chorus gradually diminishes as most birds enter their nighttime roosts. When dusk turns into darkness, the silence is broken by the loud, repetitive calls of Whip-poor-wills echoing across the valleys. Shortly after they return to their breeding territories, a full moon may prompt them to sing for the entire evening, much to the dismay of anyone trying to sleep nearby. As summer progresses and hungry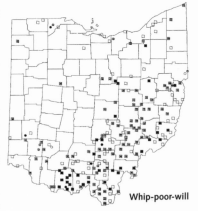

Whip-poor-will

young need to be fed, they may sing for only one or two minutes at dawn and dusk.

While detecting singing Whip-poor-wills requires little effort, observing one is another matter. With considerable luck, one may be flushed from the forest floor, or a migrant may be discovered quietly perched along a tree limb. These observations are rare, and Whip-poor-wills are most likely to be seen at night as they sit on quiet rural roads, their eyes glowing orange-red in the headlights of an oncoming car.

Breeding Whip-poor-wills reside within relatively young woods or along woodland edges bordering open fields. They occupy a variety of woodland communities, from mixed cedar-deciduous woods in southwestern Ohio to deciduous woods and pine-hemlock communities elsewhere (Mathena et al. 1984, Williams 1950). Their nests are simple scrapes on the ground, normally placed close to woodland edges where ground cover is densest. Nesting activities begin by late April, since recently fledged young have been reported as early as June 4 in southern Ohio (Braund 1940b). Elsewhere, nests with eggs are discovered between mid-May and July 1, while small young are mostly noted in June and early July, with late broods through mid-August (Campbell 1968, Mathena et al. 1984, Williams 1950).

Their breeding populations slowly declined throughout the twentieth century. In 1935, Hicks (1935a) noted greatly decreased numbers since 1900. Nevertheless, Whip-poor-wills were still recorded from seventy-four counties. They were most numerous along the Allegheny Plateau north to Washington, Athens, and Hocking Counties (Hicks 1937a). The fewest were noted within west-central and northwestern Ohio. Additional declines were apparent throughout Ohio in subsequent decades, beginning in the late 1940s in Carroll and Jefferson Counties (Buchanan 1980). Similar trends continued into the 1980s (Campbell 1968, Newman 1969, Peterjohn and Rice 1991), and statewide populations significantly declined on the Breeding Bird Survey since 1966 (Sauer et al. 1998).

Summering Whip-poor-wills are still most numerous along the unglaciated Allegheny Plateau north to Hocking, Athens, and Washington Counties. They are generally fairly common to common along this portion of the plateau, where nightly totals of 5–40 singing males can be encountered during May and June. Farther north along the plateau, they become uncommon to fairly common residents, and nightly totals seldom exceed 2–8. Within the southwestern counties, they are rare to fairly common residents but very locally distributed. Most reports are of single males, although 5–10 may be heard at a few localities. Whip-poor-wills are rare residents in northeastern Ohio, where only a few individuals remain. They have almost disappeared from the glaciated central and northwestern counties, except for a small population within the Oak Openings near Toledo (Peterjohn and Rice 1991).

Whip-poor-wills are relatively early spring migrants; any March goatsucker is probably this species. The earliest migrant returned to Marietta by March 13, 1973, and migrants have appeared at several central localities by March 24–30 (Hall 1973b). The earliest overflight in northern Ohio is April 6. Spring Whip-poor-wills normally appear in the southern counties by April 7–17 and are expected along Lake Erie by the first week of May. Breeding populations are well established by May 15–20.

Observations of migrant Whip-poor-wills have noticeably declined since the 1950s, and they are presently casual to rare spring visitors away from established breeding localities. These migrants are mostly detected between April 25 and May 15, usually as isolated individuals, although 3–8 are infrequently encountered along western Lake Erie.

Their southward migrations have always been poorly defined. Breeding Whip-poor-wills quietly depart during September, and the last individuals are usually noted between September 15 and 25. Fall migrants are accidental to casual away from established nesting localities, with most records near Lake Erie. A few individuals linger into October, and the latest records are October 15 at Dayton and October 22 in the Cleveland area (Mathena et al. 1984, Rosche 1992).

Chimney Swift *Chaetura pelagica* (Linnaeus)

With their compact cigar-shaped bodies, short tails, and long narrow wings, Chimney Swifts are designed for sustained rapid flight. In fact, they spend virtually all the daylight hours on the wing. But while they rank among the strongest of all flyers, they are poorly adapted for a terrestrial existence. With their short, weak legs, Chimney Swifts are incapable of taking off from any horizontal surface and must roost by hanging onto the vertical sides of chimneys or hollow trees.

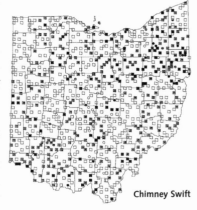

Chimney Swift

Although Chimney Swifts are normally very social birds, the first ones returning each spring are usually solitary individuals. The earliest swift appeared in Marietta on March 14, 1973 (Hall 1973b). During relatively mild springs, the first migrants may return by the first week of April. When spring temperatures are unusually cold, few swifts appear before April 15. They normally become widespread by April 20–25 and peak migratory movements are evident between April 25 and May 15. Small numbers of migrants are noted through the end of May.

These migrants are common in every county, but spring flocks are normally composed of 10–50 swifts. The largest concentrations usually total 100–400, while maxima of 1,000+ have been estimated at Findlay, Toledo, and Cleveland during the first half of May.

Breeding Chimney Swifts are equally numerous in large cities, small villages, and the rural countryside. They are fairly common to locally abundant summer residents in every county (Peterjohn and Rice 1991), and daily totals of 15–75+ are expected. Chimney Swift populations have remained reasonably stable since the mid-1960s (Sauer et al. 1998), although some local declines have been apparent since 1990. Their statewide status and distribution have not appreciably changed since the beginning of the twentieth century (Hicks 1935a, Peterjohn and Rice 1991). Chimney Swift populations undoubtedly expanded during the nineteenth century, when suitable nesting sites in chimneys became widely available (Wheaton 1882).

As their name implies, Chimney Swifts now exhibit a strong preference for nesting in chimneys. During the twentieth century, the only swifts known to breed within a natural cavity were using a large beech tree near Cincinnati on July 16, 1939 (Walker 1939b). Most available information on their nesting biology and behavior is provided by Ralph Dexter's careful studies of breeding swifts at Kent over nearly forty years. Shortly after they return in early May, their courtship flights are commonly observed and most pair bonds are formed. Nest construction normally begins during the last half of May and continues through mid-June. These nests are simple platforms composed of small dead twigs held together and cemented to the chimney with the bird's saliva. Eggs are mostly laid during the last week of May and June, with renesting efforts through mid-July. Young swifts leave the nest as early as June 20 but mostly fledge during the last half of July and early August (Dexter 1956b, Williams 1950). After the breeding season has ended, Chimney Swifts gather into large evening roosts, invariably in large unused chimneys. At first these roosts may shelter several hundred swifts, predominantly resident adults and their offspring, but expand as migrants appear from farther north. By early September, these roosts may contain 1,000–2,000+ swifts.

Their evening descent into the chimney provides quite a spectacle. The birds begin to gather about an hour before sunset, first scattered individuals and then numerous small flocks. As darkness approaches, every roosting swift gathers overhead into a swirling mass of chattering birds, flying in large circles over the chimney. Initially, only individual swifts enter the roost. But as the sunlight fades, the swirling cloud of swifts rapidly descends. In only a few minutes, most have entered the chimney, except for the straggler who quietly disappears as darkness falls.

In addition to fall roosts, migrant flocks are widely distributed each autumn. Fall concentrations tend to be larger than during spring and 50–300+ may be observed daily. Larger flights produce flocks of 500–1,000+. The largest reported fall movement totaled 5,000 along the Scioto River valley in central and southern Ohio on September 30, 1939 (Walker 1939c).

The beginning of their southward migration is difficult to establish, but migrant flocks may appear by August 5–15. This movement normally peaks during September and the first week of October. The large fall roosts normally disappear with the first strong cold front between October 5 and 14, while individuals and small flocks may remain through October 15–20. Even during relatively mild autumns, the last swifts depart by the last week of October. There are very few sightings during early November, although a flock of 12 was noted at Dayton on November 10, 1925 (Mathena et al. 1984).

Ruby-throated Hummingbird *Archilochus colubris* (Linnaeus)

Ruby-throated Hummingbirds normally return to Ohio after the spring wildflowers are abundant and many insects have emerged. While overflights appear by April 10–14, these early arrivals face an inhospitable environment. Ruby-throateds normally arrive during April 25–May 2 in southern Ohio and May 5–12 along Lake Erie. Spring totals seldom exceed 1–6 daily, with the only sizable movements totaling 35–50+ along central Lake Erie during the last half of May. Spring migrants arrive throughout May and have been observed in passage over Lake Erie into the first week of June.

As summer residents, Ruby-throateds are found in woodlands, brushy fields, fallow fields, and residential gardens—wherever suitable flowers exist. While they forage in a variety of habitats, their nests are placed in woods or along woodland edges. Breeding Ruby-throated Hummingbirds are widely distributed across Ohio (Peterjohn and Rice 1991). They are generally fairly common to common residents in the southern and eastern counties, where 3–10+ may be observed daily. Ruby-throateds become uncommon to fairly common residents in most northwestern and glaciated central counties, where summer totals seldom exceed 1–6. They can be locally rare residents within intensively cultivated portions of Wood, Henry, Defiance, Putnam, Paulding, Van Wert, Madison, and Fayette Counties.

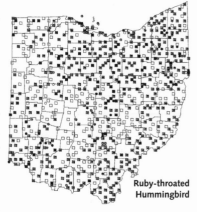

Ruby-throated
Hummingbird

Breeding populations apparently declined in portions of Ohio during the twentieth century. Jones (1903) considered Ruby-throated Hummingbirds common residents throughout the state. Their status was similar in the mid-1930s, when Hicks (1935a) recorded Ruby-throateds as "fairly common to abundant but somewhat local" residents in every county. Their declining populations were most apparent within western Ohio after 1940. Habitat destruction reduced hummingbird populations by at least 80 percent at Toledo (Campbell 1973). Similar declines probably occurred in some other western counties. In eastern and southern Ohio, suitable habitats remained plentiful and population trends were stable since the 1930s. Breeding Bird Survey data also indicated that the statewide population levels remained fairly stable since the mid-1960s (Sauer et al. 1998).

Hummingbirds are polygamous and the males provide no assistance in raising the young. After mating, the females build tiny nests of lichens and spider webs, usually at heights of six to thirty feet on large tree limbs over streams, paths, or other woodland openings. Their first clutches are normally produced by late May in southern Ohio and mid-June elsewhere. These young fledge in July. Ruby-throateds may raise two broods annually, judging from the number of late nesting records. Nest construction has been noted through July 10 and nests with eggs through mid-August (Hicks 1933a, Williams 1950). Young have remained in the nest as late as September 8 (Campbell 1968).

Since they do not participate in nesting, male Ruby-throateds normally begin their southward migration before the females and young. Migrant males appear during the last half of July and most depart by mid-August. The fall migration of female and immature Ruby-throateds generally peaks between August 10 and September 7, when they become fairly common to locally common migrants throughout Ohio. Before the advent of hummingbird feeders, these migrants preferred patches of jewelweeds in wet woods, or old fields where sunflowers, asters, and other flowers proliferate. Large concentrations were infrequently noted: 100 at Buckeye Lake on August 27, 1936 (Baird 1936d); 65–75 at Toledo on three dates between 1934 and 1940 (Campbell 1968); and 50 at Findlay on September 15, 1966 (Phillips 1980). With the recent proliferation of hummingbird feeders, fall migrants are as likely in residential yards as in natural habitats. Fall totals of 3–10 are possible at most localities, with occasional concentrations of 18–25+.

Numbers of fall migrants noticeably diminish during the second week of September, although a few Ruby-throateds are regularly observed through the end of the month. The last migrants usually depart by October 5–12, with a few acceptable records during the last half of October. Sight records during November or December require verification, since recent evidence indicates that these very late hummingbirds may be western strays rather than lingering Ruby-throateds.

Rufous Hummingbird *Selasphorus rufus* (Gmelin)

The proliferation of hummingbird feeders during the 1980s and 1990s is associated with increased numbers of extralimital reports of hummingbirds. Species that were formerly thought to occur only in western North America have been shown to regularly wander into the eastern half of the continent. Rufous Hummingbirds are the most frequently recorded western hummingbird in eastern North America, where they have proven to be regular fall and winter visitors (AOU 1998).

This accidental visitor to Ohio was initially discovered at the Westerville (Franklin County) feeders of Perry and Midge Van Sickle on August 15, 1985. It remained until August 18 and was viewed by more than 100 birders (Peterjohn 1986a). There are at least nine additional confirmed fall or early winter records. Specimens were obtained from Guernsey County on July 25, 1991 (Harlan 1991b); Maumee (Lucas County) on December 1, 1992, which had been present at the feeder since October 15 (Harlan 1993d); and in Holmes County near Loudonville on January 4, 1997 (Brock 1997b). A female banded in Lake County remained November 24–December 2, 1998 (Rosche 1998c). The other reports are of adult males observed or photographed at feeders: at Delightful (Trumbull County) on August 23–30, 1987; Parma on November 5–10, 1987 (Peterjohn 1988a); Columbus on August 9–10, 1989 (Peterjohn

1990a); Loudonville on September 11–14, 1995 (Harlan 1996a); and at Luckey (Wood County) between September 8 and November 13, 1996 (Brock 1997a).

Rufous Hummingbirds are accidental spring migrants anywhere in eastern North America. Ohio's only reports are adult males photographed at Mentor during April 29–May 1, 1995, and documented from Lake County on June 8–10, 1997 (Brock 1995c, Fazio 1997c).

The field identification of *Selasphorus* hummingbirds is challenging, especially most female and immature plumages, whose identities can only be confirmed in the hand. In addition to the confirmed reports of Rufous Hummingbirds, there are several records of immature or female *Selasphorus* hummingbirds whose identities were never positively established.

Belted Kingfisher *Ceryle alcyon* (Linnaeus)

A canoe trip down an Ohio stream or walk along a streambank is a good way to become acquainted with Belted Kingfishers. With their distinctive plumage and characteristic rattling calls, they are instantly recognized as they fly just above the surface of the water. As their name implies, kingfishers mostly subsist on minnows and other small fish, although they also capture crayfish and other invertebrates. They normally hunt from perches bordering the stream, quietly scanning the waters below for signs of life. Most prey is captured near the surface of riffles and shallow pools, frequently in water less than a foot deep.

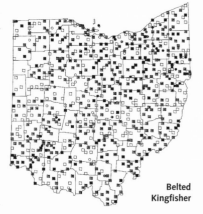

Belted Kingfisher

During the summer months, kingfishers feed in small ditches, creeks, large rivers, and along the margins of ponds and lakes. While they may forage over a large area, the number of nesting pairs is limited by the availability of suitable nest sites. Belted Kingfishers excavate their burrows in loose soil near the tops of steep, eroding streambanks. These burrows extend several feet into the bank, ending in a small chamber, where their eggs are normally laid during the last half of April or early May. The young kingfishers remain here until they fledge in June or early July. Kingfishers raise only one brood but renest if their first clutch is destroyed. Renesting attempts produce nests with eggs through July 4 and fledglings through August 6 (Peterjohn and Rice 1991, Trautman 1940).

Breeding kingfishers are most likely to be found along moderate-sized creeks and large rivers, although pairs are also scattered along small streams, reservoirs, and Lake Erie. Belted Kingfishers are fairly common summer residents in most counties, becoming locally uncommon in some western counties, where few nest sites are available (Peterjohn and Rice 1991). They are never numerous, and canoe trips produce only 3–10 daily, although counts of 15–20+ are possible after the young have fledged.

Their status remained fairly constant during the twentieth century. Hicks (1935a) considered kingfishers to be rare to abundant but locally distributed residents in every county during the 1930s. In subsequent years, kingfishers experienced local declines in some western counties, where stream channelization projects eliminated suitable habitats. Breeding Bird Survey data indicates fairly stable population trends across Ohio since 1966 (Sauer et al. 1998).

After their young fledge, kingfishers disperse to locations where suitable nest sites are unavailable. This dispersal, evident by the last half of July, marks the beginning of their fall migration. This southward movement is poorly defined, as kingfishers gradually drift through the state. Fall kingfishers are most numerous between August 15 and October 10 but are regularly encountered well into November.

As winter residents, Belted Kingfishers are very hardy. They are found wherever open water is available, normally along creeks and rivers, although a few regularly spend the winter at hot-water outlets along Lake Erie. Their wintering numbers fluctuate in response to weather conditions. Kingfishers may be fairly widespread during mild winters but scarce during seasons marked with long cold spells.

Belted Kingfishers are rare and very locally distributed winter residents in the northern counties, where daily totals seldom exceed 1–3 individuals. They become uncommon to locally fairly common winter residents elsewhere, most numerous along large rivers. While most winter counts total 1–5 daily, a canoe trip down the Scioto River in Franklin and Pickaway Counties on February 18, 1985, produced 25+ kingfishers along fifteen miles of the river.

Their northward migration is as inconspicuous as their autumn movements. Breeding kingfishers begin to appear on their territories by February 20–March 10. Most return by mid-April, although a few continue to pass over Lake Erie into the first week of May. These migrants are mostly noted as scattered individuals.

Red-headed Woodpecker *Melanerpes erythrocephalus* (Linnaeus)

A summer drive through western Ohio farmlands frequently produces sightings of this unmistakable woodpecker. Red-headeds are apparent in flight over open fields, their striking red, white, and black plumage unlike any other resident bird. When they are not in flight, their preferred perches are telephone poles and dead snags on tall trees, giving them a commanding view of the surrounding countryside. Unlike most woodpeckers, Red-headeds seldom drill for burrowing insects. Instead, their summer diet is insects captured on the wing, supplemented with acorns and other mast.

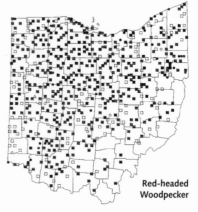

Red-headed
Woodpecker

Their statewide breeding populations fluctuated dramatically during the past centuries. Numbers increased rapidly after 1860, when open farmlands with numerous fencerows and small woodlots provided nearly ideal habitats, and Red-headed Woodpeckers became one of Ohio's most numerous breeding birds (Jones 1903). This sizable population was short-lived. By the mid-1930s, Hicks (1935a) cited "decidedly reduced numbers" within most counties. They were common to abundant throughout the western half of the state, "less common" in the northeastern counties, and uncommon to rare and locally distributed along the unglaciated Allegheny Plateau.

A brief recovery was reported during the 1950s, most notably in the western counties. But this trend was reversed during the 1960s, and Ohio breeding populations have experienced significant declines since 1966 (Sauer et al. 1998). Breeding Red-headed Woodpeckers remain most numerous within the western half of Ohio, where they are uncommon to fairly common residents (Peterjohn and Rice 1991). In recent years, summer totals are usually 2–5 daily, with infrequent reports of 10–15. They are generally uncommon residents within the northeastern counties. Daily totals usually are three or fewer, although a few locations may host 5–10 woodpeckers. Red-headeds are least numerous along the unglaciated Allegheny Plateau. They are fairly common at a few localities, including the Killbuck Creek valley and portions of Carroll County. However, these woodpeckers are casual to rare residents in most southeastern counties, usually as isolated pairs, and were not recorded from Lawrence and Jefferson Counties during the Breeding Bird Atlas (Peterjohn and Rice 1991).

Ideal Red-headed Woodpecker nesting habitats are fields with scattered open woodlots dominated by oaks and hickories. In the absence of open woods, isolated trees and telephone poles provide suitable cavities. Nesting usually begins during May, and most nests with eggs are reported between May 20 and June 15. Renesting efforts may continue into July. Recently fledged young appear by mid-June and may be noted through mid-August (Trautman 1940, Williams 1950).

The breeding population is largely migratory. Since Red-headeds are day-time migrants, their passage is conspicuous. At one time their migratory movements were prominent each spring and autumn. But as their breeding populations declined in Ohio and elsewhere, numbers of migrants have undergone a comparable decline.

Their spring migration is rather brief. Migrant Red-headeds usually appear during the last week of April and are uncommon to fairly common between May 5 and 20. Spring flights may produce tallies of 15–20+ along Lake Erie, although these flights have become less frequent in recent years. Most recent spring reports are of six or fewer daily, with the largest numbers appearing in the western counties.

As fall migrants, Red-headed Woodpeckers may leave their nesting territories by the last week of August. This movement normally peaks between September 10 and October 10, while smaller numbers are noted through November 10–15. These woodpeckers may appear and disappear from localities well into the winter months, but these late movements are the result of food availability, rather than long-distance migration. The number and distribution of fall migrants are comparable to spring.

During winter, Red-headed Woodpeckers subsist on acorns, beechnuts, and waste corn. Their distribution and relative abundance reflects the availability of these foods, particularly the mast crop. Hence, their winter distribution patterns are unpredictable and different each year, a pattern reminiscent of the food-related winter movements of most northern finches (Smith 1986). During the few winters with abundant mast, sizable influxes of these woodpeckers may produce as many as 75–250+ on Christmas Bird Counts. Such influxes were periodically noted through 1962 but have not been apparent in recent years, perhaps reflecting a westward shift in their winter distribution (Smith 1986).

These woodpeckers are now rare to locally fairly common winter residents within the western half of Ohio. During most winters, daily totals are five or fewer, with infrequent concentrations of 10–15. They become casual to locally uncommon winter residents elsewhere, generally least numerous along the unglaciated Allegheny Plateau. Most eastern Ohio winter reports involve only 1–3 Red-headeds, although as many as ten have been reported from the north-eastern counties.

Wintering Red-headeds are found within open woodlots dominated by oaks, beeches, and hickories. These woodpeckers infrequently visit bird feeders. They are very territorial and remain within a small area as long as food is available. On calm winter days, their distinctive rolling calls carry through open woods, and Red-headeds are conspicuous as they defend their food supplies from competitors.

Red-bellied Woodpecker *Melanerpes carolinus* (Linnaeus)

With their loud calls and distinctive plumages, Red-bellied Woodpeckers are familiar residents of Ohio woodlands. Mature and second growth woods invariably support resident pairs, as do extensive riparian corridors. They are not necessarily restricted to natural woodlands, however, and regularly inhabit parks, cemeteries, and shaded residential areas.

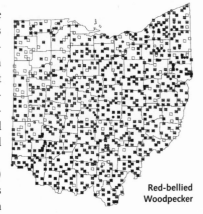

Red-bellied
Woodpecker

In the early 1900s, Jones (1903) described Red-bellied Woodpeckers as fairly common residents in southern Ohio but less common in the northern counties. As late as the mid-1930s, breeding records were known from only sixty-five counties. Breeding populations were not yet established in most northwestern counties, and these woodpeckers remained very local and rare in northeastern Ohio (Hicks 1935a). Their populations increased throughout the state during the 1950s. They appeared at Findlay in 1956 but were not regularly reported at Toledo until 1960. Nesting was first recorded there in 1963 (Campbell 1968, Phillips 1980).

Red-bellied Woodpeckers are now generally fairly common to common permanent residents, becoming locally uncommon in intensively cultivated portions of northwestern Ohio (Peterjohn and Rice 1991). Daily totals seldom exceed 1–6 in northern Ohio and 5–20 elsewhere. Although as many as 399 have been tallied on Cincinnati Christmas Bird Counts, such large numbers are not encountered by solitary birders.

Since their winter diet is mostly mast, Red-bellied Woodpeckers prefer oak-hickory and mixed oak forests. In northeastern Ohio, where oak forests are scarce, they prefer beech-maple woods (Williams 1950). If adequate mast is not available, they supplement their diet with regular visits to bird feeders or by obtaining insects and insect larvae in typical woodpecker fashion.

With the advent of warm weather in late March, male Red-bellieds become vocal as they establish their breeding territories. This conspicuous behavior lasts for only a few weeks until nesting activities are under way. Once the eggs are laid, usually during late April or early May, Red-bellieds become much less conspicuous until their young fledge in June or early July. Initiation of nesting activities may begin earlier during unusually warm springs. Trautman (1940) cited a nest with young as early as April 15, 1924, at Buckeye Lake. If the first clutches fail, Red-bellieds will renest and produce nests with eggs through June

8 and dependent young through August 14–24 (Braund 1940b, Brock 1995a, Trautman 1940).

Red-bellied Woodpeckers are essentially permanent residents. Some movement may be evident in early spring, when adults are establishing their breeding territories. Greater dispersal is evident during fall, as the young search for suitable unoccupied wintering sites and occasionally visit migrant traps along Lake Erie.

Yellow-bellied Sapsucker *Sphyrapicus varius* (Linnaeus)

As their name implies, sapsuckers have a unique feeding behavior. They drill rows of small holes into the bark of trees, then return later to these holes to feed on insects attracted to the sugary sap. While they drill into a variety of deciduous and coniferous trees, they prefer apples, cherries, and related species, whose sap is particularly attractive to insects. Contrary to popular belief, their feeding does not harm the trees.

Yellow-bellied
Sapsucker

The northward migration of Yellow-bellied Sapsuckers is associated with sap production in trees. While a few early migrants appear by the first week of March, they are expected during March 20–30 within the central and southern counties and March 28–April 5 along Lake Erie. Most sapsuckers pass through Ohio during April, becoming uncommon to fairly common migrants in most counties and locally common along Lake Erie. Spring totals of 1–5 daily are generally noted, with occasional movements of 8–15. Larger flights are infrequent and have only been encountered along Lake Erie and near Columbus, where 20–35+ have been noted on several occasions. Higher totals were 50 at Columbus on April 5, 1963, and 60 at Headlands Beach State Park on April 20, 1996 (Brock 1996c, Thomson 1983). The last migrants normally depart by May 5–10. Stragglers have remained through May 19–21 in central Ohio and Dayton (Harlan 1995c, Mathena et al. 1984), and May 25 at Toledo and in Hancock County (Campbell 1968, Whan 1999a).

While most sapsuckers breed in northern deciduous forests, Ohio hosts a small nesting population. The distribution of nesting sapsuckers may once have been more widespread, since there are nesting records from Wayne County in 1891 and Lorain County in 1901, plus probable breeders near

Toledo in 1907 (Baird 1905, Campbell 1968, Hicks 1935a). Since the 1930s, breeding sapsuckers have been restricted to the extreme northeastern counties. Hicks (1935a) cited isolated summer records from Trumbull and Geauga Counties, but the only small population resided in Ashtabula County, where summering sapsuckers were "not uncommon" but locally distributed, with records from twelve locations (Hicks 1933a).

During recent decades, there have been very few reports of summering sapsuckers from northeastern Ohio. Habitat destruction was responsible for declines in Ashtabula County (Hicks 1933a), although sporadic sightings indicated that a small population remained. During the Breeding Bird Atlas, summering and breeding sapsuckers were discovered in at least four sites in Ashtabula County and one in Geauga County (Peterjohn and Rice 1991), indicating that they remain rare and very locally distributed summer residents. Concerted efforts to locate nesting sapsuckers in the northeastern counties during 1998–1999 provided a better indication of the current size of the breeding population. At least 5–6 nests were discovered in Ashtabula County and isolated pairs were found in Trumbull, Geauga, Lake, and Cuyahoga Counties (Brock 1998d, Leberman 1999, Rosche 1999b). Summering sapsuckers were also reported from Summit and Portage Counties during the 1990s. These records suggest that this breeding population may total at least 10–20 pairs.

Breeding sapsuckers are surprisingly secretive. Hence, there is relatively little information available on their nesting biology in Ohio. Most summering sapsuckers occupy wet deciduous woods or the margins of bogs where yellow birch, beech, and aspen are prevalent (Hicks 1933a). Their nesting activities are initiated during May. Incubation begins during the first half of May, and nests with young have been recorded between June 6 and July 1. Most young sapsuckers fledge in late June or early July.

Fewer Yellow-bellied Sapsuckers are detected as fall migrants. Early migrants return to the northern counties during the first week of September but they normally appear by September 10–17. A few individuals may appear in central and southern Ohio at this time, but they are normally expected during September 25–30. Their southward migration peaks between September 25 and October 15, when they become fairly common along Lake Erie and rare to uncommon through the interior counties. Fall sightings mostly are of 1–6 sapsuckers along Lake Erie and three or fewer inland. Larger flights are unusual and restricted to the lakefront, where concentrations of 10–30 occasionally appear. Numbers decrease during the last half of October, although scattered migrants appear into the first half of November.

Before 1950, Yellow-bellied Sapsuckers were accidental winter visitors. Their winter status perceptibly changed in the 1950s, and small numbers have regularly wintered since the early 1960s. Today they are rare to locally uncommon winter residents in southern Ohio, most numerous in the counties bordering the Ohio River. While most winter records are of single sapsuckers, groups of 3–6 are occasionally encountered, with a maximum of 18 in Hamilton County on December 11, 1993 (Brock 1994b). They become casual to rare winter residents in other counties, where daily totals in excess of 1–2 individuals are unusual. While wintering sapsuckers are mostly found in deciduous or mixed woods, they may also occupy parks and cemeteries. These wintering sapsuckers are most apparent during December and early January.

Downy Woodpecker *Picoides pubescens* (Linnaeus)

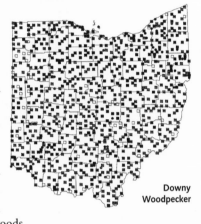

Downy
Woodpecker

As the most widespread and familiar of our woodpeckers, the Downy is an occupant of woodlands and a visitor to bird feeders throughout Ohio. These woodpeckers thrive wherever there are trees, limited only by the availability of suitable nesting cavities. Being small, Downies generally forage along smaller limbs and branches than those frequented by the larger woodpeckers. The adaptable Downy also frequently feeds on dead goldenrod stems in fallow fields or on dried cornstalks in unharvested cornfields, far from any woods.

Although they are fairly common to common permanent residents, Downy Woodpeckers are most conspicuous during winter. A full day's birding in suitable habitats might produce 20–45 during these months. Between November and early March, Downies band together with chickadees, titmice, nuthatches, and other gleaners to form the mixed species foraging flocks characteristic of our winter woodlands. These flocks cover larger areas than nesting birds, and Downies have been shown to "wander considerably" during this season (Campbell 1968).

With the advent of warm weather in March, the mixed flocks disband and Downies establish their nesting territories. Territorial activity peaks in early April. While they normally declare their territories from knotty branches or dead limbs, Downies become nuisances when they learn that gutters on houses provide equally suitable drumming sites. Their nesting chronology is similar throughout the state. Nest excavation may begin as early as the middle of March and peaks in mid-April. Their nests are normally located ten to twenty feet high, although they have been found as low as two feet in a fencepost and as high as fifty feet (Trautman 1940, Williams 1950). As with most cavity nesters, breeding information is meager, but most clutches hatch in May. The young may fledge by the end of May, although fledglings are most evident during June. Renesting attempts are responsible for nests with young through June 26 and adults with dependent young as late as September 4 (Langlois and Langlois 1964).

Once their territorial activities subside, Downies become surprisingly inconspicuous between late April and early September. While as many as 20 have been recorded during a single June day, midsummer counts generally total fewer than 10. Breeding birds are most common in the eastern half of the state, where suitable habitats are widespread. They are less numerous in intensively cultivated sections of western Ohio, but were found in every priority block during the Breeding Bird Atlas (Peterjohn and Rice 1991). Since the mid-1960s, Breeding Bird Survey data indicates that the Ohio population is stable (Sauer et al. 1998).

By early September, the adults have completed their annual molts and Downies are once again conspicuous. Although they are not known as a migratory species, some wander considerably during autumn. Trautman (1940) noted "distinct flights" at Buckeye Lake during late October and early November of several years, and single Downies occasionally appear at migrant traps along Lake Erie. Whether these woodpeckers represent irruptive movements, true migrations, or wandering individuals remains to be determined.

Hairy Woodpecker *Picoides villosus* (Linnaeus)

Hairy
Woodpecker

While the adaptable Downy Woodpecker is familiar to most people with only a passing interest in birds, Hairy Woodpeckers have more specific habitat requirements and are less likely to be encountered by the casual observer. Hairies require older, more mature trees for foraging and nest sites. They prefer extensive mature woodlands but also occupy wooded corridors along streams and residential areas if many large trees are present.

Hairy Woodpeckers are uncommon to fairly common permanent residents. Summer totals seldom exceed 1–4 daily. They are most numerous in the eastern half of the state but can be rather locally distributed in intensively cultivated portions of western Ohio, especially portions of Van Wert, Paulding, Defiance, Henry, Wood, Madison, and Fayette Counties (Peterjohn and Rice 1991). They are outnumbered by Downies everywhere. The ratio of Downies to Hairies is greatest in the western counties, where it approaches ten or twelve to one; it is reduced to four or six Downies for every Hairy in eastern Ohio.

Like Downies, Hairy Woodpeckers are most conspicuous during winter, when as many as ten may be recorded daily, although most reports are of five or fewer. Unlike Downies, Hairy Woodpeckers are very sedentary throughout the year and seldom stray from their established territories. In addition, Hairies do not normally associate with mixed species foraging flocks.

Territorial behavior is initiated with the advent of warm weather in late February or March and reaches its peak in early April. Once this activity ceases, Hairies become inconspicuous. Their nests are generally placed in the trunks of dead trees, at heights of fifteen to seventy-five feet. Most are excavated during March or early April, and their eggs are laid shortly after the nests have been completed. The first clutches normally hatch during May. Fledged young have been observed as early as May 22 but most appear during June (Trautman 1940, Williams 1950). If their first nesting attempt is unsuccessful, Hairies will renest. These renesting efforts account for nests with eggs as late as June 1, broods in the nest through June 26, and adults followed by dependent young well into July (Campbell 1968, Price 1935).

In recent years, some concern has been expressed over the trends of Hairy Woodpecker populations. Breeding Bird Survey data indicates a decline in the Ohio population since 1966, with the most significant decline occurring between 1966 and 1979 (Sauer et al. 1998). These trends may reflect land-use changes in portions of western Ohio, where intensive agricultural land-use practices have eliminated many suitable woodlots. Their numbers may be more stable in the eastern counties.

Red-cockaded Woodpecker *Picoides borealis* (Vieillot)

Red-cockaded Woodpeckers are sedentary residents of mature pine woods in the southeastern United States. Their present range extends north to southern Kentucky. They are locally distributed within this range, with few extralimital sightings (AOU 1998). Ohio's first record of this accidental visitor was provided by a specimen in the Ohio State University Museum of Zoology collected in Columbus on March 15, 1872. The collection label states that "it was in company with another of its own kind, two or three sapsuckers, nuthatches, etc., and shot from a high tree between the canal and Scioto River" (Jones 1903).

Since this species' populations seriously declined during the twentieth century, most birdwatchers assumed that it would never be recorded from Ohio again. Surprisingly, another Red-cockaded Woodpecker was discovered by park naturalist Eddie Bower at Old Man's Cave State Park, Hocking County, on April 22, 1975. It was subsequently observed and photographed by many birders through May 4 as it fed among planted pines near the main parking lot (Thomas 1980). These two records are the only acceptable reports for Ohio.

Black-backed Woodpecker *Picoides arcticus* (Swainson)

Black-backed Woodpeckers normally reside within the boreal forests of Canada and the extreme northern United States. While they are usually permanent residents in these forests, they periodically undertake defined movements southward. These invasions normally occur at seven- to ten-year intervals and occasionally produce sightings south to the lower Great Lakes (AOU 1998).

Within Ohio, Black-backed Woodpeckers are accidental visitors to the northern counties. Most records are associated with noticeable southward incursions elsewhere in the Great Lakes region. The state's first Black-backed was discovered near Painesville on October 31, 1918 (Williams 1950). Single Black-backeds were also detected in 1939 and 1940. Between 1957 and 1964, there were at least seven records from the Cleveland area (Newman 1969). In subsequent years, the only documented sighting was recorded in 1984.

There are currently eleven acceptable Black-backed Woodpecker sightings from Ohio. Ten are from the Cleveland area, mostly in Lake, Geauga, and eastern Cuyahoga Counties (Newman 1969, Williams 1950). The other is from Toledo on January 8, 1939 (Campbell 1968). There is also an undocumented sighting from Columbiana County during December 1974 and several anecdotal accounts of nineteenth century specimens from northeastern Ohio.

The earliest Black-backed Woodpecker was photographed at Lorain on September 27, 1984 (Peterjohn 1985a). Most Ohio sightings are during late fall and winter, with six reports between November 13 and February 9. There are also three spring reports, with a single woodpecker remaining at Cleveland through April 20, 1957 (Newman 1969). With the exception of two observed near Chardon on March 10, 1940 (Williams 1950), all acceptable records are of single individuals.

Northern Flicker *Colaptes auratus* (Linnaeus)

Flickers are widely distributed and conspicuous occupants of open habitats throughout Ohio. Even though they are woodpeckers, they are seldom encountered within extensive woodlands. Instead, they prefer grazed woodlots, woodland edges, parks, orchards, farmlands, and residential areas. This species is most conspicuous after dawn on spring and summer mornings,

when the males loudly declare their territories. Ascending to the tops of large
dead trees or telephone poles, they produce sharp, piercing calls, while their
constant drumming reminds other
flickers to stay away.

Their territorial activities are most
apparent during April, coinciding with
the peculiar courtship displays by
which they cement their pair bonds for
the breeding season. Nesting activities
follow shortly thereafter, beginning
with nest construction in late April and
early May. Flickers excavate cavities in

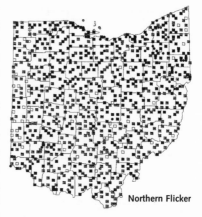

Northern Flicker

trees, fenceposts, and telephone poles, mostly at heights of ten to sixty feet, but
a few cavities have been only one or two feet above the ground (Campbell
1968, Trautman 1940). Most clutches are discovered between May 10 and June
15. The first fledglings appear by June 2, but most are noted during the last half
of June and early July (Trautman 1940, Williams 1950). Renesting attempts
produce recently fledged young through early August.

Northern Flickers rank among the most widely distributed members of our
summer avifauna (Peterjohn and Rice 1991). They are fairly common to common residents within every county, and summer totals are mostly 5–15 flickers daily, although fewer may be recorded within some intensively farmed
western counties.

Despite their widespread distribution, Northern Flicker populations have
noticeably declined during the twentieth century, including significant
declines across Ohio since 1966, according to Breeding Bird Survey data (Sauer
et al. 1998). One factor contributing to these declines is competition with
European Starlings for nesting cavities. There has also been extensive mortality caused by unusually severe winter weather, most notably following the
harsh winters of the 1970s (Robbins et al. 1986).

While flickers are permanent residents throughout Ohio, they are most
numerous during their seasonal migrations. Their spring movements normally begin during the last half of March and peak between April 5 and 20.
Flickers are fairly common to common spring migrants, becoming locally
abundant along Lake Erie. Lakefront movements of 75–150+ daily were regularly reported before 1960 but have been relatively unusual since the mid-
1970s, when most spring flights have involved only 15–50 daily. By far the
largest reported movement occurred April 15, 1972, when 1,000 were estimated in the vicinity of Crane Creek State Park/Magee Marsh Wildlife Area

(Campbell 1973). Peak lakefront movements totaled 200–325+ during other years. Within the interior counties, spring totals are mostly 25 or fewer flickers in recent years. Larger inland movements were noted before 1960, producing concentrations of 90–100 in central Ohio. Numbers of northward migrants noticeably diminish by late April, although a few individuals appear along Lake Erie into the first week of May.

Their southward migration begins between September 10 and 20 and peaks during October. Along Lake Erie, the largest fall flights total 50–150. These movements were mostly before 1960 and few flights have exceeded 20–40 in recent years. Within the interior counties, fall totals are mostly 20 or fewer daily, with infrequent reports of 40–50. Trautman (1940) recorded as many as 90 flickers daily at Buckeye Lake during the 1920s and 1930s but few inland concentrations of similar magnitude have been noted in recent decades. Their southward migration has mostly ended by November 1, although a few individuals may pass through Ohio until November 10–20.

As winter residents, Northern Flickers occupy a wide variety of habitats. Some individuals may be found in mature woodlands, feasting on acorns and beechnuts, while others regularly visit bird feeders. But most wintering flickers prefer the same open habitats they occupy during summer, especially where harvested croplands provide food during bad weather.

Wintering numbers are generally greatest during December and early January but noticeably decline with the advent of sustained cold weather. In addition to seasonal fluctuations, these numbers exhibit considerable annual variability. Wintering flickers are least numerous within the northern counties, where they are normally rare to uncommon residents. Most reports are of 1–5 flickers daily. Larger flocks are unexpected, but a few locations have hosted as many as 20–30 during relatively mild winters. In the central and southern counties, flickers are generally uncommon to fairly common winter residents. While winter totals mostly are 1–8 daily, groups of 20–40 may congregate in favorable habitats. Trautman (1940) noted as many as 100 at Buckeye Lake during some winters before 1940.

Pileated Woodpecker *Dryocopus pileatus* (Linnaeus)

A spectacular woodpecker, the Pileated is certain to impress even those people who pay scant attention to birds. Nearly as large as a crow, with a brilliant red crest and striking black and white wing pattern, Pileateds are usually observed in flight within their territories. Despite their size, they are so wary that they are seldom closely observed as they forage among large trees. They are more often heard than seen, and their loud flicker-like calls resound across the hills of southern and eastern Ohio throughout the year.

The status of Pileated Woodpeckers as occupants of extensive mature woodlands has changed tremendously within historic times. Their relative abundance reflects the changing health of Ohio's forests. When Ohio was initially settled, Pileateds undoubtedly roamed through the virgin forests. As these forests were cleared and replaced by farmland, their populations declined. The acceleration of these land-use trends during the last half of the nineteenth century caused their extirpation from many localities. They

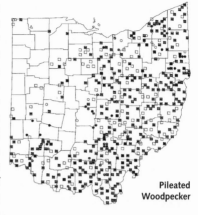

Pileated Woodpecker

disappeared from Cincinnati by the 1870s and from the remainder of western Ohio before 1900 (Campbell 1968, Clark and Sipe 1970, Langdon 1879). The last records from the Buckeye Lake area were between 1880 and 1900 (Trautman 1940).

By the turn of the twentieth century, Pileateds were largely restricted to the unglaciated Allegheny Plateau and extreme northeastern Ohio (Jones 1903). Even within these counties, they had become very scarce and the sighting of a single woodpecker or nesting pair was noteworthy. Mature woodlands were still disappearing, and Jones (1903) felt their numbers were declining and in danger of extinction.

Their fortunes started to improve during the 1920s, when abandoned farms in southeastern Ohio began to revert to woodlands. Their status was still improving in the mid-1930s, when Hicks (1935a) described Pileateds as residents in every county west to Brown, Highland, Ross, Fairfield, Licking, Knox, Ashland, Medina, and Cuyahoga. They were generally rare in most southern and eastern counties but were locally common at a few localities, especially Muskingum County, where 46 adults and four nests were located in 1935 (Hicks 1935a).

Pileated Woodpecker populations continued to increase within eastern Ohio during the 1940s and 1950s. Except for a few strays at Cincinnati in 1937 and 1938, Dayton in 1949, Toledo in 1955 and 1958, and sporadically in the Columbus area (Campbell 1968, Kemsies and Randle 1953, Mathena et al. 1984), their distribution did not appreciably change during these years.

Range expansion became apparent in the early 1960s and still continues as Pileateds attempt to reoccupy their former range. This expansion was first noted in the southwestern counties, where they returned to Dayton and Butler County in 1960 (Mathena et al. 1984, Mumford 1960b). In 1962, 26 Pileateds were counted at Cincinnati, where they have been absent only a few years earlier (Graber 1962b). Their numbers also noticeably increased in the Columbus area during the 1960s. Expansion into the northwestern counties began in the 1970s but has been slow because of a shortage of suitable woodlands within these intensively farmed counties.

Pileated Woodpeckers are now fairly common to locally common residents in most southern and eastern counties. Six or fewer individuals are expected daily, although tallies of 10–14+ are possible in areas with extensive forests. Impressive totals of 85–103 were counted on the Millersburg CBC during the late 1990s. They become uncommon to fairly common residents in the central counties bordering the unglaciated Allegheny Plateau but are absent to locally uncommon in the remainder of the state. Most reports are of three or fewer individuals in these counties. As of the 1980s, Pileated Woodpeckers had failed to recolonize twelve intensively farmed western counties (Peterjohn and Rice 1991).

While Pileateds are most numerous in extensive mature forests, they also occupy second-growth woodlands and large isolated woodlots. Their breeding territories must include suitable large trees for nesting. Their nests are placed at heights of twenty to fifty-five feet in cavities constructed during April and early May. Nests with eggs have been reported between April 18 and May 21 (Braund 1938b, Mathena et al. 1984). Their young usually hatch in May. Most dependent young have been reported in late May and early June, although re-nesting attempts produce fledglings during July.

Pileated Woodpeckers are normally sedentary. Despite their resident status, a few undertake local movements during spring and fall. These movements are hardly noticeable except when they appear at unexpected locations, such as migrant traps along Lake Erie. Their autumn movements, mostly noted in October and November, may be young birds searching for suitable territories. Their spring movements are not easily explained, but Pileateds occasionally appear along Lake Erie between March 25 and April 14.

Ivory-billed Woodpecker *Campephilus principalis* (Linnaeus)

The occurrence of this magnificent woodpecker is based solely on archaeological evidence from southern Ohio. While the bill, head, and wings might be found almost anywhere, since they were prized by Indians and actively traded between tribes, the presence of legs and other body parts is generally accepted as evidence of this woodpecker's natural occurrence in an area. It is considered unlikely that such a large bird would be carried great distances (Murphy and Farrand 1979).

Archaeological evidence of Ivory-billed Woodpeckers has been obtained from sites in Ross, Scioto, and Muskingum Counties. Leg elements (tarsometatarsi) were recovered from each site (Murphy and Farrand 1979, Wetmore 1943). Radiocarbon dating of material from the Muskingum site indicates that Ivory-billeds were present in Ohio between the twelfth and fourteenth centuries, while the Scioto County site may have been as recent as the fifteenth or sixteenth century. When they disappeared from the state is unknown. There is no evidence to substantiate their presence during historic times.

Olive-sided Flycatcher *Contopus cooperi* (Nuttall)

Sitting on a dead branch at the top of a large oak, an Olive-sided Flycatcher quietly surveys the surrounding fields for large flying insects. With its keen eyesight, it can detect prey at distances of several hundred feet and is quickly off in pursuit. Whether the chase is successful or not, it will habitually return to the same perch to wait for more insects to fly by. Olive-sided Flycatchers are frequently found near water, where insects are more plentiful, but open fields, cemeteries, and parks are equally suitable if tall perches are available. Unfortunately, this behavior cannot be regularly observed, as Olive-sided Flycatchers are normally rare migrants, becoming locally uncommon along Lake Erie. They are least numerous in the unglaciated counties, where suitable habitats are plentiful and the flycatchers are widely scattered.

Olive-sided Flycatchers are among our latest spring migrants. No reliable April records exist, although a few early individuals return during the first week of May. They are most likely to be encountered during the last half of the month. They regularly linger through June 3–7, and sightings as late as June 10–14 are not unexpected. Migrants are normally encountered as individuals or pairs. However, small concentrations are occasionally noted along Lake Erie. By far the largest reported movement involved 30 Olive-sideds at Cedar Point (Erie County) on May 13, 1907 (Jones 1910). In recent years, the largest concentrations totaled 4–6.

In eastern North America, breeding Olive-sided Flycatchers occupy boreal forests in Canada, the northern United States, and very locally at high elevations along the Appalachian Mountains (AOU 1998). At one time, a very small population may have resided in extreme northeastern Ohio. Hicks (1933a) observed summering Olive-sideds at three Ashtabula County locations between 1925 and 1932. Of these locations, the former Pymatuning Bog hosted summering Olive-sideds during three years. An incubating adult was discovered in a white pine within the bog on June 16, 1932, providing the only confirmed nesting record. With the bog's destruction, this population disappeared. Since the mid-1930s, nonbreeding Olive-sided Flycatchers have been casual summer visitors to the northeastern counties but are accidental elsewhere, producing two to four summer sightings during most decades.

Like most flycatchers, Olive-sideds begin their fall migration very early. Returning migrants may appear by the first week of August, but most are observed between mid-August and mid-September. Most depart for wintering grounds in South and Central America by the end of September. The few October records include an October 11, 1908, specimen from Hamilton County and a sighting in the Cleveland area on October 16, 1965 (Kemsies and Randle 1953, Rosche 1992). Fall sightings are of only 1–4 individuals.

Eastern Wood-Pewee *Contopus virens* (Linnaeus)

The first hint of dawn on a warm summers morning will be greeted by the plaintive whistles of the Eastern Wood-Pewee, one of our more vocal woodland songbirds. The calls continue throughout the day, although they decrease in frequency during the warm midafternoon. Sunset produces another chorus that continues until the last sunlight vanishes from the evening sky.

During summer, most pewees are detected by their distinctive calls, since these drab flycatchers frequently

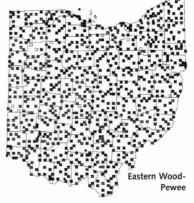

Eastern Wood-Pewee

remain hidden among the foliage of tall trees. They are among Ohio's most numerous woodland flycatchers and are fairly common to common summer residents throughout the state. Their preferred habitats are mature woodlands, from small woodlots to extensive forests, but they also occupy riparian corridors, parks, and grazed woodlots. Breeding Eastern Wood-Pewees are most numerous in southern and eastern Ohio, where mature woodlands are widely distributed. Between 12 and 25 can be recorded during a June morning within these counties. They are least numerous in intensively cultivated western Ohio, where daily totals seldom exceed 2–8 except along extensive riparian corridors.

Pewee nests are usually located at heights of twenty-five to seventy-five feet along the outer branches of tall trees. Since these nests are inaccessible, there is a paucity of nesting data from Ohio. Most nests are initiated during late May and early June, but nests with eggs have been reported as early as May 14

(Williams 1950). First broods fledge during the last half of June and July. Some pewees may raise two broods, as there are a number of nesting reports during August and early September. Nests with eggs are reported as late as August 13–15; young remain in nests through September 1, and adults feed dependent young through September 13–16 (Trautman 1940, Williams 1950).

Given their status as common summer residents, the initiation of their fall migration is difficult to detect. Records from lakefront migrant traps indicate that their passage begins during the last half of August. Eastern Wood-Pewees remain fairly common to common until the third week of September. Fall totals seldom exceed 5–10 daily. Most depart by October 9–15, with the latest documented records through October 21–24. While there are several November sight records, the identity of these individuals is uncertain.

Their spring status is also obscured by misidentifications, and all March sight records most likely pertain to phoebes. The earliest pewees return between April 18 and 25 as overflights in northern Ohio and very early residents to counties along the Ohio River. Eastern Wood-Pewees normally return by the first week of May. They become fairly common to common throughout the state by May 15–20. The largest spring movements total 20–30 daily along Lake Erie and in central Ohio, but most reports are of ten or fewer. The last migrant pewees appear along Lake Erie through May 25–June 5.

Eastern Wood-Pewee populations remained fairly stable during the first half of the twentieth century. In recent years, however, their populations suffered from the loss of mature woodlands in their North American breeding range and in South American rain forests where they winter. This habitat loss produced significant declines in pewee populations within Ohio and across North America since 1966, with the steepest declines occurring after 1980 (Sauer et al. 1998).

Yellow-bellied Flycatcher *Empidonax flaviventris* (Baird and Baird)

Of all songbirds in Ohio, *Empidonax* flycatchers are the most difficult species to identify positively in the field. All species have greenish-brown upperparts with a pair of wing bars, grayish-white underparts with varying amounts of yellowish wash, and an eye ring. Their plumage differences are subtle, and positive identification is frequently based on songs and call notes. While Yellow-bellieds are probably the most distinctive member of this group, sight records are still subject to question, especially during fall, when other species can have an extensive yellowish wash on the underparts.

Yellow-bellied Flycatchers are late spring migrants. The earliest Yellow-bellieds appear during the first week of May, although they normally arrive during May 10–15. They are most numerous during the last half of May, when they are rare to uncommon migrants through the interior of Ohio and uncommon to fairly common along Lake Erie. Daily totals are normally three or fewer individuals. Sizable movements produce as many as ten in central Ohio and 18–25 along Lake Erie. These migrants prefer dense woodlands and are frequently found near water. Yellow-bellieds normally depart by the first week of June but linger along Lake Erie through June 10–14.

These flycatchers normally breed in the boreal forests of Canada and the northern United States (AOU 1998). The only published summer sight record from Ohio is from the Cleveland area (Williams 1950). Unfortunately, the details of this sighting were never provided and the acceptability of this record is debatable.

During fall, Yellow-bellied Flycatchers are rare to uncommon migrants. In addition to mesic woodlands, they are also found in drier wooded and edge habitats during this season. They are usually encountered as isolated individuals, and the largest reported concentration is ten along Lake Erie (Campbell 1968). Since Yellow-bellieds normally return to the north shore of Lake Erie during the last ten days of July (Hussell 1982), they probably also appear in Ohio during this period. There are very few late July records, however, probably because of their inconspicuous behavior. The first Yellow-bellieds are normally detected during the second week of August. Their fall migration usually extends through the third week of September. Occasional stragglers remain into early October, and the latest acceptable report is one banded at Cleveland on October 18, 1976 (Rosche 1992). Several November sight records are not accompanied by sufficient details to allow for a positive identification.

Acadian Flycatcher *Empidonax virescens* (Vieillot)

During summer, most species of *Empidonax* flycatchers occupy different habitats, which facilitates their identification. Acadian Flycatchers inhabit mature woodlands and are unlikely to be found anywhere else. Inconspicuous when they forage silently within the understories of these forests, they are more likely to be detected by their diagnostic loud calls.

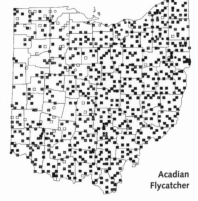

Acadian Flycatcher

While these flycatchers seemingly prefer mature beech-maple forests, they also readily occupy hemlock woods, oak and oak-maple woodlands, swamp forests, and floodplain woods. They require fairly open woodlands with well-defined understories, frequently with small creeks. Acadians become most numerous within extensive forests and normally avoid small isolated woodlots and narrow wooded corridors.

Their nests are placed at heights of eight to twenty feet, suspended between twigs on the branches of small trees. They are frequently placed over a small creek or ravine (Williams 1950). Nest construction normally begins during May and continues into mid-June. While complete clutches have been recorded by the first week of June, pairs in the southern counties undoubtedly produce clutches during May. Most clutches in northeastern Ohio are reported between June 10 and July 2 (Newman 1958, Williams 1950). Recently fledged young have been noted as early as June 6 in Warren County, but most appear during the last week of June and July (Harlan 1994d, Trautman 1940). Renesting attempts produce fledglings as late as the first week of September.

As summer residents, Acadian Flycatchers were widely distributed during the twentieth century. Jones (1903) considered them fairly common residents throughout the state. Hicks (1935a) cited summer records from eighty-five counties, noting absences only in Putnam, Allen, and Hancock Counties. While these flycatchers were "infrequent and locally distributed" within most northwestern counties, they were fairly common to abundant elsewhere.

Their status did not change appreciably in subsequent decades. Their numbers have increased in northwestern Ohio, and Acadian Flycatchers were recorded from every county during the Breeding Bird Atlas (Campbell 1973, Peterjohn and Rice 1991). However, recent Breeding Bird Survey estimates of statewide population trends indicate a significant decline since 1980 (Sauer et al. 1998).

Acadian Flycatchers are now fairly common to locally abundant summer residents throughout southern and eastern Ohio. They are most numerous along the unglaciated Allegheny Plateau, where 10–30 may be recorded daily and counts of 50–65+ are possible from tracts of extensive mature forests. Within the southwestern and northeastern counties, daily totals of 8–25+ are normal. These flycatchers are widely distributed and fairly common residents within the central counties near Columbus, where daily totals seldom exceed 5–12. They are least numerous in west-central and northwestern Ohio. While they are locally fairly common at a few northwestern localities, where 10–15 may be recorded daily, these flycatchers become uncommon to rare and locally distributed within most intensively cultivated counties.

The timing of their northward movements is fairly uniform across the state. The earliest arrivals appear by April 25–30 but they are usually detected during May 3–7. They become numerous by May 15; small numbers continue to migrate into the first half of June. These migrants are mostly breeding birds returning to their territories. Spring Acadians are uncommon visitors to lake-front migrant traps, appearing mainly during the last half of May, when daily totals are normally 1–3, with peaks of 10–14.

Their status as fall migrants is obscured by the inability to positively identify most silent *Empidonax* flycatchers. Our understanding of their relative distribution and abundance during autumn is thus incomplete. Most Acadians depart quietly from their nesting territories, and fall migrants are relatively uncommon throughout the state. All fall reports are of five or fewer. Their numbers decline during the last half of August and the last Acadians normally disappear between September 10 and 20. Only a few stragglers remain later in the month. There are several sight records into the first week of October.

Alder Flycatcher *Empidonax alnorum* Brewster

Until Alder Flycatchers were recognized as a distinct species in 1973, few birders paid any attention to them. Even after formal recognition, correctly identifying Alders proved to be a challenge. In the field, they are positively identified only by their vocalizations. Silent Alders cannot be identified in the field and frequently not even in the hand. Despite these identification problems, the status of Alder Flycatchers is becoming better established within Ohio.

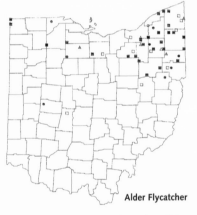

Alder Flycatcher

Alder Flycatchers are among the last migrants returning each spring. The earliest confirmed arrivals are May 8–11; they normally appear during May 15–20. They pass through the state very rapidly and most are observed between May 23 and June 7. These migrants are uncommon to fairly common along Lake Erie, where daily totals are normally six or fewer, with maxima of 8–10. Within the interior counties, Alders are casual to locally uncommon migrants, usually as scattered individuals. The last migrants remain into the second week of June, especially along Lake Erie.

Summering Alder Flycatchers are most numerous in the northeastern counties of Ashtabula, Trumbull, Lake, Geauga, eastern Cuyahoga, and Portage, where they are generally uncommon residents. Territorial males are scattered throughout these counties, normally in groups of four or fewer. They become more plentiful at only a few locations, including Grand River Wildlife

Area (Trumbull County) and Gott Fen Nature Preserve (Portage County), where 9–12+ have been reported (Peterjohn and Rice 1991), and at the Ravenna Arsenal (Portage County), where a remarkable 60–61 were estimated during 1993 and 1999. They are casual to rare and locally distributed summer residents in other northeastern counties. The southern edge of this breeding range may extend onto the unglaciated Allegheny Plateau, with isolated summering males reported from Carroll and Tuscarawas Counties (Peterjohn and Rice 1991). Elsewhere in northern Ohio, Alder Flycatchers are casual to rare summer residents and may regularly nest only in the northwestern counties of Lucas, Fulton, and Williams. They are very locally distributed in these counties, usually as four or fewer singing males. Alder Flycatchers are accidental residents elsewhere, with males apparently summering south to Champaign, Madison, Clark, Ross, and Warren Counties (Harlan 1994d, 1995d, Peterjohn and Rice 1991).

Marshes, bogs, and streambanks dominated by buttonbush, alders, dogwoods, and willows provide typical summer habitats for Alder Flycatchers—the same wet brushy thickets occupied by Willow Flycatchers. But unlike Willows, Alder Flycatchers avoid brushy successional habitats away from water. Very little information is available on their breeding biology in Ohio. The few confirmed breeding records indicate that nesting activities are initiated in early June and most young fledge by mid-July. Recently fledged young have been reported into early August (Peterjohn and Rice 1991).

Their fall status is poorly understood. Alders appear to be fairly early migrants, and most residents depart from their Ohio territories by mid-August. In addition, an influx of singing Alders is occasionally noted between July 25 and August 10. Perhaps these individuals are migrant adults from farther north. As many as 8–9 have been reported from northeastern Ohio during this period. After the adults depart in mid-August, the very few confirmed records indicate that their migration continues into the last half of September, with the latest report from Headlands Beach State Park on September 29, 1996 (Conlon and Harlan 1996a).

Willow Flycatcher *Empidonax traillii* (Audubon)

Willows are the most widely distributed *Empidonax* flycatchers of wet, brushy habitats in Ohio. While they prefer shrubby swamps and thickets bordering streams, Willows also occupy brushy wet meadows and fallow fields. Pairs may inhabit cattail wetlands if some brushy thickets are available. Their nests are usually placed within dense thickets at heights of two to twelve feet. While nests with eggs have been discovered as early as May 27 (Williams 1950), most are noted during June, with a few as late as mid-July. Recently fledged Willows reported on June 14 were exceptionally early; most young fledge during mid-July and early August (Trautman 1940). Few renesting attempts have been reported, although nests with young have been noted through August 17 (Nolan 1958d).

Willow Flycatchers are widely distributed summer residents in most counties (Peterjohn and Rice 1991). They are least numerous in southern Ohio, especially the Ohio River counties between Brown and Washington, where they are uncommon to locally

Willow
Flycatcher

fairly common. Summer totals seldom exceed 1–5 individuals daily within these counties. Elsewhere, Willow Flycatchers are fairly common to common summer residents, although they may be locally distributed within some southeastern and intensively cultivated western counties. As many as 5–25+ are reported daily away from the Ohio River. Larger concentrations of this semicolonial flycatcher are possible. Trautman (1940) reported 218 along one mile of brushy shoreline at Buckeye Lake on June 12, 1928.

Their breeding distribution was formerly more limited. At the turn of the twentieth century, nesting Willows were mostly restricted to the northern half of Ohio (Jones 1903). Their expansion into southern Ohio occurred mainly before 1930 but was poorly documented except for the first Cincinnati nesting record in 1931 (Kemsies and Randle 1953). By the mid-1930s, Hicks (1935a) cited summer records from eighty counties. While Willows were widely distributed within glaciated Ohio, they remained rare and very local along the unglaciated Allegheny Plateau north to Vinton, Muskingum, and Carroll Counties (Hicks 1937a). Populations gradually increased within most southeastern counties during subsequent decades.

During spring, an extraordinarily early singing male Willow Flycatcher returned to the Cleveland area on April 18, 1976 (Hammond 1976). A few Willows return during the first week of May, although they normally arrive during May 10–15. Most of their spring passage occurs between May 20 and June 5. These migrants are fairly common to common, and 5–20 are observed daily in most counties, with maxima of 25–32+ along Lake Erie.

Willow Flycatchers remain conspicuous until the males quit singing in mid-July. Their fall migration commences shortly after their young become independent. Southward migrants appear at lakefront migrant traps during the first week of August; migration occurs principally between August 5 and

25. This migration is hardly noticeable except for the gradual disappearance of the resident flycatchers; August sightings seldom exceed 1–10 daily. The last migrants normally depart by the first week of September. Late migrants are infrequently encountered into the first week of October.

Least Flycatcher *Empidonax minimus* (Baird and Baird)

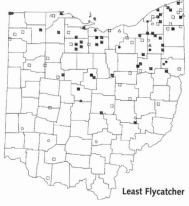

Least Flycatcher

Normally the first *Empidonax* flycatchers returning each spring, Leasts have appeared at Cleveland by April 10, 1955 (Rosche 1992), and there are scattered reports from other locations during April 11–15. These early records are exceptional. The first Leasts are expected by April 25–30 in the southern and central counties and May 1–5 along Lake Erie. Most spring migrants appear between May 7 and 23. The last migrants normally depart from interior counties before June 1, although stragglers remain along Lake Erie into the first week of June.

Migrant Least Flycatchers prefer second-growth woods but are also found in parks, cemeteries, brushy fencerows, and thickets. They are widely distributed and fairly common to common across Ohio. Between two and ten Leasts are observed daily in most counties. Larger flights are fairly regular along Lake Erie, where concentrations of 25–50+ may appear. Similar flights are unusual within the interior counties (Trautman 1940); a remarkable 300 were estimated at Greenlawn Cemetery in Columbus on May 14, 1981 (Thomson 1983).

A small breeding population has always resided in northern Ohio. Hicks (1935a) cited summer records from Lucas, Fulton, Williams, Ashtabula, Lake, Geauga, Trumbull, and Cuyahoga Counties. Only a few pairs resided in most of these counties except Ashtabula, where they were recorded from twelve localities (Hicks 1933a). Population trends were not apparent except in northwestern Ohio, where Campbell (1940) cited declines resulting from habitat destruction.

Since the mid-1930s, this breeding population has slowly expanded southward. In northeastern Ohio, increased numbers of summering Leasts were detected near Cleveland during the 1950s and 1960s (Newman 1969). They were noted south to Columbiana County by 1960 (Hall 1960d). This expansion was not apparent in the northwest, except for isolated nesting records in a few additional counties (Phillips 1980). By the mid-1970s, a few widely scattered summering Leasts also appeared in the central and southern counties.

Summering Least Flycatchers are now uncommon to fairly common residents in Ashtabula County, where 3–7 males can be recorded daily. They become generally uncommon in Lake, Geauga, Trumbull, and Portage Counties, although 36 were estimated at the Ravenna Arsenal during 1999 (Whan 1999b). They are rare east to Cleveland and south to Wayne, Stark, and Columbiana Counties (Peterjohn and Rice 1991). Elsewhere in northern Ohio, they are casual to rare summer residents south to Defiance, Henry, Wood, Seneca, and Ashland Counties, mostly as isolated pairs, although small populations are established at a few localities.

Least Flycatchers are casual summer visitors to the central counties, producing one to three reports during most years. They become accidental within the southern third of the state. Widely scattered singing males have been reported south to Butler, Brown, Ross, Hocking, Vinton, and Belmont Counties (Peterjohn 1982d, Peterjohn and Rice 1991). Most of these sightings are of isolated singing males that are probably unmated, although nesting was confirmed at Lake Hope State Park (Vinton County) in 1988 (Peterjohn 1988d).

Breeding Least Flycatchers occupy a variety of woodland habitats, from open groves and woodlots to extensive riparian corridors and young second-growth deciduous woodlands. Very little information is available on their nesting biology within Ohio. Most nests are initiated during late May and June. While dependent young have been reported by June 24, other nests have contained young flycatchers as late as August 3 (Phillips 1980).

Since adult Least Flycatchers begin their southward movements shortly after their young become independent, they are among the first songbirds returning each autumn. Migrant Leasts appear by July 20–25 in the northern and central counties and are regularly noted throughout the state during the first half of August. These migrants are most apparent between August 20 and September 15. Their numbers diminish during the last half of September, although a few remain through October 3–7. Exceptionally late migrants have been discovered in the Cleveland area through October 18–23 (Harlan 1996a, Peterjohn 1992a).

Least Flycatchers are generally uncommon to fairly common migrants, most numerous along Lake Erie. Most fall reports total 1–5 daily. Sizable movements do not normally appear in autumn; only Trautman (1940) reported as many as 25 daily at Buckeye Lake during the 1920s and 1930s.

Gray Flycatcher *Empidonax wrightii* Baird

Gray Flycatchers breed in arid sagebrush and pinyon-juniper woodland in western North America, while their winter range extends from the southwestern United States into Mexico (AOU 1998). This species has been acceptably documented from eastern North America on four occasions, including the only report from Ohio. On August 20, 1988, a Gray Flycatcher was discovered at Magee Marsh Wildlife Area in Lucas County. The bird was observed and photographed over a period of one and one-half hours as it foraged along the "Bird Trail" at the wildlife area. The plumage characteristics, vocalizations, and distinctive tail-bobbing behavior were noted at that time (Peterjohn and Gustafson 1990). This flycatcher was subsequently observed at this site through August 22.

Eastern Phoebe *Sayornis phoebe* (Latham)

Before Ohio was settled, Eastern Phoebes were very locally distributed summer residents, restricted to wooded stream valleys bordered by rocky cliffs. As people altered this environment, the modified landscape proved very acceptable for this adaptable flycatcher. Bridges over streams provided additional nest sites and populations expanded until nearly every bridge was occupied by its resident pair. Phoebes also adopted sheds, barns, abandoned houses, and other structures as nest

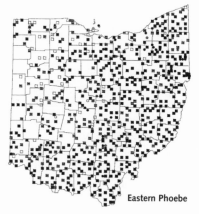

Eastern Phoebe

sites. So successful was their adaptation to man-made habitats that Jones (1903) considered them "almost a household bird" at the turn of the twentieth century.

They remained numerous through the 1930s. Hicks (1935a) described Eastern Phoebes as common to abundant summer residents in every county, most numerous along the unglaciated Allegheny Plateau. Considerable numbers of migrants also passed through the state. Trautman (1940) reported spring peaks of 30–60 daily at Buckeye Lake during the 1920s and 1930s, with fewer recorded in autumn.

Their populations declined during the 1940s, a trend that continued into the 1960s (Campbell 1968, Mathena et al. 1984). Two factors contributed to this decline: in western Ohio, intensive agricultural land-use practices eliminated many suitable nesting habitats, and periodic severe winters decimated phoebe populations throughout eastern North America. But populations have apparently stabilized since the mid-1960s (Sauer et al. 1998). While phoebes experienced short-term declines following the severe winters of 1976–1978, they fully recovered by the early 1980s.

Eastern Phoebes are now fairly common to common summer residents throughout southern and eastern Ohio, where 5–20 are expected daily. They are generally fairly common residents in the central and north-central counties, with summer totals of 3–6 daily, except within large urban areas, where they are normally scarce. Within the west-central and northwestern counties, few suitable breeding sites remain and they are rare to uncommon and locally distributed residents, usually encountered as isolated pairs (Peterjohn and Rice 1991).

Breeding phoebes prefer small wooded streams, but a few pairs nest under bridges over large rivers. Along the unglaciated plateau, they also regularly nest near upland edge habitats wherever outbuildings and abandoned houses provide suitable sites. A few pairs still use rocky cliffs, and an imaginative pair built a nest on an old coffee pot hanging on the wall of a shed (Henninger 1902). They normally raise two broods annually. Nest construction frequently begins during the last week of March, even in northern Ohio. The first clutches are normally laid in April, as early as April 8 in the central and southern counties. These young fledge by the first week of May but are more likely to appear after May 20 (Trautman 1940, Williams 1950). Second clutches are laid during June with some through July 18. These young normally fledge by late July and early August.

Our hardiest flycatchers, Eastern Phoebes may appear with the first warm weather—in the southern and central counties during the last half of February and along Lake Erie by February 25–March 2. They normally become widely distributed by mid-March, and maximum abundance is attained between March 15 and April 10. During these weeks, they become fairly common to common migrants. In recent years, most spring reports are of ten or fewer daily, with infrequent flights of 20–30+. Few migrants are detected after April 20–25.

Eastern Phoebes are uncommon to fairly common during autumn, most numerous in the eastern and southern counties. Most fall sightings are of six or fewer daily and the largest movements total 15–25. Phoebes regularly appear at lakefront migrant traps by the first week of August; the disappearance of resident pairs during late July is also indicative of an early migration. Only small numbers of migrants are detected before September, and their peak passage is expected between September 15 and October 10. Their numbers noticeably diminish after October 20–25.

Formerly accidental early winter visitors to Ohio, the number of Eastern Phoebes lingering into December and early January has noticeably increased since 1990. Statewide totals of 20–33+ have been reported on Christmas Bird Counts following mild autumn seasons, while only five or fewer may be counted when early winter weather has been harsh. Eastern Phoebes are currently casual to rare early winter visitors to the southern counties bordering the Ohio River, and casual along the unglaciated Allegheny Plateau. They are generally accidental elsewhere. Most reports are of single phoebes, although as many as 3–7 have been found on Christmas Bird Counts. These phoebes are usually observed before January 15 and disappear when extended subfreezing temperatures descend upon the state. A few phoebes overwinter within the southern counties during relatively mild seasons, producing 2–4 reports during recent decades.

Say's Phoebe *Sayornis saya* (Bonaparte)

Say's Phoebes are residents of western North America, with a breeding range extending from Alaska south into Mexico. Small numbers occasionally wander into the eastern portion of the continent (AOU 1998), primarily during fall and early winter. There are two acceptable reports from Ohio. The first Say's Phoebe was discovered by Charlotte Mathena at Hueston Woods State Park on November 26, 1989 (Peterjohn 1990a). Subsequent attempts to relocate this bird were not successful. The second record was provided by a phoebe discovered by Scott Albaugh at Kokosing Reservoir on December 11, 1997, and it was subsequently observed at nearby locations in Knox County through January 7, 1998 (Brock 1998b).

Vermilion Flycatcher *Pyrocephalus rubinus* (Boddaert)

This handsome flycatcher is known primarily as a resident of riparian woodlands in arid regions from the southwestern United States into Central America. A disjunct population is also found in South America. While the Vermilion's North American breeding range extends north to southern California, southern Nevada, western Oklahoma, and central Texas, these flycatchers exhibit a tendency to wander considerable distances from this established range. They are accidental visitors north to South Dakota, Minnesota, and the lower Great Lakes, while records extend east to the Atlantic Coast (AOU 1998).

Ohio's first Vermilion Flycatcher was discovered by William Porter, Jr., at Clark Lake Wildlife Area in Clark County on September 20, 1958. It was an immature male undergoing a pronounced molt. When collected the following day, it was found to be greatly emaciated (Trautman and Trautman 1968). There is also a spring sight record from northern Ohio: a male reported from Erie County on May 2, 1973 (Kleen and Bush 1973c). This flycatcher was closely studied by Allen Stickley, Jr., and subsequently by other birders, as it caught insects along a rural road.

Great Crested Flycatcher *Myiarchus crinitus* (Linnaeus)

Occupants of deciduous woodlands, Great Crested Flycatchers are more frequently detected by their loud, hoarse calls than by their attractive plumage. Since they prefer to forage within the canopy of tall trees, silent birds are frequently overlooked. With a little perseverance they can be observed as they quietly sit on a dead limb searching for prey or flash through the foliage in pursuit of a large insect.

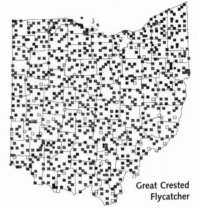

Great Crested
Flycatcher

While there are several unsubstantiated March sight records, the earliest confirmed Great Crested Flycatcher appeared at Akron on April 1, 1973 (Hammond 1973). This extremely early flycatcher was observed and heard calling as it foraged within the branches of a large tree. The first spring migrants normally return to the southern and central counties by April 20–28 and along Lake Erie by May 1–5. Great Cresteds become fairly common to common migrants by May 10. They are seldom numerous, especially within the interior counties; daily totals of 5–20 are expected throughout the state. Sizable flights are infrequent along Lake Erie, where the largest movement totaled 50 in Ottawa County on May 15, 1948 (Campbell 1968).

After returning to Ohio, Great Crested Flycatchers quickly establish their nesting territories. Mature deciduous woods are preferred but younger second-growth woodlands are occupied if a few large trees are available. Pairs are occasionally found in orchards, wooded pastures, and shade trees in city parks and cemeteries. Nesting Great Crested Flycatchers are most numerous in eastern and southern Ohio. They are common summer residents in these counties, where 5–12 are recorded daily during June. Similar numbers may also be noted in extensive woodlands elsewhere. However, Great Cresteds become locally uncommon residents within the intensively farmed western counties (Peterjohn and Rice 1991). Daily totals seldom exceed 1–5 in agricultural areas with few woodlots.

Great Crested Flycatchers have always been common and widely distributed residents (Hicks 1935a, Jones 1903). Breeding Bird Survey data indicates that their statewide population declined significantly between 1966 and 1979, but has been fairly stable since 1980 (Sauer et al. 1998). Factors responsible for this decline have not been identified.

Unlike other eastern flycatchers, Great Cresteds normally nest in tree cavities. If suitable cavities are unavailable, they have nested in telephone poles, bird boxes, and Purple Martin houses (Buchanan 1980, Campbell 1968). Their nests are normally placed at heights of twenty to fifty feet, but a few have been only five to seven feet above the ground. Nest construction normally begins during the last half of May. Great Cresteds have developed the curious and unexplained habit of lining their nests with snake skins. Most clutches are apparently laid during late May and early June. Dependent young have been observed by June 21 but most fledge during July. Renesting attempts are responsible for nest construction through June 27, which would produce young in mid-August (Trautman 1940, Williams 1950).

Once their young fledge, adult Great Cresteds become silent. Even though their populations have been supplemented by young birds, few of these inconspicuous flycatchers are observed during July and early August. They become more visible in mid-August, when their southward migration is initiated. This migration is poorly defined, but most fall Great Cresteds are observed between August 25 and September 15. These uncommon migrants are mostly noted as scattered individuals and daily totals seldom exceed 3–6. The last migrants normally depart by September 25–30. Late migrants rarely linger into the second half of October.

The phenomenon of reverse migration is not normally witnessed within Ohio during autumn. Once birds leave the state, they seldom return until the following spring. However, unusually warm temperatures and southerly winds may prompt some songbirds to migrate north during late October or early November. Hicks (1932a) witnessed a reverse migration along Alum Creek in southern Delaware County on November 16, 1931. Among the birds observed that day, he counted an incredible nine Great Crested Flycatchers, one of which was collected.

Western Kingbird *Tyrannus verticalis* Say

Western Kingbirds are widely distributed summer residents from southern Canada through the western United States to the eastern edge of the Great Plains (AOU 1998). While most migrate through the western states to and from their wintering areas in Mexico and Central America, small numbers regularly migrate eastward each autumn and reach the Atlantic Coast. These eastward migrants undoubtedly pass through Ohio and other eastern states, but relatively few are detected at inland localities as compared with the numbers appearing along the coast.

Ohio's first Western Kingbird was discovered near Lake Erie in Lucas County on September 13, 1930 (Campbell 1940). In subsequent years, they averaged one to four published records each decade through the 1970s. The number of sightings increased during the 1980s, producing published records during every year but two, with a maximum of three reports in 1989

(Peterjohn 1990a). However, numbers returned to normal in the 1990s, with only two documented records. They are considered accidental or casual migrants.

During autumn, Western Kingbirds have been detected as early as August 13 and as late as October 10 (Kemsies and Randle 1953, Kleen 1972a). Most are recorded between August 25 and September 20, with a decided peak during the first week of September. At least ten sightings are scattered along Lake Erie between Toledo and Ashtabula County. The remaining records are widely scattered through the interior counties, with at least six sightings from the Columbus area, three from the Cincinnati-Dayton area, two in the Akron-Barberton area, and singles in Holmes County, Tuscarawas County, near East Liverpool, and at Waterville. With the exception of two in Hamilton County on August 13, 1938 (Kemsies and Randle 1953), all sightings are of single individuals. These kingbirds are diurnal migrants and seldom remain in an area for very long.

Western Kingbirds are accidental spring migrants in most eastern states. There are only three published spring records from Ohio. Single Westerns were discovered at Cleveland on June 1, 1945 (Williams 1950); Holden Arboretum (Lake County) on May 11, 1959 (Newman 1969); and Columbus on May 13, 1964 (Thomson 1983).

Breeding Western Kingbirds are regularly distributed along the western edges of Minnesota, Iowa, and Missouri, with occasional nesting records east to the Mississippi River (AOU 1998). The appearance of a breeding pair in northwestern Ohio provides the easternmost nesting record in North America. Lou Campbell (1940) discovered a female Western Kingbird feeding three recently fledged juveniles on July 29, 1933, at Reno-by-the-Lake (Lucas County). The juveniles were incapable of sustained flight and undoubtedly had been raised in the area. There are two additional documented summer records. A single Western Kingbird was photographed in Adams County on June 22, 1984 (Peterjohn 1984d). The other appeared at Killdeer Plains Wildlife Area on June 30, 1998 (Brock 1998d).

Eastern Kingbird *Tyrannus tyrannus* (Linnaeus)

Few birds are as relentless and aggressive in defense of their breeding territories as Eastern Kingbirds. Whenever a crow, hawk, or other potential predator comes into view, these kingbirds immediately take flight and attack the intruder long before it approaches their nest. Calling loudly throughout the encounter, kingbirds vigorously harass the intruder until it is driven from the area. Completely fearless, they will harass perched Bald Eagles, striking the eagles on the head until they depart for a more peaceful roosting site.

This territorial behavior can be regularly observed, since Eastern Kingbirds are widely distributed summer residents, a status they maintained throughout the twentieth century (Hicks 1935a, Peterjohn and Rice 1991). While they breed in every county, they are generally most numerous within southern and eastern Ohio, where they are fairly common to common summer residents and 3–15 may be noted daily. Breeding pairs are more locally distributed within the glaciated central and northwestern counties.

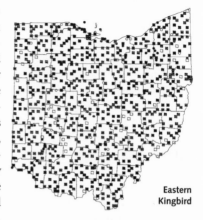

Eastern Kingbird

They become uncommon to fairly common summer residents within these counties; daily totals seldom exceed 2–7 individuals. Within a number of western counties, nesting kingbirds noticeably declined between the 1960s and 1980s. In many southern and eastern counties, however, their populations have remained fairly stable. Statewide population trend estimates from the Breeding Bird Survey do not indicate any significant changes since 1966 (Sauer et al. 1998).

Nesting Eastern Kingbirds prefer wooded corridors bordering streams, marshes, and lakes, especially corridors with tall trees providing a commanding view of the surrounding countryside. Within most Ohio farmlands, breeding Eastern Kingbirds are seldom encountered away from these habitats. In the southern and eastern counties, however, they also occupy upland areas where open fields are bordered by woodlands and wooded fencerows. A few pairs may nest in orchards, but they avoid urban areas.

Nests are normally placed on exposed branches high in tall trees but have been also located on telephone poles, fence posts, and in bushes only a few feet above the ground (Trautman 1940, Williams 1950). One pair constructed a nest on the boom of a dredge (Campbell 1968). Nest construction normally begins during the last half of May. The first clutches are laid by May 20–30 within the southern counties and June 5–15 elsewhere. Replacement clutches are noted through July 17 (Trautman 1940). The young hatch during June and the first fledglings may appear before the end of the month. Most fledglings are noted between July 10 and August 15, although a nest with young was reported from Lucas County on August 14, 1994 (Harlan 1994c).

Eastern Kingbirds are more conspicuous and numerous during their diurnal migrations. In spring, a few overflights have appeared along Lake Erie by April 6–7 (Campbell 1968, Williams 1950). These early migrants are exceptional; Eastern Kingbirds normally return to the southern counties by April 20–25 and along Lake Erie by April 28–May 3. Their maximum abundance is attained between May 10 and 25. Smaller numbers continue to pass along the lakefront into the first week of June. They are generally common along Lake Erie, where daily totals of 8–20 are expected, with occasional flights of 30–80+. The largest lakefront movements total 100–200+. Within the interior counties, Eastern Kingbirds are generally fairly common migrants and spring totals seldom exceed 5–12 individuals.

Greater numbers of Eastern Kingbirds normally pass through Ohio each autumn. When breeding populations were larger, flights of 50–100+ were detected along Lake Erie most years, especially near Toledo (Campbell 1968). Similar flights were more sporadic within the interior counties, although movements involving 50–80 individuals were reported from Dayton and Buckeye Lake (Mathena et al. 1984, Trautman 1940).

Numbers of fall migrants have noticeably diminished since 1965, although Eastern Kingbirds remain fairly common to common throughout Ohio. Recent fall totals are mostly 3–12, with occasional flights of 20–50+. Movements of 50–85+ still occur along Lake Erie, while 147 at Lake Rockwell (Portage County) on August 9, 1988, is a remarkable inland flight for recent decades (Peterjohn 1989a).

During some years, their southward movements begin by the first week of July, peak in the middle of the month, and finish by early August (Nolan 1954a). Such early fall migrations are not typical. Generally, the first migrants are noted between July 25 and August 7 and the largest movements between August 15 and September 5. The last migrants normally depart by September 14–23. Single kingbirds at Magee Marsh Wildlife Area on November 4, 1985 (Peterjohn 1986a); Seneca County on October 28, 1975, and October 28, 1995 (Harlan 1996a, Kleen 1976a); and the Cleveland area on October 24, 1976, are exceptionally late (Rosche 1992).

Scissor-tailed Flycatcher *Tyrannus forficatus* (Gmelin)

The Scissor-tailed is an attractive, slender, medium-sized flycatcher with an extremely long tail. It is usually seen hawking insects over the fields and plains of the south-central United States. It nests north to southern Nebraska and east to southwestern Missouri (AOU 1998), but frequently wanders considerable distances from this range, appearing along both coasts and in the Great Lakes region.

There are ten published records of Scissor-tailed Flycatchers from Ohio. These records include a male collected near Dunkinsville in Adams County on June 16, 1970 (Trautman and Trautman 1971); one photographed at Ottawa

Wildlife Refuge on May 13–15, 1997 (Brock 1997c); and well-described birds near Jenera in Hancock County on May 17–18, 1962, and in Wayne County on August 16, 1987 (Peterjohn 1988a, Phillips 1963). None of the other records are substantiated by written descriptions or extant specimens. Given this species' unmistakable characteristics, however, these other sightings are most likely correctly identified. The first was recorded from Marietta on May 20, 1894; a specimen of a male, it is no longer extant (Jones 1903). Another was reportedly shot near Marysville during late May 1903; it too has been lost (Jones 1905). The third sighting was in Pickaway County on July 1, 1934 (Borror 1950).

Of the ten records, six are May sightings. In addition to the four already listed, single Scissor-taileds were noted near Barberton (Summit County) on May 3, 1959, and in Adams County on May 8, 1966 (Newman 1969, Petersen 1966b). Summer records are limited to the Adams County specimen and the Pickaway County sighting. The two fall records are from Wayne County in 1987 and near Cincinnati in 1970. The exact date was not provided for the latter sighting (Petersen 1971).

Loggerhead Shrike *Lanius ludovicianus* Linnaeus

When Ohio was initially settled, the virgin forests, with few scattered openings, did not support Loggerhead Shrikes. As these forests were cleared and replaced by open farmlands, Loggerheads quickly took advantage of the newly created habitats. They apparently invaded during the mid-1800s, becoming widely distributed by 1880 (Wheaton 1882). During the first decades of the twentieth century, land-use practices produced ideal Loggerhead Shrike habitats. Farm fields were small and included

Loggerhead
Shrike

considerable acreages of grassy pastures, where Loggerheads hunted for insects, mice, and other prey. These fields were bordered by brushy fencerows and Osage orange hedgerows, whose dense vegetation provided nest sites. Shrikes thrived within these habitats, and the largest statewide populations were present between 1900 and 1930.

During the mid-1930s, Loggerhead Shrikes were rare to very common and locally distributed summer residents (Hicks 1935a). They were most frequently encountered in the central third of the state and were least numerous in the eastern counties bordering West Virginia. Trautman's (1940) report of 10–19 pairs nesting around Buckeye Lake and Jones's (1910) estimate of "about 12 pairs in each township" in Erie County may be representative of their breeding densities during these decades.

Beginning in the 1930s, land-use practices dramatically changed in the central and western counties. Intensive agricultural production eliminated most Osage orange hedgerows and shrubby fencerows, converted most pastures to cultivated crops, and greatly enlarged the size of farm fields. The ideal shrike habitat eventually disappeared and their populations plummeted.

Population declines were evident by the mid-1930s in Paulding County (Price 1935). Widespread declines became noticeable during the late 1940s at Findlay and Cleveland (Phillips 1980, Williams 1950). Campbell (1968) reported a marked decrease near Toledo during 1949. Populations continued to shrink throughout the 1950s and 1960s. By 1970, only a few widely scattered pairs remained.

Numbers of breeding pairs continued to decline in recent decades, a trend evident throughout North America (Peterjohn and Sauer 1995). Since 1980, Loggerheads have been accidental to casual summer residents, with most records from the western half of the state. During the Breeding Bird Atlas, they were reported from twenty locations in seventeen counties; half of these records were from Clark, Madison, and Pickaway Counties southwest to the Ohio River (Peterjohn and Rice 1991). Most of the remaining reports were from the northwestern counties, while the only probable breeding attempt in eastern Ohio was noted in Carroll County. A similar distribution of summer reports was evident during the 1990s, although less thorough coverage produced confirmed or probable breeding records from only ten counties. The only confirmed breeding pairs in the eastern half of Ohio during this decade were reported from Holmes and Licking Counties (Brock 1998a, Peterjohn 1991d). Since shrikes frequently do not return to the same nesting sites each year, estimating their population size is very difficult. Only one to five nesting pairs have been discovered annually since 1990, and the statewide population probably numbers fewer than ten pairs.

Loggerhead Shrikes begin their breeding activities as soon as they establish territories in late March or early April. Nests are placed at heights of four to fifteen feet in thorny trees and bushes. First clutches are normally laid during the last half of April and early May. While adults with dependent young have been noted as early as May 17, most young shrikes fledge during June (Williams 1950). Renesting efforts and second broods are responsible for nests with young through July 31 and observations of recently fledged young during late July and early August (Mathena et al. 1984).

Even when their populations were larger, most Loggerheads were only summer residents in Ohio. Their migratory movements were better defined during the early 1900s but have not been apparent in recent years, when Loggerheads became accidental or casual migrants throughout the state.

Their spring migration was formerly fairly conspicuous. The first migrants normally appeared in mid-March, and the migration continued through the third week of April. They were most numerous between March 25 and April 15, when as many as 15 daily were recorded during the largest flights (Trautman 1940). In recent decades, spring migrants are single shrikes observed during the last half of March and April.

Shrikes are diurnal migrants whose behavior is unfamiliar to most modern birdwatchers:

> Upon a few occasions, shrikes were observed migrating north in the daytime. The birds flew at a low elevation across the fields in a succession of short flights, stopping frequently to perch for short periods of time upon fences, trees, or telephone poles, and to look for food. A transient followed for three miles was still going northward in the same manner when last seen (Trautman 1940).

In contrast, their fall movements were always poorly defined. Loggerheads became very inconspicuous after the young fledged, and quietly disappeared from their breeding territories. Trautman (1940) claimed their fall migration was evident by July 23 and peaked in mid-August. Small numbers continued to pass through Ohio until late September. Very few fall migrants have been detected within the state since 1970.

During winter, Loggerhead Shrikes were always accidental to casual residents in the northern counties and casual to rare in central and southern Ohio. Not surprisingly, numbers of wintering shrikes have also declined since the late 1940s. Although they do not regularly winter at any location, wintering shrikes have been reported at a frequency of one to six sightings annually since the late 1960s. Most recent winter records are from the southern half of Ohio, with very few confirmed sightings from the northern counties.

Wintering Loggerhead Shrikes are not necessarily the same individuals breeding in Ohio, since they do not maintain their nesting territories throughout the year. In winter the Loggerheads are rather nomadic and usually establish defined feeding territories for only a few days or weeks. They mostly appear during November and December, with considerably fewer sightings after mid-January. Wintering shrikes occupy the same habitats as breeding pairs but are also found in fallow fields with considerable brushy vegetation.

Northern Shrike *Lanius excubitor* Linnaeus

The status of Northern Shrikes has been obscured by frequent misidentifications, generating a number of questionable records, especially of unseasonal and extralimital shrikes. In recent years, however, careful observations have apparently established their actual winter status.

Northern Shrikes are rare winter visitors to northern Ohio. Their normal winter range extends south to Trumbull, Portage, Medina, Seneca, and Defiance Counties. They occasionally wander south to northern Columbiana, Tuscarawas, Holmes, and central Richland Counties in northeastern Ohio and to Killdeer Plains Wildlife Area (Moore 1996). They are accidental winter visitors elsewhere, and any Northern Shrike away from this established range should be carefully identified and documented. While there are a number of sight records scattered across central and southern Ohio, most are unsubstantiated. The only confirmed records are specimens collected near Buckeye Lake in Perry County on December 26, 1954, and in Hamilton County on November 3, 1883.

The earliest Northern Shrikes have returned to the Cleveland area on October 7, 1954, and Ottawa Wildlife Refuge on October 8, 1989 (Peterjohn 1990a, Rosche 1992), but these records are exceptional. A few are noted in late October, but most Northerns appear during the last half of November and December. As winter residents, a few Northerns are nomadic, but most establish defined territories. These territories frequently include successional fields, brushy pastures, and wooded fencerows bordering cultivated fields. These shrikes are most visible on calm, sunny days when they hunt from the tops of trees or shrubs, actively pursuing rodents and small birds.

Wintering Northern Shrikes remain until the advent of warm weather in February or early March. Most depart by March 15–20, although a few remain along Lake Erie until the end of the month. Late migrants linger through mid-April, as evidenced by one photographed at Mentor Marsh Nature Preserve (Lake County) on April 14, 1979 (Rosche 1992).

Like most northern predatory birds, wintering Northern Shrikes vary considerably in numbers from year to year. During most winters, they are relatively rare, with two to six sightings from the northern counties. However, they occasionally stage southward incursions in response to food shortages within their Canadian winter range. Perhaps their largest winter invasions occurred during the mid-1950s. Unprecedented numbers appeared throughout the Great Lakes area during the winter of 1953–1954, although unusual numbers were not reported from Ohio (Nolan 1954b). A flight during the following winter produced at least ten Northerns in the Toledo area, as well as the only central Ohio specimen (Campbell 1968, Nolan 1955b). A smaller movement the next winter produced eight Northerns on the Ashtabula Christmas Bird Count. In subsequent decades, the most substantial movements were noted in the winters of 1981–1982, when shrikes were detected at fourteen locations in the northern counties (Peterjohn 1982b); and 1995–1996, when 22 were found on Christmas Bird Counts across northern Ohio, approximately ten wintered in the Toledo area, and three were reported from Killdeer Plains Wildlife Area (Harlan 1996b).

White-eyed Vireo *Vireo griseus* (Boddaert)

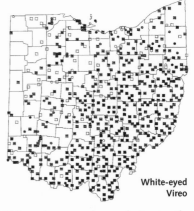

White-eyed Vireo

During the nineteenth century, the distribution and abundance of White-eyed Vireos in Ohio was the subject of contradictory information (Jones 1903). Regardless of this controversy, White-eyed Vireos were largely restricted to the southern counties at the turn of the twentieth century. They may have been rather numerous near Cincinnati but were generally rare and locally distributed in other southern counties (Henninger 1905). Elsewhere, these vireos were known only as spring migrants, regularly appearing in central Ohio and very rarely wandering north to Lake Erie.

Their breeding range slowly expanded northward. By the mid-1930s, Hicks (1935a) cited breeding records from thirty-five southern and eastern counties north to Butler, Warren, Clinton, Fayette, Pickaway, Franklin, Licking, Coshocton, Tuscarawas, and Jefferson. Along the unglaciated plateau, White-eyeds were numerous north to Hocking, Vinton, Jackson, and Meigs Counties (Hicks 1937a). They remained rare elsewhere on the plateau (Trautman 1940). Away from this breeding range, these vireos were fairly regular spring migrants within the eastern half of Ohio but accidental in the west-central and northwestern counties.

By the 1950s, White-eyed Vireos had expanded across the entire unglaciated plateau and were regularly nesting at Youngstown and Columbus. Their expansion into the Dayton area was evident by the early 1960s (Mathena et al. 1964). Within the northern counties, these vireos were regularly noted as spring migrants during the 1960s, and there were a few scattered summer records without conclusive evidence of nesting (Campbell 1968, Newman 1969). The first confirmed breeding records near Lake Erie were established during the mid-1970s. Numbers continued to increase during the 1980s, when summering White-eyed Vireos were detected in all but Paulding and Van Wert Counties for the Breeding Bird Atlas (Peterjohn and Rice 1991). This Ohio range expansion corresponded with a marked population increase throughout eastern North America (Robbins et al. 1986).

White-eyed Vireos are now fairly common to common summer residents in southern and unglaciated Ohio. Daily totals are normally 5–15 within these counties. They are fairly common residents within the central counties bordering the Allegheny Plateau, where 2–6 are expected daily, but become uncommon within the intensively farmed west-central counties (Peterjohn and Rice 1991). Nesting White-eyeds are uncommon in northeastern Ohio, where three or fewer are normally noted daily. However, an impressive 86–95 summering White-eyeds were tallied on the Ravenna Arsenal (Portage County) during 1993 and 1999 (Harlan 1993d, Whan 1999b). They become rare to uncommon residents as widely scattered pairs and singing males within the northwestern counties. This breeding population is still increasing across the state (Sauer et al. 1998).

Breeding White-eyed Vireos occupy brushy successional habitats, especially mesic areas along stream valleys. They also inhabit dry hillsides, roadside thickets, woodland clearings, and the brushy borders of woods. Their well-concealed nests are placed fairly low in dense shrubs. Within the southern counties, nesting activities are initiated in early May and clutches are discovered by midmonth. Nests with young have been noted by June 1, and these young fledge before the end of the month (Mathena et al. 1984). Their nesting chronology is normally delayed at least two weeks in northern Ohio, where young vireos may not fledge until July. In southern Ohio, reports of fledglings in early August might pertain to second nesting attempts.

Their spring migration largely consists of resident vireos returning to their nesting territories, although 70 White-eyeds in Athens County on May 10, 1994 (Harlan 1994c), probably includes local residents and migrants. Most spring totals from southern and unglaciated Ohio are 20 or fewer daily. White-eyeds are uncommon to fairly common spring migrants through the central counties and rare to uncommon in northern Ohio, with most reports of six or fewer daily.

The earliest spring migrants returned to Dayton by March 30, 1986 (Peterjohn 1986c), Pickaway County by April 1, 1950 (Mayfield 1950c), and northern Ohio by April 6–7. White-eyed Vireos normally appear in the southern and central counties during April 15–23 and are widely distributed by May 5. In northern Ohio, they are not expected to arrive until April 25–May 5, and migrants appear along the lakefront through May 20–25.

Most fall sightings are of resident vireos, with the only sizable movement totaling 25 at Cincinnati on September 13, 1981 (Peterjohn 1982a). Resident White-eyeds are regularly detected through September 20–25. In northern Ohio, they normally depart by October 1 but may remain through October 7–10 in the southern and central counties. Away from their breeding territories, these vireos are casual to rare fall migrants, mostly scattered individuals during September.

A few linger well after their normal departure dates. There are at least ten November sightings from the northern half of Ohio and reports of single vireos during December 15–18 from Lorain, Seneca County, Columbus, and Meigs County. A White-eyed Vireo photographed near Kent on February 7–11, 1998 (Saxe 1998) provides the only midwinter record and one of the most northerly wintering reports from North America.

Bell's Vireo *Vireo bellii* Audubon

Since the 1920s, Bell's Vireo has gradually expanded its breeding range eastward through the lower Great Lakes states. First moving through Illinois and then Indiana, this nondescript vireo with its distinctive rolling song did not appear in Ohio until 1962. Although it has been more regularly observed since 1980, its status is still evolving. Its eastward range expansion is somewhat surprising in view of its declining populations within the central United States (Sauer et al. 1998).

Bell's Vireo

Ohio's first confirmed Bell's Vireo was a cooperative male discovered in Whetstone Park in Columbus on May 26–27, 1962. He was widely observed and more than thirty-five minutes of his songs were recorded on tape (Borror 1970). The next Bell's Vireo also appeared in Columbus, another male whose songs were recorded at Greenlawn Cemetery on May 19, 1966 (Borror 1970). In 1968, a pair was discovered nesting near Cincinnati (Petersen 1968b). This attempt was unsuccessful, since the nest and eggs were collected.

Bell's Vireos remained accidental visitors through the 1970s, with confirmed sightings every two or three years in the western half of the state. With the exception of a summering male in Franklin County during 1972, all confirmed records were spring migrants, mostly singing males. Bell's Vireos have been reported annually since 1980, reflecting their continued expansion into

Ohio, and summering individuals or nesting pairs have been discovered each year except 1983.

Bell's Vireos are now accidental to casual spring migrants through the western half of Ohio. While they averaged one to three sightings annually during the 1980s, they were not observed annually during the 1990s. The majority of these sightings were near Toledo and Columbus, and the remainder were widely scattered. The earliest Bell's Vireos are reported during the last week of April, but most are observed between May 7 and 25. All records have been of 1–2 vireos. Bell's Vireos are accidental spring visitors to the eastern counties, where the only acceptable records are of single vireos from Holmes County on June 1–2, 1981 (Peterjohn 1981c); Headlands Beach State Park (Lake County) on May 26, 1984, and May 19–20, 1990 (Peterjohn 1984c, 1990c); Wayne County during May, 1988 (Peterjohn 1988c); Willoughby on May 15–16, 1994 (Brock 1994c); and Mahoning County on May 14, 1996 (Conlon and Harlan 1996a).

As summer residents, Bell's Vireos have been regularly encountered only at Buck Creek State Park (Clark County), where 1–2 males have resided during most years since 1986. Nesting vireos were also discovered at Irwin Prairie Nature Preserve (Lucas County) during 1980–1982, Resthaven Wildlife Area (Erie County) in 1984, and Columbus in 1985 (Peterjohn and Rice 1991). The breeding status of summering birds reported from Stark, Lucas, Franklin, Adams, Madison, Marion, Hamilton, and Butler Counties is uncertain, although each site was occupied for only a single season.

Nesting Bell's Vireos occupy successional habitats dominated by shrubs and saplings, with some weeds and grasses. They prefer dry fields. The first clue to their presence is the male's distinctive song, which may be delivered from the middle of thick cover or an exposed perch. Their nests are normally placed in dense shrubs, usually at heights of less than eight feet. Their nesting activities normally begin in late May or early June, with the young fledging by early July. A later attempt produced a nest with eggs through July 12–16+ and the young fledged August 1.

Once they quit singing, Bell's Vireos become nearly impossible to observe among the dense shrubbery. Additionally, they can be difficult to separate from immature White-eyed Vireos. Hence, their fall status is poorly understood. There are fewer than seven acceptable fall records, mostly during August and early September of single vireos at scattered locations in the western half of the state and one from Barkcamp State Park (Belmont County) in eastern Ohio (Whan, in press).

Yellow-throated Vireo *Vireo flavifrons* Vieillot.

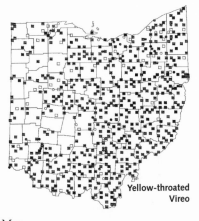

Yellow-throated
Vireo

With their colorful plumage, the Yellow-throated has a reputation as our most attractive vireo. But they can be remarkably difficult to observe in the upper branches of tall trees. The first spring migrants frequently return when the vegetation is still budding, offering little concealment for these brightly plumaged vireos. As soon as the vegetation becomes fully developed, they easily hide among the abundant foliage. Fortunately, Yellow-throateds are regularly detected by means of their vocalizations after early May.

Spring overflights have appeared as early as April 6, 1997, in Hocking County and April 7, 1947, near Toledo (Campbell 1968, Fazio 1997b). Within the southern counties, breeding vireos regularly return by April 15–20 and become fairly common before the end of the month. In contrast, there are relatively few April records from the northern counties, where they normally return during the first week of May. By May 10, these vireos are uncommon to fairly common statewide, except for some western counties where they are locally rare. These migrants are never numerous; spring counts are normally ten or fewer daily and the largest flights total 15–20. Most residents return by May 20, although occasional Yellow-throateds appear at lakefront migrant traps into the first week of June.

Breeding Yellow-throated Vireos are found almost exclusively in extensive mature woodlands. While they prefer large oaks and maples, these vireos are found in a variety of wooded habitats, from floodplain forests to woodlands covering dry ridges. Since they nest in the tops of tall trees, relatively little information is available on their nesting biology. Nest construction has been noted by the first week of May at Cincinnati (Kemsies and Randle 1953). While most nests are probably constructed during mid-May in the northern counties, nests with young have been reported as early as May 22 in the Cleveland area (Williams 1950). Within the southern counties, the first fledglings appear by June 5–15, although young vireos normally fledge during late June and early July elsewhere. These vireos apparently raise two broods, since nests with young have been reported through August 9 and dependent young as late as August 28 (Campbell 1968, Trautman 1940).

As summer residents, Yellow-throated Vireos were always widely distributed within Ohio. Hicks (1935a) cited breeding records from seventy-nine counties, noting that these breeders were often locally distributed or absent in some western counties. Breeding vireos underwent a substantial increase in the Cincinnati area after 1947 (Kemsies and Randle 1953). Similar increases were not evident elsewhere, and Breeding Bird Survey data indicates that statewide populations have remained fairly stable since 1966 (Sauer et al. 1998).

The statewide breeding distribution has not appreciably changed since the 1930s, and the Breeding Bird Atlas recorded them in every county except Clark (Peterjohn and Rice 1991). Yellow-throated Vireos are now fairly common summer residents throughout southern and eastern Ohio, most numerous along the unglaciated Allegheny Plateau. Summer totals are normally 3–12 daily. They become uncommon to fairly common summer residents in the central and northern counties adjacent to the plateau; in these counties, 2–5 are noted daily. They are least numerous in west-central and northwestern Ohio, becoming uncommon to rare residents and very locally distributed in counties where few extensive mature woodlots remain (Peterjohn and Rice 1991).

These vireos are regularly detected into the first half of July but become inconspicuous after the males quit singing. Relatively few are noted in August. They become more conspicuous during September, when the males begin to sing again. Their fall migration is poorly defined. The last fall Yellow-throateds normally depart from northern Ohio by September 15–20, although they remain in the southern counties until September 23–28. There are very few records after the first week of October and none have remained later than October 17–19. Most fall records are of only 1–3 individuals.

Blue-headed Vireo *Vireo solitarius* (Wilson)

The former Solitary Vireo has been split into three species: Cassin's and Plumbeous Vireos, whose distributions are restricted to western North America, and Blue-headed Vireo, which is widely distributed in eastern North America (AOU 1998). While Blue-headed Vireos are primarily migrants through Ohio, their status has changed in recent decades. Since the early 1950s, their breeding range has expanded throughout the Appalachian region and into woodlands in lower elevations (Brooks 1952b, Robbins et al. 1986), resulting in increased numbers of summering vireos in Ohio and other eastern states.

Ohio's first nesting Blue-headed Vireos were discovered in Ashtabula County by Hicks (1933a). Between 1928 and 1931, he observed summering vireos at four sites and located two nests. Williams (1950) cited 1–3 pairs at

Little Mountain (Lake and Geauga Counties) after 1937 and a similar number at Stebbins Gulch (Geauga County), beginning in 1947. Along the unglaciated Allegheny Plateau, breeding Blue-headeds were unrecorded until 1961, when Randle (1963) observed males at two Hocking County locations. He noted five males at these sites in 1962, the same year a summering Blue-headed Vireo was reported from Columbiana County (Hall 1962b). Additional summering vireos have been discovered since the

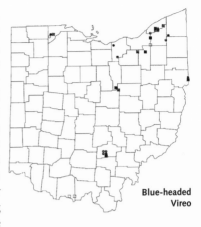

Blue-headed
Vireo

1970s. They were reported from a total of 29 locations during the Breeding Bird Atlas (Peterjohn and Rice 1991), and have been discovered at additional sites since then.

Blue-headed Vireos are now casual to rare and locally distributed summer residents in eastern Ohio, becoming uncommon in Lake County, Hocking County, and the Mohican State Forest area. In northeastern Ohio, breeding pairs are regularly found at scattered sites in Ashtabula, Lake, Geauga, Portage, eastern Cuyahoga, Summit, and Medina Counties. Summering vireos are also occasionally noted in Lorain County (Peterjohn and Rice 1991). Five or fewer pairs are present at most locations, although as many as ten have been counted at Stebbins Gulch and other preferred habitats (Brock 1994d). Along the unglaciated Allegheny Plateau, Mohican State Forest supports the largest population, where 28 were counted during a survey in 1997. Smaller numbers are scattered along the Little Beaver Creek watershed in Columbiana County and in the hemlock ravines of Hocking County, where 2–9 pairs regularly nest at six or more locations (Peterjohn 1982e). Scattered summering males or nesting pairs have also been observed in Jackson, Adams, and Scioto Counties. Recent counts indicate that the eastern Ohio breeding population may total 150–200 pairs during most summers.

In northwestern Ohio, summering Blue-headed Vireos have only been reported from the Toledo area. The first records were of nonbreeders during 1940 and 1973 (Campbell 1968, 1973). Beginning in 1983, five or fewer pairs have summered in the Oak Openings area, and nesting was confirmed in 1986 (Peterjohn and Rice 1991).

Initially, breeding Blue-headed Vireos were restricted to mature mesic hemlock forests. As their population expanded, these vireos spread into pine plantations and mixed pine-deciduous woods. These breeding vireos normally forage within the understory and lower branches of tall trees and are seldom found in the canopy. Their nests are placed in saplings or small trees, usually at heights of less than twenty feet. Nest construction has been observed during May and early June. Nests with eggs have been reported between June 12 and July 11 (Hicks 1933a, Peterjohn 1982e), and recently fledged young have been reported as early as June 15 and are expected through early August (Peterjohn and Rice 1991).

Nesting Blue-headeds return before the arrival of most spring migrants. In the southeastern counties, the first resident Blue-headeds appear by April 5–10, and they return to northeastern Ohio by April 15–22. Even though the females appear one or two weeks later, established pairs may occupy their territories for nearly one month before nesting activities are initiated.

The earliest spring overflight appeared at Headlands Beach State Park on March 29, 1998 (Rosche 1998b), and others have been discovered at scattered locations by March 30–April 4. Migrant Blue-headeds normally return to southern and central Ohio during the last week of April and along Lake Erie by May 1–5. Most migrants are observed during the first half of May, when they become rare to uncommon through the interior counties and uncommon to fairly common along Lake Erie. Generally 1–5 are noted daily. The largest flights produce only 10–20 in central Ohio and along Lake Erie. Most migrants depart by May 20–25, although a few linger along the lakefront through the end of the month.

The first fall migrants infrequently appear along Lake Erie during the last half of August, but they normally return to the northern and central counties by mid-September and to southern Ohio by September 20–25. They are mostly observed between September 25 and October 15, becoming uncommon along Lake Erie and rare to uncommon within the interior counties. Three or fewer are normally observed daily, with a maximum of ten at Buckeye Lake (Trautman 1940). While they normally depart by October 25, Blue-headeds occasionally remain into the first half of November. A late vireo was discovered at Euclid (Cuyahoga County) on November 22, 1985 (Peterjohn 1986a), but despite several reports from Christmas Bird Counts, there are no acceptable December records.

Warbling Vireo *Vireo gilvus* (Vieillot).

Unremarkable in their green and white plumage, foraging Warbling Vireos are nearly impossible to detect as they silently move along the outer branches of cottonwoods, sycamores, and other tall trees. Once their distinctive song is learned, however, Warbling Vireos are regularly detected along mature wooded corridors bordering streams and lakes throughout Ohio.

While the earliest overflight was discovered near Dayton on April 4, 1986 (Peterjohn 1986c), the first Warbling Vireos normally appear in the southern and central counties by April 22–30 and along Lake Erie by May 1–5. They become fairly common migrants during the first half of May, when 4–10 daily are found across Ohio, and flights produce counts of 20–30+ along Lake Erie and in central Ohio. Their northward migration apparently continues through May 20–25, but late migrants are difficult to distinguish from residents.

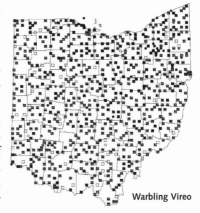

Warbling Vireo

As summer residents, Warbling Vireos were always widely distributed. Hicks (1935a) recorded them from every county but noted that they were "less frequent" in portions of southern and southeastern Ohio. He later described them as uncommon to fairly common residents along the entire unglaciated Allegheny Plateau (Hicks 1937a). Their breeding distribution did not substantially change during subsequent decades (Peterjohn and Rice 1991), but their statewide populations declined along Breeding Bird Survey routes since 1966 (Sauer et al. 1998). Warbling Vireos remain fairly common to common summer residents in most portions of Ohio, becoming locally uncommon from Hocking and Athens Counties south along the Allegheny Plateau to Adams County.

When males are most vocal in June, as many as 15–35 individuals may be tallied during a morning's canoe trip down large rivers. Such counts are exceptional, however; summer totals seldom exceed 5–12 in most areas. Warbling Vireos are decidedly less numerous in other habitats. In recent years, only a few pairs have been recorded in shade trees, orchards, and wooded groves, although they were "common" in these habitats at the turn of the twentieth century (Jones 1903).

Within riparian habitats, their nests are usually placed at heights of thirty to fifty feet along inaccessible outer branches of tall trees (Trautman 1940). Nests may be lower in other habitats and have been recorded only six feet off the ground in an apple orchard (Price 1935). Nest construction has been reported as early as April 25 but is mostly noted in May (Williams 1950). The first clutches are normally laid in the last half of May and these young fledge in late June or early July. Earlier clutches are possible, since recently fledged young have been reported along Lake Erie by June 2 (Campbell 1968). Later nesting attempts are responsible for clutches through July 15 and adults accompanied by young through August 7 (Campbell 1968, Trautman 1940).

By mid-July, the males quit singing and Warbling Vireos become inconspicuous. They are seldom observed until late August, when the first migrants appear and resident males begin singing again. Warbling Vireos are uncommon to fairly common migrants throughout Ohio until September 20–25, mostly as five or fewer daily. The largest reported flights total 15–30+, generally along Lake Erie, where these counts represent residents and migrants. Most Warbling Vireos depart by October 5, with stragglers through October 12–15. There are several reports during the last week of October, and the latest migrant was noted at Ottawa Wildlife Refuge on November 4, 1990 (Anderson and Kemp 1991a).

Philadelphia Vireo *Vireo philadelphicus* (Cassin)

During spring, migrating Philadelphia Vireos are uncommon to fairly common along Lake Erie and rare to uncommon within the interior counties. Daily totals seldom exceed three individuals inland and eight along Lake Erie. Only Jones (1910) reported concentrations exceeding 10–15, including "uncountable numbers" associated with the exceptional May 13, 1907, flight at Cedar Point (Erie County). While a Philadelphia Vireo returned as early as April 22, 1981, to Hueston Woods State Park (Peterjohn 1981b), there are very few April sightings of these late migrants. They generally arrive during the first week of May, and most reports are between May 12 and 25. Late migrants may appear along Lake Erie into the first week of June.

Their status during summer and fall is more obscure because of difficulties separating Philadelphias from other vireos. Sightings between mid-June and mid-August are especially suspect and most have proved to be Warbling Vireos, which can have extensive yellowish underparts in juvenal and fresh fall plumages.

While fall Philadelphia Vireos have appeared within the northern and central counties by August 25–30, they normally return during the first week of September. They are fairly regularly encountered into the first week of October and depart by the October 10–15. There are relatively few sightings of lingering Philadelphias, and the latest migrant remained at North Chagrin Reservation through November 17–24, 1999 (Rosche 1999c). Fall migrants are more frequently encountered along the lakefront, where they are uncommon to fairly common. Their inland status is similar to spring migration. Most reports are of three or fewer daily, with occasional flights of 5–10 along the lakefront. Concentrations of 17 at Shaker Heights on September 11, 1989, and 22 at Ottawa Wildlife Refuge on September 7, 1997, are exceptional (Brock 1998a, Peterjohn 1990a).

Red-eyed Vireo *Vireo olivaceus* (Linnaeus)

Few woodland birds can match the Red-eyed Vireo's reputation as a persistent vocalist. Their song is a monotonous series of robin-like phrases endlessly repeated throughout every summer day. A single male may sing several thousand phrases daily. While silent Red-eyed Vireos are easily overlooked, a careful count of singing males indicates that this species ranks among the most numerous occupants of Ohio's woods.

Red-eyed Vireo

Breeding Red-eyed Vireos may occupy the canopies of young forests, but most dwell within the understories of mature woods. They inhabit woodland communities varying in size from several-acre oak-hickory woodlots to extensive deciduous forests and hemlock woods. Only pine plantations are avoided. Small numbers may nest in shaded residential areas, although they avoid open park-like habitats.

During summer, Red-eyed Vireos are generally common and widely distributed residents. Totals of 25–50+ are frequently tallied throughout the state. They become abundant in the southeastern counties, where daily counts of 75–125+ are possible. Breeding Red-eyeds are least numerous in intensively cultivated western Ohio, where they are fairly common residents and daily totals seldom exceed 5–10 except along extensive riparian corridors. The statewide population has increased since 1966, and these trends are most evident after 1980 (Sauer et al. 1998). These increases are primarily a result of the maturation of eastern Ohio forests.

Their breeding biology was extensively studied by Norberg (1945) on South Bass Island in western Lake Erie. Their average territory size is approximately one acre but can be as small as three-tenths of an acre. Nests are usually placed along slender limbs near the periphery of young trees, at an average height of fifteen feet. Some nests have been reported as high as eighty feet (Trautman 1940). Red-eyed Vireos normally raise two broods. Nest construction begins by mid-May and the first clutches appear as early as May 22. Adults accompanied by young have been reported by June 9, although the first broods normally fledge during late June or early July (Trautman 1940). Second broods are normally initiated during July and are responsible for nests with eggs as late as August 16 and fledglings into late August (Williams 1950).

The earliest spring overflights have been encountered along Lake Erie on April 5 at Toledo and April 8 at Cleveland (Campbell 1968, Williams 1950). Spring Red-eyed Vireos normally return to southern Ohio by April 15–20 and can be numerous by the end of the month. The first migrants return to the central counties during the last week of April and become numerous during the first week of May. Spring migrants reach Lake Erie in numbers by May 5–10. The end of their spring migration is poorly defined, but Red-eyeds are regularly observed at Lake Erie migrant traps into the first week of June. These migrants are common to abundant, regularly producing daily counts of 25–50+. Large May flights along Lake Erie may total 50–100+, while tallies of 150–200+ in the southern counties represent a mixture of migrant and resident Red-eyeds.

Fall Red-eyed Vireos generally peak during September. Most of these silent migrants remain hidden by the vegetation and are much less conspicuous than during spring. Hence, fall migrants are fairly common throughout the state and daily totals seldom exceed 8–20. The largest reported fall concentration was 42 along western Lake Erie on August 31, 1980 (Thomson 1983). Most Red-eyeds depart by the first week of October, with only occasional stragglers after October 15. There are five November sight records along Lake Erie, including a remarkably late Red-eyed in the Cleveland area on November 25, 1931 (Williams 1950).

Blue Jay *Cyanocitta cristata* (Linnaeus)

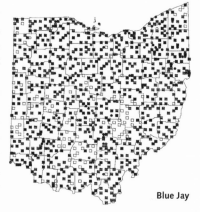

Blue Jay

Since Blue Jays regularly occupy shaded residential yards, parks, cemeteries, and other wooded urban areas as well as forests, they are among the most familiar of Ohio's resident birds. During most of the year their loud and raucous calls announce their mischievous presence. In winter they regularly visit bird feeders, boldly chasing away smaller songbirds as they fill their crops with sunflower seeds. These jays are inconspicuous only during the nesting season, when they are more intent on raising their young than creating a ruckus.

While Blue Jays are fairly common to common permanent residents, this status hides a more complex pattern of occurrence. In fact, some Blue Jay populations are migratory, producing fairly spectacular movements in portions of the state.

Their migratory movements are most evident during spring, beginning between April 15 and 22 and continuing through June 3–10. On clear days with southerly winds, large silent flocks of migrant jays continuously pass along Lake Erie. The first flocks may appear by 7:30 AM. They normally peak between 9:00 and 11:00, with smaller numbers continuing into early afternoon (Newman 1969). These flights usually occur at rates of 200–700+ per hour. With ideal conditions, flights involving 1,000–2,000+ each hour have been reported at Cleveland and along western Lake Erie, with estimates of 5,000–10,000 in a single day.

Similar spring movements are not normally apparent within the interior counties, where migrant jays are mostly observed in small flocks of 5–30 flying at low heights over fields and woods, frequently pausing to rest. With favorable winds, a number of flocks may be noted in a single morning; 200–400+ can be tallied daily. The largest reported inland spring movement totaled 2,000 at Lake St. Marys on May 26, 1969 (Petersen 1969).

Along Lake Erie, their fall migration is not nearly so spectacular, because most Blue Jays fly around the lake. Fall flights are restricted to the Western Basin and seldom exceed the numbers reported from inland counties. A flight of 4,600 along western Lake Erie on September 28, 1985, is exceptional (Peterjohn 1986a).

Fall movements through the interior counties resemble the northward migration. They are most noticeable within the western counties, where flocks of 5–40 are regularly observed passing from fencerow to fencerow. With northerly winds, daily totals of 200–400 are recorded. These movements are less noticeable within the eastern counties, where fall totals seldom exceed 30–60 daily. The first migrant flocks normally appear by September 10–20 and are noted into the first half of November.

Blue Jays were formerly rather erratic winter residents. Their abundance fluctuated with the size of the mast crop (Trautman 1940). These fluctuations were most apparent in the northern and central counties but were also evident at Dayton (Campbell 1940, Mathena et al. 1984).

Their wintering numbers have gradually increased since 1940. These wintering jays frequently take advantage of food available at an ever-increasing number of bird feeders. Blue Jays are now fairly common to common winter residents. While their wintering numbers are still somewhat variable, they do not exhibit the extreme fluctuations described by Trautman (1940). Within most counties, winter reports normally total 8–25+ daily, while as many as 40–60 are reported in years of peak abundance.

Blue Jays were always widely distributed summer residents. Jones (1903) considered them common residents, except within the southeastern counties. Hicks (1935a, 1937a) noted a similar distribution. He described them as generally fairly common to abundant residents except in the southeastern counties bordering the West Virginia panhandle, where they became locally uncommon to rare.

Since the mid-1960s, nesting jays have generally increased throughout eastern North America and the Great Lakes region (Robbins et al. 1986), but populations in Ohio have remained stable (Sauer et al. 1998). While they are widely distributed summer residents and regularly recorded in every county (Peterjohn and Rice 1991), they are still least numerous within the southeastern counties bordering the Ohio River where Blue Jays are uncommon to fairly common residents. They are generally common elsewhere. As a result of their inconspicuous behavior during summer, daily totals seldom exceed 5–20 jays.

Blue Jays normally place their nests in dense ornamental conifers in residential areas or tangles within woodlands. One pair even nested in a mailbox (Henninger 1906). Nest construction may begin during the last half of March, and the first eggs are reported during mid-April (Mathena et al. 1984, Trautman 1940, Williams 1950). Most clutches are discovered during late April and May, with the young fledging during the first half of June. Some pairs may raise two broods. Nests with eggs have been reported as late as June 30 and adults accompanied by dependent young through September 1 (Walker 1940e).

Black-billed Magpie *Pica hudsonia* (Linnaeus)

While Black-billed Magpies reside in the western half of North America, they tend to wander eastward during late fall and early winter. These wandering magpies have produced a number of extralimital records across the Great Lakes region into New England (AOU 1998). This vagrancy was most pronounced before the mid-1960s. The relatively few extralimital sightings in recent years reflect a significant decline in magpie numbers throughout western North America since 1966 (Sauer et al. 1998). Their pattern of vagrancy has also been obscured by magpies that have escaped or been released from captivity. For example, a number of magpies were accidentally released in the Pittsburgh area in the late 1950s, producing scattered sightings within nearby states during the next few years. In general, escaped magpies appear at any time of the year and frequently remain for a number of weeks or months. Few of them exhibit evidence of previous captivity. An exception is the first magpie collected in Ohio (in Lucas County on May 9, 1937), described as a "female in good condition, although primaries and tail feathers were badly worn" (Campbell 1940). This extreme feather wear and the unusual date strongly suggest that this individual was previously held in captivity.

Black-billed Magpies are accidental visitors to Ohio. There are only three acceptable winter records conforming to their established pattern of vagrancy.

These records are single magpies in Lucas County between January 29 and February 11, 1950, and on January 16, 1955 (Campbell 1968); and one near O'Shaughnessy Reservoir (Delaware County) on December 31, 1956 (Thomson 1983).

All other Ohio magpies have problematic origins. The records include three spring sightings from the Toledo area; two pairs attempting to nest near Sandusky between April 1 and May 10, 1973; a road-killed magpie found in a Columbus residential area during April 1960; a pair remaining in the Canton area for nearly a year during 1961–1962; and one at Marietta on April 19, 1997. A sight record from Lorain County during December 1972 was never adequately substantiated. Some of these records could pertain to genuine vagrants, but most were probably birds released or escaped from captivity.

American Crow *Corvus brachyrhynchos* Brehm

The sentiments of Dawson (1903) about crows are still applicable:

American Crow

> The dusky bird is a notorious mischief-maker, but he is not quite so black as he has been painted. More than any other bird he has successfully matched his wits against those of man, and his frequent easy victories and consequent boastings are responsible in large measure for the unsavory reputation in which he is held. It is a familiar adage in ebony circles that the proper study of Crow-kind is man, and so well has he pursued this study that he may fairly be said to hold his own in spite of fierce and ingenious persecution. He rejoices in the name of outlaw, and ages of ill treatment have only served to sharpen his wits and intensify his cunning.

Crows were not always widely distributed residents within Ohio. Their numbers substantially increased during the eighteenth and nineteenth centuries, coinciding with the clearing of the original forests. By the early 1900s they were well established throughout the state, although the northern counties generally supported smaller populations, especially in winter (Jones 1903). Crows continued to increase during the 1900s, attaining their maximum abundance between the 1930s and 1950s. Modern agricultural practices were detrimental to crows, producing marked declines within the western half of the state during the 1960s and 1970s. Their statewide populations increased after 1980 (Sauer et al. 1998).

While crows are permanent residents, their distribution patterns are fairly complex. The crows observed during summer are not necessarily the same individuals seen in our wintering flocks.

American Crows are common to abundant summer residents throughout the eastern half of Ohio and the southwestern counties, where 15–50 are observed daily and as many as 75–130+ may be noted. Breeding crows are uncommon to common residents within northwestern and west-central Ohio, least numerous in the counties bordering western Lake Erie (Peterjohn and Rice 1991); daily totals normally are 20 or fewer.

Nesting crows are most numerous where woodlands, farm fields, successional fields, and residences are interspersed. They are also regularly found in urban areas, nesting in parks, cemeteries, and backyards and finding a plentiful source of food in our refuse. Crows prefer to nest in woodlands, especially pine plantations, although undisturbed deciduous woods are equally suitable. Nest construction is evident in March and early April. Within the southern counties, crows have complete clutches by the last half of March. Elsewhere, nests with eggs are reported between April 10 and May 10, with renesting attempts through June 15 (Campbell 1968, Trautman 1940, Williams 1950). Young crows may fledge during the last half of May but most appear in June and early July.

Crows become common to abundant migrants throughout Ohio. Their spring movements begin with the first warm days of late winter, usually in February or early March. The largest flights occur before March 20. Within the inland counties, few migrants are noted after April 1. The lakefront migration normally continues through April 10–20, with a few stragglers into the first week of May.

The largest spring movements pass along Lake Erie. Five thousand crows have been estimated at Toledo on several dates and 10,000 moved along the Cleveland lakefront on February 28, 1931 (Campbell 1968, Williams 1950). Since 1970, 30–200 crows comprise most daily observations, and occasional flights total 500–1,000+. The largest recent movement was 2,300 at Headlands Beach State Park on March 11, 1990 (Peterjohn 1990c). Smaller numbers migrate through the interior counties; there, only Trautman (1940) reported flights of "several thousand" crows at Buckeye Lake and near Columbus during the 1920s and 1930s. Since the mid-1960s, most inland totals are 100 or fewer daily, with infrequent flights involving 200–500.

Their autumn migration is less conspicuous. Along Lake Erie, fall sightings usually are of 100 or fewer crows, with exceptional movements producing totals of 1,000–2,100+. These numbers have remained stable since the 1950s. Within the interior counties, fall concentrations are comparable to those noted each spring. The only inland movement involving 1,000 crows was reported by

Trautman (1940) at Buckeye Lake before 1940. These migrants may appear along Lake Erie by September 5–15 (Campbell 1968). The largest flights occur during October 20–December 10.

Before 1960, crows were common to abundant winter residents throughout Ohio. By day, flocks of 20–100+ were regularly encountered. Each evening these flocks returned to roosts, where several hundred to several thousand crows would gather. These roosts were scattered across the state, usually in young pine plantations or similar habitats providing dense cover. Some roosts were occupied for decades. Most roosts supported fewer than 5,000 crows, while the largest roosts hosted 10,000–25,000. As many as 100,000 crows were claimed at several northern Ohio roosts.

Since 1960, their wintering numbers have declined in the intensively farmed western counties, where they are now locally uncommon to fairly common winter residents, and daily totals seldom exceed 15–25. Wintering crows remain common to abundant in the eastern and southwestern counties. Winter totals of 30–75 are regular in these counties and flocks of 100–400+ appear most years. American Crows still congregate into winter roosts, although this behavior is less pronounced now than during the 1930s. In recent years, large roosts have been maintained at Mansfield, Springfield, Cincinnati, Lucas County, and Belmont County, and each has supported an estimated 10,000–30,000 crows during some years. Smaller roosts in other locations host 1,000–3,000 crows.

Common Raven *Corvus corax* Linnaeus

Although it is difficult to believe today, Common Ravens were probably the most numerous corvid (jays, magpies, crows) in Ohio when the state was first settled. As the human population increased and the original forests were converted to farmland, ravens rapidly disappeared and were replaced by the ubiquitous crows.

Specific information on the former abundance and distribution of ravens is difficult to find. Accounts indicate that they were common residents in the vicinity of Lake Erie, especially from Cleveland eastward. Jared Kirtland described them as common in the northeastern counties, a fact corroborated by Alexander Wilson during his visit to the area during the early 1800s (Williams 1950). They were said to be "undoubtedly present" in central Ohio, but the few records do not adequately establish their true status (Wheaton 1882). Ravens may have also resided in the southern counties, although no early naturalist specifically cited their presence.

Rapid destruction of the virgin forests extirpated ravens from the central and southern counties by the early nineteenth century. Nevertheless, ravens periodically wandered into these counties throughout the 1800s until the last central Ohio specimen was collected near Marysville on September 3, 1879 (Wheaton 1882). They were still frequently encountered near Cleveland during the 1850s but greatly declined by the late 1870s, when they were only rare winter visitors (Williams 1950). They probably disappeared from northeastern Ohio shortly thereafter. Their last stronghold was the extensive Black Swamp in northwestern Ohio. Anecdotal accounts indicate that ravens were still fairly common residents in Paulding County during 1880, outnumbering crows in winter (Price 1935). Similar accounts tell of a nest in Fulton County during the late 1800s, but the details are vague (Hicks 1935a). This northwestern Ohio population apparently disappeared between 1900 and 1905 (Jones 1903, Price 1935).

After the extirpation of this resident population, ravens became accidental visitors. One raven was carefully studied by Milton Trautman on ice-covered Lake Erie near South Bass Island on January 20, February 16, and March 6, 1946 (Trautman 1956). It was with a small flock of crows foraging for food around some ice shanties on the frozen lake. Of several reports from eastern Ohio during the 1990s, the most convincing is of two ravens in Trumbull County on April 4, 1999 (Whan 1999a). Given their recent population expansion in Pennsylvania, perhaps Common Ravens are poised to establish a permanent population in Ohio in the near future.

Horned Lark *Eremophila alpestris* (Linnaeus)

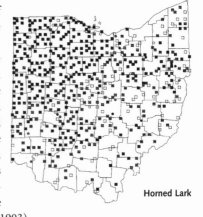

Horned Lark

Given the current abundance of Horned Larks, it is difficult to imagine that they were not always widely distributed residents. Yet, like most prairie birds, Horned Larks started nesting in the state relatively recently. Before 1880, they were strictly migrants and winter visitors. Their status changed during the 1880s, when the prairie race of the Horned Lark invaded Ohio from the west. This range expansion was fairly rapid. By 1900, they were common residents, most numerous in the northern and western counties (Jones 1903).

They remained numerous permanent residents throughout the twentieth century, although their statewide distribution patterns changed in response to habitat availability. Hicks (1935a) cited breeding records from every county, noting they were abundant in some counties and rare and locally distributed in others, with nearly equal numbers in eastern and western Ohio.

Breeding Horned Larks probably occur in every county, but were not reported from Lawrence County during the Breeding Bird Atlas (Peterjohn and Rice 1991). They are common to abundant summer residents within the northwestern and glaciated central counties, where 10–50+ daily are regularly observed and concentrations of 100–200+ are possible after nesting is completed. They are fairly common residents in southwestern Ohio, usually as 5–15 daily, although they become uncommon to rare and locally distributed in counties bordering the Ohio River. Within the northeastern counties, Horned Larks are locally rare to fairly common residents and their summer abundance rarely exceeds 5–15 daily. Breeding larks are least numerous along the unglaciated Allegheny Plateau, especially in the counties bordering the Ohio River. They are normally rare to uncommon residents along this plateau but become locally common on large reclaimed strip mines. Most daily totals are 1–5 larks except within reclaimed strip mines, where 20–35+ may be tallied.

Horned Larks thrive in open and desolate habitats occupied by few other birds. Cultivated fields provide ideal nesting territories. Short-grass pastures, reclaimed strip mines, golf courses, quarries, and vacant lots in cities may support breeding pairs. Horned Larks are remarkably inconspicuous within these habitats, their plumage providing excellent camouflage against a background of bare soil. Their presence is readily detected by their sharp call notes and distinctive tinkling song, frequently delivered as they "skylark" overhead.

This species is the first songbird to begin nesting each year. Any warm winter day prompts male larks to initiate their courtship flights. Most pairs establish territories during late February or early March. Nests with eggs have been reported as early as March 12 (Kemsies and Randle 1953), although most first clutches are laid during the last half of the month. These early nesting attempts are frequently interrupted by late winter snowstorms, and more than one incubating female has kept her eggs warm while several inches of snow fell on top of her (Campbell 1968, Trautman 1940). The first nests produce fledglings by April 5, although most appear later in the month. Horned Larks may raise two or more broods annually. Nests with eggs have been reported through June 24–30 and recently fledged young through July 20 (Mathena et al. 1984, Perkins 1935, Price 1931).

While most of our breeding population resides within Ohio throughout the year, their numbers are augmented by northern races migrating south for the winter. The first migrants are heard passing overhead during the last week of September, and this movement continues into the first half of December. These migrants are hardly noticeable among our breeding population. Most fall flocks total 50–300+; these flocks are primarily composed of summer residents through October, while the northern races become numerous by early December.

Horned Larks are most numerous during winter in the western half of Ohio. They may appear as scattered individuals or flocks of 50–250+ during mild seasons. Large flocks are most apparent during severe winters with extended snow cover; 100–500+ may be noted daily, and concentrations of 1,000–2,000 individuals are infrequently observed. Larger flocks are exceptional; an incredible 50,000 Horned Larks were estimated near Cincinnati on January 12, 1982 (Peterjohn 1982b).

Fewer Horned Larks winter in eastern Ohio. They are normally uncommon to fairly common residents within the northeastern and unglaciated counties, where most sightings are of 50 or fewer. Inclement weather occasionally produces flocks of 100–200+, but concentrations of 1,000–1,500 have only been reported from Tuscarawas and Licking Counties.

The first warm weather of February prompts Horned Larks to start moving northward. This movement is most pronounced through mid-March, although small migrant flocks may be observed through April 10–15. Migrant larks are mostly heard as they pass overhead; flocks on the ground seldom exceed 25–200 individuals. The largest reported spring movements total 500–1,000.

Purple Martin *Progne subis* (Linnaeus).

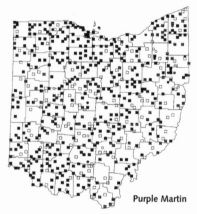

Purple Martin

Purple Martins have been closely associated with people for centuries. Indians erected gourds to attract them to their settlements. The early settlers copied this practice by erecting nesting boxes near their residences. As the human population expanded, more nesting boxes were provided and martin populations undoubtedly increased. They became abundant by the mid-1800s and remained numerous until the 1880s, when their numbers declined as a result of competition with House Sparrows for nesting sites (Jones 1903). However, Purple Martins remained common to abundant summer residents in every county into the 1930s (Hicks 1935a).

In recent decades, Purple Martin populations have exhibited marked annual fluctuations that tend to obscure long-term trends (Mayfield 1964). These fluctuations are mostly a result of their susceptibility to prolonged periods of cold, wet weather. Unusually cold spring temperatures cause considerable mortality of adults. Cold, rainy weather when young are in the nest is responsible for almost complete reproductive failure. Extensive mortality in 1960, 1968, 1972, 1977, and 1978 noticeably reduced breeding populations (Hall 1960c, Robbins et al. 1986) and contributed to a significant decline in the statewide population since 1966 (Sauer et al. 1998). Despite these recent declines, Purple Martins remain fairly common to common summer residents, though rather locally distributed, depending upon the availability of nesting houses. Summer totals are normally 10–50 individuals daily.

A few Purple Martins return very early in spring, appearing at New Bedford (Coshocton County) on February 11, 1999; Mt. Hope on February 12-13, 1999 (R. Schlabach 1999); and Cleveland by March 1, 1929 (Williams 1950). Other records are scattered across the state before March 20. These early arrivals are exceptional; martins normally return to southern Ohio by March 25–30 and Lake Erie by the first week of April. They become numerous by April 20–May 5. Large concentrations are rarely encountered. Trautman (1940) reported spring movements of 700–800 daily at Buckeye Lake during the 1920s and 1930s. Similar movements have not been apparent in recent years, and spring concentrations rarely exceed 25–100.

Upon their arrival, martins visit their nest houses briefly and may disappear for several days or weeks. Nest construction usually begins in early May and requires three to four weeks, since the adults work irregularly on these structures (Allen and Nice 1952). Eggs are normally laid in early June, although observations of dependent young during the first week of July indicate that some nests are initiated in May. Most young fledge during the last half of July. Purple Martins occasionally renest if their first clutch is destroyed. Nests with eggs have been reported through the first week of July, nests with young through August 14 (Williams 1950), and dependent young as late as August 20–27 (Harlan 1995a, Trautman 1940).

Since 1900, Purple Martins have only been known to nest in houses provided by people. At one time, they also nested in natural cavities. Wheaton (1882) cited nests in tree cavities, mostly in old woodpecker holes. Jones (1903) observed their nests in stumps at Indian Lake.

As soon as the young fledge, Purple Martins abandon their breeding colonies. During daylight hours, they are widely scattered over the countryside. At night, these flocks may gather at traditional roosts. This roosting behavior presents an impressive spectacle, as described by Langlois and Langlois (1964) on South Bass Island:

> The martins line up on telephone and power lines late each day and remain until the daylight begins to fade. Whenever one bird lands on a wire, others

come to land there too, and the wire becomes covered with birds like a string of beads … Occasionally the whole flock takes off and circles around for a while, then comes back to rest on the wires, but when darkness approaches, they leave the wires for good. They fly towards the roosting area, and the early birds come in quite low to the ground.

The would-be roosters do not go promptly into the thicket, but circle around and around above the area, and the size of the circling flock grows rapidly in the half-hour before dark. During this period, the flock rises progressively higher as if to stay in brighter light so as to be able to see each other better, and human eyes follow their movements with increasing difficulty. Presently, it seems as if there is a cloudburst of fluttering leaves as some of the birds drop hoveringly down into the thicket, and after this occurs a few times, there is a mass descent in a beeline into the thicket. Within about ten minutes the entry into the thicket is complete, and the noise of birds settling such matters as who sits next to whom is deafening to cupped ears.

The South Bass Island roost was probably the largest; as many as 250,000 Purple Martins were estimated to congregate there (Campbell 1968). Large numbers also roosted at the former state penitentiary in Columbus and at Akron, where 25,000–30,000 appeared each fall during the 1960s and early 1970s (Thomson 1983). Roosts of 3,000–10,000 were also reported near Cleveland, Cuyahoga Falls, Dayton, and Cincinnati. Most of these roosts disappeared by the 1970s, but South Bass Island has been used consistently, although only 3,000–8,000 were estimated during the 1980s and 1,000–4,000 during the 1990s (Peterjohn 1987a, Harlan 1994a). In addition, roosts of 1,000–3,000+ occasionally formed near Dayton, Columbus, Cleveland, Lorain, and in Erie County after 1980. Their abundance during autumn is related to this roosting behavior. Near roosts, 100–300+ may be observed daily. Away from these roosts, they become uncommon to fairly common migrants and daily totals seldom exceed 15–30.

These roosts begin to form during the last half of July and normally reach their maximum size by mid-August. Many martins migrate south during the last half of August, and their numbers noticeably decline by September 7. Smaller flocks are noted through the third week of September. Late migrants are very infrequently observed during October, although a few martins linger very late: through October 27–30 at three locations and November 11, 1931, at Cleveland (Williams 1950).

Tree Swallow *Tachycineta bicolor* (Vieillot)

A remarkably hardy bird, the Tree Swallow is normally the first swallow to appear each spring. Overflights have returned to Dayton and western Lake Erie by February 13 (Mathena et al. 1984, Peterjohn 1984b). While these overflights must migrate south or perish, spring Tree Swallows regularly appear during the first half of March. On warm days, the first arrivals survive on newly emerged insects, but they can subsist on dried fruit if insects are unavailable.

Tree Swallow

During warm springs, flocks of Tree Swallows may appear before April 1, with as many as 450 along western Lake Erie on March 29, 1981. Similar concentrations normally develop by April 10–20 most years. Migrant flocks are noted until May 8–15. Tree Swallows are fairly common to abundant spring migrants, most numerous along Lake Erie. The largest concentrations normally develop within Ottawa and Lucas Counties, where flocks of 500–1,700+ are expected. Similar totals are less frequently encountered elsewhere along the lakefront; flights of 2,000 at Euclid on April 14, 1983, and 1,700 at Lorain on April 8, 1980, are exceptional (Kleen 1980c, Peterjohn 1983c). Within the interior counties, most flocks total 50–400+. The largest inland concentration was 1,200 at Alum Creek Reservoir on April 24, 1981.

After May 20, only resident pairs remain. Breeding Tree Swallows were formerly restricted to marshes, ponds, and lakes, where they nested in cavities within dead snags. Where dead snags were numerous, breeding Tree Swallows became abundant. During the nineteenth century, sizable populations nested at Buckeye Lake, Indian Lake, and Lake St. Marys (Clark and Sipe 1970, Trautman 1940). Only small numbers were distributed elsewhere in the northern half of Ohio (Jones 1903).

During the first decades of the twentieth century, Tree Swallows declined at these lakes as the dead snags disappeared. By the mid-1930s, breeding pairs were locally distributed south to Mercer, Pickaway, Fairfield, Guernsey, Tuscarawas, and Columbiana Counties. They were numerous only along western Lake Erie and locally within the northeastern counties (Hicks 1935a, 1937a).

Their summer status remained unchanged until the late 1950s and early 1960s, when a southward range expansion became apparent. Tree Swallows increased within the central counties, finding suitable habitats at newly constructed reservoirs. Summering swallows also appeared near Dayton (Mathena et al. 1984). During the 1960s and 1970s, their flexibility in selecting nesting sites allowed them to expand across the state. In addition to natural cavities, they began to readily adopt Wood Duck boxes and occupy bluebird boxes miles from any body of water. They were recorded from every county except Athens during the Breeding Bird Atlas (Peterjohn and Rice 1991), and their statewide populations increased subsequently (Sauer et al. 1998).

Breeding Tree Swallows are common to abundant along western Lake Erie, where 50–200+ are noted daily. They are fairly common to common in other northern and central counties, with most reports involving 10–75. They are uncommon to fairly common in the southern third of the state; most reports now total 25 or fewer.

Tree Swallows normally begin nesting in late April or early May, but a nest with young has been noted as early as April 25 in Brown County (Harlan 1992c). Most clutches are laid during May and the young fledge between June 15 and July 10. Few nests with eggs are reported after June 15, although nests with young into the last half of July are probably the result of renesting efforts (Trautman 1940, Tuttle 1987).

As soon as their young fledge, Tree Swallows congregate in large flocks. These flocks are most apparent between July 10 and August 15, comprising the first peak of a distinctly bimodal fall migration. This early movement is most apparent along western Lake Erie, where Tree Swallows become abundant migrants. As many as 3,000 were tallied there on July 12, 1936, and August 15, 1931, although concentrations rarely exceed 1,000–1,500 in recent years (Baird 1931b, Campbell 1968). Fewer July migrants appear in the remainder of the state, where flocks of 50–500 are typical before mid-August; an estimated 5,000 at Killdeer Plains Wildlife Area on August 12, 1991, is exceptional for an inland location (Harlan 1992a).

The second peak of fall migration is apparent throughout Ohio. During most years, numbers peak between September 15 and October 20. In some years, large flocks appear by the last week of August; in others they may not develop until October. Tree Swallows become abundant migrants along western Lake Erie and fairly common to locally abundant elsewhere. This movement produced a concentration of 15,000 in Ottawa and Lucas Counties on September 30, 1934 (Campbell 1968), although peak September and October concentrations normally total 1,000–4,000 since 1960. Away from western Lake Erie, flocks of 50–500+ may develop, and the largest inland concentrations total 2,500–6,000.

While most Tree Swallows depart by October 28–November 5, a few stragglers linger well into November. Some remain until harsh winter weather prevails, becoming accidental visitors after November 20. There are at least eight acceptable early winter sightings from Ohio: six along western Lake Erie and single reports from Dayton and Seneca County. These records are of groups of five or fewer, mostly during December, although one was reported from the Ottawa Wildlife Refuge Christmas Bird Count on January 4, 1987.

Violet-green Swallow *Tachycineta thalassina* (Swainson)

Violet-green Swallows are widely distributed summer residents in western North America, and their winter range largely extends from Mexico south into northern Central America. Only a small number of vagrants have been detected in eastern North America (AOU 1998). The scarcity of vagrant records is somewhat surprising, but single Violet-greens are easily overlooked among the large flocks of Tree Swallows that congregate in eastern North America.

Ohio's only Violet-green Swallow was discovered by David Kline in Holmes County on May 16, 1990. This swallow was with a flock of swallows foraging over farm fields near his home. It was carefully observed by several birders and photographed during its brief visit (Kline 1990).

Northern Rough-winged Swallow *Stelgidopteryx serripennis* (Audubon)

Uttering a hoarse *dirt-dirt-dirt*, several Rough-winged Swallows leave their perch on a dead snag along a stream and forage for insects low over the surface of the water. After feeding for several minutes, they fly to a nearby eroding streambank, enter a small burrow, and feed their brood of hungry young. The adults remain in the burrow just long enough to care for the young before emerging to secure more food. Even after the young fledge, they remain dependent upon the adults for

Northern Rough-winged Swallow

several weeks, aggressively approaching the returning parents to obtain a share of the meal.

This behavior is a common sight along medium-sized and large streams throughout Ohio. Rough-winged Swallows prefer larger streams, which are more likely to be bordered by suitable eroding streambanks. They also regularly nest along small streams, but avoid channelized streams and ditches, whose grass-covered banks are unsuitable for nesting. In the absence of eroding streambanks, adults may nest in bridge drainpipes, the ends of blocked field tiles, and boat pontoons. Frequently they nest far from water in the steep walls of gravel pits, quarries, and rocky cliffs next to highways and railroads. Some have nested in the overflow pipes of a swimming pool, openings of an oil storage tank, and under a semi-trailer (Chapman 1938, Peterjohn and Rice 1991, E. Schlabach 1998).

Rough-wingeds are fairly common to common and widely distributed summer residents. They become locally distributed only in intensively farmed western Ohio, where most streams are small and channelized. Daily totals are normally 5–25 individuals, although float trips may produce counts of 30–50+. Totals of 100+ are possible along the Scioto, Muskingum, and other large rivers.

Since the mid-1960's, breeding populations have expanded northward in eastern and central North America (Robbins et al. 1986). These increases have not been evident within Ohio, where Breeding Bird Surveys indicate stable populations (Sauer et al. 1998). Their statewide distribution patterns have not noticeably changed during the twentieth century (Hicks 1935a, Peterjohn and Rice 1991).

Rough-wingeds nest as isolated pairs or in loose colonies of 5–20 pairs. While they may be found near large Bank Swallow colonies, the two species generally do not form mixed colonies. The adults search for suitable burrows immediately upon their return and have been observed entering burrows as early as March 30 (Mathena et al. 1984). Most nest excavation occurs during late April and early May but has been reported as late as May 25 (Trautman 1940). The few nests with eggs have been noted between early May and early June. Most young fledge between mid-June and mid-July.

Campbell (1968) described migrant Rough-wingeds as "unsocial," since they generally do not associate with other swallows. Their spring movements are not very pronounced; adults merely appear at nest sites. The earliest migrants have been noted in all portions of the state during the last week of March, but the first adults normally return to the southern counties by April 1–5 and along Lake Erie during the second week of the month. Rough-wingeds are widely encountered by April 18–24. Bad weather occasionally produces concentrations during late April or early May; the largest spring flocks total 100–350 individuals.

Their fall migration is equally inconspicuous. As soon as the young become independent, family groups congregate into flocks. These local movements normally take place during the last half of July and early August. By mid-August, Rough-wingeds have quietly disappeared from their breeding sites and formed flocks of 100–400 scattered along large rivers throughout the state. Similar concentrations also appear along Lake Erie near Huron (Erie County), at Lake St. Marys, and occasionally at other large reservoirs. These autumn flocks mostly depart by October 3–7. Small flocks have been noted through October 12–18 and a few stragglers as late as November 15–16 along Lake Erie (Conlon and Harlan 1996b, Kleen and Bush 1973a) and December 3–12, 1999, in the Toledo area (Whan, in press).

Bank Swallow *Riparia riparia* (Linnaeus)

Unlike Northern Rough-winged Swallows, which nest in aggregations of twenty or fewer pairs, Bank Swallows only breed in well-defined colonies. While the smallest colonies may have only 20–30 pairs, most total 50–100 nests, with occasional congregations of 200–400. Larger colonies are unusual; the only report of a colony with 2,000–3,000 nests was from the Toledo area in 1933–1934 (Campbell 1968).

Bank Swallows excavate their nest burrows in soft soil near the tops of eroding banks along streams and lakes, within sand and gravel quarries, and on abandoned high-walls in strip mines. A few colonies have been reported at unlikely sites such as large piles of fly ash behind a power plant (Campbell 1968). Nest excavation may begin by April 19, and nests with young have been noted by June 1 (Campbell 1968, Williams 1950). Most nests contain eggs by late May or the first week of June, and the first fledglings normally appear by June 25–30. Unsuccessful nesting attempts are frequent. Renesting produces nests with eggs during the first half of July and recently fledged young as late as August 12 (Walker 1940d).

Instability of their nesting habitats causes frequent changes in colony locations. Their colonies along lakes and rivers are particularly ephemeral, lasting for only two to five years. The most stable colonies are in quarries where constant excavation creates suitable nest sites each year.

Breeding Bank Swallows were always locally distributed. In general, they were most numerous in the northern third of the state but appeared wherever suitable nest sites were available. In the mid-1930s, Hicks (1935a, 1937a) cited breeding colonies from most northeastern counties, every county bordering Lake Erie and Sandusky Bay, and Williams and Fulton Counties. While they were locally common within these northern counties, they were rather rare and very locally distributed elsewhere, with scattered records south to Guernsey, Muskingum, Hocking, Franklin, Logan, and Mercer Counties and a few colonies along the Scioto and Ohio Rivers in Hamilton, Adams, Scioto, Lawrence, and Pike Counties. Since colony locations changed frequently, population trends were difficult to establish. Breeding Bird Survey data indicates that statewide populations have remained stable since the mid-1960s (Sauer et al. 1998), but this overall stability probably hides declines in the northern counties and increases in southern Ohio (Peterjohn and Rice 1991).

Bank Swallow

Bank Swallows are now fairly common to common summer residents along Lake Erie and throughout northeastern Ohio. They are uncommon and locally distributed elsewhere in northern Ohio and along the northern edge of the unglaciated Allegheny Plateau in Tuscarawas, Carroll, and adjacent counties. They are fairly common to locally common residents along the Scioto River south of Columbus, the lower sections of the Great Miami and Little Miami Rivers, and portions of the Ohio River. They are uncommon residents in other glaciated counties but are absent from large portions of the unglaciated Allegheny Plateau (Peterjohn and Rice 1991). Near nesting colonies, summer totals of 50–300+ are noted. Away from these colonies, most sightings are of single swallows.

The only March sightings are of single Banks in Wayne County on March 25, 1978, and near Dayton on March 30, 1980 (Mathena et al. 1984). They normally appear in the southern and central counties by April 15–20 and along Lake Erie by April 18–25. Their northward migration peaks between May 5 and 20, and migrant flocks appear through the end of the month. Most spring flocks total 30 or fewer, although concentrations of 100–900+ develop during inclement weather. Like most swallows, Banks suffer substantial mortality when unusually cold weather persists during late April or early May.

Bank Swallows attain their maximum abundance as fall migrants. These migrants become common to abundant along western Lake Erie, where spectacular concentrations formerly developed each August. Flocks of 10,000+ were regularly observed before 1940, and an incredible 1,000,000 were estimated at Cedar Point Wildlife Refuge (Lucas County) on August 8, 1931 (Campbell 1968). These concentrations noticeably declined after 1940, although flocks of 2,000–4,000+ still appear in most years and 10,000 were estimated on August 21, 1996 (Brock 1997a). Similar concentrations are not expected east of Sandusky Bay. Although Banks are generally common migrants along the Central Basin, fall flights seldom exceed 100–500 in recent years. The largest reported movement totaled 3,000 at Ashtabula on July 20–22, 1962 (Graber 1962d).

Within the interior counties, Bank Swallows are uncommon to locally abundant fall migrants. Most inland reports are of 50 or fewer, although 200–500 may appear at several localities each autumn. The largest recent flocks totaled 2,500 at Barberton on July 27, 1988, and 3,000 at Killdeer Plains Wildlife Area on August 12, 1991 (Peterjohn 1988d, Harlan 1992a).

Bank Swallows are relatively early fall migrants; the first individuals appear by June 28–July 5. Their southward movements normally peak between July 20 and August 20. They remain numerous through the end of August, but most depart by September 5–12. Only small numbers remain through the last week of September. There are very few sightings during October, and the appearance of a Bank Swallow at Cleveland on November 12, 1955, is extraordinary (Rosche 1992a).

Cliff Swallow *Petrochelidon pyrrhonota* Viellot.

Cliff Swallows were initially restricted to the Great Plains and western North America, nesting on cliffs bordering large valleys and rivers. Their populations underwent a dramatic eastward range expansion during the nineteenth century, bringing them into close association with people. In fact, this expansion was a direct result of the early settlers' creation of open farmlands that proved suitable for foraging swallows. Since natural cliffs were unavailable, Cliff Swallows developed the habit of nesting under the eaves of barns or other outbuildings.

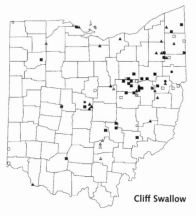

Cliff Swallow

Within Ohio, the first Cliff Swallow colonies were discovered near Cincinnati around 1820. They spread eastward to Columbiana County by 1838 (Kirtland 1838). By midcentury they were common and generally distributed summer residents (Wheaton 1882). This expansion was relatively short-lived. A decline was apparent during the 1890s, and nesting Cliff Swallows disappeared from a number of localities shortly after the turn of the twentieth century (Campbell 1968, Dawson 1903). Of all factors contributing to this decline, competition with the rapidly expanding House Sparrow was probably most important. These aggressive sparrows regularly usurped Cliff Swallow nests, seriously reducing their reproductive success.

The population decline continued during the twentieth century. By the mid-1930s, Hicks (1935a) recorded nesting Cliff Swallows from only 41 counties, mostly within southern and eastern Ohio. Most of these counties supported very small populations of fewer than six colonies and 100 pairs. These colonies were generally short-lived, existing for only two or three years before disappearing.

More declines occurred in subsequent decades. By the mid-1960s, Cliff Swallows were in danger of disappearing from Ohio. While small colonies briefly developed at scattered localities, the few sizable colonies were in Holmes and Wayne Counties, where Amish farmers encouraged their development and continued existence. But beginning in the mid-1970s, their fortunes improved as new colonies became established. The majority were discovered on dams or highway bridges over large lakes, where House Sparrows offered no competition. Once established, these new colonies were regularly occupied. This expansion happened throughout eastern North America (Robbins et al. 1986) and continued into the 1990s.

Nesting Cliff Swallows are now mostly encountered within the eastern half of Ohio (Peterjohn and Rice 1991). They are locally distributed within these counties, varying from absent to locally abundant summer residents. Their center of abundance is still the Amish farmlands in Holmes, Wayne, Coshocton, and Tuscarawas Counties; there, colonies of 50–600+ pairs nest under the eaves of barns, and the total population exceeds 2,000 pairs (Kline 1997). Colonies on dams and bridges are prevalent in the northeastern counties, where 50–100+ pairs breed at most large reservoirs. They are least numerous along the southern Allegheny Plateau, with only a small number of scattered colonies mixed with Barn Swallows in rural farmlands.

Fewer Cliff Swallows breed in the western half of Ohio, where the availability of nest sites may be a limiting factor. They are very locally distributed and are now absent to fairly common summer residents, most numerous at large reservoirs near Columbus. Their distribution extends from the Ohio River to Lake Erie and at scattered reservoirs and large rivers in between. Most of these colonies total fewer than 50 pairs.

Cliff Swallows initiate their nesting activities shortly after they return. In southern Ohio, nest construction has been noted by the last week of April. These activities are evident by mid-May along Lake Erie. Most clutches are laid between mid-May and mid-June, with renesting attempts into mid-July. The young normally fledge during July. Nesting begins later at newly established colonies and young may remain in nests through August 15–20.

Migrant status is directly related to the size of the nesting population. When numbers were exceptionally low, Cliff Swallows were rare migrants across Ohio. Since the mid-1970s, the expanding nesting populations have produced increased numbers of spring and fall migrants.

Spring Cliff Swallows are now uncommon to locally common migrants. Concentrations of 20–200+ occur near breeding colonies. Elsewhere, most spring sightings total 15 or fewer individuals. Large spring movements have not been evident since the 1940s. When breeding populations were larger, sizable flights produced concentrations of 500 at Buckeye Lake on May 10, 1934, and Lake St. Marys on May 14, 1947 (Baird 1934b, Clark 1964).

These swallows normally return during the last half of April. The largest numbers are expected during May, and detectable movements appear as late as May 24–26. A few late migrants remain into the first half of June (Trautman 1940). March records are limited to single Cliffs at Dayton on March 25, 1980

(Kleen 1980c); in Pike County on March 30, 1993 (Harlan 1993c); and at Ottawa Wildlife Refuge on March 31, 1979 (Kleen 1979c).

The fall migration is usually apparent by July 25–August 5. In general, these migrants are most prevalent between August 10 and September 6, with smaller numbers remaining through September 18–25. The latest Cliff Swallows have remained through October 9–10. Fall Cliff Swallows are rare to locally fairly common migrants. Most sightings are of ten or fewer, with occasional flocks of 15–30+. Sizable fall flocks were not apparent even when their breeding populations were larger. The largest reported fall concentrations totaled 100–150+ at lakes in Knox, Delaware, and Mahoning Counties.

Barn Swallow *Hirundo rustica* Linnaeus

The Barn Swallow is Ohio's most numerous and familiar resident swallow. There is a near-universal familiarity with this bird, owing to its close association with people. Most pairs nest in barns, sheds, abandoned houses, and under bridges, requiring only regular access to the nest sites and a minimum amount of disturbance. The only pairs occupying natural habitats are found along cliffs on West Sister Island in western Lake Erie (Campbell 1968). These active little birds are ben-

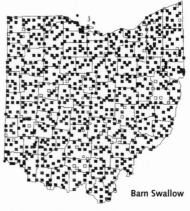

Barn Swallow

eficial occupants of farmyards, since the adults consume quantities of insects. They become a nuisance only when young are in the nest and the adults actively defend them from all intruders.

Barn Swallows nest as isolated pairs or in loosely defined colonies, normally raising two broods annually. Nest construction begins during late April or May, and nests with eggs have been observed by the second week of May. First broods fledge as early as the first week of June, although most appear during the last half of June and early July (Trautman 1940, Williams 1950). Second clutches are initiated while the adults are still feeding their first broods. These second nesting attempts produce nests with eggs as late as August 10 and nests with young through September 11 (Price 1928a, Yoder 1997), although most second broods fledge by mid-August.

As summer residents, Barn Swallows are common to abundant in every county. They are one of few species that are as numerous in the intensively cultivated western counties as in the unglaciated southeastern counties. Summer totals are generally 30–80+ daily, except in large urban areas, where they become locally scarce or absent.

This adaptable species rapidly expanded within Ohio during the eighteenth and nineteenth centuries. They became common summer residents by the mid-1800s (Wheaton 1882). While their numbers declined periodically following unusually cold spring weather, they usually recovered within one or two years. Their statewide populations remained stable during the twentieth century, but a significant decline was evident on Breeding Bird Survey routes after 1980 (Sauer et al. 1998).

Except for occasional overflights as early as March 15–16, the first Barn Swallows return between March 28 and April 5. Most years they become numerous by April 15–22. Spring migrants are most evident during cold, wet days in late April and early May, when concentrations of 300–1,000+ may appear throughout the state. As many as 3,000 were reported from central Ohio on May 8, 1960 (Thomson 1983). Large flights exceeding 5,000 per hour have passed along Lake Erie during days with favorable southerly winds (Mumford 1961c). Their spring migration normally ends by May 20–25.

Barn Swallows begin their fall passage rather early; migrants are usually evident by the third week of July. Most fall reports total 30–100 individuals, with occasional concentrations of 300–600. The largest fall flights produced 2,000 at Barberton on September 10, 1989, and 1,400 along western Lake Erie on August 18, 1987 (Peterjohn 1987a, 1990a). Fall migrants remain common through mid-September, with most departing by September 25–October 5. Stragglers occasionally linger into late October and early November. Exceptionally late birds survive into December, with at least five Ohio records. The latest Barn Swallows were noted through January 16, 1995, in Lucas County and December 25–27, 1990, near Waverly (Pike County) (Harlan 1995b, Peterjohn 1991b).

Carolina Chickadee *Poecile carolinensis* (Audubon)

While Carolina Chickadees were undoubtedly present in the southern and central counties during the nineteenth century, their status and distribution were the subjects of conflicting accounts. Wheaton (1882) may be most accurate. In the 1880s, he described Carolinas as summer residents in central Ohio and said that they migrated southward shortly after the breeding season. They were permanent residents within the southern counties.

Their status was better defined during the twentieth century, although the Black-capped and Carolina Chickadees were regularly misidentified and many extralimital or unseasonal sightings were in error. Carolina Chickadees were well-established permanent residents in southern and central Ohio by the early 1900s (Trautman 1940). Their breeding range expanded northward during the 1920s and 1930s, especially in eastern Ohio, where Carolinas eventually spread north to Columbiana, Stark, and Wayne Counties (Baker 1933, Buchanan 1980, Stevenson 1928). Their rate of expansion slowed in subsequent decades, and the northern boundary of their range has not changed appreciably since the 1970s. Their statewide populations have been increasing along Breeding Bird Survey routes since 1966 (Sauer et al. 1998).

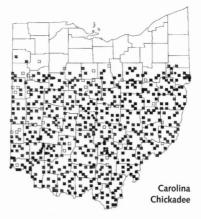

Carolina
Chickadee

Carolina Chickadees now breed north to southern Mahoning, Stark, Wayne, Ashland, Richland, Crawford, Wyandot, southern Hancock, Allen, and Paulding Counties (Peterjohn and Rice 1991). Their distribution near the northern edge of their range in western Ohio is poorly understood, and they have been reported from Putnam and Seneca Counties, where breeding has not yet been established. They are generally permanent residents, although some may retreat from the northern boundary of this range during winter.

Carolina Chickadees are accidental visitors farther north. While a number of sight records exist from the northern tiers of counties, these records lack the in-hand measurements necessary to positively distinguish Carolina Chickadees from Black-cappeds and hybrids. A few specimens were collected, however, to document the extralimital wanderings of some Carolinas: one near Oberlin (Lorain County) on April 27, 1923; two females at Solon Bog (Portage County) on May 8, 1935; and two females east of Hudson (Portage County) on May 1, 1935 (Williams 1950).

Their habitat preferences and breeding biology are very similar to those of Black-cappeds. Carolina Chickadees are most numerous in mature woodlands and wooded riparian habitats. They also occupy wooded fencerows, orchards, and shaded residential areas. They nest in cavities, usually at heights of two to fifteen feet. If suitable cavities are not present, a fence post or bird house will suffice. Most nest construction takes place in late March and early April. The first eggs are laid by mid-April, and nests with young are reported by the first week of May (Trautman 1940). Fledglings appear by May 15 but most are noted in late May and June. Renesting attempts produce nests with eggs through June 5 and dependent young as late as July 22 (Trautman 1940).

Carolina Chickadees are generally fairly common to common permanent residents. They are least conspicuous during the breeding season, when the adults are busy raising broods and daily totals seldom exceed 5–20. In winter, Carolinas are most numerous in the southern and unglaciated counties, where as many as 20–50 are observed daily. They are least numerous in intensively cultivated western Ohio. There, winter totals seldom exceed 6–15.

The periodic Black-capped Chickadee invasions may produce marked southward movements of Carolinas between mid-October and December. These movements are poorly described but have produced some noteworthy concentrations along the Scioto River in Pickaway County: 400 Carolinas on November 18, 1961 and 200 during the first week of October 1963 (Petersen 1964a, Trautman 1962). Following these southward movements, Carolinas are observed in reduced wintering numbers in central and southern Ohio. During the largest Black-capped invasions, Carolinas largely disappear from the central counties (Graber 1962b, Trautman 1962). While Carolinas undoubtedly undertake spring movements following these invasions, no sizable spring concentrations have been encountered.

Black-capped Chickadee *Poecile atricapilla* (Linnaeus)

Distinguishing between Black-capped and Carolina Chickadees always poses problems for ornithologists. Their plumages are very similar and no single characteristic consistently separates them throughout the year. The two species hybridize, and chickadees with intermediate characteristics confound these problems. Most chickadees are separated by their vocalizations and measurements in the hand, but these characteristics are not helpful for identifying silent chickadees in the field.

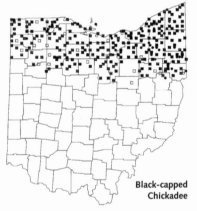

Black-capped
Chickadee

Identification problems resulted in disparate and often inconsistent statements concerning the historic status of Black-capped Chickadees. Only the account of Wheaton (1882) was reasonably consistent with recent records and provided a suitable basis for comparing historic changes in the distribution of this species. He stated that Black-capped Chickadees were resident south to central Ohio until the mid-1800s. Their breeding range gradually contracted northward during the last half of the nineteenth century as Black-cappeds were replaced by Carolinas. By the early 1900s, Black-capped Chickadees were confined to northern Ohio and were only casual winter visitors to the central counties (Trautman 1940, Wheaton 1882).

The first complete account of Black-capped Chickadees' statewide distribution was provided by Hicks (1935a). He described Black-cappeds as fairly common to abundant residents in northern Ohio, becoming locally rare within a few western counties. Their breeding range extended south to Mercer, Allen, Hancock, Wyandot, Crawford, Richland, Ashland, Wayne, Stark, and Columbiana Counties.

This breeding distribution has contracted northward only in western Ohio, where Black-cappeds now nest south to Paulding and Putnam Counties (Peterjohn and Rice 1991). Elsewhere, their distribution remains identical to that described by Hicks (1935a). A few isolated pairs may still be found slightly south of this range, but these chickadees are absent from central and southern Ohio except during periodic winter invasions. Breeding Bird Survey data indicate that the statewide population has increased since 1966 (Sauer et al. 1998).

Black-cappeds are common residents in the northeastern counties. Daily totals of 10–20+ are noted during summer and 20–40+ in winter. These chickadees are more locally distributed west of Lorain and Medina Counties. They are uncommon to fairly common residents in most northwestern counties, becoming locally rare near Lake Erie and in intensively cultivated areas. Within these counties, Black-cappeds are found along mature wooded corridors bordering streams and the few remaining extensive woodlands. Totals of 3–12+ individuals are reported during summer. Winter counts of 10–25+ are possible, except near Lake Erie, where they are absent.

Black-capped Chickadees nest in cavities at heights of two to sixty feet. If natural cavities are unavailable, they nest in fence posts and bluebird boxes. Nest construction may begin during the last week of March but is mostly noted in April. Most nests contain eggs during May, which normally hatch during the last half of the month. Young chickadees usually fledge in June (Campbell 1968, Williams 1950). Recently fledged young in the last half of July may represent successful renesting (Phillips 1980).

While most Black-capped Chickadees are permanent residents, this species undertakes periodic winter invasions south of its established range. These invasions result from food shortages in forests in Canada and the upper Great Lakes states. Although these movements probably occurred throughout historic times, the first southward invasion was noted in 1941. The largest movements were noted during the winters of 1951–1952, 1954–1955, 1959–1960, 1961–1962, and 1965–1966 (Campbell 1968). For unknown reasons these movements were less frequent after 1970. The only recent flights appeared in the 1975–1976 and 1993–1994 winters.

Away from their breeding range in northern Ohio, Black-capped Chickadees are irregular winter visitors. Their winter status in the central counties is directly related to the numbers of Black-cappeds moving south-ward. They are absent during some years, and small invasions produce only scattered chickadees in others. During massive invasions they become fairly common or common winter residents and even outnumber the resident Carolina Chickadees. These large flights may result in totals of as many as 10–30 Black-cappeds daily in central Ohio.

Black-capped Chickadees appear in the southern counties only during the largest invasions, usually as scattered individuals, although flocks of 5–10 were reported during the flights of the 1960s (Graber 1962b). The southward extent of these invasions is verified by specimens collected in Athens, Morgan, and Vinton Counties; there are sight records south to the Ohio River. Their status in southwestern Ohio is less certain. A number of reports come from Dayton, including 43 on their Christmas Bird Count during the 1954–55 flight (Mathena et al. 1984). Recent records from Cincinnati were thought to be "of extremely doubtful validity" by Kemsies and Randle (1953).

During the largest flights, the first individuals appear at lakefront migrant traps by late August or early September and are regularly observed during the first half of October. Smaller movements may not be apparent along Lake Erie until October 20–November 10. These migrations are most evident along the Lake Erie shoreline, where breeding Black-cappeds are normally very scarce or absent. Reports from Cleveland of 206 in one hour on October 23, 1954, and 507 in 2.5 hours on October 8, 1959, are representative of lakefront totals during the largest movements (Mumford 1960a, Nolan 1955a). Totals of 20–100 daily occur in smaller invasions. In the interior counties, fall sightings are of ten or fewer individuals.

Following these invasions, their northward movements are poorly defined. In the central and southern counties, the last individuals depart by April 5–15. Their lakefront passage is most apparent in April, producing flights of 75–175+ during the largest movements, although most spring totals are of fewer than 25 daily. The last spring migrants usually leave Lake Erie by the first week of May.

Boreal Chickadee *Poecile hudsonicus* (Forster)

Residents of boreal forests in Canada and the northern United States, Boreal Chickadees infrequently wander south of this range during late fall and winter. These movements, triggered by food shortages, are normally associated with massive southward flights of Black-capped Chickadees. Wandering Boreals may spread southward through New England and the lower Great Lakes states. Eleven records exist from northern Ohio, where Boreals are accidental late fall and winter visitors.

Ohio's first Boreal Chickadee was collected on Turtle Island in western Lake Erie on November 6, 1943 (Mayfield 1944). The next Boreals were associated with Black-capped Chickadee invasions during the 1950s: three northwestern Ohio records in 1951 and single 1954 sightings from Ottawa County and Ashtabula (Campbell 1968, Nolan 1955b). The winter of 1963–1964 produced three Boreal Chickadee records from the Cleveland area (Newman 1969). The most recent, during the 1972–1973 winter, were single sightings from Toledo and Cleveland (Campbell 1973, Kleen and Bush 1973b).

With one exception, these sightings occur between November 6 and January 1. The exception is a Boreal Chickadee visiting a Columbia Station feeder between March 7 and April 2, 1964 (Newman 1969). These chickadees are most likely to be encountered on islands in western Lake Erie or close to the lakeshore, wandering inland as far as the village of Holgate (Henry County) on November 17, 1951 (Campbell 1968). Most records are of single individuals, although four were reported from South Bass Island on November 19, 1951 (Campbell 1968).

Tufted Titmouse *Baeolophus bicolor* (Linnaeus)

Fairly common to common residents of woodlands throughout Ohio, Tufted Titmice join chickadees and other gleaners in mixed-species foraging flocks during the nonbreeding season. Their hoarse calls and loud, ringing songs are regularly heard throughout the year, frequently providing the first indication that a flock is in the area.

Tufted Titmice were well established in every county by the early 1900s (Jones 1903), although their numbers in northern Ohio probably

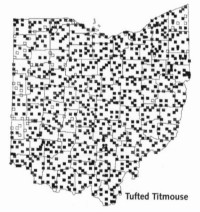

Tufted Titmouse

increased during the first decades of the twentieth century. Statewide distribution patterns have not noticeably changed since the 1930s, and Breeding Bird Survey data indicates that statewide populations have remained stable since 1966 (Sauer et al. 1998). However, short-term population fluctuations are produced by inclement winter weather. Like all gleaners, titmice suffer substantial mortality during ice storms and extreme temperatures. A single severe storm may significantly reduce their populations, as was widely noted following the winter of 1977–1978 (Robbins et al. 1986). Titmice populations generally recover quickly given one or two mild winters.

Tufted Titmice generally prefer mature woodlands and wooded riparian corridors; they are found in small open woodlots and brushy thickets only during winter (Trautman 1940). Small numbers occupy orchards and shaded residential areas. Given these habitat preferences, Tufted Titmice are most numerous in the southern and eastern counties, where daily totals of 5–35+ are regularly noted in summer and 20–50+ during winter. While similar numbers may be locally encountered elsewhere, titmice are generally least numerous in the intensively cultivated western counties and northern tier of counties. They become locally uncommon in these areas; summer totals normally are 3–15 daily and winter reports seldom exceed 20–25.

Sedentary birds, most titmice spend their entire lives within an area of only several square miles. A few titmice rarely appear at lakefront migrant traps during spring and fall. These individuals may merely be searching for suitable nesting or wintering habitats rather than being true migrants. The only indication of a defined fall movement of Tufted Titmice along Lake Erie occurred in association with the Black-capped Chickadee flight of 1993. Small numbers, generally five or fewer daily, were noted at several locations during October.

Their breeding chronology is very similar to that of chickadees. They form pairs during mid-March and begin searching for suitable nesting cavities. While they nest in fence posts and occasionally bird houses, most titmice choose natural cavities at heights of five to forty feet. Their eggs may be laid by mid-April in the southern counties and during May in northern Ohio. Renesting attempts produce clutches as late as June 10 (Trautman 1940). Most young fledge during the last half of May and June, although some fledglings accompany their parents through early July (Campbell 1968, Phillips 1980).

Red-breasted Nuthatch *Sitta canadensis* Linnaeus

These attractive little nuthatches normally reside in coniferous forests of Canada, the northern United States, and the higher elevations of the western mountains. Food availability greatly influences their seasonal movements, just as it does with other residents of these forests. When food is plentiful, most Red-breasted Nuthatches remain in these forests. But virtually all of them will desert these forests when food is scarce, producing a massive invasion in states to the

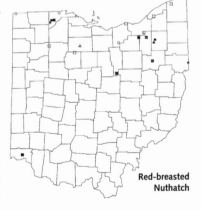

Red-breasted
Nuthatch

south. These movements are frequently associated with invasions of Pine Siskins and Evening Grosbeaks. Southward flights were sporadic during the first half of the twentieth century but generally occur at intervals of two to three years since the 1950s.

Timing of their autumn migration varies with the size of the southward flight. During sizable invasions, the first Red-breasted Nuthatches appear along Lake Erie by mid-August and within the southern counties by August 23–30. The migration normally peaks between September 10 and October 15. Their numbers decline during the last half of October and few migrants are detected after mid-November. Their fall movements are later during "noninvasion" years, when the first nuthatches return during September 10–20. A defined peak is not apparent, with only scattered sightings through late October.

Fall Red-breasted Nuthatches are most numerous along Lake Erie. During flight years, they become fairly common to common migrants and daily totals of 10–40+ are possible. In nonflight years, these nuthatches are uncommon lakefront migrants, with most reports of five or fewer. Their fall distribution is fairly uniform across the interior counties; they become uncommon to fairly common migrants during flight years and casual to rare at other times. Most fall reports are of 1–8 individuals, with occasional concentrations of 20–40+.

Wintering Red-breasted Nuthatches are most numerous within pine plantations and mixed woodlands throughout the unglaciated Allegheny Plateau and northeastern counties. They are normally uncommon to fairly common residents within these counties, usually in groups of 2–8. They become locally common following sizable invasions, when daily totals of 15–25+ are possible. Elsewhere, these nuthatches are erratic winter residents and may be absent some years, casual to rare in others, and rare to locally fairly common following sizable invasions. Winter totals normally are 1–5 daily, with local flocks of 5–20 during invasion years. These wintering nuthatches are most likely to be found at bird feeders, although some occupy conifers in parks, cemeteries, and residential areas.

The size of their spring movement is directly related to the number migrating south the previous autumn. Timing of their northward movements is reasonably consistent each year. Spring migrants are apparent by mid-April and peak between April 22 and May 15. The last migrants usually depart from the interior counties by May 20 and along Lake Erie by May 25–June 5.

These nuthatches are uncommon to fairly common spring migrants along Lake Erie, where most sightings are of ten or fewer daily. Daily totals seldom exceed 20 Red-breasteds, even during invasion years. Within the interior counties, spring nuthatches are normally rare to uncommon, becoming locally fairly common in flight years. Most inland spring records are of 1–5 individuals, with occasional concentrations of 6–20. A report of 45 at Columbus on April 23, 1981, is exceptional (Thomson 1983).

Red-breasted Nuthatches were very sporadic summer residents during the first half of the twentieth century. The first breeding records were from two Ashtabula County locations, where Hicks (1933a) discovered an adult with dependent young on July 18, 1929, and located a nest on June 13, 1931. The only other summer sightings were also from northeastern Ohio. The July 17, 1931, record from Headlands Beach State Park may have been an unusually early migrant (Baird 1932a). However, two pairs summering on Little Mountain in 1938 may have nested (Williams 1950).

A pattern of sporadic nesting records from northern Ohio continued through the 1970s, averaging one to three sightings each decade. These records invariably followed sizable winter invasions. Since 1980, summering Red-breasted Nuthatches have been recorded almost annually, with reports from as many as three to seven locations during some years.

Red-breasted Nuthatches are accidental to casual summer residents in northern Ohio, most frequently noted in the Oak Openings area of Lucas County and in Portage, Summit, Medina, and Cuyahoga Counties. Small numbers are also fairly regular in Mohican State Forest at the northern edge of the unglaciated Allegheny Plateau. Summering nuthatches are sporadic elsewhere. Breeding has been confirmed at Findley State Park (Lorain County), Tiffin, Canton, South Bass Island, and in Medina, Trumbull, and Mahoning Counties (Hall 1998, Peterjohn 1991d, Peterjohn and Rice 1991, Whan 1999a), while suspected breeders have been reported from a number of additional locations. They are accidental summer visitors in the central and southern counties, with the only confirmed nests at Cincinnati and in Hocking County (Hall 1998, Peterjohn and Rice 1991). They have also remained into summer in Miami and Hamilton Counties and at Dayton (Harlan 1994c, Kleen 1980d, Mathena et al. 1984, Peterjohn and Rice 1991).

Some summering nuthatches are found in residential areas, occupying conifers and regularly visiting bird feeders. Others inhabit conifer plantations and hemlock woodlands. Aspects of their breeding biology are described by Chasar (1998) and Kotesovec (1996). The few breeding records indicate that nesting activities are initiated in April or early May, with the young fledging by mid-June. Renesting attempts are responsible for nests with young through July 15–28 (Bittner 1965, Hicks 1933a).

White-breasted Nuthatch *Sitta carolinensis* Latham

This nuthatch is a familiar resident of deciduous woods, mature riparian corridors, parks, cemeteries, and shaded residential areas throughout Ohio. Its

territories center around mature deciduous trees providing cavities for nesting and roosting. Perhaps its most distinctive trait is its peculiar method of
foraging for food. Unlike woodpeckers
and creepers, which steadily move up
tree trunks and branches, White-
breasted Nuthatches normally walk
headfirst down the trunks and around
branches.

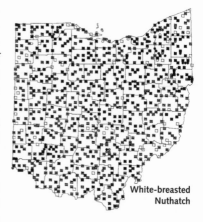

White-breasted
Nuthatch

White-breasted Nuthatches are fairly common to common permanent
residents in most counties, although
they become locally uncommon in
intensively farmed western Ohio. Their distribution and abundance have
remained fairly consistent throughout the twentieth century, and Breeding
Bird Survey data indicates that their statewide populations are stable since
1966 (Sauer et al. 1998).

White-breasted Nuthatches are fairly conspicuous during spring, especially
in late March and early April when their territorial and courtship activities
peak. They become inconspicuous later in the breeding season, when daily
totals seldom exceed ten individuals. Nest building commences in April. Their
cavities may be located ten to sixty feet high, usually in live deciduous trees.
Nesting records indicate that most eggs are laid during the last half of April
and early May, although nests with young have been reported as early as May
1 (Williams 1950). Recently fledged young have been observed as early as May
22, with most appearing during June (Trautman 1940). Young nuthatches
observed as late as August 15 are probably the result of renesting attempts
(Williams 1950).

Although they are normally sedentary, White-breasted Nuthatches periodically undertake noticeable fall movements. These influxes are most apparent
at lakefront migrant traps, where the White-breasteds are usually absent.
During the largest movements, as many as 10–15 may appear daily during late
September and October. These movements usually coincide with southward
invasions of Black-capped Chickadees.

During winter, White-breasted Nuthatches are important members of the
mixed-species flocks foraging within deciduous woods. Their nasal calls are
readily recognized above the chatter produced by these flocks. Although their
numbers are subject to annual fluctuations, winter sightings usually total 4–15
daily. As many as 60 individuals have been recorded during years of peak
abundance (Trautman 1940). Several factors are responsible for these fluctu-

ating winter populations. Influxes from farther north may raise populations to their highest levels. Conversely, winter storms may cause their numbers to decline for several years, as occurred after the severe winters of 1976–1978.

While fall influxes are apparent along the lakefront, the return flights are normally very small. Spring movements occur in April but seldom produce more than five individuals daily at lakefront migrant traps.

Brown Creeper *Certhia americana* Bonaparte

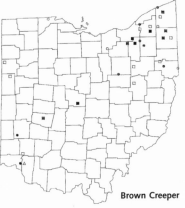

Brown Creeper

The least conspicuous members of Ohio's mixed-species flocks of wintering birds, Brown Creepers are easily overlooked as they move from tree to tree in search of food hidden among crevices in the bark. With their upperparts serving as camouflage, motionless creepers disappear against the bark of most deciduous trees. But creepers call persistently, and their presence is announced by high-pitched calls long before they are observed.

Brown Creepers are primarily migrants and winter residents. A few individuals appear at scattered localities during August, some as early as the first week. In all likelihood, these early creepers are wandering nonbreeders or postbreeding adults. In general, the first southward migrants return to Lake Erie by September 10–17 and to the central and southern counties by September 20–October 5. This movement is most pronounced during October and continues through the first half of November.

Fall creepers are uncommon to locally common visitors, with the largest numbers appearing along Lake Erie. They are seldom numerous; fall totals mostly are eight or fewer daily. The few sizable movements, restricted to Lake Erie, produce local concentrations of 25–30. Perhaps the largest movement occurred on October 14, 1928, when "scores" of creepers were grounded at Bay Point (Ottawa County), where they were observed on the ground catching insects (Campbell 1968).

Most wintering Brown Creepers inhabit woodlands, although a few individuals reside in parks and cemeteries. They are most numerous in floodplain woods but also occupy upland forests and isolated woodlots.

While they are widely distributed, wintering creepers are slightly more numerous within the central and southern counties, where they are fairly common residents. In northern Ohio, creepers become uncommon to locally fairly common. Most winter totals are 1–6 daily, with occasional reports of 8–12. These numbers exhibit considerable annual fluctuations. Some years they are scarce and few reports exceed 1–3 daily. They can be numerous in other years, when tallies of 10–15 are reported across the state. Years of peak abundance may produce Christmas Bird Count totals of 40–60+ in northern Ohio and 100–140+ in the central and southwestern counties.

Winter populations remained fairly stable during the twentieth century. The largest reported winter concentrations occurred after 1950, perhaps as a result of improved numbers in the Great Lakes breeding population since the mid-1960s (Robbins et al. 1986).

Spring migration probably begins during the last half of March. Their northward movements peak in April, when creepers become fairly common to locally common visitors. Most spring totals are eight or fewer daily, with occasional concentrations of 20–45+ in central Ohio and along Lake Erie. The largest spring movement was encountered on April 19, 1964, when "hundreds" of creepers visited the Toledo area (Campbell 1968). Most creepers depart by April 20–30, with the last migrants remaining through May 7–15.

At one time, Brown Creepers were unknown as summer residents within Ohio. The first nesting records were from Ashtabula County, where Hicks (1933a) recorded summering pairs at only two locations between 1928 and 1931. The only other northeastern Ohio summer records before 1950 were of a Geauga County nest and summering birds in Lorain and Cuyahoga Counties (Mayfield 1947c, Williams 1950).

Their status changed in the 1960s, when summering creepers became rare but fairly regular residents in northeastern Ohio. This increase was first noticed in the Cleveland area, where breeding pairs were regularly recorded after 1964 (Newman 1969). During the 1970s, summering creepers began to appear elsewhere. Nesting was recorded in Carroll and Jefferson Counties in 1972, while a singing male was recorded near Dayton in 1974 (Buchanan 1980, Kleen 1974d). This range expansion continued into the 1980s and 1990s.

Brown Creepers are now rare to locally uncommon summer residents in northeastern Ohio. They are most frequently encountered near Cleveland, where as many as seven males have been recorded from a single locality, and in Ashtabula County (Peterjohn and Rice 1991). Scattered pairs occur in other northeastern counties south to Columbiana, Stark, and Wayne, and within Mohican State Forest at the northern edge of the unglaciated plateau. In the northwestern counties, a few pairs regularly reside in the Oak Openings area of Lucas County (Harlan 1992d). Creepers are casual summer residents elsewhere, with scattered records from all portions of the state. Surprisingly, many recent sightings have been from southwestern Ohio, including nests in

Hamilton County in 1982 and Montgomery County in 1985, and as many as four in a Dayton park in 1984 (Mathena et al. 1984, Peterjohn and Rice 1991). Along the unglaciated Allegheny Plateau, summering creepers have been recorded south to Hocking County (Thomson 1983). These summering creepers can be easily overlooked, especially after the males quit singing in early June.

Breeding creepers occupy mature woodland habitats, preferring mesic woods and swamp forests. Their nests are cleverly hidden under the loose bark of dead trees. Some nests have been reported as early as April 11–16 (Fazio 1997b, Peterjohn and Rice 1991), producing fledglings by late May. Other documented attempts indicate nest construction beginning during May, with recently fledged young noted after mid-June (Hicks 1933a, Williams 1950).

Rock Wren *Salpinctes obsoletus* (Say)

Rock Wrens are widespread summer residents in western North America, from southern Canada into Mexico, but retreat from northern portions of their range during winter. Since they undertake fairly lengthy migrations, a few disoriented Rock Wrens wander east of their established range, appearing at scattered localities in central and eastern North America (AOU 1998). Ohio's only record of this accidental visitor was provided by a wren discovered at Edgewater Park in Cleveland on December 7, 1963. It remained through December 14, foraging for insects among the rocks along the breakwall and occasionally visiting weeds, scattered bushes, and rubble in an adjoining parking lot and field (Newman 1969). It was closely studied by many observers and photographed by William Klamm.

Carolina Wren *Thryothorus ludovicianus* (Latham)

Like most wrens, Carolinas are unobtrusive, spending most of their lives skulking through brushy thickets, dense undergrowth, and shrubbery. Among our most vocal songbirds, they sing throughout the year. Their loud, rolling song resounds through the otherwise silent woodlands in early February and in August after most birds quit singing.

Carolina Wrens are common and widespread residents in eastern North America. They reach the

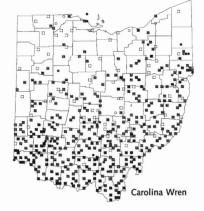

Carolina Wren

northern edge of their range in the Great Lakes and New England states, where their distribution considerably expanded after the 1880s (DeVos 1964). While these wrens always resided in the southern half of Ohio, their historic status in the northern counties is problematical. A few may have been present prior to 1880, but their numbers increased during the last decades of the nineteenth century (Jones 1903).

Their status has not appreciably changed during the twentieth century except in response to severe winter weather. Prolonged deep snow cover is detrimental to Carolina Wrens, since it buries most of their available food. When combined with subzero temperatures, this condition causes declines of 50–90 percent in wren populations. On average, severe winters reduce wren populations once or twice each decade. Exceptionally severe weather during three winters produced the most dramatic declines. Although the available information is scanty, the winter of 1917–1918 apparently eliminated Carolina Wrens from most of Ohio (Trautman 1940). Their populations recovered by 1922 at Buckeye Lake and later in more northerly locations. Smaller declines were noted in subsequent decades, but the general trend was towards increases through the 1950s and 1960s. Their numbers peaked in the early 1970s, as evidenced by a remarkable 1,801 on the 1974 Cincinnati Christmas Bird Count.

These all-time high populations were decimated by the unusually brutal winters of 1976–1977 and 1977–1978 (Robbins et al. 1986). Following the second severe winter, Carolina Wrens were reduced by more than 90 percent and eliminated from many localities. The few remaining wrens were mostly found in the extreme southern counties. With these individuals forming the nucleus, Carolina Wrens gradually recovered during the 1980s and early 1990s. Severe weather during the 1993–1994 winter produced another noticeable population decline followed by a gradual recovery, but their populations are still less than the extraordinary numbers of the early 1970s.

As permanent residents, Carolina Wrens are most numerous in the southwestern counties north to Preble, Montgomery, and Clinton and along the unglaciated Allegheny Plateau north to Muskingum, Guernsey, and Belmont Counties (Peterjohn and Rice 1991). Most years they are fairly common to locally abundant residents, and daily totals of 15–35 are regular. Following severe winters, they become uncommon to locally rare residents, with no more than 6–8 daily.

Elsewhere along the Allegheny Plateau and in the central counties near Columbus, Carolina Wrens are normally uncommon to fairly common residents, with daily totals of 3–8. They become rare within these counties following severe winters. They are rare to uncommon residents in the west-central counties, normally as isolated pairs, although 6–8 may be counted along riparian corridors. Carolina Wrens are least numerous in the northern third of Ohio, where they are casual to locally uncommon residents following mild winters and casually observed after severe winters. They are mostly observed as isolated pairs, least numerous in the northeastern counties of Ashtabula, Lake, Geauga, and Trumbull and the northwestern counties of Williams, Fulton, Defiance, and Paulding (Peterjohn and Rice 1991).

Carolina Wrens exhibit no defined spring or fall migrations. Individuals appearing between August and November at localities where they do not normally breed are wandering in search of mates and suitable unoccupied habitats. Unless a territory is established, these individuals normally disappear after several weeks.

The primary habitat requirements of Carolina Wrens are thick undergrowth and dense tangles. They are found wherever such habitats are available: woodlots, wooded ravines, riparian corridors, roadside edges, fencerows, and residential areas. Normally associated with edges, they are not encountered in forest interiors.

Carolina Wrens nest on or near the ground in brush piles, cavities, roots of fallen trees, and similar situations. While they rarely occupy bird houses, these wrens frequently nest in buildings. Their nests have been found in hanging flower baskets, mailboxes, and junk left in isolated corners of outbuildings. One pair attempted to nest inside a garden tractor. Most pairs raise at least two broods. Nest construction normally begins during the last half of March or early April and the first clutches are laid by mid-April. While fledglings have been reported by the last week of April, most first broods fledge during May (Mathena et al. 1984, Trautman 1940). Later clutches are initiated during June and July. These young fledge by mid-August, although late attempts produce young wrens through the first week of September. An exceptionally late nest with eggs was reported from Brown County on December 8, 1988 (Peterjohn 1989b).

Bewick's Wren *Thryomanes bewickii* (Audubon)

According to Trautman (1940), Ohio's first Bewick's Wren was discovered in 1879. The initial records were from the southern and central counties, where numbers increased dramatically during the next twenty years. By the turn of the twentieth century, Bewick's Wrens were common summer residents throughout southern Ohio and the central counties "nearly to Columbus" (Henninger 1902, Jones 1903). Scattered individuals were observed north to Lake Erie, although breeding populations were not established in the northern half of the state. Range expansion continued into the first decades of the century but at a slower rate.

Bewick's Wren populations apparently peaked between 1925 and 1940. During this period, they nested in every county north to Mercer, Shelby, Logan, Union, Morrow, Knox, Wayne, Stark, and Columbiana (Hicks 1935a). Only a few isolated records came from the northern counties. Summer residents were fairly common to very common along the unglaciated plateau north to Muskingum, Noble, and Washington Counties (Hicks 1937a). They were uncommon to rare elsewhere along this plateau and in most glaciated southern and central counties. Additional range expansion was hardly evident except for the first Trumbull County nest in 1932 (Skaggs 1934).

Bewick's Wren

Populations declined during the 1940s, although this trend became obvious only at the end of the decade. During the late 1940s and early 1950s, Bewick's Wren populations were subject to marked annual fluctuations in abundance (Brooks 1953d). Most remaining pairs inhabited the unglaciated counties, with small numbers regularly appearing in southwestern Ohio (Kemsies and Randle 1953).

Beginning in the mid-1950s, the remnant Bewick's Wren populations underwent rapid declines. Most of these wrens disappeared by 1960–1965, although isolated pairs were reported every year through 1970. Despite these declines, a few Bewick's Wrens appeared in the northern counties. The first Cleveland area nest was established at Kent in 1949 and nesting wrens were also recorded in 1952 and 1957 in Summit and Cuyahoga Counties (Newman 1969, Williams 1950). In the Toledo area, Campbell (1968) recorded summering males in 1956, 1957, and 1961. A nesting pair was also reported from South Bass Island in 1950 (Langlois and Langlois 1964).

During the 1970s, Bewick's Wrens were no longer annually observed. A few pairs were occasionally discovered, and nesting attempts were reported from Cuyahoga, Muskingum, Belmont, Athens, and Hocking Counties (Peterjohn and Rice 1991). Fewer Bewick's Wrens were noted subsequently. A pair successfully raised young in Brown County in 1980 and two pairs were reported from Hamilton County during May 1983, although nesting was not confirmed (Kleen 1980d, Peterjohn 1983c). In 1986, single pairs nested in Pike and Scioto Counties. The Pike County pair returned in 1987 and successfully raised two broods (Peterjohn and Rice 1991). During the 1990s, the only indisputable nesting record was from Brown County in 1995 (Lund and Weitlauf 1995).

There were a few additional sight records, most notably from Headlands Beach State Park on May 21, 1994 (Brock 1994c). Bewick's Wrens are presently accidental summer residents in southern Ohio and accidental nonbreeding visitors elsewhere.

Competition with an expanding House Wren population contributed to the disappearance of Bewick's Wrens from Ohio. Whenever territories overlapped, conflicts between these species were inevitable. As witnessed by Newman (1961) in Cuyahoga County, Bewick's Wrens invariably disappeared after repeated conflicts with the more aggressive House Wrens. But other factors were also involved, since Bewick's Wrens vanished from areas where House Wrens were scarce or absent. The disappearance of brushy edge habitats and removal of trash piles and brush from rural residences may have eliminated many formerly suitable nest sites (Smith 1980).

As summer residents, Bewick's Wrens preferred rural homesteads—typically a small unkempt residence surrounded by trash piles, open outbuildings, and brushy edge habitats. They also infrequently occupied orchards and shrubby fencerows.

Most pairs apparently raised two broods each summer (Henninger 1910d). Nest construction was recorded as early as the last week of March, but most first clutches were produced between mid-April and mid-May. These broods normally fledged by mid-June. Second clutches were initiated in late June and July, and adults with dependent young were observed into late August. Bewick's Wrens exhibited adaptability in their choice of nest sites: bird houses, natural cavities, trash piles, and a wide variety of objects, including old hats, coffee cups, and tin cans placed in undisturbed corners of outbuildings. In recent years, pairs exhibited a preference for flower baskets hanging on porches (Peterjohn and Rice 1991).

The majority of Bewick's Wrens were summer residents. Most appeared between March 15 and April 20. Scattered sightings along Lake Erie indicated their spring migration continued until May 10–20. Spring overflights were casual to accidental north of their established breeding range. Their fall migration was poorly defined as most wrens quietly disappeared from the state. The few records indicated that this migration occurred during September and early October.

While most Bewick's Wrens wintered in the southern United States, small numbers apparently remained within Ohio. Although there were few specific records, these wrens were described as rare winter residents in southern Ohio during the 1920s and 1930s (Trautman 1940). They were casual to accidental winter visitors away from the southern counties, where the few winter records included single wrens at Cleveland in 1960 and near Toledo in 1962 (Campbell 1968, Newman 1969).

House Wren *Troglodytes aedon* Vieillot

Of all wrens found in Ohio, House Wrens have most successfully adapted to edge habitats available near rural and urban residences. As their name implies, these plain wrens regularly occupy any suitable bird house erected for them, assuming adequate foraging sites are present.

House Wren

The distribution of House Wrens greatly expanded after Ohio was settled. They became common summer residents in most counties by the mid-1800s (Wheaton 1882). Their populations declined during the latter decades of the nineteenth century. Langdon (1879) attributed this decline to competition with growing numbers of House Sparrows at Cincinnati. However, sizable wren populations coexisted with House Sparrows elsewhere, so other factors were probably responsible for their reduced numbers. By the turn of the twentieth century, breeding House Wrens largely disappeared from southern Ohio and were common only in the northern counties (Henninger 1902, Jones 1903).

These reduced populations were short-lived. Increased numbers were evident during the first decades of the twentieth century. By 1935, Hicks (1935a) considered them fairly common to very abundant summer residents in every county, but least numerous in southern Ohio. Along the unglaciated Allegheny Plateau, House Wrens were rare residents in Adams and Lawrence Counties and rather rare to uncommon in other counties north to Hocking, Athens, and Washington (Hicks 1937a).

Statewide populations generally increased in subsequent decades, and significant increases have been evident along Breeding Bird Survey routes since 1966 (Sauer et al. 1998). House Wrens are fairly common to abundant summer residents in most counties. They are most numerous in the northeastern counties and locally in central and western Ohio, especially along streams bordered by mature wooded corridors. While 10–30+ daily are regularly noted in most glaciated counties, 50–75+ may be tallied in favorable habitats. These wrens are least numerous in southern Ohio from Adams and Pike Counties east to Washington and Morgan Counties (Peterjohn and Rice 1991). They are fairly common to uncommon residents within this corridor, and daily totals seldom exceed 3–10.

House Wrens thrive within wooded edge habitats, especially wooded fencerows, woodland edges and openings, orchards, riparian corridors, and shrubby thickets near residences. In addition to bird houses, House Wrens regularly nest in natural cavities. If these sites are unavailable, breeding pairs may choose pants left on a clothesline, the eaves of buildings, tin cans, clothespin bags, pipes, and mailboxes. House Wrens normally raise two broods. The first nests are initiated in early May and these young fledge by late June, although early broods appear by June 2 (Trautman 1940). Second nesting attempts begin in early July and these young normally leave the nest in August (Williams 1950). A few late nests produce dependent young into mid-September (Peterjohn 1990a). Nesting House Wrens have a reputation as quarrelsome and aggressive birds. They are particularly antagonistic towards other cavity nesters and may puncture eggs or kill young birds of other species.

During spring migration, a few early House Wrens return during the last week of March, but these overflights are unusual. The first migrants normally appear within the central and southern counties during April 12–20 and along Lake Erie by the last week of the month. They become common by the first week of May. Spring migrants are mostly individuals returning to their breeding territories, but large flights may develop during the first half of May. These flights are most noticeable along western Lake Erie, where 200 were counted near Toledo on May 14, 1949 (Campbell 1968). Counts of 40–100+ have been noted in other areas, but most reports are of 10–25 daily.

House Wrens are regularly detected until the males quit singing in late July or early August, but become inconspicuous in late summer. Their fall migration is poorly defined. It apparently begins in early September, marked by the gradual disappearance of resident wrens (Trautman 1940). The largest fall flights total 20–50, but daily tallies of these uncommon to fairly common migrants seldom exceed 1–8 individuals. House Wrens are regularly observed through October 5–15. The last migrants occasionally remain until the first week of November.

When weather conditions are favorable, lingering House Wrens may survive into early winter. They are accidental to casual visitors during December, averaging one acceptable sighting every two to four years. These early winter records are scattered across Ohio but are more likely in the central and southern counties. Most of these wrens succumb to the rigors of a typical Ohio winter. The only confirmed sightings after the first week of January are furnished by a House Wren overwintering in Hamilton County during 1949–1950 and another in Hamilton County on February 2, 1997 (Brock 1997b, Kemsies and Randle 1953).

Winter Wren *Troglodytes troglodytes* (Linnaeus)

One cannot help but be enchanted by these tiny, energetic wrens. Hardly more than a small ball of brown feathers with short wings and virtually no tail, Winter Wrens actively forage close to the ground within deciduous woods. At times they are frustrating to observe as they fly from thicket to thicket and immediately disappear into dense tangles. On other occasions they are inquisitive and react to the presence of an observer by hopping onto a log, bouncing up and down on their short legs, and repeatedly scolding with their sharp call notes.

Winter Wren

Despite their size, Winter Wrens are not daunted by a normal Ohio winter. They spend the winter in underbrush, tangles, piles of debris, and other cover in woodlands and wooded stream valleys. They are seldom found away from woody cover, although Campbell (1968) observed them in herbaceous cover at the edge of marshes.

Their winter status fluctuates in response to weather conditions. Numbers decrease following severe winters but gradually improve during successive mild seasons. In addition to these weather-induced fluctuations, their wintering numbers have gradually declined during the twentieth century. These declines are most apparent in the central and southern counties, where Winter Wrens were formerly regular residents and 3–8+ individuals could be observed daily before 1950.

Winter Wrens are now uncommon winter residents in the southern and unglaciated counties, where 1–5 are observed daily. They are generally absent from the northeastern snowbelt counties of Lake, Geauga, and Ashtabula. Elsewhere, they are casual to rare residents as widely scattered individuals. Even during the mildest seasons, their numbers are greatest before January 15 and noticeably decline by mid-February.

Winter Wrens are most numerous as migrants. They prefer brushy woodlands but are also found in parks, cemeteries, and residential areas; fallow fields with scattered bushes; and barren riprap along dams. Numbers of migrants fluctuate in response to winter mortality rates, as was evident following the severe winters of 1976–1978. In spring, the earliest Winter Wrens appear during the first half of March, although they normally return during March 20–30. Their northward movement peaks between April 5 and 22.

These migrants normally depart from the interior counties by the end of April, but small numbers remain along Lake Erie until May 7–15. Stragglers are noted at lakefront migrant traps through May 28–June 6.

These wrens are most numerous along Lake Erie, where they are fairly common to common migrants. While 3–10 are observed along the lakefront during most days, larger flights produce tallies of 20–40. A remarkable flight concentrated 200 at Magee Marsh Wildlife Area on April 15, 1972 (Campbell 1973). Fewer pass through the interior counties, where they are uncommon to fairly common migrants, and spring totals are normally six or fewer daily. Larger flights are restricted to central Ohio, where Trautman (1940) reported a maximum of 50 at Buckeye Lake and 60 appeared at Columbus on April 18, 1975 (Kleen 1975c).

The first fall migrants are detected along Lake Erie, occasionally during the first week of September but frequently not until September 15–22. They are expected in the southern counties by September 27–October 5. Peak numbers pass along Lake Erie during October 1–20 but are more likely within the interior counties during the last half of the month. A few migrants appear throughout November and until the first sizable snowstorm (Trautman 1940).

Fall migrants are also most numerous along Lake Erie, where Winter Wrens become fairly common to common. Daily totals of 3–10 are expected, while strong cold fronts regularly produce concentrations of 20–35+ and occasionally 60–75+. They are uncommon fall migrants in most interior counties, where 1–5 are observed daily. They largest inland fall flights total 10–20.

A very small breeding population exists in northeastern Ohio, largely restricted to hemlock gorges within the Chagrin River watershed in Lake, Geauga, and Cuyahoga Counties. Winter Wrens were initially recorded there in 1926; territorial males also appeared in 1938, 1947, and 1948 (Williams 1950). These wrens were believed to be unmated. Ohio's first nesting record was established in 1964, when adults accompanied by two dependent young were noted at Bedford Reservation (Cuyahoga County) on July 11 (Newman 1969). Since 1969, a few pairs have presumably nested at Stebbins Gulch and Little Mountain and sporadically appeared in other locations within this watershed (Peterjohn and Rice 1991). During the 1990s, additional males and pairs were discovered outside of this watershed in Lake, Cuyahoga, Summit, Portage, and Medina Counties. While only 5–10 males were believed to reside in northeastern Ohio during the 1980s (Peterjohn and Rice 1991), this population now totals 8–15 males during most years.

Away from northeastern Ohio, the only confirmed nesting attempt was established at Conkles Hollow Nature Preserve in 1974. Single males have been casually detected in other Hocking County hemlock woods in subsequent years, but they were probably unmated. Winter Wrens also summered in

Mohican State Forest during 1981 and annually beginning in 1991 (Hall 1981c, Harlan 1991a). As many as four males were found there in 1997, but nesting has not yet been confirmed. Winter Wrens summering in woodlots near western Lake Erie were undoubtedly nonbreeders, as was one in Columbiana County on June 16, 1992 (Harlan 1992d).

Breeding Winter Wrens are restricted to cool mesic ravines where hemlocks predominate or are mixed with deciduous trees. They prefer areas with dense underbrush, overturned trees, and similar cover. Their nests are placed on the ground, frequently hidden among tree roots or fallen logs. The few confirmed Ohio breeding attempts have been initiated in May, with the young fledging in June and early July.

Sedge Wren *Cistothorus platensis* (Latham)

The Sedge Wren has a reputation as an erratic summer resident whose movements frequently defy logical explanation. Breeding pairs are as likely to appear in mid-July as mid-May, and they seldom occupy the same nesting territories for two consecutive years. These erratic movements became more noticeable in recent decades as this wren's populations declined.

Sedge Wren

Since Ohio lies near the eastern edge of their range, Sedge Wrens were always locally distributed and relatively rare summer residents. In the mid-1930s, Hicks (1935a) cited summer records from thirty-five counties, primarily within the northern half of the state. They were usually noted at only one to three localities in each county, mostly five or fewer males, although a few "colonies" of 10–30 males also existed. The largest and most dependable populations occupied the Oak Openings area and former Pymatuning Bog, where 20–25 males were recorded most years (Aldrich 1934, Campbell 1968). They were accidental to rare within the southern counties and along the unglaciated Allegheny Plateau, usually as isolated males, although "colonies" of nine and 26 males were reported from Muskingum County in 1934 (Hicks 1936).

These populations declined in subsequent decades. In the Oak Openings, numbers of singing males were reduced to ten by 1941 and one in 1947. They disappeared by 1950 (Campbell 1968). These declines were equally dramatic within the northeastern counties, where every colony disappeared prior to

1940 (Aldrich 1934). Elsewhere, summering Sedge Wrens failed to appear in most counties. In subsequent decades, occasional "flights" produced a flurry of sightings during some years, but these movements never established permanent breeding populations.

Sedge Wrens are presently rare summer residents within wetlands bordering Lake Erie and Sandusky Bay in Ottawa and Lucas Counties. They are usually detected at one to three localities each year, mostly 1–2 territorial males, with a total population of fewer than eight males. Elsewhere, Sedge Wrens are casual summer residents within the glaciated counties, where they are usually discovered at one to five locations each year (Peterjohn and Rice 1991). Most reports are of three or fewer males and the total population is less than 15 pairs. The only recent "flight" occurred in 1994, which produced totals of 24+ in Erie County and 13+ in Sandusky County (Harlan 1994d). Summering Sedge Wrens are largely absent from the unglaciated counties, where they have been detected only in Holmes and Carroll Counties since 1980.

As their name implies, Sedge Wrens occupy sedge meadows, wet prairies, and grassy borders of wetlands. They prefer areas with damp soils or even rather dry upland fields. Their nests are globular structures located close to the ground in dense vegetation. They begin nesting in late May and early June, with the young fledging by July. After this brood is raised, they frequently shift breeding locations. These shifts may only be from one field to an adjacent one. At other times, small "flights" apparently move a number of Sedge Wrens into Ohio from elsewhere. Their second nesting attempts are initiated in late July; the latest clutches were discovered on September 9, 1936 (Campbell 1968). The young may fledge through September 15–20.

Their spring migration is poorly defined. While overflights appear at Cleveland by March 29–April 7 (Rosche 1992, Williams 1950), the first migrants return to other locations during the last week of April. Most spring Sedge Wrens are detected between May 5 and 22. These migrants are casual to rare along Lake Erie, with most sightings of 1–3 individuals. They are accidental to casual elsewhere, normally producing three or fewer reports annually. When their breeding populations were larger, spring Sedge Wrens were generally casual to uncommon migrants, but daily totals seldom exceeded six individuals (Trautman 1940, Williams 1950).

Sedge Wrens are slightly more numerous as fall migrants, most frequently observed along Lake Erie, where they are casual to uncommon in totals of three or fewer. They become accidental to locally rare migrants through the interior counties, mostly within the western half of the state. Even when the breeding populations were larger, their fall status was similar. These migrants are most likely to appear between September 15 and October 15, with a few remaining through November 5. Migrant Sedge Wrens prefer wet meadows and grassy habitats, but are also observed in dry weedy fields, especially along Lake Erie.

Sedge Wrens have always been accidental winter visitors. There are only two published December records: single wrens in Lucas County on December 24, 1939, and near Dayton on December 28, 1940 (Campbell 1968, Mathena et al. 1984). A Jackson County specimen collected on March 10, 1932, apparently overwintered. This male wren was in excellent physical condition and was found within "a small ditch on a wind and snow swept hillside" (Trautman 1933).

Marsh Wren *Cistothorus palustris* (Wilson)

Marsh Wrens might also be known as "cattail wrens" since they nest only in cattail marshes in Ohio. An aggressive and vocal bird, this wren produces a distinctive, rollicking song that carries across the marsh, while the singer remains hidden in dense vegetation.

Marsh Wren

Like most of Ohio's wetland avifauna, Marsh Wrens substantially declined in numbers during the twentieth century. In the early 1900s, Jones (1903) considered them abundant residents in most large marshes, recognizing that they were locally distributed and absent from areas lacking suitable wetlands. Their statewide distribution was better defined by Hicks (1935a). In the mid-1930s, these wrens were numerous in the western Lake Erie marshes and were regularly encountered in most northeastern counties. They were locally distributed elsewhere, with nesting records from forty-three counties south to Columbiana, Carroll, Guernsey, Muskingum, Perry, Fairfield, Pickaway, Champaign, Mercer, and Shelby.

Despite declining populations, statewide totals were substantial. For example, Trautman (1940) estimated at least 200 males at Buckeye Lake in the 1920s and 1930s. Similar numbers were probably present at Lake St. Marys (Clark and Sipe 1970). Campbell (1940) estimated 150 males in the Cedar Point marshes (Lucas County) on July 18, 1936, and remarked that summering Marsh Wrens were encountered "wherever there is a patch of cattails of any size."

The inland population substantially declined between 1940 and 1960. At Buckeye Lake, only a few pairs remained by the early 1960s. Marsh Wrens were common at Lake St. Marys through 1950 but disappeared during the next ten years (Clark and Sipe 1970). As these populations were declining, Marsh Wrens expanded into the southwestern counties. They annually nested at Spring Valley Wildlife Area after 1952 and sporadically appeared near Cincinnati (Kemsies and Randle 1953).

Populations remained stable in northern Ohio marshes into the 1960s. Marsh Wrens were widely distributed within the northeastern counties and numerous along western Lake Erie, where Anderson (1960) estimated 100 males in the Winous Point marshes (Ottawa County) in 1960. These populations mostly declined after 1970 (Campbell 1973) and may still be declining.

Marsh Wrens are now fairly common summer residents in the marshes bordering Sandusky Bay and western Lake Erie. Most marshes support five or fewer males, although 10–15+ inhabit large undisturbed wetlands. They are generally uncommon and locally distributed summer residents in northeastern Ohio, with small numbers scattered across every county. They are casual to rare and very locally distributed residents elsewhere south to Belmont, Guernsey, Licking, Madison, Warren, and Hamilton Counties (Peterjohn and Rice 1991, Harlan 1995d). While as many as 25 males reside at Spring Valley Wildlife Area, most inland marshes support ten or fewer males. Breeding Marsh Wrens are generally absent from southeastern Ohio except for a nesting record at Senecaville Reservoir in 1977 and a territorial male in Vinton County in 1991 (Hall 1977, Harlan 1991b).

Male Marsh Wrens are polygamous, frequently building "dummy nests" as they attempt to attract several females into their territories. Nesting activities are usually initiated by mid-May, but nests with eggs have been found as early as May 13–15 (Aldrich 1946). Most first clutches are noted between May 20 and June 15, while later clutches are laid through August 4 (Campbell 1968, Trautman 1940). Nests with young may be discovered by May 25, and recently fledged young appear between early June and late August.

In recent years, spring migrations mostly include birds returning to their breeding territories. The first Marsh Wrens may arrive between April 20 and 30, but they normally appear during May 5–10. This migration continues through May 25–30. These migrants are casual to rare in the southern and eastern counties, where they do not breed, appearing as scattered singles. Spring totals seldom exceed 3–10 within their established breeding range.

When populations were larger, their northward movements were impressive. Trautman (1940) regularly observed "hundreds" daily at Buckeye Lake during the 1920s and 1930s; peak movements between May 8 and 20 produced flights of "thousands." Similar numbers were not reported elsewhere. Spring movements were slightly earlier then, with individuals regularly appearing throughout Ohio by April 20–25.

Their southward migration was always less conspicuous. Even when breeding populations were larger, no sizable fall flights were reported. Presently,10 or fewer individuals are observed daily in the marshes where they regularly breed. Away from their established breeding range, Marsh Wrens are accidental to rare fall migrants, with most sightings of 1–4 wrens. According to Trautman (1940), their southward passage normally peaks during the last three weeks of September. Smaller numbers are regularly observed through October 10–20, while occasional late migrants remain into November. Fall Marsh Wrens regularly appear in weedy fields along Lake Erie. Within the interior counties, they have been observed in fallow fields and brushy edge habitats.

As early as the 1930s, Trautman (1933) believed "a few individuals winter practically every year in the Lake Erie marshes." While Campbell (1968) cited only fourteen winter records from the Toledo area through 1968, winter Marsh Wrens have been observed almost annually in subsequent years, confirming Trautman's beliefs. These wrens are casual to rare winter residents along western Lake Erie, averaging one or two sightings annually. While most are discovered during December and the first half of January, a few survive until spring. Elsewhere, the number of winter records has declined as breeding populations disappeared. Wintering Marsh Wrens are accidental to casual visitors away from western Lake Erie, averaging one record every two or three years. These records are well distributed, although there are no recent winter sightings along the unglaciated Allegheny Plateau.

Golden-crowned Kinglet *Regulus satrapa* Lichtenstein

A midwinter's walk through a cold Ohio woodlot is always enlivened by the appearance of tiny Golden-crowned Kinglets nervously moving through the bare trees. Their greenish plumage with the male's brilliant orange crown or the female's yellow crown provides a touch of color to an otherwise drab landscape. Golden-crowned Kinglets frequently associate with woodpeckers, chickadees, titmice, and other birds in mixed-species flocks foraging for insect eggs and pupae among dead leaves and barren branches. The kinglets are a bundle of energy, constantly flicking their wings and actively flitting from branch to branch in their quest for food.

Golden-crowned Kinglets are uncommon to common winter residents of pine plantations, hemlock groves, and ornamental conifers. If conifers are absent, they occupy shrubby thickets and brushy woodlots. Wintering Golden-crowned Kinglets are widely distributed, a status they have maintained since the 1800s (Jones 1903). While they tend to be slightly less numerous in the northern counties, they are locally common winter residents in cedar thickets on the western Lake Erie islands. Most locations support five or fewer individuals, although flocks of 10–15 occupy extensive groves of conifers. Daily totals seldom exceed 30, but Christmas Bird Count tallies of 100–225+ occur during winters of peak abundance.

Their wintering numbers are subject to dramatic fluctuations in response to severe weather. Prolonged cold temperatures and ice storms can take a considerable toll of these diminutive birds, and they can become scarce during February and March in severe winters. In particular, the extremely harsh winters of 1976–1978 decimated populations throughout eastern North America (Robbins et al. 1986). These populations returned to normal during the more moderate winters of the early 1980s.

The largest numbers of Golden-crowneds occur during fall, especially along Lake Erie, where they become abundant migrants. They normally return to the lakefront by September 15–22. Substantial movements may occur during October. By far the largest flight produced an estimated 25,000–50,000 on South Bass Island on October 7, 1954 (Campbell 1968). Other flights have produced 100–800+. Numbers of migrants are greatly diminished during November.

While a Golden-crowned Kinglet appeared at Cincinnati as early as September 11, 1985 (Peterjohn 1986a), the first migrants through the interior counties normally appear during the last week of September. The peak occurs by mid-October. These fall migrants are fairly common to locally common in most counties, normally producing daily totals of 5–30 individuals. The largest fall flight totaled 70 in central Ohio (Trautman 1940).

As a result of winter mortality, fewer Golden-crowneds pass through Ohio each spring, although they are still fairly common to common migrants. Most observations are of 20 or fewer, with occasional flights of 50–150+ reported from central Ohio and along Lake Erie. The largest spring flights produce counts of 250–350 from western Lake Erie. The first migrants normally appear by March 20–30, with the largest concentrations reported during the first three weeks of April. They usually depart from inland locations by April 30, but a few linger along Lake Erie through May 7–14. Migrants are very rare later in the month but have remained through May 27, 1983, at Dayton (Mathena et al. 1984).

In recent decades, Golden-crowned Kinglets have taken advantage of ornamental conifer plantings and expanded their breeding range southward in the northeastern United States (Andrle and Carroll 1988). Ohio's first breeding pairs were belatedly reported from Columbiana County during 1962–1963 (Hochadel 1999). There were two summer reports from the Cleveland area before 1970 (Flanigan 1968, Newman 1969), but these individuals were presumably nonbreeders. The next nesting records were reported from Columbiana and Portage Counties in 1989 (Hochadel 1999). A family group was discovered in the Maumee State Forest (Lucas County) in 1990 and a nest was found there the following year (Kemp 1991). Breeding was also reported in Summit County in 1991 (Reinthal 1991), Medina County in 1992 (Brock 1992b), and later in Lake County. Territorial birds were reported from Mohican State Forest during 1998 (E. Schlabach 1998). Golden-crowned Kinglets have become accidental to rare and very locally distributed summer residents in northern Ohio, especially within the northeastern counties, where the breeding population may total 3–8 pairs.

Breeding Golden-crowned Kinglets occupy ornamental spruces, pine plantations, and hemlock forests. The few reports indicate that nesting activities begin during late April or early May. Fledged young have been discovered as early as May 29 (Kotesovec 1998), but most are noted between mid-June and early July.

Ruby-crowned Kinglet *Regulus calendula* (Linnaeus).

Unlike Golden-crowneds, Ruby-crowned Kinglets are mostly known as migrants through Ohio. Since they primarily spend the winter months in the southern United States, the numbers appearing each spring reflect the severity of the preceding winter in that region. Unusually severe winters such as those of 1976–1978 cause extensive mortality and sharply reduce the numbers of migrants (Robbins et al. 1986).

Their spring arrival is announced by the loud and complex songs produced by the spritely little males. Migrant Ruby-crowneds frequently associate with Golden-crowneds, forming small flocks actively foraging through woodlands, wooded edges, parks, and shaded residential areas. Unlike Golden-crowneds, they do not show a preference for conifers. The majority of Ruby-crowneds are found in brushy thickets or dense saplings, although they also forage in the upper branches of tall trees.

While the first migrants may return during March 25–30, they are usually encountered during the first week of April. They are most numerous between April 15 and May 10, when they become fairly common to common across Ohio. Daily totals are generally 5–25, with flights occasionally producing concentrations of 40–60. The largest spring movements total 100–180+ in central Ohio and along Lake Erie. Most depart from the southern and central counties by May 16–20, although they have been recorded as late as May 27, 1983, at Dayton and May 31, 1925, at Columbus (Borror 1950, Peterjohn 1983c). Late May stragglers are more frequently reported along Lake Erie, where a few linger through June 7.

Ruby-crowneds are accidental nonbreeding summer visitors. Singles at Wooster on June 6, 1971, and in Delaware County on June 4–6, 1995 (Harlan 1995d), were most likely very late migrants. One reported from Old Man's Cave State Park in Hocking County on June 13, 1974, was described by Worth Randle as a male in full song. This individual was found within hemlock woods and may have been on territory, but could not be subsequently relocated. Other reports include one in Lake County through June 28, 1954 (Flanigan 1968), and another that apparently summered at Painesville during 1983 (Hannikman 1983).

Early migrant Ruby-crowneds return to Lake Erie by August 16–19. Other early migrants appeared in Mahoning County and Columbus by August 22 (Borror 1950, Harlan 1995a), and the southwestern counties by August 27–30 (Harlan 1996a, Kemsies and Randle 1953). Their migration normally begins during the last half of September. Fall migrants are most numerous along Lake Erie, where they become common to abundant between September 25 and October 20. The largest flights produced 650 in the Cleveland area on October 13, 1990, and 400 at Ottawa Wildlife Refuge on October 5, 1986 (Peterjohn 1987a, 1991a). Movements of 100–250+ are occasionally encountered, while daily totals normally are 5–40 along the lakefront. Fall migrants are decidedly less numerous through the interior counties. They are fairly common during the first three weeks of October, with generally 3–12 individuals daily. The largest inland fall flights total 20–40 Ruby-crowneds. The last migrants are normally observed through mid-November.

Ruby-crowned Kinglets were formerly accidental winter visitors, with very few records before 1940. Numbers of winter sightings noticeably increased after 1960, and they have become casual to rare early winter visitors across Ohio. Statewide totals from Christmas Bird Counts increased from 5–15 during the 1970s to 20–67 in the 1990s. Most reports are of individuals, although as many as 6–8 have been noted on Christmas Bird Counts. Winter Ruby-crowneds are mostly discovered within shrubby woodland thickets or shrub-dominated successional habitats. Most records are during December and the first half of January. However, a few survive the rigors of Ohio winters, with scattered late February reports from all portions of the state.

Blue-gray Gnatcatcher *Polioptila caerulea* (Linnaeus)

Blue-gray Gnatcatchers can be remarkably early spring migrants, frequently returning before there are many gnats to catch. The earliest arrivals are noted between March 25 and 31, either as residents returning to the southern counties or overflights north to Lake Erie. Small numbers regularly return to southern Ohio during the first week of April and to the central and northern coun-

ties by April 10–16. Their maximum
abundance is attained between April 20
and May 10. Small numbers are
observed at lakefront migrant traps
through May 20–28.

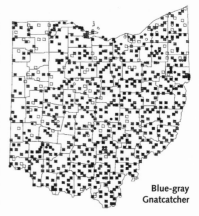

Blue-gray
Gnatcatcher

Spring gnatcatchers are generally
common migrants throughout the
southern and unglaciated counties,
where daily totals of 10–30 are frequent. Large flights produce tallies of
50–100+, which include both resident
pairs and migrants. They are fairly
common to common migrants in the
glaciated central counties and 3–20+
may be observed daily. Their spring status within the northern counties has
greatly improved since 1970, and they are now uncommon to locally common
migrants. The largest flights along Lake Erie total 40–50 in the Cleveland area
(Brock 1994c), but most lakefront reports are of 20 or fewer. Similar numbers
are not expected away from the lakefront in northern Ohio, where 1–8 individuals are normally detected.

Breeding gnatcatchers occupy mature woodlands. They prefer swamp
forests but also inhabit upland woods and riparian corridors. Their nests are
mostly placed at heights of twenty to sixty feet, anchored to fairly stout limbs.
These compact structures are composed of lichens and spider webs, although
other material is gathered for their lining. Within the southern counties, nest
construction begins during the last half of April and clutches are completed by
early May (Kemsies and Randle 1953). Fledglings may appear by the last week
of May, but most are noted during June. In the northern counties, the earliest
clutches are discovered by mid-May, and fledglings are expected during the last
half of June (Trautman 1940, Williams 1950). Renesting attempts and second
clutches produce nests with young well into July and recently fledged young
through August 20 (Peterjohn and Rice 1991).

As summer residents, gnatcatchers have increased during the twentieth
century. In the mid-1930s, Hicks (1935a) considered them uncommon to
abundant residents in the southern two-thirds of Ohio, with the largest numbers along the unglaciated Allegheny Plateau. They were rare to absent and
very locally distributed within the northern counties.

Their northward expansion was most apparent after 1960, a trend noted
throughout eastern North America (Robbins et al. 1986). Blue-gray
Gnatcatchers are now fairly common to common across southern and eastern
Ohio (Peterjohn and Rice 1991). Since they become inconspicuous once nest-

ing is under way, summer totals are normally 3–20 daily. Counts of 25–35 are possible once the young start to fledge. Breeding pairs are least numerous in the intensively farmed west-central and northwestern counties, where gnatcatchers are uncommon to fairly common summer residents (Peterjohn and Rice 1991). Most reports are of six or fewer daily, while tallies of 8–12 are possible along riparian corridors.

Their southward migration has always been poorly defined. This movement normally begins during the first half of August and continues through mid-September. The last fall migrants are usually recorded between September 20 and 30, with a few sightings during October. Fall gnatcatchers are most evident within the southern and unglaciated counties, where they are uncommon to fairly common migrants. They are generally uncommon in the glaciated central counties and rare to uncommon in northern Ohio. Most fall sightings are of four or fewer individuals, and the largest totals are 6–10.

Blue-gray Gnatcatchers are accidental visitors after late October. There are at least four November records of single gnatcatchers from northern Ohio. The six December records are from Buckeye Lake, Tiffin, Ottawa County, Lowell (Washington County), Mariemont (Hamilton County), and Lake County. The latest records are provided by gnatcatchers at Lowell on December 13, 1971 (Hall 1972a), and Mariemont on December 27–28, 1987 (Peterjohn 1988b). It is unlikely that this insectivorous species could survive an Ohio winter.

Northern Wheatear *Oenanthe oenanthe* (Linnaeus)

These members of the thrush family breed from Greenland across Eurasia to Alaska and the Yukon Territories in western North America (AOU 1998). They normally spend the winter months in Africa and southern Asia. Migrant Northern Wheatears are very rare but regular visitors to eastern North America, primarily along the Atlantic Coast in autumn. Small numbers have also been detected as spring migrants, but there are exceptionally few winter records from our continent.

Hence, the appearance of a wintering Northern Wheatear in Ohio was completely unexpected. This individual was discovered by Mark Shieldcastle on January 4, 1988, in a frozen marsh adjacent to a marina near Lake Erie in Ottawa County. It roosted in the marsh and apparently subsisted on spiders and insects captured on the boat docks. It was banded on January 17 and viewed by a number of observers through January 21. Plumage characteristics indicated that it was not an adult male. Its measurements suggested that it was a member of one of the Eurasian races or a small representative of the Greenland race.

Ohio's second Northern Wheatear was discovered by Vic Fazio at Big Island Wildlife Area on November 9, 1998. It remained at this location through November 18 and was also observed by many birders as it foraged in disturbed weedy fields (Brock 1999c).

Eastern Bluebird *Sialia sialis* (Linnaeus)

Dawson (1903) eloquently described the first spring flocks of Eastern Bluebirds:

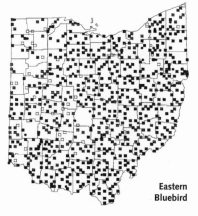

Eastern
Bluebird

> How the waiting countryside thrills with joy when Bluebird brings us the first word of returning spring. ... The cruel north wind may sweep down again and all the ugly signs of winter return, but Bluebird has kindled in our hearts the fires of an inextinguishable confidence ... Surely there is nothing in nature more heartening than the resolute courage and sublime good cheer of this dauntless bird. Reflecting heaven from his back and the ground from his breast, he floats between sky and earth like the winged voice of Hope.

Migrant Eastern Bluebirds are expected during the last half of February, except along Lake Erie, where they may appear during the first week of March. Their northward movements normally peak between March 10 and April 5, although occasional bluebirds are heard passing overhead through the first week of May. The appearance of bluebirds at lakefront migrant traps as late as May 27–June 1 is perplexing but may represent extraordinarily late spring migrants (Peterjohn 1986c, 1990c).

Spring bluebirds are normally observed as pairs returning to their breeding territories or as small flocks. These diurnal migrants may remain only long enough to catch a few insects, feed on fruits left over from the previous autumn, or rest at the top of a small tree before continuing their journey. Most spring sightings are of 30 or fewer bluebirds. Large flights are unusual, although movements of 65–120 have been reported from central and northern Ohio (Campbell 1968, Trautman 1940).

Breeding bluebirds prefer open habitats, especially grassy fields and road-sides with scattered trees, fencerows, and telephone wires. They regularly nest near rural residences but avoid developed residential areas. The most critical component of their territory is a suitable cavity for nesting, within a tree, fen-cepost, or bird house. Most territories are established during March, but nesting activities normally begin during the last week of the month within the southern counties and the first half of April elsewhere. Eastern Bluebirds normally raise two or three broods annually. While a complete clutch has been reported by March 11, most first clutches are noted after April 10. These young fledge during the last half of May and early June. Additional nesting attempts produce clutches through mid-July and dependent young well into August (Trautman 1940, Williams 1950).

Ohio's bluebird population undoubtedly expanded during the nineteenth century and became widely distributed by the late 1800s (Wheaton 1882). Since 1900,˙their populations have dramatically fluctuated in response to severe weather and intense interspecific competition for nesting cavities. Prolonged cold and snow cover cause extensive mortality of wintering bluebirds and recently returned migrants. The most famous episode occurred during the spring of 1895, when the sudden return of winter weather nearly eliminated bluebirds from the Great Lakes states and New England (Dawson 1903). Marked declines also followed the severe winters of 1958–1960 and 1976–1978 (Robbins et al. 1986). After unusually harsh weather, breeding bluebirds may become fairly scarce, with only a few pairs where they would normally be numerous. Their populations usually quickly recover, although complete recovery may require three to six years after the most severe declines.

The introduction of European Starlings and House Sparrows also caused historic declines in bluebird populations (Campbell 1968, Williams 1950). These declines were most apparent before 1950, but have been reversed since the late 1960s. The establishment of "trails" of bluebird boxes provides nest sites where none previously existed, and bluebirds have expanded in areas where they were formerly scarce. Trends from Breeding Bird Survey routes indicate that populations have increased since 1980, compensating for declines experienced during the severe winters of 1976–1978 (Sauer et al. 1998).

Breeding Eastern Bluebirds are most numerous in the southern and unglaciated counties. As common to abundant summer residents, 10–30+ are observed daily during years of normal abundance and totals of 40–50+ are possible once the young start to fledge. They become fairly common to common residents within the central and northeastern counties, where summer totals are normally 5–25 except along established nest box "trails." They are least numerous within the intensively farmed northwestern and west-central counties, where most natural cavities have been eliminated (Peterjohn and Rice 1991). Bluebirds are uncommon to fairly common summer residents, becoming common only where nest boxes are provided, with most reports of 15 or fewer daily.

Their fall migration normally begins during the last half of September; the nearly invisible bluebirds are detected by their call notes as they pass overhead.

This southward movement peaks in October, when bluebirds become fairly common to common migrants across Ohio. Fall totals seldom exceed 30 blue-birds daily, although movements of 60–120 have been detected in most por-tions of the state. The largest flights totaled 200+ near Utica (Licking County) on October 8, 1957, and a similar number near Dayton on October 14, 1932 (Mathena et al. 1984, Nolan 1958a). While their numbers diminish by early November, some southward movement is detected into the last half of December.

Numbers of wintering bluebirds fluctuate with weather conditions. They are most numerous and widely distributed during mild winters but mostly vacate Ohio when the weather is unusually harsh. During most years, Eastern Bluebirds are fairly common to locally common winter residents within the southern and unglaciated counties, where 10–60+ are noted daily. They become uncommon winter residents in the central counties near Columbus and rare to uncommon in the northern and west-central counties. After early January, daily totals seldom exceed 3–8 bluebirds away from southern and eastern Ohio. These wintering numbers have apparently increased since the mid-1960s. Wintering bluebirds occupy habitats similar to the summer resi-dents but prefer areas with brushy fencerows, thickets, or other cover. Some may visit woodlands. Since they largely subsist on berries, their abundance and winter movements are dictated by the availability of these foods.

Mountain Bluebird *Sialia currucoides* (Bechstein)

Breeding Mountain Bluebirds are widely distributed in a variety of open woodland and shrubby habitats across western North America. Some popula-tions are migratory and small numbers of these bluebirds regularly wander into portions of eastern North America (AOU 1998), where they are most like-ly to appear during late fall and winter. Ohio's only record of a Mountain Bluebird was provided by a female discovered by Dwight Miller, Ed Schlabach, and Steven Schlabach near Ragersville (Tuscarawas County) on December 14, 1989. It was associated with a small flock of Eastern Bluebirds, as they foraged within an abandoned field and adjacent wooded habitats. The Mountain Bluebird was photographed and observed by many birders, with the last obser-vation on January 13, 1990 (Schlabach 1990).

Townsend's Solitaire *Myadestes townsendi* (Audubon)

Townsend's Solitaires are occupants of the western mountains, breeding from Alaska south into Mexico. The northern populations generally retreat into the western United States and Mexico during winter (AOU 1998). Like other migratory birds from these mountains, Townsend's Solitaires have demonstrated a tendency to wander east of this range. Small numbers regularly appear from the northern Great Plains across the upper Great Lakes to New England and the Maritime Provinces during winter.

Ohio's first record of this accidental visitor fits this pattern of vagrancy. A Townsend's Solitaire was discovered on December 26, 1938, in Sylvania Township, Lucas County, during the Toledo Christmas Bird Count. It was initially reported by a group led by F. R. Flickinger and was intermittently viewed through January 14, 1939 (Campbell 1940). The second Townsend's Solitaire was an unexpected discovery at Magee Marsh Wildlife Area. It was discovered by Milton and Mary Trautman, Evelyn Gordon, and Avis Newell on the exceptional date of May 24, 1970. This individual was collected the following day, proving to be an emaciated female in "wretched plumage" (Trautman and Trautman 1971). The third record was provided by a solitaire photographed by James Seymour at Medina on November 14, 1994 (Rosche 1994). This individual could not be subsequently relocated.

Veery *Catharus fuscescens* (Stephens)

As summer residents, Veeries prefer young, moist deciduous woods dominated by dense saplings and shrubby thickets. They easily hide among the dense, woody cover and are seldom observed during summer. Their presence is readily detected, however, by their beautiful descending song, cascading from these young woodlands in the early morning and evening hours of late May and June.

Veery

Veery nests are difficult to discover in the dense vegetation, and very little information is available on their breeding biology in Ohio. Within the northeastern counties, nest construction has been reported by May 13, although most nests probably are built during late May and early June (Williams 1950). Nests with eggs are reported between May 18 and June 17 and young remain in the nest through July 18 (Campbell 1968, Williams 1950). Most fledglings appear in late June and July.

Breeding Veeries have gradually expanded their summer range southward. Jones (1903) reported only "small numbers" of summering Veeries within the northern counties and alluded to summer records elsewhere. By the mid-1930s, Hicks (1935a) considered Veeries local summer residents in northern

Ohio, citing records from twenty-four counties south to Paulding, Fulton, Lucas, Seneca, Huron, Ashland, Wayne, Stark, and Columbiana. They were common in Ashtabula County and the Oak Openings of Lucas County (Campbell 1940, Hicks 1933a). Elsewhere, they were very locally distributed and generally uncommon in the northeastern counties and rare in northwestern Ohio (Hicks 1935a, Williams 1950).

During subsequent decades, breeding Veeries noticeably increased within the northern counties and small numbers expanded into the southern half of Ohio. They are most widely distributed in Ashtabula, Trumbull, Lake, Geauga, Portage, Summit, and eastern Cuyahoga Counties, where they are fairly common to common summer residents and 5–20 may be noted daily. The 220–350 males estimated at the Ravenna Arsenal (Portage County) during 1993 and 1999 are exceptional summer totals for northeastern Ohio (Harlan 1993d, Whan 1999b). Breeding Veeries are generally uncommon to fairly common residents elsewhere in northern Ohio, becoming rare in the intensively farmed northwestern counties and locally common in the Oak Openings area (Peterjohn and Rice 1991). Five or fewer are normally recorded daily, except in the Oak Openings, where tallies of 10–20+ are possible.

Within central Ohio, Veeries have been casual to rare summer residents since the mid-1970s. Records are usually of widely scattered pairs, mostly in counties near Columbus. They are generally rare residents along the northern edge of the unglaciated Allegheny Plateau, except at Mohican State Forest, where 34 males were counted during summer 1997. They are generally absent elsewhere on the plateau except for a few pairs breeding in the Clear Creek valley of Hocking and Fairfield Counties and isolated reports from Athens and Hocking Counties during the Breeding Bird Atlas (Peterjohn 1982d, Peterjohn and Rice 1991). In southwestern Ohio, they are accidental to casual summer residents. There have been sporadic nesting records in Montgomery County since 1958 (Mathena et al. 1984), a Hamilton County summer record in 1964 and a nest in 1966 (Petersen 1964d, 1966c), a summering male at Hueston Woods State Park in 1987 (Peterjohn and Rice 1991), and summering males in Clinton County during 1991 and 1993 (Harlan 1991b, Brock 1993d).

Migrant Veeries are most evident during their northward passage. While they have been reported as early as March 31–April 5 along Lake Erie, there are no substantiated Ohio records until April 13–15. Spring Veeries usually return to the southern and central counties by April 22–28, and are expected along the lakefront during the first week of May. Spring Veeries are most numerous between May 7 and 21. Small numbers remain into the first week of June.

These migrants are most numerous along Lake Erie, where they become fairly common to common. Concentrations of 20–70+ Veeries appear during large flights, with totals of 3–8+ on other days. These thrushes are normally uncommon to locally common migrants elsewhere in the northern and central counties. Spring totals usually are eight or fewer daily, although flights produce as many as 43–50+. They are least numerous in the southern and unglaciated counties, where spring Veeries are uncommon migrants. Except for a remarkable flight of 100 daily at Cincinnati during April 20–24, 1982 (Peterjohn 1982c), most spring records are of fewer than 5.

Veeries are much less conspicuous during their autumn migration. The first migrants are expected during the last half of August. Most fall Veeries are reported between August 25 and September 20, with small numbers lingering into the first week of October. There are no substantiated sightings after October 10–19. Fall Veeries are generally uncommon migrants, and relatively few are detected as night migrants passing over the state. Most fall records are of only 1–5; no sizable movements have been reported.

Gray-cheeked Thrush *Catharus minimus* (Lafresnaye)

At the turn of the twentieth century, Gray-cheeked Thrushes were considered rare migrants throughout Ohio (Jones 1903). Their nondescript plumage and similarity to the more numerous Swainson's Thrush posed field identification problems for the early ornithologists. With the advent of better field guides and optical equipment, however, Gray-cheekeds proved to be more numerous than previously thought.

Gray-cheekeds are normally the last thrushes returning each spring. Except for an occasional overflight in mid-April, the first arrivals may be encountered during the last week of April in mild springs and the first week of May during most years. Peak numbers occur between May 12 and 25, when they are uncommon to fairly common migrants along Lake Erie and uncommon elsewhere. Fewer than ten individuals daily are normally observed along the lakefront and five inland, while movements of 15–20 infrequently occur along Lake Erie. Larger concentrations are exceptional, such as 45 at Buckeye Lake on May 15, 1932 (Trautman 1940). Occasional stragglers are noted through the first week of June.

During fall, Gray-cheekeds are most readily detected at night, when migrants utter their distinctive call notes as they pass overhead. These nocturnal migrants are most numerous following the passage of strong cold fronts, when flights over Westerville (Franklin County) produce counts in excess of 100 per hour. Rates of 25–50 per hour are more typical. These movements are not evident to daytime birders, who regard Gray-cheekeds as uncommon to fairly common fall migrants, most numerous along Lake Erie. Daily counts seldom exceed 10, and the largest concentrations on the ground total 20–25.

The first fall migrants frequently return during the last week of August.

Gray-cheekeds are distributed throughout Ohio by the first week of September, and the largest nocturnal flights normally occur during the last three weeks of the month. Numbers are normally diminished by the first week of October, although flights in excess of 50 per hour have been recorded through October 4. Gray-cheekeds normally depart by mid-October, with a late migrant banded at Cleveland on November 13, 1971 (Rosche 1992).

Their winter range normally is within the rain forests in South America; a few records come from Central America (AOU 1998). There are also a few winter sight records from North America, but most are believed to be misidentifications. One legitimate winter record is a specimen collected in Clermont County on December 28, 1947. It provides the only acceptable winter record from Ohio (Kemsies and Randle 1953). While exceptionally late birds are frequently injured, this individual appeared to be healthy.

Bicknell's Thrush *Catharus bicknelli* (Ridgway)

Formerly considered a race of the Gray-cheeked Thrush, Bicknell's Thrushes have a very limited breeding distribution in high-elevation coniferous forests of northern New England and adjacent Canada. They winter on islands in the Caribbean Ocean, and migrants are normally found along the Atlantic Coast of the United States (AOU 1998). There are very few sightings west of the Appalachian Mountains, so the appearance of a Bicknell's Thrush in Ohio was unexpected. The only record is of an individual collected along Swan Creek south of Monclova (Lucas County) on September 9, 1933 (Campbell 1934, 1968). This specimen was examined by Wallace (1939), who considered the identification to be "unquestionably authentic" but provided no additional information.

Swainson's Thrush *Catharus ustulatus* (Nuttall)

The most numerous of the migrant spotted thrushes, Swainson's Thrushes are found wherever trees and dense shrubbery are available. They abound in young woodlands and swamp forests with dense shrub layers and understories. Smaller numbers are regularly encountered in riparian corridors, parks, cemeteries, and shaded residential areas.

During spring, a few overflights have appeared in central and northern Ohio as early as April 5–6. The first migrants normally return to the southern half of the state during April 22–27 and Lake Erie by May 1. Their spring arrival is fairly erratic, however, and Swainson's Thrushes may be absent until the first week of May and then become widespread overnight. Spring migrants are most numerous between May 10 and 25, when they are fairly common to locally abundant throughout Ohio. Spring reports mostly are of 5–40 individuals daily, although large flights may produce concentrations of 300–400 in central Ohio and along Lake Erie (Campbell 1968, Thomson 1983, Trautman 1940). A few late migrants regularly linger until June 3–7. The last migrants occasionally remain along Lake Erie into the second week of June.

Since they are relatively late spring migrants, it is not unusual to hear male Swainson's Thrushes singing during early June. These males have led to reports of breeding Swainson's Thrushes, reports that have never been adequately verified. No nests have been discovered, and the only record of a "recently fledged juvenile" lacked adequate details to eliminate similar species that regularly breed in Ohio. Swainson's Thrushes become accidental nonbreeding visitors after mid-June, when the few reports include one at Cleveland on July 4, 1958 (Rosche 1992), one in Ashtabula County on June 26, 1992 (Brock 1992d), and one that apparently summered at Magee Marsh Wildlife Area during 1985 (Peterjohn 1985d).

As fall migrants, a few Swainson's Thrushes return to northern Ohio by July 25–August 10, although they normally appear along Lake Erie with the first cold front following August 20. They are normally detected in the southern and central counties by August 27–September 5. This movement peaks between September 10 and October 5, when they become fairly common to locally abundant migrants statewide. Numbers of migrants decline by October 10, and the last Swainson's Thrushes usually depart by October 15–20.

Fall Swainson's Thrush totals seldom exceed 5–40 daily. Large flights have produced concentrations of 300+ in central Ohio and along Lake Erie (Peterjohn 1986a, Trautman 1940). Their fall abundance is subject to considerable annual variation, and migrants can be scarce during some years.

Numbers observed on the ground represent a fraction of the total population passing overhead each fall. Swainson's Thrushes normally are the most numerous songbirds recorded as nocturnal migrants. Following the passage of a September cold front, the loud calls of migrant Swainson's are regularly heard from dusk to dawn and counts of 100–300 per hour are regular in central Ohio. The largest flights produce estimates of nearly 1,000 per hour.

A few Swainson's Thrushes linger into late autumn. There are a number of sightings during the last days of October and early November, with specimen records through November 13, 1976, at Cincinnati (Kleen 1977a). While Swainson's Thrushes have been occasionally reported during December and January, most of these winter records are believed to be misidentifications. The only documented early winter reports are of one found dead at Warren on December 11, 1991, and one at Cleveland on December 20, 1980 (Hall 1992b, Peterjohn 1981a). All winter Swainson's Thrushes should be carefully identified and documented to eliminate the similar Hermit Thrush.

Hermit Thrush *Catharus guttatus* (Pallas)

In a family renowned for its beautiful songs, no other North American thrush can match this inconspicuous species. Delivered from a perch near the top of a tall conifer, the Hermit Thrush's song begins innocently with several short introductory notes, followed by a brief pause and then a cascade of clear flute-like notes eloquently descending the musical scale. Each repetition produces a remarkably complex yet perceptibly different song, providing an enchanting serenade for all occupants of the cool coniferous forests preferred by Hermit Thrushes.

Hermit Thrush

The presence of breeding Hermit Thrushes is unexpected because Ohio is removed from established populations in Ontario, northern Michigan, and higher elevations of the Appalachian Mountains (AOU 1998). But they have found suitable nesting sites at a few Ohio localities closely resembling northern coniferous woodlands. Despite anecdotal nineteenth-century nesting accounts at Cincinnati and Cleveland, breeding Hermit Thrushes were initially confirmed at the former Pymatuning Bog in Ashtabula County by Hicks (1933a, 1935a). Summering birds were noted in 1928, 1930, 1932, and 1933, with nests discovered in the latter two years. The bog's destruction in the mid-1930s eliminated this small population. Summering Hermit Thrushes then went unrecorded until 1953, when two males summered at Conkles Hollow Nature Preserve in Hocking County (Brooks 1953d). Nesting was not confirmed that summer. Worth Randle revisited this site and other hemlock ravines in Hocking County during the 1960s and 1970s. Breeding Hermit Thrushes were discovered at Conkles Hollow only in 1966 and 1976 (Petersen 1966c), indicating they were not regular summer residents.

A breeding population became established when nesting Hermit Thrushes were discovered at Mohican State Forest in Ashland County in 1979 and near Old Man's Cave State Park (Hocking County) in 1982. Three to five pairs resided at both sites during the 1980s. A pair also nested in the Cuyahoga Valley Recreation Area (Summit County) during 1983 and 1984, while breeding was suspected during several summers of the 1980s in Hocking County at Conkles Hollow and Cedar Falls State Park. Additionally, unmated males or pairs briefly established territories at several other eastern Ohio locations and in Lorain County (Peterjohn and Rice 1991).

The statewide population was estimated at only 8–12 pairs in 1988 (Peterjohn and Rice 1991), but noticeably expanded during the 1990s. A total of 15 males were counted in Mohican State Forest in 1997, and 30 males were estimated in Hocking County during 1998 (Hall 1998). A few pairs apparently reside in Lake County hemlock forests. Additionally, 1–2 males summered in the Oak Openings area during 1991–1993 (Harlan 1993d, Peterjohn 1991d). Approximately 45–50 pairs now breed in Ohio, and their numbers are still increasing.

Their nesting chronology is poorly documented. Nest construction has been observed between late April and early June. The few records of fledged young during June and early July indicate that most nesting attempts are initiated during May (Chasar 1999).

Most observers recognize Hermit Thrushes as familiar migrants, more numerous during spring. They are generally fairly common or common spring migrants, but their numbers are subject to considerable fluctuations. They appear in the southern counties by March 20–30 and along Lake Erie by the first week of April. Peak numbers, normally encountered between April 15 and 30, produce daily counts of 5–30 along the lakefront and occasional flights involving as many as 250 on April 29, 1934, and 300 on April 15, 1972, near Toledo (Campbell 1940, 1973). Inland Hermits are normally encountered as daily totals of 3–15, with peaks of 25–50. While Trautman (1940) reported spring counts of 200 at Buckeye Lake during the 1920s and 1930s, similar flights have not been noted recently. Most migrants depart from inland localities by May 5–10, although a few linger along Lake Erie through May 15–20.

As fall migrants, Hermit Thrushes are generally uncommon to fairly common visitors. Daily totals seldom exceed 3–20 individuals. Largest concentrations totaled 75–95 at Buckeye Lake before 1940 and along Lake Erie (Campbell 1968, Trautman 1940). Like the spring migrants, fall Hermits are most numerous near the lakefront. Exceptionally early migrants have appeared in northern Ohio during August 22–25, but they normally arrive during the last half of September along Lake Erie and by October 1–5 elsewhere. Fall migration peaks during October, and small numbers regularly remain through mid-November.

While most Hermit Thrushes winter in the southern United States and Mexico (AOU 1998), small numbers are regular winter residents in Ohio. Their winter status is poorly documented, since they are inconspicuous, but the number of reports has increased since 1980. The only indication of their presence may be a sharp "*chuck*" note uttered from dense cover. Hermit Thrushes are locally uncommon to rare winter residents of woodlands in the southern and unglaciated counties, where 1–7 individuals may be tallied daily. They are generally less numerous elsewhere, usually casually or rarely encountered as isolated individuals. Surprisingly, the largest wintering concentration occurs on Kelleys Island in western Lake Erie, where dense red cedar and dogwood thickets provide abundant food and cover. As many as 39–63 have been recorded there during December. Like most berry-eating birds, numbers of wintering Hermit Thrushes vary annually in response to food availability.

Wood Thrush *Hylocichla mustelina* (Gmelin).

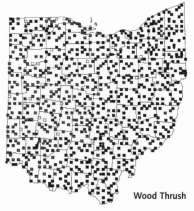

Wood Thrush

The woodlands are remarkably peaceful as another calm, warm June day approaches dusk. In the distance, the silence is broken by the clear flute-like phrases of a Wood Thrush. At this time of day, he seems to be the only living bird as his song echoes through the still woods. His serenade continues until dark, when a series of sharp call notes signals the end of another summer day. The next morning, when these woods are alive with the chorus of a multitude of birds, the Wood Thrush briefly joins this chorus, but usually only as a background voice lost among the clamor. He saves his prime vocalizations for the evening hours, when they can be fully appreciated.

Persons who appreciate quality bird songs are glad to know that Wood Thrushes are fairly common to locally abundant summer residents. While they prefer mesic woods with well-defined understories, Wood Thrushes are found in any woods that have a complete canopy and are not heavily grazed or recently cutover. They are at home in hemlock forests but avoid uniform pine plantations and seldom reside in shaded residential areas.

Like other woodland occupants, summering Wood Thrushes are most numerous within the southern and eastern counties. They are least numerous in the west-central and northwestern counties, where they remain common only along extensive riparian corridors or woodland preserves such as the Oak Openings. Within the most intensively cultivated counties, they become fairly common or even locally uncommon summer residents (Peterjohn and Rice 1991). Generally 10–40+ Wood Thrushes are counted daily in southern and eastern Ohio, although daily tallies seldom exceed 4–10 in the western counties. Breeding Bird Survey data indicate that the statewide population has remained fairly stable since 1966, although some declines are evident since 1980 (Sauer et al. 1998). Habitat destruction on their breeding range and the loss of wintering areas in Central America have contributed to declines in their continental populations (Robbins et al. 1986).

The earliest spring migrants return as overflights along Lake Erie. One was noted as early as March 22, 1953, at Cleveland (Rosche 1992), and several migrants have appeared during the first week of April. The first migrants normally return to southern Ohio by April 13–20 and are regularly encountered throughout the southern half of the state by April 25–30. Wood Thrushes are expected along Lake Erie by May 1–5. In the southern and unglaciated counties, tallies of 50–100+ are possible during the first half of May and include both local breeding pairs and migrants. Along Lake Erie, spring totals seldom exceed 5–20 daily, and the largest reported concentration is 35. The last migrants normally depart from lakefront migrant traps by May 20–25.

Upon their return, Wood Thrushes immediately initiate the process of raising their broods. Nest construction begins during the first half of May, and nests with eggs are reported as early as May 15–18 in central and northern Ohio (Trautman 1940, Williams 1950). Adults accompanied by young are found as early as the first week of June (Mathena et al. 1984, Trautman 1940), indicating that some clutches are laid in early May. Some pairs raise two broods. Later breeding attempts are responsible for nest construction during the first week of July and nests with young as late as August 18 (Williams 1950).

Once they cease singing, Wood Thrushes become inconspicuous, and considerably fewer are detected after August 1. Their fall migration is poorly defined. Few Wood Thrushes are noted as nocturnal migrants, and the largest concentrations are only 15–20, with most daily totals of five or fewer. Wood Thrushes are regularly encountered through the third week of September; most depart by the end of the month. Small numbers remain into October, a few into November. There are at least three confirmed December records and several undocumented reports. One Wood Thrush survived at a Willoughby feeder through January 10, 1975 (Rosche 1992), and another was found dead in Bellaire (Belmont County) on January 18, 1992 (Harlan 1993b).

American Robin *Turdus migratorius* Linnaeus

Our most familiar native songbirds, Robins are seen any summer day quietly gathering worms on residential lawns. Few native species have adapted so successfully to man-made habitats as the American Robin; its density may reach one pair per acre on large mowed lawns with scattered shade trees (Williams 1950). Robins are also at home in parks, cemeteries, and similar habitats. A few pairs prefer open second-growth woodlands. Unlike the suburban Robins, which are tame and easily observed, woodland nesting pairs are remarkably furtive.

Their true abundance is apparent at dawn, when every male Robin greets the new day with a brief chorus. Robins are abundant residents in every county. Generally 50–150+ individuals are counted daily, with larger numbers in urban areas.

When Ohio was initially settled, Robins were probably rather rare inhabitants of the younger woods and woodland edges. Their populations expanded during the nineteenth century as the forests were cleared. They have been common to abundant sum-

American Robin

mer residents since the mid-1800s (Wheaton 1882). However, their populations have fluctuated. Declines are apparent following unusually harsh winters. Robin populations were decimated by the widespread use of harmful pesticides during the 1950s and 1960s. Once these pesticides were banned, their numbers significantly increased (Robbins et al. 1986). Breeding Bird Survey data indicate that the statewide population has increased since 1966 (Sauer et al. 1998).

Their nesting habits are very well known. Their mud and grass nests are normally placed in trees but in rare instances are located on the ground. An adaptable species, Robins have nested on bridges, buildings, porch lights, fence posts, inside barns, and in tree cavities (Phillips 1980, Stewart 1931). They normally raise two or three broods each summer. Nest construction begins during late March or early April, and the first nests with eggs are expected between March 31 and April 15. Recently fledged young have appeared by April 18 but are most apparent during the last half of May (Trautman 1940). Second clutches are mostly reported between May 25 and June 30, with the young fledging in late July and early August. A few late pairs feed dependent young through Sepember 20 (Campbell 1968). An exceptionally late pair was incubating eggs in Columbiana County on November 10–11, 1933 (Baird 1934a). There have even been two winter nesting records. In Columbus, a pair started nest construction on December 12, 1965, and hatched their eggs during January 6–7 but abandoned the nest two days later due to cold temperatures and the absence of food (Kress 1967). Another winter Robin's nest with eggs was reported from Cincinnati on January 17, 1955 (Nolan 1955b).

Robins become even more numerous during their seasonal migrations. Their northward movements begin with the advent of warming temperatures in February. These movements usually peak during March, when as many as 100–500 are observed daily and flights of 1,000–2,000+ have been reported. Smaller numbers continue to pass northward through the first half of April.

Robins begin to move into woodlands during late July and August. By early September, most Robins abandon residential yards in favor of woods, where roosts of 100–2,000+ may be encountered. Their southward movements begin by mid-September. These migrants are most visible during October; flocks may pass through the state until late November.

Before 1940, winter Robins were regularly encountered in southern Ohio, becoming uncommon in the central counties and rather rare along Lake Erie (Campbell 1940, Jones 1903, Trautman 1940). Sizable winter roosts were only reported from the southern counties (Henninger 1902). The largest central Ohio winter flocks totaled 100–300, while most northern sightings were of 25 or fewer.

Since 1950, their wintering numbers have dramatically increased as a result of the extensive planting of crabapples, hawthorns, and other ornamental fruit trees. Their dependence on these winter fruits causes the size and distribution of wintering flocks to fluctuate annually. These flocks are frequently nomadic, remaining at a locality as long as fruits are available and then traveling considerable distances in search of food. Hence, sizable influxes during January and early February are regular occurrences.

American Robins are generally uncommon to locally common winter residents. Most winter sightings are of 50 or fewer, with occasional flocks of 100–250+. A few sizable winter roosts develop each year, frequently associated with starlings and blackbirds. These roosts have formed throughout the state. Most are composed of 500–3,000 Robins. The largest roosts include 5,500+ at Lorain, 6,000 at Utica, 6,400+ at Mentor, and a remarkable 15,000+ at Cincinnati during the winters of 1958–1959 and 1964–1965 (Mumford 1959b, Petersen 1965b).

Varied Thrush *Ixoreus naevius* (Gmelin)

Varied Thrushes normally breed in mature coniferous forests of the Pacific Northwest from Alaska to northwestern California, and winter along the Pacific Coast from southern Alaska to Mexico (AOU 1998). For many years, they were known as rare but regular winter visitors to eastern North America. These eastern winter records were centered around the upper Great Lakes and New England states, and eastern Canada. Since the mid-1970s, they have also regularly wintered near the lower Great Lakes.

Ohio's first Varied Thrush appeared at a Mentor (Lake County) feeder on December 18, 1977. This individual was observed and photographed by many birders through January 5, 1978 (Kleen 1978b). The next sightings occurred during the winter of 1979–1980, when single Varied Thrushes appeared at three widely scattered locations. Subsequently, 1–3 thrushes were recorded during six winters in the 1980s and four years in the 1990s. They are presently accidental to casual winter visitors, with at least seventeen acceptable sightings. These records are widely scattered except for the unglaciated counties: eight sightings from the Cleveland area, two from the Columbus area, and singles at Cincinnati, Dayton, Mansfield, Lima, Bluffton (Allen County), Findley State Park (Lorain County), and Ottawa County. The only fall migrant was noted at Headlands Beach State Park on October 30, 1994 (Brock 1995a). Most were noted between mid-December and late March at bird feeders. The latest remained at a Parma Heights feeder through April 6, 1996 (Conlon and Harlan 1996a).

Gray Catbird *Dumetella carolinensis* (Linnaeus)

Gray Catbirds are unobtrusive occupants of dense shrubbery, their plain gray plumage allowing them to disappear into the vegetation. Their mewing call notes may provide the first clue to their presence, but catbirds are usually very inquisitive and easily coaxed into the open. They are most conspicuous during spring and early summer, when males provide an almost nonstop chorus of disjointed notes. Unlike mockingbirds and Brown Thrashers, catbirds seldom imitate the songs of other birds.

Gray Catbird

A few Gray Catbirds have been reported in March, but these individuals may have overwintered. The first spring migrants usually return to the southern counties between April 15 and 20, and catbirds are widely encountered within these counties by the end of the month. Their migration along Lake Erie is approximately one week later, becoming numerous by the first week of May. During advanced springs, however, they may be common migrants throughout Ohio by the last week of April. Their spring migration normally peaks between May 7 and 18, when daily totals of 10–30+ are possible. Spring flights produce tallies of 40–75+ within the interior counties and 100–200+ along Lake Erie. The last migrants usually depart from lakefront migrant traps by May 25.

Gray Catbirds are fairly common to common summer residents, a status that has prevailed since the mid-1800s (Hicks 1935a, Wheaton 1882). Breeding Bird Survey data indicate that statewide populations have increased since 1966 (Sauer et al. 1998). They regularly inhabit the brushy edges of woods, streams and marshes, abandoned fields, roadside edges, shrubby fencerows, parks, and residential areas. Gray Catbirds are most numerous in the eastern half of Ohio, where shrubby edge and successional habitats are widely available. Daily totals of 15–45+ are expected during late May and June. Numbers are generally reduced in the western half of the state, where suitable shrubby habitats are more restricted. Summer reports seldom exceed 5–20 daily, except along extensive riparian corridors and in brushy habitats within the southwestern counties and the Oak Openings of Lucas County (Campbell 1968, Mathena et al. 1984).

This species normally raises two broods annually (Nickell 1965). Their nests are usually placed at heights of three to eight feet in dense shrubbery. Nest construction is under way in central and southern Ohio by the second week of May, and nests with eggs are expected throughout the state by the end of the month (Trautman 1940, Williams 1950). The first broods fledge during the last half of June and early July. Second clutches are produced during July, and nests with young have been reported as late as August 20–29 (Campbell 1968, Nickell 1965, Walker 1940e).

Their southward migration is less conspicuous. Trautman (1940) reported migrants at Buckeye Lake as early as late August, but most of their migration occurs during September and the first week of October. Fall totals are generally 5–15 daily, with occasional reports of 25–55+. Their numbers noticeably diminish by the second week of October, and only occasional stragglers are encountered after October 20.

While Gray Catbirds normally winter in the southeastern United States, a few regularly linger into winter as far north as Ohio. The number of early winter records has increased recently, from generally five or fewer annually on Christmas Bird Counts before 1985 to 6–12 annually in the 1990s. They may appear at any locality, although the majority of sightings are from the southern and central counties. Most wintering catbirds are discovered in the shrubby habitats where they spend the summer months, although a few become regular visitors to bird feeders. Most disappear following the onset of extended snow cover and cold temperatures, usually by the middle of January. A few have overwintered, usually in the southern counties during relatively mild seasons, but several have survived winter in northern Ohio.

Northern Mockingbird *Mimus polyglottos* (Linnaeus)

Northern Mockingbirds are sure to catch the attention of anybody residing within the domain of these distinctive backyard birds. Their drab grayish plumage flashes diagnostic white patches in the wings and tail as they move from perch to perch. An aggressive species, they are not afraid to chase other birds considerably larger than themselves or even small dogs and cats. Their ability to mimic bird songs is legendary, and many mockingbirds regularly repeat the songs of twenty or

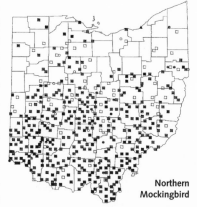

Northern
Mockingbird

more species and many other noises that they regularly hear. Persistent singers, they may repeat their repertoire throughout the day and most calm, moonlit spring nights, much to the chagrin of anybody trying to sleep in the neighborhood.

Mockingbirds initially appeared within Ohio during the mid-1800s, mostly as widely scattered individuals. By the 1870s, they were established as rare residents in the southern counties but were virtually unknown elsewhere (Langdon 1879, Wheaton 1882). At the turn of the twentieth century, Jones (1903) considered them rare residents north to Columbus, but felt that the few northern Ohio records may have pertained to escapes. They were numerous at only a few localities, as exemplified by 20 tallied in Morgan County in 1896.

Mockingbird populations noticeably expanded during the first decades of the twentieth century. By 1910, they became sporadic visitors to northern Ohio, and nesting populations were established in the Columbus area (Bales 1911a, Jones 1910). They were firmly entrenched in central Ohio during the 1920s (Trautman 1940). They invaded the extreme northeastern counties during the 1930s, with the first Ashtabula County record in 1932 (Hicks 1933a), although there were very few confirmed northern Ohio nesting records before 1940 (Campbell 1940, Williams 1950).

In the mid-1930s, Northern Mockingbirds were considered "regular residents" within the southern half of Ohio; they were locally distributed except in Adams, Lawrence, Guernsey, Muskingum, and Morgan Counties, where they became "fairly common to very common" (Hicks 1935a, 1937a). They remained rare and very locally distributed in the northern half of the state. These numbers exhibited considerable annual variation, especially after severe winters, when their populations were markedly reduced.

During the 1940s and 1950s, the widespread introduction of multiflora rose greatly benefited mockingbirds. They became widely distributed throughout the southern half of Ohio. Within the northern counties, small local breeding populations were established north to Lake Erie, and mockingbirds appeared at a number of localities where they were formerly absent. Nesting pairs were missing only from the extreme northeastern counties.

Numbers probably peaked during the late 1960s and early 1970s. Mockingbirds became common residents in southern Ohio, especially the southwestern counties near Cincinnati, where more than 400 were tallied on Christmas Bird Counts. Similar numbers were not reported from other southern counties, although 15–30 could be expected daily in most counties bordering the Ohio River. Even at Columbus, as many as 10–20 mockingbirds were observed at a few localities. Numbers remained low within the northern counties, although 3–5 individuals could be locally encountered.

The severe winters of 1976–1978 decimated mockingbird populations, and their numbers are still recovering. Moreover, multiflora rose hedgerows are no longer popular and many have been removed. This habitat loss prevented mockingbirds from returning to some counties.

Northern Mockingbirds are now fairly common to common residents in southern Ohio north to southern Preble, Montgomery, Clinton, Ross, Vinton, Athens, and Washington Counties. As many as 5–20 individuals may be recorded daily. They are uncommon to fairly common residents north to Darke, Logan, southern Morrow, Holmes, Tuscarawas, and Columbiana Counties (Peterjohn and Rice 1991). Daily totals seldom exceed 3–10 in these counties. They are casual to rare and locally distributed residents in the northern counties, usually as widely scattered pairs, least numerous in the northeastern counties. Breeding Bird Survey data indicate that the statewide populations remain fairly stable, with increases after 1980 neutralizing declines experienced in the 1970s (Sauer et al. 1998).

While mockingbirds are mostly permanent residents, a few undertake seasonal movements. Wandering individuals are most likely to appear in March and April as they search for mates and suitable breeding territories. Trautman and Trautman (1968) reported occasional diurnal migrants over western Lake Erie during April, and strays have appeared at lakefront migrant traps through May 8–11. Their fall movements are less well defined. The few lakefront migrants are mostly noted in September; other wandering mockingbirds appear during October and November as they search for suitable winter territories.

Breeding Mockingbirds are fairly numerous in urban areas, residing in ornamental plantings at residences, parks, and cemeteries. They are equally at home within hedgerows bordering rural residences. Mockingbirds also inhabit brushy pastures, especially where hawthorns, rose bushes, and similar tangles are present. If multiflora rose hedges are available, they may be found in extensively cultivated areas. Their nests are usually placed in dense shrubs at heights of two to seven feet. Mockingbirds are multibrooded and may raise three broods in the southern counties, where their nesting activities commence in April. Most young fledge between late May and August, although dependent young have been reported as late as November 16 (Peterjohn and Rice 1991, Petersen 1967a).

Brown Thrasher *Toxostoma rufum* (Linnaeus)

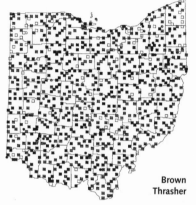

Brown Thrashers are most apparent during their spring migration, when the males perch on bushes or small saplings and sing incessantly. These migrants mostly appear along fencerows, woodland edges, and upland brushy fields but also visit wooded migrant traps along Lake Erie. The first migrants normally return to the southern counties during the last week of March and are expected in central and northern Ohio by April 3–8. Their maximum abundance is normally attained between April 15 and May 5, and a few migrants remain along Lake Erie through May 15–20.

Brown Thrasher

Spring thrashers are fairly common to common migrants throughout Ohio. They are seldom numerous, however, and only 3–12 are observed during most days. Larger flights produced totals of 75 in the Oak Openings on May 2, 1936 (Campbell 1968), and 30–40 at other locations.

Breeding thrashers occupy dry and dense shrubby cover; fencerows and other brushy corridors are as suitable as extensive overgrown fields. They are generally fairly common to common residents in the southern and eastern counties but are fairly common to locally uncommon in intensively farmed western and central counties. While 5–15+ thrashers are counted in the southern and eastern counties, daily totals seldom exceed 3–8 elsewhere. Breeding Bird Survey data show that their statewide populations have consistently declined since 1966 (Sauer et al. 1998). Despite these recent declines, the statewide pattern of distribution and abundance has not appreciably changed during the twentieth century. Both Jones (1903) and Hicks (1935a) considered thrashers fairly common or common residents statewide.

Nesting activities are initiated during the last half of April in the southern counties, and nests with eggs have been reported as early as April 30 near Youngstown (Richter 1939). Most pairs have complete clutches by mid-May. These young fledge by mid-June, although early attempts produce dependent young by the last week of May in southern and central Ohio. Brown Thrashers apparently raise two broods annually, as indicated by nests with eggs into mid-July and adults accompanied by young through August 20 (Trautman 1940).

Most thrashers nest in thorny shrubs, thickets, and other dense cover. Their first nests are normally placed on or near the ground; subsequent nests may be up to fourteen feet high (Campbell 1968, Trautman 1940). A few thrashers constructed nests in unusual locations. Phillips (1980) cited a Hancock County nest placed in a can in a juniper bush, and I discovered a pair nesting among riprap along a dam, far from any brushy cover.

By late July or early August, most thrashers become remarkably inconspicuous. Their southward migration is poorly defined. A few migrants have appeared along Lake Erie by July 25–August 10. Most of their migration apparently occurs between September 10 and October 5. The last thrashers normally depart by October 10–20. Fall observations are mostly of 1–4 thrashers daily, with occasional reports of 10–20.

Before 1940, Brown Thrashers were accidental or casual winter visitors, with the few records scattered across the state at two- to four-year intervals. Campbell (1940) cited only three winter records from the Toledo area and Trautman (1940) noted only three winter records from Buckeye Lake. Numbers increased during the 1940s and 1950s, and thrashers have been reported each winter since the 1960s.

Brown Thrashers are now casual winter visitors in northern and central Ohio and casual to rare in the southern counties. As many as 8–15 may be reported during some winters. Given their secretive behavior, a number of winter thrashers are probably overlooked. Most reports are of isolated individuals, although 3–4 have been reported on southern Ohio Christmas Bird Counts. They are normally found in the same brushy habitats where they nest, although a few regularly visit feeders. While many thrashers disappear after early January, a number have overwintered.

European Starling *Sturnus vulgaris* Linnaeus

The introduction of European Starlings into North America was a blunder whose disastrous consequences surpass even those associated with the introduction of House Sparrows. Starlings' adaptability allowed them to rapidly expand across the continent wherever man has substantially altered the natural surroundings. Pugnacious and quarrelsome, starlings normally dominate our native birds.

Starlings were initially released along the Atlantic Coast and rapidly spread westward. Their expansion across Ohio was described by Hicks (1933b). Ohio's first starling was reported from West Lafayette (Coshocton County) during January 1916. The next sightings were from Ashtabula County in 1918 and Knox County in 1919. In 1920, the first nest was discovered near Belleville in Richland County on May 11; flocks of 18–38 in Knox County during August indicated that they had also nested at

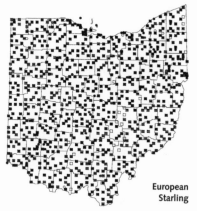

European Starling

other locations (Hicks 1933b, 1935a). Their numbers literally exploded between 1921 and 1925, when individuals or breeding pairs "had certainly appeared in every Ohio county" (Hicks 1933b). Sizable flocks formed in early autumn, including 1,800+ in Knox County on August 14, 1924. By the end of the decade, starlings became common to abundant residents throughout Ohio, and fall flocks of 1,000–5,000+ were regular. Their numbers increased during the 1930s, and a large roost of 100,000+ was discovered at Buckeye Lake as early as the winter of 1935–1936 (Trautman 1940).

Starlings are abundant permanent residents. As many as 100–500+ are observed daily during summer. Based on Breeding Bird Survey data, Ohio has the unfortunate distinction of supporting one of the largest nesting populations in North America (Robbins et al. 1986). This population remains relatively stable despite brief declines following severe winters (Sauer et al. 1998).

Breeding starlings are normally closely associated with people. They are equally at home in cities, in intensively farmed fields of western Ohio, and at rural homesteads in the southeastern counties. While they prefer urban and residential areas, nesting starlings also occupy parks, woodland clearings, riparian corridors, and wooded fencerows. They nest in natural cavities but also use bird houses, holes under the eaves of buildings, and a variety of other artificial nest sites. They normally raise two broods annually. Nest construction has been observed as early as March 28, but most first clutches are laid between April 15 and May 7 (Campbell 1968, Phillips 1980). First broods normally fledge in late May and early June. Their second clutches are laid during June, and these broods fledge in July.

As soon as the first broods fledge, juvenile starlings accumulate into small flocks. These flocks are evident by mid-June and continue to grow as more young are produced. Concentrations of 300–1,000+ are regularly observed in farm fields and along roadsides by early August.

Their fall migration probably begins in late August, but the largest concentrations are normally apparent between late September and mid-November. Immense numbers may appear, frequently mixed with blackbirds, and fall roosts of 10,000–100,000+ are frequent. These roosts are frequently located in cattail marshes during August and September but shift to pine plantations, dense deciduous woods, and even buildings as the weather turns colder. Their southward movements may continue through mid-December.

Starlings are abundant winter residents. They are most numerous in cities and farmlands, where 500–2,000+ are observed daily. Fewer are found in the rural southeastern counties; there, daily totals infrequently exceed 200–500. They also form large winter roosts, frequently in association with blackbirds. If undisturbed, winter roosts may be occupied for many years and attract concentrations of 10,000–25,000+. Larger roosts occasionally develop. For example, Dayton roosts supported an estimated 449,000 starlings in 1977 and 607,000 in 1952 (Mathena et al. 1984).

With the return of warming temperatures in February, starlings begin their northward migration. They move through the state primarily during March, when flocks of 500–5,000 are regularly observed. Large roosts are also formed—an estimated 150,000 starlings were reported at Columbus on March 12, 1972 (Thomson 1983)—but spring roosts are normally of short duration. Numbers of migrants are sharply reduced by April 7, although small flocks pass along Lake Erie until April 15–20.

American Pipit *Anthus rubescens* (Tunstall)

As spring migrants, American Pipits prefer farm fields, where they pursue insects and other invertebrates. Neither shy nor wary, they frequent plowed fields, grassy pastures, and flooded fields, relying on their somber plumage to hide them from predators. This plumage provides surprisingly good camouflage against bare soil; more than once I have scanned a field and found only 5–10 pipits on the ground but counted 100–200 as they flew away.

Given these habitat preferences, American Pipits are uncommon to fairly common spring migrants in the glaciated counties but rare to uncommon on the unglaciated Allegheny Plateau. They are erratic migrants, however, and large spring flocks may appear anywhere. Their erratic migratory behavior also results in considerable annual variability in abundance.

The first spring migrants may return during the last week of February, and are regularly encountered by mid-March. Their spring passage has two fairly distinct peaks. Large flights are observed between March 20 and April 15, most prominently after early spring snowstorms. Smaller flights are occasionally encountered around the first half of May, primarily in the northern counties.

These migrants are usually observed as flocks of 50 or fewer individuals; the largest flights produce flocks of 200–1,000+. The last spring migrants normally depart from the southern half of the state by May 10–15 and Lake Erie by May 20, with stragglers remaining through May 27–31. One at Headlands Beach State Park on June 8, 1996, was exceptionally late (Brock 1996d).

Fall American Pipits frequent open fields but are also found along the exposed margins of large rivers and reservoirs. These migrants are uncommon to fairly common in most counties. While American Pipits have returned by September 2–10, they normally appear during September 22–October 5. Most fall migrants are observed between mid-October and mid-November, in numbers comparable to spring. The largest flights are composed of 300–800 individuals. Their numbers decline during the last half of November, and the last migrants normally depart by December 5–10.

American Pipits can be surprisingly hardy. In the northern counties, they are accidental to casual early winter visitors, as lingering individuals or flocks of 30 or fewer; 1999 Christmas Bird Count totals of 200 at Wilmot and 62 at Ragersville are exceptional. They are casual to rare in central and southern Ohio through early January. Small flocks may remain until the first winter storm forces them south; late concentrations include 75 on January 6, 1983, in Pickaway County (Peterjohn 1983b) and 40 in Mercer County on January 8, 1917 (Henninger 1918). American Pipits become accidental visitors after January 15–20, although a few have overwintered north to Holmes, Geauga, and Richland Counties (Peterjohn 1992b, Rosche 1999a, R. Schlabach 1998). Twenty in Hamilton County on January 29, 1995, were remarkable for midwinter (Harlan 1995b).

Sprague's Pipit *Anthus spragueii* (Audubon)

Sprague's Pipits occupy grasslands and are unlikely to be found elsewhere. As migrants, they are very shy and furtive, preferring to remain hidden among the grasses; they take flight only when flushed underfoot. These pipits are normally found within central North America, breeding in the prairies of southern Canada and the northern United States and wintering in Texas and Mexico (AOU 1998). They are accidental visitors anywhere east of the Mississippi River.

While there have been a handful of Sprague's Pipit records from Ohio, most of these sightings are misidentifications. There are only two acceptable records of this accidental visitor. Ohio's first Sprague's Pipit was collected by Jay Sheppard at the Oxford airport in Butler County on November 15, 1958 (Sheppard 1959). It was with three other Sprague's Pipits, one of which was banded on November 25. This small flock occupied the grassy border of the airport, in an area where the grass was dead or burned out. The only other acceptably documented sighting was provided by a single Sprague's Pipit flushed by Jim Hoffman from grasses and weeds at a lakefront landfill in Cleveland on October 31, 1974 (Kleen 1975a).

Bohemian Waxwing *Bombycilla garrulus* (Linnaeus)

In the first half of the nineteenth century, Bohemian Waxwings were apparently fairly regular winter visitors to Ohio. The accounts of Kirtland and Read cited the frequent presence of winter flocks of these wanderers from western North America. Their status noticeably changed during the latter half of the century and their visits became much more sporadic (Wheaton 1882, Williams 1950).

Their sporadic winter visits continued into the twentieth century. During most winters, these waxwings were absent; in others, only widely scattered individuals or small flocks were observed. Defined flights were exceptionally rare. Probably the largest flight of the twentieth century occurred in the winter of 1919–1920, with smaller movements in the spring of 1944 and winter of 1961–1962. This status was maintained through the mid-1960s, with two to eight sightings per decade. Since 1967, there have been only four acceptable records, single Bohemians in the Toledo area on March 11–12, 1978, December 20, 1981, and February 21–25, 1990; and one at North Chagrin on December 12, 1999 (Kleen 1978c, Metcalf 2000, Peterjohn et al. 1987, Peterjohn 1990d).

The earliest acceptable winter visitor was recorded on November 29, but these waxwings normally appeared during the last half of December. Reports of wintering Bohemian Waxwings were distributed throughout January and February. Their numbers diminished during March, although a few remained through March 20–April 4. An exceptionally late Bohemian was reported from Cleveland on May 11, 1920 (Williams 1950).

During the twentieth century, most reports have been of 1–10 Bohemian Waxwings. While single individuals may be associated with flocks of Cedar Waxwings, the Bohemian flocks have been mostly segregated from their more numerous brethren. The largest flocks are most likely to appear within the northeastern counties: 75 at Painesville on January 27, 1920; 32 in Ashtabula County on December 22, 1919; 30 in Lake County on January 2, 1963; and 30 at Cleveland on March 8, 1944 (Newman 1969, Wharram 1921, Williams 1950). The largest flocks from other portions of Ohio totaled about 20 in New Bremen (Auglaize County) on January 18–22, 1910, and 15 at Findlay on March 15, 1962 (Henninger 1910c, Phillips 1980).

Since 1900, the majority of Ohio's thirty acceptable sightings have been from the northern counties: thirteen from the Cleveland area, five from

Toledo, two from Findlay and Youngstown, and one each from Ashtabula County, Lorain County, Bowling Green, and Canton. The four other sightings were of single Bohemians from Cincinnati in 1961 and 1963 (Graber 1962b, Petersen 1964a), the New Bremen flock in 1910, and one near Quincy (Logan County) on December 31, 1930 (Curl 1932).

Cedar Waxwing *Bombycilla cedrorum* Vieillot

Belying their elegant appearance, Cedar Waxwings are voracious feeders. When a winter flock descends upon a hawthorn, crabapple, or other fruit tree, these birds move from branch to branch, eating until their crops bulge. Depending on the flock size and the amount of fruit, Cedar Waxwings can completely strip a tree in a few hours or days. Then the flock moves on in search of another fruit-laden tree.

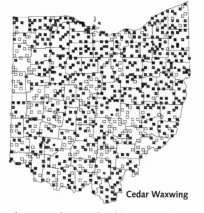

Cedar Waxwing

This nomadic behavior explains the erratic winter status of Cedar Waxwings throughout Ohio. Some years they may be nearly absent. In other winters, they may be locally distributed within a few counties. Even during periodic flights, they are generally uncommon and locally distributed winter residents. While wintering Cedar Waxwings may be observed in small groups of ten or fewer birds, they are mostly encountered in flocks of 20–50. During flight years, they become locally abundant; flocks of 75–100 are regular and concentrations of 300–500+ are infrequent. The largest winter concentrations include an estimated 1,600 at Toledo on January 6, 1985, and 2,000 in Summit County on January 3, 1990 (Peterjohn 1985b, 1990b), while Christmas Bird Counts have produced tallies of 2,700+.

Given their erratic winter status, Cedar Waxwings are also rather erratic migrants through Ohio. They exhibit a fairly complex migration pattern, with two distinct peaks during both spring and fall.

The first spring migration peak occurs between February 15 and March 15. Where these waxwings come from and where they are going has never been conclusively established. The size of this movement is variable from year to year and locality to locality. During some years, it is not evident anywhere. In other years, it may produce locally distributed flocks of 15–50 individuals and occasional large concentrations: 400 in the Ross-Pickaway county line area on March 13, 1968, and 175 in Ottawa County on February 28, 1959 (Mumford 1959c, Thomson 1983).

A second and decidedly larger spring movement occurs during May—some years by the first week of the month, other years not until after May 15. During the last half of May, Cedar Waxwings become common to abundant migrants throughout the state. They are mostly observed in flocks of 30–75; daily totals of 200–400+ are possible in every county. These migrants are most plentiful along Lake Erie, where 1,000–2,000+ can be counted daily. The last migrant flocks remain through June 5–12.

As summer residents, Cedar Waxwings formerly fluctuated considerably in numbers. These fluctuations were most noticeable in central and southern Ohio, where these waxwings might be locally absent some years and uncommon during others (Kemsies and Randle 1953, Trautman 1940). They regularly resided only within the northern counties, where they were uncommon to common (Hicks 1935a).

Their statewide populations increased on Breeding Bird Survey routes during 1966–1980 (Sauer et al. 1998), a trend evident throughout eastern North America (Robbins et al. 1986). As their numbers increased, their summer status became less variable. Cedar Waxwings are now fairly common to common and widely distributed summer residents, perhaps slightly less numerous in the southern counties bordering the Ohio River (Peterjohn and Rice 1991). They are normally encountered as pairs or small groups, and summer totals seldom exceed 10–35 daily.

Breeding Cedar Waxwings reach their greatest densities in mature wooded corridors bordering streams and lakes, although they also regularly occupy orchards, parks, roadsides, and shaded residential areas. Breeders add large quantities of insects to the usual diet of fruits.

Their breeding biology was studied by Putnam (1949). Cedar Waxwings are already mated upon arrival on their territories. Their territories are very small: a nest, a guarding perch, and between 225 and 1,100 square yards of space. Waxwings do not defend feeding territories. Nest construction begins by early June. Eggs are usually laid by mid-June and the female performs all of the incubation. While the eggs normally hatch in late June and early July, nests with young have been reported by June 20 and recently fledged young as early as June 26 (Phillips 1980, Trautman 1940). The males care for the fledglings while the females start raising another brood. These second nesting attempts produce nests with eggs through September 3 and a nest with young on October 26, 1981, near Dayton (Hicks 1934b, Mathena et al. 1984).

Flocks of Cedar Waxwings begin to develop in late July and early August. By mid-August, their fall migration has begun. These migrants are generally most numerous between August 20 and September 30, when flocks of 30–100+ are scattered across the state. Larger concentrations, such as 1,800 on South Bass Island on September 13, 1985 (Peterjohn 1986a), are exceptional.

A second migration peak between October 15 and November 7 is normally less pronounced, although flocks of 30–50 may still be regularly encountered. The report of "several thousand" along the Little Miami River on October 23, 1983, is exceptional for late fall (Peterjohn 1984a). These flocks may linger into late November, but only wintering Cedar Waxwings remain into December.

Blue-winged Warbler *Vermivora pinus* (Linnaeus)

The earliest Blue-winged Warbler returned to Clermont County by April 9, 1991 (Harlan 1991a), and other over-flights appear by April 12–17. Territorial males usually return to the southern counties during April 22–27 and along Lake Erie by the first week of May. Their northward migration is brief and most residents return by May 15–20, although stragglers remain at lakefront migrant traps through May 25.

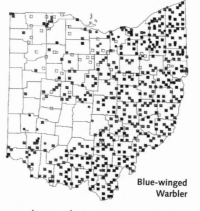

Blue-winged Warbler

Since their breeding range barely extends north of Ohio, this spring migration mostly comprises residents returning to their nesting territories. These warblers are uncommon spring visitors to migrant traps across the state, where most sightings are of six or fewer daily. Larger spring tallies are a mixture of resident birds and migrants, such as 71 in Athens County on May 10, 1994, and 42 in the Cuyahoga Valley National Recreation Area on May 9, 1998 (Harlan 1994c, Rosche 1998b).

Nesting Blue-winged Warblers prefer damp shrub-dominated habitats, including successional fields, woodland edges, and clearings. Since they occupy successional habitats, these attractive warblers invariably disappear when the shrubs are replaced by trees. The males are mostly detected by their distinctive songs and can be difficult to observe because they frequently sing from perches within dense cover.

Nests are placed on or near the ground, usually expertly concealed within dense herbaceous vegetation. These nests are frequently parasitized by Brown-headed Cowbirds, which may reduce the fledging success of some populations (Canterbury et al. 1995). Nest construction begins during the first half of May and continues into early June. Most clutches are noted between mid-May and mid-June. Dependent young appear by June 12–20, especially within southern Ohio, but most fledglings are expected in late June and July (Campbell 1968, Williams 1950).

At one time, Blue-winged Warblers were predominantly a southern species whose breeding range extended only into southern and central Ohio. This range slowly expanded northward, mostly during the nineteenth century, since nesting Blue-wingeds were widely distributed by the early 1900s (Jones 1903). Range expansion during the twentieth century was restricted to the Toledo area, where they became numerous during the 1920s and 1930s (Campbell 1940).

In the mid-1930s, Hicks (1935a) considered Blue-wingeds uncommon to rare and locally distributed summer residents, although he cited records from eighty counties. They were most numerous within southern Ohio and along the unglaciated Allegheny Plateau north to Hocking and Athens Counties (Hicks 1937a). These warblers were only locally common elsewhere in eastern Ohio. They were decidedly less numerous in western Ohio, where suitable successional habitats were scarce, and were unrecorded from eight northwestern counties.

In subsequent decades, their breeding populations increased within eastern Ohio, where Blue-wingeds are regularly distributed along the unglaciated Allegheny Plateau and northeastern counties (Peterjohn and Rice 1991). Conversely, their numbers declined within many western counties, where most shrubby habitats have disappeared. Statewide population trends have remained stable on Breeding Bird Survey routes since 1966 (Sauer et al. 1998).

Blue-winged Warblers are fairly common to common summer residents throughout southern and eastern Ohio, somewhat less numerous in the southwestern counties. Summer totals of 5–25+ daily are expected in most of these counties. They become uncommon to fairly common in the central counties, where ten or fewer are observed daily. Breeding Blue-wingeds are least numerous within the west-central and northwestern counties; while they are locally fairly common near Toledo, they are rare elsewhere and absent from intensively cultivated areas (Peterjohn and Rice 1991).

Once the males quit singing in early July, Blue-winged Warblers are infrequently encountered. Their inconspicuous behavior continues into autumn, and their fall migration is poorly defined. They become casual to locally uncommon fall migrants, with all sightings consisting of four or fewer individuals. Their southward migration apparently begins by mid-August. The last Blue-wingeds normally disappear between September 10 and 20. While a few individuals linger into the first half of October, a Blue-winged Warbler at Cleveland on November 14, 1948, was extraordinarily late (Williams 1950).

Blue-winged Warblers frequently interbreed with Golden-wingeds, producing recognizable hybrid offspring known as "Brewster's" and "Lawrence's" Warblers. When both species regularly nested within Ohio, "Brewster's" Warblers were rare but regular summer residents. In recent years, they have become accidental to casual summer residents, with sightings every two or three years, except during the Breeding Bird Atlas project when they were reported almost annually (Peterjohn and Rice 1991). Territorial males may appear anywhere, but are most frequently noted in the Oak Openings. Small numbers of "Brewster's" Warblers pass through Ohio each year, becoming casual to rare spring migrants along Lake Erie but are generally accidental within most interior counties. They become accidental to casual migrants throughout Ohio during autumn.

"Lawrence's" Warblers have always been less numerous than "Brewster's." "Lawrence's" Warblers are accidental to casual migrants and summer residents throughout Ohio (Peterjohn and Rice 1991). The migration patterns, habitat preferences, and nesting biology of these hybrids are identical to the parental species. It is not unusual to find mixed pairs, composed of hybrids mated with Blue-wingeds or occasionally with another hybrid.

Golden-winged Warbler *Vermivora chrysoptera* (Linnaeus)

Despite dissimilar appearances, Golden-winged and Blue-winged Warblers are closely related. In fact, regular hybridiz-ation between these two species has prompted some ornithologists to con-clude that they are morphs of a single species. This hybridization has signifi-cantly altered the distribution of nesting Golden-wingeds within North America. Wherever Blue-winged Warblers expand into the breeding range of Golden-wingeds, the latter species invariably declines and disappears (Gill 1980).

Golden-winged
Warbler

An expanding Blue-winged Warbler population largely replaced Ohio's locally distributed pairs of nesting Golden-wingeds. These pairs were never numerous. The only substantial Golden-winged population existed in the Oak Openings of Lucas County, where Campbell (1968) reported 37 males in 1932. Ashtabula County supported a small population; pairs were recorded at eight locations between 1928 and 1932 (Hicks 1933a). Elsewhere, breeding pairs were very sporadically encountered during the 1920s and 1930s. Hicks (1935a) cited nesting records from fifteen counties scattered across the state except for southwestern Ohio. These records were mostly of single pairs breeding for only one or two years. A few additional pairs were discovered along the unglaciated Allegheny Plateau before 1937 (Hicks 1937a).

Breeding Golden-wingeds were declining by the 1930s. In the Oak Openings, only 14 males were reported between 1937 and 1939. This number was reduced to ten by 1945 (Campbell 1968). Nesting Golden-wingeds essentially disappeared from the remainder of the state, except for occasional summering males or pairs at widely scattered northern and eastern localities. Between 1950 and 1968, only 1–3 males were annually recorded in the Oak Openings (Campbell 1968, 1973). A small population was established in Columbiana County during the 1960s but disappeared before the end of the decade (Hall 1962b, 1963b).

After 1968, the Oak Openings population vanished except for sporadic territorial males. The Breeding Bird Atlas project obtained fourteen reports from eleven counties (Peterjohn and Rice 1991). Territorial males remained throughout the breeding season at only six of these locations. The Oak Openings area hosted as many as 2–3 males, but they were not present during each year of the project. Nesting was not confirmed anywhere in Ohio during the 1980s.

Golden-winged Warblers are now casual summer residents in the Oak Openings area, where single males were sporadically encountered during the 1990s. They are accidental summer residents elsewhere. Nesting was reported from Columbiana County during 1991 (Harlan 1992d). Singing males were detected in Trumbull, Hancock, Lake, Portage, and Muskingum Counties and within the Wayne National Forest during the 1990s, but these males did not provide any evidence of nesting. This population remains on the verge of extirpation.

Nesting Golden-winged Warblers occupy the same brushy habitats preferred by Blue-wingeds. Their breeding biology is also similar. Golden-winged nests are placed on or near the ground in dense cover. Nests with eggs are reported between May 30 and June 21. The first fledglings appear during the last half of June but are mostly noted in the first half of July (Campbell 1940, 1968).

Golden-winged Warblers have always been scarce migrants through Ohio. Each spring, they are casual to rare visitors to most localities, becoming uncommon at a few migrant traps along Lake Erie. These sightings are mostly of individuals, with infrequent reports of 3–6 daily. The earliest arrivals appear during April 19–26. Most spring Golden-wingeds are observed between May 5 and 15, with a few through May 22–30.

Fewer Golden-wingeds are detected in autumn, when they become rare migrants along Lake Erie and accidental to casual inland. All fall reports have been of 1–4 individuals. They mostly pass through the state during August. The last fall migrants are normally observed between September 7 and 15, with only a few records through October 2. Remarkably late Golden-wingeds include one banded at Cleveland on October 18–21, 1978, and one observed near Toledo through November 21, 1987 (Hannikman 1978, Peterjohn 1988a).

Tennessee Warbler *Vermivora peregrina* (Wilson)

A warm morning in mid-May is invariably greeted by the loud ringing songs of Tennessee Warblers. Seemingly, every woodlot, park, and shaded residential area resounds with this distinctive song. Vibrant songs are usually produced by rather unremarkable birds, and this bird is no exception: the Tennessee is one of our plainest warblers. Its plumage of various shades of green and gray renders it rather difficult to observe in the emerging foliage.

While Tennessees are among our more numerous migrant warblers, their numbers are subject to considerable annual fluctuations. The causes of these fluctuations are poorly understood. However, relatively high numbers between the mid-1960s and 1980 reflect population increases correlated with spruce budworm outbreaks within their nesting range (Robbins et al. 1986).

While overflights appear as early as April 18–23, they return during late April only in the warmest seasons. They normally appear during the first week of May throughout Ohio, and peak numbers are encountered between May 10 and 25. When Tennessee Warbler population levels are high, daily totals are normally 10–40 in the southern and central counties and 25–100 in northern Ohio; the largest flights produced estimates of 200–250 in the Toledo area and at Buckeye Lake (Campbell 1968, Trautman 1940). When their population levels are low, daily counts are generally 15 or fewer at inland locations and 10–35 along Lake Erie; occasional flights of 50–100+ individuals may be found across the state. Most depart by June 1–4, except for stragglers through June 10 along Lake Erie.

During summer, Tennessee Warblers occupy boreal coniferous habitats across Canada and the extreme northern United States (AOU 1998). They are accidental nonbreeding visitors to northern Ohio, with at least eight widely scattered reports of single singing males between June 15 and July 6. These males remained for no longer than five days and then disappeared.

Each autumn, Tennessee Warblers are fairly common to common migrants. Since the mid-1960s, peak concentrations seldom exceed 20–65 daily, well below the fall maxima of 100 reported from the Toledo area by Campbell (1968) and 1,000 from Buckeye Lake by Trautman (1940). The first migrants have been noted at inland counties by July 21–23 and infrequently appear along Lake Erie during the last week of July. They are regularly encountered during the last half of August along Lake Erie and by the first week of September elsewhere. Tennessee Warblers are widely distributed throughout September and the first week of October, with most reports of 15 or fewer daily. They normally depart by October 10–17, with stragglers remaining through November 9–13.

Orange-crowned Warbler *Vermivora celata* (Say)

Despite the absence of distinctive field marks, the Orange-crowned is a rather attractive warbler. Its plumage is a mixture of greens and grays, with indistinct streaks on the breast. The male's orange crown is normally concealed except when he is agitated.

During spring migration, most Orange-crowneds are encountered in brushy thickets, tangles, and dense saplings; they seldom venture to the tops of tall trees. They are most frequently observed along Lake Erie, where they become uncommon migrants, mostly in groups of 1–3 individuals. A concentration of 32 on South Bass Island on May 16, 1948, was exceptional (Campbell 1968). Away from the lakefront, they are casual to rare spring migrants, least numerous in the unglaciated counties. Most inland sightings are of scattered individuals. The earliest migrants appear by April 12–18 but normally return by April 25–May 2. They are mostly observed between May 5 and 15, and the last migrants depart by May 20–23.

Confusion with Tennessee Warblers has greatly obscured the fall status of Orange-crowneds. They are actually among the last warblers returning to Ohio; reports during August and early September are most likely misidentifications. The first migrants may appear along Lake Erie between September 18 and 23 and are expected in the interior counties by September 25–October 5. They are mostly observed during the first three weeks of October, when Orange-crowneds become uncommon migrants along Lake Erie and casual to rare inland. As in spring, most fall sightings are of scattered individuals, although as many as eight have been reported along Lake Erie. Fall migrants prefer brushy thickets, tangles, and weedy fields dominated by ragweeds. The last fall migrants normally depart by October 25, with a few stragglers into November.

Orange-crowneds are accidental early winter visitors. A few sightings along Lake Erie during December 3–14 may be very late migrants. Other December records include an Orange-crowned in the Cleveland area through December 24, 1964, and near Youngstown through December 27, 1953 (Brooks 1954b, Rosche 1992). Later sightings are limited to single warblers lingering at Cincinnati through January 6, 1980, and at Toledo on January 26, 1958 (Campbell 1968, Kleen 1980b). An Orange-crowned attempting to overwinter at Greenlawn Cemetery in Columbus was discovered on December 26, 1926. This individual was regularly observed through February 10, 1927, but then disappeared (Walker 1928a).

Nashville Warbler *Vermivora ruficapilla* (Wilson).

Since Nashville Warblers retain their distinctive plumage throughout the year, they are among our more easily identified warblers. With their gray heads, white eye-rings, green backs, and yellow underparts, Nashvilles are not likely to be confused with any other warbler foraging among the branches of small or large trees.

Nashvilles are widely distributed spring migrants. An exceptionally early arrival was reported from the Cleveland area on April 8, 1945 (Williams 1950). During most years, the first migrants appear in the southern counties by April 20–25 and along Lake Erie by April 25–30. They become fairly common to common migrants between May 5 and 15, when 5–20 are observed daily. Large flights yield concentrations of 40–80 in central and northern Ohio. Along western Lake Erie, the largest movement produced 150 Nashvilles on May 13, 1961 (Thomson 1983). Their numbers sharply diminish after May 15 and most depart by May 20–25. A few stragglers remain along the lakefront into early June.

A small breeding population may once have resided in Ashtabula County. Hicks (1933a) cited summering Nashvilles in Monroe and Wayne Townships, although these birds may have been unmated. The only confirmed breeding record was provided by an adult feeding a fledgling in the former Pymatuning Bog on June 15, 1931. Summering Nashvilles were not recorded in Ashtabula County after the 1930s.

After they disappeared from Ashtabula County, Nashville Warblers became accidental summer visitors in northern Ohio. Sightings through June 13 at Cleveland pertain to late spring migrants. Single males summered near Canton during 1936 and in Lorain County during 1982, but they were probably unmated (Baird 1936c, Peterjohn and Rice 1991). There have been two confirmed nesting records: a pair raised a young cowbird in Stebbins Gulch (Geauga County) during 1969 (Flanigan 1969); and a nest with one young was discovered in the Cuyahoga Valley National Recreation Area near Peninsula (Summit County) on June 13 1996, with the young fledging on June 15 (Kotesovic and Zadar 1996). A Nashville Warbler observed near Hinckley on June 28, 1997, was close to the 1996 nest site (Brock 1997d). Summering birds were also reported from Lake County during the 1990s. Elsewhere, the only summer record is of a Nashville Warbler near Dayton on June 11, 1993, probably a very late migrant (Harlan 1993d).

While early Nashville Warblers return to Lake Erie by the first week of August, fall migrants normally appear along the lakefront with the first strong cold front after August 20. They arrive within the interior counties by the first week of September. Most Nashvilles pass through Ohio between September 15 and October 10, and the last migrants normally depart by October 18–25. A few individuals occasionally linger through November 19–26, but December reports are limited to one at Cleveland on December 1, 1980, and another on the Hamilton-Fairfield Christmas Bird Count on December 24, 1969 (Harlan 1992e).

Fall Nashville Warblers were formerly considered to be as numerous as spring migrants. September totals of ten or more daily were frequent. The largest reported concentrations totaled 60 along western Lake Erie and 100 at Buckeye Lake (Campbell 1968, Trautman 1940). Similar numbers have not been apparent since 1970. Nashvilles are now uncommon to fairly common fall migrants, with eight or fewer expected daily and flights producing tallies of 18–30 individuals. These fall migrants prefer woodlands, although a few frequent weedy fields.

Northern Parula *Parula americana* (Linnaeus)

It is unfortunate that this beautiful little warbler is an uncommon migrant. The Northern Parula is observed all too infrequently, mostly in fleeting glimpses as a small bird flits through the canopy of a tall tree. Despite this uncooperative behavior, the species' presence is frequently detected by the male's distinctive buzzy song.

Northern Parula

While the earliest Northern Parulas return during the first week of April, these overflights are unexpected. The first spring migrants are normally breeding warblers returning to the southern and eastern counties by April 15–20. These resident Parulas establish their territories by the first week of May, the same time migrants appear in the remainder of the state. These migrants are uncommon in most counties, becoming rare in the west-central and northwestern counties away from Lake Erie. Three or fewer Parulas are usually observed daily, and the largest flights produce tallies of 8–12. While 15–20+ have been reported from Hocking County in early May, these counts are mostly resident warblers. Their spring migration normally continues through May 20–25, with stragglers through the end of the month.

As summer residents, Northern Parulas were formerly restricted to hemlock forests along the unglaciated Allegheny Plateau (Hicks 1935a). They are now locally distributed along the plateau, where most are found nesting from eastern Adams County north to southern Fairfield County. Smaller numbers breed from the Little Beaver Creek watershed in Columbiana County south to Monroe County, and along the Mohican River in Ashland, Knox, and Holmes Counties (Peterjohn and Rice 1991). Parulas are rare to uncommon in most of these counties, usually encountered as scattered pairs or groups of 2–4 territorial males. They become locally fairly common in Hocking County, where 6–12+ males may be counted daily. Hocking County probably supports 75–100 pairs, more than all other unglaciated counties combined. Except for isolated reports of singing males and pairs, breeding Northern Parulas are generally absent from other portions of the unglaciated plateau.

Since the late 1950s, summering Parulas have expanded into mature sycamore-oak riparian woodlands in southwestern Ohio. The first Cincinnati area nest was discovered in 1958 (Nolan 1958d). In subsequent years, they spread throughout southwestern Ohio north to Preble, Montgomery, Clinton, and western Ross Counties. They have become uncommon to rare in most of these counties, with most reports of four or fewer daily, although as many as 11 males were counted along the Little Miami River in Warren County (Peterjohn and Rice 1991).

In the 1990s, summering Northern Parulas appeared at locations in central and northwestern Ohio where nesting was previously unrecorded. Six males were counted along Big Darby Creek during 1991. A similar number of males were detected along the Sandusky River in Wyandot and Seneca Counties during 1993 (Brock 1993d). Small breeding populations are apparently becoming established along mature riparian corridors in these portions of the state. Elsewhere, a singing male in the Oak Openings on June 11, 1992, may have been unmated (Harlan 1992d), while a nest was discovered in Delaware County on July 10, 1995 (Harlan 1995d).

A small breeding population formerly occupied hemlock woods in the northeastern counties. Hicks (1933a, 1935a) cited summering birds at seven locations in Ashtabula County and at isolated sites in Lake and Mahoning Counties. They disappeared during the 1930s, and only occasional territorial males were reported from northeastern Ohio through the 1980s. During 1993–1994, scattered territorial males were detected during surveys of the Grand River and Chagrin River watersheds, suggesting the existence of a small breeding population in portions of Lake and Geauga Counties. However, recent nesting in northeastern Ohio was confirmed only at Brecksville Reservation in Cuyahoga County, with a successful attempt in 1994 and unsuccessful nests in 1995 (Chasar 1994, 1995).

Since their nests are normally placed at inaccessible locations in tall trees, little information is available on their breeding biology in Ohio. Parulas build unique nests composed of mosses, probably during late April and May. The few breeding records indicate eggs are normally laid during May and young fledge by late June. Late nesting efforts are responsible for young leaving the nest on July 18 (Chasar 1994).

As fall migrants, Northern Parulas become casual to rare across Ohio. These migrants are mostly observed as scattered individuals, with infrequent groups of 3–6 along Lake Erie and in the central counties. The first fall migrants return to Lake Erie by the last week of August. They are most likely to be observed between September 15 and October 7. A few migrants may remain later, but the only November records are from the Cleveland area: single Parulas on November 5, 1977, and November 20, 1976 (Hannikman 1977, Rosche 1992).

Yellow Warbler *Dendroica petechia* (Linnaeus)

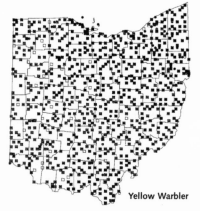

Yellow Warbler

This widely distributed species is one of our most numerous resident warblers. While overflights have appeared at Cleveland by March 25, 1942, and in southern Ohio by April 5 (Henninger 1902, Williams 1950), the first migrants are normally found in the southern counties during April 13–18, the central counties by April 22–26, and in northern Ohio between April 28 and May 2. By the first week of May, they become common to abundant migrants in brushy thickets, shrubby old fields, woodland edges, and the brushy margins of ponds and streams.

Spring migrants are most numerous along western Lake Erie, where large flights have produced 1,500 Yellows on May 15, 1948; 1,000 on May 22, 1943; and 800 on May 7, 1983 (Campbell 1968, Peterjohn 1983c). These large movements are not representative, however, and daily totals of 25–75 are expected along the entire lakefront during May, with occasional flights of 150–250+. While Trautman (1940) alluded to large flights at Buckeye Lake during the 1920s and 1930s, similar inland flights have not been evident in recent decades. Away from western Lake Erie, 15–30 are normally observed daily, with occasional movements of 50–100+. These migrants pass through the interior counties until May 15–20 and remain at lakefront migrant traps through May 20–25.

Breeding Yellow Warblers prefer unshaded shrubby thickets near lakes and wetlands and willow saplings along streams. While they are most numerous near water, they also occupy brushy old fields and abandoned orchards. Their nests are usually placed at heights of one to ten feet in shrubs and saplings, although Trautman (1940) described one nest placed fifty feet high in a sycamore. Nest construction begins during the first half of May. Nests with eggs are reported by May 12–13 in central and northern Ohio, although earlier dates are probable in the southern counties. While most eggs hatch in early June, nests with young have been noted by May 18 and recently fledged young by May 25 (Trautman 1940). Most dependent young are observed during late June and early July. Nests with young as late as July 17 and adults feeding dependent young on August 11 are probably the result of renesting attempts.

Yellow Warblers are fairly common to locally abundant and widely distributed summer residents, a status they have maintained throughout the twentieth century (Jones 1903, Hicks 1935a, Peterjohn and Rice 1991). Breeding warblers are most numerous in northern Ohio, especially in Lucas, Ottawa, Sandusky, and Erie Counties. As many as 30–75 may be counted daily during June. Similar numbers are also encountered in Ashtabula, Trumbull, Lake, Geauga, and Portage Counties. Fewer breeding Yellows are found in the central and southern counties, where daily totals seldom exceed 5–35. They are least numerous in the southern counties bordering the Ohio River, especially southwestern Ohio, where ten or fewer are observed daily.

While Breeding Bird Survey data indicate that their statewide populations have significantly increased since 1980 (Sauer et al. 1998), local populations have experienced declines. These declines are most apparent in intensively farmed areas, where most suitable habitats have been eliminated. Populations in eastern Ohio have also suffered local declines as their preferred brushy habitats underwent succession into second-growth woods.

Yellow Warblers are among the first songbirds to begin their fall migration. The first fall migrants appear along Lake Erie by mid-July and their southward movements are very noticeable by the last week of the month. This migration normally peaks during the first half of August. These migrants are most numerous along Lake Erie, where 5–20 are noted daily and the largest flights are composed of 100–225. Smaller numbers pass through the interior counties, where fall totals seldom exceed 5–15 daily. Most Yellows depart by September 10–17, with stragglers through early October. Despite this early migration, a few Yellows have appeared remarkably late. There are at least five reports during the first half of November, including four at Cleveland on November 9, 1988 (Peterjohn 1989a). An incredibly late Yellow Warbler was carefully identified during a snow squall at Cleveland on December 7, 1983 (Peterjohn 1984a).

Chestnut-sided Warbler *Dendroica pensylvanica* (Linnaeus)

Lynds Jones expressed affection for this attractive warbler:

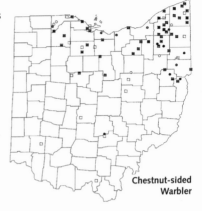

Chestnut-sided Warbler

> It is not easy for me to tell why Chestnut-sided Warbler impresses me as an exquisite. Perhaps it is on account of his small size and close-knit form, or his willingness to have me approach within speaking distance. His colors are not so bright, nor their pattern in either the contrast or harmony that may be found with other warblers, but there seems to be something about the bird which makes the day brighter, the wearing field work easier and the hours of parting forgotten when he flits into view. (Dawson 1903)

Jones's affection is shared by many who are acquainted with Chestnut-sideds as they pass through Ohio each year. These migrants are frequently encountered in brushy woods but are also regularly noted in parks, cemeteries, and shaded residential areas.

While overflights have been detected along Lake Erie as early as April 13 (Campbell 1973), Chestnut-sideds are expected to appear during April 27–30 and become widespread by the first week of May. Their numbers peak between May 10 and 22, when they become fairly common to common migrants. Spring Chestnut-sideds are most numerous along western Lake Erie, where flights of 100–200+ are occasionally detected. Lakefront totals of 8–30+ are noted during most mid-May days. Away from Lake Erie, spring totals are usually eight or fewer daily, with occasional reports of 10–20+. The largest inland movements produced 75 at Buckeye Lake on May 11, 1929, and 62 in Trumbull County on May 10, 1995 (Hall 1995c, Trautman 1940). Most Chestnut-sideds depart from the interior counties during the last week of May, but a few linger along Lake Erie through June 3–7.

A small nesting population always existed within Ohio. Breeding Chestnut-sideds are well established in Ashtabula County, where the first nest was located in 1907 (Sim 1907). Hicks (1933a) described them as "very local but sometimes common" residents in this county between 1929 and 1932, with observations from 32 localities. A small population also occupied the Oak Openings area, where 13 males were counted in 1932 but only 5–6 males in subsequent years (Campbell 1940). Except at these two localities, Chestnut-sided Warblers were rare and sporadic summer residents in northern Ohio during the mid-1930s, with records from Paulding, Defiance, Williams, Fulton, Wayne, Lake, Geauga, Cuyahoga, and Trumbull Counties (Hicks 1935a).

This population slowly expanded in subsequent decades. By the 1960s, Newman (1969) claimed that "considerable numbers of singing males were present at various localities" in the Cleveland area. This expansion continued through the 1990s.

Chestnut-sided Warblers are now uncommon to locally common summer residents in northeastern Ohio, with summering males regularly recorded south to Columbiana, Summit, and Medina Counties (Peterjohn and Rice 1991). Totals of 65 breeding on the Ravenna Arsenal (Portage County) during 1993 and 12 in Pennline Bog (Ashtabula County) during 1992 are exceptional (Harlan 1992d, 1993d); usually six or fewer are found at most localities. Chestnut-sided Warblers are fairly common summer residents in the Oak Openings area of Lucas and Fulton Counties, where 6–10 are present during most years, but become casual to uncommon and locally distributed elsewhere in northern Ohio (Peterjohn and Rice 1991). Summering Chestnut-sideds are casual visitors to central Ohio near Columbus, where they are discovered at two- to four-year intervals. Most of these males are thought to be unmated, but nesting was confirmed in Franklin County during 1997 (Fazio 1997c). They are accidental summer visitors to the southwestern counties, where nesting was documented in Montgomery County in 1992 and 1997 (Harlan 1992d, Fazio 1997c). Chestnut-sided Warblers are locally uncommon summer residents along the northern edge of the unglaciated Allegheny Plateau; small numbers are scattered south through Carroll and northern Jefferson Counties (Peterjohn and Rice 1991), and up to eight have been found in Mohican State Forest. A few pairs also reside along the Clear Creek valley in Hocking and Fairfield Counties (Thomson 1983). Singing males are casually found in clearcuts elsewhere in the unglaciated counties, with reports south to Ross, Athens, and Scioto Counties.

Breeding Chestnut-sided Warblers are encountered within brushy thickets, dense clearcuts dominated by shrubs and saplings, shrubby woodland edges, and dense overgrown fields (Miller 1930, Sim 1907, Williams 1950). Their nests are located near the ground in dense shrubs and herbaceous vegetation. Breeding activities normally begin during the last half of May. While fledglings have been reported as early as June 4 (Campbell 1968), these early nesting attempts are exceptional. Most nests with eggs are discovered between June 12 and July 20, and the young usually fledge during July and the first half of August (Campbell 1940 and 1968, Williams 1950).

Chestnut-sided Warblers have returned to Lake Erie during the last half of July and Youngstown by August 8 (Baird 1933). They regularly appear along

Lake Erie during August 15–23. The first southward migrants are normally noted in the central and southern counties by August 25–September 2. These migrants are mostly observed during the first three weeks of September. Fall Chestnut-sideds are fairly common migrants along Lake Erie but uncommon inland; daily totals seldom exceed 5–10 individuals, and the largest reported flights totaled 20–37. The last migrants normally depart by October 5, with a few lingering through October 16–22. The only later report is of one banded in Lake County on November 7, 1992 (Harlan 1993a).

Magnolia Warbler *Dendroica magnolia* (Wilson)

The Magnolia Warbler is another occupant of northern coniferous woodlands that is also a rare but regular summer resident of hemlock forests in eastern Ohio. The first Ohio breeding records were provided by Hicks (1933a) from Ashtabula County, citing summer records from eight locations into the early 1930s. With the destruction of the former Pymatuning Bog and with logging activities in other hemlock woods, this small population apparently disappeared before 1940.

Magnolia
Warbler

Breeding Magnolias were discovered at Stebbins Gulch in Geauga County during 1947 (Williams 1950). As many as four pairs nested at this location during subsequent years. A similar number occupy nearby Little Mountain (Lake and Geauga Counties) (Newman 1969). Since 1980, small numbers have been reported from other locations in Lake County, while up to five males have summered at Hinckley MetroPark in Medina County (Harlan 1993d). Isolated males and breeding pairs are sporadically reported from other hemlock woods in Cuyahoga, Summit, and Lorain Counties (Peterjohn and Rice 1991). Breeding Magnolias in northeastern Ohio now total approximately 15–25 pairs during most years.

Within the unglaciated counties, 3–8 pairs of Magnolia Warblers have nested at Mohican State Forest since the late 1970s. They also reside within Hocking County hemlock ravines, where Worth Randle discovered the first breeding pair at Conkle's Hollow Nature Preserve in 1966. One or two pairs have nested within the Clear Creek valley since 1970 (Petersen 1970d). Small numbers of summering males sporadically appeared at other Hocking County locations during the 1980s (Peterjohn 1982e), but became regular residents at

Big Rocky Hollow and near Cedar Falls State Park during the 1990s. This Hocking County population now totals 3–10 pairs. The only other summer records are from Columbiana County.

Away from the eastern counties, breeding Magnolia Warblers have only been reported from the Toledo area (Campbell 1968). This northwestern Ohio breeding record is of a summering pair near Sylvania (Lucas County) during 1965; a nest with young was discovered on July 12.

Within hemlock woodlands, breeding Magnolias prefer steep ravines and woodland edges where the understory and shrub layers are densest. Their nests are usually placed in small trees within dense cover. The few breeding records indicate that most nests are initiated during the last half of May and early June, with the young fledging by early July. An early nesting attempt was reported by Hicks (1933a) in Ashtabula County; adults were feeding dependent young on June 10, 1931. Kotesovec (1994a) provides information on the breeding behavior of Magnolia Warblers, noting young fledging from a nest near Hinckley between June 16 and 20.

This attractive warbler is fortunately a widely distributed migrant through the state. With the exception of occasional overflights during April 10–17, the first Magnolia Warblers usually return to the southern half of Ohio by May 1–4 and Lake Erie by May 3–7. They become fairly common to common spring migrants between May 10 and 24. Daily totals are generally 5–20 within the interior counties and 10–30 along Lake Erie. Large flights produce tallies of 40–75 within the central counties and 100–200 in northern Ohio. The last migrants usually depart by May 28–June 4, but a few may linger through June 13–18 in the northern half of the state.

The first fall migrants occasionally return to Lake Erie by July 19–28 and central Ohio by August 1 (Campbell 1968, Harlan 1995a, Williams 1950). Magnolias normally appear along the lakefront during August 20–25. Fall migrants may become common along Lake Erie by the last week of August but become common within the interior counties during the first week of September. Normally 5–25 Magnolias are observed daily, while infrequent flights produce totals of 50–125+ along Lake Erie and at Buckeye Lake. Most Magnolias depart by the first week of October. Only occasional stragglers remain after October 10–16, with sightings as late as November 15, 1957, at Toledo and November 19, 1972, at Cleveland (Campbell 1968, Hammond 1972).

Cape May Warbler *Dendroica tigrina* (Gmelin)

Within Ohio, Cape May Warblers are primarily migrants to and from their breeding range in the coniferous forests of northern New England and eastern Canada. Numbers of most warblers nesting within these forests, including

Cape Mays, fluctuate considerably in response to food availability. During spruce budworm outbreaks, the Cape May population increases dramatically, and this species ranks among our most numerous migrant warblers. At other times, relatively small numbers are observed.

While a few early migrants return by April 23–28, Cape Mays are normally encountered during the first week of May. Most pass through the state between May 5 and 22. These spring migrants are most numerous along Lake Erie, where they are normally fairly common to common. Generally, 20 or fewer individuals are observed daily along the lakefront, although large flights produce totals of 30–60+. They are normally rare to uncommon migrants within the interior counties but may become fairly common during years of peak abundance. Inland totals seldom exceed 3–12 daily, although as many as 40 have been reported from Buckeye Lake (Trautman 1940). Most depart during the last week of May, with stragglers remaining in northern Ohio through June 6–9. There are no adequately documented midsummer records.

Fall Cape May Warblers have returned as early as July 25–30, but the first migrants normally appear along Lake Erie during August 20–25. They may become fairly numerous along the lakefront during the last week of August, but are not expected at inland localities until August 28–September 5. They remain fairly common September migrants along Lake Erie, producing daily reports of 3–10 and occasional flights of 50–100+. Fall migrants are less numerous within the interior counties, where they are generally rare to uncommon visitors. Inland totals are normally 1–8 daily and the largest flights total 15–20. The last migrants normally depart by October 7–15.

Cape May Warblers are surprisingly hardy for a species that usually winters in the West Indies (AOU 1998). In addition to a few late migrants during November, Cape Mays are accidental early winter visitors to Ohio. There are at least ten published sight records during December and January: four in the Cleveland area, two at Youngstown, and singles at Belpre, Zanesville, Buckeye Lake, and Cincinnati. Most wintering Cape Mays disappear before January 20. However, one overwintered at a Cincinnati area feeder during January and February 1980 (Kleen 1980b).

Black-throated Blue Warbler *Dendroica caerulescens* (Gmelin)

Black-throated Blues are among our most easily identified warblers. Their distinctive plumages are identical in spring and fall, allowing for their immediate recognition as they forage within shrubs and small saplings. They mostly occur within young woodlands but may also appear in wooded parks and cemeteries.

In spring, an overflight appeared in the Cleveland area as early as April 14,

1959 (Rosche 1992), but there are few additional records before May 1. Black-throated Blues normally appear during the first week of May, and their spring movements peak between May 10 and 20. The last migrants normally depart by May 25–31 but may remain into the first week of June in northern Ohio.

These spring migrants are most numerous along Lake Erie, where they are generally fairly common, although daily totals seldom exceed 3–10 individuals. Flights in excess of 25–50 are exceptional. The largest reported flight totaled 200 in Lake County on May 4, 1936 (Williams 1950). Black-throated Blues are generally uncommon migrants in northern and glaciated central Ohio, becoming rare to uncommon in the southwestern and unglaciated counties. Most inland reports are of four or fewer individuals, although small flights of 10–15 have been encountered.

At one time, a few Black-throated Blues may have regularly nested in Ashtabula County. Hicks (1933a) observed summering birds in Wayne Township in 1928 and 1929 and the former Pymatuning Bog during 1931. Breeding was established at both sites; a nest with eggs was discovered on June 11, 1931, and adults accompanied by dependent young were observed on July 7, 1928. Since then, habitat destruction eliminated these nesting locations and breeding Black-throated Blues have not been observed in the county.

With the disappearance of these breeding pairs, Black-throated Blues became accidental nonbreeding summer visitors. Most have been detected in hemlock ravines within the Chagrin River watershed in eastern Cuyahoga, Lake, and Geauga Counties. Males have irregularly appeared within these ravines since the mid-1960s but without any evidence of nesting. During the 1980s, summer records were limited to an apparently unmated male at Mohican State Forest during 1982 and single nonterritorial birds observed briefly at five locations in northwestern and eastern Ohio (Peterjohn and Rice 1991). During the 1990s, summering Black-throated Blues were reported from the Oak Openings area in 1993 and Stebbins Gulch (Geauga County) in 1995 (Brock 1995d, Harlan 1993d). In 1997, three males summered at Mohican State Forest, where nesting was not confirmed (Brock 1997d), while a nesting report from Lake County requires additional confirmation.

While a few Black-throated Blues return to northern Ohio during the last week of August, they normally appear during September 1–5. They are noted in the central and southern counties by September 5–10. Black-throated Blues trickle through the state during September and the first week of October, while the last migrants usually depart between October 10 and 17. November records are limited to one at Cincinnati on November 8, 1975 (Kleen 1976a), and two central Ohio reports through November 11–19 (Borror 1950, Brock 1996a). One at Garfield Heights (Cuyahoga County) on December 4–5, 1993, was exceptionally late (Harlan 1993d).

Fall migrants are generally uncommon to fairly common along Lake Erie, where most reports are of five or fewer and the largest flights total 15–20. Fall Black-throated Blues are rare to locally uncommon within the interior counties and least numerous in southwestern Ohio. Daily totals are mostly three or fewer, although as many as 15 were reported from Buckeye Lake (Trautman 1940).

Yellow-rumped Warbler *Dendroica coronata* (Linnaeus)

While other warblers spend the winter in warm tropical climates, one regularly survives the harsh Ohio winters. The hardy Yellow-rumped Warbler overwinters in woodlands throughout the state, subsisting on poison ivy berries, but it also eats dogwood and other small berries. Its numbers, like those of all birds subsisting on fruit, fluctuate considerably in response to food availability.

Numbers of wintering Yellow-rumped Warblers have become more plentiful in recent years. Before 1940, they were accidental to casual winter visitors and were not reported annually. Their numbers gradually improved during the 1940s and 1950s, and they have been regularly encountered since 1960.

Yellow-rumped Warblers are normally casual to rare winter residents in northern Ohio, where they are mostly observed as individuals or small flocks of 3–11. However, they can be plentiful within red cedar groves on Kelleys Island (Erie County). Usually 30–50 winter in these groves and 300 were counted on December 5, 1984 (Peterjohn 1985b). In the central counties, Yellow-rumped Warblers are normally rare winter residents. During most winters, they are encountered as scattered individuals. Small flocks of 3–15+ are observed when fruit is abundant. As many as 118 were tallied on the 1979 Columbus Christmas Bird Count and 117 on the 1968 Buckeye Lake Christmas Bird Count. These warblers become locally uncommon winter residents in southern Ohio. They are usually observed in flocks of eight or fewer, with infrequent groups of 20–35+. Larger concentrations are possible, as evidenced by 100+ in the Forestville area (Hamilton County) during the winter of 1950–1951 (Kemsies and Randle 1953) and occasional Christmas Bird Count totals of 100–150+.

During relatively warm springs, the first migrants return by the last week of March. In other years, they may not appear until mid-April. Yellow-rumpeds are our most numerous migrant warblers, becoming common to abundant between April 20 and May 12. Their numbers decline markedly after May 15, and the last migrants normally depart by May 20–27. A few linger in the northern half of Ohio into the first week of June.

Spring migrants regularly occur in woodlands, parks, cemeteries, and other wooded habitats. During some years, only 15–40 Yellow-rumpeds are observed daily and the largest lakefront flights are composed of 100–150. In other years, their numbers can be astounding, and daily totals of 100+ are encountered throughout the state. The largest inland flights are composed of 500 at Dayton and 200–500 at Buckeye Lake (Mathena et al. 1984, Trautman 1940). These numbers are dwarfed by flights along western Lake Erie: 5,000 on May 6, 1972; 2,000 on May 7, 1983; and 1,900 on May 10, 1996 (Campbell 1973, Conlon and Harlan 1996a, Peterjohn 1983c).

Summering Yellow-rumped Warblers were unknown in Ohio until 1989, when a singing male was reported from Lucas County (Peterjohn 1989d). During the 1990s, male Yellow-rumpeds were noted at Mohican State Forest during four years beginning in 1992, including a "female or immature" in 1994 (Brock 1994d). Breeding has not been established there. Midsummer reports from the Oak Openings area in 1991–1992, Headlands Beach State Park in 1995, and Medina County in 1997 pertain to nonbreeders (Brock 1995d, Harlan 1992d, Rosche 1997c). Other reports from northern Ohio during the first half of June are probably very tardy spring migrants.

While early fall Yellow-rumpeds have been noted along Lake Erie by August 20–25, they normally return during September 8–15. They have appeared in the central and southern counties by the first week of September but are expected by September 20–27. The largest lakefront flights are noted between September 27 and October 20, while inland flights are usually about one week later. The southward migration continues through November 10–20.

Migrating Yellow-rumped Warblers are as numerous in fall as in spring. Daily totals of 25–100+ along Lake Erie and 10–50 inland are expected during October, with tallies of 200–400+ possible during larger movements. Occasional large flights have been encountered, including an estimated 7,500 at the Crane Creek State Park/Magee Marsh Wildlife Refuge complex on October 5, 1985, and 1,000–1,200+ at Buckeye Lake on several October dates during the 1920s and 1930s (Peterjohn 1986a, Trautman 1940).

Most Ohio records are of the eastern "Myrtle" race. However, the western "Audubon's" race has been well documented on three occasions. Adult male "Audubon's" Warblers were reported from the Cleveland area at Shaker Lakes on April 30–May 3, 1931, and at Richmond Heights on October 5, 1941 (Williams 1950). Another report of this accidental visitor was well described from Wooster on April 23–28, 1992 (Brock 1992a).

Black-throated Gray Warbler *Dendroica nigrescens* (Townsend)

An accidental visitor to Ohio, the first substantiated Black-throated Gray Warbler was collected on the Ohio State University campus in Columbus on

November 15, 1950. This warbler was initially discovered by Gene Rea and Edward Thomas earlier in the day as it foraged with a small flock of juncos and Ruby-crowned Kinglets (Thomas 1951). The next substantiated record was provided by a Black-throated Gray discovered near Athens on November 19, 1969. It was photographed during its daily visits to a suet feeder through December 16 (Hall 1970a). Surprisingly, single Black-throated Gray Warblers were encountered on four occasions during the 1990s: at Baldwin Lake (Cuyahoga County) during April 26–May 3, 1992 (Harlan 1992e); in Georgetown (Brown County) between November 25, 1992, and February 16, 1993 (Pasquale 1993); at Independence (Cuyahoga County) on December 11–18, 1993 (Turner and Turner 1994); and at Sugarcreek on November 11–28, 1994 (Brock 1995a).

In addition to these reports, there are at least eleven spring sightings from the Cleveland area, but only the Black-throated Gray discovered at Cleveland on April 25–26, 1967, and studied by many birders appears to be correctly identified (Newman 1969). The other records lack documentation and verification by knowledgeable observers.

Black-throated Gray Warblers normally breed in the mountains of western North America, from southern Canada to southeastern Arizona and northern Baja California (AOU 1998). They mostly winter in Mexico, with small numbers in southern Texas, southern Arizona, and southern California. This western warbler has proven to be an accidental but regular vagrant to eastern North America, primarily during late fall and early winter.

Black-throated Green Warbler *Dendroica virens* (Gmelin)

The first spring Black-throated Green Warblers are normally resident males returning to their territories within the southeastern counties. These males may appear during the first week of April and are regularly noted by April 10–16. Overflights are occasionally detected across the state during April 1–8. The first spring migrants are expected outside of their breeding range during April 20–27 within the southern and central counties and April 25–May 2 along Lake Erie. Their

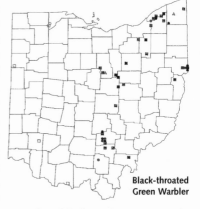

Black-throated
Green Warbler

northward migration peaks between May 5 and 20. The last migrants normally depart from the interior counties by May 25–30, but stragglers remain along Lake Erie through the first week of June.

Black-throated Greens are fairly common to common spring migrants within woods, riparian corridors, parks, cemeteries, and shaded residential areas. These migrants are most numerous along Lake Erie, where 10–30 are observed daily and flights of 50–100 are not surprising. Larger movements produced as many as 400 at Magee Marsh Wildlife Area on May 7, 1983 (Peterjohn 1983c). Similar numbers are not normally apparent within the interior counties, where daily totals are usually 15 or fewer. Spring flights may produce inland counts of 20–40, but only Trautman (1940) reported as many as 50–125 daily at Buckeye Lake during the 1920s and 1930s.

Ohio has always supported a small breeding population of Black-throated Green Warblers. Initially, nesting pairs were restricted to the northern counties, especially northeastern Ohio east of Cleveland (Williams 1950). A few pairs also occasionally summered and probably nested in Lorain County (Baird 1905, Jones 1910). By the mid-1930s, nesting warblers were very locally distributed in Ashtabula, Lake, Geauga, Cuyahoga, and Mahoning Counties (Hicks 1933a, 1935a). They were rare to uncommon except within the Chagrin River watershed, where 10–19 pairs were counted at Little Mountain between 1933 and 1938 (Williams 1950). Along the unglaciated Allegheny Plateau, Black-throated Greens were uncommon residents within the Shawnee State Forest in Scioto County, but only a few pairs were known from Adams, Jackson, Hocking, Lawrence, Fairfield, and Knox Counties (Hicks 1935a, 1937a). The only other breeding Black-throated Greens were in Ashland County, while summering males were infrequently reported from Williams and Lucas Counties in northwestern Ohio (Campbell 1968, Hicks 1935a).

Breeding populations subsequently expanded along the unglaciated Allegheny Plateau, where nesting warblers moved northward through the hemlock forests, appearing in Columbiana County by the early 1960s (Hall 1962b). Numbers of breeding pairs also increased within the northeastern counties. These increasing trends continued into recent decades. During the 1980s, the statewide population was estimated at 250–350 pairs (Peterjohn and Rice 1991). By 1997, Mohican State Forest hosted 187 territorial males, and estimates from other known breeding locations indicated that the statewide population may exceed 600 pairs.

Black-throated Green Warblers are now locally distributed summer residents along the entire Allegheny Plateau. They are fairly common to common across Hocking County, Mohican State Forest, the Little Beaver Creek watershed in Columbiana County, Hinckley Metropark in Medina County, and the Chagrin River watershed in portions of Cuyahoga, Lake, and Geauga Counties (Peterjohn and Rice 1991). As many as 10–20+ males can be counted daily at these localities. These warblers are casual to locally uncommon residents elsewhere within the eastern third of the state, with scattered records from Adams and Scioto Counties north to Ashtabula County. A few pairs may regularly nest in pine plantations in Richland County (Peterjohn and Rice 1991), but summering Black-throated Greens are generally accidental in the remainder of Ohio. Males sporadically appear in the Oak Openings area, where nesting has not been confirmed. Other reports from the western counties are of non-breeding males briefly observed in unsuitable habitats.

Breeding Black-throated Green Warblers are mostly restricted to hemlock or mixed hemlock-deciduous forests. A few males are also found within mixed deciduous-pine woodlands. They occupy the canopies of these woods and Kotesovec (1994b, 1995) provides most of the available information on their nesting biology in Ohio. Within the southeastern counties, their breeding activities begin by late April or early May and fledglings are observed by mid-June. In the northeastern counties, nesting begins during the last half of May, and the young warblers fledge during the last week of June and July.

Black-throated Greens have a protracted fall migration. Early migrants return to western Lake Erie by July 25–August 2 and Cincinnati by August 7 (Campbell 1968, Harlan 1993d, Peterjohn 1982a). During most years, they appear along the lakefront by August 25–September 2 and the interior counties during the first week of September. Their southward movements peak between September 15 and October 8. The last migrants normally depart by October 12–18, although stragglers occasionally remain as late as November 18, 1948, at Cleveland (Williams 1950).

These fall warblers are fairly common to common migrants. They are most numerous along Lake Erie, where 5–20 are observed daily. Large flights are less frequent than in spring, although as many as 200 were reported from the Toledo area on September 23, 1944 (Campbell 1968). Inland fall totals are 5–15 individuals daily, with occasional flights of 20–30. The only larger flights were reported by Trautman (1940) at Buckeye Lake, where up to 100 Black-throated Greens were tallied daily in late September.

Townsend's Warbler *Dendroica townsendi* (Townsend)

As occupants of mountain coniferous forests, Townsend's Warblers breed in western North America from Alaska to northern Oregon and Wyoming. Their winter range normally extends from California south to Costa Rica (AOU 1998). Like many other long-distance migrants, a few of these warblers wander from this established range and become accidental visitors elsewhere in North America.

The first accepted record of this accidental visitor to Ohio was a male Townsend's Warbler discovered along the bird trail at Magee Marsh Wildlife

Area, Lucas County, on April 7, 1973, by Elliot Tramer and members of his ornithology class from Toledo University (Kleen and Bush 1973c). The bird was closely studied, carefully described, and its distinctive song heard on several occasions. It was observed for twenty minutes as it foraged with several Yellow-rumped Warblers in the leafless box elders along the trail. Another singing male Townsend's Warbler was discovered near Maumee (Lucas County) on April 30, 1983. It was studied for more than 45 minutes as it foraged in riparian woods along Swan Creek with other migrant warblers and kinglets (Anderson 1998).

Blackburnian Warbler *Dendroica fusca* (Müller).

Blackburnian
Warbler

For those who enjoy birds for their attractive plumages, this species becomes an immediate favorite. Few birds match the visual impact made by a male Blackburnian Warbler in full sunlight against the bare branches of a budding tree. His vivid orange and black face pattern adds sparks of brilliant color to a somber landscape, a sure sign that spring has arrived. Yet, once the trees fully acquire their leaves, a male may be impossible to discover as he sings from the canopy of a large tree.

This attractive warbler is a widely distributed and fairly common spring migrant. Daily totals seldom exceed 5–12 individuals. While large flights produce occasional tallies of 30–50 in central and northern Ohio, the largest reported movement totaled 100 in the Toledo area on May 24, 1947 (Campbell 1968). Overflights have appeared across the state by April 15–19, but the first migrants normally return to the southern half of Ohio during the last week of April and to the lakefront during the first week of May. Their maximum abundance is attained between May 7 and 20. Smaller numbers remain through the end of the month, with lingering males along Lake Erie through June 7–15.

Fewer Blackburnian Warblers are observed during autumn. They are uncommon to fairly common fall migrants throughout Ohio; daily totals seldom exceed 3–10 individuals. The largest fall flight totaled 60 at Buckeye Lake on September 26, 1925 (Trautman 1940). They are relatively early migrants and have returned to Lake Erie during the last week of July and Greene County by July 28 (Harlan 1993d). However, the first fall migrants normally return to the lakefront by August 18–25 and to the interior counties during the last week of August. Their passage is mostly completed by September 25–30; only a few remain into the first week of October. The latest migrants have been reported through October 20–22. While there is one December sight record, it lacks supporting details.

Blackburnian Warblers were unknown as summer residents in Ohio until 1931, when males were discovered in Ashtabula County at the former Pymatuning Bog and in Kingsville Township. A nest was discovered at the latter site during 1932 (Hicks 1933a). During 1933 and 1934, one or two pairs summered at Little Mountain, within the Chagrin River watershed (Williams 1950). These records established Blackburnian Warblers as casual or accidental summer residents in extreme northeastern Ohio, a status they maintained through the 1980s. While none were reported from Ashtabula County since the 1930s, one or two pairs sporadically appeared at Little Mountain, Stebbin's Gulch, and other nearby locations in Lake and Geauga Counties. In addition, a pair nested at Lake Rockwell in Portage County between 1984 and 1986 (Peterjohn and Rice 1991), and a few nonbreeders were reported from several other locations.

Along the unglaciated Allegheny Plateau, a summering Blackburnian Warbler was discovered by Worth Randle at Old Man's Cave-Cedar Falls State Parks in Hocking County during 1954. Annual June surveys of this location between 1960 and 1975 recorded at least one male each year, with a maximum of six in 1961. They disappeared during 1976 (Peterjohn 1982e). During the 1980s, isolated Blackburnians occasionally appeared in Hocking County, Vinton County, and Mohican State Forest, but these males were most likely unmated (Peterjohn and Rice 1991).

During the 1990s, only Mohican State Forest consistently hosted summering Blackburnian Warblers; four or fewer males are noted most years, with a maximum of 13 in 1997. They remain casual summer visitors in Hocking County, where the most recent nesting attempt was documented in 1990 (Peterjohn 1990d). They are accidental to casual summer residents in the northeastern counties. They nested at Hinckley (Medina County) during 1993 (Kotesovec 1993) and sporadically appear at locations in Lake, Geauga, and Summit Counties. Blackburnians remain among our rarest breeding warblers, with a statewide population of no more than 10–15 males.

Most summering Blackburnian Warblers are found within mature hemlock forests. The only exception is at Lake Rockwell, where a nesting pair occupied an extensive stand of planted pines. There are fewer than ten confirmed nesting records, and Kotesovec (1993) provides the only detailed account of their nesting biology in the state. The few records indicate that breeding begins during late May or the first half of June; adults have been observed carrying food to nestlings during the last half of June in Hocking County and late June and early July in the northeastern counties.

Yellow-throated Warbler *Dendroica dominica* (Linnaeus)

In the nineteenth century, Yellow-throated Warblers were regarded as widely distributed summer residents, regularly encountered north to Lake Erie (Wheaton 1882). Their numbers rapidly diminished during the late 1800s (Jones 1903). Habitat availability was not a factor in this decline, but the causes were never established. By the early 1900s, these warblers had largely disappeared except for small numbers in Scioto and adjacent southern counties (Henninger 1905).

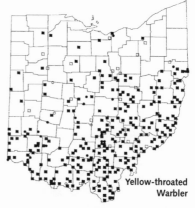

Yellow-throated
Warbler

By the mid-1920s, nesting pairs could be located along the Scioto River north to Circleville and there was a nesting attempt in Columbus during 1925 (Walker 1928d). In the 1930s, Hicks (1935a, 1937a) described Yellow-throated Warblers as very local summer residents in southern Ohio, with records from every county along the unglaciated Allegheny Plateau north to Hocking and Athens. In southwestern Ohio, he cited records from Hamilton, Clermont, and Brown Counties, although these sightings were disputed by Kemsies and Randle (1953). These warblers were rare in every county except Pike and Scioto, where 50–100 pairs may have been present. They were accidental spring visitors to the remainder of the state.

This population slowly spread northward along the unglaciated Allegheny Plateau after 1940. In southwestern Ohio, breeding pairs were recorded at Cincinnati and Dayton during the 1950s, although they did not become widely distributed until the late 1960s (Kemsies and Randle 1953, Mathena et al. 1984). Nesting pairs reappeared in central Ohio during the 1960s. Within the northern counties, spring migrants were regularly reported beginning in the 1970s, and summering pairs have been present since 1975. During the Breeding Bird Atlas, Yellow-throated Warblers were found in sixty-six counties north to Lake Erie, but were very locally distributed within the northern one-quarter of the state (Peterjohn and Rice 1991). They continued to occupy new locations in northern Ohio during the 1990s. Statewide population trends along Breeding Bird Survey routes are stable (Sauer et al. 1998), but these data are from southern and eastern Ohio, where Yellow-throated Warblers have been established for decades.

Yellow-throated Warblers are now fairly common to locally common summer residents throughout southern and unglaciated Ohio. Most reports are of 3–10 daily, with local concentrations of 12–20. They become uncommon to fairly common residents in the glaciated central counties, very locally distributed in intensively farmed areas. Summer totals seldom exceed 1–5 individuals daily in these counties. These warblers are accidental to locally uncommon residents in northern Ohio. Stream surveys produced 11 males along the Sandusky River, six along the Chagrin River, and four along the Grand River; these totals are indicative of their local abundance in northern Ohio during the 1990s. They are normally detected as scattered males and pairs elsewhere, but are absent from most intensively farmed northwestern counties.

Breeding Yellow-throated Warblers prefer large sycamores bordering creeks and rivers. They are not restricted to these habitats, however, and pairs occupy upland mixed deciduous-pine woods. Since they normally nest at considerable heights, relatively little information is available on their breeding chronology in Ohio. Within the southern counties, nesting activities are probably initiated during the last half of April, although nest construction has been reported into early June. The few nests have been discovered during May and early June, while recently fledged young appear between June 7–10 and August 11, with most before mid-July (Walker 1928d). Their breeding activities are probably delayed by one or two weeks in northern Ohio.

Spring migration is mostly resident warblers returning to their territories; the largest movements total 20–30 in the southern counties. Away from nesting locations, Yellow-throated Warblers are casual to rare spring visitors, usually as scattered individuals, with a maximum of three at lakefront migrant traps. The earliest spring migrant was reported from Pike County on March 25, 1983 (Harlan 1994f). A few migrants normally appear in the southern counties during the first week of April and are widely distributed by April 15–25. In northern Ohio, early migrants return by April 5–15, but most spring Yellow-throateds are noted between April 25 and May 15. A few stragglers are noted into early June.

Like many of our resident warblers, Yellow-throateds become inconspicuous once the males quit singing in early July. Hence, their fall migration patterns are poorly understood. These warblers begin moving southward during August 10–25. The last migrants normally depart by September 22–October 3. One in Gallia County on November 4, 1989, was very late (Hall 1990a). Fall Yellow-throated Warblers are uncommonly reported in southern Ohio but are rare elsewhere in their nesting range. These records mostly are of single warblers. They are accidental fall visitors away from known summering locations, producing an average of one report annually from the northern counties during the 1990s.

This species is an accidental winter visitor. One was reported from the Youngstown Christmas Bird Count on December 18–19, 1972. Another Yellow-throated Warbler visited a Mansfield feeder between December 6, 1981, and January 10, 1982 (Peterjohn 1982b). It disappeared during an extended period of severe weather. One survived at a Holmes County feeder through January 20, 1991 (Anderson and Kemp 1991b). The fourth winter record was provided by one that appeared at a Holmes County feeder around January 10, 1993, and was last seen alive on March 14; it was found dead a week later (Harlan 1993b). The latter individual showed characteristics of the eastern race *dominica* (Dunn 1993); all other Ohio records pertain to the *albilora* race.

Pine Warbler *Dendroica pinus* (Wilson)

As their name implies, breeding Pine Warblers are found only in tracts of mature pines. Their preferred habitats are dry ridges where tall pines are interspersed with younger deciduous trees, but they also occupy uniform pine plantations. Within these habitats, they can be inconspicuous as they forage among the outer branches of the tall pines. Only singing males are readily detected.

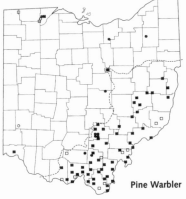

Pine Warbler

At one time, Pine Warblers were among the least known of our resident warblers. Hicks (1935a) considered them "extremely rare and local" summer residents in eastern Ohio. Scioto County hosted the largest breeding population, with an estimated 40–50 pairs. Scattered pairs and summering warblers were also known from Jackson, Hocking, Fairfield, Knox, Ashland, Lake, and Ashtabula Counties. Their breeding population increased during subsequent decades, especially along the unglaciated Allegheny Plateau. Similar trends were noted across eastern North America after 1966 (Robbins et al. 1986). These increases resulted in the establishment of small breeding populations in some glaciated counties beginning in the 1980s.

Along the unglaciated Allegheny Plateau, Pine Warblers are uncommon to fairly common but locally distributed summer residents north to Ross, Hocking, and Guernsey Counties (Peterjohn and Rice 1991). Daily totals are normally eight or fewer except in preferred areas, where 10–12 males can be counted. Elsewhere along this plateau, these warblers are generally rare residents, usually encountered as groups of three or fewer singing males, although a total of 11 were counted in Mohican State Forest during 1997.

In the glaciated counties, Pine Warblers are rare and locally distributed summer residents in northeastern Ohio. Numbers increased during the 1990s, with pairs and singing males reported from scattered locations in the Cleveland area south to Medina and Portage Counties. In northwestern Ohio, extensive pine plantations are only present within the Oak Openings, where 3–6 males have summered since 1983, and nesting was confirmed in 1987. While summering males have been reported from the Dayton area, the only breeding pairs in southwestern Ohio are known from Hamilton County (Peterjohn and Rice 1991).

Little information is available on their nesting biology in Ohio. Pine Warblers place their nests in the outer branches of tall pines, and these nests are difficult to discover. In southern Ohio, nest construction begins in mid-April. Eggs are laid by late April, and the young fledge by late May and early June. These warblers could raise two broods annually but later nesting attempts have never been reported from Ohio. Nesting activities begin several weeks later in northern Ohio, where nest construction is initiated during the first half of May, eggs are laid by late May, and the young fledge in late June and July.

The Pine Warbler is the first resident warbler returning each year. Territorial males may appear in the southern counties during the first week of March, are regularly noted by March 12–18, and become widespread by March 25–April 5. March migrants are unusual at the northern edge of the Allegheny Plateau and in the northern counties, where territorial males normally return by mid-April.

Away from their breeding range, Pine Warblers are rare to locally uncommon spring migrants. Overflights have appeared as early as March 6, 1961, at Columbus and March 15, 1986, along western Lake Erie (Mumford 1961c, Peterjohn 1986c). These overflights normally are single Pines, although 15+ appeared at Cincinnati on March 13–14, 1977 (Kleen 1977c). Most migrants pass through Ohio between April 15 and May 7, usually four or fewer daily, with occasional groups of 6–8. The last spring migrants linger into the last half of May. Unlike the resident warblers, migrant Pines are regularly observed in deciduous woods.

Their status as fall migrants is poorly understood. Other fall warblers are regularly misidentified as Pines, and many sight records have proven to be incorrect. Fall Pine Warblers are generally rare and usually encountered as scattered individuals, although small groups of 3–5 are found within their breeding range. They tend to be rather late migrants, with very few confirmed sightings before mid-September. Most appear between September 15 and October 10, with a few lingering through mid-November.

Most Pine Warblers spend the winter months in the southeastern United States. They are relatively hardy warblers, however, and a few regularly overwinter as far north as southern Missouri and southern Kentucky. The number of winter reports from Ohio has increased in recent decades. Harlan (1992e) cited approximately 30 winter sightings, of which only ten occurred before 1980. Wintering Pine Warblers have been discovered annually since 1987, with as many as three reports during some years, and there are currently more than forty records from the state. Pine Warblers are now casual early winter visitors in southern Ohio, where most records are of 1–2 individuals in pine woods during December. They are also casual winter visitors in the Toledo area but are accidental elsewhere, with reports scattered across the state. While most were noted during December, several overwintered at bird feeders.

Kirtland's Warbler *Dendroica kirtlandii* (Baird)

Kirtland's Warbler was first described from a specimen collected by Charles Pease in Lakewood (Cuyahoga County) on May 13, 1851 (Williams 1950). Pease presented the specimen to Dr. Jared Kirtland, who sent it to Spencer Baird at the National Museum in Washington. Baird named the species in Kirtland's honor, recognizing his significant contributions to our understanding of the natural history of the Ohio and Mississippi River valleys.

This warbler was known only as a very rare migrant until its limited breeding range was discovered within young jack pine woods in the northern lower peninsula of Michigan. These warblers winter in the Bahamas and adjacent islands (AOU 1998). Their migration corridor crosses Ohio, and the entire population probably passes over the state each spring and autumn.

Kirtland's Warblers are the rarest of the eastern wood warblers that regularly appear in Ohio. The exact number of sightings is uncertain, because a number of reports are undocumented and their identification is questionable, especially individuals in obscure fall plumages. There are at least forty-seven reports that are probably credible, some of which are based on specimens, photographs, and thoroughly prepared descriptions.

Most Kirtland's Warblers are detected during spring, when they are casually encountered along western Lake Erie and accidental visitors elsewhere. Mayfield (1988) reported at least thirty spring sightings, mostly from the northern half of Ohio. However, there are very few records from the northeastern counties after 1900. Six additional spring records were documented during the 1990s, four along western Lake Erie and singles at Willoughby on May 15, 1994, and in the Oak Openings on May 10, 1996 (Brock 1994c, Conlon and Harlan 1996a). Spring records are of 1–2 individuals, normally appearing between May 10 and 25. The only confirmed April record was at Tiffin on April 30, 1975 (Kleen 1975c).

Considerably fewer Kirtland's Warblers are observed in autumn. Mayfield (1988) cites only nine fall records widely scattered across the state. The only recent report was from Paulding County on September 21, 1995 (Dunakin 1996). These accidental fall migrants have been reported between the last week of August and early October, but all confirmed sightings are during September.

Kirtland's Warblers were detected more frequently before 1970, despite substantially greater numbers of birdwatchers searching for this species in recent years. Kirtland's Warblers averaged one Ohio record every two or three years during each decade through the 1960s. In contrast, there were only two published sightings during the 1970s and three reports in the 1980s. The population of this endangered warbler substantially increased during the 1990s, which is reflected in the seven records during this decade.

Prairie Warbler *Dendroica discolor* (Vieillot)

This occupant of abandoned fields overgrown with shrubs and saplings has gradually extended its breeding range northward during the twentieth century. In the late 1800s, Prairie Warblers were rare spring visitors throughout Ohio (Jones 1903). The first summer residents were recorded from Scioto County, where Prairies were considered "not common" in 1905 and the first nest was discovered in 1908 (Henninger 1905, 1908).

Prairie Warbler

Their initial northward expansion was restricted to the unglaciated Allegheny Plateau. By the mid-1930s, breeding Prairie Warblers were found in every county north to Muskingum, Morgan, and Washington (Hicks 1935a, 1937a). They were locally numerous in Hocking, Jackson, and Vinton Counties but were rather rare elsewhere. By 1960, summering Prairies reached the northern edge of the unglaciated plateau.

Prairie Warblers also expanded into glaciated Ohio. Breeding pairs initially appeared at Cincinnati in 1958 and Dayton in 1961 (Mathena et al. 1984, Nolan 1958d). Few nonbreeding summer visitors were reported from the glaciated central and northern counties until the late 1960s. Territorial males were initially recorded at Toledo in 1968 and Cleveland in 1976, although nesting was not established at either area for several years (Campbell 1973, Kleen 1976c). This gradual range expansion apparently ended during the 1980s.

Breeding Bird Survey data indicate that statewide populations have remained stable since 1966 (Sauer et al. 1998).

Breeding Prairie Warblers are most numerous on the red cedar-covered hillsides of Adams County, where they are common to abundant residents. Daily totals of 25–75+ are possible throughout the county. Elsewhere along the unglaciated Allegheny Plateau, these warblers are uncommon to locally common residents; 3–10 are noted daily, with local concentrations of 15–20+ in areas where shrubby successional habitats are plentiful. Prairie Warblers are generally uncommon summer residents in southwestern Ohio, becoming locally fairly common in portions of Highland, Brown, Clermont, and Warren Counties and locally rare in urban and heavily farmed areas. Most sightings are of five or fewer individuals, with local totals of 8–12+. The fewest Prairies inhabit the glaciated central and northern counties, where they become accidental to locally rare residents. Scattered males and pairs are regularly observed near Columbus, the Mansfield-Ashland area, the Oak Openings, and several sites near Cleveland, but are sporadically encountered in other northern counties (Peterjohn and Rice 1991).

Prairie Warblers nest in dry brushy fields adorned with pines, red cedars, and deciduous saplings less than ten feet high. They normally disappear when the woody vegetation becomes too dense and tall. In southern Ohio, nesting activities begin during May. Most clutches are reported between May 15 and June 15, and nests with young have been discovered by the last week of May (Braund 1940a, Walker 1928d). Fledglings are expected by mid-June, with late clutches producing young into July. Their breeding chronology is delayed by several weeks in northern Ohio, where the first clutches are laid in late May and early June and the young fledge during July.

As spring migrants, the earliest Prairie Warbler appeared near Wilmington on April 3, 1997 (Fazio 1997b), and overflights have been noted across the state by April 10–16. In southern and unglaciated Ohio, Prairie Warblers are regularly encountered by April 20–25, and all return by May 10–15. This movement largely comprises residents arriving on their breeding territories. Elsewhere, Prairie Warblers are casual to rare spring migrants, normally encountered as single individuals, with occasional groups of 3–5. Most migrants appear between April 25 and May 15, with stragglers along Lake Erie into the last half of May.

Prairies become inconspicuous once the males stop singing in early July, and their southward migration is poorly understood. Fall Prairie Warblers are normally rare to uncommon along the unglaciated plateau and accidental to rare elsewhere. Records mostly are of single warblers. Their southward movements may peak between August 15 and September 15, with stragglers through October 10. A few have been discovered during the last half of October, and the latest well-documented report is from Cincinnati on November 8, 1975 (Kleen 1976a).

Palm Warbler *Dendroica palmarum* (Gmelin)

During migrations, Palm Warblers are mostly encountered in brushy thickets, wooded fencerows, woodland edges, and other shrubby habitats. They also occur in weedy fields during fall. Many are found in fairly open habitats, such as shrubs along Lake Erie beaches and bushes scattered within cemeteries and parks. Palms are regularly observed feeding on the ground near bushes, constantly pumping their tails and making short flights in pursuit of insects.

While their numbers fluctuate from year to year, Palm Warblers are most numerous during spring. Overflights have been reported from several locations as early as the first week of March, but these birds may have overwintered locally. There are also sightings during March 24–April 7. They normally return by April 20–28. Palm Warblers are most numerous during the first two weeks of May, when they become fairly common to locally abundant migrants along Lake Erie but uncommon to fairly common inland. Daily lakefront totals are normally 5–25, but large flights along western Lake Erie produce estimates of 100–200+. Fewer than ten daily are noted at most interior counties, although flights produce as many as 25–50+ at scattered locations, and 132 were counted at the Cuyahoga Valley Recreation Area on May 10, 1997 (Fazio 1997b). Most Palms depart by May 17–23, with stragglers through May 30–June 4 along Lake Erie. One at the Cuyahoga Valley Recreation Area on June 13, 1992, may have been an exceptionally late migrant or nonbreeding summer visitor (Harlan 1992d).

The earliest fall Palm Warblers returned to Buckeye Lake by August 9, 1933, and Cleveland on August 10, 1997 (Rosche 1997c, Trautman 1940), but even late August records are very unusual. They normally appear between September 8 and 15. Most fall Palms pass through Ohio between September 20 and October 10. They are generally fairly common migrants along Lake Erie and uncommon inland. Daily totals seldom exceed 10, and the largest concentrations total 25–30. Most migrants depart by the third week of October, with small numbers lingering into November.

Palm Warblers are casual early winter visitors; there are more than fifty published records scattered throughout Ohio, with the greatest number from the southwestern and central counties. They are mostly encountered as individuals, with occasional flocks of 3–5, normally during December and early January. Most disappear by January 15 and very few have overwintered. One survived the winter of 1926–1927 at Greenlawn Cemetery in Columbus by feeding on the ground under dense evergreens and shrubs (Walker 1928a).

Other Palm Warblers have survived into February at Columbus (Mayfield 1947b), Buckeye Lake (Trautman 1940), and Holmes County during two winters (Harlan 1993b, 1995b).

Our Palm Warblers are normally of the western race characterized by mostly grayish underparts. The eastern race has entirely yellow underparts and is apparently a very rare migrant and early winter visitor. They are most likely to appear during spring along Lake Erie and within the northeastern counties following days with strong northeasterly winds. They have also been noted along central Lake Erie in autumn. During the 1990s, a few appeared in Holmes and Tuscarawas Counties during late autumn and winter (Dunn 1993, Yoder 1992).

Bay-breasted Warbler *Dendroica castanea* (Wilson)

Bay-breasted Warblers are occupants of boreal forests across northern New England and eastern Canada (AOU 1998). Although they nest in conifers, spring migrants are found in all types of woodlands. Overflights appear as early as April 19–21. However, they normally return during the first week of May. Their numbers reach a decided peak during the third week of May, when they become fairly common to common migrants. Spring totals are generally 3–20 daily, although large flights produce concentrations of 100–150 along western Lake Erie and 80–100 at Columbus. Most migrants depart by May 25–31, with small numbers lingering along Lake Erie through the first week of June. Late migrants remained at Toledo through June 13, 1948, and Cleveland until June 14, 1964 (Campbell 1968, Rosche 1992). This species has not summered in Ohio, but one at Headlands Beach State Park on June 23, 1996, may have been an exceptionally late migrant or nonbreeding summer visitor (Brock 1996d).

When their population levels are high, fall Bay-breasteds make up a sizable proportion of the mixed-species warbler flocks visiting woodland, edge, and shrubby habitats. While the earliest migrant returned to Cleveland by July 17 (Rosche 1992), there are few additional records before August 10. They are expected to return to Lake Erie by August 18–22 and can be fairly numerous by August 25. They regularly appear in the interior counties during the first week of September. Fall Bay-breasteds are generally fairly common to common during September but become uncommon when population levels are low. Daily totals are normally 20 or fewer, while tallies of 30–40+ are regular and as many as 100–150 have been reported along Lake Erie and in central Ohio. Most depart by October 7–12. Only occasional stragglers are noted during the last half of October, and there are no published records after October 30.

Their numbers are subject to considerable annual fluctuations, mostly the result of periodic outbreaks of the spruce budworm caterpillars within their boreal forest breeding range. When the caterpillars are abundant, warbler populations exhibit substantial increases. These high population levels are maintained for several years until the outbreak ends, followed by a rapid decline to more typical numbers.

Blackpoll Warbler *Dendroica striata* (Forster)

The status and distribution of Blackpoll Warblers is similar to the Bay-breasteds. Both warblers are relatively late spring migrants en route to their boreal forest breeding grounds. Both are subject to substantial population fluctuations in response to spruce budworm outbreaks. Even their fall plumages are very similar.

Blackpoll Warblers undergo a truly incredible fall migration. They are among the very few songbirds who fly directly from North America to their wintering grounds in South America (Nisbet et al. 1995). The initial stages of this migration are a series of relatively short flights from their breeding grounds to the Atlantic Coast. During these flights, the warblers accumulate considerable fat deposits, which eventually fuel their several-thousand-mile transoceanic flight.

Blackpoll Warblers are generally fairly common to common fall migrants, becoming uncommon in the southwestern and west-central counties. These migrants are most numerous along Lake Erie, where daily totals of 8–35 are frequent. Large flights may produce 50–100 daily; there were as many as 200 at Toledo on September 25, 1943 (Campbell 1968). Within the interior counties, daily totals seldom exceed 3–20. Only Trautman (1940) reported substantial inland movements of as many as 150 daily at Buckeye Lake during the 1920s and 1930s. While the first fall migrants return to western Lake Erie by July 21–25, they regularly appear along the lakefront during the last half of August and become common by September 1–5. Within the interior counties, there are few late August records and they normally appear between September 5 and 10. Fall Blackpolls are regularly encountered through October 5–12. Only stragglers remain until the first week of November.

Blackpolls are uncommon to fairly common spring migrants. Daily spring totals seldom exceed 5–10 individuals. The largest flights produce concentrations of 30–50. Unusually early overflights include an April 16, 1875, specimen from central Ohio and several sightings by April 17–18 (Borror 1950). However, the first migrants normally appear during April 30–May 7. Their peak spring movement occurs between May 15 and 25. Most depart before May 30, with stragglers into early June.

While migrant Blackpolls linger along Lake Erie into the second week of June, they are accidental nonbreeding summer visitors. An unmated male remained at Magee Marsh Wildlife Area into early July of 1985 (Peterjohn 1985d), while others have been noted in the Cleveland area through June 21, 1981, and June 23, 1996 (Brock 1996d, Rosche 1992).

Cerulean Warbler *Dendroica cerulea* (Wilson)

When the first Cerulean Warblers return each spring, the budding vegetation is just beginning to emerge, and these attractive warblers may be forced to feed relatively close to the ground. A migrant in Hamilton County on April 9, 1991, was early (Harlan 1991a), since they normally return to the southern counties by April 18–25 and along Lake Erie during the first week of May. Most resident Ceruleans appear by May 12–17 and very few are detected at lakefront migrant traps after May 20. This northward migration is mostly

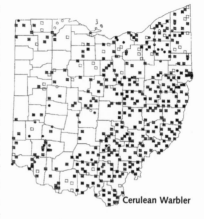

Cerulean Warbler

resident warblers returning to their territories, and tallies of 5–30+ daily are possible in the southern and eastern counties. They are uncommon spring migrants elsewhere, mostly appearing as scattered individuals, although as many as 10–15 have been reported along Lake Erie.

As soon as the foliage is fully developed, Cerulean Warblers retreat to the canopies of tall trees, where they remain throughout the summer. Breeding pairs occupy mature deciduous woodlands. While they prefer upland oak-hickory and beech forests, Ceruleans also readily occupy mesic beech-maple woodlands and mixed riparian corridors.

Their historic status and distribution reflected their dependence on mature wooded habitats. In the late 1800s, Jones (1903) considered them "not uncommon" summer residents throughout Ohio. During the twentieth century, their populations improved in most southern and eastern counties, where extensive mature woodlands became more prevalent. By the mid-1930s, Ceruleans were among the most numerous woodland warblers along the Allegheny Plateau (Hicks 1935a). They remained fairly common to common residents within these counties. In contrast, their numbers steadily declined in many west-central and northwestern counties since the 1930s (Campbell 1968). These declines were reflected in similar statewide population trends along Breeding Bird Survey routes since 1966 (Sauer et al. 1998).

Cerulean Warblers are now fairly common to common summer residents in southern and eastern Ohio west to the glacial boundary and Cuyahoga and Richland Counties (Peterjohn and Rice 1991). In southwestern Ohio, they are generally fairly common residents north to southern Preble, Montgomery, and Greene Counties. Daily totals of 5–15 are noted in most southern and eastern counties, with 20–30+ in extensively wooded areas. Elsewhere, Cerulean Warblers are generally uncommon residents in the central third of the state. They become casual to uncommon and locally distributed in the northwestern counties but are absent from the most intensively farmed western counties (Peterjohn and Rice 1991). Most locations in these glaciated counties support only 1–3 territorial males, although as many as 6–12 are counted along riparian corridors and other suitable habitats.

Since their nests are located at heights of thirty to one hundred feet in the canopies of tall trees, relatively little information is available on their breeding biology. Nest construction probably begins during the first half of May and continues into June. The few nests with eggs are reported in June, but earlier nests are likely in the southern counties. Recently fledged young appear by June 18 but are mostly noted during July (Williams 1950).

Once the males quit singing, Cerulean Warblers become very inconspicuous. Even within the southern and eastern counties they are rarely observed after July 15. Their southward movements are very poorly defined. Fall migration apparently begins in August and peaks before September 15 (Trautman 1940). These migrants are invariably observed as widely scattered individuals. Most depart before September 25, with very few sightings as late as October 7–9.

Black-and-white Warbler *Mniotilta varia* (Linnaeus)

Readily recognized by their distinctive plumages and nuthatch-like behavior, Black-and-white Warblers are familiar migrants throughout Ohio. The earliest acceptable spring migrant returned to Troy by March 25, 1991 (Harlan 1991a), and other overflights have been noted during April 2–8. They normally appear in the southern counties by April 15–20 and northern Ohio by April 25–30. Their northward migration peaks between May 3 and 18, with smaller numbers appearing through

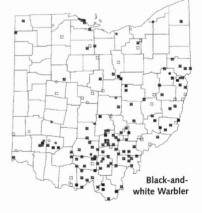

Black-and-white Warbler

May 25–28. Along Lake Erie, a few stragglers remain into the first week of June.

These migrants are fairly common to common along Lake Erie, where 3–10 are observed daily and flights produce concentrations of 25–50. Away from the lakefront, similar numbers are encountered within some southeastern counties, where migrants are augmented by breeding pairs. Elsewhere, Black-and-whites are generally fairly common migrants, with six or fewer individuals daily. In recent years, few flights from the inland glaciated counties exceed 10–15, although Trautman (1940) reported as many as 42 from Buckeye Lake in the 1920s and 1930s.

Breeding Black-and-white Warblers are fairly common residents on the unglaciated Allegheny Plateau north to Hocking, Perry, and Athens Counties (Peterjohn and Rice 1991). Most localities support five or fewer daily, although 8–15 are tallied within favorable habitats in Hocking, Scioto, Vinton, and Ross Counties. Elsewhere along the unglaciated plateau, they become uncommon to rare summer residents and are mostly encountered as widely scattered pairs. Within glaciated Ohio, Black-and-white Warblers are casual to rare summer residents within the southwestern, central, and northeastern counties, most frequently found in areas bordering the unglaciated plateau and in Warren and Clinton Counties. These summering warblers are very locally distributed and many may be unmated. They are largely absent from west-central and north-western Ohio, except for a few males occupying woodlands near western Lake Erie.

Their distribution and relative abundance have not appreciably changed since the mid-1930s, except for the disappearance of a small breeding population in northwestern Ohio (Campbell 1968, Hicks 1935a). But nesting Black-and-whites were more widely distributed during the nineteenth century. Langdon (1879) considered them common summer residents at Cincinnati, where there have been few summer records since 1900 (Kemsies and Randle 1953). Jones (1910) regularly observed a few breeding pairs in Lorain and Erie Counties around the turn of the twentieth century. This decline was probably related to habitat destruction.

Nesting Black-and-white Warblers normally prefer extensive woodlands with dense understories and shrub layers, occupying edge habitats as well as forest interiors. In southeastern Ohio, they are mostly found on dry wooded hillsides. The former population in the northwestern counties inhabited swamp forests (Campbell 1968). But these warblers are not necessarily restricted to extensive woods. Several pairs occupy young wooded corridors only 100–150 feet wide along the Scioto River in Ross County.

Their nests are expertly hidden on the ground, usually at the base of a tree or shrub. In the southeastern counties, nesting activities begin in late April or early May, since fledglings are reported by the first week of June. These activities probably begin one or two weeks later elsewhere. Nests with eggs have been discovered between May 29 and June 14 in northern Ohio, while recently fledged young appear during the first half of July (Campbell 1968, Hicks 1933a).

Black-and-white Warblers can be early fall migrants. Campbell (1968) reports probable migrants at Toledo by July 7, and they occasionally appear within the northern and central counties before the end of the month. Their southward movement normally begins by August 5–15 and continues through September 22–30. The last migrants usually depart by October 7–10, but stragglers remain into November, with at least three sightings from the Cleveland area and one at Columbus. An exceptionally late migrant was noted at Kent on December 16, 1979 (Kleen 1980b).

Fewer Black-and-whites are detected as fall migrants. They are generally fairly common along Lake Erie, where most sightings are of six or fewer individuals, with occasional flights of 18–25. These migrants are uncommon to fairly common in most inland counties, with 1–4 observed daily. The largest inland movements involve 10–12 individuals.

American Redstart *Setophaga ruticilla* (Linnaeus)

This distinctive warbler is one of our more numerous migrants. American Redstarts visit all types of woodlands, from swamp forests and second-growth woods to parks, cemeteries, and shaded residential areas. Feeding in low shrubs or high in the canopy, they are certain to be noticed as they actively flit from branch to branch.

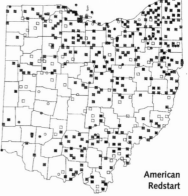

American Redstart

The earliest overflights appeared at Cincinnati on April 13, 1994 (Harlan 1994c), and elsewhere by April 18–22. Spring migrants normally return during the first week of May. Their numbers peak between May 10 and 25, and they frequently become the most numerous migrant warbler during the last half of May. Numbers diminish by May 30, but stragglers regularly remain into the first week of June. These migrants are common to abundant along Lake Erie, with 15–30 encountered daily and flights producing concentrations of 75–250+. Redstarts are fairly common to common spring migrants in most inland counties, where daily totals normally are 5–15 and sizable movements involve 30–100 individuals.

Their status as summer residents has changed considerably since the late 1800s, when American Redstarts were considered common residents throughout Ohio (Jones 1903). In 1935 Hicks (1935a) recorded breeding redstarts from 68 counties. They were most numerous within the eastern third of the state and the swamp forests of northwestern Ohio but were very locally distributed or absent elsewhere. In eastern Ohio, they were most numerous in the northeastern counties and within Lawrence, Scioto, and Adams Counties but were uncommon to rare elsewhere (Hicks 1935a, 1937a).

Redstarts experienced local declines during subsequent decades. Near Toledo, they remained numerous until 1940 but became rare after 1950 (Campbell 1968). Similar reductions were apparent in a few eastern counties. However, population trends along Breeding Bird Survey routes have been stable since the mid-1960s (Sauer et al. 1998), and the Breeding Bird Atlas discovered more summer residents than were previously thought to occur (Peterjohn and Rice 1991).

American Redstarts are uncommon to common summer residents across northern and eastern Ohio, least numerous in intensively farmed northwestern counties and east-central counties where strip mining is prevalent. Summer totals are generally 2–12 daily, although 15–20+ are counted in some northeastern counties. They are casual to rare residents elsewhere but are absent from some intensively farmed western counties. While they frequently occur as isolated pairs, nesters also form loose associations. It is not unusual to find 5–10+ pairs nesting at one locality, yet they are absent from nearby woods.

Breeding redstarts occupy young woods with dense understories and shrub layers, preferring swamp forests and mesic woods along streams. Nest construction is initiated by May 15–25 and continues into June. The first clutches are laid by May 19–28, but most are discovered in early June. Renesting attempts produce clutches into the first week of July (Sturm 1945, Trautman 1940). Recently fledged young appear by June 12 but are more likely to be detected in late June and July.

American Redstarts have a fairly protracted fall migration. The first arrivals may return to Lake Erie by the last week of July but normally appear during August 10–20. Fall migrants are expected within most interior counties by August 25–30. They are generally numerous throughout September and early October but normally depart by October 10–15. Stragglers produced two November records from Cleveland and single sightings from Cincinnati and Erie County, while an exceptionally late redstart was discovered near Cleveland through December 8, 1973 (Hammond 1973).

Along Lake Erie, American Redstarts are fairly common to common fall visitors, with most reports of 25 or fewer daily. A few large flights produce concentrations of 75–130+. They become uncommon to fairly common fall migrants within the inland counties. Most September totals are ten or fewer daily, with occasional concentrations of 15–50.

Prothonotary Warbler *Protonotaria citrea* (Boddaert)

Prothonotary
Warbler

Perched on a dead snag in a wooded swamp, a male Prothonotary Warbler looks like a golden-orange jewel in the morning sunlight. One of the most stunning warblers, he is not reticent about showing off his exquisite plumage as he forages along the margins of a swamp, nor about declaring his territory from an exposed perch. His loud song rings through the area, a distinctive *sweet-sweet-sweet-sweet* on one pitch.

Prothonotary Warblers are normally associated with wooded swamps in the southern United States. But they find suitable breeding habitats within Ohio, even though relatively few shrubby swamps remain. Fairly adaptable, the Prothonotaries also reside along the wooded margins of reservoirs, large rivers, quiet backwaters, and ponds.

Prothonotary Warblers were always locally distributed summer residents. Hicks (1935a) cited breeding records from twenty-nine counties south to Montgomery, Pickaway, Muskingum, and Guernsey and the Buckeye Lake area, plus isolated records from Washington County. While these warblers were generally rare summer residents, many pairs were concentrated at the "canal lakes" of Buckeye, St. Marys, Loramie (Shelby County), and Indian and the Muskingum River near Ellis Dam. Trautman (1940) estimated 50–80 nesting pairs at Buckeye Lake between 1922 and 1924 but only 25–45 pairs by 1933. Similar populations were found at other lakes, while 15 pairs were counted near Ellis Dam in Muskingum County during 1934–1935 (Hicks 1936).

Their statewide distribution has changed considerably since the mid-1930s. Populations at most "canal lakes" have disappeared, although Indian Lake and Lake St. Marys still host 10–15 pairs. Prothonotaries discovered a number of breeding locations at newly constructed reservoirs and along large rivers. Their range spread southward and their overall population was probably increased in recent decades.

Prothonotary Warblers remain locally distributed summer residents but were found in forty-nine counties during the Breeding Bird Atlas (Peterjohn and Rice 1991). Breeding pairs are scattered across the state but are least numerous in the northwestern and west-central counties. Breeding Prothonotaries are rare in many counties, with only five or fewer pairs at one to three locations. Where habitats are suitable, they become locally fairly common summer residents. The largest population resides within the Killbuck Creek valley in Wayne, Holmes, and Coshocton Counties, where 10–20+ males are noted daily. Other sizable populations are scattered along the Scioto River south of Columbus, the Little Miami River in Warren and Hamilton Counties, and within the western Lake Erie marshes. Daily totals of 5–15 individuals are possible at these locations.

Breeding Prothonotaries prefer natural cavities at heights of one to twelve feet over standing water. If natural cavities are unavailable, they readily occupy bird houses or other nest sites, including crevices in buildings, coffee cans, paper bags, minnow buckets, and even a mailbox (Campbell 1968, Petit and Fleming 1987, Trautman 1940). Their nesting activities are normally initiated during the first half of May. Nests with eggs are reported between May 15 and June 28 (Morse 1914, Trautman 1940). While some young leave the nest by June 5, they normally fledge during late June and early July. Nests with young reported through July 11–14 and dependent young observed between August 8 and 15 probably represent renesting attempts (Trautman 1940, Williams 1950).

Unusually early spring Prothonotaries have returned to several locations by April 6–10. The first migrants normally appear within the southern counties during April 20–27 and along Lake Erie by the first week of May. Most summer residents return by May 20. Their spring migration is largely residents arriving on their breeding territories. Prothonotaries are accidental to casual migrants away from established breeding sites.

Their southward movements are equally inconspicuous. According to Trautman (1940), fall Prothonotaries are most numerous between August 10 and 20, when he tallied as many as 50 daily at Buckeye Lake. The sizable breeding population comprised most of his August concentrations. Elsewhere, only 1–5 individuals compose most fall sightings. The last migrants normally depart by September 15–20. Since there are only two October sight records, the appearance of a Prothonotary at Columbus on November 11, 1963, is extraordinarily late (Petersen 1964a).

Worm-eating Warbler *Helmitheros vermivorus* (Gmelin)

As summer residents, Worm-eating Warblers only occupy the understory and shrub layers within the interior of extensive mature forests. Unobtrusive, they are frequently overlooked as they forage within the underbrush. Only singing males are fairly conspicuous, delivering their dry buzzing trill from a tall perch, frequently as high as forty to fifty feet.

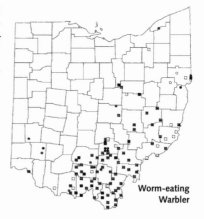

Worm-eating Warbler

Breeding Worm-eating Warblers have always been most numerous along the unglaciated Allegheny Plateau. They are uncommon to fairly common residents along this plateau north to Ross, Hocking, Athens, and Washington Counties, becoming uncommon to rare and locally distributed north to Columbiana, Holmes, and southern Ashland Counties (Peterjohn and Rice 1991). They are most numerous in Hocking, Ross, Vinton, Pike, Scioto, and Adams Counties, where 10–25+ are recorded daily. Summer totals seldom exceed 4–6 in other unglaciated counties, although a total of 19 were counted in Mohican State Forest during 1997.

Within southwestern Ohio, Worm-eating Warblers are rare and locally distributed summer residents north to Montgomery and Warren Counties. This population is composed of scattered pairs and singing males within parks and along steep wooded valleys bordering large rivers (Kemsies and Randle 1953, Mathena et al. 1984).

Breeding Worm-eating Warblers have not been confirmed elsewhere. There are no summer records from the glaciated central counties. In northern Ohio, anecdotal nineteenth-century nesting records from Cuyahoga and Ashtabula Counties are not considered valid (Jones 1903). In recent years, summering males have been located in Geauga, Summit, and Lake Counties but were believed to be unmated (Peterjohn and Rice 1991). At Toledo, the only summer record is furnished by a nonbreeder observed on June 16, 1930 (Campbell 1940).

Little information is available on their breeding biology within Ohio. Worm-eating Warblers nest on the ground, frequently near the base of small saplings. Nest construction apparently begins in May, and the first clutches are laid during the last half of the month and early June. Recently fledged young appear during the last half of June and July.

Worm-eating Warblers become difficult to locate after early July. Although their fall migration is poorly defined, these movements apparently begin by August 20–25 and continue through September 15–20. Outside their established breeding range, Worm-eating Warblers are accidental fall visitors. There are fewer than twenty published fall records from glaciated central and northern Ohio, most within their normal migration period, except for late warblers in the Toledo area through October 9–14. The only later record is provided by a specimen washed onto the Ohio River shore near the Clermont-Hamilton county line on November 1, 1947 (Kemsies and Randle 1953).

Their spring migration is better defined. The first males normally return to their territories between April 18 and 25 and the last resident pairs arrive by May 10–15. Small numbers of Worm-eating Warblers regularly appear north of their breeding range each spring. These overflights are most apparent along Lake Erie, where they have been reported as early as March 29, 1994, in Ottawa County, and others appear during the first half of April (Harlan 1994c). They are rarely encountered along the entire lakefront, with fewer than six sightings some years and as many as twelve to fifteen reports in others. Most are scattered individuals, with a maximum of seven at Magee Marsh Wildlife Area on April 28, 1974 (Thomson 1983). Spring overflights are casual to rare near Columbus and in the northeastern counties, but there are very few sightings from the west-central counties and northwestern Ohio away from Lake Erie. These inland overflights are also mostly scattered individuals, although a remarkable 12 were reported from Akron following a thunderstorm on May 6, 1975 (Hammond 1975). Most overflights appear between April 28 and May 12, with a few late migrants noted through May 25–June 6.

Swainson's Warbler *Limnothlypis swainsonii* (Audubon)

Swainson's Warblers are uncommon occupants of woodlands with dense shrub layers in the southeastern United States. They breed in cane thickets within swamp forests along the Mississippi River valley and wet shrubby woods along the Atlantic Coastal Plain, but prefer rhododendron hollows or similar impenetrable thickets in damp woods along the Appalachian Mountains. Their breeding range extends north to eastern Kentucky and central West Virginia (AOU 1998).

Ohio's first Swainson's Warbler was discovered near the village of Chesapeake in Lawrence County on May 4, 1947. This singing male was intermittently observed through June 21, when it was collected. It was believed to be unmated and did not occupy typical breeding habitat, frequenting a steep stream valley supporting honeysuckle, Virginia creeper, cross vine, and blackberry tangles, but few trees (Green 1947). Its appearance corresponded with a northward range expansion in West Virginia during the 1940s and 1950s (Brooks 1953c).

In addition to the Lawrence County specimen, summering Swainson's Warblers were reported from Jefferson County during 1964, 1966, 1970, and 1971 and Columbiana County in 1976 (Buchanan 1980, Hall 1976b). A specimen was reportedly taken from Jefferson County, but there are few additional substantiating details. Although a pair of warblers was reported from Columbiana County, nesting was never confirmed at these locations.

During the 1980s, Ohio's only summer record was of a singing male in Jackson County between May 18 and 25, 1987 (Peterjohn and Rice 1991). This male also occupied atypical breeding habitat: a cutover hillside supporting an impenetrable thicket of shrubs and saplings, but no large trees. In all likelihood, this male too was unmated. In the 1990s, the only summer report was of a territorial male at Jefferson Lake State Park (Jefferson County) during June 24–July 5, 1993 (Harlan 1993d). This male was very elusive and no evidence of breeding was reported.

Swainson's Warblers seldom overfly their breeding range. They are accidental spring visitors to Ohio; one was photographed at Greenlawn Cemetery in Columbus on April 27–28, 1985 (Peterjohn 1985c), and another was banded at Ottawa Wildlife Refuge on April 28, 1998. A Swainson's Warbler was reportedly closely observed near Dayton on April 22, 1961, but could not be relocated (Mathena et al. 1984). Other details are unavailable and the validity of this sighting is difficult to judge. There are also four undocumented spring records from the Cleveland-Akron area and one at Steubenville, but the validity of these sightings is doubtful.

Ovenbird *Seiurus aurocapillus* (Linnaeus)

Ovenbirds were named for the domed nests resembling Dutch ovens that they cleverly hide in leaf litter on the forest floor. Through a small entrance located on the side, the adults easily slip in and out of these nests without revealing their locations. These nests are usually discovered only by accident when an adult flushes at an observer's feet. Cowbirds, however, seem to easily locate Ovenbird nests and regularly parasitize them.

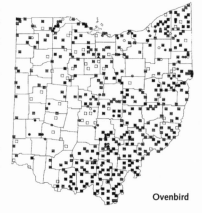

Ovenbird

Since Ovenbirds' nests are so difficult to locate, there is relatively little information on their breeding biology in Ohio. Within the southern counties, Ovenbirds begin nesting by late April or early May and recently fledged young appear during the first half of June. These pairs may raise two broods annually, since fledglings are recorded through early August. Nesting activities commence several weeks later in northern Ohio, where nest construction begins in mid-May, and nests with eggs are reported between May 20 and July 4 (Campbell 1968, Phillips 1980). These young normally fledge during late June and July (Williams 1950).

Breeding Ovenbirds occupy mature woods with open understories and a forest floor covered with leaf litter. They are equally at home on dry wooded hillsides of southeastern Ohio and in the swamp forests of the northwestern counties. Inhabitants of extensive woodlands, they are found only in shaded forest interiors.

The relative abundance of breeding Ovenbirds reflects the distribution of these wooded habitats. Throughout eastern and unglaciated Ohio, they are fairly common to abundant summer residents. Summer totals are normally 5–25+ daily, while as many as 50–125+ are counted within the heavily wooded southeastern counties. Ovenbirds are locally rare to fairly common residents in most southwestern, glaciated central, and northwestern counties, and summer totals are normally 3–10 individuals daily. They are least numerous within intensively farmed portions of western Ohio, where breeding pairs were not recorded from three counties during the Breeding Bird Atlas (Peterjohn and Rice 1991). They become locally common at a few western Ohio locations; in the Oak Openings of Lucas County, as many as 50 males have been counted in one day (Campbell 1968).

These breeding populations have remained fairly stable during the twentieth century and no significant trends are evident along Ohio Breeding Bird Survey routes since 1966 (Sauer et al. 1998). Since the 1930s, declines are apparent only in western Ohio, where wooded habitats have been extensively converted to farmlands. Populations within the eastern counties have not appreciably changed.

As spring migrants, the earliest Ovenbirds have appeared at Dayton by March 29–30 and along Lake Erie by April 12–14. These early migrants are exceptional. Within the southern counties, resident males normally return by April 12–16 and are widespread by April 20–25. In northern Ohio, Ovenbirds usually return by April 25–May 2 and become numerous by May 10. Along Lake Erie, their northward movement peaks between May 5 and 20; scattered migrants linger into the first week of June.

Within the interior counties, daily totals of 100–150+ are possible in southeastern Ohio during the first half of May and include both residents and migrants. Away from breeding locations, they are uncommon to fairly common migrants; usually six or fewer are observed daily, with a maximum of 50 at Buckeye Lake on May 11, 1929 (Trautman 1940). Along Lake Erie, Ovenbirds are fairly common spring migrants. Most lakefront reports are of ten or fewer daily, while flights produce 40–75+ individuals.

Given the inconspicuous behavior of silent Ovenbirds, their southward migration is poorly defined. It apparently begins during the last half of August. Small numbers of migrants are detected throughout September, but they normally depart by October 5–15. Stragglers have lingered into mid-November at a few localities. During autumn, Ovenbirds are locally rare to fairly common migrants. Most fall sightings are of five or fewer individuals daily, although Trautman (1940) occasionally noted 15–25 at Buckeye Lake during the 1920s and 1930s.

Ovenbirds normally winter in Central America and the Caribbean region (AOU 1998). They are accidental winter visitors in Ohio, with at least eleven records since 1965. Four Cincinnati records include at least three that overwintered. Single birds have also been reported from Dayton, Toledo, Cuyahoga Falls, Mansfield, Lorain County, Akron, and Cleveland. Most have visited bird feeders, although the Dayton individual was discovered in a pine grove (Mathena et al. 1984).

Northern Waterthrush *Seiurus noveboracensis* (Gmelin)

Northern
Waterthrush

As their name implies, waterthrushes are invariably found along small streams, quiet backwaters, ponds, and wooded swamps. They are not thrushes but rather large warblers, immediately recognized by their plain brown upperparts, striped underparts, and distinctive habit of teetering like Spotted Sandpipers. While recognizing a waterthrush is no problem, distinguishing between the two species, Northern and Louisiana, is a challenge. Singing males are readily separated, but silent individuals require careful study. Northern Waterthrushes are mostly known as transients through Ohio. Unlike our resident Louisiana Waterthrushes, Northerns prefer quieter water, including wooded swamps, brushy margins of small ponds, and backwaters along large creeks and rivers.

During their northward migration, a few Northern Waterthrushes return by April 12–16. These mid-April sightings are very unusual, and earlier sight records most likely pertain to misidentified Louisianas. The first Northerns are normally encountered during April 23–30 in the central and southern counties and April 28–May 5 along Lake Erie. Most pass through the state between May 5 and 24. Only a few stragglers remain along Lake Erie into the first week of June.

These waterthrushes are most numerous along Lake Erie, where they become fairly common migrants and 6–12 are observed daily. Maximum daily totals are 25–40. Fewer Northerns are detected within the interior counties, where they are uncommon to locally rare migrants. In recent years, most inland spring sightings are of 1–5 individuals and daily totals of 10–15 are exceptional.

A small breeding population exists in northeastern Ohio. This population was larger in the 1920s and 1930s, when suitable habitats were more widely distributed. While Hicks (1935a) cited nesting records from Lake, Geauga, Trumbull, and Ashtabula Counties, only Geauga and Ashtabula Counties regularly supported nesting pairs. Ashtabula County hosted the largest population; they were known from eleven locations, and 22 pairs were counted at the former Pymatuning Bog in 1932 (Hicks 1933a). Summering Northerns also regularly appeared at five Geauga County sites (Williams 1950). Away from these northeastern counties, the only summering Northern Waterthrushes were reported from a Huron County bog (Hicks 1935a).

Destruction of the Pymatuning Bog and other northeastern Ohio wetlands reduced this population. During the 1980s, summering Northerns were recorded from one to four locations in Summit, Portage, Geauga, and Ashtabula Counties, mostly as widely scattered pairs (Peterjohn and Rice 1991). Reports from the 1990s were primarily from Geauga County, although they apparently persisted in Portage County, and as many as two males summered in Mohican State Forest during several years through 1997. The status of this breeding population is imperfectly known, but the statewide total probably does not exceed 10–15 pairs (Peterjohn and Rice 1991).

Within Ohio, breeding Northern Waterthrushes prefer bogs and other wetlands where buttonbush, dogwood, alder, and poison sumac thickets provide dense cover along shallow water. Red maple-yellow birch swamp forests with dense shrub layers are equally suitable (Aldrich 1934, Hicks 1934b). Northern Waterthrushes nest on the ground within dense cover. The few confirmed breeding records indicate that their nests are constructed in the last half of May and early June. Nests with eggs are reported between May 17 and June 15; young normally fledge during late June and early July (Hicks 1935a, Williams 1950).

Their status as fall migrants is obscured by identification problems. A few are reported during the last half of July, but the first fall Northerns normally appear along Lake Erie during August 10–20 and within the central and southern counties by the last week of the month. Migrants are expected through September 25–30. The last Northerns normally depart by October 5–15, although a few linger into early November. They are rare to uncommon in all counties but tend to be most numerous near Lake Erie. Most fall sightings are of 1–4 daily, while as many as 10–12 have been reported from the lakefront and central Ohio.

Northern Waterthrushes are accidental winter visitors. There are at least seven sightings on Christmas Bird Counts since 1963: two at Dayton, Ashland, and Ottawa Wildlife Refuge/Magee Marsh Wildlife Area and one in Tuscarawas County. All sightings are of single birds. Most were noted on single dates during December, although the Tuscarawas County bird was also observed on January 3 and February 15, 1998, and may have overwintered (R. Schlabach 1998).

Louisiana Waterthrush *Seiurus motacilla* (Vieillot)

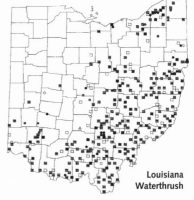

Louisiana
Waterthrush

The more widely distributed of our resident waterthrushes, Louisianas reside along small, rocky, shaded streams flowing through mature woodlands. Nesters are as numerous along the hemlock-dominated headwaters of the Chagrin River in Geauga County as along southeastern Ohio streams bordered by deciduous woods.

Louisiana Waterthrush nests are placed on the ground, usually hidden under tree roots or among herbaceous vegetation close to the stream. Their nesting activities are normally initiated during the last half of April. Nests with eggs are expected during May, although renesting attempts result in clutches through the first week of June (Williams 1950). In southern Ohio, fledglings appear by the last days of May or the first week of June. They normally appear during mid-June within the northern counties, while late nesting attempts produce young into July.

Nesting Louisiana Waterthrushes are most numerous along the unglaciated Allegheny Plateau, where forested stream valleys are widely distributed. They are fairly common to common residents, with daily totals of 3–15 in most southeastern counties. Within southwestern Ohio, Louisiana Waterthrushes are fairly common residents in the counties bordering the Ohio River but become uncommon and locally distributed elsewhere north to southern Preble, Montgomery, and Greene Counties. They are also uncommon to fairly common residents in northeastern Ohio and in the central counties bordering the Allegheny Plateau (Peterjohn and Rice 1991). Daily totals are generally eight or fewer away from the unglaciated counties. They become rare and very locally distributed residents in the west-central counties, with a few isolated pairs scattered from Miami to Logan Counties (Peterjohn and Rice 1991). These waterthrushes are largely absent from northwestern Ohio, except for breeding pairs in the Oak Openings area since 1990 and Seneca County since 1993 (Harlan 1993c, 1993d). These populations have been stable during recent decades (Sauer et al. 1998). In fact, the Ohio breeding distribution has not substantially changed since 1900 (Hicks 1935a, Peterjohn and Rice 1991).

While overflight Louisianas have appeared in southeastern Ohio by March 7, 1946, and Lorain County by March 16, 1983 (Borror 1950, Peterjohn 1983c), the first migrants normally appear by March 25–April 2 in the southern counties and April 5–10 in northern Ohio. Their migration largely takes place in April and is normally concluded by April 20–25. This movement is mostly residents returning to their nesting territories. Away from their breeding sites, Louisiana Waterthrushes are casual to rare spring migrants during late March and April, usually single individuals. While there are innumerable May sight records of migrant Louisianas, these reports primarily pertain to misidentified Northerns.

Their fall status is also obscured by misidentifications. Louisiana Waterthrushes are very early fall migrants. They quietly disappear from their breeding territories during the last half of July and most depart by August 15–22. They are accidental to casual migrants away from their established nesting locations. While a few Louisianas might linger into the first week of September, all later sight records are almost certainly misidentified Northern Waterthrushes.

Kentucky Warbler *Oporornis formosus* (Wilson)

Breeding Kentucky Warblers reside within mature deciduous woodlands. They are equally numerous in dry upland woods and more mesic communities but normally avoid swamp forests. Occupants of shrub and understory habitats, Kentuckies prefer forest interiors and usually avoid woodland edges. Hence, they are found in extensive woodlands and large woodlots, avoiding regularly timbered forests. Kentucky Warblers are fairly secretive as they skulk through the underbrush, and may not appear until an observer approaches their nest, excitedly responding to the presence of an intruder.

Kentucky Warblers nest on the ground, typically at the base of a sapling or small shrub. Their expertly concealed nests are bulky and mostly composed of dead leaves and grasses (Lloyd 1934). In southern Ohio, clutches are laid during May and the young usually fledge during the last half of June. Their nesting chronology is delayed by one or two weeks in the northern counties, where young warblers normally fledge during July. Renesting attempts produce July broods in southern Ohio (Trautman 1940).

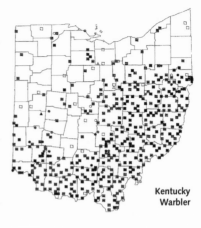

Kentucky Warbler

Their statewide distribution gradually expanded northward during the twentieth century. In the early 1900s, Jones (1903) considered Kentucky Warblers fairly common summer residents in the southern third of Ohio, although this status was disputed by Henninger (1902). They were unrecorded from the remainder of the state. Their breeding range expanded northward along the unglaciated Allegheny Plateau between 1910 and the early 1930s. Hicks (1935a) recorded breeding Kentucky Warblers in every county north to Butler, Montgomery, Clinton, Ross, Fairfield, Licking, Knox, Ashland, Wayne, Stark, and Columbiana. They were locally distributed and uncommon at the northern edge of this range and fairly common to common along the Allegheny Plateau north to Coshocton, Guernsey, and Monroe Counties (Hicks 1937a).

This range expansion continued in subsequent decades. By the 1940s, Kentuckies became rather common residents in Carroll and Jefferson Counties but remained "very infrequent" north of the glacial boundary (Buchanan 1980). Nesting Kentuckies were detected at Youngstown by 1950 and in the Toledo area in 1958 and 1963 (Brooks 1950c, Campbell 1968). A summering male appeared near Cleveland in 1960 (Newman 1969). This expansion is still producing new breeding records from northern Ohio, although statewide population trends are stable along Breeding Bird Survey routes since the mid-1960s (Sauer et al. 1998).

Kentucky Warblers are fairly common to common summer residents in southern and eastern Ohio north to Preble, Montgomery, Clinton, Highland, Ross, Licking, Knox, Richland, Ashland, Wayne, Stark, and Columbiana Counties (Peterjohn and Rice 1991). Where extensive mature woodlands are prevalent, 15–30+ individuals are noted daily. At the northern and western boundaries of this range, daily totals seldom exceed 4–6, although a total of 46 males were recorded in Mohican State Forest during 1997. In the central counties adjacent to Columbus, they become uncommon, with only 1–4 daily. Kentuckies remain casual to rare and very locally distributed elsewhere (Peterjohn and Rice 1991). Most of these sightings are of isolated pairs and summering males.

The first spring Kentuckies appear in the southern counties by April 15–25 and northern Ohio by May 5–10. Most breeding warblers return by May 15–20. This migration normally consists of warblers returning to their breeding territories, although tallies of 30–45+ in the southeastern counties during early May include migrants as well as summer residents. Away from breeding locations, Kentucky Warblers are casual to rare spring migrants. They are usually detected at lakefront migrant traps, where there are five to ten reports during most years. The earliest extralimital Kentucky appeared at Tiffin on April 19, 1976, but most are observed between May 8 and 25 (Kleen 1976b).

Like most woodland warblers, Kentuckies become inconspicuous once the males quit singing in early July. There are relatively few records after July 15. Most resident Kentuckies quietly leave between the last half of August and September 10–20. They are accidental to casual fall migrants away from their established nesting range. Most extralimital fall sightings are before September 20, but they have been reported as late as October 17, 1958, at Cleveland (Rosche 1992).

Connecticut Warbler *Oporornis agilis* (Wilson)

This elusive skulker of woodland thickets is one of the rarest warblers regularly migrating through Ohio. Discovering a Connecticut Warbler is noteworthy during either fall or spring migration, and obtaining a satisfactory view of it requires considerable patience and perseverance. Even singing males are adept at remaining hidden. With a little luck, foraging Connecticuts occasionally come into view—always near the ground or in dense tangles no more than six to eight feet high.

As spring migrants, Connecticuts are among the last warblers returning to Ohio. There are probably no valid sightings before May 7–10. The first migrants normally appear around May 15; most are recorded between May 18 and 30. Connecticuts are rare to uncommon along Lake Erie and casual to rare inland. They are generally encountered as scattered individuals, with occasional totals of 3–6 daily. The spring of 1929 brought unprecedented numbers to Buckeye Lake, where 15–25 were recorded daily between May 22 and 25 (Trautman 1940). Most depart by June 1–5, with a few stragglers into the second week of the month.

Fall migrants may inhabit weedy and brushy fields in addition to woodland thickets. They silently hide among the abundant vegetation, and their status is further obscured by the difficulty of separating Connecticuts from the similar Mourning Warblers. Fall Connecticuts are generally casual to rare migrants, normally encountered as scattered individuals. Most migrants are overlooked, and Trautman's report of 19 Connecticuts, including 14 specimens, on South Bass Island during September 1950 may be representative of the numbers actually passing through the state (Campbell 1968). The first migrants have been reported during the last week of August. They are most frequently observed between September 10 and October 5. The latest Ohio fall sightings are only October 11–12.

Mourning Warbler *Oporornis philadelphia* (Wilson)

Mourning
Warbler

The behavior and migrations of the Mourning Warbler, another skulker through shrubs and other low woodland cover, are similar to those of the Connecticut Warbler. Both species rank among the last migrants returning each spring. A few early Mournings appear during the first week of May, but they normally return during May 10–15. Most migrate between May 18 and June 3. The last migrants linger in northern Ohio until June 10–15.

These spring migrants are most numerous along Lake Erie, where they become uncommon to locally fairly common in late May. As many as 3–6 are observed daily and totals of 8–20 are possible during large flights. They become rare to locally uncommon migrants within the interior counties and daily totals seldom exceed 1–4. Occasional flights have been reported, perhaps the largest in 1929 when Trautman (1940) observed 15–50 daily at Buckeye Lake between May 22 and 25.

A small summering population of Mourning Warblers formerly existed in the Oak Openings of Lucas County. During the 1930s, Campbell (1940) considered them uncommon summer residents, with 4–7 pairs annually. Although breeding was suspected most years, a nest was discovered only in 1932. These summering Mournings remained through 1941 but were only intermittently observed in subsequent years, averaging one record every four years (Campbell 1968). Most of these later males were probably unmated. The last summering males were reported in 1960. Hicks (1935a) also cited unspecified summer records in northeastern Ohio.

Between 1960 and 1980, Mourning Warblers were unrecorded as summer residents and the small Ohio breeding population was presumably extirpated. Surveys for the Breeding Bird Atlas proved otherwise, beginning in 1983, when a territorial male summered in Geauga County (Peterjohn and Rice 1991). The following year, nesting behavior was exhibited by pairs in Summit and Geauga Counties, while a male summered in Clinton County. The Geauga County pair returned in subsequent years, and territorial males were also reported from the Oak Openings-Maumee State Forest area and Ashtabula, Lake, and Williams Counties.

In the 1990s, small numbers of summering males were reported from Ashtabula, Geauga, Lake, and Summit Counties and periodically from the Oak Openings area. A maximum of 14 territories were noted in northern Ohio during 1992 (Brock 1992b), with 5–6 males and a female carrying food at the Pennline Bog in Ashtabula County (Harlan 1992d). These sightings indicate that Mourning Warblers are casual to rare and very locally distributed summer residents in the extreme northeastern and northwestern counties. They are accidental summer residents elsewhere, although three males reported from Mohican State Forest during 1997 may indicate nesting there.

Breeding Mourning Warblers prefer dense, brushy habitats with a few scattered trees. Extensive cutover areas are ideal, although woodland clearings and edges as well as brushy fields are also occupied. Their nests are cleverly hidden near the ground in dense shrubbery. The few Ohio breeding records indicate that nesting activities begin in early June and the young fledge by mid-July.

As fall migrants, a few early Mournings are reported along Lake Erie during the first half of August; however, they normally return during August 20–25. They usually appear at inland locations by September 1–5. Most Mournings pass through Ohio during September and depart by October 4–8. The latest documented Mourning was an immature female carefully studied at Euclid on November 2, 1985 (Peterjohn 1986a).

Fall Mourning Warblers are generally rare migrants, although many are undoubtedly overlooked as they skulk through the dense underbrush. They are mostly observed as scattered individuals, with no more than 3–4 noted daily.

Common Yellowthroat *Geothlypis trichas* (Linnaeus)

Among our most numerous resident warblers, Common Yellowthroats are found wherever suitable edge and successional habitats are available. They frequent the shrubby margins of ponds, streams, ditches, and wetlands but are also commonly recorded in dry brushy fields, fallow fields, fencerows, woodland edges, and young open woodlots. The distinctive males frequently sing from exposed perches. Their song, a repetitive *wichety-wichety-wichety*, is among the first songs learned by most birders.

As summer residents, yellowthroats have been widely distributed ever since the virgin forests were cleared. Their populations have not appreciably changed during the twentieth century, and data from Breeding Bird Survey routes indicate that statewide populations have increased since 1966 (Sauer et al. 1998). They are least numerous in intensively farmed western Ohio, where edge and successional habitats are relatively scarce. Yellowthroats are fairly common to common residents in Wood, Henry, Defiance, Paulding, Van Wert, Putnam, Madison, Fayette, and Clinton Counties, where daily totals seldom exceed 8–15 except along extensive riparian corridors. They are common to abundant summer residents elsewhere and 25–100+ are recorded daily. Campbell's (1968) report of 300 in the Oak Openings on July 18, 1936, probably included many young raised that summer.

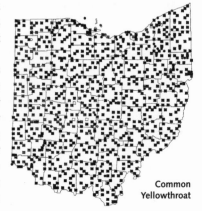

Common Yellowthroat

While observing Common Yellowthroats is fairly easy, discovering their nests is difficult (although cowbirds seemingly find them with great regularity). These nests are usually well concealed by herbaceous vegetation, on or within six inches of the ground. Nest construction is initiated during the first half of May, and the first clutches are completed between mid-May and early June. The first broods fledge by June 10–20 but are most frequently noted during early July. Second broods or renesting attempts are responsible for nests with young through July 28 and adults accompanied by young through August 22 (Trautman 1940, Williams 1950).

The first spring migrants normally return to southern Ohio during the third week of April and are commonly encountered by May 1. While a few overflights return to Lake Erie by April 15–18, they usually appear in northern Ohio during April 27–30 and are common by May 5–9. Spring totals are usually 10–50 daily, with occasional reports of 100–200. Yellowthroats may frequent lakefront migrant traps through May 22–27.

Fall yellowthroats are difficult to locate until their distinctive harsh call notes are learned; then they become numerous migrants. Daily totals are usually 10–30, with occasional reports of 50–100+. While their southward movement may begin during the last half of August, most yellowthroats pass through Ohio in September. Their numbers diminish by the first week of

October, although a few regularly linger into November.

Common Yellowthroats normally winter in the southern United States, Central America, and the Caribbean region, although they are occasionally found north to the lower Great Lakes (AOU 1998). Within Ohio, there was only one published winter record before 1940. The number of winter sightings began to accumulate in the 1940s and 1950s. Wintering yellowthroats have been reported nearly every year since the mid-1960s. This increased number of sightings may reflect greater numbers of observers as well as more yellowthroats attempting to overwinter.

Wintering yellowthroats are now casual to accidental visitors, producing one to six reports annually but are not regularly detected at any location. Most records are from the western Lake Erie marshes and the southern half of Ohio, predominantly of isolated individuals, although as many as three have been reported on Christmas Bird Counts. These records are mostly during December and the first half of January. Many yellowthroats do not survive the rigors of a typical Ohio winter, although some have been observed into March.

Hooded Warbler *Wilsonia citrina* (Boddaert)

An exquisite combination of greenish upperparts, yellow underparts, and a bright yellow face surrounded by a jet black hood, male Hooded Warblers look like feathered jewels as they flit through the understory of mature woods. Like most occupants of understory habitats, these bright warblers become remarkably inconspicuous once the foliage is fully developed, and their presence is mostly detected by their loud, rolling song.

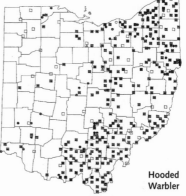

Hooded Warbler

Breeding Hooded Warblers occupy extensive mature woods, remaining within the forest interiors and seldom wandering to the edges. They prefer mesic woodlands, especially beech-maple communities. Their nests are placed in saplings, grape tangles, or similar cover, usually at heights of less than four feet (Williams 1950). Within the southern counties, clutches are produced by mid-May. These young fledge by late June. Their breeding chronology is delayed by one or two weeks in northern Ohio, where the first nests are normally discovered during late May and early June and the young fledge during July. Renesting attempts produce nests with eggs through July 4 and young into early August (Walker 1928d, Williams 1950).

Nesting Hooded Warblers are most numerous within the eastern half of Ohio (Peterjohn and Rice 1991). Along the unglaciated Allegheny Plateau, they are fairly common to common residents north to Hocking, Morgan, and Monroe Counties, where 5–30+ are noted daily. They are uncommon to fairly common along the remainder of the plateau, with daily totals of six or fewer, except at Mohican State Forest, where counts of 10–30+ are possible. Within the northeastern counties, Hoodeds are uncommon to locally common summer residents, most numerous along the Chagrin River watershed and near Hinckley, where they are as numerous as in the unglaciated counties. Considerably fewer nesting Hoodeds are found elsewhere. They are rare to uncommon and locally distributed near Columbus, the north-central counties, and southwestern Ohio, where most reports involve only 1–2 pairs. Fewer reside in the west-central and northwestern counties; they are absent from many of these counties and accidental to locally rare elsewhere (Peterjohn and Rice 1991).

At the turn of the twentieth century, Jones (1903) noted that Hooded Warblers were most numerous within the extreme northeastern and southeastern counties. Hicks (1935a) cited breeding records from twenty-nine counties, mostly within southern and northeastern Ohio, although the Cincinnati area records were disputed by Kemsies and Randle (1953). Numbers increased along the unglaciated Allegheny Plateau since the 1930s, when they were numerous only within Hocking and Scioto Counties (Hicks 1937a). The first confirmed Cincinnati nesting record was in 1958 (Nolan 1958d), and their appearance at most other localities has been since 1960. Statewide population trends estimated along Breeding Bird Survey routes are stable since 1966 (Sauer et al. 1998).

As spring migrants, Hooded Warblers are mostly known as residents returning to their breeding territories, although counts of 40–60+ from southeastern Ohio during the first half of May include both migrants and nesters. Away from their breeding sites, they are casual to locally uncommon migrants, most likely to appear along Lake Erie and near Columbus as scattered individuals and occasional groups of 2–5.

The earliest Hooded Warblers appeared during the unprecedented overflight of March 28–April 2, 1950, producing sightings at Toledo and at least three records from Columbus (Campbell 1968, Mayfield 1950c). There are few other records before April 15–20, when the first residents normally return to the southern counties. There, they are widespread by the end of April and most return by May 10–12. Elsewhere, migrant Hoodeds are most likely to appear between April 25 and May 20.

After the males quit singing, Hooded Warblers become inconspicuous, with few records after mid-July. Most Hoodeds quietly disappear during the last half of August through September 20–25. Occasional warblers linger until October 5–12. Exceptionally late Hoodeds were reported from Cleveland on October 31, 1949, and Toledo between November 25 and 29, 1961 (Campbell 1968, Rosche 1992). These fall migrants are casual to locally uncommon, most numerous within the eastern counties. Fall sightings normally involve only 1–3 individuals.

Wilson's Warbler *Wilsonia pusilla* (Wilson)

During their passage through Ohio, these handsome warblers are most likely to be found in brushy woods, willow thickets, and other habitats dominated by shrubs and saplings. Although they occupy upland habitats, Wilson's Warblers are especially fond of dense shrubby thickets near water and are readily observed as they forage within the low bushes.

Wilson's Warblers rank among the later spring migrants. The earliest over-flight appeared at Cleveland on April 23, 1978 (Hannikman 1978), but there are few other records during late April. The first migrants normally appear by May 3–7 and attain their maximum abundance between May 12 and 24. At that time, they become fairly common to common along Lake Erie, where daily totals of 5–20 are normal. The largest flights total 40–50. At inland sites within central and northern Ohio, Wilson's Warblers are uncommon to fairly common. As many as 25 have been reported from Buckeye Lake (Trautman 1940), but most observations are of six or fewer. These warblers are scarce spring migrants through southern Ohio, particularly the unglaciated counties, where they are rarely encountered. Most southern sightings involve single individuals, although 6–8 have been noted at Dayton (Mathena et al. 1984). The last migrants normally depart inland locations by May 30 and Lake Erie by the first week of June, but have remained in the Cleveland area through June 10–14 (Flanigan 1968).

Breeding Wilson's Warblers occupy bogs and damp willow thickets across Alaska and Canada south to northern New England, the upper Great Lakes, and the western mountains (AOU 1998). There are no confirmed summer records from Ohio after the last migrants depart by mid-June.

The initiation of fall migration is somewhat uncertain, since sight records during late July and early August frequently are misidentifications of similar warblers. The first confirmed fall migrants appear along Lake Erie during the third week of August and are regularly noted by September 1. Inland migrants are normally detected by September 3–7. Fall Wilson's are fairly common to common along Lake Erie and rare to uncommon inland. Concentrations sel-dom exceed ten daily, with infrequent reports of 15–30 along Lake Erie and in the central counties. Wilson's Warblers are observed through the first week of

October but become very scarce later in the month. The latest confirmed records are October 31, 1974, at Columbus and November 3, 1993, at Waterville (Kleen 1975a, Harlan 1994a). There is also an undocumented January sight record from eastern Ohio.

Canada Warbler *Wilsonia canadensis* (Linnaeus)

Another late spring migrant, the Canada Warbler is exceptional during April, although overflights have appeared by April 17–22. The first migrants normally return during May 5–10. Most migrants are observed in young woods with dense shrub layers, especially swamp forests or woodlands near water. Spring migration is fairly rapid and most depart by May 25–June 1. Late migrants pass along Lake Erie through June 8–15, but early June migrants are unusual away from the lakefront.

Canada Warbler

Spring Canadas are most numerous along Lake Erie, where they are common during the last half of May. Normally 5–20 are observed daily along the lakefront, and occasional flights of 30–40+ are reported. They are uncommon to fairly common migrants through the glaciated central and northern counties, becoming uncommon to locally rare in southern and unglaciated Ohio. Inland spring totals seldom exceed 3–10. Only Trautman (1940) reported a sizable inland flight, with 25–55 daily at Buckeye Lake between May 22 and 25, 1929.

At one time, nesting Canadas were largely restricted to Ashtabula County. Hicks (1933a) regularly observed summering pairs in the former Pymatuning Bog and cited eight records from five other locations before 1933. The only other summer Canadas appeared in the Oak Openings of Lucas County, where Campbell (1968) cited records during seven years between 1931 and 1946, including a successful nest in 1937.

In 1947, Canada Warblers expanded into Ohio's hemlock forests. This expansion was first apparent in the northeastern counties, with a territorial male at Little Mountain on June 20 (Williams 1950). In subsequent years, as many as 4–6 pairs regularly appeared there, at Stebbins Gulch, and in other hemlock ravines in Geauga, Lake, and Cuyahoga Counties (Newman 1969). Summering Canadas were first recorded from southeastern Ohio in 1963, when Worth Randle discovered a male in Hocking County. The next summering warbler was recorded from this county in 1968, and they have regularly nested there since 1970 (Petersen 1970d).

Canada Warblers are casual to rare and locally distributed summer residents within hemlock forests in eastern Ohio. They are most numerous at Mohican State Forest, where 21 males were counted in 1997, and along the Chagrin River watershed in Lake, Geauga, and Cuyahoga Counties, where 3–10 pairs regularly nest at seven or more sites. As many as three pairs regularly breed at three to five locations in Hocking County. Isolated pairs have also appeared in Summit, Medina, Lorain, Jackson, and Vinton Counties (Peterjohn and Rice 1991). No summering warblers have been found in Ashtabula County since the 1930s, and the only recent summer record from the Oak Openings area was in 1991 (Peterjohn 1991d). This breeding population exhibits marked annual fluctuations in abundance. Even when they are most numerous, this population probably totals only 50–75 singing males.

Summering Canada Warblers in the Oak Openings occupy second-growth deciduous woods (Campbell 1968), but all other records are from bogs and hemlock forests. Breeding warblers prefer openings where the shrub layer and ground cover are relatively dense, especially along small streams and springs. Nesting activities begin during the last half of May, and most pairs have complete clutches by the first half of June. Adults accompanied by dependent young are recorded between June 27 and July 28 (Hicks 1933a).

Canadas are among the first warblers returning each autumn. Southward migrants appear along Lake Erie during the first half of August and return to most interior counties by August 15–20. This passage peaks between August 23 and September 15. Fall Canadas are rare to uncommon migrants, mostly as scattered individuals, although daily totals of 7–10 have been noted. Most depart by September 22–27. October sightings are very unusual, but Canadas have reportedly remained through October 22–26.

Painted Redstart *Myioborus pictus* (Swainson)

Ohio's only record of this accidental visitor was provided by a Painted Redstart in Middleburg Heights (Cuyahoga County) between November 15 and 22, 1970 (Petersen 1971). This distinctive warbler was observed by numerous individuals and photographed during its periodic visits to a feeder at the residence of Dr. and Mrs. Joseph Hadden. Since Painted Redstarts normally nest in the southwestern United States (AOU 1998), the appearance of one in Ohio was very unexpected. These warblers have subsequently proven to wander occasionally during late fall and early winter, producing a few other extralimital records from eastern North America.

Yellow-breasted Chat *Icteria virens* (Linnaeus)

"If there is a feathered oddity in America, it is the Yellow-breasted Chat," Dawson (1903) wrote. He further elaborates:

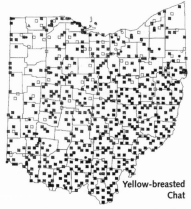

Yellow-breasted Chat

> when you listen to his quaint medley of calls, caws, squawks, pipings, and objurations, you almost feel that the scientists must be as queer as himself for having placed him among the warblers. Structurally he does belong to this family, but his vocal performances are about as far from warbling as midnight is from midday.

Dawson's sentiments have been echoed by many others who are amused by the antics of these large, handsome warblers. The breeding male's outlandish vocalizations and strange territorial displays are unlike any other North American warbler. Yet, a foraging chat is reclusive and allows only brief views before disappearing into cover.

Yellow-breasted Chats are occupants of dense thickets and tangles found in abandoned fields and woodland clearings. The red cedar-covered hillsides in southwestern Ohio provide ideal habitats, as do blackberry and rose tangles dominating clearcuts and fallow fields in the southeastern counties. They are not found along fencerows or other narrow shrubby corridors. With their preference for successional habitats, chats invariably disappear when the shrubby tangles are replaced by small trees.

Their statewide distribution reflects the availability of successional habitats. Chats have always been locally distributed within the west-central and northwestern counties, where brushy fields are scarce. Moreover, Ohio lies near the northern boundary of their range and there is a noticeable decrease in abundance from the southern to northern counties.

Hicks (1935a) provided the first detailed account of the chat's summer distribution. He cited records from eighty-one counties, noting their absence from seven northwestern counties. Chats were common to abundant throughout southern Ohio, gradually becoming uncommon to rare and locally distributed within the northern counties. Along the unglaciated Allegheny Plateau, they were most numerous north to Muskingum, Guernsey, and Monroe Counties (Hicks 1937a). In subsequent decades, Campbell (1968) described an abrupt decrease at Toledo after 1948, while Breeding Bird Surveys indicate a significant statewide decline since 1966 (Sauer et al. 1998).

Despite these declines, chat distribution patterns have changed little since the 1930s (Peterjohn and Rice 1991). Chats remain fairly common to locally abundant residents throughout southern Ohio and along the unglaciated Allegheny Plateau north to Coshocton, Guernsey, and Belmont Counties. Daily totals of 8–15+ are possible, while as many as 30–50 are tallied at a few localities. They become fairly common to locally common residents elsewhere along the unglaciated plateau, although summer totals seldom exceed 5–12 daily. Within the glaciated central counties, chats become locally distributed and uncommon to fairly common residents, with most reports of 1–6 individuals. They are casual to locally uncommon residents in northern Ohio but are absent from intensively farmed portions of the northwestern counties. While Campbell (1968) counted 20–35 daily in the Oak Openings, similar numbers have not been evident since 1950. In recent years, most northern reports are of only 1–4 chats.

For a "southern warbler," the Yellow-breasted Chat is a relatively late migrant. The earliest chats return to the southern counties by April 17–21, although they normally appear during April 28–May 3. They return to central and northern Ohio by May 5–10. Few migrants are noted after May 20–25. This movement mostly consists of resident chats returning to their territories.

Spring chats are rare visitors to lakefront migrant traps. These migrants mostly appear during May, but a few late individuals have been observed at Cleveland through June 10–11. These sightings are of only 1–3 chats daily.

The male's conspicuous territorial displays belie a secretive bird whose nests are difficult to locate, generally placed at heights of two to four feet in dense thickets. Within the southern counties, most chats have complete clutches by the last half of May. These activities are delayed in northern Ohio, where nests are mostly reported during June (Campbell 1968, Williams 1950). Recently fledged young have been noted as early as June 2 at Buckeye Lake, but most appear in late June and early July (Trautman 1940). Renesting attempts produce young into early August.

After the males quit singing in early July, Yellow-breasted Chats become inconspicuous. There are relatively few records after July 15, although chats are undoubtedly more numerous than these sightings indicate. They are casual to rare fall migrants, usually observed as single individuals. This migration apparently begins in August and is mostly completed by September 15–25. A few late chats remain through October 25–November 3.

Yellow-breasted Chats are accidental early winter visitors, with three published December sightings. These records are of single chats in Ottawa County, near Buckeye Lake, and at Brecksville (Cuyahoga County). The Brecksville chat survived until December 22 but was found dead a few days later (Nolan 1954b).

Summary Tanager *Piranga rubra* (Linnaeus)

Summer Tanagers have always had a limited distribution, primarily restricted to the southern and unglaciated counties. In 1935, Hicks (1935a) described their breeding range as extending north to Butler, Montgomery, Greene, Madison, Franklin, Licking, Coshocton, Tuscarawas, Carroll, and Columbiana Counties. Summer Tanagers were accidental north of this range. They were common only within Adams, Scioto, and Lawrence Counties and regularly encountered along the Allegheny Plateau north to Muskingum, Guernsey, and Washington Counties (Hicks 1937a). Breeding Summer Tanagers were rare and locally distributed elsewhere.

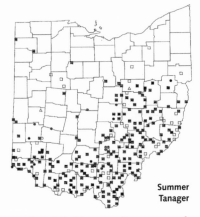

Summer Tanager

While nesting populations remain stable along Breeding Bird Survey routes (Sauer et al. 1998), evidence suggests that Summer Tanagers are slowly expanding their breeding range northward. Along the unglaciated Allegheny Plateau, Summer Tanagers are most numerous in Adams, Pike, Scioto, and Lawrence Counties; as many as 5–10 are observed daily. Summer Tanagers are fairly common elsewhere along the plateau north to Coshocton, Tuscarawas, and Belmont Counties, although daily totals seldom exceed 1–5 individuals. Breeding tanagers are uncommon and locally distributed residents along the northern edge of the unglaciated plateau (Peterjohn and Rice 1991). They remain fairly common near Cincinnati but are rare to uncommon and locally distributed in other southwestern counties north to Preble, Montgomery, and Greene (Mathena et al. 1984, Peterjohn and Rice 1991). Expanding populations are apparent near Columbus. They have become rare residents within Franklin and adjacent counties as locally distributed pairs and singing males (Peterjohn and Rice 1991).

Beginning in the 1950s, breeding Summer Tanagers appeared in northern Ohio. The first nesting records were reported at Youngstown in 1950 (Brooks 1950d), Akron in 1956–1958 (Newman 1969), and Toledo, where nesting was suspected in 1955 and confirmed at two sites between 1957 and 1961 (Campbell 1968). There were very few additional breeding records during the 1960s and 1970s, and the Breeding Bird Atlas detected only a small number of widely scattered individuals during the 1980s (Peterjohn and Rice 1991). Summer Tanagers summered in the Oak Openings area of Lucas County in

1988, and nesting was confirmed there in 1989 (Peterjohn 1988d, 1989d). One or two pairs bred there subsequently, but the Oak Openings remain the only northern Ohio location where Summer Tanagers regularly nest. They are accidental to casual summer residents in other northern counties.

Breeding Summer Tanagers prefer upland woods. While they occupy mature woodlands, they are also found in open disturbed woods and woodland edges but avoid young second-growth forests. Summer Tanagers normally remain within the canopy. However, singing males are regularly detected by their clear robin-like song, which lacks the hoarse notes characteristic of Scarlet Tanagers. Nesting activities are initiated by the last half of May within the southern and eastern counties but begin during early June in northern Ohio. The young normally fledge by late June and July, but renesting efforts produce young into the first half of August.

Resident Summer Tanagers may return to southern Ohio by April 23–30, but they normally appear during the first week of May. Their breeding populations are well established by May 15–20. This northward movement largely comprises tanagers returning to their territories, with daily maxima of 8–12 individuals.

Small numbers regularly overshoot their normal breeding range each spring. These overflights are rare along Lake Erie and near Columbus but are accidental to casual elsewhere. The number of overflights varies considerably, with only two to four sightings some years and six to ten or more in others. These records are usually of single tanagers observed between May 5 and 24, although a few have appeared through June 7.

Their southward migration is poorly defined. Summer Tanagers normally depart from the northern edge of their breeding range by September 14–18 but remain in the southern counties through September 22–27. Occasional individuals linger through October 5–8. Fall records are mostly of 1–3 daily. Summer Tanagers are accidental to casual fall visitors throughout the northern and glaciated central counties. The few extralimital fall records are mostly during September, although a late Summer Tanager appeared at Toledo on October 13, 1984 (Peterjohn 1985a).

Scarlet Tanager *Piranga olivacea* (Gmelin)

For most people captivated by birds, spring migration is made memorable by multitudes of brightly colored songbirds flitting among the branches of flowering trees. Perhaps no other songbird presents such an unforgettable image as a brilliant male Scarlet Tanager. As described by Dawson (1903):

> Never shall I forget the day, when in treading an overgrown path by the riverside I came suddenly upon four males on a single limb not twenty feet away.

The vision smote me like a blinding flash. The two oldest of the group were certainly among the most magnificent birds ever seen in Northern latitudes. Their coats were red-dyed to the point of scarlet saturation, and as they moved off slowly, the memory of the bird-man received an indelible image of these most beautiful four.

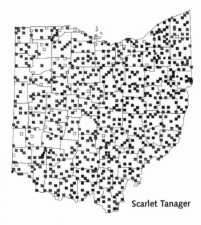
Scarlet Tanager

Fortunately, Scarlet Tanagers are fairly common to common spring migrants and summer residents. An exceptionally early male was reported from the Cleveland area on March 29, 1977 (Rosche 1992), but there are no other sightings before April 12–15. The first Scarlet Tanagers normally return to the southern counties by April 20–25 and along Lake Erie during the first week of May. During advanced seasons, the males are inconspicuous among the abundant foliage. They are much more visible during late springs, as Dawson (1903) noted:

> Those who haunt the woods in maying time are almost sure to see a vision of scarlet and black revealing itself for a moment in the higher tree tops, but swallowed up again all too soon by the consuming green. If, however, the leaves are not fully sprung the Tanager will move about quietly or sit rather stupidly in the middle branches, as tho bored by the lack of green and at a loss what to do with his brightness.

Most resident Scarlet Tanagers return by mid-May and the last migrants depart lakefront migrant traps by May 25. The largest lakefront flights produce counts of 20–40+ while totals of 40–70+ from the unglaciated counties include resident and migrant tanagers. Spring totals are normally 4–12 daily.

As summer residents, Scarlet Tanagers are most numerous in extensive mature woodlands and riparian corridors. They also occupy second-growth woods if some large trees remain. Breeding Scarlet Tanagers are most numerous in the eastern and southern counties, where 20–40+ are counted daily in heavily wooded areas. They are normally fairly common residents elsewhere but become locally uncommon in some west-central and northwestern counties (Peterjohn and Rice 1991). Summer totals seldom exceed 4–10 individuals away from southern and eastern Ohio. In recent decades, Scarlet Tanagers undoubtedly declined in many western counties as woodlands were converted to agricultural fields and residential areas. Conversely, populations probably increased in many southern and eastern counties where woodlands are maturing. The net result has been stable statewide populations on Breeding Bird Survey routes since 1966 (Sauer et al. 1998).

Their nests are normally placed at heights of twenty feet or more in tall trees. Nest construction is prevalent during May. Eggs are normally laid by late May, and recently fledged young have been reported as early as June 8 (Williams 1950). Most young Scarlet Tanagers fledge in late June and July. Second broods or renesting attempts are responsible for nests with eggs through August 3 and a nest with young on August 9 (Trautman 1940, Williams 1950).

Scarlet Tanagers are regularly detected as long as the males continue to sing. Once singing ceases, usually during the first half of July, they become inconspicuous, although a few are located by their distinctive *chip-burr* call notes. Their fall migration is poorly defined. Fall Scarlet Tanagers are fairly common in the unglaciated counties but uncommon elsewhere. Most depart by September 25–October 1, with stragglers through October 19–21. Most fall observations are of five or fewer individuals.

Western Tanager *Piranga ludoviciana* (Wilson)

Breeding Western Tanagers are widely distributed in western North America from southeastern Alaska to southern Arizona (AOU 1998). They normally winter in Mexico and Central America. In eastern North America, these tanagers are primarily accidental vagrants during late fall and early winter. These wandering individuals are frequently discovered at bird feeders, usually at localities near the Atlantic and Gulf Coasts.

There are two documented records of this accidental visitor to Ohio. A Western Tanager was photographed at East Harbor State Park on November 20, 1982 (Peterjohn 1983a). The second record was a male discovered at Magee Marsh Wildlife Area on May 16, 1996 (Brock 1996c), providing one of very few confirmed spring reports from eastern North America. In addition, there are three undocumented sight records that fit this species' known pattern of vagrancy: one at Mayfield Heights (Cuyahoga County) on November 24, 1962; one visiting a Mentor feeder during December 1–28, 1963; and another at Mentor between December 21, 1971, and January 3, 1972 (Newman 1969, Rosche 1988). The two at Mentor were observed by a number of birders.

Green-tailed Towhee *Pipilo chlorurus* (Audubon)

Green-tailed Towhees are inhabitants of the western United States that regularly wander east of their normal range. There are reports from many states and provinces in eastern North America, mostly in the Great Lakes region and the Northeast (AOU 1998). Most are discovered at feeders during winter.

There are now four records of this accidental visitor to Ohio. The first Green-tailed Towhee was discovered in the Columbus area during late

December 1963. It remained at a feeder through the following February (Petersen 1964b), but no photographs or written descriptions are available. A fall migrant was discovered in Saybrook Township, Ashtabula County, on September 24, 1964. It was captured, banded, photographed, and then released (Petersen 1965a). The third towhee wintered in Hamilton County between December 12, 1969, and March 31, 1970. It was widely observed and photographed as it regularly visited a bird feeder (Petersen 1970b). The most recent Green-tailed Towhee also wintered at a feeder (Akin 1993). It was discovered on January 10, 1993, in Amherst Township, Lorain County, and remained there through April 15 (Harlan 1993c).

Spotted Towhee *Pipilo maculatus* Swainson

Formerly considered conspecific with Eastern Towhees, Spotted Towhees are widely distributed occupants of brushy habitats in western North America. Their breeding range extends eastward to the western Great Plains, but these towhees occasionally wander into eastern North America during the nonbreeding seasons (AOU 1998).

Spotted Towhees are accidental visitors to Ohio, with three published reports. The first record was of a Spotted Towhee observed by three experienced birders along the Scioto River in Delaware County on March 29, 1946 (Borror 1950). No other details are available for this sighting. The second towhee was captured, banded, and photographed at Springville Marsh Nature Preserve (Seneca County) on May 4, 1996 (Bartlett 1996). It was last observed at this location on May 12. Another Spotted Towhee appeared in a residential yard in Lakewood (Cuyahoga County) during October 22–29, 1998 (Rosche 1998). This individual was photographed and observed by a number of birders during its visit.

Eastern Towhee *Pipilo erythrophthalmus* (Linnaeus)

With their distinctive plumages and characteristic calls, Eastern Towhees rank among our most familiar occupants of brushy habitats. They are found in successional fields, small woodlots, woodland edges, and are particularly fond of red cedar-covered hillsides in southern Ohio. They also occupy dense hedgerows if successional fields are nearby but avoid shrubby fencerows surrounded by cultivated fields.

These towhees normally raise two broods annually. Their first nests are placed on the ground and constructed during the last half of April in southern Ohio and early May in the northern counties. These broods usually fledge in late May and June. Their second nests are mostly placed in low dense shrubs and tangles but are reported as high as twelve feet in red cedars (Braund

1940b). These clutches are laid during
June and early July, with the last young
fledging in August (Phillips 1980,
Trautman 1940).

Eastern Towhees are generally fairly
common to common summer residents in the southern and eastern
counties, where 8–40+ are counted
daily. Similar numbers are encountered
locally in central and western Ohio,
such as in the Oak Openings
(Campbell 1968). However, smaller
numbers generally summer in the
western counties north of Butler,

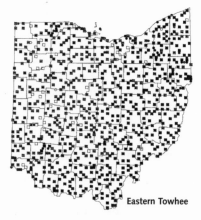

Eastern Towhee

Warren, Clinton, Highland, and Ross and daily totals seldom exceed 2–12.
They become locally uncommon summer residents in the intensively cultivated western counties where successional habitats are scarce (Peterjohn and Rice
1991).

Since the mid-1960s, breeding Eastern Towhee populations have declined
significantly in most of eastern North America, although the Ohio trends
remained stable (Sauer et al. 1998). Several factors contributed to local declines
in Ohio, most notably the loss of suitable shrubby habitats through secondary
succession and conversion into cultivated fields. Populations were also reduced
by the severe winters of 1976–1978 and did not recover until the 1980s.

Most of these towhees spend the winter months in the southern United
States. Fall migrants are generally uncommon to fairly common and produce
daily totals of 3–15 individuals and infrequent concentrations of 30–50+. The
first fall migrants appear at lakefront migrant traps by September 18–25 and
most migration occurs between October 1 and 21. The last migrants normally depart by the first week of November.

Migrant Eastern Towhees are very noticeable during spring. A few arrive in
late February but they normally appear by March 10–15. They are regularly
encountered during the last half of March, becoming uncommon to locally
common between April 15 and May 8. Spring totals are usually 3–10 daily.
Large flights produce local concentrations of 15–50 and as many as 125–150 at
Columbus and the Oak Openings (Campbell 1968, Thomson 1983). The latest spring migrants usually depart from Lake Erie by May 15.

As winter residents, Eastern Towhees are casual to rare in northern Ohio,
rare to uncommon in the glaciated central counties, and uncommon to fairly
common in southern and unglaciated Ohio. They are relatively scarce some
years, with very few sightings from the northern half of the state and only indi-

viduals or flocks of eight or fewer in the southern counties. During other years, towhees may be fairly numerous and small flocks may appear in any county. The largest reported winter concentrations include 18–25 in northern Ohio, 75 in the Salem area (Columbiana County) during the winter of 1931–1932 (Baird 1932b), and Christmas Bird Count totals of 30 at Cleveland, 74 at Oxford (Butler County), and 118–214 at Cincinnati. Wintering towhees occupy the same shrubby habitats where they are found during summer, although a few also visit bird feeders.

Bachman's Sparrow *Aimophila aestivalis* (Lichtenstein)

Bachman's Sparrow was first recorded from Ohio on August 18, 1890, when a specimen was secured at Columbus (Jones 1903). These sparrows were sporadically reported during the 1890s, although spring migrants appeared north to Lake Erie at Cedar Point (Erie County) on May 14–17, 1900 (Jones 1910). Most of their range expansion apparently occurred between 1900 and 1915, when Bachman's Sparrows were initially recorded from many locations in southern and eastern Ohio. The first nests were reported from Highland County in 1898 and Fairfield County in 1903. Nesting populations were firmly established by 1910 (Brooks 1938a, Roads 1936).

Their populations apparently peaked between 1915 and 1922 but may have declined by the 1930s (Brooks 1938a). In 1935, summering Bachman's Sparrows were recorded from every county north to Butler, Montgomery, Greene, Fayette, Franklin, Knox, Ashland, Wayne, Tuscarawas, and Belmont (Brooks 1938a, Hicks 1935a). Only a few spring overflights were reported north of these counties. These summering sparrows were generally rare to uncommon and irregularly reported from the southwestern counties. Along the Allegheny Plateau, they were rare in most counties, becoming uncommon in Vinton County and fairly common in Hocking County (Hicks 1937a).

Breeding Bachman's Sparrows were frequently encountered on the dry upper slopes of hillsides. These hillsides were generally eroded and covered with sparse herbaceous vegetation and blackberry tangles; the gullies were covered with trees, shrubs, and vines (Brooks 1938a). Despite the fairly open habitats, these sparrows were difficult to observe, since they mostly skulked along the ground. Only singing males were obvious, and their beautiful songs carried considerable distances on a calm summer evening. They nested on the ground under weeds and grasses and their nests were difficult to discover. The first nesting attempts were normally initiated during May, with the broods fledging in late June and early July. They may have raised two broods, since nests with eggs were recorded as late as August 6 (Lloyd 1931).

As spring migrants, the earliest Bachman's Sparrow returned to Portsmouth by April 2. Most males appeared on their breeding territories by April 18–30 (Brooks 1938a). Spring migration apparently continued through mid-May, based on the few extralimital sightings near Lake Erie. Singing males were regularly located into early July, but there were relatively few records once singing ceased. Their fall migration was poorly documented. Most sparrows apparently departed during August and early September. The latest reported fall sighting was September 17 (Borror 1950).

Breeding populations underwent another brief expansion between the mid-1940s and early 1950s. This expansion was most evident in northern Ohio, where the first Cleveland area records occurred in 1944 and 1949, while Toledo's first Bachman's Sparrow was noted in 1948 (Campbell 1968, Williams 1950). Increased populations were not evident within the southern and eastern counties during these years.

Their final decline apparently began during the late 1950s. They were last recorded at East Liverpool in 1963 and at Utica and Dayton in 1964 (Hall 1963b, Mathena et al. 1984, Petersen 1964d). By the mid-1960s, remnant populations remained near Cincinnati and very locally in the southeastern counties (Austing and Imbrogno 1976). These populations disappeared by the late 1960s and only isolated pairs remained. Surprisingly, the last confirmed summer sightings were from locations outside their normal range. Male Bachman's Sparrows summered in the Oak Openings of Lucas County in 1968, 1971, and 1972, although breeding was never established (Campbell 1973). Single birds were recorded from Trumbull County and Youngstown during 1972 (Hall 1972c). The last territorial male summered at Highbanks Metropolitan Park in Delaware County in 1974.

Their disappearance is perplexing; there are no apparent reasons for their decline. Suitable habitats seem to be available throughout the southeastern counties, and no species is known to compete with Bachman's Sparrows. But for whatever reasons, they disappeared from Ohio and adjacent states. The last documented sighting was from Scioto County on September 6, 1978 (Kleen 1979a).

American Tree Sparrow *Spizella arborea* (Wilson)

During the waning days of October, a strong cold front encourages most migrant songbirds to depart for warmer climates. This cold weather also prompts the return of winter residents, including the American Tree Sparrow, which breeds in the Arctic tundra and is well suited to withstand an Ohio winter. The earliest American Tree Sparrows have returned to Lake Erie by September 25 and central Ohio by September 27 (Borror 1950, Rosche 1992), but they normally appear in northern Ohio during the last half of October and in the southern counties by the first week of November. Their numbers increase rapidly and flocks of 10–100+ appear by late November. These winter residents inhabit weedy fields, roadsides, wetlands, brushy thickets, edges of woodlots, and occasionally visit rural bird feeders.

American Tree Sparrows were formerly among our most numerous wintering birds. During the 1920s and 1930s, daily counts in central Ohio regularly produced totals of 200–700 individuals (Trautman 1977). Similar numbers were encountered elsewhere, while as many as 1,000+ might be tallied under favorable circumstances. Their numbers declined in the 1940s, a trend continuing through the 1990s. This decline was attributed to the loss of successional habitats (Trautman 1977).

American Tree Sparrows remain fairly numerous winter residents, although their numbers fluctuate from year to year. Their abundance is frequently correlated with winter weather conditions. Influxes are usually associated with severe weather in Canada and the upper Great Lakes that forces birds into Ohio. Prolonged severe weather in Ohio may cause them to migrate farther south.

Wintering American Tree Sparrows are most numerous in central and northern Ohio, where they are fairly common to abundant residents. As many as 30–100 are recorded daily and totals of 150–300 are frequent. Christmas Bird Counts may produce tallies of 1,000–2,000+ during years of maximum abundance. They are fairly common to locally common in the southwestern counties. While daily totals seldom exceed 25–75, concentrations of 500–800 are occasionally reported. They are least numerous in the southeastern counties, especially bordering the Ohio River, where daily totals of these uncommon to fairly common residents seldom exceed 10–50.

A warm, sunny March day may prompt male American Tree Sparrows to produce their beautiful, clear whistled song. This song is not regularly heard within Ohio, since most begin their northward migration as soon as the weather begins to moderate. They normally depart from the southern and central counties by March 25–30, although they are regularly encountered along Lake Erie through the first week of April. The last migrants are usually recorded between April 10 and 20. A few late migrants have lingered through May 7–12 in southwestern Ohio and May 22–30 in the northern counties.

Chipping Sparrow *Spizella passerina* (Bechstein)

These handsome little sparrows are summer residents familiar to many Ohioans as a result of their preference for nesting in shrubbery around residences. They prefer large mowed lawns surrounding suburban and rural residences, but also occupy orchards, pine plantations and, in densely populated urban areas, parks and cemeteries.

Given these habitat preferences, Chipping Sparrows are fairly common to common summer residents. They are most numerous in the southern and eastern counties, where roadside surveys regularly produce counts of 20–60+ daily. Similar numbers are noted around the peripheries of large cities in the remainder of the state. Fewer Chipping Sparrows are found in the intensively farmed western and central counties, where daily totals seldom exceed 5–20.

Chipping
Sparrow

Their long-term population trends apparently varied across Ohio. Chipping Sparrows declined in the Toledo area after the early 1900s, a trend continuing into the 1970s (Campbell 1968, 1973). Similar declines were evident in other central and western counties where intensive farming practices eliminated suitable habitats. These local declines were not apparent elsewhere, and data from Breeding Bird Survey routes indicated increasing statewide populations since 1966 (Sauer et al. 1998).

As spring migrants, the earliest Chipping Sparrows appear across the state by March 12–18. They become fairly common to common migrants by April 10–20. Their spring migration is mostly resident sparrows returning to their territories. Flights of 15–50+ are occasionally encountered during April 20–May 7, while concentrations of 100–200+ are exceptional. The last migrants normally depart lakefront migrant traps by May 15–20.

Nest construction has been reported as early as April 7 and a nest with eggs by April 16, although most first clutches are laid during late April and May (Trautman 1940). The first broods may fledge during the last half of May but most are observed in June. Chipping Sparrows raise two or three broods annually; nests with eggs are reported through August 1, while adults accompanied by dependent young are regularly noted well into August (Braund 1938a, Campbell 1968).

During autumn, Chipping Sparrows frequently form flocks of 10–25+ individuals. They are locally abundant along Lake Erie and in the northeastern counties, where flights of 100–250+ occasionally occur, but are normally fairly common to common in the eastern and southern counties as daily totals of 5–50+. Fall migrants are uncommon elsewhere and produce totals of 20 or fewer daily. These migrants are most apparent during September 20–October

20, with small numbers lingering into November or December during mild autumns.

Chipping Sparrows normally winter in the southern United States and Mexico (AOU 1998). Their winter status in Ohio is obscured by numerous misidentifications on Christmas Bird Counts. Before 1970, these sparrows were accidental visitors during December and early January, but there were no confirmed overwintering records. The number of winter reports increased after 1970, producing an average of one confirmed sighting every two or three years through 1990 and nearly annual midwinter records subsequently. Wintering individuals are reported from all portions of the state, and are accidental or casual in the southern counties and strictly accidental elsewhere. Most reports are of isolated sparrows visiting bird feeders, but ten were discovered near Proctorville during late December 1989 (Hall 1990b).

Clay-colored Sparrow *Spizella pallida* (Swainson)

Before 1920, Clay-colored Sparrows were restricted to the northern Great Plains states and adjacent Canadian provinces, migrating through the central United States to wintering areas in Mexico. The 1920s marked the initiation of an eastward range expansion through Ontario, Minnesota, Wisconsin, and Michigan (DeVos 1964). These sparrows became well established around the upper Great Lakes by the mid-1960s. This range expansion continued, and they presently breed across southern Ontario to southwestern Quebec and occasionally western New York (AOU 1998).

The appearance of Clay-colored Sparrows in Ohio and the evolution of their status are correlated with this range expansion. The first Clay-colored Sparrow was collected by Charles Walker at South Bass Island on May 12, 1940 (Walker 1941). Another was sighted in Ottawa County on May 16, 1948 (Campbell 1968). There were no sight records during the 1950s and only three in the 1960s. Once a breeding population became established in southern Ontario, they became fairly regular migrants. Clay-coloreds averaged records during two of every three years during 1976–1989, but produced 1–10+ reports annually during the 1990s.

Most Ohio records are of spring migrants, with approximately forty sightings through 1999. They are casual to rare along Lake Erie but accidental visitors to inland counties, with at least fourteen sightings scattered across the state. All spring reports are of one or two Clay-coloreds observed between April 22 and May 22.

Although Clay-colored Sparrows should appear during fall migration, there are few records. These migrants casually appear in the Cleveland area, producing at least eight acceptable reports since 1980 of singles noted between

September 16 and October 14. They are accidental elsewhere, with the only inland records of single sparrows at Kent on September 14, 1980 (Kleen 1981), and two reports in Holmes County between September 17 and October 7.

There are no confirmed winter records. One Clay-colored reportedly was banded in Miami County during December 1961, but no details are available to support this record.

As sightings increased during the 1990s, Clay-colored Sparrows began to remain into summer. The first summer record was of a singing male in the Cuyahoga Valley National Recreation Area (Summit County) through June 19, 1994 (Harlan 1994d). Another male established a territory near Berlin Heights (Erie County) during May–June 1999 (Whan 1999a). While Clay-colored Sparrows remain accidental summer visitors, the establishment of a breeding population is a possibility.

Field Sparrow *Spizella pusilla* (Wilson)

Occupants of brushy successional habitats, Field Sparrows are most numerous in fallow fields where tangles, shrubs, and saplings are scattered among weeds and grasses. Breeding densities may approach one pair per acre in ideal habitats (Williams 1950). In addition to fallow fields, smaller numbers inhabit brushy pastures, shrubby woodland edges, fencerows, and the brushy borders of streams and swamps.

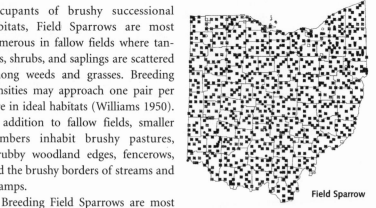

Field Sparrow

Breeding Field Sparrows are most numerous in the southern and eastern counties. They are abundant on the red cedar-covered hillsides in Adams and Brown Counties, where 50–100+ are tallied daily. They are common in other successional habitats, and 20–40+ daily are counted in other eastern and southern counties. Similar numbers are locally encountered in suitable habitats elsewhere, such as the Oak Openings near Toledo. In intensively farmed central and western Ohio, Field Sparrows are fairly common summer residents; daily totals seldom exceed 5–15. They become scarce within large urban areas.

Field Sparrows undoubtedly increased in numbers after Ohio's virgin forests were replaced by younger successional habitats. They became common summer residents by the late nineteenth century (Wheaton 1882). Their populations significantly declined during recent decades, however, a trend that was evident along statewide Breeding Bird Survey routes since 1966 (Sauer et al. 1998).

Nesting activities begin by late April in southern Ohio and early May farther north. Their nests are built on the ground or in shrubs and saplings to heights of fourteen feet. First clutches are normally laid by May 5–15, but unusually early nests produce dependent young by May 14 (Trautman 1940). The first broods normally fledge during June. Field Sparrows raise multiple broods annually. Nests with eggs have been discovered as late as August 26 at Cleveland (Williams 1950). Extraordinarily late fledglings were reported from Cincinnati on October 10, 1937 (Walker 1937b).

Most Field Sparrows spend the winter months in the southern United States. Since these sparrows are common summer residents, the beginning of their fall migration is difficult to determine. The bulk of this migration occurs between September 20 and October 20, with the last migrants departing by November 15. These migrants are uncommon to locally common and mostly observed in flocks of 20 or fewer, with occasional concentrations of 40–140+.

Before 1940, Field Sparrows were rather unusual winter residents. Since then their numbers have markedly increased. Today, winter Field Sparrows are most numerous in southern Ohio, especially near Cincinnati. They are generally uncommon to fairly common residents in these counties, with totals of 5–40 daily. These numbers are subject to considerable annual fluctuations. During years of peak abundance, 100–200+ have been reported on several southern Ohio Christmas Bird Counts. Wintering Field Sparrows are much less numerous in central Ohio, where they are rare to locally uncommon as scattered individuals or flocks of 15 or fewer. They are least numerous in northern Ohio, where they are rare winter residents, becoming casual in the extreme northeastern counties. Most northern Ohio winter records are of 1–8 individuals.

The first spring migrants appear in the southern counties in mid-March and along Lake Erie before the end of the month. Their migration peaks during April. While the largest flights formerly produced totals of 300–400 (Campbell 1968, Trautman 1940), similar movements have not been apparent since the 1960s. In recent years, the largest flights seldom exceed 50–100, and most reports of these fairly common to common migrants are of 20 or fewer daily. Their spring migration normally ends by April 20–25, although a few remain along Lake Erie into the first week of May.

Vesper Sparrow *Pooecetes gramineus* (Gmelin)

Few birds benefited more from the clearing of Ohio's virgin forests than the Vesper Sparrow. These forests were replaced by small cultivated fields, pastures, and hayfields bordered by brushy fencerows—nearly ideal habitats for this occupant of open farmlands. Numbers of Vesper Sparrows increased considerably during the nineteenth century; in its latter decades, they became abundant summer residents throughout the state. Migrants were also very plentiful, especially in spring, when Jones (1903) found Vespers "swarming over fields and pastures" in considerable numbers.

Vesper Sparrow

Sizable populations were maintained into the first decades of the twentieth century. Hicks (1935a) considered Vespers common to abundant residents in every county, somewhat less numerous and locally distributed in extreme southern Ohio. Impressive numbers of migrants also appeared. Spring flights frequently produced concentrations of 100–160 individuals (Campbell 1968, Trautman 1940). Larger numbers appeared each autumn, at least near Buckeye Lake, where Trautman (1940) regularly noted flocks of 100–300 and as many as 500 could be found.

By the 1930s, changing land-use practices already produced noticeable declines in breeding populations (Price 1935). Farm fields were becoming larger, grasslands were converted to cultivated crops, and fencerows were disappearing. In the southeastern counties, Vesper Sparrows were also losing breeding habitats to successional changes. These factors reduced Vesper Sparrow populations during subsequent decades. Their numbers were substantially reduced in most counties by 1960 (Thomson 1983), a trend that was evident across Ohio after 1966 (Sauer et al. 1998).

Despite reduced populations, Vesper Sparrows remain fairly common to common summer residents within farmlands east through Huron, Richland, Knox, Licking, Pickaway, and Ross Counties (Peterjohn and Rice 1991). Daily totals of 5–20 are possible in most of these counties and 30–50+ locally occur in western Ohio. Vesper Sparrows are uncommon to fairly common summer residents in northeastern Ohio and along the unglaciated Allegheny Plateau south to Muskingum, Guernsey, and Belmont Counties. While they become locally common in reclaimed strip mines, generally 1–6 are recorded daily within most of these counties. Elsewhere along the Allegheny Plateau and within the southwestern counties bordering the Ohio River, Vesper Sparrows are casual to rare residents as scattered pairs (Peterjohn and Rice 1991).

Breeding Vesper Sparrows prefer well-drained fields with sparse vegetation.

Their nests are placed on the ground, usually under a clump of grasses. Nests with eggs have been reported by the last week of April, although most first clutches are laid by mid-May (Trautman 1940, Williams 1950). Fledglings have been detected by May 17 but are normally expected during mid-June. Vesper Sparrows apparently raise two broods annually. Second clutches are noted through mid-July and adults accompanied by fledglings through August 13 (Price 1940a, Trautman 1940).

As spring migrants, Vesper Sparrows are mostly noted as residents returning to their territories. Small flights occasionally produce local concentrations of 20–40+, but daily totals are normally ten or fewer. Within southeastern Ohio, these migrants are rare to uncommon, with only 1–5 daily. While the first migrants have been noted as early as the first week of March, they normally appear by March 20–30. Most Vespers return during April and few migrants are detected after April 25.

Their fall migration has become poorly defined in recent years. After the males quit singing in July, Vesper Sparrows become inconspicuous. Most quietly depart between September 15 and October 20, with the last migrants lingering into the first half of November. Later migrants have become very rare since 1960. Fall Vespers are generally uncommon to rare migrants at most localities, usually reported as scattered individuals. The largest recent flocks were composed of 20–35. Fall concentrations in excess of 100 have not been reported since the 1930s.

Vesper Sparrows have always been accidental to casual winter visitors. Most are discovered before January 15, although a few have overwintered. While they have been reported throughout Ohio, they are not regularly noted at any location, and there are relatively few winter records from the northeastern counties. Wintering Vespers are almost invariably isolated individuals inhabiting brushy fencerows and woodland edges near farm fields. The number of winter records has averaged one sighting every two years since the mid-1960s.

Lark Sparrow *Chondestes grammacus* (Say)

Lark Sparrows expanded into Ohio during the nineteenth century, as the land use became predominantly agricultural. They were first recorded in 1861 and appeared east to the Scioto River and north to central Ohio by 1882 (Wheaton 1882). Small numbers expanded into northern Ohio during the 1890s. Their populations probably peaked between 1900 and 1910. In that decade, small numbers were regularly encountered in northern Ohio near Toledo, Oberlin, and Cleveland (Campbell 1968, Jones 1903). They were also "rather common" summer residents near Buckeye Lake (Trautman 1940). Lark Sparrows were widely distributed elsewhere except for the eastern third of the state (Jones 1903).

By 1935, Lark Sparrows had declined, and the center of their distribution shifted to the south-central and southeastern counties (Hicks 1935a, 1937a). Along the unglaciated Allegheny Plateau, they were very locally distributed and generally very rare or rare in every county north to Coshocton, Guernsey, and Belmont. Larger populations were noted in Adams County, where as many as 25 pairs summered during some years, and Muskingum County, where 14 pairs were located in 1935 (Brooks 1938b). Numbers were

Lark Sparrow

variable, and Lark Sparrows seldom remained at any locality for more than a few years. Elsewhere, breeding or summering Lark Sparrows were reported from four southwestern counties, twelve central and west-central counties, and six counties in the northern third of the state. While nesting Lark Sparrows were regularly encountered near Toledo and in Butler County (Campbell 1968, Kemsies and Randle 1953), their appearance in the other glaciated counties was very sporadic.

Their breeding population continued to decline. This decline was poorly documented, partly as a result of their fluctuating numbers and sporadic appearance even at traditional nesting locations. This variability produced short-lived increases during the 1950s and 1960s (Nolan 1955d, Petersen 1965c). Lark Sparrows then disappeared from most counties. By the late 1960s, breeding Lark Sparrows were restricted to isolated populations in the Oak Openings of Lucas County and southern Adams County. Only infrequent individuals were encountered elsewhere.

Their status has not changed appreciably since the 1960s. During the Breeding Bird Atlas, their total population probably did not exceed 12 pairs. As many as five pairs annually nested in the Oak Openings and adjacent portions of Fulton County. Sporadic observations indicated that a few Lark Sparrows remained in southwestern Adams County. The only other summer records were of breeding pairs in Hamilton and Auglaize Counties (Peterjohn and Rice 1991). During the 1990s, the Oak Openings population increased to 20 pairs by 1998 in response to favorable habitat management (Whan 1999b). Other breeding records were limited to 1–6 adults at Killdeer Plains Wildlife Area during 1994–1997 (Brock 1994, 1995d) and one pair near Columbus in 1993 and 1994 (Harlan 1995a). The absence of sightings from Adams County may indicate that this small population has disappeared.

Their disappearance from Ohio is perplexing. Suitable habitats are seemingly available. While Lark Sparrows are susceptible to nest parasitism by Brown-headed Cowbirds, their decline started long before cowbirds were as numerous as they are today. However, Brooks (1938b) noted that these sparrows occupied markedly different habitats within the Ohio River valley than elsewhere in their range. Perhaps these habitats are marginal for Lark Sparrows and their reproductive success was insufficient to maintain their populations.

Lark Sparrows prefer to nest in disturbed open habitats characterized by short vegetation interspersed with open soil, where there are a few boulders, fenceposts, small trees, and telephone poles for use as perches by singing males. Rocky, overgrazed pastures are preferred in southern Ohio, while the Oak Openings Lark Sparrows occupy open weedy and shrubby fields along sandy beach ridges. Nesting pairs have also inhabited abandoned quarries. Their nesting activities normally commence during May, although adults accompanied by young have been observed as early as May 29 (Grigore 1994). Most first broods fledge during June. Later breeding attempts are represented by nests with eggs through July 15 and fledglings through July 27 (Campbell 1973, Gier 1949).

These summer residents normally disappear shortly after their young fledge. Adults are seldom encountered after early August, although they have been observed into the first week of October in the Oak Openings area (Grigore 1994). They are accidental fall migrants, with only one to three reports each decade. The few fall records are mostly single sparrows observed in the vicinity of Lake Erie between the last week of August and mid-October.

Lark Sparrows are accidental winter visitors. One was closely observed at the North Chagrin Reservation in Cuyahoga County during January 25–27, 1964, but no other details are available (Newman 1969). The only documented winter reports are of one observed by many birders near Farmerstown (Holmes County) between December 30, 1997, and April 4, 1998 (R. Schlabach 1998), and another near New Bedford (Coshocton County) through December 26, 1998 (R. Schlabach 1999).

As spring migrants, most Lark Sparrows are noted between April 20 and May 15. Since the mid-1960s, this movement is primarily the few resident pairs returning to their territories. These sparrows are accidental spring migrants away from established nesting locations, producing three to six records each decade. Most extralimital spring Lark Sparrows are discovered within the western half of Ohio, although one was noted in Holmes County on April 28, 1986, and another in Muskingum County on May 2, 1997 (Fazio 1997a, Peterjohn 1986c).

Black-throated Sparrow *Amphispiza bilineata* (Cassin)

As occupants of deserts and dry shrublands, Black-throated Sparrows are widely distributed in Mexico and the western United States north to southern Oregon, southern Wyoming, and western Oklahoma. They withdraw from the northern edge of this range during winter. Black-throated Sparrows also wander into central and eastern North America (AOU 1998), where most appear during late fall and winter at bird feeders.

Ohio's first record of this accidental visitor fits this established pattern of vagrancy. A Black-throated Sparrow visited the feeder of Helen Stump in Conneaut between November 5 and December 9, 1961. It was carefully studied by Mrs. Stump and its identification corroborated by J. Paul Perkins and Paul Savage (Savage 1962).

The only other Black-throated Sparrow was discovered by Andy Fondryk at the Hambden Orchard Wildlife Area (Geauga County) on June 3, 1988. This singing male established a territory and was observed through late July (Peterjohn 1988d). Its unexpected appearance in northeastern Ohio may represent the first summer record anywhere in eastern North America.

Lark Bunting *Calamospiza melanocorys* Stejneger

Lark Buntings are widespread occupants of short-grass prairies throughout central North America. Their breeding range extends from the southern Canadian Prairie Provinces to northern New Mexico and Texas. Most wintering buntings are found in the southwestern United States and Mexico (AOU 1998). They also wander outside their normal range during all seasons. Ohio's ten acceptable records of this accidental visitor consist of four sightings during summer, two in spring, one in fall, and three in winter.

Ohio's first Lark Buntings were reported during the 1930s. Lawrence Hicks noted a flock of seven males along the Maumee River near Napolean (Henry County) on July 28, 1930, and a flock of three in Jerusalem Township, Henry County on August 9, 1937 (Hicks 1946). These sight records are supported by sketchy details, suggesting that these distinctive birds were correctly identified. These records may have been associated with the extended droughts on the North American prairies during that decade.

The first specimens were secured during the 1940s. An immature Lark Bunting was collected in South Euclid (Cuyahoga County) on September 6, 1944 (Skaggs 1945). Another was collected near the village of Deshler (Henry County) on August 7, 1945 (Hicks 1946). It was discovered the previous day in association with a second bunting.

Lark Buntings then went unrecorded until 1962, when a female was discovered near Columbus on April 28 (Thomson 1983). During the 1970s, a territorial male was reported near Conneaut on June 28, 1970, but "had been present for some time" and viewed by many observers (Flanigan 1970). A male Lark Bunting appeared at a feeder in Thurston (Licking County) during January 1971. It remained through May 8 and was closely studied as it molted into breeding plumage (Thomson 1983). Two females were discovered along a county road in Scioto Township, Pickaway County, on April 24, 1977. These birds were carefully observed on the ground and in flight as they foraged along the edge of cultivated fields. Following their absence during the 1980s, Lark Buntings have appeared twice during winter in the 1990s in Holmes County: one near Fredericksburg during January 1–4, 1992 (Peterjohn 1992b), and a first-year male near Farmerstown on January 27–February 14, 1998, that was intermittently reported through April 4 (Brock 1998c, R. Schlabach 1998).

Savannah Sparrow *Passerculus sandwichensis* (Gmelin)

Savannah Sparrows rank among the more numerous summer residents of Ohio's grasslands. Their high-pitched songs are heard wherever suitable habitats exist. Breeding pairs reside in every county but are not uniformly distributed. Savannahs are fairly common to common residents within the northern and glaciated central counties, where daily totals of 5–20+ are frequent and local concentrations of 40–100+ are possible. Within the southwestern counties, they become

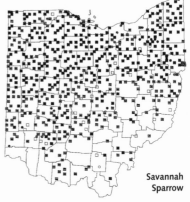

Savannah Sparrow

uncommon to rare and locally distributed, least numerous near the Ohio River. Most sightings are of ten or fewer daily, although local concentrations may develop. For example, 160 Savannahs were estimated in a single Clinton County field during 1984 (Peterjohn 1984d). Along the unglaciated Allegheny Plateau, Savannah Sparrows are fairly common south through Belmont, Guernsey, and Muskingum Counties, with most reports of ten or fewer daily. They become uncommon to rare and locally distributed along the remainder of the plateau, most likely to be encountered on reclaimed strip mines (Peterjohn and Rice 1991).

They have not always been widely distributed summer residents. In fact, they were strictly migrants through Ohio during the nineteenth century (Jones 1903). The first breeding populations were reported from several northern counties during the 1920s (Campbell 1940). By the mid-1930s, Hicks (1935a) cited summer records from thirty-two counties south to Defiance, Wyandot, Franklin, Licking, Wayne, Stark, and Columbiana.

This expansion continued during subsequent decades; nesting pairs reached Dayton and Cincinnati by 1952 (Kemsies and Randle 1953, Mathena et al. 1984). Their southward expansion along the unglaciated Allegheny Plateau continued into the 1970s. Their statewide breeding populations have apparently stabilized, and data from Breeding Bird Survey routes do not indicate any significant trends since 1966 (Sauer et al. 1998).

Savannah Sparrows breed in pastures and hayfields composed of grasses, clovers, and alfalfa. They prefer lightly grazed pastures with tall grasses but also reside in hayfields mowed once or twice a year. Their nests, expertly concealed on the ground under clumps of grasses, are usually discovered by accident. Nesting activities begin during May, and nests with eggs are reported between May 10 and July 18 (Williams 1950). Recently fledged young have appeared by June 5, but most are noted during late June and July. Late attempts produce fledglings into early August.

The spring migration of Savannah Sparrows is defined by the passage of singing males. While a few early migrants return during the first half of March, especially when temperatures are relatively mild, the first Savannahs are expected during March 23–April 3. They become widely distributed by April 8–12 and remain numerous until May 7. A few migrants are noted through May 20–25.

Spring Savannahs are generally uncommon to common migrants, most numerous within the glaciated counties. Daily totals are usually 3–25 during April. Larger flights occasionally produce concentrations of 60–150+. The largest movement occurred on April 22, 1951, when Trautman (1956) noted "hundreds" on South Bass Island in western Lake Erie.

Their status as fall migrants is not so thoroughly understood. When efforts are made to locate fall Savannahs, greater numbers are found than are normally reported during spring. Trautman (1940) routinely noted 15–50 daily at Buckeye Lake during the 1920s and 1930s and frequently noted as many as 60–180. Campbell (1968) also reported flights involving 100+ at Toledo, while 240–300 were reported from Big Island Wildlife Area during October 10–13, 1997 (Fazio 1998a). If such totals are applicable to the entire state, Savannah Sparrows may be fairly common to common fall migrants through most northern and central counties. They may be uncommon in southern Ohio, where suitable habitats are scarce.

The first fall migrants appear by September 5–15 and become widespread during the last half of the month. Their maximum abundance is normally attained between September 25 and October 20. They usually depart by November 7–10, with a few stragglers later in the month.

Savannah Sparrows were once considered accidental winter visitors, but their secretive habits probably caused them to be overlooked. During the 1980s, up to six wintering sparrows were regularly flushed from grassy fields along the Ross-Pickaway County Line Road in central Ohio. During the 1990s, as many as 12 were found in fields in Tuscarawas and Holmes Counties, while scattered individuals were noted at a few locations in western Ohio. These sightings indicate that Savannah Sparrows are probably rare and locally distributed winter residents in the southern two-thirds of the state, becoming accidental to casual farther north. While some individuals disappear when the weather conditions become harsh, others have overwintered.

Grasshopper Sparrow *Ammodramus savannarum* (Gmelin)

Named for their high-pitched insect-like song, Grasshopper Sparrows are inconspicuous, more likely to be heard than seen. Males are observed when they sing from the tops of weeds and grasses, but silent Grasshoppers remain hidden amid dense grassy cover and are observed only when flushed underfoot. Dawson (1903) once observed a male singing from the top of a sapling and sarcastically noted that this sparrow "surely must have atoned for his boldness by skulking among the grass roots for two days thereafter."

Grasshopper
Sparrow

Grasshopper Sparrows reside in hayfields, pastures, clover fields, and occasionally weedy fallow fields (Trautman 1940, Williams 1950). Their status reflects the availability of these habitats. Breeding Grasshoppers underwent a tremendous expansion during the nineteenth century, becoming widely distributed by the late 1800s. At the turn of the twentieth century, Jones (1903) considered them fairly common but locally distributed residents. Their numbers probably peaked in the 1920s and 1930s. At Buckeye Lake, for example, Trautman (1940) estimated 100–200 breeding pairs. Hicks (1935a) described them as common to extremely abundant summer residents, with records from every county. He later noted they were locally rare to uncommon in a few southeastern counties (Hicks 1937a).

Numbers of breeding sparrows declined in the 1940s and have continued to decrease (Robbins et al. 1986, Sauer et al. 1998, Trautman 1977). Factors contributing to this decline include conversion of grasslands and clover fields into cultivated crops and the more frequent mowing of remaining hayfields, which greatly reduces these sparrows' breeding success and increases the mortality of nesting adults. However, not all changes in land-use patterns have been detrimental. Along the unglaciated plateau, reclaimed strip mines have created abundant grasslands.

Breeding Grasshopper Sparrows are found in every county, although their abundance varies across the state. They are least numerous in northeastern Ohio, becoming rare to uncommon and locally distributed across Cuyahoga, Lake, Geauga, Ashtabula, and Trumbull Counties. In other northern and glaciated central counties, Grasshoppers are uncommon to locally common residents. Daily totals of 3–20 are noted in most counties, with occasional concentrations of 50–100+. They become fairly common to locally abundant summer residents in most southern and unglaciated counties, except for Hamilton and Brown Counties, where they are rare (Peterjohn and Rice 1991). While 5–20 are encountered daily, concentrations of 75–120+ develop in fallow fields in southwestern Ohio and reclaimed strip mines in the eastern counties.

Relatively little information is available on their breeding biology. First clutches are probably laid during May and early June. While fledglings have been reported by June 5 (Trautman 1940), most are observed in late June and early July. Second nesting attempts produce clutches through mid-July. These young fledge during August (Campbell 1968, Price 1932 and 1935).

Their spring migration is mostly Grasshopper Sparrows returning to their territories. The earliest overflights appeared at Cleveland by March 23 and other localities during the first half of April (Williams 1950). The first sparrows are normally detected during April 15–25 in the southern and central counties and April 25–May 3 along Lake Erie. Little migration is evident after May 15–20.

Once the males quit singing, Grasshopper Sparrows become very inconspicuous. There are few fall records after the first half of August. This paucity prompted Campbell (1968) to speculate that their southward movement is primarily during August. However, scattered sightings in September and October are indicative of southward movements similar to most sparrows. These migrants are noted into the first half of October, with a few late sightings through November 20.

Grasshopper Sparrows are apparently accidental winter visitors but would be easily overlooked. There are at least four confirmed winter records and several undocumented sightings that may be correct. These records are scattered across the state, including one banded in Ottawa County on December 14, 1983 (Peterjohn 1984a). Most winter reports are of single sparrows during December and early January. A Grasshopper Sparrow in Butler County on February 5, 1983, probably overwintered (Peterjohn 1983b).

Baird's Sparrow *Ammodramus bairdii* (Audubon)

On April 22, 1951, the passage of a cold front produced a spectacular movement of migrating birds along the south shore of Lake Erie. As Milton Trautman surveyed this movement on South Bass Island, he noticed an unusual sparrow among the multitudes of common sparrows. It was similar to a Savannah, but had an ochraceous central crown stripe and face pattern, while the streaking on its underparts was finer than the Savannah's, with only a narrow band of streaks across the upper breast (Trautman 1956). After carefully studying and describing the bird, Dr. Trautman concluded it was a Baird's Sparrow. His sighting provides the only acceptable record of this accidental visitor to Ohio and one of very few extralimital records from the eastern United States. Baird's Sparrows normally breed in the Dakotas, Montana, and adjacent southern Canada and winter in the southwestern United States and adjacent Mexico (AOU 1998).

Henslow's Sparrow *Ammodramus henslowii* (Audubon)

Most sparrows are drab brown birds that have few admirers. Nevertheless, they possess a certain charm. I have a particular affection for Henslow's Sparrows, partly because of their obscurity and partly for their attractive appearance. In fresh plumage, their olive faces, chestnut wings, and purplish-brown backs are colorful. Unfortunately, they usually remain hidden in vegetation rather than exhibiting this plumage. Even when they sing their distinctive song—which

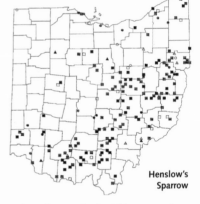

Henslow's Sparrow

is really more like a hiccup—they are as likely to be perched within vegetation as on an exposed stem.

The distribution and abundance of Henslow's Sparrows have been constantly changing, reflecting our increased ability to locate this species, as well as changes in habitat availability. Nesting Henslow's prefer grassy or weedy fields with a few scattered saplings and shrubs. They are equally at home on hillside grasslands dominated by broom-sedge and in reclaimed strip mines with extensive grasslands mixed with sweet-clovers. In northwestern Ohio, they prefer wet prairies dominated by sedges with scattered shrubs (Hyde 1939). Breeding Henslow's also inhabit cranberry bogs, timothy pastures, and clover hayfields (Walker 1928c).

As with most obscure birds, there is considerable confusion about the historic status of these sparrows. Audubon collected the first Henslow's Sparrow known to science in Kentucky, across the Ohio River from Cincinnati, in 1820. He later described the species as an accidental visitor to Ohio but provided no basis for this claim (Hyde 1939). The first Ohio specimen was collected in 1872 at Buckeye Lake (Trautman 1940). Henslow's were sporadically observed during the 1890s from Hamilton, Lorain, and Erie Counties (Kemsies and Randle 1953, Walker 1928c). Breeding was confirmed during 1904, when a nest was discovered in Seneca County (Henninger 1910a). However, they were not regularly reported until the 1920s.

Henslow's Sparrows greatly expanded during the 1920s and 1930s (Hyde 1939). By the mid-1930s, Hicks (1935a) cited summer records from forty-six counties, primarily in northern and central Ohio. He noted records from "every county north of Paulding, Henry, Wood, Seneca, Wyandot, Marion, Delaware, Franklin, Fairfield, Hocking, Perry, Muskingum, Coshocton, Tuscarawas, Stark, and Columbiana," claiming they were "locally abundant" in many counties. The only other records were from Champaign, Greene, Madison, and Jackson Counties.

Populations probably peaked in central and northern Ohio during the 1930s, when suitable grassland habitats were most prevalent. Declines were evident in the 1940s and continued through the 1950s, mostly the result of changing land-use practices and urban development. By the late 1960s, they became very rare at Toledo and uncommon at Cleveland (Campbell 1968, Newman 1969).

While Henslow's Sparrows declined in glaciated northern and central Ohio, they expanded into the southern and unglaciated counties. This expansion began during the 1940s but was poorly documented, except for the first records east of the Flushing Escarpment in Carroll and Jefferson Counties in 1944 (Buchanan 1980). These birds took advantage of habitats available in abandoned farmlands and extensive grasslands found in reclaimed strip mines.

Henslow's Sparrows were well established in southern and unglaciated Ohio by the early 1980s. Despite local fluctuations as suitable habitats appear and disappear, they remain uncommon to locally abundant summer residents in most counties southeast from Clermont, Highland, Ross, Licking, Knox, Stark, and Columbiana. They are most widely distributed along the glacial boundary, where suitable habitats are plentiful (Peterjohn and Rice 1991). They are less frequently encountered elsewhere but become locally abundant on reclaimed strip mines in Belmont, Harrison, Guernsey, Muskingum, Vinton, Gallia, and Lawrence Counties, where the largest colonies are composed of 50–130+ singing males (McCormac 1999). Similar large colonies appeared near several southwestern Ohio reservoirs during the 1980s but vanished when the habitats became unsuitable. Daily totals usually are 3–8 individuals away from large colonies. Populations have declined elsewhere, and these sparrows are accidental to rare summer residents in the glaciated central and northern counties, except along the glacial boundary. Pairs and groups of up to 5–9 males are scattered across these counties, but are very scarce in northwestern and west-central Ohio (Peterjohn and Rice 1991).

Relatively few Henslow's Sparrows are detected as spring migrants; most simply appear at their breeding territories. While they have returned as early as March 18 (Kemsies and Randle 1953), the first migrants are normally detected during April 10–20. Most return by May 15–20. The only sizable migration occurred on April 22, 1951, when "many dozens" were reported among an immense movement of sparrows on South Bass Island (Trautman 1956).

As summer residents, Henslow's Sparrows are among the few birds known to regularly switch locations between broods. Some of these movements are in response to mowing of hayfields, but this behavior has also been reported from undisturbed fields. Relatively little information is available on their nesting chronology. Nests are located on the ground and are very difficult to discover. The few reports of nests indicate that first clutches may be laid during late May, while later clutches are noted as late as August 8. The first broods usually fledge during the last half of June and early July. Dependent young have been observed as late as September 24 (Campbell 1968).

Henslow's Sparrows become very difficult to detect once the males cease singing. The relatively few records after early August indicate that migrants are most likely to appear during October, although they may remain into the first week of November at Cincinnati (Kemsies and Randle 1953). While there are two published December sight records, neither is accompanied by acceptable details.

Le Conte's Sparrow *Ammodramus leconteii* (Audubon)

The most elusive grassland sparrow, Le Conte's is a secretive skulker through dense herbaceous vegetation bordering marshes, bogs, and mudflats. Frustrating the birder's desire to get good views, Le Conte's do not normally respond to any form of attraction. Instead, they remain hidden until flushed at the observer's feet. Their flights are short and barely above the top of the vegetation before dropping into dense cover. With considerable perseverance, a Le Conte's Sparrow may be observed closely; it will prove to be one of the most handsome of all sparrows.

The status of Le Conte's Sparrow is poorly understood. The first record was provided by a specimen collected in Hamilton County on April 5, 1880

(Kemsies and Randle 1953). There were no additional records until one was observed near Toledo on September 3, 1932 (Campbell 1940).

The 1936 fall migration featured an unbelievable invasion for a species that had been recorded only twice previously. This movement was most noticeable in Lucas County, where the first Le Conte's appeared on August 30. Relatively few were detected during September, but the October movement was substantial. The largest numbers appeared in Jerusalem Township, Lucas County; 53 were counted in a single wet meadow on October 25 and several hundred were thought to be present (Campbell 1968). Six Le Conte's were collected in Clermont County between October 11 and 25 (Goodpaster and Maslowski 1937), while groups of six or fewer were reported from Wood, Franklin, Delaware, and Licking Counties (Hicks 1937c). Small numbers lingered through November 22–23 in Licking County.

That flight has never been repeated. Le Conte's Sparrows remained accidental visitors, with only one to four sightings per decade between 1940 and 1979. Greater observer activity produced seven documented records during the 1980s and at least ten reports during the 1990s, although this secretive sparrow is not detected annually.

Le Conte's Sparrows are accidental to casual spring visitors near Lake Erie, where there are at least twelve published sightings of single individuals. They are accidental migrants elsewhere, with only two records from the Cincinnati area and one in Holmes County on May 6, 1996 (Kemsies and Randle 1953, Conlon and Harlan 1996a). They have returned in March, but most records are between April 15 and May 7. The latest spring Le Conte's was noted at Toledo on May 12, 1945 (Campbell 1968).

Le Conte's Sparrows are casual fall migrants along the Cleveland-Lorain lakefront, averaging one sighting every two or three years. They are accidental elsewhere. After the 1936 invasion, the only inland records have been of single sparrows near Cincinnati on October 29, 1960 (Mumford 1961a); Pickaway County on October 9, 1978; Big Island Wildlife Area on September 29, 1984 (Peterjohn 1985a); and in Holmes County on October 20, 1991 (Peterjohn 1992a). All recent fall records are of 1–2 Le Conte's Sparrows. While one appeared at Cleveland on August 22, 1992 (Brock 1993a), most fall reports are between September 25 and October 25. The latest Le Conte's was collected in Lorain County on December 19, 1962 (Newman 1969).

Nelson's Sharp-tailed Sparrow *Ammodramus nelsoni* Allen

The behavior and habitat preferences of Le Conte's Sparrows are shared by this reclusive species. Migrant Nelson's Sharp-tailed Sparrows prefer sedge meadows, wet pastures, the grassy borders of marshes, depressions, and wet fields dominated by dense herbaceous vegetation. These brightly colored sparrows normally remain hidden within dense vegetation. Even spring migrants are unlikely to be detected, since Nelson's Sharp-taileds seldom sing away from their nesting range. Unlike Le Conte's Sparrows, which seldom offer satisfactory views, Nelson's Sharp-taileds are somewhat more obliging and respond to some forms of attraction by emerging from dense cover.

Nelson's Sharp-tailed Sparrows undoubtedly pass through Ohio each spring and autumn. Before 1960, these regular migrations went largely undetected. The majority of sightings have been reported since 1960, reflecting greater efforts to locate these sparrows.

Nelson's Sharp-tailed Sparrows are generally late spring migrants. The earliest confirmed reports are May 8–9 (Brock 1993c, Kemsies and Randle 1953), but most spring migrants are detected between May 15 and 28. These migrants are accidental to casual along Lake Erie, with at least seventeen records, mostly within the Central Basin. They are accidental through the interior counties, with four reports from central Ohio, two Cincinnati area sightings, and single records in Trumbull and Wyandot Counties. All spring reports involve 1–3 sparrows. These few records probably represent only a fraction of their numbers passing through Ohio each spring.

Their fall migration patterns are better understood. The first southward migrants appear between September 7 and 15. They are most likely to be observed during September 20–October 20, with a few stragglers into November. Nelson's Sharp-tailed Sparrows are rare to locally uncommon along the entire lakefront, with most sightings of 1–5 individuals. Within the interior counties, they are accidental to casual fall migrants through the glaciated counties, with sightings every two to four years. There are presently no sightings from the unglaciated counties. Most inland records are of five or fewer sparrows, although as many as ten were flushed near Findlay on October 8, 1961 (Phillips 1980).

During two years, Nelson's Sharp-tailed Sparrows staged pronounced invasions. In late September 1953, "flocks" were reported from the Cincinnati area. Few specific details were provided, but this movement coincided with a "substantial invasion" elsewhere in the Midwest (Nolan 1954a). A similar invasion was noted along western Lake Erie during autumn 1964. This movement was most apparent at Winous Point (Ottawa County), where 75 were counted September 30–October 1 and at least 200 were believed to be present (Campbell 1968, Petersen 1965a).

Nelson's Sharp-tailed Sparrows are accidental winter visitors. One at Cleveland on December 10, 1990 (Peterjohn 1991b), may have been an exceptionally late migrant. Three were discovered at Cleveland on December 4,

1952, and were regularly observed through February 1, 1953 (Nolan 1953b, Rosche 1992). Their subsequent disappearance may indicate that these sparrows did not overwinter.

Fox Sparrow *Passerella iliaca* (Merrem)

Fox Sparrows are among our earliest spring migrants, returning to brushy fields, dense fencerows, and shrubby woodlots with the first warm days. Their beautiful whistled song, too infrequently heard, is a welcome signal of the approaching spring. A few early migrants appear during the last half of February, but they normally return by March 3–12. This migration peaks between March 20 and April 15; they normally depart by April 20–25. Stragglers linger into the first half of May and exceptionally late birds are noted through May 20–28.

Relative abundance varies considerably from year to year. During most springs, Fox Sparrows are fairly common to common along Lake Erie, where 8–15 are observed daily and concentrations of 25–50+ may develop. They become uncommon to fairly common migrants through the interior counties; daily totals of 3–6 are expected and seldom exceed 15–25. Fox Sparrows infrequently stage sizable spring movements, becoming fairly common to common migrants in most counties. These movements produced flocks of 75 at Buckeye Lake in the 1920s and 1930s and 100 at Magee Marsh Wildlife Area on April 15, 1972 (Campbell 1973, Trautman 1940). They can also be fairly scarce, with no more than 2–10 at any locality.

Fox Sparrows normally breed in the boreal forests of Canada and Alaska (AOU 1998). They are accidental summer visitors to Ohio, with only one acceptable report. A male Fox Sparrow established a territory in Firestone Metropark in Akron, where it was initially discovered on June 4, 1989, and remained at least through June 26 (Rosche 1989).

Fewer Fox Sparrows are observed during fall migration. They become uncommon to fairly common along the lakefront but are rare to uncommon within the interior counties. Most fall sightings are of six or fewer individuals; the largest concentrations total 8–25. While migrants have appeared at Ashtabula and Cleveland by August 21–22 (Mumford 1960a, Williams 1950), these sightings are exceptionally early. They normally appear along Lake Erie during September 18–25. A Fox Sparrow in Hocking County on September 16, 1965, was very early for the southern counties (Hall 1966a), where they may not appear until mid-October. Most fall migrants are observed between October 10 and November 10, with small numbers through the end of November.

While most Fox Sparrows winter in the southern United States, small numbers regularly remain north to the Great Lakes. Within Ohio, they are rare winter residents in the southern counties, especially near Cincinnati. Most winter records are of 1–2 individuals, although small flocks of 8–10 may develop. A December 1987 concentration of approximately 100 near Cincinnati was remarkable (Peterjohn 1988b); they may have been very late migrants. Elsewhere, wintering Fox Sparrows are casual to rare residents within the central counties and accidental to casual in northern Ohio. As many as five have been reported from the central counties but most northern reports are of scattered individuals. Winter Fox Sparrow records have noticeably increased since 1940.

Song Sparrow *Melospiza melodia* (Wilson)

Few songbirds have been as extensively studied as Song Sparrows, whose life history became the subject of Margaret Morse Nice's classic monographs (Nice 1937, 1943). At a small area within the present city limits of Columbus, she carefully examined all aspects of their behavior and daily activities throughout the year. In addition to providing a wealth of information on this common species, her studies serve as a model for all other research into the life histories of songbirds.

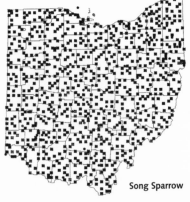

Song Sparrow

As winter residents, Song Sparrows are common to locally abundant, generally most numerous within the southern half of the state. Their numbers fluctuate in response to food and cover availability, as well as weather conditions. During years of maximum abundance, totals of 75–200+ may be encountered, although most daily counts are of 50 or fewer individuals. When they are relatively scarce, peak counts may total only 20–40. These wintering sparrows occupy all types of edge and successional habitats. The majority are males; approximately half are permanent residents within Ohio, while the remainder are migrants from farther north (Nice 1937).

Although they are classified as permanent residents, Song Sparrows undergo definite migrations each spring and fall. Their spring migration begins during February or early March. The earliest migrants are mostly males (Nice 1937). The largest movements occur between March 10 and 30, when most females return and many sparrows are in passage to more northerly breeding locations. These movements produce daily totals of 50–100+ in most counties and flights of 100–800+ along Lake Erie. The last migrants usually depart from northern Ohio by April 10–20.

Well before spring migration is underway, the resident males establish their breeding territories. Any warm weather during late January or early February prompts them to start singing, each producing a variable song that is different from his neighbor. As described by Nice (1943):

> The songs of each male are entirely distinct; as a rule they sound pleasant and "cheerful" to human ears, yet a few are disagreeable while still others are of great beauty. Many individuals have no specially distinctive songs, while some have one or two songs which are unforgettable to an attentive observer. The same individual may have songs of all degrees of quality: harsh, typical, and especially musical.

Breeding activities begin shortly after the females arrive. The nests are built solely by the females and construction may begin by the last week of March. The first nests are almost invariably placed on the ground (Nice 1937). As the season progresses, their nests are placed at greater heights; by midsummer, most nests are two to three feet above ground. The first eggs have been laid as early as April 10, but most first clutches are initiated between April 17 and 30. Nests with young have been noted by April 21, but most first broods hatch during May 5–18. Recently fledged young have appeared as early as April 25; most first broods fledge during the last half of May (Nice 1937, Trautman 1940). Second broods normally fledge during the last half of June and July (Nice 1937). The latest breeding attempts include nest construction through August 10 and nests with young as late as September 7 (Mathena et al. 1984, Walker 1940d).

During summer, Song Sparrows are common to abundant residents, occupying an array of habitats from residential yards to fallow fields, roadside thickets, brushy fencerows, woodland edges, and the margins of wetlands. Daily totals of 50–100+ are expected in most counties except the intensively cultivated western counties and large urban areas, where 20–50 are recorded daily. Data from Breeding Bird Surveys indicate that Ohio supports one of the largest Song Sparrow populations in North America (Robbins et al. 1986). This population has remained fairly constant throughout the twentieth century. Declines were evident following the severe winters of 1976–1978, but their numbers recovered by the early 1980s and subsequently remained stable (Sauer et al. 1998).

Their fall migration is normally apparent during the last week of September but their main passage is in October. Fall migrants are as numerous as spring migrants, producing movements of 50–500+ daily along Lake Erie and 25–200+ within the interior counties. The last lakefront migrants depart by November 10–15, while movements continue into early December within the interior counties.

Lincoln's Sparrow *Melospiza lincolnii* (Audubon)

This retiring species is more numerous than our sightings indicate. Spring Lincoln's Sparrows are secretive skulkers through dense brushy tangles, thickets, and woodland edges, and must be coaxed from the underbrush by pishing or by imitating a screech-owl's whistle.

Early spring Lincoln's Sparrows have appeared by April 14–21, but the first migrants are normally detected during the first week of May. Their northward movements peak between May 8 and 22, when they become uncommon to fairly common along Lake Erie but are rare to uncommon inland. Inland totals are usually 1–6 individuals daily. Along Lake Erie, eight or fewer are expected daily, but flights of 15–35 are possible. The largest movement totaled 100 at Euclid on May 11, 1984 (Peterjohn 1984c). Most depart by May 25–30, with occasional stragglers along the lakefront as late as June 12, 1986, at Euclid (Peterjohn 1986d).

Greater numbers of Lincoln's Sparrows pass through Ohio each autumn. These migrants prefer dense brushy cover but are also found in fallow fields. Lincoln's Sparrows are easily confused with juvenile Song Sparrows and August reports of Lincoln's Sparrows most likely represent misidentifications. The first Lincoln's usually return to Lake Erie by September 12–20 and to southern Ohio by the last days of the month. Most fall migrants are recorded between September 28 and October 20 as they become fairly common along Lake Erie and uncommon through most inland counties. Daily totals of 1–8 are expected inland and 1–10 along Lake Erie. Larger flights are infrequent but produced as many as 42 in one thicket and 200 daily at Buckeye Lake during the late 1920s and 1930s and 100+ at Cleveland on October 4, 1986 (Peterjohn 1987a, Trautman 1940). Occasional late migrants remain into November.

Most Lincoln's Sparrows winter from the southern United States south into Central America (AOU 1998). While there are a number of early winter sight records, especially on Christmas Bird Counts, many of them are questionable. Lincoln's Sparrows are accidental throughout Ohio during December; all winter sightings should be accompanied by thorough details. A few have been positively identified as late as December 20–30, but there are only two confirmed records of wintering individuals: one in downtown Cleveland during 1987–1988 that survived with the assistance of food provided by thoughtful birders (Peterjohn 1988b); and one in Akron during 1991–1992 that was observed into March (Harlan 1992b).

Swamp Sparrow *Melospiza georgiana* (Latham)

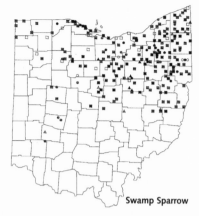

Swamp Sparrow

As their name implies, Swamp Sparrows are restricted to wetlands during the breeding season. Nesting pairs occupy cattail marshes, grassy wet meadows, shrubby vegetation bordering ponds, bogs, and lakes, and birch-maple swamp forests (Williams 1950). Their nests are placed low in herbaceous cover. Construction begins by late April or early May. Some clutches are laid during the last half of April, since fledged young have been reported by May 30 (Trautman 1940). However, most nests with eggs are noted between May 13 and June 25 and fledglings are expected during the last half of June and July (Williams 1950). Late clutches produce young into early August.

Breeding Swamp Sparrows are most numerous within northeastern Ohio south to the glacial boundary and west to Morrow, Richland, and Huron Counties (Peterjohn and Rice 1991). They are widespread and uncommon to common residents in this area. Summer totals normally are 3–10 individuals daily, although favorable habitats support 15–25+ males. They are also uncommon to fairly common residents in marshes bordering Sandusky Bay and western Lake Erie, where daily totals seldom exceed 3–8. Away from Lake Erie, they are rare to uncommon and locally distributed residents in the northwestern counties, as scattered pairs and groups of 4–8 individuals.

Along the unglaciated Allegheny Plateau, Swamp Sparrows are rare to uncommon and locally distributed south into Guernsey, Harrison, and Jefferson Counties (Peterjohn and Rice 1991). Most records are of 1–6 territorial males. They are now accidental to rare summer residents within the glaciated central counties, with records south to Clark, Pickaway, and Licking Counties. Small populations reside at Knox Lake and Indian Lake, but resident males are only sporadically encountered elsewhere. Nesting Swamp Sparrows have never been confirmed in southern Ohio, although singing males have lingered at Spring Valley Wildlife Area and other suitable wetlands into the first week of June.

Their statewide distribution and relative abundance have not markedly changed during the twentieth century (Hicks 1935a, Peterjohn and Rice 1991). The only noticeable decline is near Toledo, where Campbell (1968, 1973) reported reduced numbers in the western Lake Erie marshes and Oak Openings after 1940.

As migrants, Swamp Sparrows are most numerous within marshes and wet meadows, but they also frequent fallow fields, brushy thickets, shrubby woodland borders, parks, and cemeteries. They begin their northward movements during the last week of March. Their maximum abundance is attained between April 10 and May 7 and the last migrants depart by May 18–23. Spring Swamp Sparrows are most numerous along western Lake Erie and in northeastern Ohio. They are fairly common to common visitors to these areas; 10–30 are recorded daily and concentrations of 50–100+ are possible. Similar concentrations may develop in suitable marshes elsewhere in glaciated Ohio, but daily totals are normally 15 or fewer. Throughout the unglaciated counties, spring Swamp Sparrows are uncommon to fairly common migrants and most reports are of ten or fewer.

The first fall migrants may return by September 5–10 but are expected during September 15–22. The largest southward movements occur during October. Only wintering Swamp Sparrows remain after mid-November. These migrants become common to abundant along western Lake Erie, where 20–50 are observed daily and flights of 100–200 regularly appear in late October (Campbell 1968). The largest movement totaled 532 in Ottawa County on October 5, 1979 (Kleen 1980a). They are also common migrants through northeastern Ohio, although fall totals seldom exceed 10–50. Within the remainder of Ohio, Swamp Sparrows are locally common migrants through wetlands in the glaciated counties, where daily totals are normally 5–15 and as many as 30–80 are counted during the largest flights. Elsewhere, they become uncommon to fairly common migrants, with only 3–10 daily.

Wintering Swamp Sparrows are most numerous within wetland habitats but are regularly found in weedy fields, brushy thickets, and woodland edges. While they have wintered regularly during the twentieth century, their numbers have noticeably increased since the 1950s.

Swamp Sparrows are fairly common winter residents within the southern counties, where 3–10 are expected daily and 20–40 may congregate in favorable habitats. A concentration of 100 in Hamilton County on January 1, 1996, was exceptional (Harlan 1996b). They attain a similar status and relative abundance within the western Lake Erie marshes, where Christmas Bird Count totals of 100–150+ are possible. Within the central and interior northwestern counties, Swamp Sparrows become locally rare to fairly common winter residents; daily totals are usually six or fewer individuals. Local concentrations may develop in central Ohio near Columbus, where as many as 50–60 have been tallied. Wintering Swamp Sparrows are rare to locally uncommon in northeastern Ohio, and most sightings are of five or fewer, with occasional flocks of 10–12. Numbers noticeably diminish during winter and they may become scarce by February, especially when the weather is harsh.

White-throated Sparrow *Zonotrichia albicollis* (Gmelin)

White-throated Sparrows are found wherever migrant birds congregate, most frequently brushy fields, dense thickets, and shrubby woodland edges but also woodlands, parks, and cemeteries. They spend most of their time on the ground, scratching through the leaf litter. As they forage among vegetation or hide in thick cover, their presence is readily detected by their distinctive call notes or their pleasant whistled song.

Their northward migration begins by the last week of March in the southern and central counties. They become widespread during April 10–17, and their maximum abundance is attained between April 22 and May 10. At that time, White-throated Sparrows are fairly common to common in most counties and abundant along Lake Erie. Daily totals of 10–50 are noted at most localities, while larger movements produce tallies of 50–100+. Sizable flights produce phenomenal numbers, such as 800 at Columbus on May 6, 1975 (Thomson 1983). Along Lake Erie, concentrations of 300–500+ are infrequently recorded and more than 1,200 were estimated at Magee Marsh Wildlife Area on May 11, 1980 (Thomson 1983). The last migrants normally depart from interior counties by May 22–30, although a few linger along the lakefront through June 5–12.

White-throated Sparrows are sporadic breeders (Peterjohn and Rice 1991). There were confirmed nesting records from the Marblehead Peninsula (Ottawa County) in 1913 and Cleveland in 1929 (Campbell 1968, Williams 1950). A small population existed in Ashtabula County, where Hicks (1933a) discovered pairs in Wayne Township and the former Pymatuning Bog during 1928–1932. These pairs occupied young swamp forests, nesting on the ground among dense herbaceous vegetation (Hicks 1933c). Several nests contained eggs or young by June 14–15, while adults accompanied by dependent young were noted through July 6–16 (Hicks 1933a). A reported nesting attempt from Ashtabula County during 1997 requires confirmation.

Nonbreeding White-throated Sparrows are casual but fairly regular summer visitors to the northern tier of counties. They produced one to four reports almost annually during the 1990s, but were more sporadic during previous decades. These individuals may appear anytime during June, July, or August. Some remain for several days and then disappear, while others linger for several weeks or longer. Elsewhere, White-throated Sparrows are accidental summer visitors, with most reports during June. These reports include a singing male in Holmes County during July 15–August 9, 1993 (Brock 1993d, Harlan 1994a); the latest central Ohio record from Columbus on June 11, 1948 (Borror 1950); and one at Spring Valley Wildlife Area during June 17–29, 1999 (Whan 1999b).

White-throated Sparrows are fairly common to locally abundant fall migrants, most numerous along Lake Erie. A few very early migrants return to the lakefront by August 22–23. However, their southward movement normally begins during September 10–15 along the lakefront and September 22–30 within the central and southern counties. Most White-throateds pass through the state during October. The last migrant flocks depart by November 15. Most fall sightings are of 10–50 individuals daily; sizable movements produce concentrations of 100–200. The largest fall flights total 300–500+, primarily along the lakefront.

Before 1940, wintering White-throated Sparrows were very rare in northern and central Ohio. For example, Campbell (1940) cited one winter record in the Toledo area through 1940, while Trautman (1940) noted only one winter flock at Buckeye Lake during the 1920s and 1930s. They were regularly found in the southern counties, where they became uncommon to locally fairly common winter visitors, with most flocks totaling fewer than ten individuals. Wintering populations increased during the 1940s, resulting in additional records from central and northern Ohio. They became regular residents in these counties during the 1950s. Statewide wintering numbers substantially increased during the 1960s and 1970s. These increases are most apparent on Christmas Bird Counts. At Cincinnati, for example, the largest total on any count before 1952 was 124 individuals; by 1977, more than 1,000 were tallied. Their winter populations have stabilized since 1980.

White-throated Sparrows are now fairly common to locally common winter residents throughout southern Ohio; 5–25 are observed daily and concentrations of 30–50+ are encountered, especially near Cincinnati. They become uncommon to fairly common in the central counties, where most reports are of 25 or fewer daily. In northern Ohio, wintering White-throateds are generally uncommon residents, becoming rare in some northeastern counties and fairly common at favored localities. More than 100 winter within the red cedar thickets on Kelleys Island. Similar totals are remarkable elsewhere in northern Ohio, where most sightings are of 12 or fewer individuals. These winter numbers may be reduced by late January during years with severe weather.

Harris's Sparrow *Zonotrichia querula* (Nuttall)

These large sparrows normally reside in central North America, breeding in the taiga forests of Canada and migrating through the Great Plains to a winter range extending from Nebraska to Texas (AOU 1998). Harris's Sparrows also regularly stray to the states and provinces bordering their established range, while fewer individuals wander toward both coasts.

Within Ohio, the first Harris's Sparrow was collected at Columbus on April 29, 1889. This individual was reportedly taken from a flock of 3–5 (Jones 1903). The next sighting was recorded during 1921, but this species has been observed fairly regularly in subsequent years. Between 1920 and 1980, Harris's Sparrows were observed from three to nine times each decade, with the largest number of sightings during the 1920s, 1950s, and 1960s. Only one was reported during the 1980s, but at least twelve were found during the 1990s.

Most Harris's Sparrows are reported as migrants, usually within flocks of White-crowned and White-throated Sparrows. Harris's Sparrows also visit bird feeders during winter. They are most likely to occur within the western half of Ohio and along Lake Erie.

Harris's Sparrows are accidental to casual migrants throughout Ohio. There are at least eighteen fall records, mostly of single individuals, with a maximum of three at Toledo on October 21, 1928 (Campbell 1968). These migrants are noted between October 9 and November 12, although one at Akron on November 25, 1974, may have been a late migrant (Hall 1975a). Spring Harris's Sparrows have been reported on at least twenty-five occasions. These migrants have appeared as early as April 1, but most are noted between April 20 and May 15. The latest migrants remain through May 24–26. Spring records, like those in fall, are mostly single individuals, although 2–5 have appeared at a few locations. Small "flights" may produce three or four records during a single season.

Wintering Harris's Sparrows are accidental visitors. There are at least eleven confirmed winter sightings and a number of unconfirmed records. Seven of these records are scattered across the southern half of the state; the others are from North Canton, Wilmot, Holmes County, and Henry County. All substantiated winter records are of single sparrows.

White-crowned Sparrow *Zonotrichia leucophrys* (Forster)

As migrants, White-crowned Sparrows are regularly found along brushy fencerows, woodland edges, weedy old fields, and pastures supporting hawthorn and multiflora rose tangles. Smaller numbers also visit parks, cemeteries, and residential yards.

Spring White-crowneds appear during the first half of April and are widely distributed by April 15–22. The largest movements normally occur between April 28 and May 12. At this time, White-crowneds become fairly common to common along Lake Erie and uncommon to fairly common through the interior counties. Spring totals seldom exceed 10–25 individuals, but flights involving 40–100+ may occur in the northern half of the state. During some years, the largest flocks are composed of only 3–10. The last spring migrants usually depart by May 20–25, although stragglers remain through the end of the month.

White-crowneds appear in greater numbers during autumn. The first migrants return to Lake Erie by September 20–25 and most interior counties by the first week of October. Their maximum abundance is attained between October 7 and 25, with smaller numbers through mid-November. Fall White-crowneds are most numerous along Lake Erie, where they become fairly common to locally abundant migrants. While fall totals mostly are 5–25 daily, sizable movements are detected almost annually. Concentrations of 100–300+ appear along the entire lakefront; the largest flight totaled 628 at Cleveland on October 19, 1988 (Peterjohn 1989a). Within the interior counties, they are uncommon to locally common migrants, generally observed in flocks of 15 or fewer. Large flights are less frequently noted, although 100 were tallied at Buckeye Lake during several autumns (Trautman 1940) and 300+ appeared at Spring Valley Wildlife Area on October 24–27, 1987 (Peterjohn 1988a).

Wintering White-crowned Sparrows were unrecorded until the 1930s and became widely distributed during the 1950s. Their numbers generally peaked in the 1970s, and declined after 1980. These changes are related to the presence of multiflora rose hedges, with which wintering White-crowneds are frequently associated, especially where croplands, weedy fields, and grassy pastures are nearby. Multiflora rose was widely planted from the 1930s to the 1960s. In recent years, however, it has been labeled a nuisance and is being eradicated.

They are now most numerous within the southwestern and glaciated central counties, where they are uncommon to locally common winter residents. Concentrations seldom exceed 3–15 daily, although as many as 50–140+ are counted in areas with plentiful multiflora rose hedges. They become casual to uncommon winter residents within the northwestern counties, where daily totals normally are ten or fewer. Larger tallies are reported on Christmas Bird Counts, with as many as 95 at Toledo (Campbell 1973). Wintering White-crowneds are generally uncommon to fairly common along the unglaciated Allegheny Plateau; most reports are of 3–15 daily. A tally of 1,070 White-crowneds on the 1999 Millersburg Christmas Bird Count is remarkable for any portion of the state. They are least numerous in northeastern Ohio, where they are casual to locally uncommon residents. Usually five or fewer are observed daily, although a few localities host 10–25.

White-crowneds can be scarce one winter and fairly numerous the next, even in areas with relatively stable habitat conditions. Moreover, populations are generally larger during December than later in the winter. In fact, December reports of 100+ White-crowneds may pertain to very late migrants, since similar concentrations are very infrequent during January and February.

White-crowned Sparrows have always been accidental nonbreeding summer visitors. After the last spring migrants depart during the first week of June, the few summer records are restricted to Lake Erie: there are at least two June reports from the Cleveland area and two July sightings from Lucas County. Sparrows observed in the Cleveland area during August 13–20 are probably early fall migrants.

Most White-crowneds visiting Ohio are members of the eastern *leucophrys* race. The western *gambelli* race was initially recorded as a specimen collected near Buckeye Lake in 1928 (Trautman 1935b). This race is apparently an accidental to casual visitor during spring and fall migrations, producing two to five reports each decade since the 1970s. Because immature individuals are impossible to positively identify in the field, the *gambelli* race may be more numerous than these few sightings of adults indicate.

Dark-eyed Junco *Junco hyemalis* (Linnaeus)

Anyone feeding birds during winter has hosted Dark-eyed Juncos. Formerly known as Slate-colored Juncos for their handsome gray and white plumage, these sparrows occur wherever adequate food and shrubby cover are available. They prefer brushy thickets, fencerows, and woodland edges bordering fields. They also frequent bird feeders and are as likely to occur in suburban backyards as in the rural countryside.

Dark-eyed Junco

Dark-eyed Juncos are fairly common to common winter residents. During some years, they are relatively scarce until late January or February, when sizable numbers are driven south in search of food. In other years, they are widely distributed until prolonged snow cover forces them to leave Ohio. Wintering juncos are widely distributed in the southern and eastern counties. Between 20 and 80 are observed daily, and totals of 100–200+ are possible in some areas. They are more locally distributed in the west-central and northwestern counties, especially in intensively farmed areas, where winter totals seldom exceed 5–30 daily.

These wintering numbers represent a marked decline since the 1920s and 1930s, when Trautman (1940) regularly observed 30–300 daily at Buckeye Lake. Similar numbers were reported from other locations. On Christmas Bird Counts, reports of 700–2,500+ were frequent through the early 1970s, but became relatively unusual after 1980. These declining numbers reflect a significant reduction in their eastern North American breeding populations since 1966 (Robbins et al. 1986).

Most wintering juncos are of the eastern "Slate-colored" race. Two western races have also been reported; many of these reports remain problematical, however, since these races regularly hybridize, and the positive identification of individuals in the field is not possible under many circumstances. The "Oregon" race is apparently an accidental to casual winter visitor, producing two to six reports annually in recent years. The best-documented reports are of adult males and are scattered across the state, most frequently from the glaciated counties. Sightings of "Gray-headed" juncos from Adams and Lorain Counties require additional verification, given the difficulty in field identification and the fact that they are unknown as vagrants in eastern North America.

Fall migrants have appeared along Lake Erie during the first week of September but are expected during September 15–25. They return to central Ohio as early as September 15 (Borror 1950), but normally appear in the central and southern counties during the first week of October. Their numbers gradually increase through November. Fairly common to common migrants statewide, most recent fall reports are of 50 or fewer daily, with occasional concentrations of 100–300+. Even when populations were larger, the largest fall flocks were composed of 200–400 juncos (Campbell 1968, Trautman 1940). Hence, totals of 730 at Cleveland on October 19, 1988, and 600 at Headlands Beach State Park on November 10, 1996, are remarkable (Conlon and Harlan 1996b, Peterjohn 1989a).

Their spring migration regularly produces sizable concentrations. This migration may begin in February or early March, but the largest movements are mostly noted between March 25 and April 25. Within the interior counties, these movements produce totals of 100–500 juncos. Larger flights occur along Lake Erie, producing "thousands" at South Bass Island on April 22, 1951 (Trautman 1956); 2,000 at Magee Marsh Wildlife Area on April 15, 1972 (Campbell 1973); and 1,500 at Cleveland on April 15, 1985 (Peterjohn 1985c). But spring totals usually are 25–75 daily. They normally depart from the central and southern counties by May 1–5 and Lake Erie by May 8–12, but occasionally remain through the end of May at Columbus, Dayton, along Lake Erie, and at other locations.

During summer, Dark-eyed Juncos reside in the coniferous forests of the northern United States, Canada, and the western mountains. A small breeding population exists in Ohio—a remnant of a formerly sizable summer population. Kirtland (1838) described "great numbers" breeding in the Cleveland area during the 1830s. They were apparently widespread in northeastern Ohio, although there are few factual accounts describing their status. As the mature beech-maple forests were cleared during the 1800s, this population largely disappeared. By 1935, breeding juncos were restricted to Lake, Geauga, Trumbull, and Ashtabula Counties (Hicks 1935a). Only Ashtabula County supported a sizable population, with summer records from twelve locations and a maximum of 50 pairs in eastern Monroe Township through 1930 (Hicks 1933a). Most of these breeding juncos disappeared before 1932, and the last pairs were displaced by the destruction of the Pymatuning Bog.

Breeding Dark-eyed Juncos are largely found in the Chagrin River watershed in portions of Geauga, Lake, and Cuyahoga Counties. They are rare to uncommon and locally distributed in hemlock ravines and mature beech-maple forests, mostly as pairs, but groups of 4–10+ territorial males occur at Stebbins Gulch, Little Mountain, North Chagrin Reservation, and Hell Hollow MetroPark. Surveys conducted during the 1990s indicate that this population totals 30–50 pairs during most years. They are casual summer visitors elsewhere in northeastern Ohio, with scattered reports of summering juncos and confirmed nesting at Hinckley, Brecksville, and in Ashtabula County during the 1990s (Brock 1994d and 1996d, Peterjohn 1990d).

Breeding juncos choose forests with dense shrub layers and ground cover, frequently placing their nests on the ground at bases of overturned trees or in clumps of ferns (Hicks 1933a). Nests with eggs have been discovered as early as April 9, and adults with dependent young are observed by late May. Later attempts regularly produce clutches during June. The latest attempt produced a nest with eggs on August 21 and adults with young on September 10 (Hicks 1933c, Kleen 1976b).

Dark-eyed Juncos are accidental summer visitors elsewhere, but nesting has never been confirmed away from the northeastern counties. Summering juncos were noted in the Toledo area in 1934 and 1942 (Campbell 1968), but the only other reports have been during the 1990s. A single territorial male in Mohican State Forest during 1997 and 1998 was in potential breeding habitat (Kline 1997, E. Schlabach 1998). Other individuals were probably nonbreeding, such as one summering at Columbus during 1994 and 1995 (Harlan 1994d, 1995d); two at Strouds Run State Park (Athens County) on July 29, 1991 (Harlan 1991b); and one in Holmes County on August 13, 1993 (Harlan 1994a).

Lapland Longspur *Calcarius lapponicus* (Linnaeus)

After spending the summer on the Arctic tundra, Lapland Longspurs migrate south to winter in the open fields of Canada and the United States. Along Lake Erie, the first fall migrants return during September 20–30 and are regularly observed by mid-October. This southward passage is made up of infrequent small flocks of 20 or fewer scattered along the lakefront, with occasional concentrations of 100–200 along western Lake Erie. They remain rare to uncommon lakefront migrants into the first half of December.

Fall Laplands are casual to uncommon migrants away from Lake Erie, least numerous in the southern and unglaciated counties. Most inland records are of ten or fewer, but flights of 100–500+ have been reported from the central counties. While fall migrants may appear by September 21–26 in the northern half of the state, there are few records before the first week of November. Their inland movements are poorly understood, since these migrants are inconspicuous occupants of large farm fields, which are seldom visited by birders during this season.

Wintering Lapland Longspurs inhabit farmlands, where they usually associate with mixed flocks of Horned Larks and Snow Buntings. When snow covers the ground, these flocks wander considerable distances before congregating in fields where manure has been recently spread. The absence of snow cover allows them to disperse throughout farmlands and relatively few are observed.

Modern agricultural practices are detrimental to wintering Laplands. Clean farming techniques and fall plowing eliminate most food from farm fields and contributed to the decline in wintering numbers since the 1930s. Campbell (1940) often encountered winter flocks of 200–400 in the Toledo area, while flocks of 100–300 were regularly reported from central Ohio (Trautman 1940). In the northeastern counties, flocks of 75–200 were occasionally noted (Williams 1950).

Similar flocks may occur today but are certainly an exception. Lapland Longspurs are now rare to locally fairly common winter residents in the glaciated counties and along the unglaciated plateau south to Coshocton and Tuscarawas Counties. They became accidental to casual visitors elsewhere along the unglaciated Allegheny Plateau. They are most plentiful during cold, snowy winters, when flocks of 5–25+ are scattered across the state. Sizable flocks are most likely to be encountered under these conditions. Since 1960, the largest flocks are generally composed of 50–150 individuals. Concentrations of 400 in Marion County on January 8, 1984, and 1,176 on the 1961 Tiffin Christmas Bird Count are remarkable for recent years. In contrast, Laplands are scarce during mild winters.

While spring Laplands are generally most numerous during March, migrant flocks may appear between the last half of February and the first week of May. Stragglers remain as late as May 17–18. These migrants are most apparent as flocks moving along western Lake Erie, where they are uncommon to fairly common. They are rare to uncommon through western and central Ohio, becoming accidental to casual elsewhere. Most spring flocks are com-

posed of 15–40 Laplands, flying low overhead and producing their character-
istic rattling call notes. Sizable spring concentrations are infrequent: an esti-
mated 10,000 in Lucas County on May 1, 1949 (Campbell 1968); 4,200+ past
Maumee Bay State Park on March 21, 1997 (Fazio 1997b); 2,600 near
Celeryville (Huron County) on March 25, 1939 (Walker 1939a); and 1,800 at
Magee Marsh Wildlife Area on April 11, 1996 (Conlon and Harlan 1996a).
Flocks of 625 in Mercer County on April 13, 1986 (Peterjohn 1986c), 400 in
Greene County on March 31, 1940 (Mathena et al. 1984), and 75 near Salem
(Columbiana County) during March 26–April 9, 1933 (Baird 1933), are note-
worthy for those locations.

Smith's Longspur *Calcarius pictus* (Swainson)

Smith's Longspurs are enigmatic birds within Ohio. Even their initial status is
clouded with uncertainty. The first published account is of two specimens
collected in Portage County on January 29, 1888 (Kemsies and Austing 1950).
These specimens are no longer extant. Since these longspurs were described
as feeding on ragweeds, a very unlikely behavior for this species, in all likelihood they were not correctly identified. Additional sight records from the
Cleveland area during May 1924 were also from unlikely habitats (Williams
1950). In the absence of specimens and written descriptions, these records
and other unpublished sightings during the early 1900s are considered very
questionable.

Ohio's first confirmed Smith's Longspur was furnished by a specimen collected at Lake St. Marys on October 23, 1944 (Clark 1964). More specimens
were taken near Oxford in 1949 (Kemsies and Austing 1950). When observers
became familiar with this species' habitat preferences, they discovered that
Smith's Longspurs were fairly regular migrants in portions of western and central Ohio.

Smith's Longspurs were observed during most years between 1950 and the
early 1970s as casual to rare spring migrants through the southwestern, west-
central, and central counties. They became locally uncommon at preferred
sites, including grassy fields bordering the Oxford airport in Butler County
and several pastures in Madison County. Surprisingly, none were reported
from northwestern Ohio. Four sightings from the Cleveland area were the only
records along Lake Erie and from eastern Ohio (Newman 1969).

While spring migrants appeared as early as March 6 (Thomson 1983), most
were recorded between March 20 and April 15. A few remained into the first
week of May. They were usually observed in flocks of fewer than 30 individuals. Larger concentrations were occasionally encountered: 150 near Oxford on
March 31, 1962 (Graber 1962c); 200 in Madison County on April 20, 1965

(Petersen 1965c); and 250 in the Ross-Pickaway County Line area on April 15, 1956 (Thomson 1983). They were frequently discovered in segregated flocks, although some were with flocks of Lapland Longspurs. They preferred large open fields covered with short grasses or grasses mixed with clovers.

Smith's Longspurs were apparently accidental or casual fall migrants through the southwestern, west-central, and central counties. Most sightings were during late October and November. The few published sightings include 12 at Lake St. Marys on October 23, 1944 (Clark 1964); 13 near Oxford on November 15, 1958 (Sheppard 1959); and two in Madison County on November 30, 1968 (Little 1969).

Their winter status is problematical. Trautman and Trautman (1968) described Smith's Longspurs as accidental to rare winter visitors which may be overlooked. There are no specimens or documented sight records to substantiate this claim. The few undocumented records include one in Madison County on January 7, 1968 (Little 1969). Since Ohio is far from their established range in the south-central United States (AOU 1998), it is doubtful that Smith's Longspurs were regular winter residents.

Despite nearly annual records through the early 1970s, Smith's Longspurs mysteriously vanished in subsequent years. During the 1980s there were only three sight records of spring migrants along Lake Erie: two in Cleveland and one in Ottawa County. The most recent report was of one at Cleveland on April 6, 1991 (Peterjohn 1991c). Their disappearance was partly explained by habitat changes. Several preferred pastures and hayfields were converted to cultivated crops. But they also no longer appeared at the Oxford airport, where adjacent fields have not been visibly altered. The absence of recent sightings may reflect a shift in migration routes, or that Smith's Longspurs still regularly pass through the state but are overlooked by observers unfamiliar with their habitat preferences.

Snow Bunting *Plectrophenax nivalis* (Linnaeus)

Long before winter storms bring snow and cold temperatures, Snow Buntings return to Ohio. They first appear along Lake Erie, usually in small, compact flocks flying low over the water. These buntings are immediately recognized by the flash of their white wing coverts against the lake's dark waters, creating the impression of a small group of snowflakes blown ashore by the November winds.

The earliest Snow Buntings returned to Ashtabula on September 21, 1936 (Baird 1936d), but fall migrants are exceptional before mid-October. Small flocks are regularly observed along Lake Erie by October 25–30, the same time they arrive at inland localities in northern Ohio. They have appeared in the southwestern counties by October 29–31, but normally arrive in central Ohio during the first week of November and in the southern counties by the last half of the month. Their lakefront passage is largely completed by December 3–10, with stragglers through December 20–25.

Fall flocks are widespread along the entire lakefront, becoming fairly common during November, with daily totals of 20–200 and occasional flights of 500+ individuals. A concentration of 5,000 near Toledo on October 25, 1945, was remarkably early (Campbell 1968). These migrants are locally distributed within the interior counties, frequently detected on mudflats and riprap bordering large reservoirs. They are casual to locally fairly common in the northern half of Ohio, becoming accidental to rare within the southern counties. Inland flocks are normally composed of 50 or fewer individuals, and the largest flocks total 100–150+.

As winter residents, Snow Buntings occupy barren agricultural fields, frequently in association with Horned Larks and Lapland Longspurs. They also form large segregated flocks. Their relative abundance exhibits considerable annual variation, with occasional pronounced movements. However, their detectability is directly related to the extent of snow cover; the largest flocks are usually reported during cold, snowy weather. Throughout winter, Snow Buntings wander in search of food and large flocks tend to move southward as the season progresses.

Their complex winter distribution patterns are related to land use. Snow Buntings are most numerous in the agricultural fields of northwestern Ohio. When the fields become snow covered, these buntings are fairly common to abundant residents. They are normally encountered in flocks of 25–300; concentrations of 500–1,000 are fairly frequent. The largest flocks occur during the last week of January, with an estimated 5,500 near Toledo in 1943 and 5,000 in Hancock County in 1977 (Campbell 1968, Phillips 1980).

In northeastern Ohio, wintering Snow Buntings are generally uncommon residents in flocks of 5–50 individuals. Larger concentrations include 1,000+ near Youngstown on several dates, 2,000 near Chardon on December 25, 1930, and an estimated 5,000 near Wooster during the winter of 1981–1982 (Hall 1982b, Williams 1950).

Large wintering flocks do not normally wander into central Ohio, although concentrations of 1,000–2,000 may appear south to Lake St. Marys and Killdeer Plains Wildlife Area. Elsewhere in the central third of the state, Snow Buntings are uncommon winter residents, usually observed in flocks of 20 or fewer, while 50–450 are rarely noted near Columbus and along the northern edge of the unglaciated Allegheny Plateau.

In the southwestern counties, they are casual to rare residents; midwinter sightings normally total six or fewer, with occasional flocks of 10–50. Their largest movement occurred during the winter of 1980–1981, when as many as 400 appeared near Dayton and 100 near Cincinnati (Peterjohn 1981a). They are least numerous in the unglaciated southern counties, where they are casual visitors, usually encountered as scattered individuals or flocks of 6–12.

Throughout the year, Snow Buntings make a comfortable living in rather inhospitable surroundings. On a cold January morning, they quietly forage in open fields, oblivious of the subzero temperatures and biting winds. Only extreme weather conditions force them out of these habitats. The blizzard of the 1977–1978 winter caused many Snow Buntings to seek refuge at bird feeders. A few even appeared within residential areas in Columbus, unprecedented behavior for this hardy little bird.

The first spring migrants appear along Lake Erie during mid-February, even when winter has a firm grip on the landscape. Their passage begins in earnest with the first February thaw and continues into the last half of March. The last migrants usually depart from southern and central Ohio by the first week of March and along Lake Erie by the first week of April. Lingering Snow Buntings have remained through March 26, 1930, in Hamilton County and May 2, 1955, at Cleveland (Kemsies and Randle 1953, Rosche 1992).

This migration is poorly defined, especially inland, where Snow Buntings are casual to rare in small numbers. Spring migrants are not uniformly distributed along Lake Erie but congregate in Lucas, Ottawa, and Erie Counties; they are rare farther east. Along western Lake Erie, they are uncommon to locally fairly common migrants, usually in flocks of 30 or fewer, with occasional groups of 75–100. The largest spring movements produce 1,000–2,500.

Northern Cardinal *Cardinalis cardinalis* (Linnaeus)

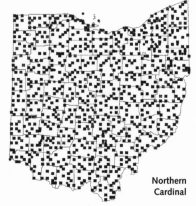

Northern
Cardinal

January thaws provide brief respites from the rigors of winter, melting the accumulated snows and encouraging the male Northern Cardinal to cheerfully proclaim the beginning of spring. A snowstorm several days later sends him back to the cover of brushy thickets to await the return of more favorable weather. As the days increase in length, the urge to proclaim his territory becomes stronger and the male Northern Cardinal sings every morning, even in the middle of a March blizzard. He is eventually correct and spring returns, but our affection for this handsome backyard visitor extends beyond his optimistic song during a January morning. As simply stated by Dawson (1903): "Not merely for the splendor of his plumage, but for the gentle boldness of his comradeship and the daily heartening of his stirring song, the Cardinal is beloved of all who know him."

Northern Cardinals rank among our most familiar native songbirds because of their preference for shrubbery in residential yards and frequent visits to bird feeders. In addition to urban areas, they are found wherever shrubby cover is available, including brushy fields, thickets, fencerows, and woodland edges. These permanent residents are most numerous during winter, when they are fairly common to locally abundant. Wintering cardinals frequently congregate into flocks of as many as 60 individuals, and 6–10 males may be observed adorning a single shrub. A winter day's birding usually produces tallies of 20–80 and totals of 100+ are not extraordinary. They are most numerous in the southwestern counties, especially at Cincinnati, where Christmas Bird Count totals frequently exceed 2,000 and an incredible 3,775 were tallied in 1970.

During late February and March, the winter flocks of Northern Cardinals disband as pairs establish their territories for the breeding season. As a result of dispersal and winter mortality, they become fairly common to common summer residents. Summer totals normally are 10–20 daily in intensively cultivated western Ohio and 30–75+ elsewhere. Their nesting activities begin during the first half of April. Their nests are usually placed in shrubs and vines at heights of three to eight feet, although some are as high as twenty to thirty-eight feet in trees (Baird 1934d, Trautman 1940). Nests with eggs have been reported as early as April 7 at Dayton (Mathena et al. 1984), but first clutches are normally laid during late April and early May. First broods fledge by mid-June. Subsequent nesting attempts produce young throughout the summer, and nests with eggs have been reported as late as September 1 (Baird 1934d). Adults with dependent young may be observed through the first week of October.

While they are primarily permanent residents, some Northern Cardinals exhibit migratory behavior. These movements are poorly understood, since migrants are difficult to distinguish from residents. Migrants are most apparent over western Lake Erie, where Trautman and Trautman (1968) reported spring movements during April and May and fall migrants in September and October.

Northern Cardinals have not always been common residents across Ohio. When Ohio was initially settled, they were restricted to the southern half of the state. They expanded into northern Ohio during the last half of the nineteenth century (DeVos 1964). At the turn of the twentieth century, they were still rather rare near Lake Erie (Campbell 1968, Jones 1903). Their northern Ohio populations continued to increase into the 1920s and 1930s, and statewide populations are still increasing along Breeding Bird Survey routes (Sauer et al. 1998).

Rose-breasted Grosbeak *Pheucticus ludovicianus* (Linnaeus)

Each spring the first male Rose-breasted Grosbeaks return when the vegetation is still budding. These attractive males are readily observed as they forage among the bare branches of tall trees. Unfortunately, by the time the rest of these grosbeaks return, the foliage is well developed. Like most colorful songbirds, Rose-breasted Grosbeaks remain hidden among the dense vegetation; most later migrants are detected by their robin-like songs or sharp call notes.

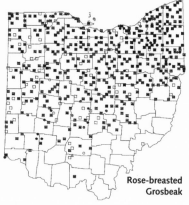

Rose-breasted
Grosbeak

Overflights have appeared as early as the first week of April, but the first Rose-breasted Grosbeaks normally return during April 20–30 in the southern and central counties and May 1–5 along Lake Erie. Their northward migration peaks between May 7 and 24, when they become fairly common to common in most counties but can be locally uncommon in southern Ohio. Only 3–10 individuals are noted most days. Concentrations of 15–30+ occur annually and the largest movements total 80–100+. The last spring migrants pass through lakefront migrant traps into the first week of June.

When Ohio was initially settled, Rose-breasted Grosbeaks may have been summer residents throughout the state. Audubon claimed he found nests in the Cincinnati area, and there were nineteenth century summer records from Columbus (Jones 1903, Kemsies and Randle 1953). The southern populations disappeared by the mid-1930s, when Hicks (1935a) cited summer records south to Paulding, Wood, Seneca, Ashland, Holmes, Tuscarawas, Stark, and Columbiana Counties. These breeding grosbeaks were uncommon to locally common and widely distributed in the northeastern counties. They were locally distributed elsewhere and common at only a few localities.

Their breeding range has been expanding southward since the 1960s. Dayton's first summer record came in 1962 (Mathena et al. 1984), and isolated sightings were reported from the central counties during that decade. Cincinnati's first recent nesting record came in 1975 (Kleen 1975d), and there were a number of other sightings from the central and southwestern counties in the 1970s. Additional range expansion was documented during the 1980s (Peterjohn and Rice 1991), but this trend may have slowed during the 1990s.

Rose-breasted Grosbeaks are now fairly common to common summer residents across northeastern Ohio, where 3–15+ are recorded daily. They are also widespread in the northwestern counties, but are generally uncommon to fairly common, least numerous in the intensively farmed counties. Summer totals seldom exceed 2–5 individuals daily. In central Ohio, Rose-breasted Grosbeaks are generally uncommon residents, regularly encountered as 1–4 individuals south to Darke, Clark, Pickaway, Fairfield, Perry, Muskingum, Tuscarawas, Harrison, and Jefferson Counties (Peterjohn and Rice 1991). They are generally rare to uncommon and locally distributed summer residents within southwestern Ohio. Breeding grosbeaks remain casual to absent along the unglaciated Allegheny Plateau from Belmont, Guernsey, Morgan, Hocking, and Ross Counties south to the Ohio River.

Breeders prefer young second-growth deciduous woods and woodland edges. They are usually found along riparian corridors, in mesic woods, and occasionally in swamp forests. Their nests are normally placed at heights of ten to twenty-five feet in young trees but have been recorded at greater heights. Nesting activities are normally initiated during the last half of May, and nests with eggs have been discovered through June 23. While recently fledged young have appeared by May 25, they are expected during the last half of June and July (Campbell 1968, Williams 1950).

Their southward migration begins during the last half of August in the northern counties and by the first week of September along the Ohio River. This movement continues throughout September. Fall migrants are generally fairly common to common in northern Ohio, most numerous along Lake Erie, and uncommon to fairly common elsewhere. Most records are of ten or fewer individuals daily. Larger flights are restricted to Lake Erie, where as many as 30–38 have been reported. Most depart by October 5–10. A few stragglers linger as late as mid-November.

Most Rose-breasted Grosbeaks spend the winter months in tropical climates. Some are accidental winter visitors in North America, with records north to New England and the Great Lakes states (AOU 1998). These wintering grosbeaks are invariably found at bird feeders. Within Ohio, there are at least 11 acceptable winter records: from the Cleveland area, Columbus, Cincinnati, Toledo, Oxford, Warren, Findlay, the Mohican State Forest area, Adams County, and Scioto County, as well as several unsubstantiated sightings. While these wintering grosbeaks are more likely to appear in December and early January, several survived into February and March.

Black-headed Grosbeak *Pheucticus melanocephalus* (Swainson)

Western counterparts of our familiar Rose-breasted Grosbeaks, Black-headeds are accidental visitors in most states and provinces east of the Great Plains. Despite their accidental status, a few Black-headeds normally appear somewhere in eastern North America each year, frequently visiting bird feeders during winter.

Black-headed Grosbeaks are accidental visitors to Ohio. Their status is obscured by the inability to accurately distinguish Black-headeds from the considerably more numerous Rose-breasted Grosbeaks. Female and immature grosbeaks are particularly difficult to identify, and even male grosbeaks can be confusing.

Within Ohio, there are two indisputable records of Black-headed Grosbeaks. A male visited an Akron feeder between January 1 and April 5, 1975, and photos taken by Robert Graham clearly establish its identity (Peterjohn et al. 1987). Another grosbeak was photographed by Karl Maslowski at a Milford (Clermont County) feeder during April 10–13, 1969 (Petersen 1970b). A male studied by Jerry Cairo, Don Tumblin, and Karen Zanders at Rising Park in Lancaster on May 6, 1978, also appears to be correctly identified. There are several other reports of Black-headed Grosbeaks visiting feeders in winter and early spring, including one at Cincinnati between January and March, 1976 (Thomson 1983), and an immature male at Sylvania (Lucas County) on March 3–15, 1965 (Campbell 1968). These grosbeaks were not photographed and written descriptions are unavailable. Hence, the accuracy of their identifications cannot be assessed.

Blue Grosbeak *Guiraca caerulea* (Linnaeus)

Blue Grosbeak

The historic status of Blue Grosbeaks in Ohio is clouded with uncertainty. While there were many reports during the late 1800s and the first decades of the twentieth century, these sightings were undocumented or supported by details suggesting the birds were misidentified. If these grosbeaks occurred in the state, they were accidental visitors.

Ohio's first confirmed Blue Grosbeak records were provided by Hicks (1945a). He discovered males in Adams County on June 9 and 30, 1940. In 1941, a pair was regularly observed during June 8–22. While the female was noted carrying food, no nest was located. Breeding was established in 1942, when a nest with eggs was discovered along Beasley Fork in Monroe Township, Adams County, on June 6. An adult accompanied by dependent young was observed on June 21. A permanent population did not become established, however, since Blue Grosbeaks could not be relocated later in the decade.

Between 1945 and the early 1970s, this species once again became an accidental visitor. As before 1940, most sightings were either undocumented or supported by inconclusive details. However, Blue Grosbeak populations were gradually expanding northward, a trend particularly evident after 1966 (Robbins et al. 1986). As they spread northward, the likelihood of occasional Blue Grosbeaks reaching Ohio increased. Hence, some reports during the 1960s and early 1970s may have been correct, constituting the vanguard of their eventual expansion into the state. This recent range expansion produced a nesting pair in Vinton County during 1975 (Hall 1976a). In 1976, a pair probably nested near Cincinnati, while 1977 produced nesting records from Vinton and Meigs Counties (Hall 1977, Kleen 1976c). Breeding pairs were recorded during every subsequent year.

During the 1980s, breeding Blue Grosbeaks were primarily restricted to southern Ohio. They were uncommon summer residents in Adams County, rare to locally uncommon in portions of Pike, Scioto, Lawrence, Gallia, and Meigs Counties, and casual to rare elsewhere north to Butler, Ross, and Noble Counties (Peterjohn and Rice 1991). They were accidental visitors to central and northern Ohio, where the only confirmed breeding record was an unsuccessful attempt in the Oak Openings of Lucas County during 1988 (Peterjohn 1988d).

Their populations continued to increase during the 1990s. Blue Grosbeaks are now fairly common to locally common summer residents in Adams, Lawrence, and Gallia Counties, where daily totals of 10–15+ are possible (Harlan 1991b, McCormac 1999). Elsewhere in southern Ohio, they are uncommon to locally fairly common residents from Brown County north to Ross and Washington Counties, with daily totals generally of three or fewer, but remain rare in the Cincinnati area. Summering grosbeaks are casual to rare farther north along the unglaciated Allegheny Plateau, with nesting established north to Tuscarawas and Holmes Counties (Kline 1997, Whan 1999b). Except for the Toledo area, where as many as three pairs have nested annually (Brock 1997d), they are accidental summer visitors in the glaciated counties, with only a few scattered sightings north of Cincinnati.

Breeding Blue Grosbeaks are occupants of brushy successional habitats and dense thickets along fencerows and roadsides. Singing males are conspicuous, delivering their rich warbling songs from telephone wires, treetops, and other exposed perches. Their nests are placed in dense cover, usually at heights of three to ten feet. Nesting activities probably begin during May, but the few nests with eggs have been discovered in early June. Dependent young are observed between the last half of June and mid-August (Peterjohn and Rice 1991).

During spring, the first resident Blue Grosbeaks return to the southern counties by April 30–May 5 and most arrive by May 15–20. Overflights involve single individuals and are most likely to appear between May 10 and 30. These overflights are rare along Lake Erie, where 1–3 are discovered during most years, but remain accidental to casual within the other glaciated central and northern counties, although they have been more frequently encountered as the breeding population expands.

Singing Blue Grosbeaks are regularly detected into August, but there are relatively few sightings once the males stop singing. Their southward migration has been poorly documented. In all likelihood, Blue Grosbeaks begin their migration during mid-August and the last individuals depart during the last half of September; the latest acceptable fall report is September 22, 1990, in Hamilton County (Peterjohn 1991a). There are no confirmed fall records away from the known nesting locations.

Indigo Bunting *Passerina cyanea* (Linnaeus)

Indigo Buntings are prime examples of the saying "familiarity breeds contempt." As they perch on a telephone wire or small tree in the sunlight of a summer morning, male Indigos are very beautiful, surpassed by few other songbirds. If they were rare, their beauty would be appreciated by anybody having the opportunity to observe one. But Indigo Buntings are common to abundant summer residents, and singing males are hardly noticed except by those who appreciate birds for their aesthetic qualities.

Indigo Bunting

Except for a few mid-April overflights, the first Indigo Buntings normally return to southern Ohio by April 20–25. They appear in the central and northern counties during the first week of May. This spring movement is poorly defined within the interior counties, where it mostly consists of returning residents. Sizable flights appear along Lake Erie, producing migrant flocks of 20–40+ and daily totals of 100–300+ during the largest movements. This migration peaks in mid-May, while the last lakefront migrants are noted through May 27–June 5.

As summer residents, Indigo Buntings are widely distributed, and the male's repetitive song resounds throughout the rural countryside. They are found wherever brushy habitats are available, including woodland edges and openings, fencerows, roadsides, and riparian corridors. They are most numerous on the red cedar-covered hillsides in Adams and Brown Counties, where 100–200+ are tallied daily. Indigo Buntings are also plentiful throughout other southern and eastern counties, where daily totals of 75–125+ are possible. Less numerous in intensively farmed central and western Ohio, 30–50+ may be noted daily but they become abundant where suitable brushy habitats are plentiful; Campbell (1968) counted 150 in the Oak Openings in a single June day. While they have been abundant throughout the twentieth century, their populations have undergone steady increases on Breeding Bird Survey routes since 1966 (Sauer et al. 1998).

Their nesting activities normally begin during May, and the first clutches are produced in the southern counties by midmonth. Fledglings have been noted as early as June 21 (Trautman 1940), and most first broods fledge during late June and July. Later attempts are responsible for nest construction through August 15 (Phillips 1980), nests with young through September 5 (Trautman 1940), and observations of adults with dependent young into mid-September.

Male Indigo Buntings are persistent singers whose songs are heard long after most other birds become silent. By mid-August, Indigos become fairly inconspicuous, and daily totals seldom exceed 3–15 individuals except when flocks are encountered and 30–40 are observed. The largest fall concentration was 300 in the Toledo area on September 6, 1941 (Campbell 1968). These buntings are regularly recorded throughout September, but their numbers noticeably decline by the first week of October. The last migrants usually depart by October 10–17. A few infrequently linger into late October or the first week of November.

Most Indigo Buntings spend the winter south of the United States. However, a few attempt to overwinter as far north as the lower Great Lakes—probably individuals that were injured or otherwise unable to complete their migration. Most are found at bird feeders. Indigo Buntings are accidental winter visitors in Ohio. In addition to reports from Christmas Bird Counts, these records include single Indigos at Barnesville (Belmont County) on December 17, 1959, and Columbus on December 25, 1924 (anonymous 1928, Hall 1960b). Another lingered in the Cincinnati area through January 29, 1960, and may have overwintered (Mumford 1960b). Still another at Lake St. Marys on March 18, 1944, was more likely a wintering bird than an exceptionally early migrant (Clark and Sipe 1970).

Painted Bunting *Passerina ciris* (Linnaeus)

These exceptionally attractive buntings are found in two disjunct populations in North America. One population breeds in the southeastern states from North Carolina south into Florida; the other occupies the southern Great Plains of the United States and adjacent portions of northern Mexico (AOU 1998). Painted Buntings have been widely reported outside of this range, but because this species is kept in captivity, some of these reports are believed to be escaped individuals rather than vagrants.

Within the midwestern United States, the few acceptable reports of vagrant Painted Buntings have been of spring overflights. Ohio's only record of this accidental visitor fits this pattern of vagrancy: one was noted at a Tiffin feeder during April 16–19, 1997 (Fazio 1997c). This handsome male was photographed and widely observed during this visit.

Dickcissel *Spiza americana* (Gmelin)

The status of Dickcissels in Ohio reflects their erratically fluctuating populations. Fretwell (1977) and others theorized that food availability on their South American wintering grounds may be largely responsible for the dramatic variation in the numbers returning to North America each summer. Drought conditions on the Great Plains may also contribute to the eastward movements of Dickcissels towards Ohio.

Dickcissel

Dickcissels spread eastward from the Great Plains during the nineteenth century, entering Ohio by the mid-1800s (Wheaton 1882). In the 1880s, they were locally abundant summer residents in some central and southern counties but less common in northern Ohio. By 1900, they were well established in the western half of the state but remained rare in the east (Jones 1903). This breeding range was maintained during the twentieth century, but their relative abundance fluctuated considerably. Sizable breeding populations were infrequent: between 1932 and 1934, when single fields supported 150 in Lucas County and 50 near Newark (Baird 1934c, Campbell 1968); between 1983 and 1988, when as many as 100 were found in a single Butler County field (Peterjohn 1983d); and 1995, with peaks of 75–100 in the northwestern counties (Brock 1995d). During these peak years, they become uncommon to locally common residents in the western and central counties, with most reports of 1–6 individuals. These sizable breeding populations are normally followed by precipitous declines. Even when populations are low, a few pairs or singing males appear in the central and western counties, although the statewide population may not exceed 10–30 males. But their summer status is not completely boom or bust. Moderate numbers were recorded in the mid-1950s, mid-1960s, and 1990s, including colonies of 10–25 and scattered males in many western and central counties.

Breeding Dickcissels are most likely to appear east to Scioto, Pike, Ross, Pickaway, Fairfield, Licking, Knox, Richland, Huron, and Erie Counties (Hicks 1935a, Peterjohn and Rice 1991). They are most numerous in the tier of counties bordering Indiana. Dickcissels have always been accidental to rare and irregular summer residents in the eastern half of Ohio. Along the unglaciated Allegheny Plateau, summering males were discovered in Morgan County in 1967 (Hall 1967). They reappeared during the 1980s, when small populations were located on reclaimed strip mines in Coshocton, Muskingum, and Gallia Counties (Peterjohn and Rice 1991). Other small populations have been noted in Vinton, Pike, Lawrence, Belmont, and Tuscarawas Counties subsequently. Within the northeastern counties, the few records include nests in Lake and Columbiana Counties (Baird 1934c, Williams 1950) and summer records from Ashtabula, Mahoning, and Geauga Counties.

Breeding Dickcissels prefer clover and alfalfa hayfields but also occupy timothy fields, the grassy borders of marshes, wet prairies, and weedy fallow fields (Campbell 1968, Trautman 1940). On reclaimed strip mines, they are found in areas supporting mixed grasses and sweet-clovers. Males attempt to mate with several females but do not help rear the young. The females build their nests on or near the ground in dense grassy cover. Most nests are constructed in June, with the young fledging in July and early August (Price 1935, Trautman 1940).

Migratory movements are not very apparent. Spring migration is largely birds appearing on their territories. The few March records most likely pertain to wintering individuals. Earliest spring migrants have appeared during the last half of April, but there are very few sightings before May 3–8. Most summering birds return during May 15–June 10. Spring Dickcissels are mostly recorded from the western half of Ohio; they are accidental in the eastern counties.

After the males quit singing in July, Dickcissels become inconspicuous. Most fall migrants are detected by their distinctive buzzy call notes as they pass overhead. Rare to casual throughout Ohio, most depart during August and the first half of September. Relatively few migrants are detected through October 5–17.

While most Dickcissels migrate to tropical climates for the winter, a few elect to overwinter within Ohio. These accidental winter visitors are mostly detected at bird feeders, frequently in urban areas. There are at least twenty winter records, from Conneaut, Cleveland, and Toledo south to Columbus, Marietta, and Cincinnati. Some appear for only a few days in late November and early December, while others remain for the entire winter. Most sightings are of singles, although two appeared at Findley State Park (Lorain County) during the winter of 1979–1980 and in Holmes County during the 1992–1993 winter (Harlan 1993b, Kleen 1980b).

Bobolink *Dolichonyx oryzivorus* (Linnaeus)

Distinctive and conspicuous, Bobolinks are certain to be noticed when they arrive each spring. Breeding males are unique, with brightly colored upperparts and uniformly black underparts. The value of this plumage pattern is not apparent until they are observed perched on the tops of grasses, and their upperparts resemble the scattered flowers in the pastures and hayfields where they reside. These blackbirds are seldom quiet for long, and males frequently declare their territories with a distinctive, loud, bubbly song.

Bobolink

During spring, exceptionally early Bobolinks were noted at Cleveland on March 28, 1965 (Newman 1965). Few other overflights have been noted, and the first flocks normally appear during April 23–30. They become widely distributed by May 5–10. This northward movement ends by May 20–23 within the interior counties and May 27–30 along Lake Erie.

Spring migrants are fairly common to common across the northern and glaciated central counties, with most sightings of 20 or fewer daily, occasional flocks of 30–50+, and peak movements of 100–350+ along Lake Erie. Trautman (1940) reported flights of 100–250 at Buckeye Lake into the 1930s, but similar movements have not been apparent in central Ohio during recent decades. Within the southern and unglaciated counties, they are uncommon to fairly common visitors. Daily totals seldom exceed ten individuals, and the largest recent flocks totaled 25–40. Larger flights were occasionally encountered in earlier decades; Kemsies and Randle (1953) reported flocks of 100–150 at Cincinnati into the early 1950s.

Like most grassland birds, Bobolinks expanded into Ohio during the nineteenth century. Breeding populations were well established by the mid-1800s (Wheaton 1882), and remained reasonably numerous through the mid-1930s. Hicks (1935a) described them as usually common to abundant but locally distributed summer residents in every county south to Butler, Montgomery, Greene, Madison, Pickaway, Fairfield, Perry, Muskingum, Guernsey, Harrison, and Jefferson. Except for rare records from Hocking County (Hicks 1937a), breeding pairs were absent elsewhere.

Their numbers markedly declined in most counties after 1940. This trend continued into the 1980s, but populations stabilized along Breeding Bird Survey routes after 1990 (Sauer et al. 1998). Habitat destruction was largely responsible for this decline, but the more frequent mowing of hayfields also contributed to their reduced populations.

Despite declining populations, their range has expanded south to the Ohio River in glaciated Ohio and Pike, Vinton, Noble, and Belmont Counties along the unglaciated Allegheny Plateau (Peterjohn and Rice 1991). Bobolinks are fairly common to locally common summer residents in the northeastern counties and 5–20+ are usually detected daily. They become uncommon to locally common in other northern and central counties, where summer reports normally are of ten or fewer, but tallies of 30–50+ are possible in some reclaimed strip mines and other preferred habitats. At the southern edge of their range, Bobolinks are generally casual to rare summer residents and very locally distributed in southern Ohio. Nonetheless, large numbers may gather in suitable habitats; there were 100+ in a Clinton County field during 1984 and 50 near Dayton in 1985 (Peterjohn 1984d, 1985d).

Nesting Bobolinks are restricted to large grassy fields and clover-alfalfa hayfields. Their nests are located on the ground, expertly concealed among the vegetation. Nest construction begins during the last half of May and continues into June. Nests with eggs are reported between May 25 and July 4; young remain in the nest into the last half of July. Dependent young have been observed by June 12–15 but are most likely to appear between late June and the first week of August (Jones 1910, Trautman 1940, Williams 1950).

Beginning in late June and continuing through August, Bobolinks accumulate into flocks within grasslands, weedy fields, and the edges of marshes. Southward migrants have been noted along Lake Erie during the first week of July, but this migration normally begins during July 20–August 5. While these migrants are inconspicuous on the ground, they are regularly detected as they pass overhead, uttering their distinctive call notes. Their fall migration peaks between August 10 and September 10. Fall Bobolinks are most conspicuous during the first few hours after sunrise and as they descend to their evening roosts. The last migrants usually depart by October 5–12. Occasional stragglers linger into November.

When breeding populations were larger, 100–500 fall migrants were noted daily in the central and northern counties (Campbell 1968, Trautman 1940), while 25–75 might appear in southwestern Ohio (Mathena et al. 1984). Occasional concentrations of 500–2,000 developed in central and northern Ohio and 100–200 in the southern counties, but the largest flight totaled 7,500 at Toledo on August 8, 1936 (Baird 1936c). Since 1960, fall Bobolinks have been fairly common to common migrants across Ohio. Daily totals of 5–30+ occur in most counties, with occasional movements of 50–400+ in glaciated Ohio and 50–150+ along the unglaciated Allegheny Plateau.

Bobolinks are accidental early winter visitors in North America. Within Ohio, the latest Bobolinks lingered at Toledo through November 28, 1953 (Campbell 1968), and into mid-December on Christmas Bird Counts at Cincinnati and Ashland.

Red-winged Blackbird *Agelaius phoeniceus* (Linnaeus)

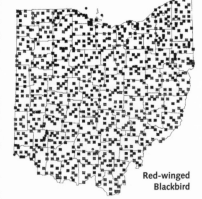

Red-winged
Blackbird

The first moderating temperatures are invariably accompanied by the return of Red-winged Blackbirds. The males rapidly spread across the state, establishing territories in wetlands and along roadsides. These territorial activities are temporarily suspended during inclement weather, but are reinitiated as soon as the sun appears and intensify when the females return later in the season.

The first migrants may return by February 5–10 but are expected during February 18–25. This passage usually peaks during March, when Red-wingeds become abundant. Daily totals of 100–1,000+ are frequent, while 10,000–20,000+ may congregate in evening roosts. Immense roosts are not normally reported during spring, although there are estimates of 500,000+ near Columbus and more than 1,000,000 at Toledo during the 1960s and 1970s (Campbell 1968, Thomson 1983). By the first week of April, most migrants have passed through Ohio, but small flocks of females may be noted through April 15–20.

Nesting Red-wingeds were once confined to cattail marshes and shrubby swamps. As their populations expanded and wetlands were drained, breeding pairs spread to upland habitats and are now more likely to occupy weedy old fields, clover hayfields, and highway rights-of-way than marshes. Red-wingeds are abundant summer residents, ranking among our most numerous breeding birds. Summer totals of 50–400+ daily are noted in most localities. Continental breeding populations increased during most of the twentieth century, especially between 1950 and 1975 (Robbins et al. 1986). This trend has been reversed since the mid-1970s in Ohio, and statewide populations exhibit significant declines along Breeding Bird Survey routes in recent years (Sauer et al. 1998).

Nesting activities begin as soon as the females arrive. Nests with eggs have been reported by April 16 in central Ohio, although most clutches are produced during early May (Trautman 1940). The earliest clutches hatch by April 28 and fledge by May 16. Most young Red-wingeds appear during the first half of June. Second clutches are laid as soon as these young fledge. Nests with eggs are regularly noted through the first week of July, and young fledge through early August (Trautman 1940, Williams 1950). A nest with eggs in Clermont County on July 31, 1938, is very late (Walker 1938c). Most nests are placed at heights of two to four feet in herbaceous vegetation, but one was found 30 feet high in a large conifer and another in a hole in a stump (Campbell 1968, Phillips 1980).

Even before many pairs finish nesting, Red-winged Blackbirds gather into large flocks. These flocks have been reported during the last half of June but are more prevalent during July. By August, the entire population gathers into evening roosts. Fall migration is most evident between mid-September and late October. Flocks of hundreds are regularly observed in every county, while evening roosts hosting 10,000–50,000+ are frequent in northwestern Ohio and more than 1,000,000 have been estimated along western Lake Erie (Campbell 1968). Numbers decline during the first half of November, and relatively few large flocks are noted after November 20–25.

Before 1940, wintering Red-wingeds were infrequently noted as scattered individuals or flocks of 20 or fewer (Campbell 1940, Kemsies and Randle 1953, Williams 1950). Only Trautman (1940) reported winter flocks of 100–200+ at Buckeye Lake. As breeding populations expanded during the 1950s and 1960s, their wintering numbers experienced a corresponding increase. These winter populations have remained stable since the 1970s.

Red-winged Blackbirds are now uncommon to locally fairly common winter residents within the southern and central counties. Most sightings are of 20 or fewer individuals and occasional flocks of 30–75+. Roosts of 500–12,000+ may develop, especially during December. Within the northern counties, Red-wingeds become uncommon to rare winter residents except along western Lake Erie, where they are fairly common to common. Most sightings are of 20 or fewer, with infrequent flocks of 30–100+. Roosts are expected only along western Lake Erie, where as many as 5,000 were reported during the winter of 1965–1966 (Campbell 1968).

Eastern Meadowlark *Sturnella magna* (Linnaeus).

On a warm spring day, male Eastern Meadowlarks are likely to pass most hours perched on fence posts, telephone wires, or tall trees, loudly proclaiming their territories. With their distinctive yellow and black breast pattern, they are readily identified and regularly observed along highways throughout the rural countryside. As their name implies, meadowlarks prefer grasslands including pastures, hayfields, fallow fields, and highway rights-of-way for nesting, although

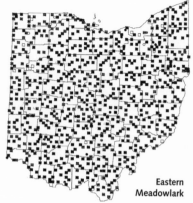

Eastern
Meadowlark

they have also been found in grain fields and grassy woodland clearings (Trautman 1940).

Eastern Meadowlarks originally inhabited prairie openings in western Ohio. As the virgin forests were replaced by small farms, they rapidly expanded across the state. They became common to abundant summer residents by the mid-1800s and retained that status through the early 1930s (Jones 1903, Trautman 1940, Wheaton 1882). Changing land-use practices beginning in the late 1930s converted grasslands into cultivated crops. This constant loss of suitable habitats produced a steady decline in meadowlark populations, a trend that continued through the 1990s (Sauer et al. 1998). Other factors contributed to this decline: more frequent mowing of hayfields significantly reduced their reproductive success, and severe winter weather during the 1970s depressed breeding populations across eastern North America (Robbins et al. 1986).

Despite declining populations, Eastern Meadowlarks remain fairly common to common summer residents. The largest numbers are found within reclaimed strip mines in the eastern counties, where 40–75+ are counted daily. While similar numbers are locally encountered in other southern and eastern locations, daily totals in the intensively cultivated central and western counties seldom exceed 15–40.

Meadowlarks nest on the ground, building domed structures hidden among the grasses. Nesting activities begin by mid-April in the southern and central counties, but most northern Ohio clutches are noted in early May (Trautman 1940, Williams 1950). Recently fledged young have been reported as early as May 16, but most appear during June. Some pairs raise two broods, since nests with eggs have been discovered through July 10, and adults feeding dependent young as late as August 26 (Phillips 1980).

After their young become independent, meadowlarks form flocks and unobtrusively forage through grasslands and harvested fields. When their populations were greater, their fall migration was very evident. Trautman (1940) regularly observed "many thousands" daily at Buckeye Lake during the 1920s and 1930s. His observations seem inconceivable today, when fall meadowlarks are uncommon to fairly common migrants, mostly as flocks of 20 or fewer, with occasional groups of 40–50. According to Trautman (1940), this migration begins by the first week of September, peaks during September 15–October 25, and the last migrants depart by mid-November.

Numbers of wintering Eastern Meadowlarks have remained fairly constant during the twentieth century. They are least numerous in northern Ohio, where they are generally rare residents, becoming casual in the northeastern counties. They are usually observed as individuals or flocks of ten or fewer. A total of 119 on the 1960 Toledo Christmas Bird Count is exceptional. Eastern Meadowlarks become uncommon winter residents in the central counties. While they are locally distributed, flocks of 10–30 are noted in preferred habitats and concentrations of 100–210 have been flushed from single fields. They are most numerous in the southern counties, where they become uncommon to fairly common residents. They are more widely distributed there than in central Ohio, although flock sizes are similar.

The advent of warm temperatures during February and early March initiates their spring migration. The first returning solitary males rapidly spread across the state. They are followed by flocks of 5–60 individuals, whose behavior was described by Trautman (1940). We may never again witness the movements of "several hundred" daily that were reported in the 1920s and 1930s (Trautman 1940). Totals of 30–50 may be noted, primarily on days with southerly winds between March 15 and April 10. These movements are most noticeable along western Lake Erie, where meadowlarks migrate around the lake. This migration continues through April 20–May 5, mostly as individuals along the lakefront.

Western Meadowlark *Sturnella neglecta* Audubon

While Western Meadowlarks are readily identified by their distinctive songs and call notes, separating Western and Eastern Meadowlarks when they are silent is a difficult identification challenge. No single plumage characteristic safely identifies all individuals. Hence, our understanding of Western Meadowlark status and distribution is based almost entirely on reports of singing males.

Ohio's first Western Meadowlark record was a specimen collected in Lakewood (Cuyahoga County) on April 8, 1880 (Williams 1950). This individual was undoubtedly a vagrant, since there were no other records for fifty years.

Beginning in the 1920s, Western Meadowlarks underwent an eastward expansion of their breeding range (DeVos 1964). Moving eastward from the Mississippi River valley, this expansion reached Ohio by 1930. During 1930 and 1931, at least 11 were discovered in Henry, Fulton, and Wood Counties, including a pair feeding fledglings in the latter county during 1930 (Campbell 1940, Hicks 1938b).

Western
Meadowlark

By 1937, Hicks (1938b) reported at least twenty-six records involving 18 individuals within eight counties, mostly in northwestern Ohio. Isolated males were also noted in Logan and Muskingum Counties. Most records pertained to unmated males, but two unspecified nesting attempts were cited.

Between the late 1930s and 1950s, small numbers regularly appeared in the northwestern counties, including annual records from Toledo after 1946 (Campbell 1968). They were accidental elsewhere; the few records included singing males at Cleveland in 1938 and Youngstown in 1939 (Walker 1939a, Williams 1950); a possible nesting pair at Bath (Summit County) in 1945 and 1946 (Williams 1950); and records from Columbus in 1946 and Cincinnati in 1959 (Borror 1950, Mumford 1959c).

The western Ohio population underwent a brief expansion during the 1960s. Summering Western Meadowlarks were regularly encountered within the northwestern and west-central counties, including a "colony" of 26 males in Oregon and Jerusalem Townships of Lucas County on May 13, 1962, and a smaller "colony" at Lake St. Marys in 1964 (Campbell 1968, Petersen 1964d). A pair nested at Cleveland in 1960, while males were reported from two other Cleveland area locations during the 1960s (Newman 1969). Their statewide population trends were then reversed and fewer Westerns were observed subsequently. The statewide summer population was 3–10 males during the 1980s (Peterjohn and Rice 1991) and 1–4 males during the 1990s, with none reported during 1999.

Western Meadowlarks are casual summer residents in northwestern and west-central Ohio. They no longer annually reside anywhere but are most likely to appear at Maumee Bay State Park and Killdeer Plains Wildlife Area. Widely scattered males and pairs are sporadically encountered south to Darke and Clark Counties. They are accidental summer visitors elsewhere, with reports from Holmes, Stark, Muskingum, Tuscarawas, Medina, and Portage Counties during the 1980s and 1990s (Brock 1995c, Peterjohn 1981c and 1990d, Peterjohn and Rice 1991). Most reports are of single singing males, although four were noted at Killdeer Plains in 1993 (Harlan 1993d). No confirmed breeding attempts were documented during the 1990s.

Western Meadowlarks occupy the same grassy fields and pastures as Easterns. Many Westerns remain at a locality for only one to three weeks before disappearing. There are few reports of pairs and even fewer confirmed breeding attempts from the Toledo area and Paulding, Seneca, Defiance, Henry, and Wyandot Counties (Peterjohn and Rice 1991, Thomson 1983). These reports suggest that nests are initiated during May and June and fledged young appear by late June and July.

As spring migrants, Western Meadowlarks are casual in northwestern and west-central Ohio but accidental elsewhere, usually as single individuals. The earliest migrants appear by February 25–March 10, although they are normally reported between the last half of March and mid-May. Numbers of spring records were greater during the 1960s, but only 1–3 have been noted during most springs since 1980.

There are very few confirmed records of Western Meadowlarks after the males quit singing. In all likelihood, the males and pairs remain near their summering territories into autumn. Their fall migration probably coincides with the southward movements of Easterns; most Westerns probably depart during October.

Their winter status remains a mystery. While there have been a few winter sight records from northwestern Ohio, none were adequately confirmed. Moreover, there are no winter specimen records from the state.

Yellow-headed Blackbird *Xanthocephalus xanthocephalus* (Bonaparte)

This distinctive blackbird was initially recorded in 1873, when a pair summered near Groveport in southern Franklin County (Wheaton 1882). Nesting was suspected but not confirmed. Yellow-headed Blackbirds remained accidental visitors in the late 1800s and early 1900s, with only eight acceptable records before 1930 (Hicks 1945b).

Their status changed abruptly in the 1930s, a result of the extended drought in the prairie states, and Yellow-headed Blackbirds were displaced from their normal breeding range. They were recorded from Ohio every year between 1931 and 1947, mostly as migrants. Most sightings were of 1–3 individuals, but small flocks were occasionally noted: 22 at Lake St. Marys on March 8, 1936; 21 at Bay Bridge (Erie County) on March 28, 1939; nine in Marion County on

March 11, 1942; and 25 in western Lucas County on October 22, 1947 (Campbell 1968, Hicks 1945b). Of the twenty-three or more reports during these years, only single sightings at Cleveland and Pymatuning Reservoir were from the eastern half of Ohio (Herman 1981).

A few pairs found suitable summer territories in the western Lake Erie marshes. The first territorial males were reported near Sandusky in 1934 and at Magee Marsh Wildlife Area in 1936, but these birds were probably unmated (Hicks 1945b, Sawyer 1934). Nesting was established at Metzger Marsh Wildlife Area (Lucas County) in 1938, when dependent young were observed during July, and again in 1940, with a nest discovered on May 18 (Campbell 1968, Hicks 1945b). This pair returned in 1941 but not subsequently.

With the return of normal water conditions on the Great Plains by the late 1940s, Yellow-headed Blackbirds quit visiting Ohio. No records were published between 1948 and 1956. Singles appeared near Barberton and Hebron in 1957 and in Ashtabula County during 1959 (Herman 1981). They returned to the western Lake Erie marshes in 1960 and have been recorded annually in subsequent years (Campbell 1968). These recent records reflect a range expansion into the Great Lakes region (Robbins et al. 1986).

Since 1960, Yellow-headed Blackbirds have been rare visitors in the western Lake Erie marshes, primarily during spring and summer. Away from these marshes, they are accidental to casual visitors and may appear anywhere at any time in habitats varying from cattail marshes to agricultural fields and residential feeders. They are frequently found in flocks with other blackbirds. Most sightings are from the western half of Ohio and along Lake Erie east to Cleveland, primarily of five or fewer individuals.

During spring, a few Yellow-headed Blackbirds return in late February and early March. These early migrants are unusual. Most are detected between April 20 and May 15, coinciding with their arrival along western Lake Erie. Since 1980, spring migrants are normally detected at one to three sites annually away from western Lake Erie.

Summering Yellow-headed Blackbirds are rare along western Lake Erie. During some years, only one unmated male may be found, while in other years they may appear in two or three marshes. Groups of 6–8 males and females were noted during 1979 and 1993 (Harlan 1993c, Herman 1981). There are no recent confirmed breeding records, but reports of adults carrying nesting material or food suggest that they periodically nest in these marshes. Summering Yellow-headeds prefer large wetlands where patches of cattails are mixed with open water. Their breeding activities probably extend from the last half of May into July. Away from these marshes, Yellow-headed Blackbirds are accidental summer residents. Records are limited to two males in Hancock

County during June 1946 (Phillips 1980), and single males at Cleveland during 1960 and 1961 and Big Island Wildlife Area during May 1986 (Newman 1969, Peterjohn and Rice 1991). These males were unmated.

Yellow-headed Blackbirds are not reported annually during fall. Two in Medina County on July 20, 1989, and five at Gnadenhutten (Tuscarawas County) on July 25–26, 1964, probably were early migrants (Herman 1981, Peterjohn 1989d). Most fall records are distributed between late August and early December, primarily along Lake Erie east to the Cleveland area and within the northwestern counties.

Yellow-headed Blackbirds do not regularly overwinter at any location, but have produced one or more records during most winters since the late 1970s. They have been detected along western Lake Erie during six winters, mixed among wintering blackbird flocks. Away from western Lake Erie, they are most likely to visit bird feeders, with reports scattered across the glaciated counties but concentrated near the larger cities.

Rusty Blackbird *Euphagus carolinus* (Müller)

Migrant Rusty Blackbirds are most frequently observed along damp wooded corridors bordering streams, lakes, and wetlands and in flooded woodlots. They are gregarious, however, and also associate with mixed flocks of blackbirds foraging in farm fields.

While the earliest fall migrant returned to Toledo by August 23, 1931 (Campbell 1968), Rusty Blackbirds normally appear along Lake Erie during September 20–30. They are expected in the central and southern counties by October 5–15. Their maximum abundance is attained between October 15 and November 15, when they become uncommon to locally common migrants but are more locally distributed than in spring. Sizable concentrations may develop in suitable habitats, and flocks of 1,000–2,000 have been reported from the northern half of the state. Most fall flocks total 50 or fewer except within the northwestern counties, where 100–400 regularly congregate. Their migration is completed by mid-December.

Before 1950, Rusty Blackbirds were casual winter visitors, with most records comprising individuals or small flocks in the southern half of the state. As other wintering blackbirds increased during the 1950s and 1960s, Rusties underwent a similar increase. The first sizable winter roosts totaled of 3,000 at Dayton during December 1952 and 2,500 near O'Shaughnessy Reservoir (Delaware County) during the winter of 1953–1954 (Mathena et al. 1984, Nolan 1954b). Similar roosts periodically appeared subsequently, with a maximum of 5,000 at Buckeye Lake during December 1979 (Thomson 1983). Winter roosts have been restricted to the western two-thirds of Ohio.

Rusty Blackbirds are now casual to rare and rather irregular winter visitors. Since the late 1980s, the largest roosts total 100–300+. Most winter sightings are of scattered individuals or flocks of 20 or fewer, generally during December and the first half of January. Some Rusties overwinter where adequate food is available, primarily in agricultural areas, where they feed in harvested fields.

The first spring Rusty Blackbirds may appear during February of mild seasons, but normally return by March 5–12. The largest concentrations are frequently noted between March 18 and April 15. Spring migrants are widely distributed and uncommon to common in most counties, becoming abundant along western Lake Erie. Most reports are of 75 or fewer, while flocks of 100–250+ appear in suitable habitats. Movements of 1,000–3,400 are occasionally encountered, while the largest reported flock totaled 10,000 near Dayton on March 18, 1967 (Mathena et al. 1984). They usually depart by the first week of May, with a few stragglers later in the month, generally along Lake Erie. Ohio's latest spring record is a central Ohio specimen collected May 31, 1941 (Borror 1950).

Brewer's Blackbird *Euphagus cyanocephalus* (Wagler)

Formerly restricted to the western half of North America, nesting Brewer's Blackbirds moved eastward into the upper Great Lakes area during the 1930s. By the 1950s, breeding populations were established east to northern Michigan and adjacent Ontario (DeVos 1964). At the same time, wintering Brewer's Blackbirds became regular residents in the southeastern United States. In subsequent years, however, additional range expansion has not been apparent.

Their status in Ohio reflects this eastward range expansion. Brewer's Blackbirds were unrecorded until April 12, 1936, when a flock of five was discovered in Spencer Township, Lucas County (Campbell 1940). At first they were known only from sporadic records in the northwestern counties. They did not appear in other portions of the state until the 1950s and early 1960s, and have been annually reported since 1960.

Two factors obscure their status. Brewer's Blackbirds can be difficult to distinguish from Rusty Blackbirds and some reports have proven to be misidentifications. Moreover, observers seldom examine large flocks in search of the few Brewer's mixed among the thousands of other blackbirds.

Brewer's Blackbirds are rare spring migrants near western Lake Erie in Ottawa and Lucas Counties, producing one to three sightings during most years. Most reports are of ten or fewer individuals. Larger concentrations are exceptional: 55 on April 3, 1938, and an incredible 300 on April 6, 1963, in Lucas County (Campbell 1968). They are accidental to casual spring migrants through other western counties and accidental within central and eastern

Ohio, normally in groups of five or fewer, although as many as 150 have been reported. Their spring migration averages slightly later than the northward passage of Rusty Blackbirds. Most reliable records are during April and the first half of May.

The latest spring migrant was reported from Kent on June 1, 1986 (Hannikman 1986). There are no acceptable summer records from Ohio, although this species might appear near the Michigan border. Within Michigan, their breeding range primarily extends across the northern two-thirds of the state, but includes a few reports from the southeastern counties (Brewer et al. 1991).

Fewer Brewer's Blackbirds are detected as migrants in fall than in spring. They are apparently accidental to casual visitors within the western half of the state, becoming accidental in the eastern half. Most fall sightings are scattered between mid-October and mid-November, usually as flocks of ten or fewer individuals. The largest reliable fall concentrations are several flocks of 20–30+ along western Lake Erie and 32 at Killdeer Plains Wildlife Area on November 8, 1987 (Peterjohn 1988a).

Their status as winter residents is poorly understood. In Ohio, most wintering Brewer's Blackbirds are found at feedlots. They are accidental to casual winter residents in the western half of Ohio, averaging one confirmed sighting every two or three years, and accidental in the eastern half of the state. Most reliable winter records are of five or fewer individuals, although small flocks occasionally develop. Campbell (1968) reported 14–15 near Toledo in 1963 and 1966, and as many as 24–30 were counted in Ross County during the late 1980s and early 1990s (Peterjohn 1991b).

Common Grackle *Quiscalus quiscula* (Linnaeus)

Few native birds have so successfully adapted to man-made habitats as Common Grackles. From western Ohio farmlands to rural roadsides of the southeastern counties and urban areas throughout the state, these grackles are abundant summer residents and seen by the hundreds each day. Smaller numbers also occupy wetlands, wooded edges, and open successional fields. Only extensive mature woodlands do not support nesting pairs.

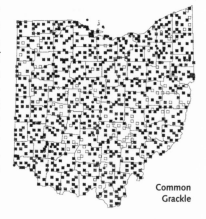

Common
Grackle

Common Grackle populations increased tremendously during the twentieth century. These increases were most evident in the 1940s and 1950s and continued into the 1970s (Robbins et al. 1986). Populations stabilized during the 1980s, and recent statewide trends along Breeding Bird Survey routes indicated significant declines (Sauer et al. 1998).

Their spring migration coincides with the early movements of other blackbirds. Warm weather during February is accompanied by the first returning flocks. They quickly spread across the entire state. Their northward movements peak during March, when daily totals of 500–2,000+ are frequent. Larger roosts host as many as an estimated 500,000 Common Grackles, but these immense flocks are unusual. Few migrant flocks are encountered after April 7.

Common Grackles begin breeding activities immediately upon their arrival. Their displays are familiar sights on residential lawns and in shade trees during March and April. As described by Dawson (1903):

> His love-making antics, too, are all the more ridiculous for being earnest.
> Perched upon the tip-top of an evergreen he thrusts his wings out, spreads his
> tail and ruffles all his feathers, and then throws his head forward like a person
> about to obtain relief from seasickness. The outcome of all this effect is a sound
> by no means ravishing …

Nest construction has been reported as early as mid-March. There is considerable variability in the nesting behavior among pairs, however, and some nests are not constructed until mid-May (Maxwell 1970). Common Grackles nest as isolated pairs but also breed in aggregations of 3–25 pairs. Large conifers near residences provide preferred nest sites, although other dense trees, shrubs, and bridge girders are regularly utilized. If these sites are unavailable, grackles have nested in cattail marshes, buttonbush swamps, orchards, Wood Duck boxes, and Purple Martin houses (Campbell 1968). One pair nested in a woodpecker cavity enlarged through decay and excavation (Lloyd 1943).

The first clutches are normally laid during the last half of April, and nests with young have been reported by April 23 (Trautman 1940). Fledged young normally appear by mid-May and are regularly encountered through late June. Renesting efforts produce nests with young through June 30 and adults accompanied by dependent young through August 3.

Breeding Common Grackles are abundant, and daily totals of 100–500+ are expected during May and early June. Once the young are independent, grackles congregate in large foraging flocks and evening roosts. Flocks of 300–1,000+ are noted by late June or early July. These concentrations steadily grow through the summer and autumn, their numbers swelled by migrants during September and October. By day, these flocks spread over the country-side, feeding on grain and weed seeds in agricultural fields and any available food in urban areas. They roost in groves of trees or cattail swamps, where 10,000–100,000+ may spend the night. Some roosts have supported an esti-mated 1,000,000 Common Grackles. Most migrate south by early November, although some roosts remain intact into December.

At one time, Common Grackles were rare winter residents. Their numbers increased after 1900, corresponding with their expanding breeding popula-tions. Between 1920 and 1940, they were casual to uncommon winter resi-dents, usually in groups of 12 or fewer, with occasional flocks of 100–400. By the 1950s, they became regular winter residents in most counties and period-ically formed sizable roosts. Their winter status has not changed appreciably in subsequent years.

Common Grackles are generally rare to uncommon winter residents in northern Ohio and uncommon to fairly common elsewhere. These wintering grackles are normally observed in flocks of 25 or fewer individuals, with occa-sional concentrations of 100–1,000+. Large winter roosts have appeared in all portions the state, but do not form every year. As many as 20,000–83,000 have been estimated at these roosts, allowing them to become locally abundant win-ter residents at some localities.

Great-tailed Grackle *Quiscalus mexicanus* (Gmelin)

Great-tailed Grackles were formerly restricted to Central and South America and the extreme southwestern United States. During the twentieth century, their nesting range expanded and they presently breed north to central California, central Colorado, Nebraska, Iowa, and Missouri (AOU 1998). Some birds occasionally wander as far north as British Columbia and Montana and east to Illinois and Ohio. Ohio's only record of this accidental visitor was provided by a male discovered by J. Kirk Alexander in Carroll Township, Ottawa County, on May 6, 1985. This Great-tailed Grackle was relocated at the same site and photographed the following day. It was also reported from sev-eral other Ottawa County locations later in the month (Peterjohn 1985c).

Brown-headed Cowbird *Molothrus ater* (Boddaert)

Brown-headed Cowbirds are brood parasites. Female cowbirds are egg-laying machines, producing an egg nearly every day during the breeding season. But rather than building their own nests, they lay their eggs in the nests of other songbirds. These songbirds dutifully incubate the cowbird eggs along with their own. The cowbird eggs hatch first, bringing forth young cowbirds that invariably thrive while the other young frequently die of starvation. Female cowbirds prefer to parasitize the nests of small songbirds, particularly Red-eyed Vireos, Yellow Warblers, Common Yellowthroats, Indigo Buntings, Chipping Sparrows, and Song Sparrows. As cowbirds expanded, their success was achieved at the expense of the parasitized species.

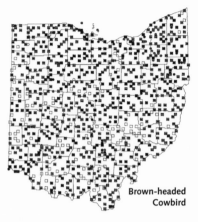

Brown-headed
Cowbird

Cowbirds are native to the Great Plains and expanded into Ohio during the 1840s (DeVos 1964). Their expansion through the state was rapid, and cowbirds became common and widely distributed summer residents by the 1880s (Wheaton 1882). Their populations remained stable into the 1930s, when Hicks (1935a) described them as common to abundant residents in every county. Additional increases were apparent during the 1950s and early 1960s, but statewide trends on Breeding Bird Survey routes show significant declines since 1966 (Sauer et al. 1998).

Brown-headed Cowbirds are common to abundant summer residents, equally numerous in woodlands, brushy fields, farmlands, and urban areas. Between 25 and 100+ are observed daily, mostly as groups of six or fewer individuals, although flocks of 20–60+ nonbreeding males may be encountered. Female cowbirds begin laying eggs during the last half of April; this activity normally peaks between May 10 and June 20. A few females produce eggs through late July (Williams 1950). The first fledgling cowbirds are reported by early June and are regularly noted into early August.

Like most other blackbirds, cowbirds accumulate into flocks shortly after the end of the breeding season. Groups of 100–200+ are noted by mid-July, and flock size increases as the season progresses. Their southward migration apparently begins during the last half of August, peaking between mid-September and mid-November (Trautman 1940). These migrants are fairly common to abundant, most numerous around feedlots and farm fields. The largest fall concentrations normally total 500–2,000+, although as many as 5,000+ have been reported.

As late as the early 1900s, Jones (1903) cited no winter records of Brown-headed Cowbirds from Ohio. The number of winter sightings grew slowly. By 1940, they were generally casual to rare and sporadic winter residents in the central and southern counties (Kemsies and Randle 1953, Trautman 1940). They remained accidental winter visitors in northern Ohio (Campbell 1968, Williams 1950). Their status changed dramatically during the 1950s and 1960s as wintering cowbirds were discovered throughout Ohio. As early as the winter of 1953–1954, 40,000 were estimated at a roost near O'Shaughnessy Reservoir in Delaware County (Nolan 1954b). These large roosts remain exceptional, although as many as 80,000 congregated at Dayton during the winter of 1980–1981 (Mathena et al. 1984). Most winter roosts contain 500–5,000 cowbirds.

Brown-headed Cowbirds are now uncommon to locally abundant winter residents. They are abundant only near their roosts. Away from these roosts, they are found most frequently in the western counties but can be scarce along the unglaciated Allegheny Plateau. Most winter sightings are of 5–100 except at the roosts.

Timing of their spring migration coincides with the movements of other blackbirds. The first migrants are expected during the first warm days of February and early March. This movement normally peaks between March 10 and April 10, with very few migrants after April 20. Spring cowbirds are common to abundant migrants. Most reports are of 50–1,000 daily, with occasional flocks of 2,000–5,000+. Large roosts may briefly form; as many as 25,000 cowbirds have been estimated at a blackbird roost near Columbus (Thomson 1983).

Orchard Oriole *Icterus spurius* (Linnaeus)

While Orchard Orioles are not as brightly colored as the more familiar Baltimore Orioles, they are still welcome additions to our breeding avifauna. Adult male Orchards are handsome in their mixed black and chestnut-orange plumage—unlike the females and immature males, whose hues are predominantly bright yellows and greens. These sprightly little orioles produce a distinctive song, an outburst of whistles and chatter unlikely to be confused with the loud, clear whistles repeated by Baltimores.

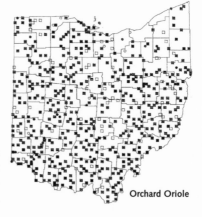

Orchard Oriole

As summer residents, most Orchard Orioles are found in young wooded riparian corridors, shade trees near rural residences, fencerows, roadside thickets, parks, orchards, pastures, and fallow fields with scattered small trees. They are equally numerous along streams and in upland habitats. Their nests are normally placed at heights of less than twenty feet in small trees. In the southern counties, nesting activities are initiated by mid-May, and adults are feeding young in the nest by the first week of June. The first fledglings are noted by mid-June. Breeding activities are delayed by one to two weeks in northern Ohio, where young Orchards are expected out of the nest during late June and early July (Braund 1940b, Mathena et al. 1984, Williams 1950). A very late nest with eggs discovered near Toledo on July 27, 1935, certainly represented a re-nesting attempt (Campbell 1968).

Their statewide distribution repeatedly expanded and contracted during the twentieth century. In the early 1900s, Orchard Orioles were apparently expanding in the northern counties, particularly near Lake Erie in Lorain and Erie Counties, where they were nearly as numerous as Baltimore Orioles (Jones 1903, 1910). This expansion was short-lived and their breeding range was markedly reduced by the mid-1930s. Hicks (1935a) considered Orchard Orioles uncommon to rare and very locally distributed summer residents, citing records from fifty-one counties, mostly in the eastern half of the state. Breeding Orchards were most numerous within Muskingum, Morgan, Athens, Hocking, Jackson, and Scioto Counties.

Their recent range expansion began in 1945, when increased numbers were apparent at Cincinnati and along the unglaciated Allegheny Plateau (Buchanan 1980, Kemsies and Randle 1953). By the mid-1960s, increasing populations were apparent throughout the western half of Ohio and some northeastern counties. This expansion continued into the 1990s. Orchard Orioles now breed in every county. They are least numerous in northeastern Ohio, where they are uncommon and locally distributed as scattered pairs (Peterjohn and Rice 1991). In other northern and the glaciated central counties, Orchards are uncommon to fairly common residents, least numerous within intensively farmed areas. Most summer reports are of 1–5 daily, although as many as 9–18 are detected at a few localities. Nesting Orchards are fairly common to common across southern and unglaciated Ohio. In counties bordering the Ohio River, 10–25+ are noted daily, but totals seldom exceed 5–15 elsewhere.

While an exceptionally early Orchard Oriole returned to Utica (Licking County) on March 31, 1965 (Petersen 1965c), they normally appear in the southern counties during April 17–25, central Ohio by April 27–May 3, and along Lake Erie by May 3–8. Breeding populations are established within the southern counties by May 15, but the last pairs appear along Lake Erie through June 2–5. This migration mostly includes resident orioles returning to their territories. At migrant traps along Lake Erie and other locations where they do not nest, Orchard Orioles are uncommon to fairly common spring migrants, with most reports of 1–7 individuals.

Orchard Orioles are among the earliest songbirds to begin their fall migration. Migrant Orchards appear along Lake Erie by July 7–12, but most are reported between July 25 and August 15. They are rare to uncommon in most counties, with no more than seven daily. The latest migrants usually depart by September 2–5. An Orchard Oriole at Toledo on September 24, 1938, was exceptionally late (Campbell 1968).

Bullock's Oriole *Icterus bullockii* (Swainson)

The western counterpart of the Baltimore Oriole, Bullock's Orioles are widely distributed summer residents across the western half of the United States and southern Canada. Most spend the winter months in Mexico and northern Central America (AOU 1998). There are reports of Bullock's Orioles from eastern North America, frequently of individuals visiting feeders during winter. Distinguishing Bullock's from Baltimore Orioles is a difficult challenge, especially since these species regularly hybridize within the central Great Plains, and many extralimital reports of Bullock's Orioles have been recently questioned (Lee and Birch 1998).

Bullock's Orioles have been reported from Ohio on two occasions. A female overwintered at a Columbus feeder during 1974–1975 and returned the following winter. This individual was studied by many observers, and my own brief notes described a female with a yellowish wash to the face, throat, and upper breast, an off-white belly, yellow undertail coverts, and a gray back.

The other reported Bullock's Oriole visited an Akron area feeder during December 1990 (Kopka 1991). However, the described field marks of an orange head, nape, and breast, an olive back, and light orange undertail coverts suggest that this individual was actually a Baltimore Oriole.

Baltimore Oriole *Icterus galbula* (Linnaeus)

With a sharp, loud whistle and a flash of brilliant orange and black, a male Baltimore Oriole announces his presence from the top of a large oak. His return is a sure sign spring has arrived. While spring overflights have appeared along Lake Erie by the first week of April, the first Baltimores normally return to southern and central Ohio during the last week of April and Lake Erie by May 1–5. Their northward movements peak between May 7 and

Baltimore
Oriole

20. During these brief weeks, the countryside and wooded residential areas come alive with the Baltimore's loud calls and colorful plumage. These migrants are fairly common to common; 5–25 are expected daily, with occasional totals of 40–75+. Large flights along Lake Erie produce tallies of 100–200+. The last stragglers leave migrant traps during May 27–June 3.

As summer residents, Baltimore Orioles have been fairly common to common and widespread throughout the twentieth century. Nesting pairs are slightly less numerous in extreme southern Ohio, especially Adams, Scioto, and Lawrence Counties, where they are uncommon to fairly common. While local populations have fluctuated during recent decades, statewide trends along Breeding Bird Survey routes indicate a slight increase since 1966 (Sauer et al. 1998).

Nesting Baltimore Orioles favor wooded riparian corridors, forest edges, and large shade trees in parks and near residences. They were formerly familiar summer residents in cities and regularly built their nests in large elms shading urban streets. The disappearance of most elms substantially reduced the numbers nesting in urban areas. Baltimores are now most numerous along wooded corridors bordering creeks and rivers. A canoe trip down any stream bordered by large sycamores and cottonwoods produces counts of 15–30 and as many as 50–60+ have been tallied. Summer totals generally are 3–12 in other habitats.

Baltimore Orioles are renowned for their nests, which hang from the outer branches of tall trees. These nests are concealed by vegetation during summer but become obvious after the leaves fall. Nest construction begins shortly after their return and has been noted by April 25 (Williams 1950). Nests with eggs are reported between May 18 and June 20, and most nests contain young during the last half of June. Most recently fledged young appear in late June and early July, but renesting attempts produce fledglings through early August (Trautman 1940, Williams 1950).

Once males quit singing in early July, Baltimore Orioles become difficult to locate. This inconspicuous behavior continues through fall migration, when they are uncommon to fairly common in most counties but can be locally common along Lake Erie. Most fall reports total eight or fewer, with occasional flights of 20–50+. Migrants are apparent by mid-July along Lake Erie and August 3–8 at inland locations. Most are found during August, with the last migrants normally departing by September 15–20.

Baltimore Orioles are surprisingly hardy and may linger into autumn, with late October and November sightings scattered across the state and an equal number during early winter. Most winter records are Baltimores visiting bird feeders during December and the first half of January, although a few individuals overwintered. Accidental anywhere after early November, there are now at least 29 winter records scattered across the glaciated counties.

Brambling *Fringilla montifringilla* Linnaeus

Snowstorms during late March or early April exasperate people anxious for the arrival of spring. But they can be productive for birding, causing birds to congregate at feeders and allowing migrants to be observed that otherwise would be missed. Such was the case in the appearance of Ohio's only Brambling, which was first observed on March 31, 1987, at the Bath (Summit County) feeder of Horace and Helen Harger after a snowstorm blanketed northern Ohio. Although the bird was a male acquiring its breeding plumage, its identity was not confirmed until April 5. During its irregular visits to the Hargers' feeder, this attractive finch was viewed by many observers through April 7 (Rosche 1987). Bramblings are Eurasian finches whose breeding range extends from Siberia to Scandinavia. In winter, they are found south to the Mediterranean region, India, and China (AOU 1998). They are accidental winter visitors to North America.

Gray-crowned Rosy-Finch *Leucosticte tephrocotis* (Swainson)

Gray-crowned Rosy-Finches normally occupy alpine tundra in the western mountains, although they move to lower elevations during winter. Periodic food shortages result in movements outside this range. While these rosy-finches occasionally wander onto the Great Plains, vagrants have appeared east to Maine (AOU 1998). Ohio's only Gray-crowned Rosy-Finch briefly visited the Joseph Croy residence near Whitehouse (Lucas County) on February 6–7, 1984. Photographs taken by the Croys clearly established its identity (Peterjohn 1984b).

Another rosy-finch frequented a feeder at the Norman Hazen residence in Conneaut during April 5–6, 1971 (Flanigan 1971). While the written descriptions definitely indicate that this bird was a rosy-finch, its specific identification cannot be established with certainty. Some field marks support the claimed identification as a Black Rosy-Finch (*L. atrata*), a species with no confirmed records from eastern North America, but the details are insufficient to eliminate one of the darker races of Gray-crowned Rosy-Finch.

Pine Grosbeak *Pinicola enucleator* (Linnaeus)

This visitor from boreal coniferous forests has always been very erratic in its movements into Ohio. Most winters, Pine Grosbeaks remain in the northern forests. Periodic food shortages prompt them to move southward, and they infrequently penetrate the northern border of the state.

There were few nineteenth-century records of Pine Grosbeaks from Ohio. The first noticeable movement occurred in the winter of 1903–1904, producing sightings along the entire lakefront (Jones 1904, 1910). These finches were infrequently reported from northern Ohio in subsequent years until the winter of 1933–1934, when a large movement into the northeastern United States produced multiple observations at Toledo and Cleveland (Campbell 1968, Williams 1950). Their winter movements were most apparent between 1950 and the early 1970s. An "unprecedented flight" appeared in the winter of 1951–1952 (Brooks 1952a). The largest numbers were noted during December, with flocks of 10–20 scattered south to Wooster and Youngstown. An adult male provided the first Cincinnati area record between December 20 and January 27 (Kemsies and Randle 1953). A smaller flight was reported during the 1954–1955 winter, while scattered Pine Grosbeaks were noted in northern Ohio during most winters of that decade.

Their largest invasion of the twentieth century was noted in the winter of 1961–1962. These grosbeaks appeared during late November and remained throughout the winter. There were flocks of 100 at Iradale (near Akron) and 60 at Akron on February 7 (Graber 1962a, 1962b), while 15–40 appeared south to Youngstown and Mohican State Forest. This flight produced the first Columbus area record and a second sighting from Cincinnati. A smaller movement during the 1965–1966 winter was limited to the counties bordering Lake Erie. The last defined flight was apparent only in the Cleveland area. The winter of 1972–1973 produced multiple records, including several flocks of 10–16 (Kleen and Bush 1973b). In subsequent years, Pine Grosbeaks became very sporadic winter visitors, averaging one record every two to four winters from northern Ohio through the early 1980s. Small flocks were only reported from the Toledo area, while other sightings were of isolated individuals. There was one sight record during the 1990s.

The earliest fall arrivals appeared by October 20–November 2, but were normally detected during the last half of November and December. The largest numbers usually appeared in December and early January, but frequently became less numerous in February. Their spring movements produced only sporadic reports between March and mid-May. While strictly accidental winter visitors now, they were formerly casually observed within the lakefront counties and south to Youngstown and Akron. Pine Grosbeaks were accidental winter visitors elsewhere, with several sightings at Findlay and the Mansfield-Wooster area, three central Ohio records, and three reports from Cincinnati.

Purple Finch *Carpodacus purpureus* (Gmelin)

Purple Finches share the erratic movements of other members of their family. They appear annually but may be fairly scarce one year and numerous the next, depending upon food availability elsewhere within their range. Whenever they appear, Purple Finches are always welcomed at bird feeders. The brightly colored males are particularly pleasing during winter when most other birds are in somber plumages.

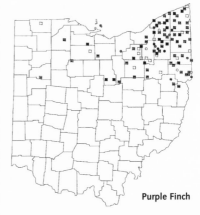

Purple Finch

Purple Finches breed in northern Ohio, and this population increased during the twentieth century. Nesting pairs were first recorded at Cleveland in 1925 (Williams 1950). By the mid-1930s, small numbers were scattered across Cuyahoga, Lake, Geauga, Trumbull, and Ashtabula Counties (Hicks 1935a). A southward and westward range extension became apparent in the 1950s, producing the first nesting records from Youngstown in 1954 and East Liverpool by 1960 (Brooks 1954c, Hall 1960d). The first Toledo nesting attempt was reported in 1955, and summering Purple Finches were noted in Mansfield by 1970 (Campbell 1968, Petersen 1970d). This expansion continued into the 1980s and 1990s in other northern counties and produced a few attempts in central and southeastern Ohio. Breeding Purple Finches are uncommon to fairly common in northeastern Ohio, with eight or fewer recorded daily east of Cleveland and south through Columbiana, Stark, and Wayne Counties (Peterjohn and Rice 1991). Small numbers reside in Carroll and Jefferson Counties at the northern edge of the unglaciated plateau. They are accidental to rare summer residents in other northern counties, with most records from Toledo, Mansfield, Lorain, Findlay, and Tiffin.

Purple Finches are accidental summer residents in central Ohio. The only confirmed breeding attempt from Columbus was discovered in 1972 (Thomson 1983). They have summered at Springfield, where nesting was suspected but never established. A female with young in Hocking County during the summer of 1990 provided the first indication of breeding in the southeastern counties (Peterjohn 1990d). A few individuals briefly appeared at several other central Ohio locations during June but were probably nonbreeders.

Ohio's first nesting pairs were discovered in hemlock ravines, bogs, and tall conifers in residential areas (Hicks 1933a, Williams 1950). In recent decades, they exhibit a preference for ornamental conifers in urban areas and rural Christmas tree farms. Purple Finch nests have been recorded as high as thirty-one feet in a tall spruce, but most are placed at heights of less than fifteen feet (Campbell 1968, Williams 1950). The few breeding records indicate that most nests are initiated in May. The young normally hatch during early June and fledge by early July. A nest with hatching young was observed as late as July 7 (Mayfield and McCormick 1956).

Very early fall migrant Purple Finches have appeared at northern and central locations by August 28–September 5. The first migrants are normally reported during September 25–October 5; most pass through Ohio during October as uncommon to fairly common migrants in deciduous woods and occasionally in weedy fields. Despite annual fluctuations in abundance, 1–8 are noted most days, with occasional totals of 15–25. Flocks of 50–120+ are exceptional. The last migrants normally depart during early November, although stragglers are noted through December 5–10.

The distribution and abundance of wintering Purple Finches varies from year to year. On rare occasions, they are absent from the entire state. But a few are detected during most winters. They infrequently stage pronounced movements and become widely distributed. These winter invasions have occurred once or twice per decade since the 1950s. Perhaps the largest recent movements were in the winters of 1959–1960 and 1982–1983, when flocks of 25–150+ were reported from a number of locations.

Their winter movement patterns are fairly complex. During some years, Purple Finches remain throughout the winter. In others, they are numerous in December and become scarce by late January and February. But if they are scarce in December, they will remain scarce throughout the season.

Wintering Purple Finches are normally most numerous near Cincinnati, where they are uncommon to fairly common residents. They are usually observed in groups of 3–15, with occasional flocks of 25–50+. During influxes, as many as 165 have been counted in one tree (Peterjohn 1983b). Small numbers also regularly winter along the unglaciated Allegheny Plateau, especially south from Hocking, Perry, and Belmont Counties. They are uncommon winter residents, generally noted as individuals or totals of 12 or fewer. Flocks of 25–40+ are possible during influxes.

Fewer Purple Finches normally winter in the remainder of Ohio, except on Kelleys Island, where December flocks of 30–60+ are regular and as many as 193 have been counted (Peterjohn 1983b). Elsewhere, they are casual to rare winter residents in the glaciated central and northern counties, usually as individuals or small flocks during December. They regularly remain through the winter only during influxes, when flocks of 5–25+ may appear. Larger concentrations are infrequent but include as many as 250 at Toledo on December 27, 1959, and 186 on the 1956 O'Shaughnessy Reservoir Christmas Bird Count (Campbell 1968, Thomson 1983).

As spring migrants, Purple Finches may be numerous some years and almost absent in others. Sizable winter influxes are frequently followed by strong spring movements, but large migrations may follow winters with relatively few residents. When they are plentiful, spring migrants appear in late March and peak during April 15–May 5, when 10–50+ are observed daily and tallies of 100–200+ are possible. During a "normal" spring, the timing of their migration is similar but daily totals seldom exceed 5–20. When they are scarce, Purple Finches may not appear until April 15–20 and are usually observed in groups of ten or fewer. These migrants depart by May 15–20.

Despite a slowly expanding breeding population, their future is uncertain. Since the 1980s, Purple Finches have faced increased competition from introduced House Finches for breeding sites and winter food supplies. House Finches are more aggressive and have displaced Purple Finches from many bird feeders during the winter months, forcing them to feed on tree and weed seeds found in natural habitats. Similar displacements have not been evident during the breeding season.

House Finch *Carpodacus mexicanus* (Müller)

The story behind the introduction and spread of House Finches through eastern and central North America is well known (Bock and Lepthien 1976). From a handful of finches liberated from a New York pet store in 1940, they rapidly spread westward and eventually merged with the native western populations during the early 1990s. Their populations are still expanding in portions of their range, and have become well established across Ohio.

Ohio's first House Finches appeared at Holden Arboretum near Cleveland on January 5, 1964 (Newman 1969). As many as four were reported throughout the winter (Petersen 1964b). By the end of 1965, they had appeared at four Cleveland area locations (Newman 1969). Small numbers were sporadically reported from this area in subsequent years, but none were recorded elsewhere until October 29, 1972, when one was found at Marietta (Hall 1973a). These finches appeared at Dayton in 1973, East Liverpool and Columbus in 1974, Holmes County in 1975, Mansfield in 1976, Toledo in 1978, and Cincinnati in 1979 (Hall 1974c, Kleen 1975c, Thomson 1983). The first records were mostly of finches visiting urban feeders during winter and spring.

Establishment of a breeding population involved a rapid westward expansion across Ohio. Breeding finches were initially restricted to cities and towns. In eastern Ohio, nesting was suspected or confirmed at several localities from Cleveland south to Belmont County in 1976–1977. By 1978, a few pairs were nesting at Columbus. Breeding populations were established in the Cincinnati-Dayton area and Toledo by 1981–1982.

Through the mid-1970s, most reports were of only 1–5 individuals at each locality. The first sizable flock at Cleveland totaled 125 on January 2, 1978

(Kleen 1978b). At other northeastern locations, the largest reported flocks were composed of 5–12 in the winter of 1977–1978, 15–25 in the winter of 1978–1979, and 40–80 in the winter of 1979–1980. A maximum of 200 appeared at Lorain during the fall of 1980. Elsewhere, House Finches were mostly reported as groups of 15 or fewer until the autumn of 1980, when 40 were counted at Columbus (Kleen 1981). Their populations expanded rapidly, with 100 counted in Butler County on January 7, 1983, and flocks of 30–45 at Cincinnati and Toledo that year (Peterjohn 1983b). As numbers increased within urban areas, House Finches spread across the rural countryside during the mid-1980s (Peterjohn and Rice 1991). Statewide populations increased through the mid-1990s (Sauer et al. 1998), but apparently stabilized by the late 1990s.

House Finches are common to abundant summer residents. In urban areas, 50–100+ are noted daily, while tallies of 20–50+ are possible in rural areas. Breeding pairs are closely associated with residences, and their preferred nest sites are ornamental shrubbery and young conifers. Nesting activities begin in late March and early April; first clutches are laid in April and early May. Adults with dependent young have been reported by April 15–25, but the first broods normally appear in May and early June. Later nesting attempts are responsible for nest construction through the first week of July and observations of dependent young as late as August 25.

House Finches are also common to abundant winter residents, regularly forming flocks of 15–50+ at bird feeders and occasional concentrations of 100–200+. In addition to flocks found at feeders, some forage in fallow fields and croplands. Winter flocks of 300–400+ are unusual, and the largest reported flock is 2,000+ near Ashville (Pickaway County) on December 8, 1985 (Peterjohn 1986b).

Not all House Finches are permanent residents. There are definite migrations each spring and autumn, but migrants are difficult to distinguish from the large breeding population. These migrants are most evident as flocks passing along Lake Erie. Their fall migration apparently peaks between September 25 and November 10, with smaller numbers moving southward into December. Most spring migrants are detected between March 15 and April 15, with a few noted through the first week of May.

Red Crossbill *Loxia curvirostra* Linnaeus

Renowned for their erratic movements, Red Crossbills invariably appear in Ohio as a result of food shortages within their traditional range. But the origin of these flocks is as unpredictable as their presence within the state. Invading Red Crossbills are as likely to have wandered east from the Rocky

Mountains as south from Canada. Hence, their statewide distribution varies from flight to flight. During some years, they are restricted to the western counties; in other years, flocks only appear along Lake Erie. A statewide movement is rare, usually part of massive regional invasions. During the phenomenal invasion of 1972–1973, the first flocks were detected during the last half of August, and Red Crossbills were fairly numerous by mid-September. This early fall migration is exceptional; there are few records earlier than October. The first fall migrants normally appear during November, and their movements continue into January.

Their fall abundance depends upon the size of the invasion. Red Crossbills are absent some years. They are normally casual fall visitors to most counties, usually as individuals or flocks of ten or fewer. During small invasions, they become locally rare migrants in the northern counties, but casual elsewhere. Only during massive invasions do they become rare to locally fairly common migrants, and flocks of 20–50+ may appear in any county.

Red Crossbills are unrecorded in approximately one out of every four winters. During most years, wintering flocks appear at one to three scattered localities, most frequently in the northern counties near Toledo and Cleveland, and also in pines along the Allegheny Plateau. Wintering Red Crossbills are generally accidental elsewhere. Following large fall invasions, they become rare to locally fairly common winter residents in northern and eastern Ohio but casual to locally uncommon elsewhere. Most winter flocks total ten or fewer individuals; concentrations of 30–50+ occur during large invasions.

Some flocks may spend the entire winter within a cemetery or small park. Other flocks visit a location for only an hour or a day, then disappear. Wintering flocks are most likely to appear within pine plantations or ornamental conifers planted in parks, cemeteries, and residential areas. A few crossbills subsist on sunflower seeds at bird feeders. When food is widely available, Red Crossbills spend the entire winter within Ohio. If pine cone production is poor, wintering numbers diminish by late January or February.

As spring migrants, their distribution and relative abundance are usually related to the size of the previous autumn's flight. On a few occasions, however, Red Crossbills have staged detectable movements into the state. They are normally casual spring migrants, but become rare to locally fairly common following invasions. Most flocks total ten or fewer individuals, with groups of 20–40+ during flight years. These movements are erratic but are generally most pronounced between March 15 and May 10. Flocks linger into late May, especially following large winter movements.

Red Crossbills are accidental summer visitors, usually following major flights. Most are recorded during June, although there are July and early August sightings from Cleveland and Canton. These summer reports are of scattered individuals or flocks of 5–40, primarily near Cleveland but also from the Toledo area, Columbus, and Hocking County. These summering crossbills are assumed to be nonbreeders, an assumption that is not necessarily valid. Red Crossbills may nest any time food is abundant, even in the middle of winter. They also breed outside of their normal range. Within Ohio, there is only one confirmed nesting record, following the invasion of 1972–1973. An incubating pair was discovered by Al Staffan at Tar Hollow State Forest in Ross County during April 1973 (Thomson 1983). This nest was subsequently abandoned. There is a probable breeding record from Cleveland, where two juveniles were reported along the Rocky River on July 12–13, 1970 (Petersen 1970d).

The pattern of erratic Red Crossbill flights has been apparent since the nineteenth century. Jones (1903) considered these crossbills "irregular" winter visitors with "considerable flights sometimes during winter or early spring, followed abruptly by total disappearance." Nineteenth century flights were indicated during the winters of 1868–1869 and 1874–1875, but additional movements almost certainly occurred (Kemsies and Randle 1953).

During the twentieth century, sizable flights occurred during the winters of 1920–1921, 1931–1932, and 1940–1941, with only sporadic encounters during intervening years (Campbell 1968, Williams 1950). In the 1950s, the only substantial movement was noted in the winter of 1954–1955 (Brooks 1955b). Their flights became more frequent during the 1960s and 1970s. The flight in 1972–1973 produced the largest numbers of crossbills recorded from Ohio (Kleen and Bush 1973b). There have been no widespread Red Crossbill movements during the 1980s and 1990s.

White-winged Crossbill *Loxia leucoptera* Gmelin

A series of call notes resembling the chatter of redpolls announces the presence of a small flock of White-winged Crossbills as they descend upon the upper branches of a tall hemlock tree. White-wingeds prefer hemlocks, with their relatively small cones, but also feed on pine cones and deciduous trees such as sweet gums, alders, and sycamores.

White-winged Crossbills are very sporadic and casual winter visitors, normally less frequently reported than Red Crossbills. Their movements into Ohio are also a result of food shortages within the northern coniferous forests where they reside. Since the two crossbills have different food preferences, the southward movements of the two species are normally unrelated. While a few White-wingeds associate with large flights of Reds, the largest White-winged movements usually are accompanied by relatively few Reds.

The first major White-winged Crossbill flight occurred during the winter of

1868–1869, but little information is available concerning the magnitude of this movement. A smaller flight was reported during the winter of 1901–1902 (Jones 1903). Except for a small movement during the winter of 1919–1920, only isolated individuals and small flocks were irregularly noted until the winter of 1940–1941, when a number of flocks appeared in the Cleveland area (Williams 1950). Additional small flights were noted during the winters of 1948–1949, 1954–1955, and 1958–1959. The next defined movement occurred in 1963–1964, when "unprecedented numbers" appeared in eastern Ohio and small flocks were scattered across the state (Hall 1964). A similar statewide invasion was detected during the winter of 1965–1966 (Hall 1966b, Petersen 1966a). Small movements were reported during the winters of 1971–1972, 1975–1976, 1977–1978, 1980–1981, and 1981–1982, but there were few reports in subsequent years until another small flight occurred in the winter of 1997–1998 (Fazio 1998a).

The largest concentrations are reported during invasion years, including flocks of 50–100 near Cleveland and Youngstown, 75 at Cincinnati, and 20–30 elsewhere (Hall 1964, Williams 1950). Most flocks total 15 or fewer individuals. During noninvasion years, these crossbills are noted as individuals and flocks of five or fewer. While White-winged Crossbills have returned as early as September 5, 1977, to Genoa (Ottawa County) (Kleen 1978a), the first migrants normally return during November. Flocks appear anytime during winter, and sizable movements may not be evident until the last half of February. Most spring migrants depart by mid-April, but a few linger into May. The latest migrants include one at East Liverpool through May 20, 1966; another at Cincinnati through May 27, 1955; and two at Lorain through June 9, 1981 (Hall 1966c, Nolan 1955c, Peterjohn 1981c).

Common Redpoll *Carduelis flammea* (Linnaeus)

The first returning Common Redpolls are normally encountered as small flocks in migration along Lake Erie. These flocks may land in fallow fields where they consort with goldfinches and feed on sunflowers, evening primrose, and other weeds. They may also join goldfinches and Pine Siskins as they devour seeds of alder, birch, sweet gum, and sycamore. These redpolls readily accept food supplied at bird feeders.

Like all northern finches, Common Redpolls are erratic winter visitors. They are very rare or absent during some years but almost abundant and widespread in others. They may be numerous by late November during some flights but may not appear until February or even March in other movements. The timing of their appearance may be a function of the distance traveled to reach Ohio. Some redpoll flights originate in Arctic Canada directly to our north. But some Common Redpolls banded in Ohio have been recaptured in Alaska, indicating a northwestward migration after leaving the state. Other flights have included small numbers of "Greater" Redpolls from Greenland.

In the northern counties, their relative abundance generally follows a cycle of fairly high numbers one winter followed by relatively few the next (Newman 1969, Williams 1950). When they are scarce, individuals or flocks of ten or fewer are rarely noted near Lake Erie. When they are fairly numerous, flocks of 10–50+ are uncommonly observed along the lakefront and smaller numbers filter inland. During large invasions, they become fairly common to locally abundant, with flocks of 20–350+ appearing south to Youngstown and Findlay (Phillips 1980, Thomson 1983); as many as 500–1,000+ have been reported near Lake Erie.

While Common Redpolls have returned to Lake Erie by October 20–24, they normally appear during November 10–December 15. Early flights produced 1,000 at Cleveland on November 8, 1980, and 200 at Youngstown on November 1, 1959 (Hall 1960a, Kleen 1981). During some years, they inexplicably disappear after early January; in others, flocks are encountered throughout the winter. Redpolls normally depart during the first half of March, with stragglers lingering into April. Following large invasions, they were noted through May 11, 1978, at Findlay and May 13, 1978, at Cleveland (Hannikman 1978, Phillips 1980).

In central and southern Ohio, Common Redpolls are accidental to casual winter visitors except during periodic invasions. Only a few sizable flights were reported during the nineteenth century in the winters of 1836–1837 and 1868–1869 (Kemsies and Randle 1953, Williams 1950). Another major movement occurred in the winter of 1906–1907. Sizable influxes were noted during the winters of 1933–1934, 1935–1936, 1943–1944, and 1946–1947 (Campbell 1968, Mayfield 1947b). The winter of 1959–1960 witnessed the "heaviest invasion in recent years" (Hall 1960b). Large flights subsequently appeared at a frequency of three to ten years, with the most recent invasion during the 1993–1994 winter (Brock 1994b, Hall 1994b).

During some invasions, Common Redpolls only wander south to Columbus. In others, flocks appear south to the Ohio River. One of the largest movements occurred during 1981–1982, with flocks of 100–150 near Columbus, 113 at Dayton, and 54 at Cincinnati (Peterjohn 1982b). The 1993–1994 flight produced a maximum of 360 in Holmes County (Harlan 1994b).

Within these counties, the earliest fall migrants are noted during the last half of October and small flocks appear by mid-December. The largest numbers are usually encountered during late January and February. Most Common Redpolls depart by early March, but may remain later following invasions:

until April 12, 1982, at Dayton and April 25, 1969, at East Liverpool (Hall 1969, Mathena et al. 1984).

Hoary Redpoll *Carduelis hornemanni* (Holböll)

Hoary Redpolls occupy the Arctic tundra, normally remaining there throughout the year. Periodic food shortages prompt southward movements during some winters, invariably in association with massive invasions of Common Redpolls. While Hoaries are presently accidental winter visitors to Ohio, they may eventually prove to be more frequent visitors than the few existing sightings indicate. Their status will always be obscured by the inability to positively identify most Hoary Redpolls in the field. Only typical frosty-appearing males are readily identified on sight. The identities of other Hoaries are difficult to confirm except in the hand.

Ohio's first Hoary Redpoll was collected in Lucas County on March 16, 1931 (Hicks 1934a). The species then went unrecorded until the redpoll invasions of the 1960s. Each major redpoll movement between 1977 and 1996 was accompanied by one to three sightings of Hoaries. Approximately fifteen confirmed records now exist from the northeastern counties and Toledo, and there is one report from Columbus. Hoary Redpolls are recorded between December 16 and April 6, mostly as visitors to bird feeders. There are also a number of unconfirmed sight records from the northern half of Ohio, mostly near Lake Erie.

Pine Siskin *Carduelis pinus* (Wilson)

Before 1950, wintering Pine Siskins were regularly recorded only within the northern counties, mostly as scattered individuals and small flocks (Campbell 1968, Williams 1950). Sizable flocks were irregularly encountered during periodic invasions. They only sporadically appeared within the central counties, usually as small flocks during invasion years (Anonymous 1928, Trautman 1940). Wintering siskins were almost unknown within the southern counties; Kemsies and Randle (1953) cited no Cincinnati records between 1869 and 1947.

Pine Siskin

Beginning in the 1950s, Pine Siskins initiated a pattern of regular invasions at two- to three-year intervals, although there were occasional flights during successive winters. These pronounced invasions, evident throughout Ohio, were frequently associated with movements of Evening Grosbeaks. This pattern of periodic winter invasions continued into the 1990s. During some invasions, a few siskins appear along Lake Erie in September and flocks are reported statewide by the first half of October. Other invasions are characterized by movements beginning in mid-October, with sizable numbers appearing in November. Nonflight years produce only scattered sightings during October and November. Fall movements continue through mid-December during sustained invasions, when flocks of 15–100+ appear as fairly common to common fall migrants. Nonflight years produce scattered individuals and flocks of 5–20, primarily in the northern counties.

Pine Siskins are casual to rare and locally distributed winter residents in the northern and unglaciated counties during nonflight years. They are normally found in flocks of 20 or fewer individuals, visiting bird feeders or in parks, cemeteries, and pine woods. They are casual elsewhere, infrequently appearing in small flocks. During invasion years, Pine Siskins become uncommon to locally abundant winter residents in the northern and unglaciated counties, where preferred localities support 50–200+. These large flocks are unusual; only 8–30+ are noted at most locations. Elsewhere, they become rare to locally common winter visitors. Flocks of 100+ have wintered at Columbus and Cincinnati, but most winter totals are of 20 or fewer in the southwestern and glaciated central counties.

Spring Pine Siskins also undertake erratic movements. During some years, large flocks appear in March and disappear by mid-April. In other years, siskins are absent until late April and early May. Spring siskins are generally most apparent between April 15 and May 15. Small numbers linger into early June. Numbers of spring migrants are directly related to the size of the previous autumn movement. During nonflight years, Pine Siskins are rare to locally fairly common migrants, most numerous along Lake Erie. Most reports are of 1–20 individuals. Following sizable invasions, siskins become uncommon to locally abundant spring migrants. Flocks of 50–200+ may appear in late April and early May. A report of 500 at Youngstown on May 7, 1961, is indicative of the numbers that accumulate under favorable conditions (Hall 1961b). Even during these flights, most spring sightings are of fewer than 50 siskins.

Pine Siskins are opportunistic breeders when food is plentiful. Southerly breeding records normally follow large invasions. Initially, Ohio breeding records followed a pattern of very sporadic breeding attempts. Hicks (1933a) indicated Pine Siskins "almost certainly" nested at the former Pymatuning Bog in Ashtabula County between 1928 and 1930, but breeding was not confirmed before the bog was destroyed. Kemsies and Randle (1953) recorded courtship behavior at Cincinnati in April 1953, but a nest was not located. The first published nesting attempt was unsuccessful at Columbus following the invasion of 1972–1973 (Thomson 1983). Nesting attempts were recorded following every large flight during the 1970s, with reports from Toledo, Cincinnati, Columbus, and Cleveland, and midsummer sightings at other areas.

Their status as a breeding bird changed following the sizable invasion of 1977–1978. Siskins probably nested during every year but two between 1978 and 1994, but none were noted later in the 1990s. During the 1980s, summering and nesting siskins were found in the glaciated counties from the Cleveland area to Cincinnati (Peterjohn and Rice 1991). A similar distribution is evident during the 1990s, except for a Hocking County attempt during 1991 (Peterjohn 1991d). They are now accidental to casual summer residents, usually noted before June 20, with very few reports during July and August. Most nests are in ornamental conifers within parks, cemeteries, and residential areas. These attempts are mostly initiated in April. While their success has been very poor, a few pairs have produced young, as evidenced by fledglings observed between April 12 and June 17.

American Goldfinch *Carduelis tristis* (Linnaeus)

Dawson (1903) expressed great admiration for these attractive finches:

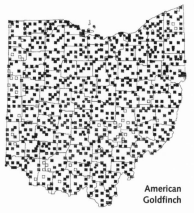

American Goldfinch

> One is at a loss to decide whether nature awarded the Goldfinch his suit of fine clothes in recognition of his dauntless cheer or whether he is only happy because of his panoply of jet and gold. At any rate he is the bird of sunshine the year around, happy, careless, free. Rollicking companies of them rove the countryside, now searching the heads of last year's mullein stalks and enlivening their quest with much pleasant chatter, now scattering in obedience to some whimsical command and sowing the air with their laughter.

Dawson's admiration is shared by all who come in contact with American Goldfinches. Fortunately, they rank among our more numerous residents, equally well known to the ornithologist and the backyard birder.

American Goldfinches are common to abundant summer residents, with daily totals of 30–75+ except in intensively farmed counties, where 15–40+ are noted. These populations remained fairly stable during the twentieth century; both Jones (1903) and Hicks (1935a) described them as among our most abundant nesting birds. Breeding Bird Surveys indicate stable statewide trends since 1966 (Sauer et al. 1998), although brief declines were attributed to the severe winters of 1976–1978 (Robbins et al. 1986).

Breeding goldfinches inhabit fields dominated by weeds and brush, thickets, fencerows, woodland edges, and cutover woods. In intensively farmed areas, they occupy weedy rights-of-way along highways and railroads, ditch banks, wooded riparian corridors, and the edges of woodlots.

American Goldfinches begin raising young when most other songbirds have completed nesting. Pairs may be formed as early as the last week of April, although this process continues into June. Nest building has been reported by May 30, but serious breeding attempts usually begin during mid-July (Nice 1939). Trautman (1940) reports nests with eggs by June 19 and dependent young by July 12 at Buckeye Lake, but these early nesting efforts are exceptional. Most clutches are discovered between July 20 and August 15, with re-nesting attempts through September 14 (Trautman 1940, Williams 1950). Young generally fledge between mid-August and mid-September, with a few as late as the first week of October.

Before 1940, most goldfinches migrated south after the breeding season. Wintering numbers exhibited considerable variability. During extended inclement weather, they became rare visitors within most counties. Conversely, relatively warm weather and plentiful food allowed flocks of 100–200 to winter north to Lake Erie, although these concentrations were unusual (Campbell 1940, Trautman 1940).

Their winter status has gradually changed since the 1940s. Annual fluctuations are less evident and American Goldfinches are fairly common to common winter residents. Flocks of 5–30 are regularly encountered, with occasional concentrations of 50–300 individuals. These numbers remain fairly constant throughout winter, although decreases are evident following extended inclement weather. Increased food availability at bird feeders contributed to their changing winter distribution patterns.

American Goldfinches migrate across Ohio each spring, but these movements are not particularly evident except along western Lake Erie. Their northward movements normally begin by April 10–20, peak between April 28 and May 18, and continue through May 25–30. During the first half of May, daily totals of 50–300 are noted along western Lake Erie and 1,000–1,500 have been estimated during sizable flights. A report by Campbell (1968) of 2,000 passing near Toledo during three hours on May 1, 1954, is indicative of the sizable numbers migrating along western Lake Erie some years. Along the lake's Central Basin, spring totals seldom exceed 100–250. Away from the lakefront, spring movements exceeding 50–100 are rarely reported. Sizable flocks of American Goldfinches formerly migrated through the interior of Ohio each spring. Trautman (1940) observed 25–250 daily and occasional movements of 500 at Buckeye Lake.

Their fall migration is normally less apparent. It produces totals of 30–60 daily at most localities, with occasional movements involving 100–200+. A few migrants are noted along Lake Erie by the first week of September, and they appear in most counties by September 20–October 5. The largest numbers are observed between October 10 and November 5. Their southward movements are largely terminated by mid-November.

Evening Grosbeak *Coccothraustes vespertinus* (Cooper)

Before 1900, breeding Evening Grosbeaks were restricted to western North America and their winter movements seldom extended east of the Mississippi River. They were accidental visitors to Ohio. The only reports were from the Cleveland-Lorain area in 1860 and during the winter of 1890–1891 (Williams 1950). A small flight in the winter of 1910–1911 produced several sightings from northeastern Ohio and the first records from the northwestern, south-western, and central counties (Jones 1911).

During the first decades of the twentieth century, Evening Grosbeaks expanded their breeding range across Canada to the Maritime Provinces and New England (DeVos 1964). As they spread eastward, wintering grosbeaks appeared more frequently within Ohio. Between 1910 and 1930, they were reported at two- to four-year intervals, mostly from the northern and central counties as small flocks or scattered individuals. More records accumulated during the 1930s. Wintering Evening Grosbeaks became fairly regular visitors to Toledo and Cleveland and produced scattered sightings elsewhere, but were not detected annually (Campbell 1968, Williams 1950).

By the early 1940s, Evening Grosbeaks exhibited winter movements into the lower Great Lakes states of sizable invasions at two- to three-year intervals, with smaller numbers during other winters (DeVos 1964). The incursion of 1945–1946 produced scattered sightings across Ohio, with a maximum of 125 at Cleveland (Williams 1950), while the movement of 1954–1955 was charac-terized by many flocks of 75–195 in the northeastern counties. The winter of 1959–1960 produced the first sizable invasion of the southeastern counties (Hall 1960b, Shaub 1963). During the 1960s, local concentrations increased to 200+ at scattered northern and eastern locations. Periodic invasions high-lighted some winters of the 1970s and 1980s, but were less frequent during the 1990s. The largest flocks increased to 300–500 in northern and eastern Ohio during these decades.

In nonflight years, Evening Grosbeaks become casual to rare near Toledo, the northeastern counties east of Cleveland, and along the unglaciated

Allegheny Plateau. They are absent elsewhere. Sightings usually are of scattered individuals and flocks of 20 or fewer.

Wintering Evening Grosbeaks generally produce two distribution patterns. During some invasions, they are fairly common to locally abundant only along the unglaciated Allegheny Plateau, where flocks of 50–200+ are widespread. They become rare to uncommon in northern Ohio and casual to rare in other glaciated counties. Most reports are of 30 or fewer individuals away from unglaciated Ohio. During other invasions, these grosbeaks are fairly common to common near Toledo, in the northeastern counties, along the unglaciated plateau, and near Cincinnati. Flocks of 100–500 appear in the northern and southeastern counties but seldom exceed 50 at Cincinnati. Elsewhere, they are casual to rare in flocks of 15 or fewer individuals.

Initially, wintering grosbeaks resided in deciduous woods, preferring box elder, ash, and maple seeds. Since the late 1960s, they are seldom found away from bird feeders, where they eagerly devour large quantities of sunflower seeds.

Their migrations are equally unpredictable, especially in autumn. During some years, the largest movements occur in October and early November; in other years, large numbers appear during late November and December. Flocks may pass into Ohio during January and February. The earliest fall migrants returned to Lake Erie by September 8–10, but there are relatively few northern Ohio records before the first week of October. During flight years, flocks of 15–40 frequently appear in northern Ohio by October 5–15 and become uncommon to common statewide by October 20–27. These movements frequently show a bimodal pattern, with one peak between October 10 and November 15 and another in December. In nonflight years, fall migrants are casual to rare along Lake Erie and in eastern Ohio, becoming casual elsewhere.

Spring migrants appear during the last half of March but most are noted between April 5 and May 10. Following sizable fall flights, Evening Grosbeaks become rare to fairly common spring migrants, most numerous along Lake Erie and the eastern counties in scattered flocks of 10–50+. Following winters when these grosbeaks are scarce, spring migrants are casual to rare and few flocks total more than 10–15. Most depart by May 10–20, although individuals have remained until June 1, 1996, in Hocking County (Conlon and Harlan 1996a); June 8, 1911, at Cincinnati (Kemsies and Randle 1953); and June 24, 1962, at Toledo (Campbell 1968). An unmated female was observed building a nest at Mineral Ridge (Trumbull County) during the first week of April 1979, but she disappeared before completing her nest (Kleen 1979c).

House Sparrow *Passer domesticus* (Linnaeus)

Dawson (1903) accurately summarized the attitude of most people toward this Eurasian native:

> Without question the most deplorable event in the history of American ornithology was the introduction of the English Sparrow. The extinction of the Great Auk, the passing of the Wild Pigeon and the Turkey—sad as these are, they are trifles compared to the wholesale reduction of our smaller birds which is due to the invasion of that wretched foreigner, the English Sparrow.

House Sparrow

According to Hicks (1935a), House Sparrows were initially released in Cleveland, Cincinnati, and Warren in 1869. They were also released at Marietta in 1870, Coshocton and Portsmouth in 1874, Steubenville in 1880–1881, and Wapakoneta in 1882. They rapidly spread throughout the state by 1885–1890, becoming common residents by the turn of the twentieth century, and their numbers were still increasing (Jones 1903).

Their rapid expansion resulted from their close association with people. During the 1800s, House Sparrows thrived on refuse in cities, waste grain in farm fields, and grain found in horse manure. Moreover, their aggressive behavior allowed them to readily dominate native songbirds by usurping nesting locations and food sources.

Throughout eastern North America, their populations peaked between 1900 and 1920. Small declines were noted during the 1920s as populations stabilized. These sparrows also lost an important food source when horses were replaced by cars and mechanized farm machinery. Their populations slowly declined in subsequent decades, a result of the "clean farming" practices that have been so harmful to most wildlife.

Since 1966, House Sparrow populations have experienced significant declines throughout eastern North America (Sauer et al. 1998). These declines reflect the effects not only of unfavorable farming practices but also of severe winter weather. During the 1980s and 1990s, House Sparrows also had competition from another introduced and aggressive occupant of residential habitats, the House Finch.

Despite their reduced populations, House Sparrows remain common to abundant permanent residents. In fact, Ohio supports one of the largest populations of any state (Robbins et al. 1986). They are most numerous in cities, villages, and farmlands, where 50–500+ are counted daily. Fewer House Sparrows are encountered in the southeastern counties, where daily totals of 25–100+ are expected, although larger numbers are present within cities.

House Sparrows nest as isolated pairs or semicolonially. As described by Dawson (1903):

> The Sparrow exhibits a most cosmopolitan taste in the matter of nesting sites. The normal half-bushel ball of trash in the tree-top is still adhered to by some builders, but the cavity left by a missing brick, a Woodpecker's hole … will do as well. Of late the choicest rural sites have been appropriated, and the cliffs once sacred to the gentle Swallow, now resound with the vulgar bletherings and maudlin mirth of this avian blot on nature.

These nests are normally placed near houses, but House Sparrows also nest far from any residence. One pair built a nest at the base of a large Bald Eagle eyrie (Campbell 1968).

Nest construction has been observed as early as January 7 but usually begins during March (Campbell 1968). These sparrows produce multiple broods and are almost constantly incubating eggs or raising young. Nests with eggs have been reported by March 8 and young accompanying adults by April 10. Fledgling House Sparrows have been noted as late as September 23 (Campbell 1968, Williams 1950).

As soon as the young fledge, they form small flocks. This postbreeding behavior was described by Trautman (1940):

> At first the flocks consisted principally of young, but as June advanced, the percentage of adults increased and by mid-July the flocks averaged about 60 percent young and 40 percent adults. Throughout the last two-thirds of July and all of August flocks of 15 to 200 individuals could be found in grain fields and along roads.

The largest roosts occur in winter. While 20,000 House Sparrows congregated at Dayton during the winter of 1953–1954 (Mathena et al. 1984), similar concentrations have not plagued other communities.

Although House Sparrows are considered permanent residents, Trautman and Trautman (1968) reported visible migrations over western Lake Erie. These movements are poorly understood, but small flocks were noted passing over the lake during March and April and again in September and October.

Bibliography

Ahlquist, J. 1964. Rufous-necked Sandpiper, *Erolia ruficollis*, in northeastern Ohio. Auk 81:432–433.

Akin, W. 1993. Green-tailed Towhee in Lorain County. The Ohio Cardinal 16:30–31.

Aldrich, J. W. 1934. Observations on a few breeding birds in northeastern Ohio. Wilson Bull. 46:96–103.

_____. 1936. European Woodcock (*Scolopax rusticola rusticola*) in Ohio. Auk 53:329–330.

_____. 1946. White eggs of the Long-billed Marsh Wren. Auk 63:442–443.

Allen, R. W., and M. M. Nice. 1952. A study of the breeding biology of the Purple Martin. Am. Midland Nat. 47:606–665.

American Ornithologists' Union. 1957. Checklist of North American birds, 5th ed. Lord Baltimore Press, Baltimore, MD. 691 p.

_____. 1983. Checklist of North American birds, 6th ed. Allen Press, Lawrence, KS. 877 p.

_____. 1998. Checklist of North American birds, 7th ed. Allen Press, Lawrence, KS. 829 p.

_____. 2000. Forty-second supplement to the American Ornithologists' Union check-list of North American birds. Auk 117:847-858.

Anderson, J. M. 1960. Summer birds of Winous Point in 1880, 1930, and 1960. 21 pp (mimeo).

Anderson, M. 1998. A second Ohio record of Townsend's Warbler. The Ohio Cardinal 21:35.

Anderson, M., and T. Kemp. 1991a. The fall season, 1990. The Ohio Cardinal 14(1):10–21.

_____, and _____. 1991b. The winter season, 1990–1991. The Ohio Cardinal 14(2):1–8.

Andrews, D. A. 1973. Habitat utilization by Sora, Virginia Rails, and King Rails near southwestern Lake Erie. M.S. Thesis, Ohio State Univ., Columbus. 112 pp.

Andrews, R. 1952. A study of waterfowl nesting on a Lake Erie marsh. M.S. Thesis, Ohio State Univ., Columbus. 153 pp.

Andrle, R. F., and J. R. Carroll, eds. 1988. The atlas of breeding birds in New York state. Cornell Univ. Press, Ithaca, NY. 551 p.

Anonymous. (Thomas, E. S., C. F. Walker, and M. B. Trautman). 1928. The winter birds of central Ohio. Ohio State Mus. Sci. Bull. 1:24–28.

Armstrong, H. 1999. A Western Grebe at East Fork State Park. The Ohio Cardinal 22:95–96.

Ashley, C. 1992. West Sister experience. The Ohio Cardinal 15:92–95.

Austing, G. R., and D. A. Imbrogno. 1976. Birds of the Hamilton County Park District and southwestern Ohio. Hamilton County Park District, Cincinnati. 52 pp.

Averbach, B. F. 1925. Hudsonian Curlew near Youngstown, Ohio. Auk 42:580.

Baird, R. L. 1905. Bird migration at Oberlin, Ohio. Wilson Bull.17:75–83.

_____. 1931a. Oberlin Region. Bird-Lore 33:268–270.

_____. 1931b. Oberlin Region. Bird-Lore 33:335–337.

_____. 1932a. Oberlin Region. Bird-Lore 34:14–16.

_____. 1932b. Oberlin Region. Bird-Lore 34:140–142.

_____. 1932c. Oberlin Region. Bird-Lore 34:275–276.

_____. 1932d. Oberlin Region. Bird-Lore 34:343–344.

_____. 1933. Oberlin Region. Bird-Lore 35:330–331.

_____. 1934a. Oberlin Region. Bird-Lore 36:115–116.

_____. 1934b. Oberlin Region. Bird-Lore 36:183–184.

_____. 1934c. Oberlin Region. Bird-Lore 36:310–311.

_____. 1934d. Oberlin Region. Bird-Lore 36:372–373.

_____. 1935a. Oberlin Region. Bird-Lore 37:141–142.

_____. 1935b. Oberlin Region. Bird-Lore 37:224–225.

_____. 1935c. Oberlin Region. Bird-Lore 37:291–292.

_____. 1935d. Oberlin Region. Bird-Lore 37:468–469.

_____. 1936a. Oberlin Region. Bird-Lore 38:245–246.

_____. 1936b. Oberlin Region. Bird-Lore 38:275–276.

_____. 1936c. Oberlin Region. Bird-Lore 38:388–389.

_____. 1936d. Oberlin Region. Bird-Lore 38:468–470.

_____.1937. Oberlin Region. Bird-Lore 39:169–170.

Baker, W. C. 1933. Some sight records from Ohio. Wilson Bull.45:35–36.

_____. 1946. Notes on summer resident Wilson's Snipe in Columbiana County, Ohio. Auk 63:446–448.

Bales, B. R. 1911a. Some notes from Pickaway County, Ohio. Wilson Bull. 23:43–48.

_____. 1911b. An Ohio nest of the Black and White Warbler. Wilson Bull. 23:55–56.

Ball, R. E. 1946. White Pelicans in northeastern Ohio. Auk 63:104.

Banko, W. E. 1960. The Trumpeter Swan, its history, habits, and population in the United States. U. S. Fish and Wildlife Service, N. Am. Fauna No. 63. 214 p.

Bartlett, H. T. 1996. A Spotted Towhee in Seneca Co. The Ohio Cardinal 19:75–76.

Beardslee, C. S. 1944. Bonaparte's Gull on the Niagara River and eastern Lake Erie. Wilson Bull. 56:9–14.

Bildstein, K. L. 1987. Behavioral ecology of Red-tailed Hawks (*Buteo jamaicensis*), Rough-legged Hawks (*Buteo lagopus*), Northern Harriers (*Circus cyaneus*), and American Kestrels (*Falco sparverius*) in south central Ohio. Ohio Biol. Surv., Biol. Notes No. 18. 53 p.

Bittner, E. C. 1965. Two nestings of Red-breasted Nuthatch. Cleveland Bird Calendar 61:30–32.

Blincoe, B. J. 1930. Leach's Petrel in Ohio. Auk 47:72.

Blockstein, D. E., and H. B. Tordoff. 1985. Gone forever—a contemporary look at the extinction of the Passenger Pigeon. Am. Birds 39:845–851.

Blokpoel, H., G. D. Tessier, and A. Harfenist. 1987. Distribution during post-breeding dispersal, migration and overwintering of Common Terns color-marked on the lower Great Lakes. Jour. Field Ornith. 58: 206–217.

Bock, C. E., and L. W. Lepthien. 1976. Growth in the eastern House Finch population, 1962–71. Am. Birds 30:791–792.

Borror, D. J. 1950. A checklist of the birds of Ohio with the migration dates for the birds of central Ohio. Ohio Jour. Sci. 50:1–32.

_____. 1970. Tape recordings as evidence of a bird's occurrence in an area. Wheaton Club Bull. No. 15.

Bownocker, J. A. 1965. Geologic map of Ohio. Ohio Geol. Surv., Columbus.

Brackney, A. W., and T. A. Bookhout. 1982. Population ecology of Common Gallinules in southwestern Lake Erie marshes. Ohio Jour. Sci. 82:229–237.

Braund, F. W. 1938a. Nesting records for Ohio birds: June 1–Sept. 1, 1937. Oologist 55:81–83.

_____. 1938b. Status of the Northern Pileated Woodpecker in Ashtabula County, Ohio. Oologist 55:128–130.

_____. 1939a. The versatile nesting habitats of the American Woodcock. Oologist 56:69–70.

_____. 1939b. Breeding records of Ohio birds: March 1–October 1, 1939. Oologist 56:110–112.

_____. 1940a. Nesting records for Ohio birds: January 1–September 1, 1940. Oologist 57:134–135.

_____. 1940b. The birds of Smoky Creek valley, Adams County, Ohio. Oologist 57:62–72.

Brewer, R., G. A. McPeek, and R. J. Adams, Jr. 1991. The atlas of breeding birds of Michigan. Michigan State Univ. Press, East Lansing, MI. 594 p.

Brock, K. J. 1992a. Middlewestern Prairie Region. Am. Birds 46:429–433.

_____. 1992b. Middlewestern Prairie Region. Am. Birds 46:1140–1143.

_____. 1993a. Middlewestern Prairie Region. Am. Birds 47:98–103.

_____. 1993b. Middlewestern Prairie Region. Am. Birds 47:261–266.

_____. 1993c. Middlewestern Prairie Region. Am. Birds 47:417–421.

_____. 1993d. Middlewestern Prairie Region. Am. Birds 47:1112–1115.

_____. 1994a. Middlewestern Prairie Region. Am. Birds 48:114–117.

_____. 1994b. Middlewestern Prairie Region. Nat. Audubon Soc. Field Notes 48:212–215.

_____. 1994c. Middlewestern Prairie Region. Nat. Audubon Soc. Field Notes 48:302–306.

_____. 1994d. Middlewestern Prairie Region. Nat. Audubon Soc. Field Notes 48:946–950.

_____. 1995a. Middlewestern Prairie Region. Nat. Audubon Soc. Field Notes 49:52–56.

_____. 1995b. Middlewestern Prairie Region. Nat. Audubon Soc. Field Notes 49:152–155.

_____. 1995c. Middlewestern Prairie Region. Nat. Audubon Soc. Field Notes 49:256–260.

_____. 1995d. Middlewestern Prairie Region. Nat. Audubon Soc. Field Notes 49:932–937.

_____. 1996a. Middlewestern Prairie Region. Nat. Audubon Soc. Field Notes 50:60–65.

_____. 1996b. Middlewestern Prairie Region. Nat. Audubon Soc. Field Notes 50:175–179.

_____. 1996c. Middlewestern Prairie Region. Nat. Audubon Soc. Field Notes 50:286–290.

_____. 1996d. Middlewestern Prairie Region. Nat. Audubon Soc. Field Notes 50:954–957.

_____. 1997a. Middlewestern Prairie Region. Nat. Audubon Soc. Field Notes 51:62–67.

_____. 1997b. Middlewestern Prairie Region. Nat. Audubon Soc. Field Notes 51:754–757.

_____. 1997c. Middlewestern Prairie Region. Nat. Audubon Soc. Field Notes 51:875–880.

_____. 1997d. Middlewestern Prairie Region. Nat. Audubon Soc. Field Notes 51:1002–1005.

_____. 1998a. Middlewestern Prairie Region. Nat. Audubon Soc. Field Notes 52:66–71.

_____. 1998b. Middlewestern Prairie Region. Nat. Audubon Soc. Field Notes 52:203–207.

_____. 1998c. Middlewestern Prairie Region. Nat. Audubon Soc. Field Notes 52:335–339.

_____. 1998d. Middlewestern Prairie Region. Nat. Audubon Soc. Field Notes 52:461–464.

_____. 1999a. Middlewestern Prairie Region. N. Am. Birds 53:58–61.

_____. 1999b. Middlewestern Prairie Region. N. Am. Birds 53:169–172.

_____. 1999c. Middlewestern Prairie Region. N. Am. Birds 53:284–288.

_____. 1999d. Middlewestern Prairie Region. N. Am. Birds 53:391–394.

Brooks, M. 1938a. Bachman's Sparrow in the north-central portion of its range. Wilson Bull. 50:86–109.

_____. 1938b. The Eastern Lark Sparrow in the Upper Ohio Valley. The Cardinal 4:181–200.

_____. 1949. Appalachian Region. Audubon Field Notes 3:14–15.

_____. 1950a. Appalachian Region. Audubon Field Notes 4:14–15.

_____. 1950b. Appalachian Region. Audubon Field Notes 4:200–202.

_____. 1950c. Appalachian Region. Audubon Field Notes 4:240–242.

_____. 1950d. Appalachian Region. Audubon Field Notes 4:274–276.

_____. 1951a. Appalachian Region. Audubon Field Notes 5:203–205.

_____. 1951b. Appalachian Region. Audubon Field Notes 5:287–289.

_____. 1952a. Appalachian Region. Audubon Field Notes 6:194–196.

_____. 1952b. Appalachian Region. Audubon Field Notes 6:280–282.

_____. 1953a. Appalachian Region. Audubon Field Notes 7:15–17.

_____. 1953b. Appalachian Region. Audubon Field Notes 7:212–213.

_____. 1953c. Appalachian Region. Audubon Field Notes 7:272–273.

_____. 1953d. Appalachian Region. Audubon Field Notes 7:307–309.

_____. 1954a. Appalachian Region. Audubon Field Notes 8:17–19.

_____. 1954b. Appalachian Region. Audubon Field Notes 8:250–252.

_____. 1954c. Appalachian Region. Audubon Field Notes 8:344–345.

_____. 1954d. Appalachian Region. Audubon Field Notes 8:344–345.

_____. 1955a. Appalachian Region. Audubon Field Notes 9:24–26.

_____. 1955b. Appalachian Region. Audubon Field Notes 9:256–259.

_____. 1955c. Appalachian Region. Audubon Field Notes 9:329–332.

_____. 1956. Appalachian Region. Audubon Field Notes 10:22–25.

_____. 1958. Appalachian Region. Audubon Field Notes 12:278–280.

_____. 1959a. Appalachian Region. Audubon Field Notes 13:28–30.

_____. 1959b. Appalachian Region. Audubon Field Notes 13:429–431

Browning, M. R. 1974. Comments on the winter distribution of Swainson's Hawk (*Buteo swainsoni*) in North America. Am. Birds 28:865–867.

Bruce, J. 1931. Yellow-crowned Night Heron in Ohio. Auk 48:593–594.

Buchanan, F. W. 1947. Red Phalarope in eastern Ohio. Wilson Bull. 59:36.

_____. 1980. The breeding birds of Carroll and northern Jefferson Counties, Ohio, with notes on selected vascular plants and animal species. Ohio Biol. Surv., Biol. Notes No. 12. 50 p.

Campbell, L. W. 1934. Bicknell's Thrush taken near Toledo, Ohio. Auk 51:241.

_____. 1938. Phalaropes of the western Lake Erie region. Auk 55:89–94.

_____. 1940. Birds of Lucas County. Toledo Mus. Sci. Bull. 1(1):1–225.

_____. 1944. Glossy Ibis near Toledo, Ohio. Auk 61:471.

_____. 1947. American Egrets nesting on West Sister Island in Lake Erie. Auk 64:461–462.

_____. 1968. Birds of the Toledo area. The Toledo Blade Co.,Toledo. 330 p.

_____. 1973. Additions to the birds of the Toledo area for years 1968 through November 1973. Toledo Nat. Assn. Yearbook 1973:13–45.

Canterbury, R. A., N. J. Kotesovec, Jr., and B. Catuzza. 1995. A preliminary study of the effects of Brown-headed Cowbird parasitism on the reproductive success of Blue-winged Warblers in northeastern Ohio. The Ohio Cardinal 18:124–125.

Carver, G. 1998. First inland nesting attempt by the Great Egret. The Ohio Cardinal 21:31-33.

Chapman, F. B. 1931. An Ohio heron colony. Bird-Lore 33:256–257.

_____. 1938. An unusual nesting site of the Rough-winged Swallow. Wilson Bull. 50:203.

Chapman, F. B., H. Bezdek, and E. H. Dustman. 1952. The Ruffed Grouse and its management in Ohio. Ohio Dept. Nat. Res., Div. Wildl. Cons. Bull. No. 6. 24 p.

Chasar, D. W. 1994. The first confirmed Northern Parula nest in Cuyahoga Co. The Ohio Cardinal 17:120–122.

_____. 1995. Northern Parula nest building in Cuyahoga County. The Ohio Cardinal 18:121–123.

_____. 1998. Confirmed nesting of Red-breasted Nuthatch in Brecksville Reservation. Cleveland Bird Calendar 94:21–22.

_____. 1999. Confirmed nest of Hermit Thrush in Summit County. Cleveland Bird Calendar 95:30–31.

Clark, C. F. 1944a. Forster's Tern in central-western Ohio. Auk 61:474.

_____. 1944b. Summer occurrence of Holboell's Grebe in Ohio. Wilson Bull. 56:169.

_____. 1946. Rare birds in west-central Ohio. Auk 63:594.

_____. 1964. Bird records from the vicinity of Lake St. Marys, Mercer and Auglaize Counties, Ohio. Ohio Jour. Sci. 64:25–26.

Clark, C. F., and J. P. Sipe. 1970. Birds of the Lake St. Marys area. Ohio Dept. Nat. Res., Div. Wildl. Publ. No. 350. 93 p.

Clark, R. J. 1975. A field study of the Short-eared Owl *Asio flammeus* (Pontopiddan) in North America. Wildl. Monogr. No. 47. 67 p.

Coale, H. K. 1915. The present status of the Trumpeter Swan (*Olor buccinator*). Auk 32:82–90.

Coles, V. 1944. Nesting of the Turkey Vulture in Ohio caves. Auk 61:219–228.

Colvin, B. A. 1985. Common Barn-Owl population decline in Ohio and the relationship to agricultural trends. Jour. Field Ornithol. 56:224–235.

Conlon, B., and R. Harlan. 1996. The reports—spring 1996. The Ohio Cardinal 19:84–97.

_____, and _____. 1997. The reports—autumn 1996. The Ohio Cardinal 20:19–31.

Courtney, P. A., and H. Blokpoel. 1983. Distribution and numbers of Common Terns on the lower Great Lakes 1900-1980: A review. Colonial Waterbirds 6:107-120.

Curl, A. L. 1932. The Bohemian Waxwing in Ohio. Auk 49:225.

Cuthbert, F. J., J. McKearnan, and L. Wemmer. 1997. U.S. Great Lakes tern and cormorant survey: 1997 progress report. Unpubl. Rept., U.S. Fish and Wildlife Service.

Dawson, W. L. 1903. The birds of Ohio. Wheaton Publ. Co., Columbus. 671 p.

Deane, R. 1905. Two additional records of the European Widgeon (*Mareca penelope*). Auk 22:206.

DeVos, A. 1964. Range changes of birds in the Great Lakes region. Am. Midland Nat. 71:489–502.

Dexter, R. W. 1952. Banding and nesting studies of the Eastern Nighthawk. Bird-Banding 23:109–114.

_____. 1956a. Further banding and nesting studies of the Eastern Nighthawk. Bird-Banding 27:9–15.

_____. 1956b. Ten-year life history of a banded Chimney Swift. Auk 73:276–280.

_____. 1961. Further studies on nesting of the Common Nighthawk. Bird-Banding 32:79–85.

Dister, D. C. 1995. Ohio's fourth inland record of Purple Sandpiper, with thoughts on the species' distribution in Ohio. The Ohio Cardinal 18:1–5.

Dolbeer, R. A., and G. E. Bernhardt. 1986. Early-winter population trends of gulls on western Lake Erie, 1950–1984. Am. Birds 40:1097–1102.

Dolbeer, R. A., P.P. Woronechi, T. W. Seamans, B. N. Buckingham, and E. C. Cleary. 1990. Herring Gulls, *Larus argentatus*, nesting on Sandusky Bay, Lake Erie, 1989. Ohio Jour. Sci. 90:87–89.

Donohoe, R. W. 1990. The Wild Turkey: Past, present, and future in Ohio. Ohio Dept. Nat. Res., Div. Wildl. Fish and Wildl. Rep. No. 11. 47 p.

Donohoe, R. W., and C. McKibben. 1973. History of the Wild Turkey (*Meleagris gallopavo*) transplants in the Ohio hill country. Ohio Jour. Sci. 73:96–102.

Donohoe, R. W., W. P. Parker, M. W. McClain, and C. E. McKibben. 1983. Distribution and population estimates of Ohio Wild Turkeys (*Meleagris gallopavo*), 1981–82. Ohio Jour. Sci. 83:188–190.

Doolittle, E. A. 1924a. Record of Brunnich's Murre for Lake County, Ohio. Auk 41:148.

_____. 1924b. Little Gull at Lake County, Ohio. Wilson Bull. 36:62–63.

Dunakin, M. 1996a. A Kirtland's Warbler in Paulding County. The Ohio Cardinal 19:6.

_____. 1996b. The winter of Paulding County's Gyrfalcon. The Ohio Cardinal 19:38–39.

Dunn, J. L. 1993. Comments on the 1992–93 Holmes County wintering warblers. The Ohio Cardinal 16:70–74.

Dwyer, C. P., J. L. Belant, and R. A. Dolbeer. 1996. Distribution and abundance of roof-nesting gulls in the Great Lakes region of the United States. Ohio Jour. Sci. 96:9–12.

Earl, T. M. 1918. Harris' Hawks in Ohio. Wilson Bull. 30:15–16.

_____. 1934. Observations on owls in Ohio. Wilson Bull.46: 137–142.

Fazio, III., V. W. 1997a. The winter 1996–1997 season. The Ohio Cardinal 20:35–57.

_____. 1997b. The spring 1997 season. The Ohio Cardinal 20:80–115.

_____. 1997c. The summer 1997 season. The Ohio Cardinal 20:125–140.

_____. 1998. The autumn 1997 season. The Ohio Cardinal 21:1–31.

_____. 1999. The summer 1999 bird review. Ohio Birds and Natural History 1:2-17.

Fazio, III, V. W., and D. Webb. 1997. A Long-billed Murrelet (*Brachyramphus perdix*) in Ohio. The Ohio Cardinal 20:1–6.

Fisher, G. C. 1907a. Bald Eagle's nest at Lewistown Reservoir. Wilson Bull. 19:13–16.

_____. 1907b. A Brant at the Lewistown Reservoir. Wilson Bull. 19:33.

Flanigan, A. B. 1968. Early and late dates for birds of the Cleveland region. 7 p. (mimeo).

_____. 1969. Thirteen visits to Stebbins Gulch. Cleveland Bird Calendar 65:48–52.

_____. 1970. Noteworthy records. Cleveland Bird Calendar 66:41–43.

_____. 1971. From adjoining locations. Cleveland Bird Calendar 67:28–29.

Fordyce, G. L. 1914. The Western Grebe in Ohio. Auk 31:243.

Franks, R. W. 1928. A Champaign County heronry. Ohio State Mus. Sci. Bull. 1:36–39.

Fretwell, S. 1977. Is the Dickcissel a threatened species? Am. Birds 31:923–932.

Garver, G. 1998. First inland nesting attempt by the Great Egret. The Ohio Cardinal 21:31–33.

Gibbons, M. 1966. Short-eared Owl nesting in northwestern Pickaway County. Wheaton Club Bull. 11:36–37.

Gier, H. T. 1949. Lark Sparrow nesting in southeastern Ohio. Auk 66:209–210.

Gilbert, W. N. 1953. Chuck-will's-widow in central Ohio. Wilson Bull. 65:43.

Gill, F. B. 1980. Historical aspects of hybridization between Blue-winged and Golden-winged Warblers. Auk 97:1–18.

Glick, B. D. 1999a. The summer 1999 season. Bobolink 3(2):1–6.

_____. 1999b. A Long-billed Curlew in Holmes County. Bobolink 3(3):11.

Godfrey, W. E. 1943. Eared Grebe in Ohio. Auk 60:452

Goldthwait, R. P., G. W. White, and J. L. Forsyth. 1961. Glacial map of Ohio. U. S. Geol. Surv. Misc. Geol. Invest. Map I–316.

Goodpaster, W., and K. H. Maslowski. 1937. Le Conte's Sparrow in Clermont County, Ohio. Auk 54:397.

Gordon, R. B. 1969. The natural vegetation of Ohio in pioneer days. Ohio Biol. Surv. New Series Bull. 3:1–109.

Graber, R. R. 1962a. Middlewestern Prairie Region. Audubon Field Notes 16:35–37, 41–43.

_____. 1962b. Middlewestern Prairie Region. Audubon Field Notes 16:332–336.

_____. 1962c. Middlewestern Prairie Region. Audubon Field Notes 16:413, 417–420.

_____. 1962d. Middlewestern Prairie Region. Audubon Field Notes 16:478–480.

Green, N. B. 1947. Swainson's Warbler in southern Ohio. Wilson Bull. 59:211.

Greider, M., and E. S. Wagner. 1960. Black Vulture extends breeding range northward. Wilson Bull. 72:291.

Grigore, M. T. 1994. Lark Sparrow observation in the Oak Openings area. The Ohio Cardinal 17:5–7.

Gustafson, M., and B. Peterjohn. 1994. Adult Slaty-backed Gulls: variability in mantle color and comments on identification. Birding 26:243–249.

Hall, G. A. 1959. Appalachian Region. Audubon Field Notes 13:292–294.

_____. 1960a. Appalachian Region. Audubon Field Notes 14:35–38.

_____. 1960b. Appalachian Region. Audubon Field Notes 14:309–311.

_____. 1960c. Appalachian Region. Audubon Field Notes 14:386–388.

_____ 1960d. Appalachian Region. Audubon Field Notes 14:448–451.

_____. 1961a. Appalachian Region. Audubon Field Notes 15:328–331.

_____. 1961b. Appalachian Region. Audubon Field Notes 15:409–412.

_____ 1962a. Appalachian Region. Audubon Field Notes 16:31–34.

_____. 1962b. Appalachian Region. Audubon Field Notes 16:475–477.

_____. 1963a. Appalachian Region. Audubon Field Notes 17:401–404.

_____. 1963b. Appalachian Region. Audubon Field Notes 17:459–461.

_____. 1964. Appalachian Region. Audubon Field Notes 18:353–356.

_____. 1965. Appalachian Region. Audubon Field Notes 19:470–473.

_____. 1966a. Appalachian Region. Audubon Field Notes 20:41–45.

_____. 1966b. Appalachian Region. Audubon Field Notes 20:422–425.

_____. 1966c. Appalachian Region. Audubon Field Notes 20:506–511.

_____. 1966d. Appalachian Region. Audubon Field Notes 20:568–570.

_____. 1967. Appalachian Region. Audubon Field Notes 21:506–510.

_____. 1968a. Appalachian Region. Audubon Field Notes 22:525–528.

_____. 1968b. Appalachian Region. Audubon Field Notes 22:606–609.

_____. 1969. Appalachian Region. Audubon Field Notes 23:589–592.

_____ 1970a. Appalachian Region. Audubon Field Notes 24:47–51.

_____. 1970b. Appalachian Region. Audubon Field Notes 24:601–604.

_____. 1972a. Appalachian Region. Am. Birds 26:604–607.

_____. 1972b. Appalachian Region. Am. Birds 26:760–763.

_____. 1972c. Appalachian Region. Am. Birds 26:857–860.

_____. 1973a. Appalachian Region. Am. Birds 27:59–63.

_____. 1973b. Appalachian Region. Am. Birds 27:614–617.

_____. 1974a. Appalachian Region. Am. Birds 28:52–56.

_____. 1974b. Appalachian Region. Am. Birds 28:638–641.

_____. 1974c. Appalachian Region. Am. Birds 28:800–804.

_____. 1975a. Appalachian Region. Am. Birds 29:57–61.

_____. 1975b. Appalachian Region. Am. Birds 29:690–693.

_____. 1976a. Appalachian Region. Am. Birds 30:67–71.

_____. 1976b. Appalachian Region. Am. Birds 30:841–844.

_____. 1977. Appalachian Region. Am. Birds 31:1138–1142.

_____. 1978. Appalachian Region. Am. Birds 32:203–206.

_____. 1979. Appalachian Region. Am. Birds 33:862–864.

_____. 1980. Appalachian Region. Am. Birds 34:894–896.

_____. 1981a. Appalachian Region. Am. Birds 35:299–301.

_____. 1981b. Appalachian Region. Am. Birds 35:822–825.

_____. 1981c. Appalachian Region. Am. Birds 35:938–940.

_____. 1982a. Appalachian Region. Am. Birds 36:176–179.

_____. 1982b. Appalachian Region. Am. Birds 36:293–295.

_____. 1984a. Appalachian Region. Am. Birds 38:200–204.

_____. 1984b. Appalachian Region. Am. Birds 38:316–318.

_____. 1986a. Appalachian Region. Am. Birds 40:111–114.

_____. 1986b. Appalachian Region. Am. Birds 40:279–282.

_____. 1986c. Appalachian Region. Am. Birds 40:469–472.

_____. 1986d. Appalachian Region. Am. Birds 40:1202–1205.

_____. 1987a. Appalachian Region. Am. Birds 41:281–284.

_____. 1987b. Appalachian Region. Am. Birds 41:430–433.

_____. 1988a. Appalachian Region. Am. Birds 42:263–266.

_____. 1988b. Appalachian Region. Am. Birds 42:1286–1289.

_____. 1989a. Appalachian Region. Am. Birds 43:100–104.

_____. 1989b. Appalachian Region. Am. Birds 43:1314–1317.

_____. 1990a. Appalachian Region. Am. Birds 44:88–92.

_____. 1990b. Appalachian Region. Am. Birds 44:266–269.

_____. 1990c. Appalachian Region. Am. Birds 44:424–428.

_____. 1990d. Appalachian Region. Am. Birds 44:1132–1134.

_____. 1991a. Appalachian Region. Am. Birds 45:444–446.

_____. 1991b. Appalachian Region. Am. Birds 45:1114–1117.

_____. 1992a. Appalachian Region. Am. Birds 46:263–266.

_____. 1992b. Appalachian Region. Am. Birds 46:1134–1136.

_____. 1993a. Appalachian Region. Am. Birds 47:91–95.

_____. 1993b. Appalachian Region. Am. Birds 47:412–414.

_____. 1994a. Appalachian Region. Nat. Audubon Soc. Field Notes 48:207–209.

_____. 1994b. Appalachian Region. Nat. Audubon Soc. Field Notes 48:942–944.

_____. 1995a. Appalachian Region. Nat. Audubon Soc. Field Notes 49:248–252.

_____. 1995b. Appalachian Region. Nat. Audubon Soc. Field Notes 49:926–929.

_____. 1996. Appalachian Region. Nat. Audubon Soc. Field Notes 50:168–171.

_____. 1997a. Appalachian Region. Nat. Audubon Soc. Field Notes 51:51–56.

_____. 1997b. Appalachian Region. Nat. Audubon Soc. Field Notes 51:747–750.

_____. 1997c. Appalachian Region. Nat. Audubon Soc. Field Notes 51:867–871.

_____. 1998. Appalachian Region. Nat. Audubon Soc. Field Notes 52:453–456.

Hammond, W. A. 1972. Noteworthy records. Cleveland Bird Calendar 68:45–49.

_____. 1973. Noteworthy records. Cleveland Bird Calendar 69:10–16.

_____. 1974. Noteworthy records. Cleveland Bird Calendar 70:7–10.

_____. 1975. Noteworthy records. Cleveland Bird Calendar 71:20–25.

_____. 1976a. Noteworthy records. Cleveland Bird Calendar 72:7–10.

_____. 1976b. Noteworthy records. Cleveland Bird Calendar 72:20–25.

Handley, D. 1953. Ancient Murrelet (*Synthilboramphus antiquus*) taken in Erie County, Ohio. Auk 70:206–207.

Hannikman, R. 1977. Noteworthy records. Cleveland Bird Calendar 73:43–45.

_____. 1978a. Noteworthy records. Cleveland Bird Calendar 74:6–9.

_____. 1978b. Noteworthy records. Cleveland Bird Calendar 74:19–22.

_____. 1978c. Noteworthy records. Cleveland Bird Calendar 74:41–45.

_____. 1979. Noteworthy records. Cleveland Bird Calendar 75:6–8.

_____. 1983. Noteworthy records. Cleveland Bird Calendar 79:27–29.

_____. 1984. Noteworthy records. Cleveland Bird Calendar 80:34–47.

_____. 1985. Noteworthy records. Cleveland Bird Calendar 81:5–7.

_____. 1986a. Noteworthy records. Cleveland Bird Calendar 82:16–19.

_____. 1986b. Noteworthy records. Cleveland Bird Calendar 82:29–31.

_____. 1987a. Noteworthy records. Cleveland Bird Calendar 83:16–18.

_____. 1987b. Comment on the season. Cleveland Bird Calendar 83:24–27.

_____. 1989. Noteworthy records. Cleveland Bird Calendar 85:33–34.

_____. 1992. Long-tailed Jaeger from Headlands Beach State Park, with a discussion of other Ohio occurrences. The Ohio Cardinal 15:6–8.

_____. 1993. Snowy Plover at Headlands Beach State Park: A first Ohio record. The Ohio Cardinal 16:67–69.

_____. 1999. Twenty-six Little Gulls on the twenty-seventh. Cleveland Bird Calendar 95:9.

Harlan, R.. 1991a. Spring 1991. The Ohio Cardinal 14(3):12–26.

_____. 1991b. The reports—summer 1991. The Ohio Cardinal 14(4):11–22.

_____. 1992a. The reports—autumn 1991. The Ohio Cardinal 15:11–26.

_____. 1992b. The reports—winter 1991–1992. The Ohio Cardinal 15:34–43.

_____. 1992c. The reports—spring 1992. The Ohio Cardinal 15:72–88.

_____. 1992d. The reports—summer 1992. The Ohio Cardinal 15:103–115.

_____. 1992e. Ohio's winter warblers. The Ohio Cardinal 15:30–31.

_____. 1992f. A Black-throated Gray Warbler in the Cleveland area. The Ohio Cardinal 15:63–64.

_____. 1993a. The reports—autumn 1992. The Ohio Cardinal 16:14–26.

_____. 1993b. The reports—winter 1992–1993. The Ohio Cardinal 16:37–47.

_____. 1993c. The reports—spring 1993. The Ohio Cardinal 16:80–94.

_____. 1993d. The reports—summer 1993. The Ohio Cardinal 16:106–119.

_____. 1994a. The reports—autumn 1993. The Ohio Cardinal 17:12–29.

_____. 1994b. The reports—winter 1993–1994. The Ohio Cardinal 17:38–48.

_____. 1994c. The reports—spring 1994. The Ohio Cardinal 17:90–109.

_____. 1994d. The reports—summer 1994. The Ohio Cardinal 17:130–145.

_____. 1994e. The Red-necked Grebe invasion of 1994. The Ohio Cardinal 17:75–78.

_____. 1994f. Ohio's earliest published spring warbler arrival dates. The Ohio Cardinal 17:85–87.

_____. 1995a. The reports—autumn 1994. The Ohio Cardinal 18:18–36.

_____. 1995b. The reports—winter 1994–1995. The Ohio Cardinal 18:48–56.

_____. 1995c. The reports—spring 1995. The Ohio Cardinal 18:88–103.

_____. 1995d. The reports—summer 1995. The Ohio Cardinal 18:127–137.

_____. 1996a. The reports—autumn 1995. The Ohio Cardinal 19:19–33.

_____. 1996b. The reports—winter 1995–1996. The Ohio Cardinal 19:45–53.

Hasbrouck, E. M. 1944. Apparent status of the European Widgeon in North America. Auk 61:93–104.

Hazard, F. O. 1947. An Ohio record for the Wood Ibis. Wilson Bull. 59:110.

Hennessy, T. E., and L. Van Camp. 1963. Wintering Mourning Doves in northern Ohio. Jour. Wildl. Manage. 27:367–373.

Henninger, W. F. 1901. A new bird for the state of Ohio—*Ardea caerulea*. Auk 18:392.

_____.1902. A preliminary list of the birds of middle-southern Ohio. Wilson Bull. 14:77–93.

_____. 1905. Further notes on the birds of middle-southern Ohio. Wilson Bull. 17:89–93.

_____. 1906. Notes on the birds of Seneca County, Ohio. Wilson Bull. 20:57–60.

_____. 1908. Nesting of the Prairie Warbler in Ohio. Wilson Bull. 20:213.

_____. 1910a. Henslow's Sparrow nesting in Ohio. Wilson Bull. 22:125.

_____. 1910b. Notes on some Ohio birds. Auk 27:66–68.

_____. 1910c. Horned Lark and Bohemian Waxwing in middle-western Ohio. Wilson Bull. 22:55.

_____. 1910d. Notes on the nesting of Bewick's Wren. Wilson Bull. 22:57.

_____. 1911a. *Falco rusticolus* in Ohio. Wilson Bull. 23:58.

_____. 1911b. Records from the Tri-Reservoir Region in Ohio in 1910. Wilson Bull. 23:61–62.

_____. 1916. Notes on some Ohio birds. Wilson Bull. 28:86–88.

_____. 1918. Notes on some Ohio birds. Wilson Bull. 30:19–21.

_____. 1919. An overlooked record of the Trumpeter Swan. Auk 36:564–565.

Herman, J. 1981. Ohio records of the Yellow-headed Blackbird (*Xanthocephalus xanthocephalus*). The Ohio Cardinal 3:31–34.

Herrick, F. H. 1924a. An eagle observatory. Auk 41:89–105.

_____. 1924b. Nest and nesting habits of the American Eagle. Auk 41:213–231.

_____. 1924c. The daily life of the American Eagle: late phase. Auk 41: 389–422.

_____. 1924d. The daily life of the American Eagle: late phase (concluded). Auk 41:517–543.

_____. 1927. The American Eagle at Vermilion, Ohio. Western Reserve University, Cleveland, Ohio. 34 p.

Hicks, L. E. 1931. The American Egret and the Little Blue Heron in Ohio during the summer of 1930. Wilson Bull. 43:268–281.

_____. 1932a. Crested Flycatchers in Ohio in mid-November. Auk 49:222.

_____. 1932b. The Snowy Owl invasion of Ohio in 1930–1931. Wilson Bull. 44:221–226.

_____. 1933a. The breeding birds of Ashtabula County, Ohio. Wilson Bull. 45:168–195.

_____. 1933b. The first appearance and spread of the breeding range of the European Starling (*Sturnus vulgaris*) in Ohio. Auk 50:317–322.

_____. 1933c. Some breeding records for Ohio. Auk 50:448–449.

_____. 1934a. The Hoary Redpoll in Ohio. Auk 51:244–245.

_____. 1934b. Some additional Ohio breeding records. Wilson Bull. 46:201–202.

_____. 1935a. Distribution of the breeding birds of Ohio. Ohio Biol. Surv. Bull. No. 32, 6(3):125–190.

_____. 1935b. The Louisiana Paroquet in Ohio, Kentucky, and Indiana. Wilson Bull. 47:76–77.

_____. 1936. Notes on the breeding birds of southeastern Ohio. Wilson Bull. 46:96–103.

_____. 1937a. Breeding birds of unglaciated Ohio. The Cardinal 4:125–141.

_____. 1937b. Avocet taken in Ohio. Auk 54:538.

_____. 1937c. An Ohio invasion of Le Conte's Sparrow. Auk 54:545–546.

_____. 1937d. Western Willet in Ohio. Auk 54:536–537.

_____. 1938a. Piping Plover taken in central Ohio. Wilson Bull. 50:141.

_____. 1938b. The Western Meadowlark in Ohio. Auk 55:544–545.

_____. 1945a. Blue Grosbeak breeding in Ohio. Auk 62:314.

_____. 1945b. Yellow-headed Blackbird breeding in Ohio. Auk 62:314–315.

_____. 1945c. Hooded Merganser breeding in Ohio. Auk 62:315–316.

_____. 1946. Lark Bunting records for Ohio. Auk 63:256–257.

Hochadel, D. 1999. The Golden-crowned Kinglet breeding in Ohio. Ohio Birds and Nat. Hist. 1:20–28.

Hochadel, D., and J. Hochadel. 1992. Golden-crowned Kinglets nest in Columbiana County. The Ohio Cardinal 15:96.

Hoffman, R. B. 1983. Herring Gulls nesting in artificial goose-nesting structures. Ohio Jour. Sci. 83:34–37.

Hussell, D. J. T. 1982. The timing of fall migration in Yellow-bellied Flycatchers. Jour. Field Ornith. 53:1–6.

Hyde, A. S. 1939. The life history of Henslow's Sparrow, *Passerherbulus henslowi* (Audubon). Univ. Michigan Mus. Zool. Misc. Publ. No. 41. 72 p.

Jehl, Jr., J. R. 1979. The autumnal migration of Baird's Sandpiper. *In* Shorebirds in marine environments. F. A. Pitelka, ed. Stud. Avian Biol. No. 2.:55–68.

Jones, L. 1903. The birds of Ohio, a revised catalogue. Ohio State Acad. Sci. Spec. Papers No. 6. 241 p.

_____. 1904. Additional records of Ohio birds. Ohio Nat. 4:112–113.

_____. 1905. Additions to the birds of Ohio. Wilson Bull. 17:64.

_____. 1907. *Catharista atrata*, Black Vulture, in Harrison County, Ohio. Wilson Bull. 19:33–34.

_____. 1909. The birds of Cedar Point and vicinity. Wilson Bull. 21:55–76, 114–131, 187–204.

_____. 1910. The birds of Cedar Point and vicinity. Wilson Bull. 22:25–41, 97–115, 172–182.

_____. 1911. Exceptional Ohio records. Wilson Bull. 23:60–61.

_____. 1914. Nineteen years of bird migration at Oberlin, Ohio. Wilson Bull. 26:198–205.

_____. 1918. Some Ohio records and notes. Wilson Bull. 30:120–121.

_____. 1941. Prairie Falcon at Oberlin, Ohio. Wilson Bull.53: 123.

Kaatz, M. R. 1955. The Black Swamp: A study in historical geography. Ann. Assn. Am. Geogr. 45:1–35.

Kemp., T. 1991. The first Golden-crowned Kinglet nest for Ohio. The Ohio Cardinal 14:1–2.

_____. 1997. Fall Golden Eagle passage over western Lucas County. The Ohio Cardinal 21:36–37.

Kemsies, E., and G. R. Austing. 1950. Smith's Longspur in Ohio. Wilson Bull. 62:37.

Kemsies, E., and W. Randle. 1953. Birds of southwestern Ohio. Ann Arbor, Michigan. 74 p.

Kendeigh, S. C. 1933. Abundance and conservation of the Bobwhite in Ohio. Ohio Jour. Sci. 33:1–18.

Kimes, E. D. 1912. A few Stark County, Ohio, notes. Wilson Bull. 24:156–157.

Kirtland, J. P. 1938. Report on the zoology of Ohio. Second Ann. Rept., Geol. Surv. Ohio. pp.:157–177.

Kleen, V. M. 1973. Middlewestern Prairie Region. Am. Birds 27:874–878.

_____. 1974a. Middlewestern Prairie Region. Am. Birds 28:58–63.

_____. 1974b. Middlewestern Prairie Region. Am. Birds 28:645–649.

_____. 1974c. Middlewestern Prairie Region. Am. Birds 28:807–810.

_____. 1974d. Middlewestern Prairie Region. Am. Birds 28:908–911.

_____. 1975a. Middlewestern Prairie Region. Am. Birds 29:64–68.

_____. 1975b. Middlewestern Prairie Region. Am. Birds 29:696–700.

_____. 1975c. Middlewestern Prairie Region. Am. Birds 29:858–862.

_____. 1975d. Middlewestern Prairie Region. Am. Birds 29:978–982.

_____. 1976a. Middlewestern Prairie Region. Am. Birds 30:77–82.

_____. 1976b. Middlewestern Prairie Region. Am. Birds 30:846–850.

_____. 1976c. Middlewestern Prairie Region. Am. Birds 30:961–965.

_____. 1977a. Middlewestern Prairie Region. Am. Birds 31:182–186.

_____. 1977b. Middlewestern Prairie Region. Am. Birds 31:336–339.

_____. 1977c. Middlewestern Prairie Region. Am. Birds 31:1006–1010.

_____. 1978a. Middlewestern Prairie Region. Am. Birds 32:210–215.

_____. 1978b. Middlewestern Prairie Region. Am. Birds 32:357–361.

_____. 1978c. Middlewestern Prairie Region. Am. Birds 32:1012–1017.

_____. 1978d. Middlewestern Prairie Region. Am. Birds 32:1166–1171.

_____. 1979a. Middlewestern Prairie Region. Am. Birds 33:181–185.

_____. 1979b. Middlewestern Prairie Region. Am. Birds 33:285–287.

_____. 1979c. Middlewestern Prairie Region. Am. Birds 33:775–778.

_____. 1979d. Middlewestern Prairie Region. Am. Birds 33:866–869.

_____. 1980a. Middlewestern Prairie Region. Am. Birds 34:166–169.

_____. 1980b. Middlewestern Prairie Region. Am. Birds 34:277–279.

_____. 1980c. Middlewestern Prairie Region. Am. Birds 34:781–785.

_____. 1980d. Middlewestern Prairie Region. Am. Birds 34:898–902.

_____. 1981. Middlewestern Prairie Region. Am. Birds 35:187–191.

Kleen, V. M., and L. Bush. 1971. Middlewestern Prairie Region. Am. Birds 25:750–753.

_____., and _____. 1971. Middlewestern Prairie Region. Am. Birds 25:862–865.

_____., and _____. 1972a. Middlewestern Prairie Region. Am. Birds 26:70–73.

_____., and _____. 1972b. Middlewestern Prairie Region. Am. Birds 26:610–614.

_____., and _____. 1973a. Middlewestern Prairie Region. Am. Birds 27:66–70.

_____., and _____. 1973b. Middlewestern Prairie Region. Am. Birds 27:622–625.

_____., and _____. 1973c. Middlewestern Prairie Region. Am. Birds 27:777–781.

Kline, D. A.. 1990. Ohio's first Violet-green Swallow. The Ohio Cardinal 13(3):1–2.

Kline, D. 1997. The summer 1997 season. Bobolink 1(2):3–7.

_____. 1999. The spring 1999 season. Bobolink 3(1):2–11.

Kopka, L. 1991. December Northern Oriole—in Ohio? Cleveland Bird Calendar 87:9–10.

Kotesovec, Jr., N. J. 1993. Blackburnian Warbler and other rare nesters at Hinckley MP. The Ohio Cardinal 16: 96–101.

_____. 1994a. Nesting Magnolia Warblers at Hinckley MP. The Ohio Cardinal 17:116–119.

_____. 1994b. A brief study of the nest life of Black-throated Green Warblers at Hinckley MP. The Ohio Cardinal 17:79–84.

_____. 1995. Further observations of summering Black-throated Green Warblers at Hinckley MP. The Ohio Cardinal 18:113–116.

_____. 1996a. Breeding Red-breasted Nuthatches at Hinckley MP. The Ohio Cardinal 19:77–82.

_____. 1996b. Nesting Nashville Warblers in Summit County, Ohio. Cleveland Bird Calendar 92:30–32.

_____. 1998. Early nesting Golden-crowned Kinglets at Hinckley Metropark. Cleveland Bird Calendar 94:20–21.

Kotesovec, Jr., N. J. and S. Zadar. 1996. Nesting Nashville Warblers in Summit County, Ohio. Cleveland Bird Calendar 92:30–32.

Kress, S. W. 1967. A Robin nests in winter. Wilson Bull.79: 245–246.

Langdon, F. W. 1877. Occurrence of the Black Vulture, or Carrion Crow in Ohio. Bull. Nuttall Ornithol. Club 2:109.

_____. 1879. A revised list of Cincinnati birds. Cincinnati Soc. Nat. Hist. Bull. 1:167–193.

Langlois, T. H., and M. H. Langlois. 1964. Annotated list of the birds of South Bass Island, Lake Erie. Wheaton Club Bull. 9:29–55.

Leberman, R. C. 1999. Appalachian region. N. Am. Birds 53:385–387.

Lee, C., and A. Birch. 1998. Field identification of female and immature Bullock's and Baltimore Orioles. Birding 30:282–295.

Leedy, D. L., and W. B. Hendershot. 1947. The Ring-necked Pheasant and its management in Ohio. Ohio Div. Wildl. Cons. Bull. No. 1. 16 p.

Leopold, A. 1947. On a monument to the pigeon. *In* Silent wings—memorial to the Passenger Pigeon. Wisconsin Soc. Ornith.. pp.:3–5.

LePage, T. 1995. A Royal Tern at Lorain—a new species for Ohio. The Ohio Cardinal 18:112.

Lindahl, J. 1899. The Black-capped Petrel (*Aestrelata hasitata*) on the Ohio River at Cincinnati. Auk 16:75.

Little, R. S. 1969. Field observations of the Wheaton Club. Wheaton Club Bull. Vol. 14.

Lloyd, C. K. 1931. Nesting of Bachman's Sparrow in Butler County, Ohio. Wilson Bull. 43:145.

_____. 1934. Nesting of the Kentucky Warbler in Butler County, Ohio. Wilson Bull. 46:257–258.

_____. 1943. An unusual nest of the Bronzed Grackle. Wilson Bull. 55:56.

Lund, B. A., and B. Weitlauf. 1995. Bewick's Wrens nest in Brown County. The Ohio Cardinal 18:84.

Marshall, R. O. 1931. Birds observed in eastern Ohio, 1930. Oologist 48:43.

Maslowski, K. H. 1934. An aerial nest of the Turkey Vulture (*Cathartes aura septentrionalis*). Auk 51:229–230.

Mathena, C., J. Hickman, J. Hill, R. Mercer, C. and B. Berry, N. Cherry, and P. Flynn. 1984. The birds of Dayton. Landfall Press, Dayton. 189 p.

Maxwell, II, G. R. 1970. Pair formation, nest building and egg laying of the Common Grackle in northern Ohio. Ohio Jour. Sci. 70:284–291.

Mayfield, H., 1943. Glaucous and Great Black-backed Gulls at the western end of Lake Erie. Wilson Bull. 55:129–130.

_____. 1944. First Hudsonian Chickadee for Ohio. Wilson Bull. 56:46.

_____. 1947a. Ohio-Michigan Region. Audubon Field Notes 1:7–8.

_____ 1947b. Ohio-Michigan Region. Audubon Field Notes 1:131, 135.

_____. 1947d. Ohio-Michigan Region. Audubon Field Notes 1:176–177.

_____. 1948. Ohio Region. Audubon Field Notes 2:179–180.

_____. 1949a. Middlewestern Prairie Region. Audubon Field Notes 3:17–19.

_____. 1949b. Middlewestern Prairie Region. Audubon Field Notes 3:171–172.

_____. 1950a. Middlewestern Prairie Region. Audubon Field Notes 4:17–19.

_____. 1950b. Middlewestern Prairie Region. Audubon Field Notes 4:203–205.

_____. 1950c. Middlewestern Prairie Region. Audubon Field Notes 4:243–245.

_____. 1951a. Middlewestern Prairie Region. Audubon Field Notes 5:207–208.

_____. 1951b. Middlewestern Prairie Region. Audubon Field Notes 5:257–259.

_____. 1964. Yearly fluctuations in a population of Purple Martins. Auk 81:274–280.

_____. 1988. Do Kirtland's Warblers migrate in one hop? Auk 105:204–205.

Mayfield, H. F., and J. M. McCormick. 1956. Purple Finch nesting at Toledo, Ohio. Wilson Bull. 68:249.

McLean, E. B., A. M. White, and T. O. Matson. 1995. Smooth-billed Ani (_Crotophaga ani_ L.), a new species of bird for Ohio. Ohio Jour. Sci. 95:335–336.

McCormac, J. 1999. Ohio grassland breeding bird survey. The Ohio Cardinal 22:125–130.

McKinley, D. 1977. Records of the Carolina Parakeet in Ohio. Ohio Jour. Sci. 77:3–9.

McLaughlin, V. P. 1979. Occurrence of Large-billed Tern (*Phaetusa simplex*) in Ohio. Am. Birds 33:727.

Metcalf, K. J. 1998. Documentation of the Long-tailed Jaeger (*Stercorarius longicaudus*). Cleveland Bird Calendar 94:45–46.

_____. 1999. Documentation of a late Philadelphia Vireo (*Vireo philadelphicus*). Cleveland Bird Calendar 95:44–45.

_____. 2000. Documentation of a Bohemian Waxwing at North Chagrin Metro Park. Cleveland Bird Calendar 96:10-11.

Miller, L. 1930. The Chestnut-sided and other warblers nesting in Geauga County, Ohio. Wilson Bull. 42:56–57.

Mizanin, J. 1999. Ohio's first Common Ground-Dove. Cleveland Bird Calendar 95:9-10.

Mlodinow, S. G. 1997. The Long-billed Murrelet (*Brachyramphus perdix*) in North America. Birding 29:461–475.

Moore, N. J. 1996. An annotated checklist of the birds of Killdeer Plains Wildlife Area. Ohio. Biol. Surv. Inform. Publ. No. 2.

Morse, H. G. 1914. Nesting of Prothonotary Warbler near Huron, Ohio. Wilson Bull. 26:212.

Moseley, E. L. 1908. Brunnich's Murre on Lake Erie, 1907. Wilson Bull. 20:104.

Mumford, R. E. 1959a. Middlewestern Prairie Region. Audubon Field Notes 13:33–37.

_____. 1959b. Middlewestern Prairie Region. Audubon Field Notes 13:295–298.

_____. 1959c. Middlewestern Prairie Region. Audubon Field Notes 13:373–376.

_____. 1960a. Middlewestern Prairie Region. Audubon Field Notes 14:38–41.

_____. 1960b. Middlewestern Prairie Region. Audubon Field Notes 14:312–314.

_____. 1960c. Middlewestern Prairie Region. Audubon Field Notes 14:452–454.

_____. 1961a. Middlewestern Prairie Region. Audubon Field Notes 15:44–46.

_____. 1961b. Middlewestern Prairie Region. Audubon Field Notes 15:332–334.

_____. 1961c. Middlewestern Prairie Region. Audubon Field Notes 15:413–416.

Mumford, R. E., and C. E. Keller. 1984. The Birds of Indiana. Indiana Univ. Press, Bloomington, IN. 376 p.

Murphy, J. L. and J. Farrand, Jr. 1979. Prehistoric occurrence of the Ivory-billed Woodpecker (*Campephilus principalis*), Muskingum County, Ohio. Ohio Jour. Sci. 79:22–23.

Mutter, D., D. Nolan, and A. Shartle. 1984. Raptor populations on selected park reserves in Montgomery County, Ohio. Ohio Jour. Sci. 84:29–32.

Newman, D. L. 1958. A nesting of the Acadian Flycatcher. Wilson Bull. 70:130–144.

_____. 1961. House Wren and Bewick's Wren in northern Ohio. Wilson Bull. 73:84–86.

_____. 1965. Noteworthy records. Cleveland Bird Calendar 61:16–19.

_____. 1969. A field book of the birds of the Cleveland region. Cleveland Mus. Nat. Hist., Cleveland. 46 p.

Nice, M. M. 1937. Studies in the life history of the Song Sparrow. Vol. 1: A population study of the Song Sparrow. Trans. Linnaean Soc. New York, Vol. 4. 246 p.

_____. 1939. "Territorial song" and non-territorial behavior of Goldfinches in Ohio. Wilson Bull. 51:123.

_____. 1943. Studies in the life history of the Song Sparrow. Vol. 2: The behavior of the Song Sparrow and other passerines. Trans. Linnaean Soc. New York, Vol. 6. 328 p.

Nickell, W. P. 1965. Habitats, territory, and nesting of the Catbird. Am. Midland Nat. 73:433–478.

Nisbet, I. C. T., D. B. McNair, W. Post, and T. C. Williams. 1995. Transoceanic migration of the Blackpoll Warbler: Summary of scientific evidence and response to criticisms by Murray. Jour. Field Ornithol. 66:612–622.

Nolan, Jr., V. 1953a. Middlewestern Prairie Region. Audubon Field Notes 7:18–20.

_____. 1953b. Middlewestern Prairie Region. Audubon Field Notes 7:215–216.

_____. 1954a. Middlewestern Prairie Region. Audubon Field Notes 8:21–23.

_____. 1954b. Middlewestern Prairie Region. Audubon Field Notes 8:254–256.

_____. 1954d. Middlewestern Prairie Region. Audubon Field Notes 8:314–316.

_____. 1954c. Middlewestern Prairie Region. Audubon Field Notes 8:347–349.

_____. 1955a. Middlewestern Prairie Region. Audubon Field Notes 9:28–31.

_____. 1955b. Middlewestern Prairie Region. Audubon Field Notes 9:261–262.

_____ 1955c. Middlewestern Prairie Region. Audubon Field Notes 9:333–335.

_____. 1955d. Middlewestern Prairie Region. Audubon Field Notes 9:380–382.

_____. 1958a. Middlewestern Prairie Region. Audubon Field Notes 12:33–36.

_____. 1958b. Middlewestern Prairie Region. Audubon Field Notes 12:282–284.

_____. 1958c. Middlewestern Prairie Region. Audubon Field Notes 12:356–358.

_____. 1958d. Middlewestern Prairie Region. Audubon Field Notes 12:415–417.

Norberg, A. H. 1945. The nesting cycle and behavior of the Red-eyed Vireo. M.S. Thesis, Ohio State Univ., Columbus. 48 p.

Novotny, E. 1961. Long-tailed Jaeger in Ohio. Wilson Bull. 73:280–281.

Oberholser, H. C. 1974. The bird life of Texas. Vol. 1. Univ. Texas Press, Austin, TX. p: 266.

Osborn, D. R., and A. T. Peterson. 1984. Decline of the Upland Sandpiper (*Bartramia longicauda*) in Ohio: An endangered species. Ohio Jour. Sci. 84:8–10.

Owen, D. F. 1963. Polymorphism in the Screech Owl in eastern North America. Wilson Bull. 75:183–190.

Pasquale, E. 1993. A Black-throated Gray Warbler diary. The Ohio Cardinal 16:34–35.

Payne, R. B. 1983. A distributional checklist of the birds of Michigan. Univ. Michigan Mus. Zool. Misc. Publ. No. 164. 71 p.

Perkins, III, S. E. 1935. Late date for Prairie Horned Lark nesting in central Ohio. Auk 52:453.

Peterjohn, B. G. 1981a. Middlewestern Prairie Region. Am. Birds 35:304–307.

_____. 1981b. Middlewestern Prairie Region. Am. Birds 35:828–832.

_____. 1981c. Middlewestern Prairie Region. Am. Birds 35:943–947.

_____. 1982a. Middlewestern Prairie Region. Am. Birds 36:182–186.

_____. 1982b. Middlewestern Prairie Region. Am. Birds 36:298–301.

_____. 1982c. Middlewestern Prairie Region. Am. Birds 36:857–861.

_____. 1982d. Middlewestern Prairie Region. Am. Birds 36:981–985.

_____. 1982e. Breeding avifauna of the South Bloomingville Quadrangle, Hocking County, Ohio. Report submitted to Ohio Dept. Nat. Res., Div. Nat. Areas and Preserves. 34 p.

_____. 1983a. Middlewestern Prairie Region. Am. Birds 37:185–189.

_____. 1983b. Middlewestern Prairie Region. Am. Birds 37: 306–309.

_____. 1983c. Middlewestern Prairie Region. Am. Birds 37:874–878.

_____. 1983d. Middlewestern Prairie Region. Am. Birds 37:992–995.

_____. 1984a. Middlewestern Prairie Region. Am. Birds 38:207–211.

_____. 1984b. Middlewestern Prairie Region. Am. Birds 38:322–325.

_____. 1984c. Middlewestern Prairie Region. Am. Birds 38:916–920.

_____. 1984d. Middlewestern Prairie Region. Am. Birds 38:1024–1028.

_____. 1985a. Middlewestern Prairie Region. Am. Birds 39:59–63.

_____. 1985b. Middlewestern Prairie Region. Am. Birds 39:171–174.

_____. 1985c. Middlewestern Prairie Region. Am. Birds 39:305–310.

_____. 1985d. Middlewestern Prairie Region. Am. Birds 39:917–920.

_____. 1986a. Middlewestern Prairie Region. Am. Birds 40:118–123.

_____. 1986b. Middlewestern Prairie Region. Am. Birds 40:285–289.

_____. 1986c. Middlewestern Prairie Region. Am. Birds 40:476–481.

_____. 1986d. Middlewestern Prairie Region. Am. Birds 40:1208–1212.

_____. 1987a. Middlewestern Prairie Region. Am. Birds 41:93–99.

_____. 1987b. Middlewestern Prairie Region. Am. Birds 41:286–290.

_____. 1987c. Middlewestern Prairie Region. Am. Birds 41:437–441.

_____. 1987d. Middlewestern Prairie Region. Am. Birds 41:1440–1444.

_____. 1988a. Middlewestern Prairie Region. Am. Birds 42:80–85.

_____. 1988b. Middlewestern Prairie Region. Am. Birds 42:270–274.

_____. 1988c. Middlewestern Prairie Region. Am. Birds 42: 440–444.

_____. 1988d. Middlewestern Prairie Region. Am. Birds 42: 1293–1298.

_____. 1989a. Middlewestern Prairie Region. Am. Birds 42:108–114.

_____. 1989b. Middlewestern Prairie Region. Am. Birds 42:319–323.

_____. 1989c. Middlewestern Prairie Region. Am. Birds 42:485–491.

_____. 1989d. Middlewestern Prairie Region. Am. Birds 42:1320–1325.

_____. 1990a. Middlewestern Prairie Region. Am. Birds 43:88–92.

_____. 1990b. Middlewestern Prairie Region. Am. Birds 43:273–278.

_____. 1990c. Middlewestern Prairie Region. Am. Birds 43:432–439.

_____. 1990d. Middlewestern Prairie Region. Am. Birds 43:1138–1142.

_____. 1991a. Middlewestern Prairie Region. Am. Birds 44:108–112.

_____. 1991b. Middlewestern Prairie Region. Am. Birds 44:277–282.

_____. 1991c. Middlewestern Prairie Region. Am. Birds 44:451–455.

_____. 1991d. Middlewestern Prairie Region. Am. Birds 44:1114–1117.

_____. 1992a. Middlewestern Prairie Region. Am. Birds 45:95–101.

_____. 1992b. Middlewestern Prairie Region. Am. Birds 45:270–274.

Peterjohn, B. G., and M. E. Gustafson. 1990. Gray Flycatcher in northwestern Ohio. Am. Birds 44:37–38.

Peterjohn, B. G., R. L. Hannikman, J. M. Hoffman, and E. J. Tramer. 1987. Abundance and distribution of the birds of Ohio. Ohio Biol. Surv., Biol. Notes. No. 19. 52 p.

Peterjohn, B. G., and D. L. Rice. 1991. The Ohio breeding bird atlas. Ohio Dept. Nat. Res., Div. Nat. Areas and Preserves, Columbus. 416 p.

Peterjohn, B. G., and J. R. Sauer. 1995. Population trends of the Loggerhead Shrike from the North American Breeding Bird Survey. Pages 117–121 In Shrikes (Laniidae) of the world: Biology and conservation. R. Yosef and F. E. Lohrer, eds. Proc. West. Found. Vert. Zool. No. 6.

Peters, S. J. 1998. Ohio Peregrine synopsis. Cleveland Bird Calendar 94:43-44.

Petersen, Jr., P. C. 1963. Middlewestern Prairie Region. Audubon Field Notes 17:407–409.

_____. 1964a. Middlewestern Prairie Region. Audubon Field Notes 18:42–44.

_____. 1964b. Middlewestern Prairie Region. Audubon Field Notes 18:359–360.

_____. 1964c. Middlewestern Prairie Region. Audubon Field Notes 18:454–456.

_____. 1964d. Middlewestern Prairie Region. Audubon Field Notes 18:511–512.

_____. 1965a. Middlewestern Prairie Region. Audubon Field Notes 19:44–46.

_____. 1965b. Middlewestern Prairie Region. Audubon Field Notes 19:383–385.

_____. 1965c. Middlewestern Prairie Region. Audubon Field Notes 19:480–482.

_____. 1965d. Middlewestern Prairie Region. Audubon Field Notes 19:551–552.

_____ 1966a. Middlewestern Prairie Region. Audubon Field Notes 20:429–431.

_____. 1966b. Middlewestern Prairie Region. Audubon Field Notes 20:513–515.

_____. 1966c. Middlewestern Prairie Region. Audubon Field Notes 20:574–575.

_____. 1967a. Middlewestern Prairie Region. Audubon Field Notes 21:44–45.

_____. 1967b. Middlewestern Prairie Region. Audubon Field Notes 21:513–514.

_____. 1967c. Middlewestern Prairie Region. Audubon Field Notes 21:577–578.

_____. 1968a. Middlewestern Prairie Region. Audubon Field Notes 22:443–445.

_____. 1968b. Middlewestern Prairie Region. Audubon Field Notes 22:612–614.

_____. 1969. Middlewestern Prairie Region. Audubon Field Notes 23:596–597.

_____. 1970a. Middlewestern Prairie Region. Audubon Field Notes 24:54–55.

_____. 1970b. Middlewestern Prairie Region. Audubon Field Notes 24:509–511.

_____. 1970c. Middlewestern Prairie Region. Audubon Field Notes 24:608, 613–615.

_____. 1970c. Middlewestern Prairie Region. Audubon Field Notes 24:689–691.

_____. 1971. Middlewestern Prairie Region. Audubon Field Notes 25:64–66.

Peterson, A. T. 1986. Rock Doves nesting in trees. Wilson Bull. 98:168–169.

Petit, L. J., and W. J. Fleming. 1987. Nest-box use by Prothonotary Warblers (*Protonotaria citrea*) in riverine habitat. Wilson Bull. 99:485–488.

Phillips, A. S. 1975. Semipalmated Sandpiper: identification, migrations, summer and winter ranges. Am. Birds 29:799–806.

Phillips, R. S. 1963. Scissor-tailed Flycatcher in Ohio. Wilson Bull. 75:273–274.

_____. 1967. Buff-breasted Sandpiper in northwestern Ohio. Wilson Bull. 79:340.

_____. 1980. Birds of the Hancock County, Ohio, area. Findlay College, Findlay. 154 p.

Pierce, E. 1994. Totally unexpected: A Fulvous Whistling-Duck at Magee Marsh WA. The Ohio Cardinal 17:123–124.

Price, H. F. 1928a. Late nesting of Barn Swallow. Oologist 45:11.

_____. 1928b. Notes on the Turkey Vulture. Oologist 45:62–63.

_____. 1931. Persistence in nesting of the Prairie Horned Lark. Oologist 48:146.

_____. 1932. Destruction of birds' nests on two Ohio farms. Oologist 49:102.

_____. 1934a. The hawks, eagles, and vultures of northwestern Ohio. Oologist 51:29–35.

_____. 1934b. Herons and bitterns of northwestern Ohio. Oologist 51:77–79.

_____. 1935. The summer birds of northwestern Ohio. Oologist 52:26–36.

_____. 1940a. Some Ohio and Indiana nesting dates for 1940. Oologist 57:98–101.

_____. 1940b. Notes on a Black Rail. Oologist 57:54.

_____. 1941. Nests and eggs of the Cooper's Hawk. Oologist 58:26–27.

_____. 1946. Burrowing Owl in Ohio. Auk 63:450–451.

_____ 1972. The nesting birds of northwestern Ohio. Wheaton Club Bull. (New Series) Vol. 17.

Putnam, L. S. 1949. The life history of the Cedar Waxwing. Wilson Bull. 61:141–182.

Putnam, L. S., G. Maxwell, and S. Tilley. 1964. Sight record of the Glossy Ibis for the Bass Islands, Lake Erie, Ohio. Wilson Bull. 76:98.

Randle, W. 1963. Solitary Vireo found nesting in south-central Ohio's Hocking County. Wilson Bull. 75:277–278.

Randle, W., and R. Austing. 1952. Ecological notes on Long-eared and Saw-whet Owls in southwestern Ohio. Ecology 33:422–426.

Reinthal, M. 1991. Second nesting record of Golden-crowned Kinglet in Ohio. The Ohio Cardinal 14:3–4.

Renfrow, F. 1999. Red-breasted Nuthatches nesting at Hocking Hills: the first records for southeastern Ohio. The Ohio Cardinal 22:131–133.

Richter, G. W. 1939. Ohio nesting dates for 1938. Oologist 56:40–41.

Roads, M. K. 1931. Doves use an old Robin's nest. Auk 48:265.

_____. 1936. An early Ohio record of the Bachman's Sparrow. Wilson Bull. 48:310.

Robbins, C. S., D. Bystrak, and P. H. Geissler. 1986. The breeding bird survey: Its first fifteen years, 1965–1979.U. S. Fish and Wildlife Service Res. Publ. No. 157. 196 p.

Rogers, G. T. 1955. Red Phalarope in Ohio. Wilson Bull. 67:63–64.

Rosche, L. 1987. First Ohio record of Brambling (*Fringilla montifringilla*). Cleveland Bird Calendar 83:19–20.

_____. 1988. A field book of the birds of the Cleveland region, second edition. Cleveland Mus. Nat. Hist., Cleveland.

_____. 1989. Noteworthy records. Cleveland Bird Calendar 85:33–34.

_____. 1992. Extreme date occurrence for selected migrants. Cleveland Bird Calendar 88:7–11.

_____, 1994. Noteworthy reports. Cleveland Bird Calendar 90:43–44.

_____. 1997a. Noteworthy reports. Cleveland Bird Calendar 93:8–9.

_____. 1997b. Noteworthy reports. Cleveland Bird Calendar 93: 17–19.

_____. 1997c. Noteworthy reports. Cleveland Bird Calendar 93: 30–33.

_____. 1998a. Noteworthy reports. Cleveland Bird Calendar 94: 7–8.

_____. 1998b. Noteworthy reports. Cleveland Bird Calendar 94: 18–20.

_____. 1998c. Noteworthy reports. Cleveland Bird Calendar 94:40–43.

_____. 1998d. A Ross's Gull (*Rhodostethia rosea*) at Headlands Beach State Park. Cleveland Bird Calendar 94:47–48.

_____. 1999a. Noteworthy reports. Cleveland Bird Calendar 95:6-8.

_____. 1999b. Noteworthy reports. Cleveland Bird Calendar 95:28-30.

_____. 1999c. Noteworthy reports. Cleveland Bird Calendar 95:41–44.

Rosche, L. O., and R. L. Hannikman. 1989. A wintering Sabine's Gull in Ohio. Birding 21:241–246.

Sauer, J. R., J. E. Hines, G. Gough, I. Thomas, and B. G. Peterjohn 1998. The North American Breeding Bird Survey Results and Analysis. Patuxent Wildlife Research Center, Laurel, MD. (http://www.mbr-pwrc.usgs.gov/bbs/bbs.html)

Savage, P. H. 1962. Black-throated Sparrow (*Amphispiza bilineata*) occurrence in northern Ohio. Redstart 29:75.

Sawyer, E. 1934. Yellow-headed Blackbird (*Xanthocephalus xanthocephalus*) in Ohio. Auk 51:527.

Saxe, S. 1998. A February White-eyed Vireo (*Vireo griseus*). Cleveland Bird Calendar 94:8.

Scharf, W. C. 1998. Distribution and abundance of tree-nesting heron and marsh-nesting tern colonies of the U.S. Great Lakes, 1991. Lake Superior State Univ., Gale Gleason Environ. Inst. Publ. No. 2. 44 p.

Scharf, W. C., and G. W. Shugart. 1998. Distribution and abundance of gull, tern, and cormorant nesting colonies of the U.S. Great Lakes, 1989 and 1990. Lake Superior State Univ., Gale Gleason Environ. Inst. Publ. No. 1. 56 p.

Schlabach, E. 1990. Ohio's first Mountain Bluebird. The Ohio Cardinal 13(2):1–3.

_____. 1991. Second confirmed record of Swainson's Hawk (*Buteo swainsoni*) for Ohio. The Ohio Cardinal 14:10–11.

_____. 1998. The spring 1998 season. Bobolink 2(1):3–12.

_____. 1999. Seasonal Report. Bobolink 3(4):2-7.

Schlabach, R. 1998. The winter 1997–1998 season. Bobolink 1(4):3–8.

_____. 1999a. The winter 1998–1999 season. Bobolink 2(4):2–10.

_____. 1999b. The fall 1999 season. Bobolink 3(3):2-10.

Schorger, A. W. 1955. The Passenger Pigeon, its natural history and extinction. Univ. Wisconsin Press, Madison, WI. 424 p.

Shaub, M. S. 1963. Evening Grosbeak winter invasions—1958–59, 1959–60, 1960–61. Bird-Banding 34:1–22.

Sheppard, J. M. 1959. Sprague's Pipit and Smith's Longspur in Ohio. Auk 76:362–363.

Shieldcastle, M. C. 1980. First state nesting record of Wilson's Phalarope. The Ohio Cardinal 3(2):1–2.

Shields, M. A., and T. W. Townsend. 1985. Nesting success of Ohio's endangered Common Tern. Ohio Jour. Sci. 85:45–49.

Sim, R. J. 1907. The Chestnut-sided Warbler nesting at Jefferson, Ashtabula County, Ohio. Ohio Nat. 8:209–210.

_____. 1908. Another Brunnich's Murre record for Ohio. Wilson Bull. 20:54.

Skaggs, M. B. 1932. Rare bird visitors at Youngstown, Ohio. Bird-Lore 34:389.

_____. 1934. A study of the Bewick's Wren in northeastern Ohio. Bird-Lore 36:301–302.

_____. 1936a. The Mute Swan and European Wigeon in Ohio. Wilson Bull. 48:131.

_____. 1936b. The occurrence of white herons in the Youngstown, Ohio, region. Wilson Bull. 48:269–272.

_____. 1945. First Ohio record of the Lark Bunting. Auk 62:313.

Smith, J. L. 1980. Decline of the Bewick's Wren. Redstart 47:77–82.

Smith, K. G. 1986. Winter bird population dynamics of three species of mast-eating birds in the eastern United States. Wilson Bull. 98:407–418.

Snyder, L. L. 1947. The Snowy Owl migration of 1945–46. Wilson Bull. 59:74–78.

Stahler, K., D. Frevert, N. Moore, and B. Stahler. 1991. Northern Saw-whet Owls and other raptors wintering at Killdeer Plains. The Ohio Cardinal 14(2):9–11.

Stevenson, J. 1928. Additional notes from Wayne County, Ohio. Auk 45:226–227.

Stewart, P. A. 1931. Cavity nesting robins. Wilson Bull. 43:59.

_____. 1952. Winter mortality of Barn Owls in central Ohio. Wilson Bull. 64:164–166.

_____. 1957. Nesting of the Shoveller (*Spatula clypeata*) in central Ohio. Wilson Bull. 69:280.

Stoll, Jr., R. J., and M. W. McClain. 1986. Distribution and relative abundance of the Ruffed Grouse in Ohio. Ohio Jour. Sci. 86:182–185.

Stout, W., K. Ver Steeg, and G. F. Lamb. 1943. Geology of water in Ohio. Ohio Geol. Surv. Bull. 44. 694 p.

Straw, Jr., J. A., D. G. Krementz, M. W. Olinde, and G. F. Sepik. 1994. American Woodcock. Pp: 97–114 *In* Migratory Shore and Upland Game Bird Management in North America, T. C. Tacha and C. E. Braun, eds. Allen Press, Lawrence, KS.

Sturm, L. 1945. A study of the nesting activities of the American Redstart. Auk 62:189–206.

Swales, B. H. 1918. The Purple Sandpiper at Cleveland, Ohio. Univ. Michigan Mus. Zool. Occ. Papers No. 57. 2 p.

Thomas, E. S. 1928a. Nesting of the Black Vulture in Hocking County, Ohio. Ohio State Mus. Sci. Bull. 1:29–35.

_____. 1928b. The Snowy Owl invasion of 1926–1927. Ohio State Mus. Sci. Bull. 1:64–69.

_____. 1932. Chuck-will's-widow, a new bird for Ohio. Auk 49:479.

_____. 1951. Black-throated Gray Warbler in Ohio. Wilson Bull. 63:206.

_____. 1980. Rare woodpecker at OSU Museum. The Ohio Cardinal 3(4):4–5.

Thomas, M. W., and E. P. Hengst. 1949. Little Gull at Columbus, Ohio. Wilson Bull. 61:236.

Thomson, T. 1983. Birding in Ohio. Indiana Univ. Press, Bloomington, IN. 256 p.

Tramer, E. J., and L. W. Campbell. 1986. Laughing Gull nesting attempt on Lake Erie. Wilson Bull. 98:170–171.

Transeau, E. N. 1935. The prairie peninsula. Ecology 16:423–437.

Trautman, M. B. 1926. Kittiwake in Ohio. Auk 43:228.

_____. 1928. Notes on Ohio shorebirds. Ohio State Mus. Sci. Bull. 1:40–44.

_____. 1933. Some recent Ohio records. Auk 50:234–236.

_____. 1935a. Notes on some Ohio birds. Auk 52:201–202.

_____. 1935b. Additional notes on some Ohio birds. Auk 52:321–323.

_____. 1940. The birds of Buckeye Lake, Ohio. Univ. Michigan Mus. Zool. Misc. Publ. No. 44. 466 p.

_____. 1946. A second Ohio record for the Eared Grebe. Wilson Bull. 58:216.

_____. 1956. Unusual bird records for Ohio. Auk 73:272–276.

_____. 1962. The 39th Buckeye Lake Audubon Christmas Bird Count and notes concerning the Black-capped Chickadee invasion of 1961–62. Wheaton Club Bull. 6:14–17.

_____. 1977. The Ohio Country from 1750 to 1977: A naturalist's view. Ohio Biol. Surv. Biol. Notes No. 10. 25 p.

_____.1978. Autumn migrations of selected species of ducks at Buckeye Lake, Ohio. Ohio Biol. Surv. Biol. Notes No. 11. 10 p.

_____. 1981. The fishes of Ohio. The Ohio State Univ. Press, Columbus. 782 p.

Trautman, M. B., and S. J. Glines. 1964. A nesting of the Purple Gallinule (*Porphyrula martinica*) in Ohio. Auk 81:224–226.

Trautman, M. B., and T. W. Nye. 1968. An Ohio record of the Magnificent Frigatebird (*Fregata magnificens*). Wilson Bull. 80:487–488.

Trautman, M. B., and M. A. Trautman. 1968. Annotated list of the birds of Ohio. Ohio Jour. Sci. 68:257–332.

_____., and _____. 1971. Three additions to the "Annotated List of the Birds of Ohio". Ohio Jour. Sci. 71:216.

Troyer, H. 2000. Jaeger in a hayfield. Bobolink 4(2): 11.

Turner, L., and A. Turner. 1994. Black-throated Gray Warbler in Independence, Ohio. The Ohio Cardinal 17:34–35.

Tuttle, C. 1895. Some uncommon and rare birds of Erie County, Ohio. Auk 12:190–191.

Tuttle, R. M. 1987. A six year study of nesting Tree Swallows in Delaware State Park, Delaware, Ohio 1979–1984. Sialia 9:3–7, 34.

Van Camp, L. 1974. The Bald Eagle. Toledo Nat. Assn. Yearbook 1974:11–17.

Van Camp, L., and C. J. Henny. 1975. The Screech Owl: Its life history and population ecology in northern Ohio. U. S. Fish and Wildlife Service, N. Am. Fauna No. 71. 65 p.

Van Camp, L., and H. Mayfield. 1943. Two Long-eared Owl nests near Toledo, Ohio. Wilson Bull. 55:54–55.

Walker, C. F. 1928a. Wintering Mniotiltidae in central Ohio. Auk 45:231–233.

_____. 1928b. The Yellow-crowned Night Heron nesting in Logan County, Ohio. Auk 45:370.

_____. 1928c. Henslow's Sparrow in Ohio. Ohio State Mus. Sci. Bull. 1:45–46.

_____. 1928d. Notes on the breeding warblers of central Ohio. Ohio State Mus. Sci. Bull. 1:53–58.

_____. 1931. An Ohio record for the European Teal. Wilson Bull. 43:69

_____. 1937a. Dayton Region. Bird-Lore 39:395–396.

_____. 1937b. Dayton Region. Bird-Lore 39:472–473.

_____. 1938a. Dayton Region. Bird-Lore 40:222–223.

_____. 1938b. Dayton Region. Bird-Lore 40:289–290.

_____. 1938c. Put-in-Bay Region. Bird-Lore 40:462–463.

_____. 1939a. Dayton Region. Bird-Lore 41:188–189.

_____. 1939b. Put-in-Bay Region. Bird-Lore 41(5):7–8 (supplement).

_____. 1939c. Put-in-Bay Region. Bird-Lore 41(6):7–9 (supplement).

_____. 1940a. Put-in-Bay Region. Bird-Lore 42:217–218.

_____. 1940b. Put-in-Bay Region. Bird-Lore 42:304–305.

_____. 1940c. Put-in-Bay Region. Bird-Lore 42:385–386.

_____. 1940d. Ohio Region. Bird-Lore 42:464–465.

_____. 1940e. Ohio Region. Bird-Lore 42:575–576.

_____. 1941. Clay-colored Sparrow in Ohio. Wilson Bull. 53:46.

Walker, C. F., and R. W. Franks. 1928. Birds of an Ohio cranberry bog. Ohio State Mus. Sci. Bull. 1:59–63.

Walkinshaw, L. H. 1960. Migration of the Sandhill Crane east of the Mississippi River. Wilson Bull. 72:358–384.

Wallace, G. J. 1939. Bicknell's Thrush: Its taxonomy, distribution, and life history. Proc. Boston Nat. Hist. Soc. 41(6):211–402.

Webb, L. G. 1949. The life history of the Mourning Dove, *Zenaidura macroura carolinensis* (Linnaeus) in Ohio. Ph.D. Thesis, Ohio State Univ., Columbus. 147 p.

Westerkov, K. E. 1949. A comparative study of the ecology and management of the European Partridge (*Perdix perdix*) in Ohio and Denmark. M.S. Thesis, Ohio State Univ., Columbus. 339 p.

_____. 1956. History and distribution of the Hungarian Partridge in Ohio. Ohio Jour. Sci. 56:65–70.

Wetmore, A. 1943. Evidence of the former occurrence of the Ivory-billed Woodpecker in Ohio. Wilson Bull. 55:55.

Whan, B. 1995. A Northern Lapwing in Adams Co., Ohio. The Ohio Cardinal 18:38–39.

_____. 1999a. Spring 1999 overview. The Ohio Cardinal 22:62–83.

_____. 1999b. Summer 1999 overview. The Ohio Cardinal 22:101–121.

Wharram, S. V. 1921. Notes from Ashtabula County, Ohio. Wilson Bull. 33:146–147.

Wheaton, J. M. 1877. The Ruff and Purple Gallinule in Ohio. Bull. Nuttall Ornithol. Club 2:83.

_____. 1879. Occurrence of birds rare to the vicinity of Columbus, Ohio. Bull. Nuttall Ornithol. Club 4:62–63.

_____. 1882. Report on the birds of Ohio. Ohio Geol. Surv. Bull. 4:187–628.

Williams, A. B. 1950. Birds of the Cleveland Region. Kirtland Soc. Bull. No. 2. Cleveland Mus. Nat. Hist., Cleveland. 215 p.

Wright, A. M. 1912. Early records of the Carolina Paroquet. Auk 29:343–363.

_____.1915. Early records of the Wild Turkey, part IV. Auk 32:207–224.

Yoder, L. E. 1992. Palm Warbler. The Ohio Cardinal 15:27.

_____. 1997. The fall 1997 season. Bobolink 1(3):3–9.

Young, J. P. 1914. A flight of shorebirds near Youngstown, Ohio. Wilson Bull. 26:193–195.

Index

Please note: breeding map references are in old-style figures

Parula americana (Northern Parula), 422–424, 422
Parula, Northern, 422–424, 422
Passenger Pigeon, 257–258
Passer domesticus (House Sparrow), 565–566, 565
Passerculus sandwichensis (Savannah Sparrow), 494–496, 494
Passerella iliaca (Fox Sparrow), 503–504
Passerina ciris (Painted Bunting), 528
Passerina cyanea (Indigo Bunting), 526–527, 526
Pectoral Sandpiper, 196–197
Pelecanus erythrorhynchos (American White Pelican), 12–13
Pelecanus occidentalis (Brown Pelican), 14
Pelican, American White, 12–13
     Brown, 14
Perdix perdix (Gray Partridge), 136–137
Peregrine Falcon, 133–135
Petrel, Black-capped, 11
     Leach's Storm-, 11
Petrochelidon pyrrhonota (Cliff Swallow), 355–357, 355
Pewee, Eastern Wood-, 306–307, 306
Phaetusa simplex (Large-billed Tern), 250
Phalacrocorax auritus (Double-crested Cormorant), 14–16
Phalarope, Red, 213–214
     Red-necked, 212–213
     Wilson's, 211–212
Phalaropus fulicaria (Red Phalarope), 213–214
Phalaropus lobatus (Red-necked Phalarope), 212–213
Phalaropus tricolor (Wilson's Phalarope), 211–212
Phasianus colchicus (Ring-necked Pheasant), 137–139, 138
Pheasant, Ring-necked, 137–139, 138
Pheucticus ludovicianus (Rose-breasted Grosbeak), 522–523, 522
Pheucticus melanocephalus (Black-headed Grosbeak), 524
Philadelphia Vireo, 336
Philomachus pugnax (Ruff), 203
Phoebe, Eastern, 315–317, 315
     Say's, 317
Pica hudsonia (Black-billed Magpie), 340–341
Picoides arcticus (Black-backed Woodpecker), 300
Picoides borealis (Red-cockaded Woodpecker), 299–300
Picoides pubescens (Downy Woodpecker), 297–298, 297
Picoides villosus (Hairy Woodpecker), 298–299, 298
Pied-billed Grebe, 4–6, 4

BRUCE G. PETERJOHN's interest in birds developed in the mid-1960s, and he has been actively watching and studying birds for more than 35 years. After graduating from a Columbus, Ohio, high school, Bruce received degrees from The College of Wooster in 1974 and from Southern Illinois University in 1976. Returning to Ohio in 1976, Bruce Peterjohn's employment as a biologist with the Ohio Department of Transportation provided him with ample opportunity to develop a thorough background on the status and distribution of birds across the state. Since 1991, Bruce has been employed at the Patuxent Wildlife Research Center in Laurel, Maryland, initially as coordinator of the North American Breeding Bird Survey and currently as the coordinator for all operational monitoring programs at the center.

Bruce Peterjohn's extensive background with the state's bird communities, and tenure as the Middlewestern Prairie regional editor for *American Birds*, culminated in the publication of the first edition of **The Birds of Ohio** in 1988. During the 1980s, Bruce served as co-coordinator with Dan Rice for the Ohio Breeding Bird Atlas project. The atlas was published in 1991, marking the first comprehensive summary of breeding bird distribution in Ohio in over fifty years. Bruce currently resides in Maryland, but makes annual visits to Ohio to conduct Breeding Bird Survey routes, and visits on other occasions allow him to remain familiar with the changes occurring in the state's bird communities.